Henry William Herbert

Typographical Antiquities

An Historical Account of the Origin and Progress of Printing in Great Britain and Ireland

Henry William Herbert

Typographical Antiquities
An Historical Account of the Origin and Progress of Printing in Great Britain and Ireland

ISBN/EAN: 9783741182082

Manufactured in Europe, USA, Canada, Australia, Japa

Cover: Foto ©Thomas Meinert / pixelio.de

Manufactured and distributed by brebook publishing software
(www.brebook.com)

Henry William Herbert

Typographical Antiquities

The Widow of JOHN HARRINGTON.

HER husband printed with Tho. Raynald in the year 1549. See p. 583. I find only the following book set forth by her; begun perhaps before her husband's decease.

" Psalmes of David, as Tho. Sternhold grome of the Kinges Maiesties Robes didde in his lifetime draw into English metre. Imprinted at London, by the wydowe of Jhon Harrington, M D. & L." Dedicated to the king. 1550.

EDWARD SUTTON, stationer,

WAS an original member of the Stationers' company; and on "A collecceion to be gathered of the cōpanye, by cōmaundmēt of the Lorde Maior and the Courte of Aldermen, for the howse of Brydewell," he gave xijd. Also, as a benevolence towards the charges of their hall, xijd. And towards the necessary expenses for establishing the corporation iijs. iiijd. He was one of the " vj men which was taken into the lyuera—agaynst the feaste daye," 1561; served Junior Collector of the Quarterages in 1566, and Renter, or Upper Collector in 1567; but he was fined, for negligence, xxs. He dwelt at the sign of the cradle, in Lombard-street.

" A treatyse of the newe India, with other new founde landes and Ilandes, aswell eastwarde, as westwarde as they are knowen and found in these oure dayes, after the descripcion of Sebastian Munster in his boke of vniversall Cosmographie: wherein the diligent reader may see the good successe and rewarde of noble & honeste enterpryses, by the which not only worldly ryches are obtayned, but also God is glorified, & the Christian fayth enlarged. Translated out of Latin into Englisb, by Rycharde Eden. Præter spem sub spæ." Dedicated " To the right hyghe & mighty Prince, the Duke of Northumberlande hys grace." See an extract from it below.* 1553.

7 P

Then

* "—wheras one death is dewe to nature, the same is more honourably spent in such attemptes as may be to the glorye of God & commoditie of our countrey, then in soft beddes at home,—. Which manlye courage (like vnto that which hath ben seen & proued in your grace, aswell in forene realmes, as also in this oure countrey) yf it had not been wanting in other in these our dayes, at suche time as our soueraigne Lord of noble memorie Kinge Henry the viii. about the same yere of his raygne, furnished & sent forth certen shippes vnder the gouernaunce of Sebastian Cabot yet liuing, & one syr Thomas Perte, whose faynt heart was the cause that that viage toke none effect: yf (J say) such manly courage wherof we haue spoken, had not at that tyme bene wanting, it myghte happelye haue comen to passe, that that riche treasurye called Perularia, (which is now in Spayne in the citie of Ciuile, and so named, for that in it is kepte the infinite ryches brought thither from the newe-found land of Peru) myght longe since haue bene in the towre of London, to the kinges great honoure & welth of this his realme. What riches the Emperoure hath gotten out of all the newe founde landes, it may wel appeare, whereas onlye in the Jlandes of Hispana or Hispaniola, & Cuba & other Jlandes there aboute, were gathered in two monethes twelue thousand poundes weyght of gold,—Yet speake J here nothynge of perles, precious stones, and spices."

Then a preface, and a table. The treatise contains M 6, in eights; beginning with B. On the last leaf, "Thus endeth the fyfth boke of Sebastian Munster of the lădes of Asia the greater, and of the newe founde landes & Ilandes. 1553. Imprinted—in Lombarde strete by Edward Sutton." On the back 12 couplets of verses "To al aduenturers, and such as take in hande greate enterpryses." Concludes, "Omnis iacta sit alea." W.H. Octavo.

1555. "The Decades of the newe worlde," &c. as p. 587, and 733.

1562. "The Destruction and sacke cruelly committed by the Duke of Guyse" &c. as p. 845. "Imprinted—for *him* dwellyng in Lumbard-strete at the signe of the cradell. The fyrst of May." Licensed. W.H. Octavo.

1562. "Truth tried, very comfortable to the faithful, but a discomfort to the enemies of God, by I. S." Printed for him. Licensed. Octavo.

1563. "An answere to the examination, that is sayde to haue bene made of one named John de Poltrot," &c. as p. 805. Licensed.

1565. "Toxaris, or the frendshyp of Lucian," &c. as p. 845. Octavo.

—— "Dolefull dealing of the pittielesse papists." Maunsell, p. 46." Octavo.

—— "A Discourse vpon the Libertie or captiuitie of the King" (of France.) H. Sutton for him. Licensed. Octavo.

He had license, in 1561, for printing "A declaration made by the prynce of Condee, &c.---The ijde Declaration of the prynce of Condee to make knowen the causes of the Trubbles, &c." In 1564, "The Joyes of Jeloosey." In 1566, "A moste pleasaunt worke of the whole arte of physiogme.---A book entitled, Italion, Frynshe, Englesshe and Laten.---How to playe of the lute, by Rob. Ballarde."

Tho. Hill, Londoner, in a list of his books in readiness to be imprinted, annexed to his Art of Gardening, printed by T. Marshe in 1568, has the following: "1. A large historie and discourse of the whole art of Physiognomie, now the second time encreased, vnto whiche is anneexed sundrie rare Examples of dyuers forreine Princes that came to straunge happes, accordinge to the foretelling of the Phisiognomer Cocles, which notes do not a lytle healpe to the furtherance of the arte, with other rare Secretes adioyned, not the lyke extant in the Latine Tungue, whiche worke loke for at the handes of Edw. Suttone stacioner in Lumbarde strete. 2. A pleasaunt Treatise intituled the Pathe way to knowledge, teaching all such principles as necessarilie sarue to the better vnderstanding of the arte of Astronomie & Astrologie, with other pleasaunt rules, &c. Which looke for at the handes of the sayd Suttone. 3. Also, a proper Treatise intytuled the Myrroure of Tyme, contayning manye woorthie maters and predictions ryghte necessarie to bee vnderstanded, which is in the handes of the foresayd Suttone."

NICHOLAS ENGLAND.

IN the Wardens account for the year from July 1558 to July 1559 is this entry, "Received of Nych. Ynglande for his reriges this year, xd." So that as there is no prior memorial of his being admitted either a freeman or a brother, he feems to have been an original member of the Stationers' company, though his name is not mentioned on the Rolls lift; for there are inftances of fome original freemen whofe names are not found in that lift. Perhaps he might be only a Brother, as he neither binds nor makes free. In whichfoever of thefe relations he flood to the Company, he appears to have been a very orderly member; but i do not find his name among the benevolent contributors towards the charges of the Hall, &c. though moft of the original members contributed fomewhat according to their ability or good-will. He dwelt in Pater nofter row, and had the following books printed for him.

"Brevis et perfpicua Ratio iudicandi Genituras," &c. as p. 843. 1558.

"A Famous cronicle—Sleidanes Commentaries," &c. as p. 633. 1560.

"The Arte of warre, written firft in Jtaliā by Nicholas Machiauell, 1560. and fet forthe in Englifhe by Peter Whitehorne, ftudient at Graics Jnne: with an addiciō of other like Marcialle feates and experimentes, as in a Table in the ende of the Booke maie appere. Anno. M.D.LX. Menfs. Julij." In an elegant military compartment, cut on wood: a trumpeter feen half length, at top; a foldierr on one fide, a drummer on the other; in a tablet at bottom, a fharp engagement of horfe-men. The engraver's initials W. S. Beneath all, in types, "Niclas Inglande," omitted in the fubfeqnent editions. Contains H h i, in fours, befides the dedication to Q. Elizabeth. On the back of the laft leaf is England's device, as p. 780. Licenfed. W.H. Quarto.

"Certain waies for the orderyng of Souldiers" &c. as p. 835. Where 1562. it is faid to be annexed to The Arte of warre, by miftake; my copies of them being bound together. It was annexed in after editions.

"The Nyne fyrft Bookes of the Eneidos of Virgil," &c. as p. 804. L. 1562.

"The fecretes of—Maifter Alexis," &c ib. Licenfed. 1562.

"The fecond part," &c. ib. 1563.

"The thyrde and laft parte," &c. as p. 780. 1566.

"The fecond Tome of the Palace of Pleafure," &c. as p. 967. L. 1567.

He had alfo licenfes in 1560, for "An almanacke and pronoftication of Mons Lady." In 1568, "An almanake and pronofticac'on of Doctor Bomelious."

ROBERT EALIE.

"A Difcourfe, wherein is debated, Whether it be expedient that the 155 Scripture fhould be in Englifh, for all men to read that will. Printed at London by Robert Ealie." See Strype's Eccl. Memorials, Vol. III; p. 170. This was printed alfo by Rob. Caley in December this fame year; and again in 1555. Catal. Bibl. Bodl. Vol. II; p. 536. 8°.

RICHARD HARVY, or HARVEY,

WAS an original member of the Stationers' company, gave viij d. to Bridewell, & a benevolence of xviij d. and afterwards of ij s. vj d. to the company; but i find no mention of him after 1563. He was fined in 1558 " for byndynge of greate bokes in shepes Lether, at xij d." Also, in 1562, he, with others " for sellynge of Nostrodamus, iij s. iiij d." He dwelt in Foster-Lane; and printed, in verse,

— " A Decree betwene Churchyarde the Poet and Camell."

Begins: " A decree vpon the dreame made by Davy Dicar,
with answer to Camell, whose taunts be more quicker."

A broad-side.

In 1557, he had license, to print " Devote Prayers."

NICHOLAS WYER

Was probably related to Robert Wyer, but in what degree is not certain; however he succeeded him in his house in St. Martin's parish, as appears by the following book, the only one we have met with of his printing. See p. 711, &c.

— " A pleasaunt and delightfull History of Galesius, Cymon and Iphigenia, describing the ficklenesse of fortune in love, Translated out of Italian into Englishe verse by T. C. gentleman. Printed by Nicholas Wyer in saint Martins parish besides Charing Cross." In stanzas. See Hist. of Eng. Poetry. Vol. III; p. 469.

Between July 1565 and July 1566 he had license to print these two ballads, viz. " The lamentation of Churchyardes fryndshippe.—The Courtior and the Carter."

JAMES ROBOTHOM, or ROWBOTHUM,

WAS a citizen of London, but it does not appear that he was free of the Stationers' Company; though he had licenses from them to print almanacs and prognostications, as well as other books and ballads. These perhaps were allowed him on account of a patent,[b] at least

[b] From a M.S. penes Sir John Evelyn Bart.

" Elizabeth by the grace of God, &c. To all prynters of books, and booksellers, and to all other of our offycers, mynisters and subjects greeting. We lett you to witt that for certeyne considerations us moving of our special grace and mere mocyon, we have graunted privilege, and geven lycens, and by these presents, for us, our heires, and successors, do graunte privilege, and geve lycence, unto our well beloved subjecte James Robothom, citezein of our citie of London, and to his assignes, to ymprinte or cause

least intended for him; but when, or whether executed is not so certain. He seems to have been rather a binder and bookseller than a printer, for in 1563 he was fined for that he "bounde ij hundreth of premers in skabertes—contrary to orders, ijs. vid." He kept shop first at the Rose and Pomegranate under Bow Church, and afterward in Pater-noster-Row.

"THE vvell Sprynge of Sciences vvhich teacheth the perfect worke and Practise of Arithmeticke, bothe in whole numbers and fractions, with such easie and compendious instruction into the sayde arte, as hathe not heretofore bene by any set out nor laboured. Beawtified with moste necessarye Rules and Questions, not onely profitable for Marchauntes, but also for all Artificers, as in the table doth partlye appeare: set forthe by Humfrey Baker Citisyn of London. Printed—by Rouland Hall, for James Rowbothum and are to be solde at his shop in Cheapeside vnder Bowe churche, at the sygne of the Rose and Pomegranet. 1562." On the back is "An advertisment to the louing reader," in 8 English distichs. It is dedicated "To—Maister John Fitzwilliam Gouernour of the most famous societie of Marchauntes Adventurers into Flaunders, and to the—Consuls, Assistents," &c. Besides; 160 leaves. Licensed, Alexander Dalrymple, Esq; Sixteens. 1562.

"The Pleasaunt and wittie Playe of the Cheastes," &c. as p. 80. 1562.

"The most ancient—play, called the philosophers game," &c. as p. 805. Concerning this book see The goodly Gallery, p. 923. 1563.

"A Briefe and easye instruction," &c. as p. 837. Licensed thus, —"the breffe and playne instruction to learne to play on the the gyttron and also Cetterne." 1568.

"A briefe and plaine Instruction to set all Musicke of eight diuers tunes in Tableture for the Lute. With a briefe Instruction how to play on the Lute by Tableture, to conduct and dispose thy hand vnto the Lute, with certain easie lessons for that purpose. And also a third Booke containing diuers new excellent tunes. All first written in French by Adrian le Roy, and now translated into English by F. Ke. Gentleman. Jmprinted at London by James Rowbothome, and are to be 1574.

cause to be ymprinted, all and every suche almanacks and prognostications, as are, or shall be tollerable, and authorised by our iniunctions in the Englishe tonge, together withe the breef cronycles. And that it shall not be lawfull for any manner of other person or persons of our said subiects, except such as by letters patents be specially priviledged already to emprinte, or to procure to be emprynted, uttered, or solde, any almanack, prognostication or brief cronycle, by whatsoever title the same shall or may be called, or sett forthe, with out the assignement of the same James Robothom, or his assignes, during the naturall lyf of the said James, upon pain to forfeit for every suche almanack, or prognostication, or briefe cronycle, so printed, uttered, and solde, the summe of three shillings and four pence, of lawfull money of England, the one moitie thereof to our use, and the other moitie unto hym, that will sue for the same by bill, information, plainte, or otherwise, in any of our courts of record. Any thinge to the contrary in any wise notwithstanding. Yeuen, &c."

c This should have been entred under his name, but the book did not come to my hands before the account of him was printed off.

be sold in Pater noster row at the signe of the Lute. Anno 1574." On the back is "The Bookes verdict," in 5 English couplets. Dedicated "To—the Lord Edward Seamour, Viscount Beauchamp, Erle of Hertford.—J. R.---To—my Ladie the Countesse of Kent. Adrian le Roy.---The Preface of Jacques Gohory, vnto the curteous Reader." Contains as erroneously numbered 78, but really 90 leaves. The 2d part begins at fo. 62; the 3d part at fo. 75. At the end, "Imprinted —by Jhon Kyngston for James Robothome, Anno 1574." W.H. 4°.

He had also licenses in 1561, for "an almanacke." In 1562, "An almanake of Nychelsons, with a prognostication.---Another "of Chrestoferus Stathunioys.—Arcandum." In 1563, "A prognostication of Victorius Sconsfyldes." In 1564, "The Medecyne for certayne malydyes in horses, &c.---A prognost. of Victorius Sconsylte." Also for 3 ballads.

GILES GODET, GOODET, or GOODHED, Printseller,

WAS admitted and sworn a Brother of the Stationers' Company, 16 May (1555) before the date of their Charter.

1562.} 1563.} Sometime between July 1562 and July 1563 he had license for the following prints, &c. viz "An abstracte of the geneologe and Race of all the Kynges of Englonde from the floude of Noe vnto Brute.—The picture of the prynce of Condee.---The Carde of London.—The picture of the devell and the pope.---The geneolige or lyne of our Savyor Christe, as touching his humanyte from Noee to Davyd.—The pycture of kynge Henry the eighte.—The mappe of Englonde and Skotlande.—The story of the emperours.—The story of the iij cheldren.---The pycture of Kynge Eddwarde the vi.---The pycture of quene Elysabeth.---The tenne Cõmandementes.—The confyrmation of the olde Testament.—The Creation of the worlde.---The heavenly veryte.—The pycture of Paule the appostell.---The pycture of Saloman the wyse.---The pycture of *the* Kyng of Swathwande.—The natyme of the inwarde p'tes of man and woman.—The instruction of a very faythfull man.---The dyscryption of the howse of an harlott.—The Armes of Englonde.—The example of Justice.—The pycture of Charyte.—The Rememberaunce to dye.---The fygure of Tru Religion.--- The pycture of Tru sobryete."

1565.} 1566.} Between 1565 and 1566, "A pycture made vpon the Vth of Saynte Pawle to the Romaynes.—The historye of the prodigall chylde."

WILLIAM PYCHERYNG, or PICKERINGE, ſtationer,

WAS an original member of the Stationers' company; who on a collection for Bridewell gave xij.d. and towards the eſtabliſhment of the company 5ſ. See p. 1309. Alſo, at another collection the next year, a further benevolence of xijd. He does not appear to have been taken on the Livery. It is remarkable of him that he is the firſt perſon on the liſt licenſed by the company to print. In 1558, he was fined vid. for ſome contentious words with Wm. Griffith. See p. 922. In 1562, he was fined, with ſeveral others, "for ſellynge of Noſtrodamus iijſ. iiijd." In 1566, for arreſting Anth. Kytſon, without conſent of the Maſter and Wardens, ij.ſ. vid. but this article is obliterated; perhaps becauſe Kytſon was not free of the company. In 1567, he was fined for printing a ballad without licenſe, xvj.d. Tho. Eſt was fined alſo at the ſame time xij.d. for printing a ballad for him. He appears to have printed only ballads himſelf; but had ſome books printed for him. An apprentice of his was made free by James Roberts, 8 Nov. 1571; probably his executor or adminiſtrator, there being no entry of any turnover. He dwelt on London Bridge. *(One Richard Pycheringe bound an apprentice in 1586.)*

"The copye of the ſelf ſame wordes: That my Lorde †Sturton ſpake presently at his Death, beyng the vi. day of March, in the yeare of our Lord 1556 amonge the people as his Confeſſion, deſireing the People to take Example by hym, and to kepe no Enuy in their hartes for that is the roote of all Euylles. Printed by William Pickeringe, dwellynge vpon London Brydge." (1556.)

"The Popiſh Kingdome," &c. as p. 945. See Hiſt. of Eng. Poetry, Vol. III; p. 458, note u. 1566.

A Dialogue between Experience and a Courtier, &c. as p. 994. Licenſed to him to print it both in Engliſh and Scotch. 1566.

"An almanacke and prognoſtication," &c. as p. 939. 1568.

"A declaration of ſuch tempeſtous and outragious Fluddes, as hath been in diuers places in England, 1570." See p. 890. 1571.

"Generall Pardon geuen long agone, and ſith newly confirmed by our almightie father, with many large priuiledges, grantes, and Bulls granted for euer. Drawen out of French by VVilliam Hayward." For him. Maunſell, p. 78. —— Octavo.

"A ſonge

† "Charles Lord Sturton and his men cruelly murthered Mr. Argile and his ſon; he cauſed them to be broken downe with clubs, then their throats to be cut, and after to be buried in his owne houſe 15 foot deep; for the which he was arraigned and condemned at Weſtminſter; and after conveyed from the Tower of London through the city, and ſo to Saliſbory, and was there hanged with four of his men ſervants, 6 March, 1557, ſilu Angie." M. S. on the margin of one of the copies.

—— " A songe betwene the Quenes maiestie and England." A sheet.
His first licensse was in 1557 for printing " a ballett called aRyse and wake," for which he gave to the house iiij d. He had licenses also, for " iij dialogues contanynge very honeste learned pleasaunte and nete *matter*.---The epitaph vpon the Death of kynge Edwarde the vj." In 1560, " A playe of quene hester.---A ballet of Toth'am crosse." In 1562, " A ballet entitled, god morowe to yō good syster Jone." In 1564, " Waltham Crosse, &c.---The dysputation betwene Love & monye.---Loo here I ly synner: with a prayer to the same.---The story of Jobe the faythfull servaunte of god, &c.---A dyalogue vpon christes byrth.---A neweyeres gyfte by John markante.---A Epytaph of John Philpotte.---An almanake & pronostic' of Joakin Hubrygh." In 1565, " The Lamentation for ẏ Towne of Chensford, Wrekell, Spryngfylde, vpwych and Waltham.---A bref declaration of the cruell batry and horryble warre both by see and lande which fell betwene ij monsterus nations in the lande of gryngurt.---An almanake and pronost. of Henry Rocheforth, for the yere of our lorde god, 1566.---of Mr. Joachim Hewbryghr, with the breffe and profytable Rule for marynors to knowe the ebbes, floddes, Soundynges, Landynges, markes, and dangers.---A mery and pleasaunt history donne in tymes paste by Erasmus Roterdamus.---The maryage of Jhesu christe & the sowle of man.---The preface of & vpon the dyscours of the warre of the ij gramer speches, that is to say, the nowne and the verbe." In 1566, " The examynation of certen wyches at Chensforde before the quenes maiesties Judges in the countye of Essex.---The secounde examynation and confessyon of Agnues Waterhowse and Jone her doughter, &c.---A mery pronost'. for—1567, by J. Dernyll.---A warnynge to all englonde by casualtis of fyre, for all howsholders to take warnynge there at." In 1567, " An almanake &c. of Joachym Hubryghte, for 1568." The same in 1568; also, " An exortation wherby englonde may knowe." In 1569, " A dysputation betwene Lady Jane and Dr. fack'ham, with other necessaryes by my lorde of London.---Lenton stuffe.---Lenton pēnaunce.---The ende and confession of Tho. norton and Christofer norton Rebelles in yorkeshyre," &c. In 1570, " The begynnyng and endynge of all popery." Also many ballads, at various times.

LEONARD MAYLARD

DWELT at the sign of the Cock in St. Paul's Church-yard.
1567. " The Manuell of Epictetus," &c. as p. 966.
1568. " The Enemie of Idlenesse," &c. as p. 968.
He had also license in 1567 for " A playne path waye to perfycte vertu &c."

WILLIAM JONES.

I Find three persons named William Jones, each of them free of the Stationers' Company, before the year 1600.

The first of them seems to have nearly, if not quite, served his apprenticeship before the Company had their charter, as he does not appear to have been presented as others were. See p. 1322. He was apprentice with Robert Toye, and made free 11 March 1557-8. In 1558 he was fined "for that he solde a Communion boke of kynge Edwards for one of the newe, xx d." In 1561, "for that he came into the Hall in his cloke, xij d.---for that he kepte an apprentice and not bounde, xij d." Again, "for that he kepte open his shoppe on sondayes and holydayes, ij s." In 1562, "for sellynge of Nostradamus, iij sh. iiij d." In 1564, "for that he ded stech bokes which is contrary to the Orders of this howse, and also for mysusynge of hymself before the Master & Wardens, iij sh. iiij d." In 1570, "for that he kept open his shope on St. Andrewes daye, vj d." Henry Dysele was apprentice to him. He kept the new long shop at the West door of St. Paul's church. Afterwards in the Churchyard, at the South-west door of St. Paul's church, joining unto Lollards tower.

"The Foreste, or collection of Histories," &c. as p. 838. Licensed. 1571.

"A confutation of a Popishe,—libelle," &c. ib. 1571.

"ΟΥΡΑΝΟΜΑΧΙΑ, hoc est, astrologorum ludus," &c. as p. 1007. 1572.

"The Benefit of the auncient Bathes of Buckstones," &c. ib. 1572.

"The Bathes of Bathes Ayde:" &c. as p. 1008. This and the foregoing article were afterward annexed to 1572.

"A Briefe, excellent, and profitable Discourse, of the naturall beginning of all growing and living things, heate, generation, effects of the spirits, gouernment, vse and abuse of Phisicke, preseruation, &c. No lesse pleasant and acceptable to the students of Philosophie and Phisicke, then beneficiall and necessarie for all others desirous either of knowledge, health, youth, and long life. Collected and traduced aswel forth of the best olde Wryters, as out of the new, and most approued in our daies. In the ende wherof is shewed, the order and composition of a most heauenly Wate.,* for the preseruation of Mans lyfe. By Iohn Iones Phisicion. 1574.

7 Q Hereunto

* Which "may iustly be called the Water preseruing youth, prolonging life and defending from sicknesses. Right profitable for many yonge and olde, because it helpeth nature, strengtheneth the Stomache, causeth Appetite, comforteth the Brayn, assisteth the Liuer, reuiueth the Hart, by means wherof ther foloweth good digestion, puer blood, and fine Spirites:—In fine a sweete breath it yeeldeth, youth, Bewtie and Liuelines it maintaineth, &c. But albeit that it had an hundred vertues more answerable to the manifold Vertues of the worthie and notable simples entring into the composition wel knowen, and approued of your Lordship, Yet would I haue remembred that learned saying of Fernel. Ambianus lib. 2 de Abdit. rerum causis, cap. vii. Wher he saith that greeuous is the impudencie of them, and also intollerable, which hauing gotten an excellent Medicine, without Arte, without all iudgement, offereth it to the curation of the sick. A thing in these our dayes to common,—and therefore I haue written it in Latine."

Herevnto is anexed, a right learned, and profitable work, entituled, Galens booke of Elements, by the same Author: in the ende whereof is adioyned two other bookes, containing the nature, propertie and effects of all the Bathes in England, aswel the Bathes of the Citie of Bathes, as the Bathes or wells at Buckstone in Darbyshyre, by the same Author. Seene and allowed. Jmprinted—, by william Iones, dvvelling in Paules Churchyard, at the Southvvest doore of Paules, and are ther to be fold. 1574." On the back is a cut of a talbot inclosed in a border. On the next leaf are commendatory verses in Latin, "Ad: Squieri Baliolensis in laudem Authoris---Carmen Kinderi Medici---Aliud eiusdem---In Zoilum eiusdem." Dedicated "To the—most loyall Earle, George, Earle of Shrewsbury, Earle Marshall of England, Lord Talbot, Furniuall, Vardon, and Strange of Blackmire, Knight of—the Garter, and one of the Lords of the Queenes magesties—Priuy Counsell, and Iustice in Oyre from Trent Northward, &c." G 3, in fours. Colophon, "Jmprinted —by william Iones, dwelling in Paules Churchyard, at the Southvvest doore of Paules, and are ther to be fold. 1574." WH. Quarto.

1574. "Galens Bookes of Elementes, as they be in the Epitome (which may very aptly, in my iudgement, be Entituled, for the better vnderstanding of the Readers, The Originall of all thinges naturall in the vvhole vvorlde: Confuting, as well the errours of all them that went before time, as that hath or shal folowe hereafter of the Paracelcians: marueilous pleasaunt, and most acceptable for all sharpe wittes desirous of wisedome,) published foorth of Latine into English. By John Jones Phisition Jmprinted— by VWilliam Jones, dwelling in Paules Churche Yarde,—1574." Dedicated "To the—moste trustie Earle, George, Earle of Shrewsbury" &c. as above. C 2, in fours. Colophon "Jmprinted &c. loyning vnto Loulards Towre, and are there to be solde." I have a copy of the same edition without this colophon. Quarto.

—— "The pilgrimage of Princes, penned out of sundry Greeke and Latine aucthours, by Lodovvicke Lloid Gent. At London. Printed by VVilliam Iones, and are to be solde at his nevve long Shop at the VVest doore of Povvles." In the compartment with Moses and David on the sides. See p. 1246. My Copy has 1597 in M.S. under the title; evidently a mistake,[h] as by the printer's direction this book must have been printed before 1574 when he dwelt at the S. W. door of St. Paul's. On the leaf next the title is an acrostic in English alexandrines, Christophoros Hattonus, to whom the book is also dedicated, being then "Capitaine of the Queenes Maiesties Garde, and Gentleman of her highnesse priuie Chamber.—Lodovvicke Lloide.---To the Reader.---In librum de Principum perigrinatione, Johannis Coci, Scholæ Paulinæ magistri hendecastichon cum versu quodam Homerico ad lectorem.---In Laudem Lodovici

[h] The mistake seems to have happened thus: Mr. Ames has entred it under Richard Jones, the last article, and without date; but a little above is the date 1597 in the margin, belonging to another book; the former possessor therefore probably concluded the following books should have the same date. See Ames p. 348.

Ledovici Flodi, Thomas Dranta, Archdiachonis Leuuicensis.---Christoforus Carlilus in Flodum. 4 *Sapphics*.---Ed. Grant, in Lud. Flo.—Thomas Churchyard, Gent. of Lodo. Fl." *in English alexandrines*. Then the treatise on 214 pages. At the end, The pilgrimage of queens, in alexandrines, and "The Aucthour to his booke," in the same verse; and a Table. W.H. It was printed by John Wolf in 1586. Quarto.

He had also licenses to print a considerable time before we have met with any of his performances. In 15 2, "The Cytie of Cyvelite, translated into Englesshe by william paynter." In 1565, "An almanake and pronostic. of Cunnyngham, for an. 1566.---Sixten historyes collected oute of dyuers Ryght good and profitable authours by William Paynter." In 1570, "An answere to a polige Thrawyn abrode in the Courte to fulkes." Also for some Ballads.

I find nothing more of this Will. Jones. Probably somethig might be found in the Clerk's Book; but as that remains still missing, and thereby occasions a chasm of 5 years, we must take leave of him here. This however we may be assured of, that nothing of him or his interferes with either of his two namesakes following; whom, for distinction sake, i shall denominate *the Elder*, and *the Younger*.

WLLIAM JONES, *The Elder*, stationer,

THE Son of Simon Jones of Tilfeld, Northamptonshire, yeoman, was bound apprentice to John Judson, for 9 years, from Michaelmas 1578; and was made free 19 Octob. 1587, when the said Mr. Judson was Master of the Company. He appears to have been a more orderly member than the forementioned Will. Jones, since he is once only fined xvj.*d.* in 1593; for what is not mentioned. How long he continued in business after 1597 is not easy to determine, as there is no distinction made in the Company's Register, between the identity of him and another Will. Jones, whom i call *the younger*, except at the entry of their apprenticeship, when the names, &c. of their fathers are specified. Such books as mention the residence realize the person sufficiently. There can be no doubt of such as were printed after 1587, and before 1596, when the younger one was made free. This Will. Jones *the Elder* dwelt at the sign of the Gun, near Holborn conduit.

"Rich. Greeneham, Preacher, his most sweet and assured comfort, for all those that are afflicted in conscience, or troubled in mind: with 2 comfortable letters to his frends that way greeued." For him. L. 24°. 1595.

—his 2 sermons: 1. On Prov. 22; 1. 2. On 1. Thes. 5; 19. For him. Licensed. Octavo. 1575.

"Jo. Mores Liuely Anatomy of Death: wherein you may see from whence it came, what it is by nature, and what by Christ; tending to teach 1596.

teach men to live and dye well, in the Lord. Will. Jones." Taken from Archb. Harsnet's copy of Maunsell, p. 74. Licensed 25 Oct. 1595.

1597. "The Woman in the Moone," &c. as p. 1050. "Imprinted at London[1] for *him*, and are to be sold at the signe of the gun, neere Holbourne Conduict. 1597." W. H. Quarto.

1598. "The troublesome raigne and lamentable death of Edward the second, King of England:—by Chri. Marlow Gent." Rd. Bradock, for him. K 2, in fours Licensed in 1593. Quarto.

1598. "The Blinde begger of Alexandria." F, in fours. Licensed. Quarto.

These, either by their dates, or the printer's residence, were doubtless his peculiar copies. That which follows might probably be so, but finding it described only as "printed for William Jones," it must remain in suspence till i may have an opportunity of seeing it.

1598. Mucedorus, a comedy; ascribed to W. Shakespeare as the author, but without any good authority. See the prefixes to Shakespeare's plays, by Johnson and Steevens, p. 241. Where it appears they were printed again for him in 1610, and in 1615; so that perhaps this especially might belong to W. J. *the younger*.

All licenses granted before 1596 must be designed for W. J. *the Elder*, after that time it is uncertain to which of them they belong. In 1589, license was granted him for a ballad, "Descrybing the vallures of our Eng. Archers and shott that accōpanied the blacke prince of Portugall their gov'nor into the feilds on twesdaie the 12 of Aug. With the welcome into Lyme streete by Mr. Hugh Offley." In 1590, "An hundreth godly instructions: provided &c.---The Shepherdis Starre, &c. Dedicated by Tho. Bradshaw to Therle of Essex." In 1594, "The schoole of good manners."

In 1597, "St. Peter's Ten teares, supposedly wrytten vppon his weepinge sorrowes for denyinge his Master Xpiste; Conditionally—to no other man.---Greene in conceyt newe raised from his graue to wryte the tragique storye of his faire Valeria of London."---He assigned to R. Dexter, "Mr. Greenham's Treatise of thafflicted conscience: And his 2 sermons, all in one book." In 1598, "The mynt of deformities.---Spiritual phisicke to cure the diseases of the Soule," &c.

WILLIAM JONES *the younger*.

WAS the son of William Jones of the town of Northampton, Clothworker, bound apprentice to John Windet, for 9 years from Midsummer 1587; and made free 5 July 1596; but finding nothing for certain that he printed before 1601, i shall but just mention that he dwelt in Ship-alley Red-Cross street, and continued printing till 1634; at least one of the name did.

HENRY

[1] Mr. Ames ascribed this to Richard Jones as the printer, for him, but there is no indication of that on the book.

HENRY KIRKHAM, stationer,

SERVED his apprenticeship with William Marten, stationer, from Christmas 1561, and was made free in 1568. He kept shop at the sign of the Black Boy, at the little North-door of St. Paul's Church.

"Three Sermons by Thomas Lever. 1. On Rom. 13; 1—7. Preached in the Shrowds. 2. On John 6; 5—14. Before king Edw. vi. 3. On 1 Cor. 4; 1. At Paules Crosse." Octavo. 1573.

"An Invective Againste vices taken for Vertue." &c. as p. 839. 1579.

Maunsell mentions an edition 1589, for him. I have also an edition without date, as p. 342; but it has not the necessary instructions &c. annexed as to the edition 1579.[k]

"The hurt of hearyng Masse: Sette forthe by the faithfull seruaunt of God, and constant Martire of Christ Ihon Bradford, when he was prisoner in the Tower of London. 3 Kynges 18. How long will ye halte betweene twoo opinions, &c. Imprinted at London for H. Kirkham, and are to be sold at his Shop, at the little Northdore of Sainct Paules churche, at the signe of the blacke Boye. 1580." In a border of metal flowers. F 4, in eights. WH. Sixteens. 1580.

"A blazynge Starre or burnyng Beacon," &c. as p. 839. Licensed. 1580.

"An Ansvvere vnto certaine crabbed questions," &c. as p. 1171. 1582.

"Instructions with certain Articles to be knowen of all those that come to the communion by D. W. Archdeacon. Printed for *him*. 1586." Maunsell, p. 30. Licensed in 1578. See note k. Octavo. 1586.

"A Work worth the Reading:" &c. as p. 1246. 1591.

"BACCHVS BOVNTIE: Describing the debonaire Deitie of his bountifull Godhead, in the Royall obseruance of his great Feast of Penticost. Necessarie to be read and marked of all, for the Eschuing of like Enormities. Fœcundi calices quem non fecere disertum? By Philip Foulface of Alesfoord Student in good Felloship. Printed—for *him*,—[l]1593." Three sheets. Harleian Miscellany, ii; 285. Quarto. 1593.

"A Dialogue betweene the penitent sinner and Sathan, wherein Sathan moueth vnto desperation; the sinner comforteth himselfe with the sweet promises of the holy scriptures. Set forth by T. B." Printed for him. Maunsell, p. 43. Octavo. ——

"The practice of the Diuell." &c. as p. 684. ——

He had license in 1569 to print "A dyscription of Nortons in Yorkshire, by Gybson." In 1576, "A little thinge/ Newe tydynges of a huge & ougly childe borne at Arnheim in Geldland.---These iij thinges/

j. The

[k] These were printed alone in 1586, perhaps enlarged; as they occupied only 2 leaves; unless The invective was reprinted this year also.

[l] This book must have been printed before the 5th of March 1592-3, when William the son of Hen. Kyrkham, deceased, was made free by patrimony: who also succeeded him in his shop and business.

j. The ſtrange aduentures of ij Italian Knightes. ij. Wharton's nouels. iij. A pamphlet/ Trigos dreame or viſion." In 1578, "Paul Buckes praier for Sir Humfrey Gilbertte.---An epitaphe vpon the deathe of Marmaduke Lacye e q; Juſtyce of peace within the eſt rydinge of—York, who died the xiiij of Decemb. 1578." In 1579, "An Epitaph vpon the deathe of Arthure Gaiter gent.---A fatherly admonyc'on and louinge warnynge to England; but ſpecially to London by the reaſon of a mooſt fearfull earthquake, which he ſent as a fayre token of his ſpeedie comynge to Judgement: the vj. of Aprill, 1580.---A true & terrible example of Gods wrath ſhewed by the gen'all earthquake through England.---Preparac'on to the croſſe and deathe: and of the comfort of the croſſe and deathe." In 1580, "A report of certen trauellers touchinge the age and captiuitie of a Grecian borne in Candia." In 1581, "The diſcours of Johan Powell." In 1587, "A dialogue of encouragement to Engliſhmen to be bold to fight in defence of prince and cũtrey." In 1585, "A ballet of thankes gyuing vnto God for his m'cy toward hir maieſtie, begynning Reioyce England," &c. In 1589, "A ſorowfull newe ſonette, intitled Tarltons Recantac'on vppon this theame gyuen him by a gent. at the Bellſauage without Ludgate (nowe or never) being the laſt theame he ſong.---The type or figure of frendſhip:" with Tho. Orwin. Alſo, at times for ſeveral ballads.

THOMAS CADMAN, ſtationer.

WAS preſented 13 Octob. 1556 as the apprentice of Nicholas Cliſton, an original member of the Stationers' Company; and made free 16 June 1560. Which evinces what i have elſewhere intimated, that thoſe apprentices who had been bound before the Company's charter from Phil. and Mary was granted, were preſented afterwards in order to be regiſtered, for which they payed vid. In 1562 he was fined with ſome others for ſelling Noſtrodamus, iijſ. iiij.d. Alſo, "for gyvinge John Hynde unſemely wordes, ii ſh. vj d." Again, "for that he* ded dyſobey the Wardens cõmandement, ijſ." In 1567, he was fined vi ſh. viijd. but no mention for what: after this however he is found no more on the Black Liſt. He kept ſhop at the Bible, next to the great North door of St. Paul's church.

1574. "Articles—preſented to the French king," &c. as p. 1056.

1584. "A moſt Excellent Comedie of Alexander, Campaſpe,* and Diogenes.

* His maſter Nich. Cliſton was fined at the ſame time, "for that he called Conrad Mytter d unkerd in the preſens of the Maſter and Wardens, iiijd."

* See it as played before the queen, p. 1203. Which copy has 2 prologues, and 2 epilogues; one part "at the black Friers," the other "at the Court:" the running title, "A tragicall Comedie of Alexander and Campaſpe." G, in fours.

genes. Imprinted for *him.*" At this time it appears to have been played at the Black Friars. Quarto.

" A scourge for Rebels: wherein are many notable Services truly set out, with every particular point touching the troubles of Ireland, as farre as the painful and dutiful Service of the Earle of Ormond. Written by Tho. Churchyard Gent." For him. Quarto. 1584.

" A—Treatise—of the disease called Morbus Gallicus," &c. as p. 1015. 1585.

" Rob. Greene his Planetomachia. or the firste part of the generall opposition of the 7 Planets, wherein is Astronomically described their essence, nature and influence: diversly discouering in their pleasaunt and Tragicall histories, the inward affection of the mindes, &c. containing also a briefe Apologie of the misticall science of Astronomie." For him. Quarto. 1585.

" Albion's England," &c. as p. 1237. Licensed. 1586.

"——the trewnesse of Christian Religion, *&c.* by Ph. Mornay," &c. ib. 1587.

" The Worthines of Wales:" &c. ib. 1587.

" The Politicke and Militarie Discourses," &c. as p. 1167. 1587.

"—— of curing woundes In the head, *&c.* by Fr. Arceus," &c. as p. 1016. Licensed. 1588. 1588.

" An Oration Militarie to all—Englishmen," &c. as p. 1242. 1588.

" A prooued practice for all young Chirurgians," &c. as p. 1243. L.

" A Briefe Delcription of vniuersal Mappes," &c. as p. 1192. 1589.

" The Spanishe masquerado, by Rob. Grene." L. See p. 1193. 1589.

" The French Kinges Declaration vpon the Riot," &c. as p. 1193. L. 1589.

" Repuestas, contra los Falsedades," &c. as p. 1212. Licensed. 1589.

" An Answer to the vntruthes published—in Spaine," &c. as p. 1219. 1589.

" The Birth, purpose, and mortall Wound of the Romish holie League. Describing in a Mappe the enuie of Sathans shauelings, and the follie of their wisedome through the Almighties prouidence. By I. L." For him. 32 stanzas; with a half sheet map. Lambeth Library. Quarto. 1589.

He had also licenses as follows, " 6 Apr. 1583, Yt is granted vnto him that if he gett the cōmedie of Sappho lawfully allowed vnto him, Then none of this cōpanie shall Jnterupt him to enioye yt." In 1586, " A mirror of the life, deathe and vertues of Sir Phillip Sydney knight, being a myrror for the followers of Mars and Mercurye." In 1587.. " The patheway to martiall discipline, vpon condition that yt belong to no other.---Twon Copies: whereof he is to bring the titles." In 1588, " Declaration du Roy sur l'attentāt, felonine & Rebellion du Duc de Mayēne, Duc & Chevalier d'Aumalle, & ceux qui les assisterent.---Declaration du Roy sur l'attentant—des villes de Paris, Orleans, Amyens, & Abbeuille, & autres leurs adherāts."

RICHARD

RICHARD SMITH, or SMYTHE,

I cannot find assuredly of what company he was free. If of the Stationers' he probably took up his freedom in the interval of the chasm in that company's Register, as there is no entry of his being apprenticed: in that case he must have been the son of Anth. Smith, an original member thereof, seeing there is not found any other freeman of the name of Smith before that chasm, except Sir Thomas Smith, Privy Counsellor, who was admitted a freeman just before that time. See p. 1063. But he seems rather to have been free of some other company, since I do not find him either binding or making free in the Stationers'. He kept shop at the West door of St. Paul's; and used for his device, Time bringing Truth to light.

1575. " The Poesies of George Gascoigne Esq;" &c. as p. 978.
1576. " The Steele Glas." &c. ib.
1592. " The wonderfull Combat"* &c. as p. 1101.
1592. " Archaioplutos. Or the riches of elder ages," &c. as p. 1102.
1592. " The masque of the League." &c. ib.
1593. " A Discourse of Horsmanshippe." &c. ib.
1595. " The most honorable Tragedie of Sir Richard Grinuile knight." &c. as p. 1033.
—— " An hundreth sundrie Flowres," &c. as p. 970.

I do not find either book or ballad licensed to him, except the following, viz. In 1556, " The xiij questions composed in the Italen by master John Boccace." See p. 1109.

THOMAS STIRRUP, or STIRROP, stationer,

WAS made free 16 Jan. 1560-1, came on the Livery 7 May 1582, served Renter in 1588, Under Warden in 1592, and again for the remainder of T. Woodcock's time, as p. 1106, Upper Warden in 1596, again 1597. In 1564, he was fined ij s. for quarrelling with Nic. Cleston, who also was fined iv s. at the same time. Again, in 1570, " for keeping his

* This book seems to have occasioned him some trouble; however it gave the Stationers' Company some; for in the Warden's account of expences from 15 July 1592 to 15 July 1593 are the following articles, viz. " John Wolf, 23 Nov. when he rode to Croydon about Dr. Andrews sermons printed for Mr. Smythe, 4 sh.—John Wolf to and fro Lambeth about Dr. Andrews's sermons for Rich. Smythe, who appeared 25 Nov. 10d. —A link for the Mr. and Wardens the same night going to search for Mr. Andrews's bookes." What the result of this was does not appear among the decrees and ordinances of the Company.

his ſhop open on St. Andrew's day, iiijd." Alſo, 12 May 1589, "for not attending my lord maior[p] with the company on Saturday laſt, xijd." Mr. Stirrop was preſent at a Court of Aſſiſtants, 8 Octob. 1599. "Jan. 3. 1599-60. Received the Benevolence of Mrs. Stirrop vpon her huſband's deceaſe, which was p'cell of her loan money."

"The Chriſtian Manuell," &c. as p. 1094. Licenſed. 1576.

"The Caſtell of Chriſtians," &c. as ib. Where the date[q] in the margin is to be corrected. Licenſed. 1577.

He had alſo licenſe, in 1576, for "The Cōmon places of Peter Martyr in Engliſhe of the tranſlation of Mr. Bridge a gent. of Kent." In 1596, "The Accidence and the Grāmer whiche by publique auethoritie are taught in the Scholes," were licenſed to him and Tho. Dawſon as the Wardens of the Company. See p. 1296.—"Preces in vſum ſcholæ Paulinæ." In 1597, (22 Aug.) "The victorie againſt Ryneheck the xxth of Auguſt, 1597. Item, any ballad that ſhalbe made thereof.—Moſt true and moſt admirable Newes, expreſſinge the miraculous preſeruation of a yonge mayden of the towne of Glabbichein in the dukedom of Guliſche/ And of the ſtrange yet worthie execution of Jo. Honauer of Brunholf at Wittemberghe this preſent yere, 1597." In 1599, "Paulinū Catechiſmū."

FRANCIS GODLIFF, or GODLYFE, ſtationer,

WAS made free 20 Jan. 1561-2; but the Regiſter does not inform us by whom. Next year he paid 5*ſh*. for the vſe of the Hall at his marriage; and rented a room therein, at the rate of xiij*ſh*. iiij*d*. per an. In 1564 he was fined for that he "bounde premers in parchmente/ and alſo for that he bounde them vnJuſtely, and contrary to the orders of this howſe, iiij*ſh*." In 1591, he borrowed of the Company £3. 13. 4 on his bond with ſureties, which he paid next year; when the Company returned him the 13ſh 4d. and lent him at the ſame time £7 to pay on the 29th of Sept. but i find no diſcharge of it. He appears to have been in buſineſs in July 1596, when he had an apprentice put over to him.

"The Judgement of God vppon a periured perſon dwelling in Gunne alley in the Pariſhe of Saint Buttolphs, who ripped his own belly: printed for Frances Godliſe, 1577." Maunſell, p. 113. Octavo. 1577.

He had licenſe in 1562, for "The pycture of a monſtrus chylde, which was bourne at Checheſter." Alſo, for ſome ballads at times.

7 R GREGORY

[p] This year the Lord Maior died on the 3d of May, a new one was choſen on the 5th, and probably was ſworn into office on the Saturday preceding this 12th of May. See Stow's Summary of Chronicles.

[q] Maunſell, p. 123, gives the date 1561; but as the dedication is dated in May 1577, without any intimation of a former edition he muſt have been miſtaken. The colophon is dated 1577.

"The Common welth of England," &c. as p. 1228. 1589.

Again, as p. 1288. 1594.

"The Backesliding estate of the world, shewing that the people ware worse and worse, as appeareth in these our last daies." For him. 8°.

He had also licence, in 1579, for "A briefe discours of ẏ impayringe: translated out of Frenche by W. P." In 1591. "Salustius du Bartas his weeke, or Seven Dayes work." In 1599. "Two sermons of Assise, thone a prohibition of Revenge, thother a sweorde of Maintenaunce: by Mr. Westerman."

GABRIEL CAWOOD, stationer,

SECOND son of John Cawood esq; of whom see p. 785, &c. Probably he took up his freedom by Patrimony in the time of the chasm in the Company's register. He came on the Livery 30 July, 1578; served Renter in 1586; Under Warden in 1589, again 1590; Upper Warden in 1593, again 1594; and Master in 1597, again 1599. Sept. 11, 1587, he was fined "For none appearance at a Court holden this day for vrgent busynes, xijd." As this is the only instance, he may be deemed a worthy member of his company, and to have served all their offices with reputation. He lived in St. Paul's Church-yard, at the sign of the Holy Ghost, where his father had dwelt. I do not find any books printed by him, but all that have appeared were printed for him.

"A ryght fruitfull Monition," &c. as p. 796. 1577.

"A Godly treatise—of prayer," *&c.* as p. 980. 1577.

"Euphues. The Anatomy of Wit." &c. as p. 1012. Also without date, or printer's name; but has Rowland Hall's device, as p. 801. Licensed. 1578. 1581.

"The Droomme of Doomes Day." &c. as p. 1224. Also, without date. 1586.

"The second part of the booke of Battailes, fought in our age: Taken out of the best authors and writers in sundrie languages. Published for the profit of those that practise armes, and for the pleasure of such as loue to be harmlesse hearers of bloudie broiles. At London Printed for *him*, 1587." It is introduced by "A preface to the Reader" by the collector and translator of these narratives, which begins with an invective[1] against the printer of the former part. At the end of this preface 1587.

1 "Loe here I present vnto thee (gentle Reader) a continuation of the booke of all the famous Battailes, fought in our age, and I doe hope with better hap than the first came forth, if the Printer haue done his dutie in reforming the faults noted and corrected in his proues. For as for the first part it was so misused mangled and marred by the Printer, I will not saie of purpose, but certes of pride and negligence, that---I would neuer acknowledge it for mine owne, but account it a changeling."

face is the grotesque mask frequently used by T. East, who probably might be the printer of this part. On the back, " Faultes escaped." Then, " A table of the Battailes." C c 2, in fours. Licensed. See p. 971, and p. 990. W.H. Quarto.

1588. " Euphues and his England." &c. as p. 1012. This is printed by T. East, but a different edition from that, which wants the title page.

1592. " Marie Magdalens Funerall teares. By S. W." L. Again, 1594. 8°.

1592. " The true vse of Armorie," &c. as p. 1220. Licensed.

1595. " Saint Peter's Complaint," &c. as p. 1033. L. Again 1599.

1597. " The Decree for Tythes, to bee payde in London. Anno M.D.LXXX. At London, Printed for *him* 1597." 7 leaves. W.H. Sixteens.

—— " Orders—for Orphans and their portions." See p. 1011. W.H. 16°.

—— " The Conuersion of a sinner, exhorting sinners to repentance." 8°.

He had also licenses for the following, viz. In 1581, " Watson's Passions, manifesting the true frenzy of loue." In 1584, " A Comœdie of Titirus and Galathea." See Hist. of Eng. Poetry, III; p. 406. In 1589, " Pollices of Warre, collected out of sundrie authors." In 1592, " Boetius de Consolatione Philosophiæ." In 1594, " Vrbis Hierosolimæ quemadmodũ ea Christi tempore floruit et suburbanorũ eius breuis descriptio, &c. To be printed in English." With Isaac Binge, his brother Warden. Query, if not in their names for the Company.---" La Nobilta del L'asino; di Attabalitta dal Peru prouincia del mondo nouo. To be translated into English." In 1597, " Psalmi, seu precationes D. Juan. Fisheri Roffensis. Accessit imploratio Diuini Auxilij contra tentationẽ, ex Psalmis, Dauid. Per Th. Morum.--- De ciuili & Christiana institutione Liber, Laelio Zeccho Brixiano Theologo & Jur. vtr. Doct. auctore. To be printed in English."

HENRY COCKEN, or COCKYN, stationer,

SON of Henry Cocken of West Ham, Essex, yeoman, was apprenticed to George Buck, for 8 years from the Purification 1564,5; and probably made free in the interval of the chasm in the Company's Register. He succeeded Henry Wykes at the Elephant in Fleet Street.

1577. " Beavtifvll Blossomes gathered by John Byshop from the best trees of all kyndes, Diuine, Philosophicall, Astronomicall, Cosmographical, historical, and Humane that grow, in Greece, Latium and Arabia, and some also in vulgar orchards, as wel frõ those that in auncient time were grafted, as also from them which haue with skilful head and hand beene of late yeares, yea, and in our dayes planted: to the vnspeakable both pleasure and profite of all such as wil vouchsafe fafe to vfe them. The firft Tome* Jmprinted at London for Henrie Cockyn, dwelling in Fleteftreate at the figne of the Elephant, a litle aboue the Conduit. 1577." It has prefixed, "The Author vnto his Booke: borrowed and tranflated out of Martial his epigrammes.---The Authour vnto the Reader.---A Table fhewing what is conteined in euery Chapter of this booke." Befides; 154 leaves, and The errata. W.H. 4°.

It was printed again, or republifhed with the following title, "A GARDEN of recreation plenteoufly furnifhed with all kindes of delectable flowers, tending greatly to the vtilitie and profite of all eftates. Wherein (for the moft parte) is fhewed all the notable actes, endes, and variable chaunces of all the famous Princes that haue reigned thoroughout the world vntill this day, with diuers other pleafaunt varieties, collected out of the moft auncient and beft writers in all ages by John Bifhoppe Gentleman. Imprinted at London for Henrie Cockin, dwelling in Fleeteftreate at—the Elephant, a litle aboue the Conduite. Anno 1578." The prefixes, &c. as in 1577. The Rev. Dr. Farmer, Mafter of Emanuel Coll. Cambr. Quarto. 1578.

THOMAS MAN, ftationer,

THE fon of John Man, of Weftbury in Gloceftershire, Butcher, was apprentice to John Harrifon the elder for 8 years from Midfummer 1567; made free fome time before 17 July 1576; came on the livery 4 July 1586; ferved Renter in 1594; Under Warden in 1597; Upper Warden in 1599; and Mafter in the years 1604, 1610, 1614, 1616. In 1579 he was fined "for keeping his prentice—before he prefented him aboue the tyme appointed by thordinance, v f." Alfo, "for printinge The holie fafte vnduly, and without licence, v f." And he was ordered "no further to deale with thimprintinge of the faid booke: and to pay to Mr. Daie for a recompence x f. To fell this impreffion, and Mr. Daie to be at libertie to enioye the faid copie & and to fell thofe he hath already printed." See p. 668. In 1582, for that he and John Harrifon the younger had begun to print "An Anfwere vnto the Confutation of Iohn Nichols" &c. as p. 1156, xii d. Where by miftake it was placed to John Harrifon the elder. Again, in 1584, "for printing a book diforderly x f. which he promifes to pay next Court Day. Solut. iij f. iiij d. the reft remitted." He dwelt at the Talbot in Paternofter-row. It does not appear that he printed much, if at all, himfelf; moft of the following articles being printed for him, either alone or in fhares: and fometimes

* The author feems to have defigned to continue this work on fufficient encouragement; but does not appear to have done it.

sometimes when the title-page indicates only his name, the license has been granted to him jointly with some other person; and then, when his quota has been worked off, the name of the other inserted in like manner.

1578. "John Fountein his Catechisme, translated by T. W." (*Tho. Wilcox.*) 8º.

(1578.) "A dolorous discourse of a—Bloudy Battel" &c. as p. 1095.

1579. "Thirteene Sermons of Maister John Caluine," &c. as p. 1117.

1579. "Foure Sermons of M. Iohn Caluin," &c. as ib.

1580. "Certayne short Questions and Answeres. Very profitable and necessarye for all yong Children, and such as are desirous to be instructed in the principles of the Christian Fayth. Printed by Hen. Middleton for *him*. 1580." On 8 leaves. Trinity Coll. Camb. Licensed. Again, 1590. Sixteens.

1580. "A Godly and learned sermon," &c. as p. 1059. By Wm.* Fulke.

1580. "A Treatise:—of English Medicines," &c. as ib. Licensed.

1580. "Sermons (22) of Maister Iohn Caluin:" &c. as p. 1118. Licensed.

1581. "A Godly—sermon preached—at Greenwich," &c. as p. 1059.

1581. "An Exposition of the Symbole of the Apostles," &c. as p. 1060.

(1581.) "A Caueat for Parsons Howlet," &c. as p. 1145. Licensed.

1581. "The vnfoldinge of sundrie vntruthes and absurde propositions propounded by one Banister, a fauourer of the Libertins. By Tho. Wilcox." Licensed. Octavo.

1581. "A Glasse for Gamesters, and namely for such as delight in Cardes & Dice, wherein they may see not onely the vanitie, but also the vilenes of those plaies plainly discouered and ouerthrowne by the word of God: by T. W." (*Tho. Wilcox.*) Licensed. Octavo.

1581. "The substance of the Lords Supper shortly and soundly set forth together with the principall pointes in controuersie discussed, by Tho. Wilcox." Licensed. Also without date. It is annexed to Beza's 2 sermons, in 1588. Octavo.

1582. "A—Treatise on 1 Pet. 4, 12—19. By O. Pigge." &c. as p. 1140.

1582. "A treatise of the Church, wherein the godly may discerne the true Church from the Romish, and all other false counterfait Churches, aswell in matters of doctrine as discipline: by Bertrand de Ioques.[a] Translated by T. W." (*Thomas Wilcox.*) With an epistle prefixed; said to be written by John Aylmer, bishop of London, and objected to by the puritans. See A dialogue against bishops: Pub. Libr. Camb. Clas. 19.7.4. Licensed. Octavo.

1583. "Certaine—sermons vpon the 5th Chap. of the Songs of Solomon:—By Bartimeus Andreas." See p. 1140. Sixteens.

1583. "An Answere vnto the confutation of John Nichols," &c. as p. 1156.

1583. A sermon by Eusebius Paget on Gen. 14, 20, 21. What provision ought to be made for ministers. John Wolf, for him. Sixteens.

"A

* Licensed thus in the Register, "Mr. Fulkes sermon preached before the queene in Lent last."

[a] See it printed for Richard Langton, 1581.

" A preparation to the way of Life," &c. as p. 1159. By Wm. Hop- 1583.
kinson.

" A notable—exposition of M. Iohn Knoxes vpon the fourth of (1583.)
Mathew," &c. as p. 1141 Licensed.

" Two Sermons—by Richard Bishop of Chichester," &c. as p. 1203. 1584.

" Amendment of life;—by John Vdall," &c. as p. 1141. 1584.

" A comfortable letter for afflicted consciences, written to a godly man greatly touched that way: by T. W." (*T. Wilcox.*) Sixteens.

" A Compendious Chirurgerie:—by John Banister," &c. as p. 1203. 1585.

" An exposition vppon the Booke of the Canticles, otherwise called 1585.
Schelomons Song. Published for the edification of the Church of God. By T. W." (*Tho. Wilcox.*) Waldegrave's device of the Swan. " Printed for Tho. Man. 1585." Dedicated " To—his very good friendes in Christ, Sir Iohn Brockette and Sir Iohn Cuttes Knights, and M. Charles Morison Esquire.—London, the 25 of this Maie. 1585." Besides; 285 pages. Licensed. W.H. Octavo.

" An A. B. C. for Layemen," &c. as p. 1142. Licensed. 1585.

" A right godly and learned Exposition, vpon the whole Booke of 1586.
Psalmes: Wherein is set forth the true Diuision, Sence, and Doctrine contained in euery Psalme: for the great furtherance and necessarie instruction of euery Christian Reader. Newly and faithfully set forth by a Godly Minister and Preacher of the word of God. 2 Tim. 3 Ver. 16, 17. For the whole Scripture is giuen by inspiration of God, &c. London: Printed for T. Man, and W. Brome 1586." Dedicated " To—his very louing friends in Christ, Walter Herlackinden, and Roger Herlackinden, Esquiers: and Maister William Herlackinden.—At London the 28 of April 1586. Your worships—T. W.---The printers—to al godly and Chrystian readers." Wherein they inform us that the book came into their hands " amongst the writings of that religious and worshipful Gentlemã M. (*Martin*) Herlakinden of Kent, esquier, late deceased," &c. Further, " that the framer of this work—had speciall respect to that english text of the Psalmes and Bible that was Imprinted at Geneua, which was as it shoulde seeme, the first y yere of the raygne of our gracious Queene." Besides; 550 pages; each page having " Fol." before the number. Licensed. W.H. Again 1591, as p. 1246. Quarto.

" A Godly Sermon: Preached at Detford in Kent, on Monday the 1586.
ix of June, in Anno. 1572. At London, Printed for *him*. An. 1586." The text, 1 Cor. vii; 1, 2. Contains C, in eights. W.H. Sixteens.

" Tho. Wilcox, his exposition on the 8 Rom. vers. 19—23. Printed 1587.
for *him*." Maunsell, p. 106, and p. 121. Licensed. Octavo.

" Two—Sermons of M. Beza," &c. as p. 1144. 1588.

" The true remedie against Famine" &c. as p. 1143. Where the date (1588)
in the margin should be as here; being licensed 6 Mar. 1587-8.

" An

y Probably it might have been begun then, but it does not appear to have been printed before 1560. The dedication to the queen is dated 10 April 1560.

1588. "An Admonition out of the Prophet Ioel, concerning that hand of God that of late was vpon vs, and is not cleane taken of as yet. And otherwise also very fitly agreeing (in diuers pointes) vnto these daies wherein we liue. Printed for *him*, and Thom. Gubbin. 1588." By Ed. Bunnie. Maunsell p. 25. Octavo.

1588. "A Treatise of the principles of Christes doctrine, and Antichristes doctrine, with a comparison betweene these two regiments." Ib. p. 3. 16°.

1589. "P. Rami professoris regii Grammatica," &c. as p. 1243.

1589. "The Christian's Sacrifice," &c. as ib. Again, 1591, as p. 1164.

1589. "Prayers by Oliuer Pigge, when the Spaniardes were come to the narrow seas." Octavo.

1589. "Three large letters for instruction and comfort of such as are distressed in conscience by feeling of sinne, and feare of Gods wrath." By Tho. Wilcox. Also without date. Octavo.

1589. "The French Historie of 3 bloodie broiles," &c. See p. 1244.

1589. "A short—Commentarie on the Prouerbs of Salomon," &c. as ib.

1589. "Two Sermons on Peter's fall: the text on S. Mathew and S. Luke conferred, viz. The first, Mat. 26; 34, 35, with Luke 22; 54—58; the second, Mat. 26; 72-74, with Luke 22; 60-62. Wherein we may see the causes of mens falling from God." Octavo.

1589. "The Combat betweene Christ and the Deuill, in 4 sermons on Mat. 4; 1—11." Again without date, as p. 1244.

1589. "Sophronistes. A dialogue" &c. as p. 1245.

1589. "A supplication for the sinfull, to be exhibited by all estates, to the cheefe iudge and redeemer of the world, Christ Jesus, &c. by H. R." Maunsell, p. 87. Licensed. Twelves.

1589. "Iohn Banister his Antidotarie chirurgicall, containing varietie of all sortes of medicines that commonlie fall into the Chirurgians vse, &c." Licensed. Octavo.

1589. "Instructions for the warres," &c. as p. 1243.

1589. "The Practise of Fortification:" &c. as ib.

1590. "Of the markes of the children of God," &c. as p. 1228. Again 1591, as p. 1253; and 1599, as p. 1294.

1591. "Comfort for an afflicted conscience, wherein is contained both consolation and instruction for the sicke, against the fearfull apprehension of their sinnes, of death, of the Deuill, of the curse of the law, and of the anger and iust iudgement of God. By Iohn de l'Espine: translated by Peter Allibond." Octavo.

1591 "A shorte Sōme of the whole Catechisme, gathered by Mr. John Craig minister of the worde of God in Scotland." Licensed in 1581. 8°.

1591. "The preparatiue to marriage." &c. as p. 1254. Licensed.

1591. "Sermons, Vpon the 101 Psalme," &c. as p. 1246.

1592. "A Case of Conscience, &c. By Wm. Perkins." See p. 1247. L.

1592. "Thirteen sermons—By Hen. Smith," &c. as p. 1165. Licensed.

1592. "The Sermons—gathered into one volume," &c. as p. 1247.

1592. "Three Prayers: one for the morning, another for the euening, the third

third for a ficke Man. Whereunto is annexed a godly Letter to a ficke friend: and a comfortable fpeech of a Preacher vpon his death bed. Anno 1591." Device: the loft fheep. 24 Pages. W.H. Octavo.

" A confutation of Popifh tranfubftantiation: alfo a narration how the Maffe was patched together by fundry Popes, and a briefe fumme of the reafons which they render that will not receiue the Maffe: by John de L'Epine; tranflated by Pet. Allibond." Octavo. 1592.

" Nich. Coult his hiftorie of Thomas Didimus incredulitie, being a fermon on the 20 John, ver. 24, 25." Licenfed. Octavo. 1592.

" Jurifprudentiæ Medicinæ & Theologiæ" &c. as p. 1271. 1592.

" Andr. Willet his fermon on Zach. 5; 1—4." Licenfed. Octavo. 1592.

" A Motiue to good workes, wherein is not only fhewed how farre wee are behinde our forefathers in good workes, but alfo many other creatures, in the endes of our creation. With the difference betweene the pretended good woorkes of the Papiftes and—of the Proteftants. By lip Stubs." Licenfed. Octavo. 1592.

" The Seduction of Arthington by Hacket," &c. as p. 1093. (1592.)

" A Commentarie vpon the Lamentations," &c. as p. 1250. 1593.

" Tetraftylon Papifticum," &c. as p. 1235. 1593.

" The—difcouerie of the 3 witches of Warbois," &c. as p. 1250. 1593.

" Spirituall preferuatiues againft the peftilence:" &c. as p. 1255. 1593.

" A Treatife of a Chriftian life, which is an inftruction and patterne to all thofe which profeffe chriftianitie to gouerne their life accordinge to the order of our maifter Chrift. By M. John Caluin: tranflated by John Shutte." Licenfed. Octavo. 1594.

" Sinopfis Papifmi," &c. as p. 1250. Licenfed 1594.

" An Expofition of the Lords Prayer," &c. as ib. Licenfed. 1594.

" The Holy loue of heauenly wifdome. 2. the Epiftle of S. Bafile of a folitarie life. 3. an exhortation to a ciuile life. 4. a meditation on the 7 pfalmes of Dauids repentance. 5. a meditation on the 7 pfalmes of Dauids confolation. 6. a meditation on the Lords praier. 7. a meditation on the Lamentations of Jeremy. 8. the fong of Ezechias. Tranf. by Tho. Stocker." 12°. 1594.

" The Doctrine of the Sabbath," &c. as p. 1250. Licenfed. 1595.

" A fhort—narration of the fearfull fire," &c. as p. 1251. Licenfed. 1595.

" The arraignment and conuiction of vfurie." &c. ib. 1595.

Sermons &c. by Hen. Smith. Maunfell, p. 104, 105. Quarto. 1595.

" A Pleafaunt Satyre or Poefie:" &c. as p. 1251. 1595.

" Wm. Burton his 7 fermons entit. the Rowfing of the fluggard; on Prouerbs 6; 6—11." 1595.

" Wm. Goldfon minifter his Catechifm." Octavo. 1595.

" A fermon of Baptifme by Wm. Hubbock, on 1 Pet. 3; 21, 22." 8°. 1595.

Sermons upon the—Revelation, &c. as p. 1257. Licenfed to him and Toby Cooke. Again 1599; Licenfed to him with R. Field and Felix Kingfton: " Mr. Man to haue one moyte, and Mr. Field & Mr. Kingfton the other moyte thereof." Quarto. 1596.

Lectures on Pro. 22; 6. The vertuous education of youth. Licenfed. Octavo. 1596.

1596. "Certaine Sermons,—By John Vdall." &c. as p. 1286.
1596. "The Order of Houshold instruction:" &c. as p. 1251. Licensed.
1597. "A true Chronologie," &c. as p. 1291. Licensed.
1597. Geo. Gifford's sermons on divers texts of Scripture. See p. 1251.
1597. "A sermon preached by Tho. Wilcox at Southwell, 8 Mar. 1596, on Mat. xi; 28—30." Octavo.
1597. "The Mirror of Honor:" &c. as p. 1251.
1598. "The moral Philosophie of the Stoicks." &c. as p. 1293. Licensed.
1598. "A godlie Forme of Householde Gouernment:" &c. as p. 1294.
1598. "A preparation to the most Holie Ministrie:" &c. as p. 1231.
1598. A Commentary upon the Canticle of Canticles; written in Italian by Ant. Brucioli, translated into English by Tho. James, F. New Coll. Oxford. Licensed Octavo.
1599. "The Sermons of Mr. Henry Smith," &c. as p. 1294.
1600. "A Sermon preached at great Yarmouth," &c. as p. 1301.
1600. "The treasurie of Catechisme," &c. as p. 1260. Licensed.
1600. "A Godly sermon preached before the right worshipfull Edward Coke Esquier, Attorney Generall vnto the Queenes most excellent Maiestie & others of worship in Tittleshall in Norfolke by F. B. (*Francis Bradly*) Imprinted—by Felix Kingston for *him*. 1600." Sir John Fenn.
1600. "A toile for two legged foxes." &c. as p. 1288. Licensed.
—— "A sermon of Election," &c. as p. 1145.
—— "A Worthy Treatise of the eyes," &c. as p. 1144.

He had also licenses to print in 1578, "An hospitall for the diseased;" with Wm. Hoskins: sold afterwards to Edw. White. See p. 1198. In 1579, "A catechisme—for children, which prepare themselues to come to the Holie Scripture: translated by a French copie." Perhaps Fountein's.---"The treatise of the *holy*-Fast:" about which he had a controversy as above, with John Day, who printed it in 1580; but afterwards was turned over to John Harrison jun. and him. In 1580, "A cõmunication betwene a preiste and a gentlemanne.---Pro mildapetti de vnica methodo defensione Contra diplodophilum Cõmentatio Gulielmi Templei a Regio Collegio Cantabrigiensis." In 1581, "Sanitate tuenda medicinæ, pars prima: authore Timotheo Brighto, Medicinæ Doctore.---Beza on Predestination.—Lambertus Danæus on the Lords praier." In 1583, "Medicinę Therapeutice pars, per Timotheũ Brighte.—Logica ad P. Rami Dialecticam conformata, *&c.*---P. Rami—Gramatica, *&c.*---P. Rami—Grãmatica græca," &c. With Wm. Broome. See p. 1203. In 1585, "Senecas tragedies, in Latin.---Chilias secunda—in English." See p. 1203. In 1586, "Mr. Wilcoxe Catechisme." In 1587, "Histoire du grand Royaume de la Chine, translated into English:" with J. Harrison junior." In 1588, "A medytac'on concerning prayers to God for the safetye of England." In 1590, "Le vray Discours: de la victoire merueilleuse obteine par Le Roy de france & de Nauarre Henry Quatrieme en la bataille donne contre les rebelles ligues Pres le bourg D'iury en la Plaine St. André le ix. Mars 1590.---A sermon vpon the wordes that Josyah the sõne of Amon sayd vnto

vnto Judah and Jeruſalem/ with other ſermons thereunto ãnexed." In 1591, " Three ſermons by Hen. Smith, Of Nebuchadnazar, his pride, his fall, and his recovery/ another on the Weddinge garment :" with the conſent of Wm. Wright and Tho. Scarlet." In 1593, " The holie philoſophie, with many other treatiſes of pietie/ A newe edition reviſed and augmented by Thauctor, Wm. du Vaix.". In 1594, " Jacobs Ladder, or the way to Heauen, a ſermon on 1 Cor. 9: 24." In 1595, " The Lawyers queſtion/ The anſwere to it/ The cenſure vpon the anſwere.---Twoo ſermons vpon 1 Peter, 5: 8, 9: wherein is ſhewed that the devill is to be reſiſted onely by a ſtedfaſt faith, howeſoeu' he cometh, either againſt ſoule or bodye." In 1597, " The Colonyes of Bartas, with the cõmentarye of S. G. S. engliſhed and enlarged by Wm. Liſle.---Sermons on the Songe of Salomon: dedicated to the Erle of Eſſex by Geo. Gifford.---The firſte Booke of the Maſſe* and all the partes thereof, ſett forthe by Philip de morney lord of Pleſſes." In 1598, were " aſſigned ou' vnto him, by cõſent of a Court, from Toby Cooke and John Hardie, —Burtons catechiſme. Gods woyng his Churche. 7 ſermons, called Davies evidence. Two ſermons called the caveat for ſuertyſhip. A treatiſe called the concluſion of peace betwene God and man.---Reſponce a l'examen du docteur Boulenger par laquelle ſont Juſtifiees les allegations par luy pretendues ſuneſtes, & verifies ſes calomnies contre la preface du Liure de la Saincte Euchariſtie par Philipe de Mornaye ſeigneur de Pleſſis Marli, &c. To be tranſlated and printed in Engliſh.—Meditations vpon the C1 Pſalme, written firſt in French by Philip de Mornay lord of Pleſſis, and tranſlated into Engliſh by Tho. Wilcox.—Edict du Roy & declaration ſur les precedents edicts de pacification publiè a Paris en parlement, le 25 de Feb. To be printed in Engliſh." In 1599, " Giffords 4 ſermons on 1 Tim. 6, by aſſignment from Toby Cooke, &c.---Les CL. pſeaumes de Dauid mis en Rime Frãcoiſe par Clem. Marot & Theod. de Beza. To be printed in French onely: payinge aliwaies from tyme to tyme 20 ſhillinges at euery impreſſion thereof, as well the firſt as the reſt, to thuſe of the Company.—-Foure ſermons preched by Mr. Ric. Leke at Killington in the barony of Kendall and countie of Weſtm'land, after the great viſitac'on of the peſtilence in that countie: With Hũſr. Lownes.---Verification des lieux impugnez de faux tant en la preface, qu'aux liuures de l'inſtitution de la Saincte Euchariſtie de noſtre Seigneur, par le docteur du Puy, chantre de l'egliſe de Bezas, le docteur Boulenger, & les Theologiens de Bordeaux, en leur diſcouu're, Reſponſe & Jnuentaire: par Meſſure Philippes de Mornay. To be tranſlated into Engliſh, and ſo printed." In 1600, " Newes out of Cheſhire concerning the newe found well."

* Licenſe was afterwards granted to Meſſ. Bing and Ponſonby to print a tranſlation of the ſame book out of French; whereupon a controverſy enſued between Mr. Man and them, which was ſubmitted to the deciſion of the Company; when it was ordered and agreed that the ſaid parties ſhould " parte and partelyke—haue and enioye the ſaid copye nowe and at all tymes hereafter, bearinge ratable charges for the ſame accordingly."

RICHARD SERGIER, or SERGYR, ſtationer,

SON of Thomas Sergyr, late of Naton in Norfolk, yeoman, deceaſed, was apprenticed to Luke Harriſon for 7 years from Midſummer, 1571; and made free 2 Octob. 1578, by Rob. Farmer & his wife, late wife of L. Harriſon.

1579. " An Aunſweare vnto certaine aſſertions, tending to maintaine the Churche of Rome to bee the true—Church." &c. as p. 1116. Licenſed.

1579. " A Confutation of—hereſies—by H. N." &c. as ib. Licenſed.

1579. " A Sermon Preached at Yorke—: By Mathewe Hutton," &c. as p. 1117. Licenſed.

1580. " Papa confutatus." &c. as p. 1120. Licenſed.

1580. " The Pope confuted." &c. as ib.

1582. "—expoſition vpon the prayer of our Lorde," &c. as p. 1060. Where the date in the margin is to be corrected.

1594. " The Preſent ſtate of Spaine." &c. as p. 1208. Licenſed.

He had alſo licenſe, in 1581, for " A ſermon of repentaunce by Arthure Dent," but afterward aſſigned to Mr. John Harriſon the elder.

ABRAHAM KYTSON, or KITSON,

SUCCEEDED Anth. Kytſon, at the ſign of the Sun in St. Paul's Church-yard. See p. 473. He ſeems to have been but a looſe Hand, as in the Wardens account of diſburſements from July 1585, to July 1586 is this charge, " To a purſivant about Kytſon's matter, 10ſ." As he was not free of the Stationers' company he was obliged to have ſuch as were free to print for him. See p. 1138.

1580. " Almanacks for 34 yeeres, with the reuolutions of euery yeere, gathered out of Cipr. Leouitius by Phillip Moore." Octavo.

1581. "—Naturall and Artificiall concluſions:" &c. as p. 840. Sixteens.

1591. " The Aproued order of Marſyall diſcipline, in two Bookes. Newley write by Gilles Claton. Jmprinted by J. G. for Abrã Kitſon, in Paules Churchyard at the—Sun." Bagford's MSS. Quarto.

1593. " A Direction for the Government of the Tongue according to Gods word." A ſhield with S. P. Q. R. on a feſſe, over which is a ducal coronet; St. Peter and St. Paul as ſupporters. " Printed by John Legate Printed to the Univerſitie of Cambridge. And are to be ſolde by Abraham Kitſon at the—Sunne in Paul's Church-yarde in London. 1593." Prefixed is an epiſtle " To the reader—CIͻ.Iͻ.XCII. Decemb. 12. W. Perkins." Beſides; 73 pages. W.H. Octavo.

Legat is ſaid to have printed almanacs for him, as he did for his predeceſſor.

HENRY

HENRY CAR, or CARRE, ſtationer,

SON of John Carre, late of Berwick, draper, was bound apprentice to Henry Kirkham for ſeven years from Michaelmas 1569, and made free 28 Jan. 1576-7. A very orderly member. See p. 1261.

The pain of Pleaſure. In verſe. By Ant. Munday. The Rev. Dr. Farmer, Maſter of Emanuel Coll. Camb. Quarto. 1580.

"Praiers vſed by M. John Caluin" &c. as p. 1136. 1583.

"Gods Judgment ſhewed at Paris Garden," &c. as p. 1141. 1583.

The intended Treaſon of Dr. Parry againſt Q. Elizabeth: with the Pope's letter. For Hen. Carre. See p. 1082. 1584.

"The Theatre of the Popes monarchie, wherein aſwell the vncleane liues of that wicked generation, as alſo their Anti-chriſtian gouernment is deſcribed, &c. by Phil. Stubs." Octavo. 1584.

"Two godly and learned Sermons, made by that famous and woorthy inſtrument in Gods church, M. Iohn Caluin. Which Sermons were long ſince tranſlated out of Latine into Engliſh, by M. Robert Horne late Byſhop of Wincheſter, at what time he ſuffered exile from his Country, for the teſtimony of a good conſcience, as his Apology in the beginning of the booke will witnes. And becauſe theſe Sermons haue long lyen hidden in ſilence, & many godly and religious perſons haue beene very deſirous of them: at their earneſt requeſt they are nowe publiſhed by A. M. At London Printed for Henry Car, and are to be ſold in Paules Churchyard, ouer againſt the ſigne of the blaſing Starre." On the back is the earl of Leiceſter's creſt gartered; over it, "The glory of the Honourable, is the feare of God," and under it, 1584. The dedication is inſcribed to the ſaid "Lord Robert Dudley, Earle of Leiceſter, *&c.*—Anthony Munday." In the firſt ſermon "Chriſtians are admoniſhed to flie outward Idolatrie." Pſal. 16, 3. "I will not communicate with their bloody ſacrifices, neither will I take their names in my mouth." The ſecond is An exhortation to ſuffer perſecution, *&c.* Heb. 13, 13." Contains K, in eights, the laſt leaf blank: and ſignature A has only 4 leaves; the firſt before the title, with only A j, and the fourth blank. W.H. Octavo. 1584.

"Io. Carpenter his ſorrowfull ſong for ſinfull ſoules, compoſed vpon the ſtrange and wonderfull ſhaking of the earth the 6. of Aprill. 1586. printed for Henry Car." Maunſell, p. 28. Octavo. 1586.

"Iſaack Colſe, his ſermon on the 17 of Nouember, 1587, on the 118 pſalme, verſ. 22,—26. For *him*." Ib. p. 98. At Lyd, in Kent. L. 8°. 1587.

"Steph. Iunius his Apologie for Chriſtian ſouldiers, wherein is contained, how we ought to defend by force of Armes, the Church of Chriſt againſt the tiranny of Antichriſt. tranſlated by H. P. Prin. for Henry Carre. 1588" Ib. p. 63. Octavo. 1588.

"A briefe Treatiſe—of the late 14 Traitors," as p. 1174. Licenſed. 1588.

"A Dreame of the Deuill and Diues, moſt terrible and fearful to the ſeruants seruaunts of Sathan, but right comfortable to the children of God. By Thomas Lupton." Ib. p. 46. Dedicated to Fran. E. of Bedford, 1586. For him. Licensed. 6 May 1583; "provided he get the Bishop of Londons allowance to it." Octavo.

1590. "A looking glasse for England, wherein those enormities and foule abuses may most euidently be seene, which are the destruction of euery Christian commonweale, likewise, the meanes to preuent the same, &c. Printed for *him* and Tho. Butter. Ib." p. 61. Octavo.

—— "Tho Settle his Catechisme." For him. Ib. p. 31. Licensed. 22 May, 1587, to him and Hen. Hasselup. Octavo.

He had also licenses for the following. In 1580, "A dialoge betwene Adge & Youthe." In 1581, "A lamentac'on for the deathe of Mr. Christopher Watson, minister." In 1586, "A dolefull ditty of the death of Sir P. Sydne." In 1588, "A miraculous—discourse of a woman" &c. at p. 1054. In 1589, "A thing in prose of the entertaynment of the Scottish king and his Queene at their entring into Scotland, with the Q. cornnac'on." In 1590, "A pleasant ditty, dialoguewise betweene Tarlton's ghost and Robyn good fellowe." Also for many ballads, from 1570 to 1593.

THOMAS GOSSON, stationer,

WAS made free by Thomas Purfoot 4 Feb. 1576-7

1580. "A Contention betweene three Brethren, that is to say, the Whoormonger, the Dronkard, and the Dice-player, to approue which of them three is the worst, By reason that their deceased Father had giuen his succession from the worst of them three. A worke no lesse profitable then pleasurable to read, for so much as the vilenesse of those three vices is herein set out at large. Compiled by Tho. Salter. Tout a l'honneur de Dieu. Imprinted—for *him*, dwelling in Pater noster Roe, next to the signe of the Castell. 1580." Contains 48 leaves. L. 8°.

1580 "A True Report of a straung and monsterous Child, born in Aberwick, in the Parish of Eglingham, in the County of Northumberland, this Fifth of January 1580. London, Imprinted for *him*, dwelling in Pauls Church Yard, neat the Gate, the Corner Shop to Cheapeside, at the Sign of the Goshawke in the Sonn." In the title-page is a portrait of that child, drawn by Raphe Cooke, painter in Berwick upon Tweed. One sheet. See Oldys's Catal. of Pamphlets in the Harl. Libr. No. 517. L.

1591. "Nine obseruations how to read profitably and to vnderstand truely, euery booke, Chapter and verse of the holy Bible: By Edw. Vaughan Printed for Tho. Gossen." Licensed. Octavo.

1592. "Lewes of Granada his exercises" &c. See it under John Perrin.

"The

" The Praise of a good name." &c. as p. 1231. Licensed. 1594.
" Piers Plainnes seauen yeares Prentiship," &c. as p. 1271. 1595.
" The true Copie of a Lamentable Petition" &c. as p. 1272. 1595.
" Geo. Phillips his Aprill of the Church: a sermon on Acts 5; 17 —19." For him. Licensed. Octavo. 1596.

" PLAYES Confuted in fiue Actions, Prouing that they are not to be suffred in a Christian commonweale, by the waye both the Cauils of Thomas Lodge, and the Play of Playes, written in their defence, and other obiections of Players frendes, are truely set downe and directlye aunsweared. By Steph. Gosson, Stud. Oxon. S. Cyprian. Non diserta, sed fortia. London Jmprinted for *him* dwelling in Pater noster row at the signe of the Sunne." Dedicated " To—Sir Francis Walsingham Knt. one of the principall Secretaries to her excellent Maiestie, of her highnesse moste honorable Priuy Counsell, and Chauncellor of the order.— To the—Gentlemen and studentes, of both Vniuersities, and the Innes of Court.—Yours Stephen Gosson." G, in eights, and five leaves before A. Licensed. W.H. Sixteens. —

" A Dolefull Ditty, or sorowfull Sonet of the Lord Darly, sometime King of Scots, Neuew to the Noble and worthy King, King Henry the eyght, and is to be song to the tune of Blacke and yallowe." It begins —

" My hand and pen proceed to write, A wofull tale to tell
My pen it cannot halfe indite, Alas how it befell."

Ends, " Wo worth, wo worth to them alway. Finis. H. C." Licensed, 24 March 1578-9. A broadside.

He had also licenses in 1579, for " Meditac'ons vpon the 32 Psalm." With Mr. Barker; assigned from Toby Cooke. In 1580, " The Curtin of Consolac'on." In 1589, " A manuel of Godly praiers." With the three following articles in p. 1249. In 1593, " The famous Cronicle of Henrie the first, with the life and death of Belliñ Dũn, the firste thief that euer was hanged in England." In 1594. " A true discourse of a most cruell and barbarous murther," &c. as p. 1130.—" Newes from Rome, Venice and Vienna, touchinge the procedinges of the Turke against the Christians in Austria, Hungarie and Heluetia.---Lamentable newes from Cesillia a Island of the Spanish kingis, which lately was assaylled and spoyled in sundrie places by the Turkish gallies, being 107 sayle.—An enterlude of Valentyne and Orson, plaid by hir maiesties Players. With Raffe Hancock." In 1595, " The Cakephachisma doctrinall, and confession of the liguers faithe: translated out of French.— A preparac'on to the Lords supper by Geo. Phillips.---The horrible murder of Tho. Catcher cõmitted by Wm. Norman, with the cõfession aragnement & execuc'on of the said W. Norman." With Toby Cooke. —" The first parte of the famous historye of Chinãn of England." With John Danter. In 1596, " An Exposition on the Lordes praier," &c. as p. 1270. With Wm. Blackwall. In 1598, " Granados spiritual and heavenly exercises," &c. as in 1592. With Mr. Binge, warden. Also for several ballads, at times.

HUGH

HUGH CORNE, ſtationer,

SON of John Corne, late of Kuton, Shropſhire, yeoman, deceaſed, was apprenticed to Tho. Chapman for 8 years from Chriſtmas 1567; and made free 20 Jan. 1577. A very orderly member of his company. See p. 1261.

1580. "The Plowmans* complaint of ſundry wicked liuers, and eſpecially of the bad bringinge vp of children: written in verſe by R. B. prin. for Hugh Corne. 1580." Maunſell p. 81. Licenſed. Octavo.

HENRY TURNER, or TURNOR, ſtationer,

SON of Richard Turner of Sheffield, Yorkſhire, huſbandman, was apprenticed to Tho. Marſhe for 8 years from All-ſaints day 1564; and as his apprenticeſhip expired within the time of the chaſm in the Stationers' Regiſter, he probably was made free within that interval.

1580. "A memoriall of the famous monumentes and charitable Almes deedes of the right worſhipfull Mr. Willm. Lambe eſquier, ſometime gent. of the Chappel in the reign of the moſt renowned kinge Henry theight, &c. late citizen of London, and free of the Right w'ſhipfull cõpany of Clothw'kers, *who* deceaſed the xxi. of Aprill, 1580. By Abr. Fleming."—for him. Licenſed. Mr. Lamb ſtands at the head of the liſt of Benefactors to the worſhipful company of Stationers ſet up in their dining-hall. Octavo.

NICHOLAS LYNGE, or LING, ſtationer,

SON of John Lynge of the city of Norwich, parchment-maker, was bound apprentice to Henry Binneman for 8 years from Michaelmas 1570, made free 19 Jan. 1578-9, and came on the livery 1 July, 1598, but i dont find he ever ſerved any office in the company. In 1584, he was fined for

* Under this character the Religious had been laſhed from Longland's time; here the vicious in general. Maunſell mentions, p. 80. "Pierce plowman in proſe." &c. as p. 876.

for printing Calvin on the Philipians without order, xijd. but it was licensed to him at the same time. In 1593,—for buying and dispersing Psalm-books disorderly printed, iijs. iiijd. Also, in 1600, "—for buying books of Humors letting blood in the head vayne, beinge newe printed after it was forbydden & burnt, ijs. vjd." He dwelt sometime at the West end of St. Paul's church yard, at the sign of the Mermaid; afterwards in St. Dunstan's church-yard.

"A warning to the wife," &c. as p. 891. 1580.

"The English Romayne lyfe:" &c. as p. 1096. 1582.

"A commentarie of Iohn Calvine vpon the Epistle of Paule vnto the Philippians." This is the head title; my copy wanting the title-page and prefixes. Maunsell says it was translated by Wm. Becket. Licensed. W.H. Quarto. 1584.

"Amendment of life—by John Vdall." &c. as p. 1141. 1584.

"Peters fall. Two sermons—by John Vdall," &c. as p. 1224. 1584.

"An exhortation and fruitful admonition to vertuous parentes and modest Matrones, to the bringing vp of their children in godly Education and houshold discipline: by R. G." For him. Octavo. 1584.

"A fruitfull sermon—by Henrie Smith:" &c. as p. 1113. Licensed.

"The Affinitie of the faithfull." &c. ib. 1591.

"Euphues shadow" &c. as p. 1301. 1592.

"The Triumphs ouer Death:" &c. as p. 1289. 1595.

"Pierce Pennilesse his Supplication to the Diuell. Barbaria grandis habere nihil. Written by Tho. Nash, Gent." Ling's device. "London. Printed for *him*, and are to be sold at his shop, at the Northwest doore of S. Paules. 1595." J, in fours. Colophon. "Imprinted by T. C. for *him*." See p. 1049 and 1163. Quarto. 1595.

"The Tragicall Legend of Robert, D. of Normandy, surnamed short thighe, eldest son of William the Conqueror." See p. 1033. L. 1596.

"Politeuphnia. Wits commonwealth." &c. as p. 1034. Licensed. 1598.

"Wits Theater of the little World," &c. as p. 1035. 1598.

"Three sermons by M. Hen. Smith." &c. as ib. 1599.

"Nashes Lenten Stuffe, Containing the Description and first Procreation and Increase of the towne of Great Yarmouth, in Norffolke: With a new Play neuer played before, of the praise of the Red Herring. Fitte of all Clearkes of Noblemens Kitchins to be read: and not vnnecessary by all Seruing men, that haue short boord-wages to be remembred. Famam peto per vndas. London, printed for N. L. and C. B. and are to be sold at the west end of Paules, 1599." Dedicated "To his worthie good patron, Lustie Humfrey, according as the townsmen doo christen him, little Numphs as the nobilitie and Courtiers do name him, and Honest Humfrey, as all his friendes and acquaintance esteeme him, King of the Tobacconists hic & ubique, and a singular Mecænas to the Pipe and the Tabour (as his patient liuery attendant can witnesse) his bounded orator T. N. most prostrately offers vp his tribute of inke and paper.—Yours for a whole last of redde Herrings. Th. Nashe.—To his 1599.

Readers hee cares not what they be." Besides: 75 pages. Concludes with, "But no more winde will I spend on it but this, Saint Denis for Fraunce, S. James for Spaine, S. Patrike for Ireland, S. George for England, and the red Herring for Yarmouth." Quarto.

1600. "England's Parnassus:" &c. as p. 899; but it ought not to have been inserted there, being licensed to "Mr. Lynge, Mr. Burby & Tho. Haies." The title-page in Mr. Mason's copy and mine giving only the initial letters, and not having seen the Stat. Register C. at the time that sheet was printed, i presumed the T. H. to indicate Tho. Hacket, he being the only printer to whom they then appeared applicable. There were three or four editions of the book about this time. 8°.

—— "Doomes Day book, or Alarum for Atheistes, by Sam. Gardiner."

—— "The Combate betweene Christ and the Deuill displayed: or a Commentarie vpon the Temptations of Christ: Preached in Cambridge by that reuerend and iudicious Diuine M. William Perkins." See it in his Works, Vol. III. My copy has no title-page or other prefixture whereby to ascertain the author, printer, or date of this book, but has on the outer leaf the stamp of a shield with a tasselled cord knotted, N on one side, L on the other, by which i suppose it to have been printed for him. W.H. Quarto.

He had licenses also to print, in 1582, "A woofull warning to our wanton willes, &c.---Billes for the shippinge of marchants goodes, &c." In 1590, "Euphues golden legacye" &c. as p. 1302. In 1591, "A sermon by Mr. Heurye Smithe vppon Luke viii; 19—21." In 1593, "Pierse Gaviston Erle of Cornewall his life," &c. as p. 1302. "A book called Cornelia," &c. as ib.—"The famouse tragedie of the Riche Jewe of Malta." With Tho. Millington.---"Ideas myrrour, &c.---A spiders webbe." In 1596, "Orchestra, or a poeme of Dauncinge." In 1597, "England's Heroicall Epistles by Michaell Drayton.—Wittes cōmonwealthe.—A book called The figure of Foure." In 1598, "A shadowe of truthe in certaine epigrās and satyres.---Rodomanthus infernall, or the Devill conquered.---Ariastos conclusions of the marriage of Rogero and Rodomantho, the never conquered Pagan; Written in Frenche by Phillip de Portes, and paraphrastically translated by G. M.---The portrature of the Prodigall sōne." In 1599, "The Harmonie of the Holy Scriptures, with the seu'all sentences of sundry wryters, &c.---The Legend of Hūfrey duke of Gloucester, by Chr. Middleton.---The straūge fortunes of twoo excellent prynces in yeir lyves and loves to their Ladies, in all the tides of true honor.--Kemps morris to Norwiche." Val. Simmes printed for him in 1607.

JOHN PERIN, or PERRIN, stationer,

AT the Angel in St. Paul's Church-yard, was made free by Francis Coldock, 18 Jan. 1579-80.

A posie

A posie of Gilly flowers by Hum. Gifford. For him. Licensed. 4°. 1580.
"The rooting out of the Romishe Supremacie:" &c. as p. 1058. L. 1580.
"A Godlie and profitable treatise, conteining a declaration of Christe (1582.)
and his Office. Compiled 1547 by the reuerend father, and faithfull Minister of Christe, and constant martyre in the truthe Maister Ihon Hoper: and newly corrected, and purged by the Godlie industrie of C. R. from a multitude of grosse faultes, where withall it was pestered, through the corruption of the print, and greate vnskilfulnesse of the Printer, beyng a mā of an other Nation. Matth. vii. This is my beloued sonne—, heare hym. Imprinted at London for Ihon Perrin, and are to be sold at his shop in Paules Churchyard at the Signe of the Aungell." Dedicated "To Edwarde Seimer Earle of Hertforde," &c. Wherein we are informed that it was then about 35 years since it was printed *at* [a] *Zurych.*— "Christofer Rosdell.---To the most noble and victorious Prince Edwarde Duke of Somerset: Erle of Hertforde, *&c.*—Ihon Hooper." L 4, in twelves, half sheets. My copy wants the last leaf, which probably might give the printer's name, and date. Licensed. W.H. 24°.
"The Worlde possessed with Deuils," &c. as p. 1124. Both parts. L. 1583.
"Confutation of the Popes Cannons, viz. 1. Of the Supper. 2. Of 1585.
the only mediatour. 3. Of Purgatory. 4. Of the councell of Toleta. 5. Of confession to God. 6. Of the Church. 7. Of free will. 8. Of marriage and vowes. 9. Of fasting and meates. 10. Of Images. By Theod. Beza; translated by Tho. Stocker Gent. Printed for Io. Perrin. 1585." Maunsell, p. 10. See it in 1587.
"The Vertue of Balsame, with an instruction for those that haue 1585.
their health to preserue the same: also Doctor Bulleins dyet.—for John Perin 1585." Octavo.
A sermon before the queen on Mat. 16; 17—19. Octavo. 1585.
Another, on Mark 14; 66—72. Octavo. 1586.
"The Englishman's Treasure:" &c. as p. 1237. 1587.
"The Popes Canons: VVherein the Venerable and great Masters of 1587.
the Romish Church are confuted in these ten discourses following, with diuers other matters, as appeareth in the Page next ensuing. Of the holy Supper. Of the one onely Mediatour. Of Purgatory. Of the councell of Tollete. Of the confession vnto God. Of the Church. Of Free-will. Of Mariage and Vowes. Of Fasting and Meates. Of Images. Written in the French tongue by Theodore de Beza, and translated into English by T. S. Gentleman. Beware of false Prophets *&c.* Mat. 7. c. verse 15. Seene and allowed *&c.* Imprinted—by George Robinson for Iohn Perin,—in Paules Church-yard, at—the Angell, and are there to be sould. 1587." Dedicated "To—Sir William VValdgraue Knight.—London this 10 day of Nouember 1584.—T. S." *(Tho. Stocker.)* Contains G, in eights. W.H. Sixteens.
"The Coronation of Dauid:" &c. as p. 1242. Licensed. 1588.
"The Serpent of Deuision. Wherein is conteined the true History 1590.
or Mappe of Romes ouerthrowe, gouerned by Auarice, Enuye, and Pride, the decaye of Empires be they neuer so sure.

7 T 2 Three

[a] See our General History, An. 1547.

Three thinges brought ruine vnto Rome,
  that raignde in Parces to their ouerthrowe:
Auarice and Pride, with Enuies cruell doome,
  that wrought their sorrow and their latest woe.
England take heede, such chaunce to thee may come
Fœlix quem faciunt aliena pericula cautum.

Whereunto is annexed[c] the Tragedye of Gorboduc, sometime King of this Land, and of his two Sonnes, Ferrex and Porrex. Set foorth as the same was shewed before the Queenes most excellent Maiesty, by the Gentlemen of the Inner Temple. At London. Printed by Edward Allde, for John Perrin, and are to be sold in Paules Church yard, at the signe of the Angell. 1590." Prefixed is an epistle "To the Gentlemen Readers." The Serpent of Deuision concludes on C 4. W.H. Quarto.

1591. " D. Saravia. Of the – Ministers of the Gospell." &c. as p. 1178.

1591. " The trumpet of the Soule sounding to iudgement." A sermon by Henry Smith on Eccl. 11 9. Licensed. Sixteens.

1592. " Lewes of Granada his exercises of praiers and meditations, containing 14 meditations; 7 for morning, and 7 for euening: also a treatise of consideration and praier. Translated *by Richard Hopkins.* Printed for Tho. Gosson and *him*, "1592." Licensed. Twenty-fours.

—— " William Chancie Esq; of the Conuersion of a Gentleman misled in Poperie to the true and sincere profession of the Gospell, with an exhortation to his countreymen to embrace this truth. Printed for *him*." 4°.

—— " John Marconuile, of the good and euill tonge, with the vnstablenes of the same, also the abuses thereof, also the punishmentes of God against swearers and periured persons." For him. Octavo.

He had also licenses in 1579 "for Maclins mishappe." In 1580, "The copie of a letter sente out of Ireland." In 1581, "A shadowe of Samazar, the noble Neapolitane." In 1586, "Strange newes out of Calabria, prognosticated—vpon the yere 1587." In 1587, "The hystorye of Apolonius and Camilla." In 1590, "The Tectonicon."

HANS, or JOHN STELL, or STILL.

1580. " The Bee hive of the Romishe Churche." &c. as p. 1119. Licensed.[e]

1590. " Swithune Butterfield his Catechisme, or Principles of the true Christian Religion, briefly selected out of many good books. Printed for John Still. 1590." Octavo.

In 1568 he had license with one Arnold Van Gulke for "An Almanacke in Duche." Sept. 5, 1580 is this entry: "Hans Stell. Rec'd of him for the content of the world, xijd."[d]

WILLIAM

[c] My Copy is without the Tragedy of Gorboduc; but that is reprinted in Dodsley's Collection of old plays, Vol. II.

[d] See it in our General History, under 1580.

[e] To him by the name of John Skall.

WILLIAM WRIGHT, or WRYGHTE, stationer,

SON of Matthew Wryghte of London, carpenter, deceased, was bound apprentice to Anne Heister for ten years from St. Bart. 1564, and seems to have been made free of the Stationers' Company in the interval of the chasm in their Register. I find also among the Decrees &c. in April 1584, a matter in controversy between one Mr.—Wright, Draper, and Mr.—Dawson and his partners in Seres's Privilege for Primers; but besides the omission of the Christian name, he must have been a different person from the above-mentioned William Wright, who bound apprentices, both before and after that time, in the Stationers' Company, and therefore most probably was the same for whom the following articles were printed and licensed.

"A breefe discourse of the taking Edm. Campion and diuers other Papists in Barkeshire, &c. Gathered by A. M." *(Anth. Munday)* For him. Licensed. Octavo. 1581.

"Two Judgments of God, one vpon a wicked Blasphemer in Lincolnshire: the other vpon Joane Bowser in Leicestershire to whom the Deuill appeared. Written by Philip Stubbs." 1581.

"A breefe and true reporte of the Execution of certaine Traytours at Tiborne, the xxviii, and xxx dayes of Maye, 1582. Gathered by A. M. who was there present. Honos alit Artes. ¶ The names of them executed on Monday, the xxviii. of Maye. Thomas Foord. Iohn Shert. Robert Iohnson. ¶ The names of them executed on Wednesday, the xxx. of Maye. VVilliam Filbie. Luke Kirbie. Lawrance Richardson. Thomas Cottom. Imprinted at London for William[f] VVright, and are to be solde at his shop adioyning vnto S. Mildreds Church in the Poultrie, the middle shop in the rowe. 1582." Dedicated "To the godly and woorshipfull Maister Richard Martin, Sherife, and one of the—Aldermen of this Cittie of London.—A. Munday." 10 leaves. "God saue the Queene." Licensed. W.H. Quarto. 1582.

"The second part of the Anatomie of abuses." For him. L. 8°. 1583.

"A Plaine Confutation of a treatise of Brovvnisme," &c. as p. 1164. 1590.

The Wedding Garment, by Hen. Smith. For him. L. Sixteens. 1590.

"The Royal Exchange. Contayning sundry Aphorismes of Phylosophie, and golden principles of Morrall and naturall Quadruplicities. Vnder pleasant and effectuall sentences, dyscouering such strange definitions, deuisions, and distinctions of vertue and vice, as may please the grauest Citizens, or youngest Courtiers. Fyrst written in Italian, and dedicated to the Signorie of Venice, nowe translated into English, and offered to the Cittie of London. Rob. Greene, in Artibus Magister. At London, Printed by J. Charlewood[g] for *him*. Anno Dom. 1590." Dedicated "To—Sir Iohn Hart, Knight, Lorde Mayor of the Cittie of London 1590.

[f] See p. 1166. [g] It was omitted by overfight under his name.

London: and to—Mr. Richard Gurney, and Mr. Stephen Soame, Sheriffes of the same Cittie—Rob. Greene.---To the—Citizens of the Cittie of London." Besides; J, in fours. W.H. Quarto.

1591. " The Pride of King Nabuchadnezzar." &c. as p. 1164.

1591. " The Restitution of King Nabuchadnezzar." &c. ib.

1591. " Newes from Scotland, Declaring the Damnable life and death of Doctor Fian, a notable Sorcerer, who was burned at Edenbrough in January last, 1591. Which Doctor was regester to the Diuell, that sundry times preached at North Barrick Kirke to a number of notorious Witches. With a true examination of the saide Doctor and Witches, as they vttered them in the presence of the Scottish King. Discouering how they pretended to bewitch and drowne his Maiestie in the Sea cōming from Denmarke, with such other wonderfull matters as the like has not been heard of at any time. Published according to the Scottish Coppie." For him. D, in fours, with cuts. Richard Gough, Esq; 4°.

1591. " The Rare Trauailes of Iob Hortop, an Englishman, who was not heard of in three and twentie yeeres space. Wherein is declared the dangers he escaped in his [b]voyage to Gynnie, where after he was set ashoare in a wildernesse neere to Panico, hee endured much slauerie and bondage in the Spanish Galley. Wherein also he discouereth many strange and wonderfull things seene in the time of his trauaile, as well concerning wilde and sauage people, as also of sundrie monstrous beasts, fishes and foules, and also Trees of wonderfull forme and qualitie." For him. Dedicated to the queen. C, in fours. Licensed. Quarto.

(1591.) " Newes from France." &c. as p. 1165.

1592. " The second and last part of Conny-catching," &c. as p. 1180.

1592. " Greenes Groats worth of witte bought with a million of Repentance." Licensed. Sir John Fenn. Quarto.

—— " Kinde Harts Dreame. Containing five Apparitions with their Inuectiues against abuses raigning. Deliuered by seuerall Ghosts vnto him to be publisht after Piers Penilesse Post had refused the carriage. Inuita Inuidia. By H. C." *(Hen. Chettle.)* Licensed. 1592. Hist. of Eng. Poetry, III, 291. Quarto.

—— " The Garden of felicity, containing most godly prayers and confessions to be vsed for the sicke, with diuers comfortable consolations to perswade them to be willing to die and not to feare death." For him and Tho. Butter. Licensed. 1582. Twenty-fours.

—— " Leon. Fioruante, his ioyfull Iewel, containing excellent orders, and preseruatiues against the Plague, as also marueilous Medicines for diuers maladies being his owne inuention translated by Ioh. Hester." For him. Licensed. 1579. Quarto.

He had also licenses for the following articles. In 1579, " A dolefull discourse of a mayd ỳ suffred at Westminster for buryinge hir child quicke.---An example by ỳ deathe of M'maduke Glou'.---A rufull report

[b] Of which Sir John Haukins was general.

report of ỹ grieuous mischance.—A viewe of examples meete to be perused of all faithfull Christians.---Three sundry wonders that chaũced of late." In 1580, " A true Report happened in Germany at Melwing by a mayd 14 yeres old.—William Witte, wittes will, or wills witt, chuse you whether." In 1588, " A farewell entitled to the famous generalls of our English forces, Sir John Norreys and Sir Francis Drake knights, &c. done by Geo. Peele." In 1589, " Strange newes from Hanborough.---A recitall touching the cause of Bales, a seminary priest, who was hanged and quartered in Fleetstrete on ashwensday: whereunto is added the true cause of the death of Annys (*Agnes*) Bankyn, who the same day was burnt in St. Georges Feild.—The copie of a l're concernyng the French king his victory against *the* Duke de Mayn, and the Romishe Rebels.---A triumphant dittie, shewing the victories of the French king, the wyning of the Subburbes of Parris, the Joyes of his frendes, and the fightes in the ayre.—An epitaphe in verse vpon the complaint of the people for the death of Sir Fr. Walsingham.---The trauelles of Edward Webber.--A mournfull ditty on the deathe of certen Judges and Justices of the peace and diu'se other gent. whoe dyed ymediatelie after the assises holden at Lyncolne laste paste.—An excellent ditty made vpon the arryuall of the king of Skottes with his ladye from Denmarke vppon Maye daie laste with her Coronac'on." In 1590, " The fight on the sea by 10 m'chantes shippes of London against 12 Spanishe gallies which assalted them in the Straightes of Jublitor, where the Spaniards with their gallies were spoyled, &c. With a recitall of the newes of the Abraham and the Red Lyon, with their fight against 10 gallies whom they mightely spoiled.---The copie of a l're sent into England by a gent. from the towne of St. Denys in Fraũce, wherein is set forthe the good successe of the kingis maiesties forces against the leguers and Pr. of Parmas power, with the taking a conuoy of victualls sent to Paris, and the miserable estate of Paris at this presente.—The true newes fraũce broughte by the laste poste, the 23 of Sept. 1590.---The description of the holieleage, both when yt was in his pride, and also since in his fall, &c.—A rare and due cõmendac'on of the quenes most excellẽt maiestie, with the happie and blessed estate of England: and how God hath blessed her highnes from tyme to tyme.—The strange and greuous martirdome of Thomas Williams an Englisheman, done in the towne of Dunkerk vppon the 13 Jan. 1590.—Fraũcis Fayre Weather.—A wonderfull and true reporte of strange Birdes seene in Flaũders, neere vnto the Cittie of Gaũt, &c." In 1591, " The ou'throwe of the Duke of Sauoye the 18 of Sept. 1591.---A fygge for the Spanyard." In 1594, " Newes from the Leuant seas." Also, for several ballads, at times.

THOMAS

THOMAS BUTTER, stationer.

SON of Robert Butter, late of Ludlow, Salop, yeoman, deceased, was apprenticed in 1564 to William Norton for 10 years from St. Bartholomew's. Probably he took up his freedom in the time of the chasm in the Company's Register. He was fined, 4 Sept. 1581, for having a book printed without the Wardens Hands to it, ijsh. vid; and Tho. Dawson was fined in the same sum for printing it for him. Again, 19 Apr. 1585-6, he was fined ijsh. vid. for keeping an apprentice unpresented, contrary to orders. He seems to have been succeeded by his widow in 1589, for whom Dr. Andrews's sermon on 1 Tim. 6; 17—19, was printed according to Maunsell,[1] p. 96. His son Nathaniel was made free by her, 20 Feb. 1603-4, by the name of Mrs. Newbie, late wife of Tho. Butter.

1581. " John Niccols Pilgrimage," &c. as p. 1121. Licensed.

1583. " The great Cicle of Easter:" &c. as p. 1097.

1584. A sermon of Magistracy, on Deut. 10; 18, by John Stockwood 8°.

1588. " An admonition to all Ploughholders, exhorting them to hold fast, and to labour therein diligently, for the Harvest wil come shortly, &c. by J. H." For him. Octavo.

1588. " Three sermons on James 1; 9, 10, wherein the different states of the poor and rich man are cōpared; preached at Cicester, by Phill. Jones, preacher there. Dedicated to John bishop of Glocester, and commendatory of Bristow." For him. Licensed. Octavo.

1590. " A looking glasse for England," &c. as p. 1338.

—— " The Garden of Felicity," &c. as p. 1346. Licensed, 1582.

He had also licenses for the following, viz. In 1579 " The Triall of truethe." See p. 1120. In 1580, " A petie schole of spellinge and writinge Englishe.---Certaine notes howe Reuerie māne maye trie themselues whether they be the children of God or noe." In 1581, " Morall Documentes by Wm. Wollock." In 1583, " An admonition, written by Paule vnto Timothie, iij chapt. wherein he declareth the manners of men in these latter daies."

JOHANE BUTTER, his widow.

1589. " Lanc. Andrewes Doctor, his [k]Sermons, published without his consent, on 1 Tim. 6. ver. 17. 18. 19. printed for VViddow Butter. 1589." Maunsell p. 96. Octavo.

1590. " A looking glasse for England,—Printed for Henry Carre and Tho.[l] Butter. 1590." Maunsell, p. 68.

She

[1] And yet, in p. 68 he mentions the " Looking glasse for England—printed for Hen. Carre and Tho. Butter, 1590." See p. 1338.

[k] Preached at St. Mary's Hospital, the 10th of April, 1588, being Wednesday in Easter-week.

[l] This must be a mistake; either by Maunsell, or by the printer of this book, in omitting *the widow of* before Tho. Butter; or somewhat of like purport.

She had license 9 July 1590 for "A lamentable reporte of a greate tempeste of haile that fell in Kent, 19 June 1590." Also, 24 Aug. 1592, "A sermon of M. Andrewes called the Richmans Scripture." Licensed by the bishop of London. In 1594, "A true report of the baptisme of the prince in Scotland.---The tryumphant and princelie newe ballad, declaringe the royaltie and magnificence performed at the baptisme of the Prince of Scotland."

RICHARD LANGTON.

"A Treatise of the Churche, conteining a true discourse, to knowe the true Church by, and to discerne it from the Romish Church, and all other false assemblies, or counterfet congregations. Written by M. Bertrande de Loque of Dolphinee, and dedicated vnto my Lord the Vicount of Turenne. And faithfully translated out of French into English by T. W. Imprinted at London, for Richard Langton, dwelling in Swythins Lane: and there they are to be solde. 1581." Prefixed are "The Summe of the Chapters &c.---To—Lorde Henry de la Tour, Vicount of Turenne, Countie of Monfort, Baron Mongacon, Oliergues, Bonfolz, Fey, Seruissac, Croe, &c. Captaine of fiue hundred men at armes of the kings armies.—From Turenne this xxv. of March, 1577.—Bertrand de Loque.---An admonition to the Reader." Besides, 384 pages, and a Table. W.H. See it printed for Tho. Man, 1582. Sixteens. 1581.

GEORGE PENNE, or PEN, stationer,

SON of Thomas Penne of Hackesburye, Glocestershire, weaver, deceased, was apprenticed to John Day for 7 years from All Saints, 1564, and probably made free in the interval of the chasm in the Company's Register.

"A Compendium of the rationall Secretes" &c. as p. 841. Licensed. 1582.

"Food for Families" &c. See it under Ralph Jackson.

He had also license in 1589 for "A methode to teach to write in shorte tyme: provided that if this copy apperteyne to any other, Then this Entrance to be voide."

THOMAS NELSON, stationer,

WAS made free by Mr. Dewce *(Gerrard Dewes)* 8 October, 1580. He dwelt against the great South door of St. Paul's.

1584. "The Judgement of God vpon a man that forsware himselfe at Warminster in the Countie of Wilt. 1584." For him. Octavo.

1585. "An account of Margaret Hacket a notorious witch, who consumed a young man to death, rotted his bowells and back bone assunder, who was executed at Tiborn 19 Feb. 1585. Printed for *him* and Tho. Law."

1590. "The miserable estate of Parris, with strange visions lately seene in the ayre vpon the coastes of Brittayne," &c. Licensed.

This was censored in p. 75 of a libel, entitled "A declaration of the true causes of the great troubles, presupposed to be intended against the realme of England, 1592;" of which Parsons the jesuit is supposed to have been the author. It attributes to Nelson the printing also of another tract in 1591; but i have not met with any other account of it: "And whereas there was one Caçalla and others of his company executed for Heresy and Apostasie at Validolid in Spaine 30 yeares past: the manner of this execution is an English libell newly set foorth, and said to be for the profession of the Gospell, and to be donne but late." See our general History, under 1592.

1591. "TRVE Intelligence sent from a Gentleman of Account. Concerning, The estate of the English forces now in Fraunce, vnder the Conduct of the Right Honorable the Earle of Essex. Particularly expressing what hath been doone since his departure from England, vntill the second of September last, 1591." Device: a mask. "Printed for *him*, and are to be solde at his shop—1591." Concludes on p. 8, "From Arques this 2. of September, 1591. Your louing friend and nephew, Fabian Johnson." Quarto.

1591. News from Scotland, &c. See Gent. Magazine, for Aug. 1779; p. 393. It was also printed for Will. Wright. See p. 1340. Query, whether the same edition; each having his own name only to his proper quota?

1592. "A notable Discouery of Coosenage." &c. as p. 1165. Licensed.

He had also licences for the following, viz. In 1586, "A prayer or thankesgyuing made by the prysoners of Ludgate in the 29th yere of the quenes Reign.---An inuectiue agaynst Ballard and Babington, and other their adherentes, discou'ing their treasons, and the treacheries of the Scottyshe quene, and the sentẽce pronounced against her at Foderinghay: set furth by W. K." See p. 1046. In 1588, "Certen poesies vpon the playing Cards.---An excellent dyttie of the Quenes cõming to Paules Crosse the 24th daie of Nouember, 1588." In 1589, "Newes from Rome, Spayne, Palermo, Geneuæ & Fraunce, with the miserable estate of the Citie of Parris, and the late yeilding vp of sundrie Townes of great strength vnto the King: translated out of Jtalyan and French into English.---Comucopia, or the Royall Exchange.---A futile practise wrought in Parris by frere Fraunceis against frere Donnet concerning a Nunne, &c." In 1590, "A dittie of the fight vppon the seas the 4. of June last in the straytes of Jubraltare, betwene the George and the Thomas Bonauenture and viij gallies with three fregates.—To be printed in Fr. and Eng.

Eng. Ce qui est aduenneu la traicte de Duc de Parma depuis le 10 Nouembre Jusques au 27 dudict mois 1590, Auec les novelles d'Auphine." In 1591, "A maydens dreame vpon the Death of my late Lord Chancelor.---The Pathwaie to knowledge, teaching the perfect worke and practise of Arethmetick in whole nõbers and fractions both by pen and coũters, together with the order and mãner of kepinge a m'chantes booke by waye of Debitor and Creditor/ Where vnto is ãnexed the second parte of Arethmetick truly layeinge open the rules of Algebre, Cossick number, and the extraction of Rootes, with the booke of Geometry and mathematicall examples/ set forth by Nicholaus Peters de Daventer. Provided" &c. In 1592, "Good Councell against the Plague." Also, for several ballads, at times.

SAMPSON CLARKE, stationer,

SEEMS to have been bound apprentice to Geo. Buck, and turned over to W. Broome, in the time of the chasm in the Stationers' Register; however he was made free by them, 26 March, 1583; and came on the livery 1 July, 1598.

"Tho. Lodge Gentleman his Alarum against Vserers, containing tried experiences against worldly abuses: also the Historie of Forbonius and Prisceria, with truthes complaint ouer England.—for *him*, 1584." Maunsell, p. 120. Quarto. 1584.

King John, 2 parts.—for him. Steevens on Shakspeare, p. 235. 4°. 1591.

He had also licenses for the following, viz. In 1587, "An enemy to nature." In 1589, "Menophon Camillus alarum to slumbering Ephewes in his melancholy cell Silexedria."

YARATH JAMES.

"A Godly learned and fruitfull Sermon Made vpon the Fourteenth of John, (v. 23.) in which is plainely set fourth the true looue of Christ, the markes wherby the Children of God are knowen, and the comoditie which that looue bringeth. By D.S. 1584. John 15. 13. Christ so deerly loued vs that he gaue his life for vs. At London Printed for Yarath Iames, and are to be solde in Newgate Market over against Christe Church-gate." Dedicated "To—William Pelham Knight, Liestenant of the Queenes Maiesties Ordinaunce, &c.—John Iordan." Who declares he put it to print, though the author was unknown to him, on account of its excellency. Contains C 4, in eights. The first leaf with only signature A. W.H. Sixteens. (1584.)

"The Haven of Hope:" &c. as p. 1211. 1585.

He had alſo licenſes for the following, viz. in 1580, "The Parlour of pleaſaunt Delights." In 1582, The hiſtory of Semerides, declaring the fall of his inordinate life, where vnto is ioyned The tryumphe of Truthe, &c." Alſo for ſundry ballads to the year 1586.

WALTER MANTELL, ſtationer,

WAS made free by Francis Godliff 21 Jan. 1582-3.

1585. "A prayer for the preſeruation of the Earle of Leiceſter, Lieutenant General of her Maieſties Army in the Low Countries. Printed—by *him*, 1585." Quarto.

THOMAS LAWE, ſtationer,

Was made free 18 Feb. 1583-4, by William Seres ſen.

1585. "An account of Margaret Hacket" &c. as p. 1350.

1589. "The execution of three notorious witches at Chelmisford ſizes laſt." Stat. Reg. B. fol. 246. See p. 1198. where the date 1579 muſt be a miſtake.

JOHN WINNINGTON, ſtationer,

SON of Gilbert Winnington of Terne, Salop, Carpenter, was bound to Richard Watkins for 8 years from St. Bartholomew's day 1578; with this memorandum annexed: Ordered and agreed that he ſhall ſerve his whole apprenticeſhip with Andrew Maunſell, Draper, exerciſing the art of a Stationer. He was made free by Mr. Watkins 5 Sept. 1586.

(1582.) "John Holme, his ſermon on 6 Gallath. verſ. 1. Printed for *him*, *1582." Maunſell, p. 120. Octavo.

1587. "A Sermon—at the Courte at Greenevviche," &c. as p. 1226. Alſo, without date. Maunſell, p. 106.

1588. "The Reſtitution of a ſinner, entituled the reſtoration againe of him that is fallen, by St. John Chriſoſtome; tranſlated by Robert Wolcombe." See a former tranſlation, p. 828. Twenty-fours.

1589. "A Maruaile deciphered, being an expoſition on the 12 Chapter of the Reuelation: by E. H. Printed for *him* 1589." Quarto.

"—diſ-

* This date is probably a miſtake, as his apprenticeſhip was not expired.

" —discouerie of the three witches of Warbois" &c. as p. 1250. It was licensed to Tho. Newman and him. 1593.

" The Sinners salue, which applied and practised, as well of impenitent, may bee mouued to conuersion, as the penitent armed against desperation: whereunto is annexed, the Armour for the soule against the assaultes of death. By Rob. Wolcomb: printed for *him*, 1595." Maunsell, p. 122 Twenty-fours. 1595.

HUMPHREY BAET, or BATE, stationer,

WAS made free by Mr. John Harrison sen. 8 Octob. 1579.

" Lamentable paraphrase on the Lamentations of Jeremy, by Daniell Tousain; translated by Thomas Stocker, Gent. printed for Humfrey Bate, 1587." Licensed. Maunsell, p. 115. Twenty-fours. 1587.

He had licenses also for the following, viz. in 1586, " A true report of the late woorthie fight p'formed in a voiage from Turkie by fyve shippes of London against xj galies and ij fregates, the strongest of Christiandō in the passage of the Straightes, 13 Julye, 1586."

THOMAS GUBBIN, stationer,

WAS made free by John Walley 31 Jan. 1585-6. In Feb. 1593-4, he was fined 2l sh. for buying and dispersing Psalms disorderly printed, which he promised to pay before next Quarter-day. Some others were also fined at the same time for the like offence, in proportion probably to the quantity of books so bought. See p. 1233, note r. To the entries is subjoined " And yt is ordered that eu'y of them shall bring into the Stac'oners hall so many of the said bookes disorderly printed as remayne in their handes vndispersed at the time of their examinac'ons."

" A short declaration of the end of Traytors" &c. as p. 1099. 1587.

" Amorous Fiammetta." &c. ib. Licensed. 1587.

" A Sermon—at Greenevviche,—By M. Peter Wentworth," &c. as p. 1226. 1587.

" Two very lerned Sermons of M. Beza," &c. as p. 1144. 1588.

" The lawers logike," &c. as p. 1038. For him and Tho. Newman. L. 1588.

" The Education of Children in learning:" as p. 1242. 1588.

" Abrahami Fransi, Insignium—explicatio" &c. as ib. Licensed. 1588.

" The Coronation of Dauid:" &c as ib. 1588.

" Elizabetha Triumphans." &c. as p. 1243. Licensed. 1588.

" An Admonition out of—Joel," &c. as p. 1332. 1588.

" The recantations of Will. Tedder and Anthonie Tirrel, pronounced 1588.
at

at Paul's crosse, sometime Seminarie priestes of the English colledge at Rome." For him. See p. 1100. Quarto.

(1588.) "The true remedie against Famine and Warres," &c. as p. 1143. L.

1589. "P. Rami professoris regii Grammatica, &c. as p. 1243.

1589. "A Treatise touching Antichrist, wherein the place, the time, the forme, the workemen, the vpholders, the proceeding, and lastly, the ruine and ouerthrow of the kingdome of Antichrist is plainly laid open out of the Worde of God: where also many darke places, both of Daniell and the Reuelatiō are made manifest: By Lambertus Danæus; translated by John Swan." Printed for John Porter and him. Licensed. 4°.

1590. "William Perkins his treatise tending vnto a Declaration, whether a man bee in the estate of damnation, or in the estate of grace. If he bee in the first, how he may come out of it, if in the second, how he may discerne it, and perseuere in it to the end." Printed for John Porter and him. Octavo.

1591. "Spirituall desertions, seruing to terrifie all drowsie protestants, and to comfort them which mourne for their sinnes. By Will. Perkins." Printed for John Porter and him. Sixteens.

1592. "Will. Perkins his Catechisme, gathered into six principles, and is to bee learned of the ignorant people that they may bee fit to heare sermons with profit, and receiue the Lords supper with comfort." For him. 8°.

1596. "Vlysses vpon Aiax. Written by Miso-diabolus to his friend Philaretes." Device: a Griffin. For him. F 3, in eights. This is the third part of The Metamorphosis of Ajax. Mr. Reed. Octavo.

He had also licenses for the following articles, viz. In 1587, "A brief answere vnto those ydle and frivolous quarrels of R. P. against the late edition of The Resolution by Ed. Buny; Whereunto are prefixed the booke of Resolution, and The tretyce of Pacificac'on perused and noted in the m'gent ou' all the places as are misliked of R. P. Shewing in what section of this answere following those places are handled." With Tho. Newman.---"The Arcadian Rethorick, or the preceptes of Rhethoricke made plaine by examples, greeke, latyne, englishe, Italyan, Frence and Spanishe by Mr. Abr. Frauce." With Tho. Newman. In 1588, "Three Treatises necessarye to be considered of all Christians." With John Porter.—"A thing intytled, A premonition for euerye disposytion." In 1589, "Linguæ Latinæ exercitatio: Joāne Ludouico Viuo auctore.---Tarlton's Newes out of Purgatorye, or a caskett full of pleasaunt conceiptes, stuffed with delightfull devises and quaint myrthe as his humor maye afforde to feede gentlemens fancies." In 1590, "The life of long Megg of Westminster.—Armilla aurea: To be printed in English." This and the two preceeding articles with Tho. Newman. In 1591, "The defence of Conye Catchinge, or a consutac'on of those ij Iniurious pamphlets published by R. G. (*Rob. Green*) against the practitioners of many nymble wytted and misticall sciences." With John Busby. In 1593, "A Remembrance of the late Righte Hon. Erle of Derby, deceased."

THOMAS

THOMAS NEWMAN, ſtationer,

SON of John Newman of Newbury, Berks, Clothworker, was apprenticed to Ralph Newbery for 8 years from Michaelmas 1578; and made free 15 Aug. 1586. He had frequent connections in trade with Tho. Gubbin, eſpecially at their firſt ſetting out.

" A ſhort declaration of the end of Traytors" &c. as p. 1099. 1587.

" Amorous Fiammetta." &c. as ib. Licenſed. 1587.

" The lawers logike," &c. as p. 1038. Licenſed. For T. Gubbin and him. 1588.

" Abrahami Franſi, Inſignium—explicatio." &c. as p. 1242. Licenſed. 1588.

" Elizabetha Triumphans." &c. as p 1243. Licenſed. 1588.

" Tho. White Doctor his ſermon at Pauls Croſſe on the Queens day 1589, on Luke 3; 10—14. Printed by Rich. Robinſon and *him*." Maunſell, p. 106. Licenſed 22 Nov. 1589 to Robert Robinſon; therefore finding no other mention of Richard Robinſon as a printer, apprehend it a miſtake in Maunſell. Octavo. 1589.

" A Godly garden out of the whiche moſt comfortable hearbs may be gathered for the health of the wounded conſcience of all penitent ſinners." For him. Twenty-fours. 1590.

" Syr P. S. *(Philip Sidney)* His Aſtrophel and Stella.* Wherein the excellence of ſweete Poeſie is concluded. To the end of which are added, ſundry other rare Sonnets of diuers Noblemen and Gentlemen. At London, Printed for *him*. Anno Domini. 1591." Dedicated " To the worſhipfull and his very good Freende, Ma. Fruncis Flower Eſquire, increaſe of all content.—Tho. Newman.---Somewhat to reade for them that liſt.—Tho. Naſhe." Beſides; 80 Pages. W.H. Quarto. 1591.

" Chriſtian praiers and holy meditation, aſwel for priuate as publique exercise, gathered out of the moſt godly learned of our times by Henry Bull." For him. Sixteens. 1592.

" Greenes Viſion: Written at the inſtant of his Death. Conteyning ——
a pe-

* This book, by the following charge in the Wardens account of expenditures from July 1591 to July 1592, appears to have been diſorderly printed, viz. " Sept. 18. Carrying Newman's books to the Hall, 4d." It is not eaſy to aſſign a reaſon for this ſeiſure, as if the book contained treaſon, &c. there being no mention in the decrees concerning it, or what became of the copies afterwards. In the ſaid account a little further on is charged, *To* " John Wolf when he rid with an anſwer to *the* L. Treaſurer, being with her maieſtie in progreſs for taking in of books, P. S. Aſtrophell and Stella, 15ſh." By which it ſeems as if Mr. Newman had made application to the Lord Treaſurer, who had demanded of the Company their reaſon for this extraordinary behaviour, to which they were obliged to ſend an immediate anſwer after him. The only crime to appearance was the printing this book without licence, for which the tranſgreſſor was uſually ſined a few ſhillings only. Mr. Newman in all other reſpects appears to have been a very orderly member, not once named in the Black Liſt. Indeed that liſt ſeems very deficient for this year.

a penitent Passion for the folly of his Pen. Sero sed Serio." For him. Dedicated by T. N. To—Nicholas Sanders of Ewell, Esq; The authour in his preface, expresses himself to be in great sickness and sorrow, and concludes, with—Yours dying, Robert Greene. In his introduction of the pamphlet is a copy of verses entitled "Greene's ode, of the vanity of wanton writings." The purport of what proceeds is an account of the vision he had, as he was sitting in a fair meadow under an Oak Tree, of Chaucer and Gower, who came and sat down by him; and they fell into a colloquy on a very important subject: Chaucer maintains the pleasant and humorous manner; Gower, the serious and grave. When they first sat down by him, he surveyed them so earnestly that he could not forbear describing their persons and attire; which because remarkable, and somewhat in their own Style; and might proceed from something more authoritative than bare invention; shall therefore in respect to those two worthy bards insert below.* In 31 leaves. Harleian Pamphlets, N°. 522. Quarto.

— "Everard Digbie his dissuasive" &c. as p. 1236. Licensed in 1589 with T. Gilberd.

He had licenses for several books with T. Gubbin. See p. 1354. Also, in 1593, for "Tharraignement Judgement and execuc'on of three wytches in Huntingdonshire, beinge recōmended for matter of Truthe by Mr. Judge Fenner vnder his hand wrytinge, shewed in a Court, or assemblie holden this daye. The note vnder Mr. Juson Fenners hand is layd vp in the Wardens cupboard:" With John Wynnington. See p. 1250.

JOHN

* *The description of* GEFFERY CHAWCER.

His stature was not very tall,
Leane he was, his legs were small.
Hos'd within a stock of red;
A button'd bonnet on his head,
From under which, did hang I weene,
Silver haires, both bright and sheene.
His beard was white, and trimmed round,
His count'nance blithe, and merry found;
A sleeveless Jacket large and wide,
With many pleights and skirts side,
Of Water Chamlet did he weare.
A Whittle by his belte he beare.
His shooes were corned broad before;
His Inkhorne at his side he wore;
And in his hand he bore a Book,
Thus did this ancient Poet look.

The description of JOHN GOWER.

Large he was, his height was long;
Broad of breast, his limbs were strong.
But couller pale, and wan his looke:
Such have they that ply'n their booke.
His head was gray and quaintly shorne;
Neately was his bearde worne.
His visage grave, and stern, and grim;
Cato was most like to him.
His bonnet was a Hat of blew,
His sleeves straight, of that same hew.
A surcoat of a tawnie die,
Hung in pleights over his thigh;
A breeche close unto his Dock,
Handsomed with a long Stock;
Picked before were his shoone,
He wore such as others doone.
A bag of red was by his side,
And by that, his napkin tide.
Thus John Gower did appeare,
Quaint attir'd, as you heare.

JOHN HILL, ſtationer,

WAS made free by John Harriſon the elder 8 Aug. 1586. He dwelt at the three pigeons in Pater-noſter-row.

" A godly and profitable Sermon—ſhewing the true fruites of peace and warre, &c. By Adam Hill." &c. as p. 1241. Licenſed. Sixteens. 1588.

" The principles of the true Chriſtian Religion briefly ſelected out of many good bookes by S. B." For him. Licenſed. Octavo. 1590.

JOHN DALDERNE, or DALDREN, ſtationer,

SON of Roger Dalderne, late of London, hackneyman, deceaſed, was apprenticed to Toby Cooke for 9 years from Chriſtmas 1579; and made free 9 Jan. 1587-8.

" A ſermon preached at Brocket Hawl. by Edm. Harris, on Deut. 11 29, 30. *to encourage the ſoldiers againſt the papiſh invaſion.* Printed for John Daldren." Maunsell, p. 100. W.H. Octavo. 1588.

" Giles Wiggington his Catechiſme. For *him.*" Ib. p. 32. Octavo. 1589.

" Rules or weapons concerning the ſpiritual battel, together with an expoſition on the 16 pſalme. With two Epiſtles written by Ioh. Picus Mirand. Tranſlated by W.H. Printed for Iohn Dalderne 1589." Ib. p. 92. Quarto. 1589.

" Steph. Egerton his lecture (taken by Characterie) on Gen. 12; 17—20. Printed for John Daldren." Ib. p. 99. Octavo. 1589.

" The Portraiture of Hypocriſie," &c. as p. 1234. 1589.

He had entered for his copy, 23 June 1589, " A Catechiſme to be learned and practized of all thoſe profeſſors who may be reckoned for true Xpians to receaue the Lords ſupper worthelye;" Probably Wiggington's.

WILLIAM YOUNG,

WITH about a dozen others, was ſworn and admitted free of the Stationers' company, 3 June, 1600, by tranſlation from the Drapers' with the conſent of both companies, according to the conſtitution of the City, and for which they paid iij*ſh.* iiij*d.* each. He dwelt near the great North door of St. Paul's.

" Gaſp. Oleuian on the Creede," &c. See it under Ra. Jackſon. 1589.

" Rich. Saintbarb his Catechiſme," &c. ib. 1589.

" The excellencie of the miſtery of Chriſt Ieſus," &c. ib. 1590.

" Arth. Dent his expoſition of the Articles of our faith," &c. ib. 1591.

1596. "Daniel his Chaldie visions," &c. as p. 1257.

1596. "Hen. Hollands Christian exercise of Fasting, private and publick: whereunto is added certain meditations on the 1st and 2d chapters of the Book of Job. Printed for *him* 1596." Quarto.

RALPH JACSON, or JACKSON,

SON of Thomas Jackson of the city of Coventry, Draper, was apprenticed 8 July, 1579, to Garret Dewce *(Gerrard Dewes)* for 10 years from Michaelmas next; made free 17 Octob. 1588; and came on the livery 1 July 1598. In Feb. 1593-4 he was fined "for buying and dispersing of Psalmes disorderly printed, 10sh. which he promised to pay the first monday of the next month." See p. 1353. He was one of the witnesses to William Norton's will. I learn, from his books, that he dwelt in St. Paul's Church-yard at the sign of the White Swan, from 1595 to 1600. I have not seen any before 1595.

1589. "Gasp. Oleuian on the Creede, Commandementes, Lords praier, and Sacramentes translated by Rich. Saintbarbe. Printed for Will. Young and *him*. 1589." Maunsell, p. 31. Octavo.

1589. "Rich. Saintbarb his Catechisme, wherein are chiefly handled such things as are omitted in other Catechismes. Printed for Will. Young and *him*. 1589." Licensed. Ibid. Octavo.

1590. "The Excellencie of the mistery of Christ Iesus declared in an exposition vpon 1 Tim. 3; 16, by P. M. *(Peter Muffet)* Printed for *him*, 1590." Licensed. Ib. p 48. It appears to have been printed also this year for him and Will. Young. Ib. p. 74 Octavo.

1591. "Arth. Dent his exposition of the Articles of our faith, by shorte questions and answeres printed for W. Young and *him*. 1591." L. Ib. p. 29. 8°.

1591. "R. Rawlins consort of the creatures with the creator, and with themselues.—for *him*. 1591." Ib. p. 89. Octavo.

1591. His "Perswasion to doe good cheerefully, and to beare euill patiently.—for *him*. 1591." Ibid. Octavo.

1594. "An Abridgement of the holy history of the old Testament, from Adam to the incarnation of Christ, by Simon Wildome.—for *him*." 8°.

1595. "A Comparison betweene the auncient fayth of the Romans, and the new Romish Religion." &c. as p. 1275. Licensed.

1595. "A Suruey of the Popes supremacie:" &c. as p. 1289.

1595. "Truth and Falshood:" &c. as p. 1288. Licensed. To which is annexed

1595. "A Short Answer to the Reasons—Popish Recusants—alleadge," &c.

1596. "The Coucnant betweene God and Man," &c. as p. 1235.

1596. "A Treatise of the threefolde state of man" &c. as p. 1268. Licensed.

1596. "The Contents of Scripture:" &c. as p. 1285. Licensed to him, and R. Dexter.

"Two

" Two treatiſes concerning Regeneration," &c. as p. 1268. Licenſed. 159-.
" An Expoſition of the Lords prayer :" &c. as p. 1293. 1597.
" The grain of Muſtard ſeed, or the leaſt meaſure of Grace that is, or can be effectual to Saluation. By Wm. Perkins. Printed for *him*, and Hugh Burwell." Licenſed to him alone. Octavo. 1557.
" The Works of—Richard Greenham," &c. as p. 1294. Licenſed. 1599.
" An Apologie or Defence of the Watch-vvord," &c. as p. 1295. I. 1600.
" Foode for Families: Or, An wholſome Houſhold Diſcourſe: In which all eſtates and ſorts of people whatſoeuer are taught, Their duties towards God, Their Alegeance to their King, And Their Brotherly loue and Charitie one to another. Written, For the plainer and better vnderſtanding, in a dialogue betweene the Father and the Sonne. Printed —by G. P. for R. Iackſon, and are to be ſold at his Shop, neere the Conduit in Fleet ſtreet." Dedicated " To All ſound Members,—whereof her ſacred Maieſtie is ſupreme head.—Yours in the L. if you be Cæſars in the L. E. N." Running title to this addreſs, " To the Reader." K 5, in eights. The running title to the treatiſe " Cæſars Dialogue." W.H. Sixteens. ——

He had alſo licenſes, in 1596, for " Eſopes Fables, in Latin verſe.—Johannis Apocapſioſordi Apocalipſis, ſiue Apocalipſis Jeſu Chriſti.—The Engliſh Schole maiſter, teaching all his ſchollers of what age ſo euer the moſt eaſie ſhort and perfect order of diſtinct readinge, and true writinge of our Engliſh tongc." In 1597, " When it ſhalbe lawfully auctorised. A true declaration of the 7 perſons whiche in the pariſhe of Cleworth in Lancaſhire were ſtrangely and really poſeſſed of Sathan, and of their deliu'ry by praier and faſtinge.—A true Cronology," &c. as p. 1334.—" Certen godlie ſermons vpon—Exodus 16; 2. Pro. 4; 13,—16. Pro. 17; 21. Pro. 18; 12, and 21.—Propoſitions, conteyninge certen obſeruac'ons and counſelles on diuerſe ſpiritual matters.—The deſcription of a righteous man; vpon Gen. 18.—A treatiſe of a good name.—Profitable notes for readinge and vnderſtanding the Scripture.—Sundry cõfortable letters, with certen notes to cõforte the afflicted.—Certen profitable notes vpon the booke of Exodus.—Meditations on the 119 pſalme.—A ſermon on Luke 12; 32. *All* theſe by Mr. Ric. Greenham, late preacher of Drayton." In 1598, " Graue counſelles and godly obſeruations —principally to inſtruct and comfort all afflicted conſciences.—Jehoua, or a treatiſe of the nature of God.—A treatiſe of Juſtificatiõ—by Mr. Marton."—In 1600, " The 2d and 3d partes of the w'kes of the rev. and faithfull ſervant of Chriſt, Mr. Ric. Greenham." This, and the two foregoing articles, with R. Dexter.—" A newe handling of a Planiſphere, diuided into three ſections." With Sim. Waterſon.

p It may be queried whether this be our Ralph, or one Roger Jackſon, who ſerved his apprenticeſhip with Ralph Newbery, and was made free to Aug. 1599, eſpecially conſidering the different abode; however the book appears evidently to have been printed in the time of Q. Elizabeth. G. P. may probably mean Geo. Pen, or Penne, bound to John Day in 1564. John Kingſton printed for him, in 1582. See p. 841. If our Ralph lived in Fleet ſtreet it muſt have been before 1595.

FRANCIS BOWIER.

1589. "Francisci Vietæi Opera Mathematica, in quibus tractatur canon mathematicus, seu ad triangula. Item canonicon triangulorum laterum rationalium: vnà cum vniuersalium inspectionum ad canonem Mathematicum, libro singulari. Quæ quidem omnia illustrantur Tabulis & Appendicibus ab eodem authore recognitis. Londini. Apud Franciscum Bouuier. M.D.LXXXIX." Contains 79 leaves. Bodleian. Folio.

WILLIAM LOWNES, stationer,

WAS made free by Mrs. Toy, late wife of Humphrey Toy, 19 Jan. 1578-9. Humphrey Lownes, of whom some account will be given by and by, was an apprentice to him: as was one Tho. Lownes, who was made free by him 7 Aug. 1578; after which i find no more of him.

(1590.) "A Godlie sermon of obedience on Luke 20, 25, preached in the Cathedrall Churche at Norwich, by Edmonde Sucklinge, one of the prebendaries of the same churche, 27 Feb. 1589-90. Printed for Tho. Chard,* and *him*." Licensed 6 Apr. 159 . Octavo.

HENRY HOOKE, stationer,

AS no entry is found of his being bound, or made free himself, he must have been made free by purchase in the time of the chasm in their Register. In 1592 he was fined "for keeping a p'ntise vnp'sented, ij*s.* vj*d.* And shall put the said p'entice from him by cause he is not capable of him." He was taken on the Livery 3 July 1598.

1590. "Chr. Hooke his childbirth, or womans lecture, on Luke 11 57, 58. Printed for Henry Hooke, 1590." L. Maunsell, p. 100. Quarto.

JOHN MORRIS, and JOHN BOWEN, stationers,

WHO appear at this time to have been partners, and dwelt together in St. John's street. John Morris was made free by R. Watkins 1 May 1580. See John Bowen, p. 1301.

"A

* See p. 1196; where the article was taken from Mr. Ames, and supplied from Maunsell: this from the Stationers' Register.

"A sermon preached at Hitchin in the yeare of our Lord 1587. the 1590.
17. day of Nouember, being the first day of the 29. yeare of the Queenes Maiesties reigne. By Edmond Harris, Master of Artes and Preacher of the word of God. Printed at London by John Morris and I. B. dwelling in S. Iohns streete 1590." Inscribed "To the faithfull and beloued in the Lord his brethren knowne to him in Hertford-shire, &c.—From my chamber at North Mimmes, this 16 of October, 1590." The text, 1 Peter, 2; 17. Contains 79 pages. Licensed to them. W.H. Sixteens.

John Morris had licensed to him, 26 Apr. 1587, "A treatise of Apostasy, made by Mr. Jo. de L'espine, minister of the Word of God in the church of Angiers." See p. 1075.

RICHARD OLIFFE, or OLIVE, stationer,

SON of Thomas Oliffe of Edgecote, Northamptonshire, yeoman, was apprenticed to John Perrin for 8 years from Midsummer, 1580; and made free 28 June 1588.

"Fennes Fruits: which booke is diuided into three seueral partes; 1590.)
The first, a Dialogue between Fame and the Scholar. The second, Of the lamentable Ruins which attend on War. The third, That it is not requisite to deriue our pedigree from the vnfaithfull Troians. By Thomas Fenne. London imprinted for Richard Oliffe." Quarto.

"Humfr. Barwicke, his discourse concerning the force and effect of 1591.
all manner of weapons of fier, and the disabilitie of the Long-bowe, or Archerie, in respect of others of greater force, now in vse, with probable reasons for verifying thereof, done of dutie to his soueraigne, and Contrey, &c. Printed for Ric. Olyffe, 1591." Maunsell, P. II; p. 27. 4°.

I have a copy of like import, if not the same edition, wanting the title-page and prefixes, with this head-title, "Certaine discourses written by Humfry Barwicke Gentleman, with his opinion concerning the seuerall discourses written by S. Iohn Smith, & S. Roger Williams Knightes, and of their contrarie opinions, touching Muskets and other fierie weapons, and the long bowe: with diuers other pointes of war by some others afore time mistaken."

"Axiomata philosophica" &c. as p. 1207. Licensed. 1592.

"The Mirror of Alchimy," &c. as p. 1281. 1597.

"Greens Groatsworth of wit." &c. as p. 1293. Licensed. ——

"The VVeakest goeth to the Wall. As it hath bene sundry times 1600.
plaide by the right honorable Earle of Oxenford, Lord great Chamberlaine of England his seruants." Device: Truth, &c. as p. 1279. "—Printed by Tho. Creede for *him*, dwelling in Long Lane, 1600." I, in fours. Quarto.

"The VVisdome of Doctor Dodypoll. As it hath bene sundrie times 1600.
Acted by the Children of Powles." Truth, &c. "—Printed by Tho. Creede for *him*," &c. H, in fours. Quarto.

He

He had alfo licenfes for the following, viz. In 1590, " A recitall of the victory obteined in Fraüce by the King in his late battell, and likewife what hath happened fince." May 13, 1598, " A little booke of newes out of Hungary, of an exploit and outhrowe againft the Turkes, 18 Marche 1598, at Rab, and the taking of Rab by the Chriftians.--- Caltha poetarum, or Chrifanthemon." In 1600, " Two plaies, or thinges, thone called the maides metamorphofis: thother Gyue a man luck and throw him into the Sea.---The wifdom of Dr. Dodepople, plaied by the children of Paules.---John Dromes entertainment as yt hathe ben acted by the Children of Paules.---The weakeft goethe to the walles."

WILLIAM HULME, or HOLME, ftationer.

SON of Thomas Hulme of the city of Chefter, fmith, was apprenticed to another Wm. Hulme or Holme, (who appears to have ferved his apprenticefhip with John Harrifon the elder) for 9 years from Chriftmas 1581; and was made free by the faid Mr. Harrifon, then mafter of the company, 25 June 1589. This feems rather irregular, as there is not any intimation of his being turned over to him. I find him on the Livery in 1604. In 1594 he was fined " for printing twoo pamphletes without licence jfh." In 1596, " for buying Pfalmes and Prymers diforderly printed againft her maieflies priuilege and prohibitions, iij fh. iiij d." He kept fhop near the great North door of St. Paul's.

1590. " The Touchftone of true religion, deciphering the right vfe and finall end thereof, againft the impietie of Atheifts, Epicures, Libertines, Hippocrites and Temporifours of thefe times, by A. D. printed for Willi. Holme 1590." Maunfell p. 115. Octavo.

1590. " Edw. Vaughan, his methode for the reading and vnderftanding of the olde and new Teftament, the one expounding the other according to the meaning of our Lord Jefus Chrift, printed for *him*: 1590." Ibid. p. 117. Octavo.

A

* A remarkable one, with its defcription is on the back page of fol. 12, " of men and women dauncing together, byformed or faced, the formoft fmiling, the hynmoft weeping; and dauncing in a ring, with their armes fpred abrode, and banfalled man with man, and woman with woman. One arme of the man vnder that of the woman, and the other aboue, and thus clofing together and houlding by the hands, they flowng about one after another, that alwayes ftill in one place, a fmyling countenance incountered a foregoing fad. Their number was feauen and feauen fo perfectly and fweetely counterfeited with liuely motions, their veftures whifking vp and flying abroad, that the workman could not be accufed of any imperfection, but that one had not a liuely voyce to expreffe their mirth, and the other brinifh teares to manifeft their forrow; the faid daunce was in fafhion of two Semicircles, with a feparating partition put betwixt." The margin gives us this moral; " None liue in this world in that pleafure, but they haue alfo their forrowes in time."

" A treatiſe againſt Traitors:" &c. as p. 1239. 1591.
" HYPNEROTOMACHIA THE ſtriſe of Loue in a Dreame." Device: a 1592.
caduceus as deſcribed in p. 552. " At London. Printed for *him*,—near the great North doore of Paules 1592." Contains 100 leaves, with ſeveral neat wood-cuts.' George Maſon, Eſq; Quarto.

1596. " The Honor of the Lawe." &c. as p. 1213.

He had alſo licenſes for the following, viz. In 1593, " A moſt great wonderfull and miraculous victorie obteyned by the Xpians againſte the Turkes in Hungrie, with the copie of his Letters ſent to Monſ. de Baron de S[illegible]ey, gouernor of Lille, Douay and orches." In 1596, " Sinetes [illegible]full madrigalls vpon his diſcontented fortunes." In 1599, " A comicall Satyre of eu'ry man out of his humour."

THOMAS PAVIER

WAS tranſlated, with Will. Young and others, from the Drapers' company to the Stationers', by conſent of both companies, 3 June 1600. He was one of 27 who were fined 2ſh. 6*d*. each for buying Humours letting blood &c. as p. 1266. He dwelt at the Cat and Parrots, over againſt Popes Head alley, Cornhill.

" The firſt part of the true and honorable Hiſtory of the life of Sir John Old-caſtle, the good lord Cobham. As it hath bene lately acted by the right honorable the Earle of Notingham, Lord high admirall of England, his ſervants. Written by William Shakeſpeare.—for T. P." Bibl. Croſts. No. 5129, Licenſed. Quarto. 1600.

The ſecond part—with his martyrdom, licenſed to him at the ſame time, was very probably printed alſo.

" The whole contention betwene the two famous houſes of Lancaſter and York: With the tragical ends of the good duke Humfrey, Richard Duke of Yorke, and King Henrie the ſixt. Divided into two parts. And newly corrected and enlarged. Written by William Shakeſpeare Gent.—for T. P." Ibid. No. 5130. Quarto. ——

" The Rare and moſt wonderful thinges whiche Edward Webbe —hath ſeene & paſſed in his troubleſome trauailes," &c. as p. 1305. L. ——

He had alſo licenſes in 1600, for " The 2d p'te of Tarltons Jeſtes.---The ſynner to his ſad ſoule.---The hiſt. of the life and deathe of Capt. Tho. Stucley, with his mariage to ald. Curtis his daughter, and his valiant endinge of his life at the battell of Alcazar.---Theſe copies, being thinges form'ly printed and ſet over to the ſaid T. P. 1. The pathway to Knowledge. 2. The hiſt. of Henry the 5th, with the battell of Agencourt. 3 The Spaniſh tragedie. 4. An Jnterlude called Edward longe-ſhakes. 5. The fyrſt p'te of the Gentill craſte. 6. An Jnterlude of Jack ſtrawe. 7. Mother Red caps will and teſtament. 8. Webbs travells. 9. Halleton's travelles. 10. The looking glaſs for London. 11. Solempne paſſion of the ſoules love. 12. Gods Arrow againſt Atheiſtes."

JOHN PENNIE or PENNY, stationer,

SON of John Pennie of Bobbington, Cheshire, yeoman was a prenticed to John Harrison the elder for 8 years from Christmas 1573; and made free 17 Octob. 1588, Mr. Harrison being then master of the Company. He dwelt at the Greyhound in Pater-noster-row.

1591. "O UTINAM." &c. p. 1206. This was licensed by the title of "A private mans potion for the health of England," which indeed is the running title. It is thus inscribed, "To the most noble famous, renowmed, invincible and victorious Realme of England: Be all florishing felicitie, happie prosperitie, and matchles tranquilitie longe to endure.—He that is alwaies prest to die to shield thee from danger: Iohn Dauies." The Welsh poet, author of Nosce teipsum. At the end, is the author's praier for the Queen; and his submission, or apology for writing, concluding with a poem of seven six-lined stanzas, addressed to the queen, with this head title, "Haile sacred soveraigne, the comfort of Israell." G 4, in eights, the last leaf blank. W.H. 16°.

CUTBERT BURBEE, or CUTHBERT BURBY, stationer.

SON of Edmund Burby of Ersley, Bedfordshire, husbandman, was apprenticed to William Wright for 8 years from Christmas 1584; made free 13 Jan. 1591-2; and came on the Livery 1 July 1598. He was fined in 1592 for keeping an apprentice unpresented, contrary to Orders, ijs. vjd. and in 1600 for disorderly buying books of Humours letting bloud, &c. as p. 1266. ijs. vjd. In 1592 he kept shop in the Poultry by St. Mildred's Church. In 1596, adjoyning to the Royal Exchange. In 1604, at the Swan in St. Paul's church-yard. He was a benefactor to the Stationers' Company; and his name stands the 5th on the List of benefactors set up in their dining-hall.

1592. "Maries choise." &c. as p. 1165. Licensed.

1592. "The sinfull mans search:" &c. Ib.

1592. "The Thirde and last Part of Conny-catching. With the new Devised knauish Art of Foole-taking. The like Cosenages and Villenies neuer before discouered. By R. G." Device: A man with a fool's cap, taking a gay woman round the waist with his left hand, she holding a dead rabbit by the hind legs; the three of spades between them; the ace of clubs, a knife and a pick-lock on the fore-ground. "Imprinted—by Tho. Scarlet for Cutberd Burbie, and are to be solde at his shoppe in the Poultrie by S. Mildreds Church, 1592." F, in fours. See p. 1165, and p. 1180. Quarto.

"The

" The Repentance of Robert Greene, Master of Artes: Wherein by 1592.
Himself is laid open his loose life, with the manner of his Death." For him. 15 leaves. See Oldys's Catal. of Pamphlets, N°. 47. Quarto.

" Exhortatiō to Salomon, or an exposition of Davids exhortation to 1594.
his sonne Salomon, taken out of the 1. of Chron. 28. ver. 9. Printed for *him*. 1594. By Hen. Arthington." Maunsell, p. 5. Quarto.

" The Coblers Prophecie. Written by Robert Wilson, Gent. Printed 1594.
at London by John Danter for *him*:—nere the Royall Exchange. 1594." G 3, in fours. Quarto.

" The Vnfortunate Traveller. Or the life of Iacke Wilton. Qui 1594.
audiunt audita dicunt. Tho. Nashe." Device: the phœnix.—" printed by T. Scarlet for *him*,—adioyning to the Exchange 1594." Dedicated " To—Lord Henry Wriothsley, Earle of South-hampton," &c. O, in fours. Concludes, " Farewell as manie as wish me well. June 27. 1593."

" Corn. Shilander his Chirurgerie:" &c. as p. 1050. Licensed. 1595.

" Edward the Third, and the Black Prince, their warres with kinge 1596.
John of Frañce." Licensed. Again 1599. See p. 1300.

" Wits Miserie, and the VVorlds madnesse: Discovering the Deuills 1596.
Incarnat of this Age.—Printed by Adam Islip, and are to be sold by Cutbert Burby at his shop by the Royall Exchange, 1596." Dedicated " To—Nicholas Hare of Stow Bardolse Esq; and Recorder of Lyn, and Hugh Hare Esq; Bencher of the Inward Temple; and John Hare Esq; Clarke of her Maiesties Court of Wardes—Tho. Lodge." See p. 1286.

" A Pleasant conceited Comedie, called a Knacke to know an honest 1596.
Man. As it hath beene sundrie times plaied about the Citie of London." Scarlet's device, as p. 1164. " London, Printed for *him*,—by the Royall Exchange. 1596." H, in fours. Mr. Malone. Quarto.

" Palladis Tamia. Wits Treasury." &c. as p. 1210. Fol. 333, and 1598.
a table. Licensed.

Loves labour lost, by Wm. Shakespeare, &c. as p. 1266. 1598.

" Mother Bombie."—by John Lylie, &c. as p. 1282. Licensed. 1598.

Granada's Devotions. See Gen. History, under 1582. Licensed. 1598.

The Mirror of Knighthood. The 7th book. See Gent. Mag. Vol. 54, 1598.
p. 254. Quarto.

The same. The 8th book.—The 9th book, in 1601. Ibid. Quarto. 1599.

" The English Secretarie," &c. as p. 1210. 1599.

" Foure Sermons*—by M. Henry Smith." &c. as ib. 1599.

Romeo and Juliet by Wm. Shakespeare, &c. as p. 1283. 1599.

" Nashes Lenten Stuff, &c. as p. 1599.

7 X " The

* Concerning these four sermons, and two others with three prayers printed for Wm. Leake; " 13 Aug. 1599. Yt is ordered, by their consent, that they may sell out this imp'ssion which they have last printed (whereof they have about a thousand left vnsold) at xxd. the booke: And that all imp'ssions thereof after this, they shall sell it at ij shetes a penny and not above. Viz. The book called Mr. Smythes sermons lately printed by Rob. Dexter and them." N. B. Tho. Man also had the copy-right of 40 sermons, besides The preparative to marriage; and N. Ling of three sermons, with some account of Rob. Dickons, a pretender to visions; all by the same author, printed in like manner, though at different presses, but no Order appears for regulating the price of these.

1599. "The Raigne of King Edward the third. As it hath bene sundry times played about the Citie of London."—Opportunity stan ling on a wheel, &c. as p. 1299. Imprinted by Simon Stafford for *him:*" &c. I, in fours. Mr. Kemble. Quarto.

1600. "Englands Parnassus:" &c. as p. 1283. Licensed.

He had also licenses, viz. In 1591, "The first sermon of Noahs drunkennes.---Axiochus of Plato.---Direction for Travellers." In 1593, "The seconde Reporte of Dr. John Faustus: with the ende of the wagners life.---With the consent of John Danter, The historie of Orlando furioso.—The said J. D. to haue the impryntynge thereof.---The dutie of all degrees described by kinge David.---The Coblers prophesie." In 1594, "Histoire de Primalion de Grece.—Seconde liure, *&c.*---Assigned to him from Edw. Allde, The trumpet of the soule sounding to Judgement. (*Eccl.* xi; 9.) by Hen. Smythe. The yong mans taske, Eccl. xii; 1. Remember thy maker in the daies of thy youthe. The said E. A. to have the printing of them for him so often as they shall be printed hereafter.---A book shewing the miraculous Judgement of God shewen in Herefordshire, where a mightie barne filled with corne was consumed with fire last Christmas Eeue, and duringe 15 dayes after. A ballad of the same.---An Enterlude called The Pynder of Wakefeilde.—Chiromancie, wrote in Latyn by John Rothman Phisician and Philosopher, to be translated into English." In 1595, "The most rare and pleasant historie of a knack to know an honest man.---Maroccus extaticus, or Bankes bay horse in a trance.---The Countesse of Bedfordes Temple: *if* lawfully aucthorised." In 1596, "By assignment from the wydowe Searlet, Twoo sermons of Mr. Smythes, viz. Maries Choice: and The sinfull mans serche.—By assign. from John Danter, Twoo books, viz. The first parte, and the second parte of the vij Champions of Christiandom: Referuinge the workmanship of the printinge at all tymes to the said J. D.---The 1, 2, 3, and 4 partes of the third booke of the Myrror of knighthood. Vppon condic'on—no mans, and authorised; and then doo share it at the Hall to the Master and Wardens so authorised." In 1597, "The trymynge of Tho. Nasshe gent. by the highe tituled patron Don Richardo de Medico campo, Barber Chirurgeon to Trinitie College in Cambridge.---An Edict of the Fr. kinge vpon the Articles agreed with Mons. the duke of Monceur for the reducinge of the Cytties of Nantes and others of Brytayne into the obedience of his maiestie." In 1598, "Disputatiuncularũ grãmaticaliũ libellus, ad puerorũ in scholis trivilibus, &c. Auctore Jõhis Stockwood, schole Tunbridgensis, olim ludy magistro. whiche was entred to John Harrison the younger, 14 Aug. last, and now by order entred for T. Dawson, Edw. White, Wm. Leeke and Cuth. Burby.---The praise of the Redd Herringe." In 1599, "By assign. from Mr. Dexter, Twoo sermons of the punishment of Jonah: by Mr. Smithe.---The great pardon, in opposition to the pope's Jubyle.--The plaie of Patient Grissell.---The true and present declarac'on of the mightie armie by Sea, prepared by the gen'all estates, and sent to hinder the proceedinges procedinges of the kinge of Spaine, &c.---To print when he doth get further aucthoritie for it, A true Relation of the victorie at Chieneds, neere Newport, against the Achduke Albertus, &c. by Graue Maurice, &c." In 1600, "Eu'ry man in his humor. (*By Ben Johnson.*) With Walter Burre.---The famous tragicall history of the Tartarian crippell, Emp'or of Constantinople.---Christes checke to St. Peter for his curious question:—Quid hoc ad te? In four Sermons by Mr. Leonard Barker.---A merrye meetinge: Or t'ys mery when knaues meete: Sonnettes compyled by the famous Fraternities of knaues.---Sõmers laste will and testam. presented by Will. Sõmers. With Wa. Burre.---The Journall, or daylie Register, cõteyninge a true manifestac'on accomplished by 8 ships of Amsterdam vnder the cõduct of Jacob Cornelyson, &c. An. 1598. With John Flasket.---A true report of the blacke galley of Dort, the 30 of Nov. 1600, which at that tyme took the Adm. of Andwerp with 7 other ships.---A true discours of the receauinge of the quene of Frañce into Marcelles and Lyons.---The First Savoyan, wherein ys sett forth the Right of the cõquest of Savoy by the french, and the ymportance of holdinge yt.---Three copies which were before entred and allowed to Mr. Woolf, who now hath signified his consent vnder his hand wrytinge to haue Mr. Burby Joyned with hym in the said copies, viz. A book called Learne to dye. the Sanctuary of a troubled soule. Godly meditations vpon the Lordes supper."

HUMPHREY LOWNES, stationer,

SON of Hugh Lownes of Rode in Astbury, Cheshire, husbandman, was bound apprentice to William Lownes for seven years from Midsummer 1580; made free 26 June 1587; He was fined 1 Feb. 1593-4 "for buying and dispersing of Psalmes disorderly printed, xxsh. which he hath promised to pay before the next Court-day: Paid vsh. and the rest remitted, 15 July 1594." See p. 1353. Also, 11 Feb. 1593-4, "for ij Psalm bookes disorderly printed: the counterfet leaues to be taken out, and the bookes m'ked: ijsh." July 1, 1598, he was taken into the Livery; and served Renter in 1605; Under Warden in 1608, again in 1611; Upper Warden in 1617. He appears to have immediately succeeded Rich. Smith in his shop at the West door of St. Paul's; and in 1613, if not before, dwelt in Peter Short's house, the Star, on Breadstreet-hill. He was a benefactor to the Stationers' Company; and his name stands the 8th on the List of Benefactors, set up in their dining-hall.

"The nine VVorthies of London;" &c. as p. 1249. 1592.

"The perfect path to felicitie, containing godly meditations and praiers, fit for all times, &c. by Phillip Stubbs." For him. L. 16°. 1592.

"The Gentlemans Academie." &c. as p. 1289. Licensed. 1595.

1596. "The Affectionate Shepherd, by Richard Barnefielde." For him. 16°.

1596. Again, with his Cynthia, and Legend of Cassandra. For him. Licensed. See Hist. of Eng. Poetry, Vol. III; p. 405, note p. Sixteens.

1599. "A Direction to Death: teaching man the way to die well, that being dead, he may liue euer. Made in the forme of a Dialogue, for the ease and benefite of him that shall reade it. The speakers therein are Quirinus and Regulus. Syrach, 38; 20, 21, Remember the laste ende, forget it not, for there is no turning againe. Mors sceptra ligonibus æquat." For him, 1599. Dedicated "To—Sir Thomas Vane, Knight, Lieutenant of her Maiesties Castle of Douer—William Perneby. —To the Christian Reader." Besides; 493 pages. Licensed. W.H. 8°.

—— "SAINT PETERS COMPLAINT, Newly augmented With other Poems." Device; A laureated death-head with wings, on a terraqueous globe, over it an hour-glass before a book with this motto, "I liue to dy, I dy to liue." This device enclosed in a square frame. "London. Printed by H. L. for William Leake: and are to be sold at his shop in Paules Churchyard, at the signe of the holy Ghost." This title is in a compartment with the Queen's arms at top, the Stationers' at bottom, and 4 naked boys playing on different musical instruments, two on each side, with Seres's cypher between them, who frequently used it. These poems were printed by I. R. for G. C. in 1595, see p. 1033; as also by John Wolf the same year, see p. 1182. Again by I. R. for G. C. 1599. W.H. which edition concludes on p. 66, with the poem, "From Fortunes reach." That poem stands also on p. 66 of this edition: from whence, tho' the signatures proceed regularly, there is a mistake in the paging, 59 to 77, instead of 67 to 87. At the end is a mask with three rings pendent: the same as at the end of the author's epistle prefixed. W.H. Quarto.

He had also licenses for the following, viz. In 1596, "Jacke of Newbery:—if it be lawfully aucthorised." In 1597, "The cures of the diseased in Remote Regions." In 1599, "Foure sermons preached by Mr. Rich. Leke at Kellington," &c. as p. 1335. With Mr. Man, warden.—"The first and second partes of Edw. the iiij and the tāner of Tamworthe, with the history of the life and death of Mr. Shore and his wife &c. Assigned from John Busby: all his moyte."

JOHN OXENBRIDGE, stationer,

SON of John Oxenbridge of Croydon, Surry, baker, was apprenticed to George Bishop for 12 years from All Saints, 1579; and made free 3 Nov. 1589: "Howbeit yt is agreed that he shall serve his said Master one whole yere from this day for xl.sh. wages for the yere, viz. xx sh. at euery every half yere end." He dwelt at the sign of the Parrot, in St. Paul's Church-yard; and used the rebus of an Ox passing over a bridge, with the letter N on its back.

"Tabulæ analiticæ," &c. See p. 1255. Licensed to T. Adams and him. 1593.

A looking-glass of Mortality, very profitable for all sorts of people: made by I. B. For him. 1595. Quarto. 1595.

"The substance of Christian religion soundly set forth in two bookes, by definitions and partitions, framed according to the rules of a naturall method, by Amandus Polanus: the first booke concerneth Faith: the second good workes. Translated by Elijahu Wilcockes.—for *him*, 1595." Licensed. Maunsell, p. 111. Octavo. 15 5.

"A Comfort against the Spaniard." &c. as p. 1231. 1596.

"A Progresse of Pietie," &c. as ib. Again, without date. 1596.

"The—Historie of Lazarillo de Tormes," &c. as p. 1281. Licensed. 1596.

"The most wonderfull and true storie of a certaine Witch, named Alse Gooderige of Stapenhill, who was arraigned and conuicted at Darbie, at the assises there. As also a true report of the strange torments of Thomas Darling, a boy of thirteene yeres of age, that was possessed by the Deuill, with his horrible fittes and terrible apparitions by him vttered at Burton upon Trent, in the Countie of Stafford, and of his maruellous deliuerance. Printed at London for I. O. 1597." At the end, "Printed—for John Oxenbridge dwelling in Paules Churchyard at—the Parrot, 1597." 6 sheets. Licensed. Lamb. Libr. Quarto. 1597.

A looking glass for Ireland: By Barnaby Rich. Bagford. MS. 1599.

He had also licenses for the following, viz. In 1591, "The adventures of Brusun* prince of Hungaria, &c." With Tho. Adams.---"Tell trothes Newe yeres gifte.---Green's newes bothe from Heauen and Hell;" With T. Adams. In 1594, "The pensive mans Complaint and comfort: The 2d. parte of the pensive mans practice." In 1597, "Trewe and dreadfull newe tydinges of blood and brymston which God hath caused to rayne from heaven, within and without the Cytie Strale Sonet, with a wonderfull apparition seene by a citizen of the same cytie, named Hans Geemer, whiche mett him in the filde, as he was travaylinge ou' the waie.---The lost sheep is founde; To him which calleth himselfe Elias, prentize to a glover in Mansfield, by Henry Smyth.---The trumpet of warre, by Mr. Gosson, pastor of greate Wickburrowe, in Essex." In 1599, "Twoo playes, beinge the 1st and 2d partes of Edw. the iiijth, and the Tanner of Tamworth, with the hist. of the life and deathe of Mr. Shore and Jane Shore his wyfe, as it was lately acted by the Right hon. the Erle of Derbye his servants." Q. by Tho. Heywood? He wrote on the same subjects.

WILLIAM

WILLIAM LEEKE or LEAKE, ſtationer,

WAS made free by Mr. Caldock 6 Octob. 1584; and came on the Livery 1 July, 1598. He ſerved Under Warden in 1604, again in 1606; Upper Warden in 1610, again in 1614; and Maſter in 1618. In 1600 he was fined ijſh. vjd. for buying the book of Humours letting blood &c. as p. 1265. He dwelt ſome time at the Greyhound in St. Paul's church-yard: probably went there when John Harriſon the elder removed into Pater-noſter-row. See p. 1156. Afterwards he lived at the ſign of the Holy Ghoſt, late Gabr. Cawood's. Apr. 16, 1599, he was drawn treaſurer of Seres and Day's truſt.

1594. "The Exerciſe of a Chriſtian life, written by G. L.[t] being the firſt ground and foundation whence the two treatiſes appertaining to reſolution, were made and framed by R. P. *(Rob. Perſons)* Printed by Wm. Lecke. 1594." Licenſed. Octavo.

1594. "The ſinners conuerſion. a ſermon by Hen. Smith, on Luke 19; 1—5. Printed for Wm. Leake, 1594." Licenſed. Octavo.

1594. "The ſinners confeſſion: "—on Luke 19; 6—9. Printed for *him*. 1594." Maunſell p. 105. Licenſed. Quarto.

1595. "Gods General Sūmons to his laſt Parliament: a ſermon by Geo. Phillips, on 2 Cor. 5; 10. Printed for *him*, 1595." Licenſed. Octavo.

1595. "The Paines of a painfull Paſtor.—on Eccl. 12; 9." L. Octavo.

1599. "Two ſermons[a] by Mr. Hen. Smith," &c. as p. 1210. Quarto.

1599. "The Paſſionate Pilgrime: by W. Shakeſpeare. At London, Printed for W. Jaggard, and are to be ſold by W. Leake at the Greyhound in Paules Churchyard, 1599." This ends on C 7. Then, on a ſeparate title-page, "Sonnets to ſundry notes of Muſicke." With the ſame direction. The whole on D 7, in eights. Capel's: Trin. Coll. Cambr. Sixteens.

—— St. Peter's Complaint, &c. as p. 1368.

He had alſo licenſes for the following, viz. In 1591, "A Meditac'on to be exerciſed daye and nighte: to be tranſlated into Engliſh, and after p'uſed, and lawfully allowed before it be put to printe." In 1594, "The Thirde booke of Palmeryn of Englande." In 1595, "Newes out of Vienna in Auſtria, 17 June, 1595, in what ſorte Ferdinandus Erle of Hardeck beinge generall of the ſtrong citie of Raab in Vngaria, with his Colonel Perlin, which was Capteyne over the Italian ſoldiers, were both at Vienna before the Emperors caſtell, brought before the barre, and for their treaſons and delevery of the ſaid Cyttie of Raab into the Turkes

[t] Query whether this be not a miſtake for L. G. Lewis de Granada. See Ath. Oxon. Vol. 1. col. 358.

[a] Both theſe ſermons by Mr. Smith were licenſed to W. Leake in 1592; and probably both printed in the ſame ſize, as they were again for him in 1599. Though as Mr. Smith was a very popular preacher in his Time, 'tis not unlikely that each ſermon might be printed both in Octavo and Quarto the ſame year.

[b] See the Company's Order, for the price of theſe, &c. p. 1365, notes.

Turkes possession found giltye, had Judgement, and were executed.-Venus and Adonis: assigned ouer to him by Mr. J. Harrison the elder." In 1596, "The embasse of Gods Angell: a sermon by Geo. Phillips.---The effect of the last Daie: wrote in Latyn by Dyonisius Carthusianus, and Englished by Geo. Phillips.---Sir Martin Frobisher his chivalrye, and lyves lamented tragedie.---A comfortable treatise" &c. as p. 1279. Assigned from R. Boyle. In 1597, "Hecatonphila. The Arte of Loue, or Love discou'ed in an hundred seu'all kindes.---By assignment from T. Gosson, A preparative to the Lordes Supper, with an Exercise thereof, by Geo. Phillips.---The Aprill of the Church," &c. as p. 1329. In 1598, "Disputatiuncularū grāmaticalū," &c. as p. 1366. In 1599, "By assignment from Rob. Dexter, Foure sermons of Mr. Hen. Smythes, videlicet, Twoo sermons of the songe of Symeon, one of the calling of Jonah, the 4th of the Rebellyon of Jonah.---The heroicall adventures of the Knight of the Sea." In 1600, "The soules heauenly exercyse.---The downefalle of Robert Erle of Huntingdon, after called Robin Hood.---The death of Rob. E. of Hūtingdō, with the lamētable tragidye of Chaste Mathilda." The last two articles were printed in 1601, and are among Garrick's books, in the Brit. Museum.

WILLIAM JAGGER, or JAGGARD, stationer,

SON of John Jagger, citizen and Barber-Surgeon of London, deceased, was apprenticed to Henry Denham for 8 years from Michaelmas 1584; and made free 6 December 1591. Apr. 23, 1593, he made request to have the printing of the bills for the players as John Charlewood had. "Granted, if he can get the widowes consent, or if she die, or marry out of the Company, he will be prefered before another." In 1600 he was fined with Ralph Blower for printing—Sir Anthony Shellies voiage, &c. See p. 1305.

"John Doue his sermon at Paules Crosse, on the 1. John. 2. vers. 18. Printed for Will. Iagger. 1594." Maunsell, p. 98. Octavo. 1594.

"The Passionate Pilgrime: by W. Shakespeare. At London, Printed for W. Iaggard, and are to be sold by W. Leake." &c. as p. 1370. Sixteens. 1599.

"The Schoole of Skil:" &c. as p. 1297. 1599.

He had also licenses for the following, viz. In 1594, "The book of secretes of Albartus magnus, of the vertues of herbes, stones, and certen Beastes: Also a book of the same author of the maruaylous thinges of the world, and of certen effectes caused of certen beastes: being all in one booke." In 1597, "The true perfection of Cuttworkes."

JOHN

JOHN JAGGER, or JAGGARD, ſtationer,

SON of John Jagger citizen and Barber-Surgeon, deceaſed, and brother of the abovementioned Will. Jagger, was apprenticed to Richard Tottel for 7 years from Michaelmas 1584; and made free 7 Aug. 1592, with this remarkable voucher annexed in the Company's regiſter, "Who hath ſerved out his yeres as reported by John Wolf, *(Beadle)* who had the report frō yonge Mr. Totell, dealer for his father." He ſeems to have continued as a journeyman to Mr. Tottel ever ſince he was out of his Time; and perhaps continued in that capacity with Charles Yetſweirt who ſeems to have come into Mr. Tottel's houſe about 1593, or 1594. See p. 1130. J. Jaggard, for ſo he printed his name, dwelt there however, and carried on buſineſs for himſelf after Mrs. Yetſweirt's time. He was ſworn on the Livery 3 July 1601. His device was a hand holding a ſceptre with the portcullis at top, and two ſprigs of laurel: a ſerpent about the wriſt with the tail in its mouth, forming a ſmall circle, within which is the word PRUDENTIA.

1594. "Giacomo Di Graſsi his true Arte of Defence," &c. as p. 326.[x] L.

1600. Godfrey of Bulloigne, &c. as p. 1214. Licenſed.

He had alſo licenſes for the following, viz. In 1599, "Ouidius Naſo His Remedie of Loue." With John Brown.[y] In 1600, "The Trauaylers breviate, or the diſcription of the world."

ANDREW WYSE, or WISE, ſtationer,

FOR ſo he muſt have been, ſeeing he bound three or four apprentices, at times, in that company; and yet i cannot find the regiſtry of either his being bound or made free; unleſs thoſe tranſactions were done in the name of Andr. Wythes, which being pronounced in one ſyllable will be found not ſo widely different as to the ſight may appear. The name Wythes never appears after his being made free. Greater miſtakes of the like kind have happened in thoſe times when orthography was governed by the ear, or rather whim, as inſtances are not wanting of the ſame word being ſpelt variouſly on the ſame page, and of men ſigning even their own names differently. One of the circumſtances of his being bound, or being made free might happen during the chaſm in the company's regiſter, from 1571 to 1576; which being only 5 years, both could not. Suppoſing thoſe names to indicate the ſame perſon, he was "the

[x] Where it was aſcribed to Richard Tottel as the printer for I. I. which i then ſuppoſed to mean John Jackſon, and accordingly placed it to him in p. 1220; but now find them intended for John Jaggard, being licenſed to him.

[y] As there are copies with the name of John Brown, only, it is not improbable but there were others, having John Jaggard's name alone.

" the son of Henry—of Ollerton Mallyverie, Yorksh. yoman," first bound to Henry Smith for 8 years from Lady-Day 1580, put over to Tho. Bradshawe of Cambridge, 3 Apr. 1581, and made free by him 26 May 1589. He was " fyned in full Court (28 June 1595) at Fortye shillings to be presentlie paide, for cõmittinge twoo seu'all offences in printinge Mr. Playfordes (Playsere's) sermon[a] twice without aucthoritie, contrarie to the decrees of the highe Courte of starre chamber and the ordinances of this Company. Neuertheles Respite is gyven vnto him at his request for the payment thereof till Michlemas next, at which daie he promiseth to paie the same. Pd. v s. in full payment vi pz. 18 Apr. 1597." He dwelt at the Angel in St. Paul's church-yard. All his copies were printed for him.

" CHRISTS TEARES OVER JERVSALEM. VVhereunto is Annexed a comparative admonition to London. A Jove Musa. By Tho. Nashe." R. Field's device, Anchora Spei. "—Printed for *him*—in Pauls Church-yard, at—the Angell. 1594." Dedicated " To the most honored, and vertuous beautified Ladie, the ladie Elizabeth Carey: Wife to the thrice magnanimious and noble discended Knight, Sir George Carey Knight Marshall, &c.—To the reader. Gentlemen my former epistle vnto you in this place began with Nil nisi flere libet, &c." This evinces there having been a former edition. Besides: 92 leaves. Quarto. 1594.

A sermon[a] by Tho. Playsere, D. D. on Luke 23; 28. Bodleian. 8°. 1595.

" The Pathway to Perfection." &c. as p. 1251. Text, Phil. 3; 14. L. 1596.

" The Meane in Mourning." &c. as ib. Text,[c] Luke 23; 28. L. 1596.

" The Pathway to Perfection." &c. as p. 1034. Also, 1597.

" THE MEANE IN MOVRNING. A Sermon preached at Saint Maryes Spittle in London on Tuesday in Easter weeke, 1595. By Thomas Playsere, Doctor of Diuinitie. At London, Printed by James Roberts for Andrew VVise, dwelling in Paules Church-yard, at the—Angel. 1597." The former of these two sermons is dedicated " To—Sir George Carey Knight Marshall of her Maiesties—householde, and gouernour of her Ile of Wight, &c.—From Saint Johns Colledge in Cambridge the first day of February, 1595.—Thomas Playsere." An abstract of which may be seen [b]below. This latter sermon was dedicated " To—the Lady Elizabeth 1597.

[a] This seems to be the sermon for which he was fined as above.

[c] Mr. Tho. Baker has added at the end of this article, in his copy of Maunsell, " That unhappy sermon."

[b] " Sir, as soone as I had preached this Sermon, it pleased the L. Bishop of London last deceased, both by his letter, and by word of mouth, to request a copie of it for the presse. The like did diuers other also. But in trueth I had then no copye of it Or if I had beene possessed of any, yet I was resolute to yeeld to no such motion. VVhich some (I knowe not who) vnderstanding, that being by so many, and so many times importuned, to print this or some other Sermon, I alwaies vtterly refused to doe, haue presumed to print the Meane in Mourning; altogether without true iudgement, or crauing me to counsell therein. And that so falselie, and in most places so quite contrary to my meaning, that I may say to him, whosoeuer was the procurer thereof, as Martiall the Poet sayd to one

Quem

Elizabeth Carey, vvife to the thrise noble Sir George Carey, knight Marshall, &c.—From Saint Johns Colledge in Cambridge the first day of Februarie 1595.—Thomas Playfere." An abstract of this also you will find in the notes.[c] W.H. Sixteens.

1597. Richard II.[d] (By Wm. Shakspeare.) &c. as p. 1290. Licensed.

1597. Richard III.[e] &c. as ib. Licensed. Again 1598, as p. 1282.

1598. Henry IV.[f] First part. &c. as p. 1210. Licensed.

1598. "William Alabasters seuen motiues," &c. as p. 1209. Licensed.

1599. "The historie[g] of Henrie the fourth," &c. as p. 1300. Licensed.

1600. Henry IV. Second part. &c. as p. 1291.

1600. "Much Ado about nothing." &c. as ib.

He had also license in 1600 for "The Paradise of prayers, gathered out of the spirituall workes of Lewys Granada: Englysshed by T. L."

EDMUND MATTES, or MATTS, stationer,

SON of Robert Mattes of Kingsey, Bucks, yeoman, was apprenticed to William Lownes fur seven years from the fifteenth of April, 1583; and

Quem recitas meus est, ô Fidentine, libellus.
Sed male dum recitas, incipit esse tuus.
—Certes I may be bold to auere, that as much diuersitie as there is betweene yuorie and woode: so much there is betweene that Sermon which was first once preached, and that which was afterward twise printed. Therefore after I was not onely perswaded by the aduise of all my friendes, but euen enforced by the necessitie of the thing itselfe, to print that Sermon, as it was preached, I thought good likewise to let this goe with it. That as the grauer of images in Æsop telleth Mercurie, if hee would giue a greate for the image of Jupiter, hee should haue his owne image for nothing: so if any one who hath cast away his mony vpon the former editions, will bestowe a groate vpon the true copie now sette out by myselfe, he may haue this sermon with it for nothing, in surplussage ouer and besides the bargaine."

[c] "Madam, It is reported that Demonax hauing his head broke with a stone, and being aduised to complaine to the Proconsull of that iniurie, answered that he had more neede goe to a Surgeon to heale his heade, then to a Magistrate to redresse his wrong. I must also confesse, I had rather haue had my head broken, then my sermon so mangled. For thys Sermon hath beene twise printed already without my procurement or priuitie any manner of way. Yea to my very greate greefe and trouble. Neuerthelesse I had thought good to complaine to no man. For in whom the fault resteth I cannot learne certainly. This I am sure, not any whit in my selfe.—Finding in the first editions so many broken-ended sentences, I haue (as it were) gone to a Surgeon, or rather indeed haue played the Surgeon my selfe, and by setting out the Sermon a newe, haue salued the matter as well as I could.—The gate (as I may say) and the first entrance into thys Sermon was before very lofty and stately, the Sermon it selfe very simple, and poore. Such a Styrre they kept, in terming it very vainely and most fondly *A most excellent Sermon*; as if they woulde haue cast the house out of the window, or the Citty out of the gate." Alluding to the city of Myndus. "Wherefore I haue made the gate lesser, and the Citty greater. The gate lesser, by entitling it *The meane in mourning*; which is the very dryft indeede, and the right scope of the whole Sermon. And the Citty greater, by adding diuers notes, in sundry places of the Sermon, as I haue since thought best."

[d] See prefaces to Shakspeare's plays, (1778.) p. 236, and p. 256.

[e] Ibid. p. 235.

[f] Ibid, p. 235. and p. 256.

[g] Ibid.

and made free 30 April, 1590. Apparently the brother of Wm. Mattes: perhaps his elder brother, as he was bound and alſo made free before him; however his ſucceſſor at the Hand and Plough in Fleet-ſtreet. And though he does not appear in the publiſhing way, he muſt have been in ſome manual branch, as he had an apprentice in 1594, another in 1595.

"The Metamorphoſis of Pigmalions Image," &c. as p. 1034. L.. 1598.

"The Common wealth—of Venice." &c. as p. 1231. Licenſed. 159 .

"Eſſays by Sir William Cornewaleys the younger knight." A ſecond part was publiſhed by him the next year. W.H. Twenty-fours. 1600.

"The Spaniſh Mandeuile of Miracles," &c. as p. 1035. Licenſed. 1600.

He had alſo licenſes for the following, viz. Octob. 7, 1597, "The devout mans meditations or purpoſes, which was the copy of Willm. Mattes deceaſed, entred this yere. Provided alwaies that he ſhall kepe the book himſelf without alieninge or aſſigning yt over to any p'ſon or p'ſons: and that vpon eu'y imp'ſſion thereof he ſhall pay vid. in the li. to thuſe of the poore." In 1600, "Diſcourſes vpon Seneca the Tragedian."

WILLIAM MATTES, or MATS, ſtationer,

SON of Robert Mattes of Kingſey Oxfordſhire, gent. was apprenticed to Simon Waterſon for nine years from All Saints, 1583; and made free 7 Nov. 1592. He dwelt at the Hand and Plough in Fleet-ſtreet, where he was ſucceeded by Edm. Mattes, who ſeems to have been his brother, notwithſtanding the miſtake of the entry, aſſigning different abodes and qualities to the father; for Kingſey, though on the borders of Oxfordſhire, is in Buckinghamſhire, as is rightly deſcribed under Edm. Mattes; and gent. and yeoman are nearly ſynonymous terms; modern and ancient.

"AN OVID FACIONED LOVE. Or a loue of the Ould facion. By I. T. gent." Device the braſen ſerpent, &c. "Printed by Peter Short for *him*,—1594." See p. 1208. Dedicated "To the Worſhipfull and my ſingular good friend, miſtres Anne Robertes.—To the courtious and friendlie." Beſides; 39 pages. In verſe. Capel's: Trinity Coll. Camb. Quarto. 1594.

"The Divel coniured." &c. as p. 1286. 1596.

"Aſtrolabium Vranicum Generale." &c. as p. 1001. (1596.)

He had alſo licenſes for the following, viz. Feb. 22, 1593-4, "The lamentac'on of Troye for the death of Hector; With an old womans tale in a ſolitarie Sell." Sept. 24, 1597, "The devout mans purpoſes, &c." This was granted to Edm. Mattes on the 7th of Oct. following, he the ſaid Wm. Mattes being then deceaſed.

CHRISTOPHER HUNT, ſtatinoer,

SON of Walter Hunt of Blandford, Dorſetſhire, cordwainer, was bound to Thomas Man for eight years from Michaelmas 1584; and made free 2 Octob. 1592. Feb. 1. 1593-4, He was fined "for buying and diſperſinge of Pſalmes diſorderly printed, iiijli. Whereof he hath paid xxſh. preſently, and hath gyuen his bill to Mr. Woodcock (*Wardon*) for the other xlſh. payable the xth of Maye next." See p. 1353.

1594. "Godfrey of Bulloigne," &c. as p. 1231. Licenſed.

1596. "Examen de ingeniis." See p. 1286.

—— "The force of Faith, containing a moſt ſweet and comfortable treatiſe, of the diuine talke betweene Chriſt and the woman of Canaan. Alſo a Dialogue between a ſorrowfull ſinner, and Gods word comforting him. Written in Latin by Nicholas Selneccerus. Tranſlated by R. M. Print. for Chriſtopher Hunt."

—— A ſermon on Mat. 15; 21—28, and Mark 7; 24—30. Octavo.

JOHN HARDIE, ſtationer,

SON of Chriſtopher Hardie of Barnet, Middleſex, yeoman, was apprenticed to Toby Cocke for eight years from Lady-day, 1587; but was made free 5 Aug. 1594. In 1596 he was fined "for printinge a booke of Mr. Burtons without aucthoritie and entrance, xſh. Alſo he is forbidden to ſell the book till it be aucthoriſed: and his Jmpriſonment for this offence is referred till another tyme." In October 1599, he officiated as Beadle of the company for his quondam maſter Toby Cocke, being infirm; and afterwards ſucceeded him in that office. See p. 1261. He dwelt at the Tiger's Head in St. Paul's Church-yard.

1594. "A Treatiſe of true fortitude, by Geo. Gifford." For him. L. 8°.

1594. "Concluſions of peace betweene God and man: a ſermon preached by Wm. Burton, on Prov. 7; 1, 2." For him. Octavo.

1595. "The Old Wiues Tale." &c. as p. 1272. At the End, "—to be ſolde at the ſhop ouer againſt St. Giles his Church without Criplegate. 1595." F 3, in fours. Quarto.

1596. "God wooing his Church:" as p. 1293.

He had licenſes alſo, in 1594, for "Satyre Manippee de la vertu du Catholicon D'Eſpagne, & de la Tenne des Eſtatz de Paris. To be printed in Englyſhe.---The tragedie of Ninus and Semarimis: the firſt monarche of the world."

ISAAC BINGE, ſtationer,

SON of Thomas Binge of the city of Canterbury, yeoman, deceaſed, was apprenticed to Henry Denham for ſeven years from Chriſtmas

1565;

1565; probably made free in the time of the chasm in the Company's Register; came on the Livery 7 May 1582; served Renter in 1591; Under Warden in 1595, again, 1598; and Master in 1603. He was fined 12 May 1582 for not attending the Lord Mayor with the Company, xijd. See p. 1325. note p.

"Certain very proper and most profitable Similies wherein sundry most foul vices, and dangerous Sins are plainly layd open and displayed, &c." For him. Licensed. Quarto. 1595.

He had also license in 1594 for "Vrbis Hierosolimæ—descriptio," &c. as p. 1328. In 1598, "De l'institution, vsage, & Doctrine du Saint Sacrament de l'eucharistie en l'eglise Armenne Ensemble Cõment quand, & per quels degrez La Messe s'est introdyte en sa place. To be translated into English, and so printed. With Wm. Ponsonby.---Granados spirituall —exercises, &c. as p. 1339.

PAUL LINLEY, stationer,

SON of William Linley of Lyllingston Darrell, Bucks, yeoman, was apprenticed to William Ponsonby for ten years from Lady-day 1576; and made free 16 May, 1586. He succeeded Thomas Woodcock at the Black Bear in St. Paul's Church-yard; where John Flasket seems to have been in partnership with him; and yet the third article below was printed for him alone, and all licenses entered to him only.

"Nennio, or a Treatise of Nobility: Wherein is discoursed what true Nobilitie is, with such qualities as are required in a perfect Gentleman. Written in Italian by that famous Doctor and worthy knight Sir John Baptista Nenna of Bari. Done into English by William Jones Gent. Printed by P. S. for Paule Linley, and John Flasket, and are to be sold at their shop in Paules church-yard, at the signe of the blacke Beare, 1595." Dedicated "To—Robert, Earle of Essex," &c. whose arms are on the back page.—"At my house by Charing crosse, this first of Nouember 1595.---Wm. Jones.---To the courteous Reader."---Verses by "Ed. Spenser; Sa. Danyel; G. Chapman; and Ang. Day." 98 leaves. Licensed. Trin. Coll. Cambr. Quarto. 1595.

"The Sinners Guyde." &c. as p. 1034. Licensed. 1598.

"A true Coppie of the transportation of the Lowe Countries, Burgundie, and the Countie of Charrolois: Doone by the King of Spayne, for the Dowrie of his eldest Daughter. Giuen in marriage vnto the Cardinall Albert, Duke of Austria with the Articles and Conditions of the same, signed by the King in Madrill. Translated out of Dutch by H. W. Nouember. 1598. At London, Printed by I. R. for Paule Linley, dwelling in Paules Church-yard, at—the Blacke Beare." See p. 1035. D, in fours. Licensed. W.H. Quarto. ——

Feb.

Feb. 9. 1595-6, were "assigned ou' vnto him from Mrs. Woodcock, by consent of the Company, all the Interest in and to the pryntinge of all and eu'y bookes and partes of bookes whatsou' which lawfully appertayned to her late husband Tho. Woodcocke, and after his decease to her." He had licenses also for the following, viz. in 1596, "Parentesis; Or an exhortac'on to good Life, Englished by John Turner.---Newes in a letter to Mr. White of the ouerthrowe of the Enemyes in Brabant, &c.---Sir Martin Frobisher his Chiualrye, and lives lamented tragedie." In 1597, "Assigned ouer vnto him from Edw. Blount, by the consent of the Wardens, a book in English called Hero and Leander." See p. 1287.

On the 26 June 1600 he appears to have been dead, according to an entry then made of his copies, licensed to

JOHN FLASKET, now stationer,

HAVING been on the 3 June 1600 translated from the company of Drapers, with Hugh Astley, Tho. Pavier, &c. He succeeded Paul Linley in his house and business, with whom he had connections in trade before. In 1600 he was fined ij sh. vj d. for buying The letting of Humours blood, &c. as p. 1266. He had printed for him within my limited period, besides the 2 articles abovementioned with P. Linley.

1600. "Hero and Leander. by Chr. Marloe." See it in p. 1287. Licensed.

He had also licensed to him, 26 June, 1600, "These books and partes of books which were Paule Lynlayes, viz. 1. Mr. Deringes Lectures. 2. Mr. Knewstubbes Lectures. 3. Holybandes dictionary, Fr. and Eng. 4. Agreement of the Scriptures. 5. Preparac'on to the Lordes Supper. 6. Those partes of Calvin vpon Deuteronomie, Job, the Psalmes, Himingius postill, Hollinsheads cronicle,—before Mr. Woodcockes. 7. Florio his 1st and 2d. fruites. 8. Mamillia, j parte. 9. The 3d parte of the Countesse of Pembroke. 10. Her Ivye churche. 11. A treatise for bees. 12. The Shepheardes Garland. 13. Virgillis Bucolikes and Georgickes. 14. Synners Guyde. 15. Shootinge in great ordinance, by Bourne, with his inventions and devices. 16. The 1st and 2d. comedie of Terence, in Inglish. 17. Cupydes Journey to hell, with the tragedie of Dido. 18. Treasure for travailers. 19. Hero and Leander, with the j booke of Lucon, by Marlowe. 20. Sir Tho. Cockains booke of Hūtinge. 21. Butterfields catechisme: 22. Moses his catechisme. 23. Diall of Dreames.—Englands Helicon.---The king of Fr. declarac'on of warre againste the duke of Savoie, warning his subiectes, &c.---The Journall, &c. of Jacob Cornelyson, &c." With Cuthbert Burby.

MATTHEW

MATTHEW LOWNES, stationer,

SON of Hugh Lownes of Astbury, Cheshire, fletcher, and brother of Humphrey, was apprenticed to Nicholas Ling, for ten years from Michaelmas 1582; made free the 11 Octob. 1591, by John Busby, to whom he had been put over 6 Dec. 1585; and came on the Livery 3 July, 1602. He served Renter in 1609; and Under Warden in 1616. He was fined 2 Oct. 1598 " for keeping a prentice vnpresented, contrary to Order, xijd."

" The Poem of Poemes,—by I. M." (*Jarvis Markham*). Octavo. 1595
Again, as p. 1033. Sixteens 1556..

" MORTIMERIADOS. The Lamentable ciuell warres of Edw. II. and the Barrons.—Printed by I. R. (*James Roberts*) for *him*, and are to be solde at his shop in S. Dunstons Church-yard, 1596." Dedicated " To the excellent and most accomplished Ladie, Lucie Countesse of Bedford. —Michaell Drayton."---To the same, signed E. B. Contains T 2, in fours. Trinity Coll. Cambr. Capel's books, R. 18. Licensed. Quarto. 1596.

" A Herrings Tayle: Contayning a Poeticall fiction of diuers matters worthie the reading." The device, Fortune blindfolded, standing on the ball of the Earth, holding out in her right hand a Palm branch, and in her left a naked Sword: the motto, Fortuna. " At London. Printed for Matthew Lownes, 1598." E 2, in fours. W.H. Quarto. 1598.

" Godfrey of Bulloigne," &c. as p. 1214. Licensed. 1600.

He had also licenses for the following, viz. In 1597, " A viewe of the present state of Ireland: a discourse by way of dialogue between Eudoxus and Irenius." Conditionally. In 1600, " Ciuile considerations vpon many and sundry histories aswell ancient as moderne, and principally vpon those of Guiccardin, handled after the man' of a discours, &c. by the Lord Remy, Florentin, and done into French by Gabriell Chappuys, and englished by—."

THOMAS MILLINGTON, stationer,

SON of Wm. Millington of Hamptongay, Oxfordshire, husbandman, was apprenticed to Henry Carre for eight years from St. Bartholomew's, 1583; and made free 8 Nov. 1591. He was fined 27 Aug. 1596, for printing a ballad contrary to orders, ijs. vjd. Again, 7 Feb. following, for printing a ballad, not licensed, to the wrong of T. Creed, ijs. vjd. and to pay T. C. ijs. iiijd. for amends, and then he may enjoy the said ballad. Again, 7 March, for printing a book before it was authorised and entered, ijs. vjd. He kept shop under St. Peter's in Cornhill.

" The Copie of a Letter from the French King" &c. as p. 1208. 1595.

Henry

1600 "The Cronicle History of Henry the fift, With his battell fought at Agin Court in France. Togither with Auntient Pistoll. As it hath bene sundry times played by the Right Honorable the Lord Chamberlaine his seruants.—Printed by Tho. Creede for *him* and John Busby, And are to be sold at his house in Carter Lane, next to the Powle head. 1600." G, in fours. See p. 1283. - Quarto.

1600. Henry VI. &c. as p. 1291.

1600. "The True Tragedie of Richard Duke of Yorke, and the death of good King Henrie the sixt: With the whole contention betweene the two houses, Lancaster and Yorke; as it was sundry times acted by the Right Honorable the Earle of Pembroke his seruantes. Printed—by W. W. for *him*, and are to be sold at his shoppe vnder St. Peter's Church in Cornewall. 1600." H, in fours. See p. 1267. Quarto.

He had also licenses for the following, viz. In 1593, "A booke entituled the Firste parte of the Contention of the twoo famous houses of Yorke and Lancaster, with the deathe of the good Duke Humfrey, and the banishment and deathe of the duke of Suff. And the tragicall ende of the proude Cardinall of Winchester, with the notable rebellion of Jack Cade, and the duke of Yorkes first clayme vnto the Crowne.---The famouse tragedie of the Riche Jewe of Malta." &c. as p. 1342. In 1594, "A true discourse," &c. as p. 1339. Newes from Brest, being a true reporte of the takinge of the forte called Croyden, three leagues from Brest.---The sentence of the Court of Parliament against John Castell, scholler in the Colledge of the Jesuites for the parracide by him attempted against the Kinges person." And for which he was executed. In 1595, "The Norfolk gent. his will and testament howe he comitted the keeping of his children to his owne brother, whoe delte moste wickedly with them: and howe God plagued him for it.---Jack of Newbery: so it be lawfully auctorised." Also, for sundry ballads.

HENRY OLNEY, stationer,

SON of John Olney, citizen and Turner, of London, was apprenticed to John Harrison the elder, forteen years from Michaelmas, 1584; and made free 4 Febr. 1593-4.

1595. "An Apologie for Poetrie. Written by the right noble, vertuous, and learned, Sir Phillip Sidney, Knight. Odi profanum vulgus, et arceo. At London, printed for Henry Olney, and are to be sold at his shop in Paules Church-yard, at the signe of the George, neere to Cheap-gate. Anno 1595." This title is on a separate leaf; the Apologie begins on signature B, and ends on L 3, in fours. This had been entered as his

copy

copy 12 Apr. 1595, and afterwards obliterated with this note, "This belongeth to Mr. Ponsonby by a former entrance: and an agreement is made between them, whereby Mr. P. is to enioy the copie according to the former entrance." See p. 1275. W.H. Quarto.

"DIELLA. Certaine Sonnets adioyning to the amorous poeme of Dom Diego and Gineura. By R. L. Gentleman. Ben balla à chi fortuna suona. At London, Printed for *him*, *&c.* 1596." The sonnets are 28 in number. See Hist. of Eng. Poetry, Vol. III; p. 480, note m. 16*. 1596.

If this book was licensed it must have been entred for the printer, whose name does not appear. I find nothing licensed to Olney.

RICHARD OCKOULD or OCKOLDE, stationer,

WAS made free by Tho. Scarlet, 12 Decemb. 1593. This appears to be the apprentice that Scarlet kept incog. for seven years, and for which he was fined. See p. 1164.

"A sermon preached at Pauls Cross, 7 June, 1596 by I. T. on James 4; 8. Printed for Rich. Ockolde, 1596." Quarto. 1596.

HUGH ASTLEY,

SON of Roger Astley of Maptock, Warwickshire, yeoman, deceased, was apprenticed to Mr. Will. Seres for 7 years from St. James's day 1576. It was however agreed that he should serve his time with Abr. Veale, Draper, also a brother of the Stationers' company. Accordingly he appears to have taken up his freedom in the Drapers' company: but, 3 June 1600, he, with Will. Young and others, was sworn and admitted free of the Stationers' by translation from the Drapers', &c. as p. 1357.

"The arte of Navigation." &c. as p. 1240. This copy, with others, was entred 1 March 1595-6 to Mr. Dawson, then warden, "to print for Hughe Astley,—viz. The art of Nauigation by Martin Curtis. The safegard of Saylers. The Attractiue. The Pathway to saluation. The godly exhortation to England. Item, yt is ordered that if Mr. Dawson decease, then the said Hugh shall haue his choyse of any printer, free of this company, to print the said copies for him." But, in the margin, "5 April 1596. Striken out by authoritie of a Court holden this day. The art of Nauigac'on is Mr. Watkins copy. The rest, that no partie hath no *(any)* right to it. To be printed by Mr. Dawson to thuse of the Company, that will Lay on, and pay vid. in the li." The art of Navigation was therefore now printed by assignment from Mr. Watkins. But this, with the other four copies, and "The poore mans rest. The newe Inuention 1596.

uention of Arithmetique. The garden of the Muses." were allowed him in full Court, 3 Nov. 1600; "sauynge the right of eu'y man" &c.

1600. "Belvedere, or The Garden of the Muses." Device: A tree between two high mountains; without which, a pink on one side and an hearts-ease on the other; the sun at top: the whole in an oval with this motto, Parnasso et Apolline Digna." "Imprinted—by F. K. for *him*, dwelling at Saint Magnus corner. 1600." Prefixed are an epistle "To the Reader.---To his louing and approoued good Friend, M. John Bodenham." In verse, signed A. M. Bodenham's arms on the opposite page. Guillim p. 431.---"Of this garden of the Muses.—W. Rankins, Gent.—Of the Booke.—R. Hathway.---To the Vniuersitie of Oxenford.—Stat sine morte decus.---To the Vniuersitie of Cambridge.—Sua cuique gloria." These also in verse. R, in eights. See Hist. of Eng. Poetry, Vol. iii; p. 280. Capel's: Trinity Coll. Cambridge. Licensed. Sixteens.

CLEMENT KNIGHT

WAS, with Hugh Astley and others, translated from the Drapers' company to the Stationers' 3 June 1600: yet he had licenses granted, and the following book printed for him before the said transfer. He was one of the 27 who were fined ij*sh.* vi*d.* each, for buying the letting Humours blood, &c. as p. 1260. "being newe printed after it was forbydden and burnt." He came on the Livery in 1604.

1596. "The Historie of Heaven: containing the poetical fictions of all the Starres in the Firmament, Gathered from amongst all the poets and astronomers, by Chrystopher Middleton. Printed for *him*, 1596." 4°.

He had licenses also for the following, viz. Apr. 2. 1595, "A figge for Momus." Decemb. 30. "The first p'te of the nature of a Woman." June 25, 1600, "The French Scholemaster wherof Claudius Holyband was aucthor. To pay vi*d.* in the li. for paper and printinge, according to thordinance for the poore, as often as he shall prynt it." June 26. "These bookes following, allowing vi*d.* in the li. to thuse of the poore of the company, accordinge to the ordinance in that behalf, viz. Virgilles Aeneidos in English.---The Regyment of life.---The Regiment of healthe.—Lucius Apulei, of the golden asse, in English.—Vocabula Stãbrigij."

EDWARD BLOUNT, or BLUNT, stationer,

SON of Ralph Blunt of London Merchant-taylor, deceased, was apprenticed to William Ponsonby for 10 years from Midsummer 1578; and made free 25 June 1588.

"A Worlde

" A Worlde of Wordes," &c. as p. 1213. Licensed. 1598.

" Hero and Leander." &c. as p. 1287. 1598.

" The Hospitall of incurable Fooles:" &c. as p. 1218. Licensed. 1600.

He had also licenses for the following, viz. In 1593, " The profitt of imprisonment. A parradox, first written in French by Odet de la Noue, lorde of Teleigine, and translated by John Silvester." In 1598, " Astrea. The miracle of the peace of France." In 1599, " The vnyting of the realme of Portugall to the Crown of Castile.---To be translated out of French and Latyn into Englissh: Annaei Senecae philosophi Stoicorũ omniũ opera.—The Essaies of Michell lord of Montaigne, translated into English by John Florio." In 1600, " The naturall and morall historie of the Indies: written first in the Spanishe tonge by Joseph Acosta, Jesuit, and translated into Englissh by E. G."

JOHN BROWN, stationer,

SON of John Brown of Reading, Berks, mercer, was apprenticed to Ralph Newbery for nine years from Michaelmas 1586; and made free 5 Aug. 1594. He dwelt first at the sign of the Sugar-loaf, afterward at the Bible, in Fleet-street.

" A hedgerow of bushes," &c. as p. 1266. 1598.

" A Discourse vpon the catalogue of doctors" &c, as p. 1293. L. 1598.

" A briefe description of the whole world." &c. as p. 1297. Licensed. 1599.

Again in 1600. R. Braddock for him. See p. 1299. 1600.

" Ouidius Naso his Remedie of Loue." &c. as p. 1283. Licensed to him and John Jagger, who perhaps had his quota with his own name separate also. 1600.

" The Tears of the Beloued," &c. as p. 1301. 1600.

" A true report of the most tryumphant and ryall accomplisment of the baptisme of the most excellent right high and mighty prince Henry Frederick, by the grace of God, prince of Wales, as it was solemnized August 30, 1594." Printed by Thomas Creed for him.[a] ——

He had also licenses for the following, viz. In 1597, " A shorte discourse of the valientnes of the mynde, called the Anatomie of the proper man." In 1598, " A most fragrant flower, or devoute exposition of the Lordes prayer, full of Godlye affectes. Devided into seaven meditations and prayers; Compiled by Granado a fryer, and translated out of Latyn into Englissh by I. G."---with John Herbert, " Iris, or Three sev'all boxes of sportinge familiars.—Astrea. The miracle of the Peace of France.—By assignment

 from

[a] It had been printed in Scotch at Edinburgh by Rob. Waldegrave, 1594; wherein the prince is rightly styled Prince of Scotland. His being in this edition styled Prince of Wales evinces that it was not printed till after King James came to the Crown of England.

f.om Val. Syms, The table of good Coũsell, with a singuler psalme so the syck soule."—In 1600, " The poesie, or meditac'on and prayer of a pensiue harte.—The lyse and death of our Saviour."

JOHN SMYTHICKE, or SMETHWICKE, stationer,

SON of —— Smythicke citizen and Draper of London, deceased, was apprenticed to Thomas Newman for nine years from Christmas 1589; and was made free 17 Jan. 1596-7, by Mrs. Newman. He first kept shop in Fleet street, near the Temple gate; afterward under the dial of St. Dunstan's; and used the device of a Duck, having a label in its mouth with " wick," in a compartment with this motto, " Non altam peto. I. S."

1599. " Of Mariage and Wiuing." &c. as p. 1283. See Harl. Pamphlets, N°. 273.

He had also licenses for the following, viz. Octob. 6, 1597. " The newes of the Cardinalles coming to relieve the citie of Amiens in Pickardie, 5 Sept. 1597." May 29, 1600, " Pasquilles passe and passe not, sett downe in 3ppp." Aug. 22, " Pasquilles swullerd humors." He printed till 1637.

WILLIAM ASPLEY, stationer,

SON of William Aspley of Royston, Cambridgeshire, Clerk, deceased, was apprenticed to Geo. Bishop for nine years from Christmas 1587; and made free 4 Apr. 1597. He dwelt at the Tiger's Head in St. Paul's Church-yard: afterward at the Parrot, there.

1599. An answer to Wm. Alabaster's motives, by Roger Fenton, preacher at Gray's Inn. F. Kingston, for him. See p. 1209. Licensed. Quarto.

1600. " Much Ado about Nothing." &c. as as p. 1374.

1600. Henry IV. Second part. &c. as ib.

1600. " The Pleasaunt Comedie of Old Fortunatus. As it was plaied before the Queenes Maiestie this Christmas, by the Right Honorable the Earle of Nottingham Lord high Admirall of England his seruants.—Printed by S. S. for *him*,—in Paules Church-yard, at—the Tygers head. 1600." L 3, in fours. Licensed. Quarto.

He had also licenses for the following, viz. In 1598. " The tragick Comedye of Celestina, wherein are discoursed, in most pleasant stile many philosophicall sentences and advertisementes, verye necessarye for younge gentlemen, Discoveringe the sleightes of treacherous servantes

vantes, and subtile cariages of filthye bawdes.---A brief and true declarac'on of the sycknes, last wordes, and death of the kinge of Spayne, Phillip the 2d.---A triplicitie of the Myndes passion/ The first expressinge Mary Magdalens vij Lamentac'ons for the love of Jesus. The 2d discoursinge of the excedinge Joirs of Heaven and thextreme sorowes of hell/ The third coteyninge the birthe, life and passion of our Lord and Savior." In 1599, "Of the takinge of the Jlande of the Grand Canaryes, and the Jland of Gomera, by the Hollanders, Provided, yf it cotain any thinge offensive to the State of England, this entrance to be void.---The secret last Instructions that kynge Philip the 2d kinge of Spayne, left to his son Kinge Philip the 3d of that name, conteininge howe to governe himself after his fathers death. Brought to light by a servant of his Treasorer, Don Christofer de Mora, called Roderige D. A. A. So it cotaine nothing against the State here.---A warnynge for fayre women. A comedie called Old Fortunatus in his newe liu'rie." In 1600. "Smythes Jewell, wherein the brief of the whole Bible, not onely p'ticularly but sumaryly, is conteined by analyticall methode and alphabeticall v'se: translated out of Latin into Englissh.—These viij copies, savynge the right of eu'y man that hath right, viz. 1. The Art of navigation by Martin Curtis. 2. The safegard of Saylers. 3. The newe Attractive. 4. The patheway to Saluation. 5. The Godly exhortac'on to England. 6. The poore mans rest. 7. The newe Invenc'on of Arithmetique. 8. The garden of *the* Muses."

JOHN BAYLIE

WAS translated from the Draper's Company to that of the Stationers' 25 June, 1600.

"Acolastus, or After wit. A poem, by Samuel Nicholson. At London. Imprinted for *him*, and are to be sold at his shop, neere the little North doore of Paules Church. 1600." Licensed. Quarto. 1600.

OF

OF

PRINTING

AT

OXFORD.

WHAT the noble art of printing was very early introduced into this university, is allowed; but by whose means it was brought in, who was the first printer there, or when the first book was printed, are questions that cannot be decisively answered at this distance of time. They have occasioned much altercation, originating from a quarto pamphlet, published in 1664, by one Richard Atkyns, or Atkins, of good family and considerable estate in Glocestershire, entitled "The Original and Growth of Printing: collected out of History, and the Records of this Kingdome. Wherein is also demonstrated, that printing appertaineth to the Prerogative Royal; and is a Flower of the Crown of England. By Richard Atkyns,[a] Esq. White-Hall, April the 25th, 1664. By Order and Appointment of the Right Honourable, Mr. Secretary Morice, Let this be printed. Tho. Rychaut. London: Printed by John Streater, for the Author, MDCLXIV." A faithful transcript from which, so far as it affects a MS. or Record, said to have been in the Lambeth Library, the very hinge on which the whole controversy turns, is inserted below,[b] the tract being very scarce. What has been asserted on one side, and

[a] There are two epistles prefixed to this book; one, "To the King's most Excellent Majesty;" the other, "To the Right Honourable, the Lords, and to The Honourable the Commons assembled in Parliament;" to both which his name is printed Richard Atkins.

[b] "Concerning the time of bringing this Excellent ART into *England*, and by whose Expence and Procurement it was brought; Modern Writers of good Reputation do most erroniously agree together. Mr. *Stowe* in his *Survey of London*, speaking of the 37th year of King *Henry* the Sixth his Reign, which was *Anno Dom.* 1459, saith, That the Noble Science of PRINTING was about this time found in *Germany* at *Magunce* by one *John Cutenbergus* a Knight. And that *William Caxton* of *London*, Mercer, brought it into *England* about the year 1471. And

Eli

To the most Noble Prince ALGERNON *Duke of* SOMERSET *dedi:*
this Specimen *of the first* Printing *at* OXFORD *and* CAMBRIDGE
is with great humility Inscribed by Joseph Ames F.R.S. *and Secr. to the Antiq. Soc.*

Explicit exposicio sancti Jeronimi in
simbolo apostolorum ad papam laurẽ
cium Impressa Oxonie Et finita An
no domini . M . cccc . lxviij . xvij . die
decembris .

Explicit opus magistri wil
helmi lyndewoode Super con=
stitucões prouinciales laus deo

Fratris laurencij guilelmi de saona ordinis
mioꝝ sac^e theo^e doctõis pꝓhemiũ ĩ nouã rthõrcã

Compilatũ aut̃ fuit hoc opus in alma uniuersitate Cantabrigie . Anno dñi . 1478 . die et . 6 . Julij . quo die
festum Sancte Marthe recolit̃ . Sub protectione Serenissi
mi regis anglorum Edwardi quarti .

I S

Impressum apud preclaram Cantabrigiam per
Ioannem Siberch Anno M.D.XXI.

and objected to on the other, may be ſeen in Eſſays on the Origin of Printing, by Bowyer and Nichols, with the Appendix and Supplement, octavo.

firſt practiſed the ſame in the Abby of St. *Peter* at *Weſtminſter*; With whom Sir *Richard Baker* in his Chronicle agrees throughout. And Mr. *Howell* in his *Hiſtoricall Diſcourſe* of *London* and *Weſtminſter*, agrees with both the former in the Time, Perſon, and Place in generall; but more particularly declares the Place in *Weſtminſter* to be the Almory there; And that *Iſlip* Abbot of *Weſtminſter* ſet up the firſt Preſs of Book-Printing that ever was in *England*. Theſe three famous Hiſtorians having fill'd the World with the ſuppoſed truth of this Aſſertion, (Although poſſibly it might ariſe through the miſtake of the firſt Writer only, whoſe Memory I perfectly honour) makes it the harder task upon me to undeceive the World again: Nor would I undertake this Work, but under a double notion; As I am a Friend to Truth, and ſo it is unfit to ſuffer one Man to be intituled to the worthy Atchievements of another. And as a Friend to myſelf, not to loſe one of my beſt Arguments of Intituling the King to this ART In his Private Capacity.

" Hiſtorians muſt of neceſſity take many things upon truſt, they cannot with their own but with the Eyes of others ſee what things were done before they themſelves were; *Bernardus non vidit omnia*: 'Tis not then impoſſible they ſhould miſtake. I ſhall now make it appear they have done ſo, from their Own, as well as from other Arguments: Mr. *Stowe* his Expreſſions are very dubious, and the matter expreſt very Improbable; He ſaith PRINTING was found in *Magunce*, which preſuppoſes it was practiſed ſome where elſe before, and loſt: And further, That 'twas found in the Reign of *Henry* the Sixth, *Anno Dom.* 1459. and not brought into *England* till Eleven years in the ſucceeding Reign of *Edward* the Fourth, being 12 years time after, as if it had been loſt again. If this be true, there was as little Rarity as expedition in obtaining it, the age of 12 years time having intervened, and ſo indeed it might be the Act of a Mercer rather than a more eminent Perſon; But when I conſider what great advantage the Kingdome in general receives by it, I could not but think a Publique Perſon and a Publique Purſe muſt needs be concerned in ſo publique a Good. The more I Conſidered of this, the more inquiſitive I was to find out the truth of it: At laſt, a Book came to my hands Printed at *Oxon. Anno Dom.* 1468. which was three years before any of the recited Authours would allow it to be in *England*; which gave me ſome reward for my Curioſity, and encouragement to proceed further: And in proſecution of this Diſcovery, the ſame moſt worthy Perſon who truſted me with the aforeſaid Book, did alſo preſent me with the Copy of a Record and Manuſcript in *Lambeth*-Houſe, heretofore in his Cuſtody, belonging to the See, (and not to any particular Arch Biſhop of *Canterbury*) the Subſtance whereof was this, (though I hope, for the publique ſatiſfaction, the Record it ſelf, in its due time, will appear.)

" *Thomas Bourchier*, Arch-Biſhop of *Canterbury*, moved the then King (*Henry* the 6th) to uſe all poſſible means for procuring a Printing-Mold (for ſo 'twas there called) to be brought into this Kingdom: the King (a good Man, and much given to Works of this Nature) readily hearkened to the motion; and taking private Advice, how to effect His Deſign, concluded it could not be brought about without great Secrecy, and a conſiderable Sum of Money given to ſuch Perſon or Perſons, as would draw off ſome of the Work-men from *Harlein* in *Holland*, where *John Cuthenberg* had newly invented it, and was himſelf perſonally at Work: 'Twas reſolv'd, that leſs than one Thouſand Marks would not produce the deſired Effect: Towards which Sum, the ſaid Arch-Biſhop preſented the King with Three Hundred Marks. The Money being now prepared, the Management of the Deſign was committed to Mr. *Robert Turnour*, who then was of the Robes to the King, and a Perſon moſt in Favour with Him, of any of his Condition: Mr. *Turnour* took to his Aſſiſtance Mr. *Caxton*, a Citizen of good Abilities, who Trading much into *Holland*, might be a Creditable Pretence, as well for his going, as ſtay in the *Low Countries*: Mr. *Turnour* was in Diſguiſe (his Beard and Hair ſhaven quite off) but Mr. *Caxton* appeared known and publique. They having received the ſaid Sum of One Thouſand Marks, went firſt to *Amſterdam*, then to *Leyden*, not daring to enter *Harlein* it ſelf;

for

octavo, 1774, &c. The whole seems to be impartially summed up by Sir James Burrow, in his Reports; therefore, as that book may probably be but in few hands, except those of gentlemen in the Law Department, I shall give it in his own words.

Having given an account of the Original Invention of Printing, and its earliest advances in foreign Countries, he proceeds.

" It

for the Town was very jealous, having imprisonned and apprehended divers Persons, who came from other Parts for the same purpose: They staid till they had spent the whole One Thousand Marks in Gifts and Expences. So as the King was fain to send Five Hundred Marks more, Mr. *Turnour* having writen to the King, that he had almost done his work; a Bargain (as he said) being struck betwixt him and two *Hollanders*, for bringing off one of the Work-men, who should sufficiently discover and teach this new Art: At last, with much ado, they got off one of the Under-Workmen, whose Name was *Frederick Corsells* (or rather *Corsellis*) who late one Night stole from his Fellows in Disguise, into a vessel prepared before for that purpose; and so the Wind (favouring the Design) brought him safe to *London*.

" 'Twas not thought so prudent, to set him on Work at *London*, (but by the Arch-Bishops meanes, who had been Vice-Chancellor, and afterwards Chancellor of the University of *Oxon*.) *Corsellis* was caryed with a Guard to *Oxon*; which Guard constantly watched, to prevent *Corsellis* from any possible Escape, till he had made good his promise, in teaching how to Print: So that at Oxford Printing was first set up in *England*, which was before there was any Printing-Press, or Printer, in *France*, *Spain*, *Italy*, or *Germany*, (except the City of *Mentz*) which claimes Seniority, as to Printing, even of *Harlein* it self, calling her City *Urbem Moguntinam Artis Typographicæ Inventricem primam*, though 'tis known to be otherwise, that City gaining that Art by the Brother of one of the Workmen of *Harlem*, who had learnt it at Home of his Brother, and after set up for himself at *Mentz*.

" This Press at *Oxon* was at least ten years before there was any printing in *Europe* (except at *Harlein*, and *Mentz*) where also it was but new born. This Press at *Oxford*, was afterwards found inconvenient, to be the sole Printing-place of *England*, as being too far from *London*, and the Sea: Whereupon the King set up a Press at St. *Albans*, and another in the Abby of *Westminster*, where they printed several Bookes of Divinity and Physick, (for the King, for Reasons best known to himself and Council) permitted then no Law-Books to be printed; nor did any Printer exercise that ART, but onely such as were the King's sworn Servants; the King himself having the Price and Emolument for Printing Books.

" Printing thus brought into *England*, was most Graciously received by the King, and most cordially entertained by the Church, the Printers having the Honour to be sworn the King's Servants, and the Favour to Lodge in the very Bosome of the Church; as in *Westminster*, St. *Albans*, *Oxon*, &c. By this meanes the ART grew so famous, that *Anno prim. Rich* 3. *cap.* 9. when an Act of *Parliament* was made for Restraint of Aliens, from using any Handicrafts here (except as Servants to Natives) a special *Proviso* was inserted, that Strangers might bring in Printed or Written Books, to sell at their pleasure, and Exercise the ART of Printing here, notwithstanding that Act: So that in the space of 40 or 50 years, by the especial Industry and Indulgence of *Edw.* the Fourth, *Edw.* the Fifth, *Rich.* the Third, *Henry* the Seventh, and *Henry* the Eighth, the *English* prov'd so good proficients in Printing, and grew so numerous, as to furnish the Kingdome with Books; and so skilfull, as to print them as well as any beyond the Seas, as appears by the Act of the 25 *Hen.* 8. cap. 15. which abrogates the said *Proviso* for that Reason. And it was further enacted in the said Statute, That if any Person brought Foreign books bound, he should pay 6*s.* 8*d.* *per* Book. And it was farther provided and Enacted, That in case the said Printers and Sellers of Books, were unreasonable in their Prices, they should be moderated by the Lord Chancellor, Lord Treasurer, the two Lord Chief Justices, or any two of them, who also had power to Fine them 3*s.* 4*d.* for every Book whose price shall be enhanced."

" It is now time to examine how, when, and by whom, it was first introduced into *our own*.

" Concerning this matter there are different accounts.

" It was formerly the general opinion and belief, and seemed to be agreed to by all our historians, that the art of printing was introduced and first practised in *England* by Mr. *Wm. Caxton*, a citizen of *London*, who had been bred a Mercer, having served an apprenticeship to *Rob. Large* in that branch of business: which *Rob. Large* died in 1441, after having been sheriff and Lord Mayor of *London*; and left a legacy to Caxton, in testimony of his good character and integrity. From the time of his master's death, Mr. Caxton spent the following thirty years (from 1441 to 1471) beyond sea, in the business of merchandize. In 1464, he was employed by King *Edward* the fourth in a public and honorable negotiation to transact and conclude a treaty of commerce between that King and his brother-in-law the duke of *Burgundy*.—By his long residence in *Holland*, *Flanders*, and *Germany*, he had opportunity of being informed of the whole method and process of this art: And returning to *England*, and meeting with encouragement from great persons, and particularly from the then abbot of *Westminster*, he first set up a press in that abbey, (in the *Almonry* or *Ambry)* and began to print books soon after the year 1471, and is said to have pursued his business there with extraordinary diligence till the year 1494; in which year Dr. *Middleton* says he died; " not in the year following, as all who write of him affirm." But Mr. *Ames* says, if not proves, that was no longer than the year 1491. He was probably upwards of fourscore years of age when he died. The " Recuyel of the historyes of *Troye*," is supposed to have been the first book that he printed in *England*. Dr. *Middleton* is a very strenuous advocate for *Caxton*; and professes a desire " to do Justice to his memory, " and not suffer him to be robbed of the glory so clearly due to him, of " having first imported into this kingdom an art of great use and benefit " to mankind; a kind of merit, that, in the sense of all nations, gives " the best title to true praise, and the best claim to be commemorated " with honour to posterity." The doctor states the positive evidence in proof of his assertion, as well as the negative and circumstantial: And he observes " that all our writers before the Restoration, who mention " the introduction of the art among us, give *Caxton* the credit of it, without any contradiction or variation." He cites *Stowe*, *Trussell*, Sir *Richard Baker*, *Leland*, and *Howell*, and the more modern authorities of Mr. *Henry Wharton* and M. *Du Pin*; all strong in favour of his opinion.

" In opposition, however, to all these great and seemingly invincible testimonies and authorities on behalf of Mr. *Caxton*, a book which had been scarce observed before the Restoration, was soon after that time taken notice of, and looked upon as a strong argument, if not a full and clear proof, " that the art of printing had been exercised in the university of *Oxford*, *before Caxton exercised it at Westminster, in* 1471." This book bears for its title, " *Expositio Sancti Jeronimi in Simbolum Apostolorum ad Papam Laurentium*;" and at the end—"*Explicit Expositio, &c. Impressa Oxonie, & finita Anno Domini* M.CCCC.LXVIII. xvii *die Decembris*." Yet history was quite silent about this very remarkable fact of a printing in *England* prior to Caxton's; nor was there any memorial to be found in the university of a circumstance so honourable to them, and so beneficial to Literature. It has been urged, that notwithstanding this long silence concerning such a very extraordinary event, the matter is now cleared up, by the discovery of a Record which had long laid obscure and unknown at *Lambeth-Palace*, in the Register of the See of *Canterbury*, which record contains a *narrative* of the whole transaction, drawn up at the very time. An account of this record was first published by *Rich. Atkyns* Esq. in the beginning of 1664 in his "Original and growth of printing, collected out of the history and records of this kingdom." It sets forth, "that *Thomas Bourchier*, Archbishop of *Canterbury*, moved King *Henry* "the Sixth to use all possible means to procure a printing-mould to be "brought into this kingdom. &c. nor did any printer exercise the art, "but only such as were the king's sworn servants; the king himself "having the price and emolument for printed books."

"Upon the authority of this record, all our later writers have declared *Corsellis* to have been the *first* printer in *England*. This is admitted by Dr. *Middleton*: And he specifies *Antony Wood* and Mr. *Mattaire*, and *Palmer*, and *Bagford*, by name, as persons who were clear in that Opinion. But he says, "it is strange that a piece so fabulous and carrying such evident marks of *forgery*, could impose upon men so knowing and inquisitive." He asserts, "that as it was never heard of before the publication of *Atkyns's* book, so it has never since been seen or produced by any man." He cites *Palmer* himself as owning "that it is not to be found there *now*;" And he thinks it clear, that Archbishop Parker must have very carefully examined the registers of *Canterbury*, and that it was not in *his* time. In fine, he declares in express terms, "That we may pronounce this record a *Forgery*."

"But though he seems to exult in having cleared his hands of this *Record*, yet he admits "that the book itself stands firm as a monument of the exercise of printing at *Oxford* six years older than any book of *Caxton* with *Date*." He acknowledges the fact to be strong, and what in *ordinary* cases passes for certain evidence of the age of books: But he says, "that in *this*, there are such contrary facts to balance it, and such circumstances to turn the scale, that he takes the date in question to have been falsified originally by the printer, either by design or by mistake, and an X to have been dropt or omitted in the age of its impression." And he argues with his usual sagacity and acuteness, to shew not only the possibility of his conjecture, but the probability of it, and (as he says) "to make it even certain."

"Mr. Bowyer, whose learning and particular knowledge in his profession

‡ The first Work that is known to have a date to it, was the *Psalter* published at Mentz in 1457.

ſeſſion ſeem to qualify him for being at leaſt as good a judge of this diſpute as any man that ever lived, does by no means agree with Dr. *Middleton* in this point of *Caxton's* priority to the *Oxford*-Book, or in the arguments adduced by the doctor in ſupport of his opinion; any more than he does in the former point, of the place where the art was firſt invented and practiſed abroad.—He is of opinion, that the *Oxford*-Preſs was prior to Caxton's; and thinks that thoſe who have called Mr. *Caxton* the "firſt printer in *England*," and *Leland* in particular, meant that he was the firſt who practiſed the art with *fuſile* types and conſequently brought it to *perfection*:" Which is not inconſiſtent with *Corſellis*'s having printed earlier at *Oxford* with *ſeparate types cut in wood*, which was the only method he had learnt at *Harlem*. The ſpeaking of Mr. *Caxton* as the firſt printer in *England*, in *this* ſenſe of the expreſſion, is not irreconcileable with the ſtory of *Corſellis*.

"Theſe facts and opinions being thus laid before the Reader, he will judge for himſelf, concerning their Truth or Probability. The Diſputants on both ſides have agreed in one Poſition, which will be eaſily aſſented to; namely, "that it is very unſafe to truſt to Common Hiſtory; and neceſſary to recur to Original Teſtimonies, if we would know the ſtate of the Facts with Exactneſs." Vol. IV. p. 2413, &c.

"Incipit expoſicio ſancti Jeronimi in ſimbulum apoſtolorum ad papam laurecium." This book is avouched by good judges to be printed with metal types, has ſeveral double letters and contractions, the long ſ is frequently uſed at the end of words; the paper has different marks, ſome like what Caxton printed on, and the book has a large margin. It contains by ſignatures e 9, in eights, 25 lines on a page, the firſt four leaves of each are marked, the reſt are left blank. The leaves are not numbered, neither are there running titles, nor catch words. At the end, "Explicit expoſicio ſancti Jeronimi in ſimbolo apoſtolorum ad papam laurecium Impreſſa Oxonie Et finita Anno domini. M.cccc.lxviij. xvij.die decembris." It is without printer's name or cypher, but the date is undoubtedly fair and compact. See copper-plate facing p. 1386. We know of only 5 copies of this book remaining; thoſe are in his Majeſty's library,* the earl of Pembroke's, the Bodleian, and All Souls college libraries in Oxford, and in the Public library, Cambridge. Quarto. 1468.

The next book with a date hitherto diſcovered, is Leonardus Aretinus in Ariſtot. ethic. comment. "Incipit prefacio leonardi arretini in libros ethicorum. Colophon "Explicit textus ethicorum Ariſtotelis per leonardū arretinū luciſſime tranſlatus, correctiſſimeq; impreſſus Oxoniis Anno dñi. M.CCCC.LXXIX." Y 6, in eights. The Rev. Dr. Lort, and Mr. Alchorne. Quarto. 1479.

"Incipit tractatus ſolennis fratris Egidij de ordine fratrum Auguſtinenſium de peccato originali." It begins, "Ego, cum ſim puluis & cinis, loquar ad dominum meum dicens—Domine Deus iudex—ſi omnes anime 1479.

* That mentioned by Mr. Ames as in the poſſeſſion of James Weſt Eſq; was bought after his deceaſe, in 1773, by Mr. M. C. Tutet; and after his, in 1786, for his Majeſty.

tue sunt, sicut animae patris sic et anime filii. Sed tu per tua pietate miserere nobis, vt facie ad faciam te videre possimus, qui es benedictus in secula seculorum, Amen." The Colophon in red ink. "Explicit tractatus breuis et vtilis de originali peccato, editus a fratre Egidio Romano, ordinis fratrum heremitarum sancti Augustini. Impressus et finitus Oxonie. A natiuitate dnī. MCCCCLXXIX.[f] xiiii. die mensis Marcii." See some further account of this book in Catal. Bibl. Harleianæ, Vol. iii; N°. 6674.

"All these books, *says Mr. Lewis*, agree together in every thing; they are manifestly all three printed with the same German types, or letter; they all have the signatures placed at the bottom of the page, and end of the line thus, *a i*, *a ii*, *a iii*, *&c.* they all want the direction word," *&c.* Anthony Wood says of them, "Perspicuis magis et pulchrioribus quam recentiores nonnulli," more plain and beautiful than some more modern ones.

He also intimates that Wynkin de Worde succeeded [g]John Scolar at Oxford, and that Grope Lane had its name changed to Wynken lane on account of Wynken de Worde's living and printing there.[h] If ever he did at all, it must have been in Caxton's life-time; for it evidently appears that he printed in Caxton's house after his death, and perhaps a considerable time before; and we have books of his printing at Westminster and London every year from 1494, 3 years after Caxton's death, to the time of his own, in 1534, besides many without date; therefore 'tis not likely he should have succeeded Scolar, as supposed. Changing the name of a street or lane, one would think, should not be on so trivial an account. Why not name the lane after Scolar, Rood, Hunt, or indeed rather after Corsellis. But though W. de Worde might not live at Oxford, he printed at London many grammatical books, written by Wittington, &c. which might be sold by some agent of his in Oxford; and though Pinson and Travers printed the same also, yet there does not appear near so many of theirs, and those perhaps not so correct. This has some appearance of probability. However this might be; if ever W. de Worde really lived at Oxford, and the name of Grope Lane changed to Wynkyn Lane on account of his dwelling there, why may not he be supposed to be the person who printed the Exposicio sancti Jeronimi, &c. A deed worthy such a commemoration. I objected to myself the great age he must then have lived to; but on examination it will be found not surpassing credibility, even supposing the date 1468 no mistake; for had he been 24 years of age at that time, he would not have exceeded 90 when he died; but supposing the omission of an X in the date, a circumstance which must be acknowledged probable, as it has not

[f] That is, as A. Wood paraphrases it, "Inchoatus ad festum nativitatis An. Dom. 1479, absolutus autem XIV Martii proxime sequentis."

[g] Bagford says, about 1500; and if so he must have preceded Scolar.

[h] Hist. & Antiq. Univ. Oxon. p. 227, &c.

not unfrequently[1] happened, he would then have been no more than 80 at the time of his death.

Other books have been fuppofed to be printed by Fred. Corfellis, or however by the fame perfon who printed the forementioned books.

In the late Tho. Ofborne's catalogue of books for fale in June 1756, No. 1345 " Plinii Secundi Epiftolarum, Liber primus. Exemplar elegans, literis initial. colorat. corio turcico, fol. deaur. lineis rubris & auro elegans ornat. 15 l. 15 s. Oxon. apud F. Corcellis. 1469." To which is added this note, " Hocce unicum eft exemplar notum, a variis allegatum, et vix uni vifum adeo ut Phoenix librorum dici mereratur, certe primus eft ex libris a Corcellis impreffis, cui nomen fuum adjunxerit, fecundus vero ordine omnium quos unquam ille impreffit, priorem fcilicet fcimus fuiffe, Jeronymi Expofitionem in Symbol. Apoftol. Oxoniae 1468. Anno 1470, varia idem typographus impreffit Opufcula, addito in fine nomine, fed nec unicum eorum reperitur hodie integrum. Poffident quidem amatores fragmenta aliqua poematum Latinorum, ut Gerardi Lyftrii Rhenenfis, &c. Carmen Liftrii lividorum hominum venenofas linguas, &c." This raifed the curiofity of the book-collectors, who confidered this article as a confirmation of what R. Atkins had afferted about printing at Oxford.[k] They all flocked to Ofborne's fhop, who inftead of the book, produced a letter from a man at Amfterdam, filled with frivolous excufes for not fending them to him. They were difappointed, and looked on the whole as a HUM; however, the Plinii Epiftolae, and Ger. Liftrii Oratio, &c. afterwards appeared at an auction at Amfterdam, and were bought for the late Dr. Ant. Afkew; and were fold again at an auction of his books, by Baker and Leigh, in Feb. 1775. Lot 2064, and 2622, to which articles are annexed, viz. to Lot 2064, " Ad finem haec verba, *Impr. Oxon. apud F. Corfellis*, 1470, Manu recentiore exarata funt." Alfo to lot 2622, " Haec verba, *Imprim. Oxon. ap Corfellis*, 1469, Manu recentiore exarata funt." To thofe who are at all converfant in early printing, the dates will appear at firft fight a bungling forgery.[l]

The printer of the three firft mentioned books, whoever he was, either dying or removing, was fucceeded here by Theodore Rood, a native of Cologne in Germany.

" Guido de Columnia de hiftoria Trojana, per T. R." (*Theodore Rood.*) Quarto. 1480.

Alexander

[1] Mr. Ames mentions, among others alike circumftanced, two books in his poffeffion, viz. " Formalitates de mente doctoris fubtilis Scoti." At the end, " Venetis impreffa in contrata fancti Caffiani per Simonem de Luere, 14 menfis Decembris 1051." Evidently for 1501. And, " Flores divi Bernardi," printed at Paris by Philip Pigonchet, " 1099;" whereas by his name, and there being no printing known fo early, one cannot imagine it true; but that it fhould be 1499. I fhall add to thefe a very extraordinary one in my own, wherein the date is not given in numerals or figures, but in words at length. The book is intituled, " *Practica Valefci de Tharanta que al's Philoniu dicitur*" &c. Colophon, " Impreffum lugd' per Joh'em Cleyn alemann. Anno noftre falutis Millefimo quadringentefimo primo, decimo octavo, Kal' Decembris." Similar miftakes, or omiffions, are not wanting, but thefe may fuffice.

[k] See note b, in p. 1390.

[l] See Origin of printing by Bowyer and Nichols, p. 174.

1481. Alexander de Alexandria in III libros Aristotelis de anima. A fine copy of this book is in the British Museum, but it wants the general title page. The first book ends on signature g 5. "Explicit Expositio venerabilis Alexandri super primū librū de aīa." g 6 is a blank leaf, the paper mark a pair of sheers. On sig. h i, "Incipit—Super secundū librum de anima." On y 7, "Explicit elucidantissima expositio egregii Alexandri super secundū librū de anima." y 8 is blank; the paper mark, a hand pointing with a cross, and a cross on the top of the flag-staff. On z i "Incipit—super tercium librū de aīa." On H 8, "Explicit sentenciosa atq; studio digna expositio venerabilis Alexandri super terciū librū de anima. Impressum per me Theodoricū rood de Colonia in alma universitate Oxōn. Anno incarnacionis dnice. M.cccc.lxxxi. xi. die mensis Octobris." This book is neatly printed in double columns, with the lines spaced out to the end, and has many contractions; but the types are rather inferior to those of the Expositio S. Jeronimi. It is the size of a modern quarto, but properly is a small folio, having as many leaves without paper marks as there are with them in every signature. On the first leaf of this copy, a ii, is Thomas Cantuarien'. The authograph of Arcbp. Cranmer.

1482. Joh. Latterburius in Threnos Jeremiæ. Colophon, "Explicit exposicio ac moralisacio tercii capituli Trenorum Jheremie prophete, Anno dnī MCCCCLXXXII, ultima die mensis Julii." At the end of the index, "Explicit tabula super Opus Trenorum compilatum per Johannem Latterbury, ordinis Minorum." About the middle of the book is this passage: "Item Anno Domini M.CCCC.XLIII. in capitulo provinciali London. celebrato, et etiam Oxon. pluribus vicibus, prius et post in studio secum commoranti, frater Hermanus de Colonia, fratri Johanni de Latterburii retulit viva voce, quod in patria sua est quedam Villa, que vulgariter vocatur Engere, de qua Anglia vocaliter derivatur." This is a thick folio, in the dean and chapters' library, Westminster, and printed partly on paper, and partly on vellum; it has signatures, but neither catch-words, nor numbers to the leaves, and is without name of place or printer; but from a comparison of its letter with Hunt's, or Rood's, it is judged to be one of theirs, as is the following:

—— Provincial constitutions. This is a large thick folio, in two columns, and two sorts of letters, begins with a wooden cut of Lindwood setting before a writing desk, and at the end of the book, "Explicit opus magistri Wilhelmi Lyndewoode super constitutiones provinciales: laus Deo." But at the end of the table, "Explicit tabula compendiosa super librum, qui intitulatur Provincialis, compilata per Wilhelmum de Tylia, nemore completa. In festo conuersionis sancti Pauli. Anno Domini millesimo CCCCLXXXIII." No printer's name, place, nor time put down.*

THEODORE

* Primum Isidis in Vado typis excusum est. Leland de script. p. 444.

THEODORE ROOD and THOMAS HUNT.

"Francisci Aretini Oratoris Phalaridis epistolarum e greco in latinum (1485.) versio." On the back of this title page are the following Latin verses.

"Carmelitani Brixiensis poete ad lectorem Carmen
Hunc precor atque precor, lector studiose, libellum
Perlege, qui passim gemmea verba refert.
PHALARIS hunc scripsit creteis editus oris
Si patriam queras Allipalensis erat.
Missus in exilium siculas peruenit ad oras,
Se faciens dominum qui relegatus erat.
Protinus has scripsit celebres, mihi crede, tabellas
Hostibus ac populis morigerisque simul.
Quas decus eloquii grecias facit esse latinas
Franciscus noster hic Aretinus erat.
Munificum queris, doctum, iustumque, piumque,
Jnvenies unum, Phalaris ille fuit."

Next follows an epistle to the reader, thus entitled: "Francisci Aretini Oratoris preclarissimi in eloquentissimas Pharidis tyranni epistolas per ipsum e greco in latinum versas." Contains M 3, in eights. At the end, "Hoc opusculum in Alma vniuersitate Oxonie a naturali Christiano ducentesima et nonagesima septima Olimpiade* foelicitur impressum est."

"Hoc Teodoricus Rood, quem Collonia misit,
Sanguine Germanus, nobile pressit opus;
Atque sibi socius Thomas fuit Anglicus Hunte.
Dii dent vt Venetos exuperare queant.
Quam Jenson Venetos docuit vir gallicus artem,
Ingenio didicit terra Britannia suo.
Celatos, Veneti, nobis transmittere libros
Cedite, nos aliis vendimus, O Veneti:
Que fuerat vobis ars primum nota Latini,
Est eadem nobis ipsa reperta prestans.
Quamuis semotos toto canit orbe Britannos
Virgilius, placet his lingua Latina tamen." *

Which may be thus Englished: "Theodoric Rood, by birth a German, from Cologne, printed this noble work; and Thomas Hunt, an Englishman, was his partner. God grant they may excell the Venetians. The art,

* Dr. Stack, and others, think from the Olympiades, this must be in the year 1481, being the first year of that Olympiad, but Dr. Middleton 1485, the last year. The printers here take it for granted, that there were five years from the celebration of one Olympic game to another, or that an Olympiad consisted of five full years; whereas though it is generally allowed that it was only at the beginning thereof, after the completion of four years.

* See these verses with some variation in Dr. Middleton's Dissertation on the origin of printing p. 10 and 11.

art, which Jenson a Frenchman taught the Venetians, Britain learnt by her own genius. Cease ye Venetians to send us printed books, we sell them to others. The art of printing Latin, which was known to you Venetians, is itself found out by us. Though Virgil sings the Britons separated from the whole world, they are neverthelefs pleased with the Latin tongue." All we know for certain of the said Rood and Hunt is contained in this account of them. The book was in the possession of the Rev. Herbert Randolph, rector of Deal in Kent. Octavo.

From these we are obliged to descend to Pinson's, or perhaps Wynken de Word's printing for them[p] till 1518, as in the following instance.

1506. " Principia, seu introductiones, fratris peregrini ytalici de lugo in via doctoris subtilis adipisci eiusdem doctoris doctrinam cupientibus." This title is over Duns Scotus's picture, and beneath; " Venundantur autem in alma ac florentissima vniuersitate Oxoniense, intactate virginis ac immaculate vico; sancti Johannis Euangeliste ad inter signium, per R. Pinson, cuz solerti cura ac diligentia honestissimi iuuenis ac prudentissimi Hugonis Meslier. Expensis autem Georgii Castellani, Oxonii morantis, ad intersignium sancti Johannis Euangeliste; in quo venundatur opus hoc. Finis, laus Deo, & beato Francisco, Amen, ac beate virgini.' London." See p. 252. Quarto.

J O H N S C O L A R.

ANTHONY Wood says that Theodore Rood was succeeded by John Scolar, a German, as he supposes, who set up his printing press in St. John's Street, over against Merton Church or chappel, where he printed several books from the latter part of Hen. VII, to the former part of the reign of Hen. VIII. however he mentions only two.

(1512.) " Tractatus expositorius super libros posteriorum: preclarissimi philosophi Walteri Burlei artium liberalium & trium philosophiarum magistri meritissimi: ac in sacra theologia doctoris perspicacissimi planissimiq; suis posteris Oxoniensibus admodum vtilis incipit feliciter cum summa diligentia recognitum." Colophon, " Explicit scriptum planissimi doctoris Walteri Burlei super libros posteriorum. Impressum in academia Oxonie anno Dominice incarnationis Mcccccxii die vero Decembris quarto ad laudem dei et profectum studentium.

" Fata

p Mr. Baker (in a letter to Mr. Ames, containing copies of some of Mr. Bagford's papers, mentions among other anecdotes, that Wynken de Worde printed at Oxford about 1500; but see p. 1342, note g. Mr. Bagford appears to have been the first who collected materials for a history of printing, and for that purpose to have made memorandums of all he heard, without exception; which doubtless would have been revised before they had been communicated to the public, he being esteemed very exact, as far as he could procure materials.

q Mr. Wood intimates that this book was printed this year also at Oxford; but query. See Hist. &c. Oxon. p. 217.

" Fata regunt finem: spero dii cepta secundent."

Then the king's, and the university's arms. This is taken from Mr. Lewis's MSS. Though Scolar's name does not appear to this, it probably was printed by him, as he used the same arms afterwards. 'Tis not improbable but a v may have been dropt or omitted in the date, after the x.

" Questiones moralissime super libros ethicorum eruditissimi viri, Joannis Dedicus, artium liberalium, triumq; philosopharum magistri optime meriti et in moralibus pre ceteris satis periti, feliciter incipiunt, subtilissimis Oxoniensibus in Philosophia morali lucubrare cupientibus non magis utiles quam necessarie." Colophon, " Explicitum est Joannis Dedici Oxoniensis in morali philosophia eruditissimi preclarum opusculum questionum subtilissime discutientium (licet sparsim cum quadam tamen dependentia) singulas materias in decem libris ethicorum Aristotelis investigatas, vel summa industria lucubranti patebit. Impressumq; in celeberrima universitate Oxoniensi per me Johannem Scolar in viculo Sancti Joannis Baptiste moram trahentem. Anno Dnī. mcccc. decimo octavo, mensis vero Maii die decimo quinto. Cum privilegio. Vetitum est per edictum sub sigillo Cancellariatus, ne quis in septennio hoc insigne opus imprimat, vel aliorum ductu impensis venditet in universitate Oxonie: aut infra precinctum eiusdem: sub pena amissionis omnium librorum et quinq; librarum sterlingorum pro singulis sic venditis ubiubi impressi fuerint, preter penam pretaxatam in decreto.' Cornicum occulos configere noli." In the Pub. Libr. Cambridge. Quarto. 1518.

" Tractat, perbreuis de materia & forma Mag'ri Walteri Burlei doctoris planissimi." This is over a neat wood-cut of a tutor, and his pupil presenting an open book to him, in his study; beneath which, " Aliud perbreue cōpendiū de relatiuis eiusdem doctoris vtile tamen admodum nouellis logicis." Concludes thus, " Finit tractatus duorum principiorum et de ralatiuis Mag'ri Walteri Burley Oxoniensis. Finis." On the back of this leaf, B 3, is the king's arms. On the last leaf, " Jmpositus est finis tractatui doctoris planissimi de duobus principijs. s. materia et forma et de relatiuis cum speciali priuilegio per septēniū ex edicto dignissimi cancellarij Oxonie." This over the Oxford Arms: beneath, " Impressum est presens opusculum in celeberrima vniuersitate Oxoniensi per me Joannem Scolar in viculo diui Joannis Baptiste moram trahentem Anno dnī.Mcccc. decīo octavo. Mensis vero Junij die septimo." It has much the appearance of W. de Worde's grammatical tracts. Quarto. 1518.

" Editio Whittintoni Lichfeldiensis de heteroclitis nominibus, et gradibus comparationis, Oxonie impressa per Joannem Scolar, in viculo diui Joannis Baptiste moram trahentem, anno Domini Mcccc. decimo octauo, mensis vero Junii die vicesimo septimo." With the arms of the university. " Vetitum est per edictum" &c. as above. Quarto. 1518.

 " Com-

' By this it appears that the chancellor of this famous university had, and exercised a power within his jurisdiction of granting the privilege of printing to such as he thought fit by his edict under the seal of his chancellorship; and of restraining and forbidding others on such penalties as he thought proper.

1518. "Compendium quaestiuncularum de luce & de lumine." At the end, "Cum privilegio dignissimi cancellarii vniuersitatis Oxonie." The university arms, and underneath, "Finit compendium quaestiuncularum de luce & de lumine, nouiter recognitum. Impressumq; in celeberrime vniuersitate Oxoniensi per me Johannem Scolar, in viculo diui Johannis baptiste moram trahentem, Anno domini M ccccc decimo octauo. mensis vero Junii die quinto." Thus in Mr. Lewis's MSS. A. Wood has "Junii xv." Mr. Ames, "Julii die v." But in the catalogue of English and Irish MSS. Tom. II; p. 380, this book is dated the 15th of June 1510." Neither of them mention the size of this book.

All these books have signatures, but neither numbers to the leaves, nor catch words.

CHARLES KYRFETH,

A Dutchman, seems to have succeeded John Scolar at Oxford, dwelling in the same street, and perhaps in the same house. The only book we have yet met with, printed by him, is the following:

1519. "Compotus manualis in vsum Oxoniensium." In Latin verse. Colophon, "Impressum est praesens opusculum in celeberrima vniuersitate Oxoniensi per me Karolum Kyrfeth in vico diui Johannis Baptistae moram trahentem, anno Domini M CCCCCXIX. 5 die Februarii." Quarto.

The following book, printed at the charge of cardinal Wolsey; with the king's arms on one side, and the cardinal's on the other; though it has neither date nor printer's name, was probably performed about this time at this place.

"Libellus prim. epistol. M. Tullii Cicer. Decus Oxoniensium, finitum universitate Oxoniensi." Quarto.

1569. An account of the Lithuanian translation of the Bible, is in the Brit. Museum. Quarto.

I have not met with any other account of books printed here till the year 1585, when a new printing press was erected at the expence of their chancellor the earl of Leicester, who made a present of it to the university.

JOSEPH BARNES

WAS appointed printer to this famous university; and continued so till 1617.[1] He frequently used for his device the arms of

[1] From that time John Lichfield and James Short, were printers to the university till 1624. whose books have not always both their names. John Lichfield and William Turner

of the university; an open book, with the words SAPIENTIA ET FELICITATIS, with seven seals between three ducal coronets; and about the whole OXONIENSIS ACADEMIA. Sometimes, in miniature, on a shield, with only Ox. on one side, and Ac. on the other. Sometimes he vsed a copper-plate, with emblematical figures about the arms, and JOSEPH BARNESIVS underneath.

The first book printed at the new press was "Speculum moralium Quæstionum in vniuersam Ethicam Aristotelis. Authore Johanne Caso." Which he dedicated to the chancellor. Quarto. 1585.

"A Booke of Christian Exercise, apertaining to Resolution, that is, shewing how that we should resolue our selues to become Christians indeede. By R. P. *(Robert Parsons)* Perused, and accompanied now with a treatise tending to Pacification, By Edmund Bunny. Heb. 13. 8. Jesus Christ yesterday, and to day, and the same for euer.. At Oxford, Printed by Joseph Barnes, Printer to that famous Vniuersitie. 1585." In a border. Dedicated to Edwin archbishop of York by Edm. Bunny. The epistle to the reader is dated "At Bolton Percy, in the ancienty or liberties of Yorke, the 9. of July, 1584." The Christian Exercise is divided into two parts; the first ends on page 193, and the second on p. 493. The treatise for pacification is printed so as to sell separately on occasion, with this title-page, "A treatise tending to pacification: by laboring those that are our aduersaries in the cause of religion, to receiue the Gospel, and to ioin with vs in profession thereof. By Edm. Bunny. Hosea 3. 4. 5. The children of Israell shall sit a great while without King," &c. And this, which Mr. Ames seems to have taken for the second part of the Christian Exercise, contains 140 pages. Mr. Ames, or rather his printer, seems to have made another mistake in calling this book a quarto, as the number of pages would not agree with that size. I have two editions of this book, both printed this year, page for page; the signatures of both are in twelves, half sheets; and therefore may properly be styled in Twenty-fours. 1585.

I have another edition printed also this year in octavo, without printer's name or place. It was first printed in 1584. See p. 783. The continuation of this book entitled, The second part of the book of Christian Exercise, &c. See p. 1222.

"Hyppolitus Ouidianae Phaedrae respondens, per Joannem Schepreuum Someto-christianum." Octavo. 1585.

"A Sermon preached at Chennies the 14. of September, 1585. at the burial 1585.

Turner were university printers to the year 1635. Then William Turner with Leonard Lichfield, to about 1658, when one A. Lichfield, who printed for the society of stationers is called university printer with Leonard; but typis Lichfeldianis took place about 1660, and continued a while after 1700. In the year 1648 Henry Hall is called printer to the university, and with William Hall in 1662, printed till 1676. Wood in his Athenae, mentions Samuel Clark, M. A. as elected May 14, 1658, Architypographus, who was succeeded by Martin Bold, in 1669. Books printed è Theatro Sheldoniano from 1671, have usually no printers name to them. Henry Crottenden printed a book at Oxford, in 1684, wherein he calls himself one of his majesties printers.

burial of the right Honorable the Earle of Bedford, by Thomas Sparke Doctor of Diuinitie." The university's arms. "Imprinted at Oxford by *him* Printer to that famous Vniuersitie." My copy is cut so close at bottom that it is uncertain whether there was any date added.[t] Dedicated "To—Arthur Lord Gray of Wilton, knight of—the Garter.—At Bletchley the 25 of September,[u] 1585.—Thomas Sparke." The text, "Apocal. 14. 13. I heard a voice from heauen" &c. At the end of the sermon, "September 22. An. Do. 1585." Besides, 110 pages. W.H. 16°.

1585. "A sermon briefly comparing the estate of king Salomon and his Subiects togither with the condition of Queene Elizabeth and her people. Preached in Sainct Maries in Oxford the 17. of Nouember, and now printed with some final alteration, By John Prime, 1585. Imprinted at Oxford by Joseph Barnes Printer to the Vniuersitie. 1585." Text, 1 Kings x, 9.---B, in eights, half sheets. W.H. Sixteens.

1585. "The true difference between Christian subiection and vnchristian rebellion," &c. See p. 1219. Quarto.

1586. "Reglas gramaticales para aprender la lengua Espannola y Francesa, confiriendo la una con la otra, segun el orden de las partes de la oration Latinas." Octavo.

1586. "D. Joannis Chrysostomi archiepiscopi Constantinopolitani homiliae sex, ex manuscriptis codicibus noui collegii Joannis Hannari, eiusdem coll. socii, et Graecarum litterarum in inclyta Oxoniensi academia professoris regii," &c. This in a beautiful Greek letter. Octavo.

1586. "A sermon vpon part of the eighteenth psalm (*verses* 47—51): Preached to the publick assemblie of Scholers in the Vniuersitie of Oxford, the last day of August, 1586. By John Rainolds: Vpon occasion of their meeting to giue thanks to God for the late detection and apprehension of Traitours, who wickedlie conspired against the Queenes Maiestie, and the state of the Realme." Mr. Rainold's epistle to the reader is dated, "At Corpus Christi College in Oxford, Octob. 24. 1586." C 3, in eights. W.H. Sixteens.

1586. "A comfortable sermon for all such as thirst and desire to be ioined with their head Jesus Christ, &c. Preached at the funerals of Syr Gawen Carewe, very worshipfully buried in the Cathedral Church of Exeter, 22d April, 1584, By John Charden[w] bachelor of Diuinity." The text: 1 Thes. 4, 13—18. Octavo.

1586. A Sermon preached at St. Mary's in Oxford by the foresaid John Charden,[x] on John 9, 1, 2 3,. Octavo.

1586. "A sermon preached in St. Peter's Church, at Westchester, 25 September 1586, containing matter fit for the time. By Edward Hutchins, maister of arts, and fellow of Brazennose college."[y] Sixteens.

(1586.) "A sermon preached in Westchester the viii of October, 1586, before

[t] Mr. Ames mentions this sermon in quarto.

[u] December, in the edition 1594.

[w] Chardon, or Charldron, bishop of Down and Connor in 1596.

[x] He preached another at the same place, 11 Dec. 1586, on the four following verses.

[y] See p. 1216.

ſore the Judges and certain Recuſantes: Wherein the conditions of al hereciques, but eſpeciallie of ſtubborn and peruercing Papiſts, are diſcouered, and the duty of al magiſtrats concerning ſuch Perſons, applied and opened By Edward Hutchins, *M. A. &c.* At Oxford printed by *him*, and are to be ſolde in Pauls Church-yard, at—the Tyger's head." Dedicated "To—Maſter Thomas Egerton Eſq; and ſollicitour to the Queenes moſt excellent Maieſtie." The text, Cant. 2; 1. B, in eights. W.H. Sixteens.

1586. "A ſermon preached at Trafforde in Lancaſhire, at the marriage of a Daughter of Sir Edm. Trafforde knight, Sept. 6. 1586, by Wm. Maſſie, B. D. Fellow of Braſen-noſe coll. Oxon." Sixteens.

1586. "Solomon's Sermon: of man's chief felicitie: called in Hebrew Koheleth, in Greeke and Latin Eccleſiaſtes. With a learned, godly, and familiar paraphraſe vpon the ſame: gathered out of the Lectures of A. C. (*Ant. Corranus*) and now engliſhed for the benefit of the vnlearned." About an ornament of metal flowers, "Viue pius moriere pius." Underneath, "Imprinted —1586." Dedicated, "To—the Lady Marie Dudley.—From my ſtudy in Oxford. 8. of March, 1586.—T. P." Then, "To the Chriſtian Reader Th. Pie B. D. wiſheth," &c. Beſides, 219 pages. W. H. Sixteens.

1586. In Catilinarias proditiones, ac proditores domeſticos, Odæ 6." The univerſity arms. "Oxoniæ, ex Officina Typographica Joſephi Barneſii, & veneunt in cœmeterio Paulino ſub ſigno capitis Tygurini. Anno 1586." On the back, in a lozenge form, "Odæ ſex ornatiſſimis viris D. Doctori Jameſo Ædis Chriſti Oxon. decano, et doctori Hetono prodecano, cæteriſque clariſſimis atque optimis viris eiuſdem eccleſiæ præbendariis, & privatæ obſervantiæ, et publicæ pietatis ergô dicatæ." 8 leaves, the firſt has only ſignature A. Brit. Muſeum. Octavo.

1586. "Jacob's troubleſome Journey to Bethel, containing a briefe expoſition of the 4 firſt verſes of the 33 chapter of Geneſis. Set forth by John Ouerton, Maiſter of Arts." Dedicated to maiſter Wm. Brent, from the author's ſtudy at Welborne. Rev. Dr. Lort. Sixteens.

1586. "The Praiſe of Muſicke: Wherein beſides the antiquitie, dignitie, delectation, and vſe thereof in ciuill matters, is alſo declared the ſober and lawfull vſe of the ſame in the congregation and Church of God. Hieron. in Pſal. 64.—.Printed at Oxenford—1586."—Dedicated "To—Sir Walter Rawley Knight.—From Oxenford—Joſeph Barnes.—The preface to the Reader." Contains beſides, 152 pages. W. H. Octavo.

1586. "Reflexus ſpeculi moralis, ſeu commentarius in magna moralia Ariſtotelis. Authore Johanne Caſo." Again 1596. Octavo.

(1586.) "Articles Eccleſiaſticall to be inquired of by the Churchwardens and the Sworne-men within the dioces of Hereford in the firſt viſitation of the reuerend father in God, Harbart Biſhop of the ſaid dioces: this preſent yeare M.D.LXXXVI. and the XXVIII. yeare of the raigne of our moſt gracious ſoueraigne Lady Queene Elizabeth, &c. And ſo hereafter, till the

7 See Ath. Oxon. 1; 299. Oldys's Life of Sir Walter Ralegh.

the next visitation, and from time to time to be presented." B, in fours: 70 articles. W.H. Quarto.

1587. "Thesaurus oeconomiae, seu commentarius oeconomica Aristotelis. Authore Johanne Caso." Again 1598. Quarto.

1587. "The summe of Christian Religion: Deliuered by Zacharias Vrsinus, in his Lectures vpon the Catechism autorised by the noble Prince Frederick, throughout his dominions.—Translated into English by Henrie Parrie, out of the last and best Latin Editions, together with some supplie of wants out of his Discourses of Diuinitie, and with correction of sundrie faults and imperfections, which ar as yet remaining in the best corrected Latine. At Oxford, Printed—and are to be sold in Pauls Churchyard at the signe of the Tygres head, (Chr. Barker's) 1587." Dedicated "To—Henrie Earle of Penbrooke, Lord Harbert of Cardiff, &c. Knight of—the Garter, and Lord President of Wales.—Henry Parrie.---To the Christian Readers" &c. Contains besides 1047 pages, and a table. W.H. Again 1591, and 1595. Quarto and Octavo.

1587. "Peplus illustrissimi viri D. Philippi Sidnaei supremis honoribus dicatus.—Oxonii Excudebat Josephus Barnesius, anno salutis humanae 1587.---Excellentissimo Domino, D. Henrico Herberto, Penbrochiae comiti, &c. Ioannes Luidus S. D.—Vale Oxonij. E Collegio Nouo. vii. KL. Septemb. CIƆ.IƆ.LXXXVII." The whole on 54 pages. Lambeth Libr. and W.H. Quarto.

1587. "Exequiae illustrissimi equitis, D. Phillippi Sidnaei, gratissimae memoriae ac nomini impensae." The university arms. "Paulum sepultae distat inertiae Caelata virtus. Oxonii, ex officina typographica Josephi Barnesii,—1587. Dedicated, Praecellentissimo Domino D. Roberto Dudleio, Leicestriae comiti, &c.—Vale, Oxonij, ex Aede Christi, vndecimo Kalendas Nouemb. 1587.—Guilielmus Gagerus.—Ad vtramque academia Philippi Sidnaei vmbra.—Laur. Humfredus." Contains besides, L, in fours. W.H. Quarto.

1587. "Master Bezaes sermons vpon the three first chapters of the Canticle of Canticles: wherein are handled the chiefest points of religion controuersed and debated betweene vs and the aduersarie at this day, especially touching the true Iesus Christ and the true church, and the certaine and infallible marks both of the one and of the other. Translated out of French—by John Harmar, her highnes professor in the Greeke toung in the vniuersitie of Oxford, and felowe of the newe College there. At Oxford, Printed—, and are to be sould in St. Pauls Church-yard at the Tyger's Head, 1587." Dedicated "To—Lord Robert Dudley, Earle of Lecester, &c.---The argument of the XLV Psalme, seruing for an Argument and preface or abridgement of this booke of the Canticle—or sung of songes of Salomon." 31 sermons: 435 pages. W.H. 4°.

1587. "An exposition, and obseruations vpon saint Paul to the Galathians, togither with incident Questions debated, and Motiues remoued, by John Prime. 1 Cor. 10. 15. I speake to them which haue vnderstanding: Iudge yee what I saie. At Oxford, Printed—, and are to bee sold in Pauls Church-yard &c. 1587." Dedicated "To—Iohn Pierce, the Lord

Lord Bishop of Sarum.—From new Colledge in Oxford, 1587. Ianuar. 30.—Iohn Prime." Besides; 317 pages. W.H. Octavo.

" A treatise containing the equity of an humble supplication, which is to be exhibited vnto hir gracious maiesty, and this high court of Parliament, in behalf of the countrey of Wales, that some order may be taken for the preaching of the gospel among those people." 61 pages 8°. 1587.

" Orationes duæ in Coll. Corp. Christi per Joh. Rainoldum Octavo. 1587.

" A treatise to proue that ministers publikely, and householders priuatly, are bound to catechise their parishioners and families: and that parishioners and families are bound carefully to submit themselues thereunto. By Tho. Sparkes, D. D." Octavo. 1588.

Zach. Ursinus's Catechism abridged by John Seddon. Octavo. 1588.

" The consolations of Dauid breefly applied to queene Elizabeth: in a Sermon preached in Oxford the 17. of Nouember. By Iohn Prime, 1588. —Imprinted at Oxford—, and are to be fold in Paules Church-yard,— 1588." Dedicated " To—Thomas Cooper the L. Bishop of Winchester. —From New Colledge in Oxford, Decemb. 7. 1588." The text, Psal. 23; 4. B 7. in eights. On the last page, " 2 Kings 6; 15, 16. Elizeus seruaunt seeing a great Hoast" &c. W.H. Sixteens. 1588.

" Sphæra ciuitatis, Authore magistro Johanne Caso Oxoniensi, olim collegii diui Iohannis Præcursoris socio." The university arms. " Psalm. cxxvi. Nisi Dominus custodierit ciuitatem, &c. Oxoniæ Excudebat—, 1588." On the back, Q. Elizabeth is represented behind an emblematical sphere: in the centre of which is the Earth with this motto, Justitia immobilis; then follow in the Ptolemean order, the sphere of the Moon, with libertas rerum;—Mercury, with Facundia;—Venus, with Clementia;—the Sun, with Religio;—Mars, with Fortitudo;—Jupiter, with Prudentia;—Saturn, with Maiestas; The starry region, with Camera, Stellata, Proceres, Heroes, Consiliarii; and without all, as the Primum mobile, Elizabetha D. G. Angliæ Franciæ, et Hiberniæ Regina, Fidei defensatrix." Dedicated Illustrissimo—D. Christophero Hattono, magno Angliæ Cancellario, aureæ Periscelidis equitis clarissimo, &c.—Joh. Case.---Ad Christianum lectorem Politices Studiosum.—Anno Salutis 1588, mensis Maij die 11."---Several Commendatory verses, with a table of contents. The work in eight books on 740 pages; at the end " Peroratio operis, and an alphabetical table. W.H. Quarto. 1588.

" Laur. Humfrey, his 7 sermons against treason, on 1 Sam. 26; 8—11." Maunsell, p. 100. Octavo. 1588.

" Apologia musices tàm vocalis, quam instrumentalis et mixtae. Iohanne Caso authore." Octavo. 1588.

" A Skeltonical salutation," &c. as p. 1261. Quarto. 1589.

" A sermon concerning the true comfort of God's Church truly militant, &c. on the Song of Solomon 4; 7. By Edw. Hutchins. With which is printed An Apology for the church truly militant." Ath. Oxon. 1; 531. Octavo. 1589

" Harmiaca Gymnasmata," &c. Brit. Museum. Octavo. 1589.

" De

1590. " De iniuſtitiâ bellicâ Romanorum actio." By Albericus Gentilis. Dedicated to Rob. Earl of Eſſex. Ath. Oxon. 1; 363. Quarto.

1590. " Libellus Rogerii Baconi Angli, doctiſſimi mathematici & medici, De retardandis ſenectutis accidentibus, & de ſenſibus conſervandis. Item, Libellus Vrſonis medici, de primarum qualitatum arcanis & effectibus. Vterq; affixis ad marginem notulis illuſtratus, & emendatus, in lucem prodijs, operâ Iohannis Williams Oxonienſis, cuius ſequitur Tractatus Philoſophicus, de humorum numero & natura, complexionis, morbi, perturbationum origine, caloris & humidi natiui virtute & munere in humano corpore, & de aëris infectione, vndè non rarò humores & ſpiritus coinquinantur: Oxoniæ, Ex Officina Typographica—1590." Dedicated " Inclytiſſimo—Domino Chriſtophoro Hattono, magno Angliæ Cancellario, &c.—Iohannes Williams.---Ad Lectorem.---R. Baconi vita:" in 9 diſtichs of Latin verſes, from Bale's Script. Britan. Cent. 4. cap. 55. Bacon's treatiſe on 31 pages, Brevier Roman. The two other treatiſes are printed on Small Pica Italic, with ſome Roman. Urſo's on 29 pages, and Williams's from p. 33 to p. 134. The paging of theſe beginning afreſh, but the ſignatures are continued throughout. W.H. Octavo.

1590. " Flavius Joſephus de Maccabæis; ſeu de Rationis imperio. Gr. et Lat.." Octavo.

1591. " Roger Hacket, his ſermon at Paules Croſſe on 1 Sam. XI; 5, 6, 7." Maunſell, p. 100. Octavo.

1591. " The ende of Nero and beginning of Galba. M.D.LXXXXI." See p. 1217." Pages 267. Annexed are Annotations on the four books of the hiſtory of Tacitus, and his life of Agricola, with " A view of certaine militar matters, for the better vnderſtanding of the ancient Roman ſtories." &c. 82 pages; and on a ſeparate leaf " Printed at Oxforde by *him* for Richard Wright. Cum privilegio." W.H. Folio.

1591. " An anſwer to Maſter John de Albines, notable diſcourſe againſt hereſies (as his frendes call his booke) compiled by Thomas Spark paſtor of Blechley in the County of Buck. And I heard a voice &c. Revelat. 18; 4. Put yourſelues in aray &c. Jerem. 50; 4." The univerſity arms. " Printed at Oxforde by *him*, Printer to the Vniverſity. 1591." Dedicated " To—Arthure Lord Grey of Wilton, Knight of —the Garter, &c.—Thomas Sparke.---preface to the Reader; *Anonymous* ---An anſwere to the preface ſet before John de Albines booke entituled &c.—Tho. Sparke." D'Albines treatiſe as printed at Douay 1575. is inſerted in the work, and anſwered chapter by chapter. Beſides: 426 pages; an alphabetical table, and faults corrected. W.H. Quarto.

1591. " Zach. Vrſinus his Catechiſme, wherein are debated and reſolued the queſtions of whatſoeuer moment, which haue beene or are controuerſed in Diuinitie, tranſlated by Henry Parry." Maunſell, p. 119. Octavo.

1591. " ΗΡΟΔΟΤΟΥ ΑΛΙΚΑΡΝΑΣΣΕΩΣ ΙΣΤΟΡΙΩΝ ΠΡΩΤΗ, ΚΛΕΙΩ. Herodoti Halicarnaſſenſis Hiſtoriarum liber primus, Clio." The univerſity arms. Oxoniae In officinâ—M.D.LXXXXI." On the back, or page 2, " Herodoti

" Herodoti vita ex Suida." In Greek, as is the whole book, in very neat Pica type. 69 pages, including the title. W.H. Quarto.

" A Sermon preached at Pauls Crosse the thirteenth of Iune, the second sunday in Trinitie tearme 1591, by Thomas Barne student in Diuinity. Brethren I exhort you to watch those that make Diuisions &c. —Rom. 15.—" The university arms from a copper-plate, badly engraved. " Printed at Oxford by *him*, Printer to the University. 1591." 4°. 1591.

" ΤΟΥ ΣΟΦΩΤΑ' ΤΟΥ ΒΑΡΛΑΑΜ ΛΟΓΟΣ ΠΕΡΙ' ΤΗΣ ΤΟΥ ΠΑΠΑ'ΡΧΗΣ. Barlaami De Papae Principatu Libellus. Nunc primùm Græce & Latine editus opera Iohannis Luidi Procuratoris Academiæ Oxoniensis. Ad illustrissimum Dominum Bucchurstium eiusdem Academiæ Cancellarium amplissimum." The university arms, as in the foregoing article. " Oxoniæ. excudebat—1592." On the back are the Sackville arms, with crest and supporters, from copper-plate also, and badly engraved. Contains 19 leaves. Lambeth Library. Quarto. 1592.

" Willelmi Thorni Tullius, seu ΡΗΤΩΡ in tria stromata divisus, è novo beatae Mariae Winton, in Oxon. collegio, Oxon. dicat. Heroi Filio Thorno. Visuntur insignia Gentis Herbert." Octavo. 1592.

" Lycophronis Alexandria, Græce. Oxon. ap. Barnesium." Quarto. 1592.

" Summa veterum interpretum in Vniversam Dialecticam Aristotelis." Ath. Oxon. 1; 299. See it in 1598. Quarto. 1592.

" ΑΡΙΣΤΟΦΑΝΟΥΣ ΙΠΠΕΙΣ. Aristophanis Equites." Quarto. 1593.

" A sermon preached at Whaddon in Buckinghamshyre the 22 Nouember 1593, at the buriall of the right Honorable Arthur Lorde Grey of Wilton, Knight of the most Honorable order of the Garter, by Thomas Sparke Pastor of Blechley, At Oxford, Printed by *him* Printer to the Universitie. 1593." Dedicated " To—the Countesse of Bedford, and the Ladie Grey her Honours Daughter, and to the Right honorable Thomas Lord Grey of Wilton.—At Blechley this first of December, 1593.—Tho. Sparke.---In obitum clarissimi herois, Domini Arthuri Greij. Θρηνῳδία.—Ioannes Sandfordus." The text, Isaiah 57; 1, 2. The sermon on 87 pages. W.H. Sixteens. 1593.

" Alberici Gentilis Commentarii de Maleficis & Mathemat. & aliis similibus." Quarto. 1593.

" Demosthenis Orationes 15, cum interpretatione Nicholai Carri; 3 Olynthiacarum, 4 Philippicarum." Quarto. 1593.

" Solon his Follie, or a politique discourse, touching the reformation of common-weales conquered, declined or corrupted. By Richard Beacon Gent. student of Grayes Inne, and sometimes her Maiesties Attorney of the province of Mounster in Irelande." The queen's arms. " At Oxford, Printed by *him*, Printer to the Vniversitie,—1594." Dedicated " To her most sacred Maiestie.—The author to the Reader.---The booke vnto the Reader." Besides; 114 pages. W.H. Quarto. 1594.

" A sermon preached at Cheanies" &c. as p. 1399. W.H. Sixteens. 1594.

" Franc. Trigge, his sermon at Grantham on Esay 24; 1, 2, 3." Maunsell, p. 106. Octavo. 1594.

" A sermon preached at Paul's Cross, entit. Isaac his Testament, &c. 1594.

on Gen. 21; 1—10. By Richard Lewes, B. D. Dedicated to Sir Henry Unton of Wadley in Berks." See Fasti Oxon. c. 127. Octavo.

1595. "Diarium Historicopoeticum, in quo praeter constellationum vtriusque hemisphaerii, et zodiaci, ortus, et occasus, numerum stellarum, causarumq; ad poesin spectantium, varietatem, declarantur cuiusque mensis dies fere singuli, Regum, Imperatorum, Principum Pontificum, virorumq; doctorum, natalibus, nuptiis, inaugurationibus, morte deniq;, aut re alia quacunq; insigniore, celebriores, sic, vt nihil paene desiderari possit, ad perfectam rerum gestarum Chronologiam, cum exauctoribus probatissimis, accurata quoq; annorum ratio margini ascribatur.—Suasu & permissu superiorum. Oxonii. Excudebat—1595." Dedicated "Honoratissimo viro Domino Ioanni Wollaeo, Regiae Maiestati a sanctioribus consiliis, Ornatissimæq; ipsius coniugi, Dominæ Elisabethæ, &c.—Valete Oxonij e Collegio Novo, pridie nonas Iulij, 1595.—Robertus Moore.---Ad Lectorem Benevolum.---Auctoris ad libellum paræneses." Besides, 102 pages, and an index. W.H. Quarto.

1596. "Reflexus speculi moralis," &c. as p. 1401. Quarto.

1596. "Funebria nobiliss. ac præstantiss. Eq. D. Henrici Untoni, ad Gallos bis legati regii, &c. à Musis Oxon. apparata." Ath. Ox. 1; 284. 4°.

1596. "Johannis Rainoldi, De Romanæ Ecclesiæ idololatria, in cultu sanctorum, Reliquiarum, imaginum, aquæ, salis, olei, aliarumq; rerum consecratarum & sacramenti Eucharistiæ, operis inchoati Libri duo. In quibus cum alia multa variorum papismi patronorum errata patefiunt: tûm inprimis Bellarmini, Gregoriiq; de Valentia, calumniæ in Calvinum ac ceteros Protestantes, argutiæq; pro Papistico idolorum cultu discutiuntur & ventilantur. Jerem. 51; 9. Curavimus Babylonem, &c. Oxoniæ, Apud Jos. Barnesium, M.D.XCVI." Dedicated "Illustrissimo comiti Essexiæ Roberto Devreuxo.—Oxon. e Collegio Reginæ, Jul. 7. 1596.---Index tractatuum," &c. Besides, 646 pages. W H. Quarto.

1596. "A Discovery of discontented Minds; wherein their several Sortes and Purposes are described; especially such as go beyond the Seas. At Oxford, printed by *him*, Printer to the university, 1596." Dedicated to Robert Earl of Essex, by James Perrott. See Oldys's Catalogue of Pamphlets in the Harleian Libr. No. 12. Quarto.

1597. Demosthenis Orationes XV. Græcè. Quarto.

1597. "A sermon preached at Eggington, in the County of Darby, concerning the right vse of things indifferent, the 8 Day of August. 1596. By Symon Presse Minister there. Feare God, honour the Kinge. 1 Pet. 2; 17. Printed at Oxford—, and are to bee solde in Paules Church-yard at the signe of the Bible. 1597." Dedicated "To his loving Parishioners Mr. F. Cooke," &c. The text, 1 Cor. 8; 10—13. Pages 28, including the title. W.H. Sixteens.

1597. "A sermon preached at Marlborow, 6 October. 1596, to the publick assembly of ministers at the visitation, on 1 Tim. 4; 16, by Charles Pinner minister at Wotton-basset." See Ath. Oxon. 1; 291. Octavo.

1597. "Lectures vpon Ionas, delivered at Yorke in the year of our lord 1594, By Iohn Kinge. Newly corrected and amended." Dedicated to sir fir Thomas Egerton, knight, lord keeper of the great feal. Again 1599, 1600, and frequent. Quarto.

1597. "De Chrifti Juftitia & in regno fpirituali Ecclefiæ paftorum officio, concio ad clerum. Rev. 10; 1." Ath. Oxon. 1; 388. Quarto.

1597. "Vitæ Sanctorum evangelift. Iohannis & Lucæ, à Symeone Metaphrafte, olim concinnatæ, iam recens traductæ à Rich. Bretto. Oxoniæ, Ex officina typographica Iofephi Barnefii, & veneunt Londini in Cœmiterio D. Pauli, ad infigne Bibl. M.D.XCVII." Dedicated, "Graviffimo prudentiffimoq; viro Mro. Thomae Owino ex infigni Iudicum ordine fælicitatem.—Oxoniæ è Collegio Lincolnienfi, Decemb. 23. 1596.—Richardus Brett." Contains 95 pages befides; Greek on one fide, Latin on the other. Brit. Mufeum. Sixteens.

1597. "Agatharchidis et Memnonis Hiftoricorum, quæ fuperfunt, omnia, è Græco iam recèns in Latinum traducta: per Rich. Brettum, Oxonienfem, è Collegio Lincoln. Oxoniæ, Ex officinâ typographicâ Iofephi Barnefii. 1597." Dedicated, "Honoratiffimo viro D. Thomae Egertono, Cuftodi Magni Sigilli Angliæ, *&c.*—20 Augufti, 1597.—Rich. Brett." Contains befides 128 pages, all Greek. To which is annexed, "Excerpta quaedam ex Agatharchide de rubro mari." Only a a head title. On p. 72, begins "Memnon de ftatu Heracl. ponticæ," which concludes on p. 140. "Finis eorum quæ è decimofexto Memnoniæ hiftoriæ libro excerpta funt." Brit. Mufeum. Sixteens.

1597. "Thefaurus oeconomiæ, feu commentarius in oeconomica Ariftotelis; in quo veræ divitiæ familiarum, earumq; leges, partes, & officia defcribuntur: Johanne Cafo Authore." The univerfity's arms. "1 Tim. 5; 8, Si quis autem fuorum *&c.* Oxoniæ Ex officina Typographica—, & veneunt Londini—1597." Dedicated "Illuftriffimo—Domino Thomae Sackvillo Buckhurftio Baroni,—almæ Academiæ honoratiffimo Cancellario, *&c.*—Epiftola ad lectorem."—Some commendatory verfes by Tho. Holland, and H. P.—An analytical table. Befides; 278 pages, and an index. W.H. Again 1578. Quarto.

1598. "Summa veterum interpretum in univerfam dialecticam Ariftotelis; quam vere falfoveramus in Ariftotelem inuehatur, oftendens. Auctore Ioanne Cafe Oxonienfi, olim Collegij D. Ioannis Præcurforis focio. Omnibus Socraticæ, Peripateticæq; philofophiæ ftudiofis in primis utilis ac neceffaria. Recognita & emendata. Cum indice rerum & verborum locupletifs." The univerfity's arms, fmall, with AC: on one fide, and OX on the other. "Oxoniæ Excudebat—1598." On the back, "Ioannis Readi carmen," &c. Dedicated "Illuftriffimo viro, Domino Roberto Dudleio, comiti Leiceftriæ, *&c.*—Ad benevolum lectorem.—Vale, Idibus Auguft." Befides; 201 pages, and an index. W.H. 8°.

1598. Quæftiones fex, totidem prælectionibus in fchola theologica Oxoniæ, pro forma habitus, difcuffæ & difceptatæ. Anno 1597. In quibus, è Sacra Scriptura & Patribus antiquiffimis, quid ftatuendum fit, definitur. Per Georgium Abbatem tunc Collegij Baliolenfis focium.—Ex officina —M.D.XCVIII." Befides; 224 pages, and an index. Quarto.

(1598.) "A tracte containing the artes of curious Paintinge Caruinge and

 Buildinge

Buildinge written first in Italian by Jo: Paul Lomatius painter of Milan and englished by R. H. student in Physik. In the handes of the skilfull shall the worke be approued Eccl. 9: 19." This title-page, engraved on copper-plate, is adorned with the author's portrait at top, and the translator's at bottom, with his arms over it; the university's arms on one side, and William of Wykeham's, founder of New College, on the other; the corners are supplied with sketches from poetical fiction. Dedicated "To the right Worshipfull Thomas Bodley Esquire.—since it hath pleased God to mooue your harte to the erecting and restoring of this worthie Pambiblion, or Temple to all the Muses; as I holde it the parte of every studious minde to offer vp the picture of his private Muse in carefulliest written bookes, to this shrine: So I the meanest amongst many, haue conceived not a little hope, that this shaddow of my Shaddowing Muse shall finde some place there, though it bee but that, which wee see the silly Sparrowes and Swallowes haue in the greatest Churches.—From S. Marie Coll. (Commonly called New Coll.) in Oxford, August the 24. Anno Dom. 1598.—Richard Haydocke.—To the ingenuous reader. R. H.—John Case D. of Physicke to his friende of New Colledge.—The titles of the bookes.—A table of the chapters of the whole volume in order." This work was designed to have contained seven books as appears by this table exhibiting the contents of them all, and the epistle to the reader: "Of the 7 bookes mentioned, I have now published but 5, which insomuch as they comprehend the whole contemplatiue part, I haue sent alone before, as precursors of the rest. According to the acceptance whereof, I purpose (if God permit) to gratifie you with the others with all such speede as my leasure and priuate occasions will afford." As none such are found it is pretty evident that this part did not meet with such acceptance as to encourage the translator to publish the two remaining books, though he lived, as we are told, till near the breaking out of the Grand Rebellion. Ath. Oxon. 1; c. 296. Contains 338 pages, that is to say, the first book contains, besides the prefixes, 120 pages; and the four following books, which have fresh signatures and paging, are on 218 pages, with copper-plate cuts. These were both drawn and engraved by Mr. Haydocke, as himself intimates in his address to the reader. On a separate leaf, the university's arms over this colophon, "Printed at Oxford by *him* R. H. Anno Domini, M.D.XC.VIII." Under it, the arms of William of Wykeham on a shield, with a W on each side. W.H. Folio.

1599. "Philobiblon Richardi[y] Dunelmensis sive De amore librorum, et institutione bibliothecæ tractatus pulcherrimus. Ex collatione cum varijs manuscriptis editio jam secunda; cui Accessit appendix de manuscriptis Oxoniensibus. Omnia hæc, opera & studio T. I. Novi Coll. in alma Academia Oxoniensi Socij. B. P. N. Non quæro quod mihi vtile est, sed quod multis. Oxoniæ, Excudebat—1599." Dedicated "Clarissimo et literarum ac literatorum amantissimo viro Thomæ Bodlæo.—Ex Musæo meo in Collegio Novo Iulij. 6. 1599.—Thomas James.—Vita ex Balæo.

[y] Robertus Holcot de ordine Prædicatorum Philobiblon sub Nomine Ricardi de Bury Epi. Dunelm. contexuit."—Hearne's preface to Q. Eliz. pag. cxxix.

Et ex libro quodã vetusto de Antiquit. Dunelmensibus." Besides, 62 pages, and the Appendix 4 leaves.* W.H. Quarto.

" Oratio cum Henricus Episc. Sarisburiensis graduum Doctoris susceperit habita." By Tho. Holland. Ath. Oxon. 1; c. 377. Quarto. 1599.

" Ancilla Philosophiæ, seu Epitome in VIII libros Phisicorum Arist." 1599.

" Lapis Philosophicus, seu Comm. in VIII libros Physicorum Arist." 1599.
This and the foregoing article by John Case; and both in Quarto.

" Lectures upon Ionas," &c. as in 1597. The university arms. 1599.
" Printed at Oxford by *him*, and are to be solde in Paules Church-yarde at the Bible 1599." The 48 and last lecture ends on p. 660. To which is annexed,

" A sermon preached at the funeralles of the most reverend father 1599.
John (*Piers*) late Arch-bishoppe of Yorke, Novem. the 17. in the yeare of our Lorde, 1494." (1594) By Dr. John King, one of his chaplains, afterwards bishop of London. The university arms. " Printed at Oxford by *him*. 1599." This is paged from 661 to 683. W.H. Again, 1600, with this addition after Barnes's name, " and are to be solde in Paules Church-yarde, at—the Bible."

" A sermon preached in Yorke the seventeenth day of November in 1599.
the yeare of our Lorde 1595, being the Queenes day." The university arms. " Printed at Oxford by *him*. 1599." This was annexed also to the Lectures on Jonas, following the preceding article, and paged from 684 to 706. Brit. Museum. Quarto.

" Rhetoricæ libri duo, quorum Prior de Tropis & Figuris, Posterior 1600.
de Voce & Gestu, Præcipiti in vsum scholarum accuratiùs editi. Oxoniæ, Excudebat—1600.—Viro virtutis & honoris nomine nobilissimo, Thomae Egertono, Equiti, Domino Custodi magni sigilli Angliæ, Carolus Butler Magdalensis, S. D.—Basingstochiæ, 5 Idus Martii. 1600."—Some commendatory verses; Lat. & Gr.—Ad lectorem." I 3, in eights, besides the prefixes. W.H. Sixteens.

" A collection of certaine learned discourses, written by that most famous 1600.
man of memory Zachary Vrsine; Doctor and Professor of Divinitie in the noble and flourishing Schoole of Neustad. For explication of divers difficult points, laide downe by that Author in his Catechisme. Lately put in Print in Latin by the last labour of D. David Parry: and now newlie translated into English, by I. H. for the benefit and behoofe of our Christian countrey-men. At Oxford, Printed by *him*, and are to be solde in Pauls Church-yard at the—Bible. 1600." It has prefixed a short address to the reader, (which intimates that the translation was performed at the importunity of this printer) and a table of the nine discourses, which are contained on 341 pages. W.H. Octavo.

" Theological Logic: Or, the tryal of truth, containing a discovery 1600.
of the chiefest points of the Doctrine of the great Antichrist, and his Adherents the false Teachers of the Times." The first part. By John Terry. The second part was printed in 1602. The third part was not published till 1625. Ath. Oxon. 1; 510. Quarto.

" Joh. Schepreví Hippolytus Ovidianæ Phædræ respondens, à Geo. ——
Edryco editus.—excudit Jos. Barnesius Oxoniensis." Bibl. Bodleianâ. 8°.

O F

OF PRINTING AT *CAMBRIDGE.*

IN this famous university they received the art of printing among them soon,[a] though which was their first book is difficult to ascertain, or who were the persons that brought it there. Mr. Bagford, in a letter of his to the late bishop Tanner, dated in November 1707, and communicated to Mr. Ames by his brother, a worthy promoter of his work, has these words. "I cannot but impart unto you, that very lately good Mr. Strype hath gave me an account of a booke, which archbishop Parker gave to the publick library of Bennet college, and is a piece of rhetorick, by one Gull. de Saona, a minorit, printed at Cambridge 1478." Afterwards the late reverend Mr. George North, sent Mr. Ames a perfect transcript[a] of part of it, thus, "Fratris Laurencii Guilelmi de Saona ordinis minorum, sacre theologie doctoris, prohemium in nouam rhetoricam." It is in folio, without the number of page, catch word, or signatures; the types very much like Caxton's largest. At the end, "Compilatum autem fuit hoc opus in alma universitate Cantabrigie, anno Domini 1478, die et 6 Julii, quo die festum sancte Marthe recolitur. Sub protectione serenissimi regis Anglorum Edwardi quarti." See this book in quarto, printed at St. Alban's, 1480.

Time may probably discover others.

JOHN SIBERT.

There was one John Sibert, a printer at Lyons, in the year 1498,[b] who possibly was the John Siberch that was settled here, and stiled himself who

[a] See Hist. & Antiq. Oxon. Lib. I; p. 218.

[a] See the Fac-simile in the plate facing p. 1386.

[b] "Explicit hoc opus Distinctionum praestantiss. utriusq; Juris Interpretis &c. Dni Henrici Bouhic super Decretal. &c. Arte impressoria Lugdun. per Magistrum Johannem Sibert, An. MCCCCXCVIII." Bibl. Pub. Cantab. Folio.

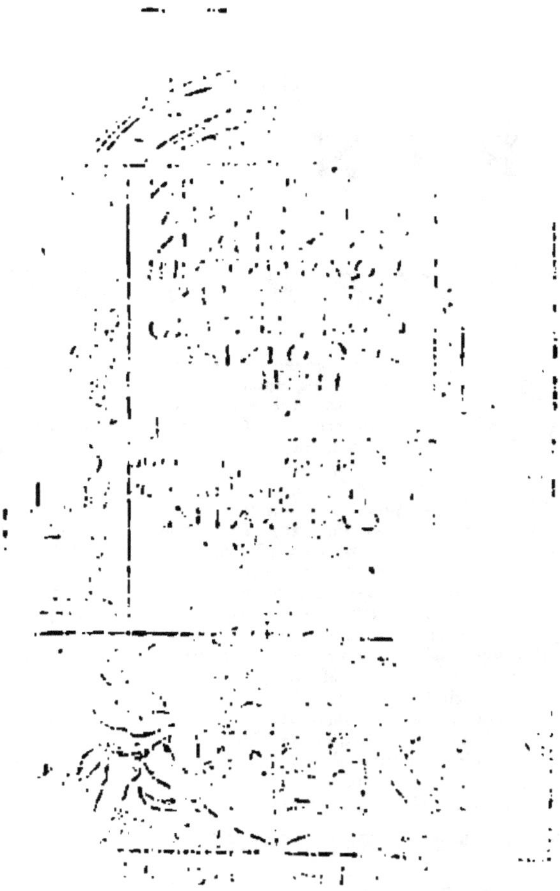

GALENI PERGAMEN-
SIS DE TEMPERA-
MENTIS, ET DE IN-
AEQVALI INTEMPE
RIE LIBRI TRES
THOMA LINACRO
ANGLO INTER-
PRETE.

Opus non medicis modo, sed et
philosophis oppido q̃ necessarium
nunc primum prodit in lucem
CVM GRATIA
& Privilegio.

Impressum apud preclaram Cantabrigiam per
Ioannem Siberch. Anno. M.D.XXI.

the first in England that printed both Greek and Latin. Yet, though there is much Greek letter in his books, we have not found any one, that is wholly of that character. He was acquainted with Erasmus, who mentions him in these words: "Saluta mihi veteres sodales, Phannum, Omfridum, Vachanum, Garardum, Nicholaum et Johannem Siburgum, bibliopolas. Datum Basileae, 25 Dec. anno 1525."[c]

"CALENI[d] PERGAMENSIS DE TEMPERAMENTIS ET DE INAEQUALI INTEMPERIE LIBRI TRES THOMA LINACRO[e] ANGLO INTERPRETE: Opus non medicis modo sed et philosophis oppido quam necessarium nunc primum prodit in lucem. CUM GRATIA & Privilegio." The whole is engraved within an architective compartment, which if designed by Hans Holbein is very badly executed, both as to the drawing and engraving; but this is the more excusable, as probably being the first copper-plate printing in England, notwithstanding what has been mentioned in p. 578, and p. 581: this title-page escaping my notice at that time. See a Fac simile opposite this page. Beneath, "Impressum apud preclaram Cantabrigiam per Ioannem Siberch Anno M.D.XXI." Then follows the dedication. "Sanctissimo domino nostro papae Leoni decimo, Thomas Linacer medicorum minimus, S. D. Londini anno Christianae salutis. Nonis Septembris." Then, "Elenchus sequentis operis," in alphabetical order. The book is printed on a good Roman Letter, with some Greek[f] words, and colon, full point, and catch words. At the end is a cut of the arms of France and England, quarterly within the garter, crowned with a French crown, abbreviations; and contains 74 leaves, besides the table. It has the comma, above a label, with "Dieu & mon droyt;" under it, a rose and pomegranate; the supporters a dragon and grey-hound, and beneath; a flower de lis, and a port-cullis with chains. The paper of several sorts; as, hand, star, pt, and beasts, &c. The colophon, "Impressum apud preclaram Cantabrigiam, per Johannem Siberch, M DXXI."[g] Quarto. 1521.

In the Bodleian Library is a copy of this work printed on vellum; the title in a compartment exactly similar to the engraved one, but printed on very neat types, without mention where, or by whom, the book was printed, as in the copper-plate.

"Libellus de conscribendis epistolis, autore D. Erasmo,[h] opus olim ab eodem caeptum, sed primâ manu mox expoliri caeptum sed intermissum, nunc primum prodit in lucem. Apud preclaram Cantabrigiensem academiam. Cum gratia & privilegio." Dedicated by Siberch, printer of Cambridge, to J. Fisher, bishop of Rochester. At the end, "Impressum Cantabrigiae per Joannem Siberch, anno MDXXI. mense Octobri." See Knight's Life of Erasmus, p. 86, 87. Quarto. 1521.

Concio

[c] See letter DCCLXXXII. to R. Aldrise.

[d] CALENI for GALENI.

[e] See Ath. Oxon. 1; 22.

[f] Hist. of Eng. Poetry, II; 124.

[g] A book very like the same letter, was printed 1520, at Colon, in the shop of Eucharius Cervicornus, intituled, "Richardi Croci Britanni introductiones in rudimenta Graeca," and dedicated by Cook to Archbishop Warham, "Mense Maio expensis providi viri, Domini Johannis lair de Siberch, wherein is shown the letters, moods, tenses, verbs, &c. of the Greek language," from hence one might think, that printing of Greek was not to perfection here before this time.

[h] Erasmus then living at Cambridge, no doubt took care of his own work. Fuller's history of Cambridge, p. 59. See Knight's Life of Erasmus, p. 49, and p. 187.

1521. "Concio reverendiss. Johãnis Fisheri episcopi Roffensis in Job. xv. 26. habita Londini eo die quo Lutheri Scripta flammis commissa sunt; latine versa per Ric. Pacæum. Cantab. per J. Siberch. 1521." Quarto.

1521. "Lepidissimum Luciani opusculum ΠΕΡΙ ΔΙΨΑΔΟΣ, &c. Henrico Bulloco interprete, &c. Ex preclarâ academia Cantabrig. anno M DXXI. Impressum est hoc opusculum Cantabrigiae, per J. Siberch." Quarto.

1521. "Reverendissimi in Christo Patris ac Domini, Domini Baldivini Cantuariensis achiepiscopi, de venerabili ac divinissimo altaris sacramento sermo devotissimus, sacraeque scripturae floribus undiquaque respersus, &c. Ex praeclara Catabrigiensi academia, anno M DXXI. finis adest felicissimus." In the dedication to Nicholas West, bishop of Ely, the printer stiles himself, "Johannes Siberch, primus utriusque linguae in Anglica impressor." Quarto.

1521. Cuiusdam fidelis Christiani epistola ad Christianos omnes, eos salubriter admonentis, atque ad penitentiam salutarem adhortantis. Subsequitur & Divi Augustini de miseria, ac brevitate hujus mortalis vitae, sermo devotissimus, et ad mundi contemptum efficacissimus, ΠΑΝΤΩΝ ΜΕΤΑΒΟΛΗ Apud praeclaram Cantabrigiam, anno M.DXXI." At the end, "Impressum in alma Cantabrigia, per me Johannem Siberch, anno XXI post millessimum quingentesimum." On the last leaf, "Joannis Duncelli, Hammelburgensis, in saeculi hujus amatorem, Decastychon." This singular piece contains only three sheets, finely printed in English Roman letter; omitting the initials. Quarto.

1521. "Doctissimi viri Henrici Bulloci, theologiae doctoris, oratio habita Cantabrigiae, in frequentissimo cetu, precentibus caesaris oratoribus, et nõnullis aliis episcopis, ad reuerendiss. D. Thomam Cardinalem, titulo sanctae Ceciliae, legatum a latere, archiepiscopum Eboracensem, et Angliae supremum cancellarium." Dedicated, "Doctissimo ac cum primis claro Joanni Talero, Henricus Bullicus salutem dicit plurimam. Mense Feb." Two sheets. See the Collections to Fiddes's Life of Cardinal Wolsey, p. 43; and p. 250. Quarto.

1522. "Papyrii Gemini Eleatis Hermathena, seu de eloquentiae victoriâ, ex preclara Cantabrigia." Quarto.

1522. The last leaf of a book ending, "Impressum In alma Cantabrigia, per me Joannem Siberch, anno Domini M DXXII. 8 Decembris." With his mark.

In the apology of Sir Thomas More, knt, p. 200. Edit. 1533. there is mention made of one SEGAR, a bookseller of Cambridge, who was prisoner in his house for heresye four or five days; and tho' it was reported, that he had used him ill, Sir Thomas vindicates himself. Of this man I have seen no books, either printed by or for him; but in the year of our Lord 1533, "mense Julii," king Henry VIII. granted to the university of Cambridge for ever under his great seal, authority to name, and to have three stationers, or printers of books, alyants and strangers, not born within, or under his obedience, and they to be reputed

puted and taken as denyſons.[1] And "21 Auguſti, anno ſupradicto univerſitas conceſſit Nicolao Spirinck, Garetto Godfray, et Sygar, hoc privilegium pro termino vitae."

Ex epiſtola Buceri ad Checum dat. Cantab. 29 Aug. 1550, in bib. coll. Corp. Chriſt. Cant. Miſc. 2. pag. 306. "Typographus noſter ille, cui cum mutuo dediſti, advenit ante hos dies, nunc, et res allatae ejus Sc. quam primum eas expedierit, veniet ab te, et exhibebit tibi formam pro molendino ad faciendum chartas, et pro typographica. Habet hic homo[k] indubiae artis abunde, et inſtrumenti ſatis."

Miſc. p. pag. 674, mention is made of a Paper-mill at Fen Ditton, near Cambridge, 1562.

Notwithſtanding the favourable licenſe for the encouragement of the preſs, granted the 20 July 1534, we have found no books printed here, after the year 1522, to the year 1584, in the ſpace of 62 years.

[1] Pro univerſitate Cantabrigia de licentia conceſſa. Pat. 26. Hen 8. p. 2 m. 14.

Rex omnibus, ad quos &c. ſalutem.

Sciatis quod de gratia noſtrâ ſpeciali, ac ex certâ ſcientiâ, et mero motu noſtris, conceſſimus et licentiam dedimus, ac per praeſentes concedimus, et licentiam, damus pro nobis et heredibus noſtris, dilectis nobis in Chriſto cancellario, magiſtris, & ſcolaribus, univerſitatis noſtrae Cantabrigiae, quod ipſi, et ſucceſſores ſui, imperpetuum, per eorum ſcripta, ſub ſigillo chancellarii dictae univerſitatis ſigillata, de tempore in tempus, aſſignent, eligant, et pro perpetuo in ſe, et infra univerſitatem noſtram praedictam perpetuo manentes et inhabitantes, tres ſtationarios, et librorum impreſſores, ſeu venditores, tam alienigenas et natos extra obedientiam noſtram, tam conductitias, quam proprias domus habentes et tenentes. Qui quidem ſtationarii, ſive impreſſores librorum in forma praedicta aſſignati, et eorum quilibet, omnimodos libros, per praedictum chancellarium, vel ejus vicem gerentem, et tres doctores ibidem approbatos, ſeu impreſſeriùm approbandos, ibidem imprimere; et tam libros illos, quàm alios libros ubicùnque, tam infra quàm extra regnum noſtrum impreſſos, ſic, ut praedicitur, per dictos chancellarium, ſeu ejus vicemgerentem, et tres doctores ibidem approbatos, ſeu approbandos, tam in eadem univerſitate, quàm alibi infra regnum noſtrum, ubicùnque placuerint, venditioni exponere licite valeant, ſeu valeat et impune. Et quod iidem ſtationarii, ſive impreſſores, etiam extra obedientiam noſtram oriundi, ut praedicitur, et eorum quilibet, quam diu infra univerſitatem praedictam moram traxerint, et negotio praedicto intendant, in omnibus et per omnia, et tanquam fideles ſubditi, et ligei noſtri reputentur, habeantur et pertractentur, ac quilibet eorum habeatur et pertractetur, ac omnibus et ſingulis libertatibus, conſuetudinibus, legibus, et privilegiis gaudere poſſit, ac lots, et ſcots, taxa, tallagia, et alias conſuetudines, et impoſitiones quaſcùnque, non aliter, nec alio modo, quàm caeteri fideles ſubditi, et ligei noſtri nobis ſolvunt & contribuunt, ſolvant & contribuant.

Aliquo Statuto, &c.

Proviſo ſemper, quod dicti ſtationarii, ſive impreſſores, extra obedientiam noſtram ſic, ut praemittitur, oriundi, omnia et omnimoda cuſtumas, ſubſidia, et alia deveria, pro rebus et marcandiſis ſuis, extra vel infra regnum noſtrum educendis, ſive inducendis, nobis debita, de tempore in tempus ſolvant prout alienigenae nobis ſolvunt, et non aliter.

In cujus, &c.

Teſte rege apud Weſtmonaſterium, viceſſimo die Julii, 1534.

Per breve de privato ſigillo.

[k] His name was Remigius. See Gent. Mag. Sept. 1781, p. 405.

THOMAS THOMASIUS, or THOMAS, M. A.

FORMERLY a fellow of King's College, Cambridge, had a license for being printer to this university, 3 May, 1582, but nothing from his press appears before 1584. This procrastination was occasioned by the Stationers' company[k] of London having seized his press, notwithstanding the privilege granted to this university. He seems to have had another license, dated 11 Feb. 1584. See Mr. T. Baker's MSS. Vol. 24; p. 207. A particular account of this affair may be seen in Strype's Annals, Vol. III: p. 194, &c. Thomas was a scholar, which the author of the dictionary which bears the name of Thomas Thomasius, which was in great esteem for many years. It was first published in 1588, and dedicated by him to sir William Cecil, knight, as we are told by Legate his successor as university printer, in his dedication of the fifth edition of it to the said noble Lord; also, that he took such pains as suited ill with his health; for he employed his thoughts so wholly upon it, as to spare neither his time, his fortune, nor himself, so he might procure wherewithal to improve his design; by which solicitude for the service of learning and the public, he fell into a grievous disease, which put an end to his life. He died a married man, and was buried in the church of St. Mary Major, 9 Aug. 1588, as Mr. T. Baker informed Mr. Ames.

1584. "A full and plain declaration of Ecclesiastical discipline out of the word of God, and of the declining of the Church of England from the same." See Strype's Life of Whitgift, p. 151. The account there given seems to imply that the book had not been printed in English[l] before. Possibly it may be the same with that bearing date M.D.LXXIIII, and an X (perhaps designedly) omitted, especially as neither printer's name nor place are mentioned:[m] besides, we have no intelligence of an edition dated 1584. It is said indeed that it was suppressed and most or all the copies seized. It is however a translation from the Latin, which was printed, 1574, as supposed at Geneva;[n] but in the late Mr. T. Baker's MS. additions to Maunsell's catal. p. 116, the title is transcribed entire, as in the notes.[o] I have a perfect copy of the book, with the same title-page, except the name of the place and the date being cut out from it. Walter Travers is generally announced to have been the author of this treatise, and Thomas Cartwright of the epistle set before it. See Strype's Annals of the reformation, III; 194, 285.

1584. "P. Rami Dialecticae libri duo, scholiis G. Tempelli Cantabrigiensis illustrati. Quibus accessit, eodem authore, De Porphyrianis praedicabilibus

[k] About this time they paid Mr. Norton for his counsell in Camb. matters, 10 s.

[l] But it is found printed at Geneva, 1580. See our General Hist. under that year.

[m] See this also ib. under the year 1574.

[n] See Neal's Hist. of the Puritans, I; 499.

[o] "Ecclesiasticae Disciplinae, et Anglicanae Ecclesiae ab illa aberrationis, plena è verbo Dei, et dilucida explicatio. Rupellae, excudebat Adamus de monte, An. 1574."

libus Disputatio. Item: Epistolæ de P. Rami Dialectica contrà Johannis Piscatoris responsionem defensio, in capita viginti novem redacta." The university arms. "Cantabrigiae, Ex officina Thomæ Thomasij, 1584." Dedicated "Nobilissimo viro et modis omnibus generosissimo Philippo Sidneo equiti aurato.—Lincol. 4 Febr.—G. Temple." The epistles have a separate title page, but the signatures and pages are continued to p. 344. W.H. Octavo.

"Fabularum Ovidii Interpretatio, Ethica, Physica, et Historica, tradita in Academia Regiomontana à Georgio Sabino, & in vnum collecta & edita studio & industria T. T. Accessit etiam ex Natalis Comitis Mythologijs de fabularum vtilitate, varietate, partibus & scriptoribus, deq; apologorum, fabularum, anorumq differentia, tractatio. Cum indice &c. Cantabrigiæ, Ex officina Thomæ Thomæ celeberrimæ Academiæ Cantabrigiensis Typographi. 1584." Dedicated "Illustriss. Principi—Alberto, Marchioni Brandeburgensi, Prussiæ, &c.—Datæ Idibus Junij. Anno M.D.LIII. in Academia Regijmontis.---Ex natalis comitis mythologiis.---G. S. De vtilitate, argumento, ac titulo operis." Besides, 638 pages, and the index. W.H. Octavo. 1584.

"Disp. de prima generatione corporum simplicium & concretorum, per Jac. Martinum, Scotum." Bibl. Bodl. Octavo. 1584.

"Antonii Sadeelis viri clarissimi vereque theologi de rebus grauissimis controuersis Disputationes accuratæ theologice et scholastice tractatae. Quarum Catalogum* sequens pagina demonstrabit.—Ex officina Thomæ Thomasij inclitæ Academiæ Cantabrigiensis Typographi 1584." W.H. imperfect at the end. Quarto. 1584.

"Two treatises of the Lord his Holie Supper: the one instructing the seruants of God how they should be prepared when they come to the holy Supper of our onely Sauiour Iesus Christ: Whereunto is annexed a Dialogue conteining the principall points necessarie to be knowne and vnderstood of all them that are to be partakers of the holy Supper. The other setting forth Dialoguewise the whole vse of the Supper: Whereunto also is adioyned a briefe and learned treatise of the true Sacrifice and true Priest. Written in the French tongue by Yues Rouspeau and Iohn de l'Espine Ministers of the word of God, and latelie translated into English.—Imprinted by Thomas Thomas Printer to the Vniuersitie of Cambridge. 1584." The former of these treatises, containing 58 pages, 1584.

 was

* "Meditationes in psal. 32. De verbo Dei scripto adversus humanas traditiones. De vero Christi Sacerdotio & Sacrificio adv. commentitium missæ sacrificium. De vera peccatorum remissione, adv. humanas satisfactiones & commentitium Eccl. Romanæ purgatorium. Sophismata F. Turriani, & responsionis ad eadem repetita, de Ecclesia & ordinationibus ministrorum Ecclesiæ. *Pertas duas*. Index Elencticus repetitionum Turriani, ex eius libro, quem bipartitum inscripsit, collectus. Centum flosculi Turrianicæ disputationis, ex vtroq; eius libro decerpti, & in Jesuitarum gratiam collecti. De legitima vocatione pastorum eccl. reformatæ, adv. eos qui in hoc tantùm capite fr. b eccl. reformata dissentire profitentur. Ex libro disciplinæ Ecclesiasticæ. Posnaniensium assertionum, de Christi in terris ecclesia, quænam & penes quos existat. Analysis & Refutatio."

was written by Yves Rouſpeau, who has introduced it with an epiſtle "To the Chriſtian reader;" the latter, by J. de L'eſpine, on 70 pages. a very elegant type, and as carefully printed. W.H. Quarto.

1584. On the parchment leaf of an ancient MS. "De excidiis et reparacionibus:" among other articles, "Anno dnī predicto, 1584. Matheus Stokys Bedellus armiger et Regiſtrarius vniu'ſitatis (argumētū aggreſſus quod nemo ante cū tractavit) edidit, et Cantebrigie per Thomā Thomaſiū typographum vniu'ſitatis imprimi procuravit catalogū Rectorū et Cancell'iorū vniu'ſitatis Cantebr. a Maurico ſive Mauricio Rectore, qui rexit ſcholares imperante Conſtantino magno ad dūm Cancellariū qui modo preſidet. Idem Matheus Stokys āno ſequenti edidit et

1585. aliū catalogū procancell'iorū procuratorū et g'duatorū ab anno dnī 1500 ad annū 1585 ex annalibus vniu'ſitatis regiſtris per eū diligenter perſcrutatis ordinatiſq; recollectū. Anno eodē ſenio gravatus etatis ſue anno . . . . . Bedelli officiū reſignavit quod magna cū laude et totius Academie cōmodo, per annos 27 adminiſtrav'at, videl't ab āno 1558 ad annū 1585."

1584. Z. Urſini Doctrinæ Chriſtianæ compendium. Octavo.

1585. "A godlie expoſition vpon certain chapters of Nehemiah, written by that worthie Byſhop and faithfull Paſtor of the Church of Durham Maſter Iames Pilkington. And now newlie publiſhed. In the latter end, becauſe the Author could not finiſh that treatiſe of Oppreſſion which he had begonne, there is added that for a ſupplie, which of late was publiſhed by Robert Some, D. in Diuinitie.—Imprinted by Thomas Thomas printer to the Vniuerſitie of Cambridge 1585." It is introduced by "A preface of M. Iohn Fox, to the Chriſtian Reader." Beſides; 82 leaves, numbered only 7: ; many other leaves are incorrectly numbered. W.H. Maunſell mentions it without date. Quarto.

1585. "An aunſvvere to a certaine Booke, written by M. VVilliam Rainoldes Student of Diuinitie in the Engliſh Colledge at Rhemes, and Entituled, A Refutation of ſundrie reprehenſions, Cauil's, &c.[1] By William Whitaker, profeſſor of Diuinitie in the Vniuerſitie of Cambridge. Imprinted by Thomas Thomas, Printer to the Vniuerſitie of Cambridge, and are to be ſold at the ſign of the white Horſe in Canon-lane, ouer-againſt the North Doore of Paules, 1585." Dedicated "To—Syr VVilliam Cecill, Knight of the Garter, Baron of Burghley, Lord high Treaſurer of England, and Chancelor of the Vniuerſitie of Cambridge." Beſides; 419 pages. W.H. Sixteens.

1585. "The Latine Grammar of P. Ramus Tranſlated into Engliſh. Whereunto is joyned, for the more eaſie underſtanding of the rules herein conteyned, a Grammatical Analyſis uppon an Epiſtle of Tullie." Very neat Roman and Italic letter, 188 pages. W.H. Octavo.

1586. "A treatiſe againſt the Defenſe of the Cenſure given vpon the books of W. Charke, and Meredith Hanmer, by an vnknowne Popiſh Traytor, In maintenance of the ſeditious challenge of Edmond Campian, lately condemned and executed for high Treaſon. In which the reader ſhal wonder

[1] See it in our Gen. Hiſt. under the year 1583.

wonder to see the impudent falsehoode of the Popish defender, in abusing the names and writinges of the Doctors, olde and new, to blinde the ignorant. Hereunto are adioyned two treatises, written by D. Fulke: the one against Allens booke of the authoritie of Priesthode to remitte sinnes, of confession of sinnes to a Priest, and the Popes Pardons: The other against the Railing declamation of P. Frarine.' Alowed by publike authoritie. Imprinted—' 1586." On the next leaf is a list of "Faultes escaped," &c. The first tract contains 359 pages; the second, with a separate title-page, 531 pages; the third, with a separate title-page also, 54 pages. W.H.

"An Harmony of the Confessions of the Faith of the Christian and reformed Churches, which purelie professe the holy doctrine of the Gospell in all the chiefe Kingdomes, Nations, and Prouinces of Europe: the Catalogue and order whereof the pages following will declare. There are added in the ende verie shorte notes: in which both the obscure thinges are made plaine, &c. All which thinges, in the name of the Churches of Fraunce and Belgia, are submitted to the free and discrete iudgement of all other Churches. Newlie translated out of Latine into English. Also in the end is added the Confession of the Church of Scotland. Alowed' by publique authoritie. Imprinted—1586." There are prefixed, "A preface in the name of the churches of Fraunce and Belgia, which professe the reformation of the Gospell.---A catalogue of the confessions &c.—An admonition to the reader," &c.—The articles of each confession---" The contentes of the book following, according to the sections, which are in number 19, and of how many confessions ech Section doth consist." The last section is concluded on p. 608. The notes or observations upon the harmony are on 21 leaves, told over. The confession of the faith of Scotland is printed separate and entitled "A general confession of the true christian faith and religion, according to Gods word and actes of our Parliaments, subscribed by the Kings Maiestie and his household, with sundrie others. To the glory of God, and good example of all men. At Edinborough the 28 day of Ianuarie. The yeare of our Lord 1581. And in the 14 yere of his Maiesties Raigne." D 2, in fours. W.H. 1586.

Octavo.

" Gram-

General Hist. under 1567.

Ibidem—1595.

In some copies this date is omitted; but otherwise the very same.

See Strype's Annals, III: 412. Also, Martin Marprelate's first epistle dedicated to the Confocationhouse "Which Harmonie was translated and printed, by that puritan Cambridg printer Thomas Thomas. And although the booke came out by publike auth[ority] yet by your leave, the Bishops have called them in, as things against their state. And trust me his grace will owe that puritane printer as good a turney as hee paide vnto Robert Walde-graue for his sawciness in printing my frend, and deare brother, Diotrephes his Dialogue. Well frend Thomas, I warne you before hand, look to yourselfe." &c. In the Stationer's Register A is this memorandum, Anno 1589—1590. "Whereas all the seis'd books were sold to Mr. Byshop, he is remembered that 40 of the being Harmonies of the Churches, rated at ijs. le peece, were had from him by warrant of my Ld. of Cant. and remain at Lambeth with Mr. doctor Cosen."

1587. "Grammatice Latine, de etymologia, liber secundus, ex vetustissimis artis et lingue auctoribus depromptus, ea methodo, quam senatus literatorum, regia auctoritate Sterlingi habitus, Scotice iuventuti facillimam censuit. Addita sunt, sed minoribus characteribus, in provectiorum gratiam, ex intimis artis penetralibus, pleràque à nemine prius congesta, quibus auctor pueris properantibus interdici velit." It contains 52 pages, beside six leaves at the beginning for the title, dedication, some poems, &c. The author, whose name is not mentioned on the title-page, dedicated this treatise thus: "Jacobo, eius nominis sexto, Scotorum regi Christianissimo, gratiam et pacem à Domino." And concludes his dedication, consisting of two leaves, thus: "Cantebrigie, ex edibus Thome Thomasii, idibus Septembris 1587. Tue M. in Domino Jesu, cliens ex animo observantissimus, Jacobus Carmichael." 4°.

1587. "Explicationum catecheticarum, quae tractationem locorum Theologicorum κατ' ἐπιτομὴν complectuntur, sicuti illae ex repetitionibus D. Zachariae Vrsini, aliquot deinceps annis, Heidelbergae in Sapientiae collegio, ab ipsius discipulis collectae sunt; editio altera:" freed from the errors of our former edition. Printed at the expence of Thomas Chard. "Ex officina Thomae Thomasii inclytae academiae typographi." 8°.

1588. "Disputatio de Sacra Scriptura, contra huius temporis papistas, imprimis, Robertum Ballarminum iesuitam, pontificium in collegio Romano, et Thomam Stapletonum, regium in scholae Duacena controuersiarum professorem. Sex questionibus proposita et tractata, a Gulielmo Whitakero, theologiae doctore, ac professore regio, et collegii D. Joannis in Cantabrigiensi academia magistro. Cantabrigiae, ex officina Thomae Thomasii, florentissimae Cantabrigiensis academiae typographi, Maii 2." Quarto.

Very probably he printed other books, especially the dictionary of his own compiling; but i have not met with any assurance thereof.

JOHN LEGATE, or LEGATT, Citizen and stationer of London,

WAS made free 30 April, 1586, and appointed printer to the university of Cambridge, 2 Nov. 1588. See T. Baker's MSS. Vol. 24; p. 93. He had not long enjoyed this office before he was disturbed by the Londoners as Thomas his predecessor had been, but on whose death all proceedings had ceased. I cannot say what might be the real cause of their controversy with the university printers, and seemingly through them, against the privileges of the university itself; for which cause several

ſeveral letters[x] were written by their orator to Lord Burghley, their Chancellor, Sir Chriſtopher Hutton their High Steward, the archbp. of Canterbury, and the bp. of London, intreating their intereſt and favour in Legate's behalf, and the ſupport of their own privileges. Thomas's Dictionary and Terence are the only articles ſpecified in them: the former of theſe Legate had printed with ſome additions of his own. I have no account when the firſt four editions were printed, but the 5th was publiſhed in 1596. The Terence was printed ſmaller than it had been for cheapneſs and commodiouſneſs. Theſe it ſeems, having been ſent to London for ſale, were ſeized, and ſent to Stationers' hall; but the company's Regiſter is ſilent in this affair, as well as in Thomas's. However, in a minute, 6 Dec. 1591, it is acknowledged that diſorders and troubles had ariſen; and, in order to prevent them for the future, a motion[y] was made, liked and agreed to, for quietneſs and good order to be had, and continued between the univerſity of Cambridge and their printers, and this *(Stationers')* company. He married Agatha, the daughter of Chriſtopher Barker, eſq. the queen's printer, by whom he had a ſon of his own name, who followed the ſame buſineſs after the death of his father.

M. T. Ciceronis de oratore ad quintum fratrem libri tres. Cantabrigiae, ex officina Johannis Legat. Octavo and Quarto. 1589.

"Pub. Terentii Afri comoediae ſex. Cantabrigiae, Ex officina Iohannis Legatt. 1589." Very neatly printed in Nonpareil Roman. W.H. Twenty-fours. 1589.

An expoſition of the catechiſm taught in the Low Countries, &c. By Jer. Baſtingius. Again frequently. See it in 1595. Quarto. 1589.

"Armilla aurea, a Guil. Perkins. Cantab. ex officina," *&c.* Octavo. 1590.

"Expoſition on Iob, and Eccleſiaſtes, by Theod. Beza." Maunſell, p. 10. See it without date. Octavo. 1590.

"Henr. Holland his treatiſe againſt Witchcraft, wherein the greateſt doubts, concerning that ſinne are briefly anſwered, the Sathanicall operatiuely proued, preſeruatiues againſt ſuch euils are ſhewed: whereunto is added, certaine meanes ordained of God to diſcouer and confound all Sathanicall inuentions of VVitchcrafte, *&c.* Maunſell, p. 122 Quarto. 1590.

"De Vniverſali et Noviſſima Judaeorum Vocatione, ſecundum apertiſſimum Divi Pauli prophetiam, in vltimis hiſce diebus praeſtanda. Liber 1590.

[x] Copies of which may be ſeen in Ward's Lives of the profeſſors of Greſham College. Appendix No. XI.

[y] "That yt mighte be Lawfull for the ſaide vniu'ſitye and printers of Cambridge for the ſpace of one monethe after the Retorne of every Frankford mart, to haue the choice of anie ſtrayne Books cominge from the ſaide marte, the ſame to be allowed to the ſaide printers of Cambridge, and by them to be printed; So alwayes that euerie ſuche Book within the ſaid monethe be orderlye allowed, and thereupon entered in the Companie of Stacioners *(Hall book)* for the ſaid printers of Cambridge, or ſome of them; And that the ſame being done, the Wardens of the ſaid company of Stationers ſhould Reſtrayne all their Company to printe the ſame, and vſe all theire power to that effecte as is vſed in like caſes to freemen in theire owne Company."

Liber vnus." Dedicated by Andr. Williat to Lord Burghley. Quarto.

1592. " Syntaxis et Prosodia, versiculis compositae, studio & labore Johannis Greenwood, Cantabrigiensis, olim socii Aulae Divae Katherinae." 8°.

1591. " Series causarum Salutis & damnationis." Octavo.

1592. " Tho. Sampsons praiers and meditations Apostolike: gathered and framed out of the Epistles of the Apostles." Sixteens.

1592. " IVSTI LIPSI TRACTATVS AD historiam Romanam cognoscendam apprimè vtiles. 1. De Magistratibus veteris P. Romani. 2. Pecunia veterum Romanorum. 3. Nominibus Romanorum. 4. Ritu conviviorum apud Romanos. 5. Supplicio Crucis. 6. Censura & censu. 7. Anno, ejusque ratione & interlocatione. Cantabrigiæ Ex officina—, Inclytæ Academiæ Typographi.—1592." G 5, in eights. W.H. Octavo.

1592. " George Sohn D. in Diuinitie in Hidelberge, his treatise contayning the true description of Antichrist, who was foretold by the prophets and apostles, and an euident proofe that the same agreeth vnto the Pope. translated by N. G. *(Nich. Grimald)*—1592." Maunsell, p. 3. 8°.

1592. " Hier. Zanchius his Treatise of the spirituall marriage betweene Christ and the church, and euerie faithfull man." Maunsell, p. 123 8°.

1592. " A very excellent and learned discourse, touching the Tranquilitie and Contentation of the minde: conteining sundry notable instructions, and firme Consolations, most necessarie for all sortes of afflicted persons in these latter dayes. Distinguished into seven Bookes, 1. Against Covetousness. 2. Against Ambition. 3. Against Anger. 4. Against Envie. 5. Against Pleasure. 6. Against Curiositie. 7. Against Feare. Written in French by the famous and learned M. I. Del'Espine, and newly translated into English by Ed. Smyth. Printed by *him*, Printer to the Vniversitie of Cambridge. 1592. And are to be solde at the—Sunne in Paules Church-yard in London." Dedicated " To—Sir Francis Hynd, Knight, and M. Thomas Wendy, Esquire; two of her maiesties Iustices of peace in her Countie of Cambridge.—Edward Smyth.—Ad Academicam Iuventutem parænesis.—G. J."—Sixteen Alexandrine verses by T. W.—" A compendious and short summe of this whole discourse." &c. Each book has also a separate syllabus prefixed to it. Folios 188. W.H. Quarto.

1592. " Prophetica, sive, de sacra et unica ratione concionandi tractatus. Editio secunda, auctior et correctior ab authore facta." Octavo.

1592. " A Golden Chaine, or description of Theologie, containing the order of the causes of saluation and damnation. Also the order which Theod. Beza vsed in comforting troubled consciences: the seconde edition. Translated by Rob. Hill." Maunsell, p. 80. See it in 1597. Octavo.

1593. " Antisanderus, duos continens dialogos, non ita pridem inter viros quosdam doctos Venetijs habitos: in quibus variae Nicholaj Sanderi, aliorumque Romanensium calumniæ, in hæc Anglorum ab excusso Pontifice tempora vafèrrimè confictae, licèt obiter & fortuitò, verè tamen candideque refelluntur.—Excusum Cantabrigiae cum consensu Primariorum hominum, quorum authoritas chartâ regiâ ad hoc requiritur, M.D.XCIII."

M D.XCIII." Dedicated "Viro illustrissimo honorifico; Domino suo Thomæ Sacvilo Baroni Buckhurstiæ, splendidissimi Garterij ordinis Equiti, &c. —Aureliæ, octavo calen. Maij. Anno 1593. Honoris tui observantissimus A. L.---Typographus lectori." The first dialogue ends on p. 110; the second on p. 196. Annexed are sundry vouchers to p. 200. The late Mr. T. Baker, from the MS. of the late earl of Oxford, has shewn Dr. Cowel to be the author. W.H. The late Dr. R. Rawlinson had a copy of this book, with MS. notes. Quarto.

1593. "Eratosthenes, hoc est, Brevis & luculenta defensio Lysiæ pro cæde Eratosthenis, prælectionibus illustrata Andreæ Duneï in Academia Cantabrigiensi Græcæ linguæ professoris: in quibus fusè explicantur multa quæ tum ad ejus linguæ cognitionem, tum ad alias res attinent. Excudebat Johannes Legatus, inclytæ Academiæ Cantabrigiensis Typographus. Anno Dom. 1593." Dedicated, "Ad nobilissimum & illustrissimum Dominum, Robertum Essexiæ comitem, pro comite Herefordiæ, Equitem auratum insignissimum honoratissimi ordinis Garterij, &c. literatorum & bonorum omnium benignissimum protectorem.—Cantabrigiæ e Collegio Sanctæ & individuæ Trinitatis 3 Cal. Octobris. 1593.—A. D. ---Ad iuventutem Græcarum literarum studiosam Cantabrigiæ.---Argumentum orationis.---Λυσίου ὑπὲρ τοῦ Ἐρατοσθένους φόνου ἀπολογία.---Lysiæ pro cæde Eratosthenis defensio Latine Reddita ab. A. D.---Praelectiones ad Lysiam de cæde Eratosthenis." Besides, 248 pages. W.H. Octavo.

1593. Tho. Bell his motives concerning the Romish faith and Religion. 4°.

1593. "A direction for the government of the tongue according to God's word." &c. as p. 1336. Maunsell mentions an edition 1598; taken probably from the date of the epistle to the reader. W.H. Octavo.

1593. Two treatises. 1. Of repentance. 2. Of the combat between Flesh and Spirit. See them in 1595. Octavo.

1593. "A table from the beginning of the world to this day. Wherein is declared in what yeere of the World every thing was done, both in the Scriptures mentioned, and also in prophane matters. Written by that worthy member of the Church of God, M. Iohn More Preacher at Norwich. Seene and allowed by publike authoritie. Printed &c. And are to be sold at the—Sunne in Pauls Churchyard—1593." In a compartment with the queen's arms at top, the Cecil arms and crest on the sides, and at the bottom. Dedicated "To—Edmond Lord Bishop of Norwich, and to the Worshipfull M. Major of the same citie, with the Aldermen his brethren, the Sheriffes, and the whole corporation.—Norton in Suffolke, 24 August. 1593.—Nicholas Bovvnd." I have given an extract from this epistle below.[a] Next is a short note for adducing the prophane

[a] "Seeing that by God's providence the workes and labours of this Reverend and Godly learned man came unto my handes, and not onely were committed unto me, but the whole care and disposition of them by a certaine hereditarie right did fall unto me: I thought it my bounden duetie both to the dead, and especially to the Church of God, that as much as did lye in me, they should attaine unto that ende, for which principally they were begunne and ended by him: which was the greatest profite and good, that

to the ſcriptural chronology. Contains beſides 237 pages, and an index. W.H.

1594. "Grammatica Anglicana, præcipuè quatenus à Latina differt ad unicum P. Rami methodum concinnata. Authore Paulo Graues Cantabrigiæ, Ex officina—1594. Extant Londini ad inſigne ſolis in Cœmeterio D. Paulini." The rev. Dr. Lort.

1594. "John More his three ſermons, 2 of them on 2. Cor. 5. ver. 10. the 3. Iohn 13 ver. 34. 35. whereunto is annexed for the comfort of the afflicted a ſermon on Romanes 8. ver. 26. to 30. Alſo a treatiſe of a contented minde: by Nich. Bounde.—1594." Maunſell. Quarto.

1594. "The death of vſury, or the diſgrace of vſurers. Compiled more pithily then hitherto hath bene publiſhed in Engliſh. Wherein Vſury is moſt lively vnfolded, defined, and confuted by Divines, Civilians, Cannoniſts, Statutes, Schoole-men, olde and new Writers. VVith an Explanation of the Statutes now in force concerning Vſury, very profitable for this preſent age.—Printed &c. 1594. And are to be ſold at the—Sunne in Paules Church-yard in London." On the next leaf is a liſt of "Authours and Writers vſed in this booke beſides the authority of the holy Scriptures." 42 pages beſides. W.H. Quarto.

1594. "A fruitfull commentarie vpon the twelue Small Prophets, briefe, plaine, and eaſie, going over the ſame verſe by verſe, and ſhewing euery where the Method, points of doctrine, and figures of Rhetoricke, to the no ſmall profit of all godly and well diſpoſed Readers, with very neceſſarie fore-notes for the vnderſtanding both of theſe, and alſo all other the Prophets. The text of theſe Prophets, together with that of the quotations omitted by the author, *are* faithfully ſupplied by the Tranſlator, and purged of faults in the Latine coppie almoſt innumerable, with a table of all the chief matters herein handled, and marginall notes very plentifull and profitable; ſo that it may in manner be counted a new Booke in regard of theſe additions. VVritten in Latin by Lambertus Danæus, and newly turned into Engliſh by John Stockwood Miniſter and preacher at Tunbridge.—Printed &c. 1594. And are to be ſold" as above. On the back, "The order—they are placed in this booke, And—in what page they are to be found." Dedicated "To the no leſſe vertuous then honourable Perſonages Henrie Earle of Huntindon, &c. and the Lady Katherine his deare and welbeloued wife Counteſſe of the ſame &c.—Tunbridge this 20 of June, 1594.

that by publiſhing of them might redound unto the Church thereby. Which as it evidently appeared to be the authours meaning—in time to have committed ſome of them to the preſſe: ſo my ſelfe in his ſtead have laboured to effect this good purpoſe of his, by commending to the Church of God theſe firſt fruits of his labours: hoping in time that the reſt may folow, If the ſcarcitie of Hebrue and Greeke characters in this land do not hinder ſome, and the great coſt and charges of Printing Maps, be a ſtay and bane to others. For in both theſe kindes there are certaine of his labours finiſhed, and have bene longe ſince readie for the preſſe.—the bare name of him that was the authour of it ſhall purchaſe ſufficient credite for it with all thoſe, who knewe him to bee a man for his great varietie of learning, beſides his excellent wiſedome and godlineſſe, with his continual—paynes in preaching the Goſpell, (*moſtly at Norwich*) for—20 yeares at the leaſt,—worthie to bee reverenced &c."

1594.—John Stockwood.---To the courteous and Christian Reader.---To his very singular good Friend the Right Worshipfull, and for many vertues most renowmed M. Antony Bacon, sonne of the most Noble and Honourable Syr Nicholas Bacon Chauncelour of England.—At Orthesium, which is a town in the cuntry of Bearne, vnder the mountains called Pyrenæi, nere vnto Spaine, where is an Vniversitie erected by the most courteous King of Navarre Henry the second. Calend of May, in the yeare of the last time 1585. Your W. most bounden. Lamb. Danæus, Professor of Diuinitie.—A table of the chiefe figures of Rhetoricke mentioned in this Treatise." Besides; 1136 pages, and a table. W.H. Quarto.

" Polimanteia, or The meanes lawfull and vnlawfull, to iudge of the fall of a Common-wealth, against the friuolous and foolish coniectures of this age. Whereunto is added, A letter from England to her three daughters, Cambridge, Oxford, Innes of Court, and to all the rest of her inhabitants, perswading them to a constant vnitie of what religion soever they are, for the defence of our dread soueraigne, and natiue cuntry: most requisite for this time wherein wee now live.—Printed *&c.* 1595. And are to be sold" as above. Dedicated " To—Robert Devorax Earle of Essex and Ewe, Vicount of Hereforde, &c.—W. C.—The Preface to the Reader;" which concludes with some Latin verses. F f 3, in fours. W.H. Quarto. 1595.

" An exposition or commentarie vpon the Catechisme of Christian religion, which is taught in the schools and churches both of the Low Countries, and of the dominions of the Countie Palatine. By Ieremias Bastingius Minister of the Word of God. Translated out of Latine into English. With three Tables. Cambridge. Printed by *him*, and are to be solde at the—Sunne *&c.* 1595." Prefixed are An admonition to the reader; and a preface to the catechism. Besides; 275 leaves, and the three tables. W.H. Also without date. Octavo. 1595.

" Two Treatises. I. Of the nature and practise of repentance. II. Of the combat of the flesh and spirit. A second Edition* corrected. Printed by *him*, 1595. And are to be sold" as above. Inscribed " To the Reader whosoever.—Written Anno 1593. the 17. of November, which is the Coronation day of our dread Soueraigne Queene Elizabeth; whose raigne God long continue. W. Perkins." Besides; 55 pages. W.H. 4°. 1595.

" A Direction for the government of the tongue according to God's worde. Printed by *him* Printer to the Vniuersitie of Cambridge, 1595." Besides; 37 pages. See it in 1593. W.H. Quarto.

" A Solace for this hard season; published by occasion of continuance of the scarcitie of corne, and excessive prise of all other kind of provision; wherein we may see the cause of this scourge for our grief, and the remedy for our comfort." Printed for him. Octavo. 1595.

" Solace for a sickman, or a Treatise containing the nature, differences and kinds of Death; as also the right manner of dying well. And it may serve 1595.

* The same inserted again in the edition 1597.

ferve for fpiritual Inftruction, 1. To Mariners, on the Seas. 2. To Soldiers in the Wars. 3. To women travailing with Child." See it in 1597. Quarto.

1595. A Golden chain, or—the order of the caufes of Salvation, &c. as p. 1420. 302 pages and a table. W.H. See it in 1597.

1595. "A Cafe of Confcience, the greateft that euer vvas; Hovv a man may know whether he be the childe of God, or no. Refolued by the word of God. Whereunto is added a briefe difcourfe, taken out of Hier. Zanchius.—London,[b] Printed for *him* 1595." Zanchius has a feparate title-page, but the pages are continued to p. 48. W.H. Quarto.

1595. "A treatife—whether a man be in the eftate of damnation or—grace:" &c. as p. 1251. Quarto.

1596. "An Expofition of the Symbole or Creede of the Apoftles, according to the tenour of the Scriptures, and the confent of Orthodoxe Fathers of the Church: reuewed and corrected By William Perkins. They are good Catholickes, vvhich are of found faith and good life. Auguft. lib. quæft. in Math. cap. 11. Printed &c. 1596. Dedicated "To—Edward Lord Ruffell, Earle of Bedford.—Ann. 1595. April 2. —William Perkins." Befides; 442 pages. W.H. Quarto.

1596. "Thomae Thomafii Dictionarium fumma fide ac diligentia accuratiffime emendatum, magnaque infuper Rerum Scitu Dignarum, Et Vocabulorum acceffione, longè auctius locupletiufque redditum. Huic etiàm (præter Dictionarium Hiftoricum & Poeticum, ad prophanas hiftorias, poëtarumque fabulas intelligendas valdè neceffarium) [c]noviffimè acceffit vtiliffimus de Ponderum, Menfuarum, & Monetarum veterum reductione ad ea, quæ funt Anglis iam in vfu, Tractatus. Quinta editio fuperioribus cum Græcarum dictionum, tum earundem primitivorum adiectione multò auctior. Cantabrigiæ, Ex officina—1596. Extant Londini, ad infigne Solis in Cœmiterio D. Pauli." Dedicated "Honoratiffimo atque excellentiffimo viro Gulielmo Cecilio, Baroni Burghleienfi, &c.—Cantabrigiæ, quinto Idus Februarii. Anno verbi incarnati Millefimo quingentefimo nonagefimo fexto.—Iohannes Legatt. ---Typographus Lectori." B b b b, in fours. See Ainfworth's preface to his firft edition. W.H. Quarto.

1596. "The Apocalyps, or Revelation of St. Iohn the apoftle and evangelift of our Lord Iefus Chrift. With a briefe and methodicall expofition vpon euery chapter by way of a little treatife, applying the words of S. Iohn to our laft times that are full of fpirituall and corporall troubles and divifions in Chriftendome. Lately fet forth by Fr. Du Ion, and newly tranflated into Englifh for the edification and confolation of the true members of our Lord Iefus Chrift in his Catholike Church." The fhield with S. P. Q. R. as p. 1336. Printed by *him*,—1596." Dedicated

[b] Thefe appear to have been printed with the fame types as the Golden Chain, of which my copy wants the title-page.

[c] This word (noviffimè) omitted in the edition 1600.

dicated "To—M. Iohn Boyse Esquire.—T. B.—To the most Christian King Henrie the fourth, King of France and Navarre.—Fr. Du Ion.—A briefe chronicle of the Apocalypse, according to the times wherein the histories thereof were done." A folding sheet with five analytical tables, according to the order of the chapters, &c. Besides; 286 pages, W.H. Quarto. 1596.

"A Watch-worde for Warre. Not so new as necessary: Published by reason of the dispersed rumors amongst vs, and the suspected comming of the Spanyard against vs. Wherein we may learne how to prepare our selues to repell the Enemie, and to behaue our selues all the tyme of that trouble. Compendious for the memorie, comfortable for the matter, profitable for the tyme. Ezekiell, 21, 12. The terrors of the sword shall be vppon my people: smyte therefore vpon thy thigh. ¶ Printed by *him*,—1596." On the next leaf, under the queen's arms, an acrostic in Alexandrines, "Elizabetha Regina." Dedicated "To—the Mayor of—Kings Lynne, and to his Associats or Bretheren the Aldermen of the same Towne.—C. G.—To the Reader,." H 2, in fours. W.H. Quarto. 1596.

"A declaration of the true manner of knowing Christ crucified." 16°. 1596.

"Rob. Some, D. D. and Mr. of Peters Coll. Camb. &c. his 3 questions wherein is handled that Christ dyed for the Elect alone. Also a proposition, that they who have most greviously offended the Majesty of God ought not to despair of his mercy.[a]—1596. Octavo. 1596.

"A discourse of Conscience; wherein is set down the nature, properties, and differences thereof, as allso the way to get and keep a good Conscience." This and the foregoing article were reprinted with 1597.

"A salve for a sickeman: or, A treatise" &c. as in 1595. "And it may serve for spirituall instruction to 1. Mariners when they goe to sea. 2. Souldiers when they goe to battell. 3. Women when they trauell with childe." Dedicated "To—the Ladie Lucie Countesse of Bedford.—Septem. 7. 1595.—W. Perkins." This discourse on Eccles. 7; 3. contains 56 pages. 1597.

"A declaration of the true manner of knovving Christ crucified. Galat. 6; 4. God forbid that I should reioyce but in the Crosse of our Lord Jesus Christ, &c." On the back is an epistle "To the Reader.—Jan. 3. 1596. William Perkins." The pages and signatures are continued from the foregoing article to p. 73. 1597.

"A discourse of Conscience:" &c. as in 1595. "The second Edition." On the back, "The contents." Dedicated "To—Sir William Piryam Knight, Lord chiefe Baron of her Maiesties Exchequer.—1596. June 14.—Wm. Perkins." The signatures and pages continued to p. 145. Each tract has a separate title-page, "Printed by *him*, printer to the Vniuersitie of Cambridge. 1597. W.H. Quarto. 1597.

"An

[a] This was translated into Latin, and printed, Hardrovici, 8vo, with some other little treatises on the same subject, by Math. Hutton, Archbp. of York, Geo. Estey, B.D. Fellow of Caius Coll. Laur. Chaderton, Mr. of Emanuel, and Andr. Willet, Coll. Chr. Rob. Some's three treatises were likewise printed in Latin at Basil, 1602. published by W. M. (Wolphang Meyer, as I suppose) with Mr. Perkins's Prophetica, sive de concionandi ratione. 8vo. T. Baker.

1597. " An Exposition of the Symbole or Creede of the Apostles," &c. as in 1596. Contains 775 pages. W.H. Octavo.

1597. " Hæc sunt verba Dei, &c. Praecepta in monte Sinai data Iudæis sunt 613, quorum 365 negativa, et 248 affirmativa, collecta per Pharisæum, magistrum Abrahamum, filium Kattani, et impressa in Bibliis Bombergiensibus, anno à mundo creato 5288, Venetiis, ab authore vox Dei appellata: translata in linguam Latinam per Philippum Ferdinandum, Polonum. Cum licentia omnium primariorum virorum in inclyta, et celeberrima Cantabrigiensi academia.—Cantabrigiæ, Ex officina."* H 4. 4°.

1597. " A Golden chaine, or the description of Theologie, containing the order of the causes of Saluation and Damnation, according to Gods word. A viewe whereof is to be seene in the Table annexed. Written in Latine, and translated by R. H. Hereunto is adioined the order which M. Theodore Beza vsed in comforting afflicted consciences. The second* edition, much enlarged, with a table at the end." Felix Kingston's device. " Printed by Iohn Legate, Printer to the Vniuersitie of Cambridge 1597." Dedicated, " To—M. D. Cesar, Judge of the Admiraltie Court, and Master of her Maiesties Court of Requestes.—Cambr. S. Iohns Coll. Julie 23. 1592.—Robert Hill.---To the Christian Reader.—Iulie 23. the yeere of the last patience of Saints. 1592.—W. P." *(William Perkins)* 218 pages besides schemes interspersed, and the table. W.H. Quarto.

1597. " Tvvo Treatises." &c. as in 1595. " A second edition corrected." Field's device. 40 pages. W.H. Quarto.

1597. " A direction for the government of the tongue according to Gods word." Field's device. Printed by *him*,—1597." On 27 pages. See it in 1593. W.H. Quarto.

1597. A reformed catholike; &c. Again, Octavo.

1598. " A reformed Catholike: or, A Declaration shewing how neere we may come to the present Church of Rome in sundrie points of Religion: and vvherein we must for euer depart from them: with an Aduertisement to all fauourers of the Romane Religion, shewing that the said religion is against the Catholike principles and grounds of the Catechisme. Printed by *him*,—1598." Dedicated " To—Sir William Bowes knight, &c.—Cambr. Iune 28. 1597.—Wm. Perkins.—The author to the Christian Reader." Besides; 375 pages. W.H. Octavo.

1598. " The Lectures of Samuel Bird of Ipswidge vpon the 8. and 9. chapters of the second Epistle to the Corinthians. Printed by *him*,—1598." In the compartment with the Queen's arms at top, as p. 1421. Dedicated " To the worshipfull M^r. Moore at Talmage Hall in Brist.—1597. Decemb. 16. Samuel Bird.—To the Christian Reader." Besides; 97 pages. W.H. Sixteens.

1598. " De Prædestinationis modo & ordine; et de amplitudine Gratiæ Divinæ. Authore Gul. Perkinsio." Bodl. Libr. Octavo.

" Specimen

* As the same was mentioned in 1591, this probably refers to the Latin edition.

" Specimen digesti, sive Harmonicæ Vet. & Nov. Testimentorum." 1598.
Brit. Museum. Folio.

" Terence in *English. Fabulae comici facetissimi et elegantissimi 1598.
Poetæ Terentii omnes Anglicæ factae primúmque hac nova forma nunc editæ: opera ac industria R. B. in Axholmiensi insulta Lincolnsherij Epvvortheatis. Ex Horatio.

Sunt delicta quidem, quibus ignovisse velimus:
Nam neque chorda sonum reddit, quem vult manus & mens:
Poscentiq; gravem persæpe remittit acutum.
Nec semper feriet, quodcunque minabitur arcus.
Prodesse non obesse.
Illud ex animo fiet, hoc præter voluntatem accidet.

Cantabrigiæ. Ex officina—1598." Dedicated " To the worshipful yong gentleman, and of vertuous education M. Christopher Wray, son and heyre to—Sir William Wray knight, and to the rest of the toward yong Gentlemen his brethren, nephewes to the vertuous and true religious Ladies, the Lady Bowes, and the Ladie Sainctpoll his very bountifull Patronesses.—Epworth in Lincolneshiere this 30. of Maie. Yours in the Lord Rich. Bernard.—Ad Lectorem. Besides, 455 pages. W.H. 4°.

" A general treatise against poperie by Thomas Stoughton Minister of 1598.
the Word." The late William Bayntun, Esq;

" A discourse touching the doctrine of doubting. In which not only 1598.
the principall arguments, that our popish aduersaries vse, for the establishing of that disconfortable opinion, are plainley and truely answered: But also sundrie suggestions of Sathan, tending to the maintenance of that in the mindes of the faithfull, fully satisfied, and that with singuler comfort also. VVritten long since by T. W. and now published for the profit of the people of God. Printed by *him*,—1598." Dedicated " To—the lord Edward Earle of Bedford, and the ladie Lucie his wife. And to—Sir John Harrington knight and the ladie his wife.—At Wooburne the 14 of Aprill. 15 8.—Thomas Wilcocks the Lords vnworthy servant." At the head, " Lord Jesus begin and make an ende." Besides, 306 pages. W.H. Sixteens.

The Judgement of Urins. Octavo. 1598.

" Praelectiones doctissimi viri Guilielmi Whitakeri, nuper sacrae 1599.
Theologiae in academia Cantabrigiensi doctoris, et professoris regii, et collegii S. Iohannis Evangelistae in eadem academia praefecti. In quibus tractatur controversia de ecclesia contra pontificios, inprimis Robertum Bellarminum iesuitam, in septem quaestiones distributa, quas sequens pagina indicabit. Exceptae primum ab ore authoris, deinde cum aliis exemplaribus collatae, et post eius mortem ad breves illius annotatiunculas examinatae. Opera & cura Ioannis Allenson, sacrae Theologiae baccalaurel, et collegii praedicti socii. His accessit eiusdem Doct. Whitakeri ultima concio ad Clerum, una cum descriptione vitae & mortis, authore

* Rather Latin and English. Each scene first in Latin, then the same in English.

anthore Abdia Assheton, Lancastrensi, sacrae Theologiae baccalaureo, et eiusdem collegii socio; quam sequuntur carmina funebria." Quarto.

1599. "A treatise of Amandus Polanus, concerning Gods eternal predestination. Wherein both this excellent doctrine is briefly and sincerely delivered, and many hard places of Scripture are opened and maintained against the corrupt expositions of Bellarmine and other adversaries." The tabl &c. as p. 1330. Printed by him,—1599." Dedicated "To—Sir Edward Ratcliffe knight; high Sheriffe—in Bedfordshire, and the vertuous and good Ladie his wife.—Camb. this 24 of Jan. 1598.—Roger Goswyke.—The authors epistle. To—I. Andrew Nanstl ke—. From Basil, Feb. 3. 1598.—Amandus Polanus of Polensdorf." Besides; 260 pages. W.H. Octavo.

1599. "H. Zanchius his confession of Christian Religion. Which nowe at length being 70 yeares of age he caused to bee published in the name of himselfe and his family. Englished in sense agreeable, and in words as answerable to his owne latine copie, as in so graue a mans worke is requisite: for the profite of all the vnlearneder sort of English christians, that desire to know his iudgement in matters of faith. Rom. 10. 10) Withe the heart man beleeveth &c. Let all things bee subiect to the iudgement of the true Catholike church. Printed by him,—1599. Dedicated by the author "To Vlisses Martinengus earle of Barchen.—At Neustade Cal. April. 1585." Besides; 442 pages. W.H. Octavo.

1599. "A Disswasive from poperie, containing twelve effectual reasons, by which every Papist, not wilfully blinded, may be brought to the truth, and euery Protestant confirmed in the same: written by Francis Dillingham Master of Arts, and fellow of Christs Colledge in Cambridge, necessarie for all men in these times.—Printed by him,—.599." Dedicated "To—Oliver L. S. John, Baron of Bletsoe.—A preface to all English Papistes whatsoeuer.—To the Christian reader.—Catalogus authorum." Besides; 152 pages. W.H. Octavo.

1600. "Thomae Thomasii Dictionarium" &c. as p. 1424. "Sexta editio superioribus multò auctior." Ccc, in eights. W.H. Octavo.

—— "The New Testament of our Lord Jesus Faithfullie translated out of Greeke." Twenty-fours.

—— Sacra emblemata. Quarto.

—— Ogerii Bellehachii sacro-sancta Bucolica. Quarto.

—— "Gulielmi Perkinsi problema de Romanae fidei ementito catholicismo. Estque antidotum contra Thesaurum catholicum Jodoci Coccii, et ΠΡΟΠΑΙΔΕΙΑ iuventutis in lectione omnium patrum. Editum post mortem authoris, operâ et studio Samuel Ward. Cantabrigiae, ex officina Joannis Legat, anno Domini M DCIII." Quarto.

—— "Iob expounded by Theodore Beza, partly in manner of a Commentary, partly in manner of a Paraphrase. Faithfully translated out of Latine into English. Printed by him,—And are to be sold at the—[a]Sunne" &c. In

a By this direction, it may be supposed, this and the following book were printed between 1593 and 1595.

In the compartment with the queen's arms at top, &c. as p. 1421. Dedicated "To the most mightie and gratious Princesse Elizabeth—Queene of England, Fraunce, Ireland, and the Ilands neere adioyning, nourcing mother to the French, Duch and Italians, exiles for the profession of Christ, and the victorious defendresse of the whole true Christian religion." In this epistle he mentions his translation of the N. Testament as having now been five times corrected, and sent abroad under her majesty's name and protection, and concludes with seven distichs of Latin gratulatory verses, and a translation of "The same in English." Dated, "From Geneva, besieged by the Duke of Sauoy, 12 of August 1589. Your Maiesties most humble Orator Theodore Beza. —The preface of Master Beza before his readings vpon Iob begunne the 23 of Januarie 1587." The whole, A a, 2, in eights. W.H. 8°.

"Ecclesiastes, or the Preacher. Solomons sermon made to the people teaching euery man howe to order his life, so as they may come to true and euerlasting happines. With a Paraphrase, or short exposition thereof made by Theodore Beza. Translated out of Latine into English. Cambridge. Printed" &c. as the foregoing article. D, in eights. W.H. Octavo.

In the year 1626, John Legate being lately deceased, leaving eleven children, licence was granted to John Legate his son, to print Thomas Thomas's dictionary, &c. How long his son printed, does not appear, but we find him a printer at London in the year 1637, and 1648, when he was one of the twenty,[f] appointed by decree of the star-chamber, to print for this kingdom.

[f] Some of them being printers before 1600. I have taken their Names from the Decree, as follows: Felix Kingstone, Adam Islip, Thomas Purfoot, Miles Flesher, Thomas Harper, John Beale, John Legate, Robert Young. John Haviland, George Miller, Richard Badger, Thomas Cotes, Bernard Alsop, Richard Bishop, Edward Griffin, Thomas Purslow, Richard Hodgkinsonne, John Dawson, John Raworth, Marmaduke Parsons. Besides his majesties printers, and the printers allowed for the universities.

OF

PRINTING

AT

St. ALBANS.

ALBON's, or St. Alban's, before called Holmehurſt, derived its name from being the burying place of that ſaint and protomartyr of England, whoſe bones, after having been concealed 500 years, were found here about A. D. 793; when Offa, king of the Mercians, is ſaid to have built a monaſtery to his memory, and endowed the ſame with poſſeſſions for the maintenance of 100 Benedictine monks. It was afterwards further enriched by royal charters, with lands and peculiar privileges; its abbots having precedence of all others in England. The noble art of printing was encouraged and practiſed here about the year 1480; no book printed here with an earlier date having yet been diſcovered. What was the name of the perſon who firſt performed it, we know not, as he has not notified it in his works. Sir Henry Chauncey calls him John Inſomuch: on what authority he has not told us. His being a monk is very probable, and W. de Worde[a] denominates him "ſometime a ſcholemaſter;" but both theſe names ſeem to be mere conjecture, eſpecially his ſurname, *Inſomuch*; for which there appears no better foundation than its being the firſt word in the two Engliſh books printed by him. Bale, and Pits after him, mention a certain ſchoolmaſter, or reader of hiſtory in the monaſtery of St. Alban's, who had collected materials for an hiſtory of England, but died before he had compiled the ſame; which papers coming to Mr. Caxton's hands, he is ſaid from them to have printed the Engliſh[b] chronicle, which goes under his name. However erroneous the latter of theſe aſſertions may be, as will be ſhown by and by, it evinces

[a] See p. 133. [b] In 1480. See p. 26.

This Plate of **SPECIMENS** *of the first Printing at* **S^T. ALBANS** *is humbly Inscrib'd to their Representatives in Parliament*
James West Esqr. and Sr Peter Thompson K^t. *by Jos. Ames.*

A B C D E F G H I K L

Compilatum autem fuit hoc opus in Alma universitate Cantabrigie Anno domini 1478° die 6. Julii Quo die Festum sancte Marthe recolitur Sub protectione Serenissimi Regis Anglorum Edwardi quarti.

Impressum fuit hoc presens opus Rethorice facultatis apud villam sancti Albani Anno domini M°. CCCC°. lxxx°.

.1 .2 . 3 . 4 . 5 . 6 . 7 . 8 . 9 .

Explicit liber modorum significandi Alberti apud villam sancti Albani a°. m°. cccc° lxxx°

M N O P Q R S T U W Y

Armes of Seynt Albons 1486.

Imprynted at S. Albons by me Joes Herforde for M. Rychard Stevenage.

evinces that it must have been another schoolmaster who printed the following books here.

" Rhetorica nova fratris Laurentii Gulielmi de Saona, ordinis Minorum. Compilatum autem fuit hoc opus in alma universitate Cantabrigie, anno Domini 1478, die et 6 Julii, quo die festum sancte Marthe recolitur; sub protectione serenissimi regis Anglorum Eduardi quarti.—Impressum fuit hoc presens opus Rhetorice facultatis apud villa sancti Albani, Anno Domini M CCCCLXXX." See the copper-plate annexed. It is divided into three parts, or chief heads, and printed in red and black ink. See Orig. e progr. della Stampa, p. 192. The late R. Mead, M. D. Reg. Med. After whose death it was sold for two shillings. A small Quarto. 1480.

Alberti Liber modorum significandi, &c. It seems to have had no distinct title-page, but begins thus " Quoniam autem intelligere, & scire contingit, in omnia scientia ex cognitione principiorum, ut scribitur primo phisicorum; nos ergo volentes habere scientie grammaticam noticiam, circa ejus principia, cujusmodi sint modi significandi per se primo ordine instare." At the end, " Explicit liber modorum significandi Alberti, impressus ad villam sancti Albani, anno m.cccc.lxxx." See the specimen in the copper-plate. The leaves are numbered at the bottom a i, a ii, &c. 46 leaves. The type &c. made Mr. Ames doubt whether this book was printed in England; however he had not observed any printed here with the same. Michael Wodhull Esq; Octavo. 1480.

" Incipiūt exēpla sacre scripture ex utroque testamēto, secund. ordinē literarū collecta. Et primo de Abstinentia." It contains by signatures, a, and b, 8 leaves; c, 6; d, e, f, 8; g, 6; h is omitted; i, k, and l, 8. Note a 1 is a blank leaf. The treatise ends on l 6, " Expliciūt exēpla sacre scripture ex ueteri et nouo testamēto collecta secund. ordinē literarū. Jnpressaq; apud uillā sancti Albani. Anno dnī m.cccc.lxxxi." Then, an alphabetical table on two leaves, entitled " Rubrice h' libri, videlicet exēplorū biblie, & quoto unaqueq; ptinent' folio: hic ānotātur —Explicit breuis tabula secund. ordinē alphabeti collecta." The articles in this table severally refer to some folio, thus, " Abstinentia folio ii; Acceptio muneris, iii: Adoratio, vi." &c. though the leaves are not numbered; neither has it catch-words nor running titles. Printed on papers with different marks. His Majesty; also in the Middle Temple library. Octavo. 1480.

" In Aristotelis physica, lib. VIII. Pr. pr. Venite ad me omnes, qui laboratis. Impressa in villa St. Albani." Bibl. Tanneri; (Johannes) Canon. Octavo. 1481.

The St. Albans Chronicle: so called, not only because it was first printed there, in its present form; but also, as being compiled by a schoolmaster (perhaps historiographer) of the monastery. So much as concerned the English affairs had been printed by Caxton, as abovementioned, but now interwoven with scripture and foreign histories, collected (1483.)

 chiefly

chiefly from the Fasciculus temporum, printed[i] 1481. and named Fructus temporum. It begins with the table; then on sig. a ij, "The Prolog," thus: [k]"N so myche that it is necessari to all creaturis of criston religyon. or of fals religyon: os gētyles and machomites: to knaw theer prince, or prynces that regne a pon them. and therin to obey. So it is commodyus to knaw their nobull actis or dedys. and the circumstās of theer lyues. Therfoor ī the yeer of our lorde. m. iiijc.lxxxiij. And in the xxiij. yeer of the regne of kyng Edward the fourth at Saint Albons so that all men may knaw the actys naemly of our nobull kyngys of Englond is cōpylit[l] together thys book. And moor ouer, is translayt owt of latin ī to englich froom the begīyng of the world. the lynage of crist: from Adā till it be cūmyn to Dauid. & from Dauid the kyngys of israel & of Juys: the hegh byschoppys in theer days wyth the Juges and prophettis. The iiij principall Reames of the worlde, that is to say of Babulon: of Perces. of Grekys. and of Romans. & all the Emperoures of Rome or Popys by ordyr and their namys. and many a notabull sadyr: wyth cermen of ther actys, breuyatly as moor plaaly is declarit in the chapytur next aftyr. And heer be rehersit the namys of the autors. of whom thees cronyclys ben translatte mooste. naamly: Galfridus Munmoth monke in hys boke of Brute. Saynt Beed in the actys of Englond. Item Beed in his boke of tymys. Gyldas in the actys of Bretan. Wylliam Malmisbery monke in the actys of kyngys of Englond. and bisshoppys. Cassiderus of the actys of emperours. and bisshoppys. Saint Austyn de Ciuitate dei. Tytus Lyuyus de gestis Romanorum. Martyn Penytenciary to the pope in his cronyclys of emperours. and byshoppys. And namly Theobaldus Cartusiensis contenyng in hys boke the progresse off all notable sadyres from the begynyng off the worlde vnto oure tyme. wyth the notabull actys of the saem. ¶ In thys neew translacion ar contened many notabull and maruelles thyngys: and thoo been legged by auctoryte of mony famous clerkys. And that eu'y man may knaw how thes croniclis be ordyrt ye shall vnderstond that this boke is deuidit ī to vij partys. Off the wych the fyrst parte cōtenys from Adam till Brute cam in to Bretan ¶ The secūd parte contenes from brute came fyrst in to England vn to the cyte of Rome was byld be Romol' ¶ The therd part cōtenes sethyn rome was byld vn to Crist was born of our lady mari ¶ The fourth from thēs vn to the cōyng of the saxons ī to englond ¶ The

[i] See Maittaire, Vol. 1; p. 462.

[k] A vacancy is left here for an I, to be supplied by the illuminator; though all the rest of the initials, except B, the first of the chronicle, are printed in red, as are also the paragraph marks. One Alan Strayler, an illuminator, is mentioned among the benefactors to the abbey of St. Albans, for that he forgave three shillings and four pence of an old debt, owing to him for colours. Bagford's MSS. See also Weaver's Anc. Fun. Monuments, p. 577, &c.

"Nomen Pictoris Alanus Strayler habetur,
Qui sine fine choris coelestibus associetur."

[l] Hence it seems not improbable but that The chronicles of England, first printed by Caxton, were originally compiled here, and continued from time to time by some of the abbey appointed for that purpose; which being in general well approved might occasion the plenty of MS. Copies, which are even at this day found amongst us.

¶ The fyst part from thēs vn to the cōīg of the danys ¶ The sect part from thens vn to the cōmyng off the normās ¶ The seuīt part from the Normās vn to owr* tym the wich is vndir the regne of kyng Edward the fourth xxiij yer whos nobull cronīclis be custū may not be sern ¶ And so in eu'y part of thes. vij. partes is shewed the most and necessary actis of all the kyngis of England & ther namys wrettyn aboue in the margent that euery man may synd them soon. And afor the kyng of englond actis be writi. ther is writi ẏ linage of crist from Adā til that crist was borne of our lady with the egh bysshopp and the juge that war in that tyme: and certan of their actis necessari till it be cummyn to Crist was borne. And aftir that Cryst was borne. and Peter was pope of Rome. is shewed be order the namys of all the popys, and emprouris of Rome afoor and aftir. wyth certan off their actis breuyatly: and mony other dyuers thyngis and maruellus in thes mens days fallyng. And it is shewid eueri thing in his place. how meny yere it fell aftyr the begynyng of the world. and how long afvor that Crist was borne. And when that I cum to Crist was born. then it is wrettyn how long any thyng fell aftyr the natiuite of Christ. And this is the ordyr off thys boke and the thyngis that be spoken of." The prologue ended; "Hic incipit fructus temporum." The seven parts into which this chronicle is divided are marked on the tops of the leaves throughout, thus: Ps. on the outer edge of the left hand page, and its number in antique figures, in like manner, on the right hand page. This may be one reason why neither pages nor leaves are numbered: it is also without catch-words. The running-titles, containing the name of the reigning monarch, are not general till after William the conqueror: before that, many pages are without; but such as have them are in a line with Ps. and its number. The type is very rude, much like Caxton's English Chronicles, 1482. The signatures are in eights, marked throughout, a, i—viij, &c. After z are the signatures &, 9, and the character for con. The second alphabet is by capitals to K viij. The initial letters &c. except the first of the prologue, and the first of the chronicle are printed in red: the first I have observed. "¶ Here ende the Croniclis of Englōde with the frute of timis." The device, the arms of St. Albans. A fine copy of this book is in his Majesty's library. W.H.. Folio.

A book, containing three separate treatises, has been ascribed in general to dame Juliana Bernes, or Berners, abbess of Sopwell nunnery, near St. Alban's, though her name appears only at the end of the 2d book, or that of hunting. The first book treating of hawking is thus introduced on signature a ii, "In so moch that gentill men and honest persones, 1486.

haue

* This seems as if the English chronicles were at least designed to have been continued to the 23d year of Edward IV; but what follows appears to me as only explanatory of "owr tym," for the reason give with it, "whos nobell chroniclis be custum may not be sern." I offer this opinion in great deference to Mr. Lewis, who explains these words by "or are not commonly known." However, they certainly are continued only, as Caxton's editions, to the coronation of Edward IV.

haukyng and huntyng with other plesuris dyuerse as in the boke apperis and also of Cootarmuris a nobull werke. And here now endyth the boke of blasyng of armys translatyt and compylit togedyr at Seynt albons the yere from thincarnacion of owre lorde Ihesu Crist M.CCCC.LXXXVI." On the next or last leaf "Hic finis diu'sorū gen'osis valde utiliū, vt intuētibus patebit." Over the St. Alban's arms as in the plate facing p. 1430. The back blank. This 3d book contains f 10, in eights. The principal initials and coats of arms are printed with inks of various colours, as black, red, blue, and yellow. Mr. Bagford says it was printed here in 1481; and at London reprinted in quarto, 1486. But no such *editions have been yet met with. Pub. Libr. Cambridge; and George Mason Esq; Folio.

At this place, as well as at Oxford and Cambridge, there is a great chasm in time. The late Mr. T. Baker thought Cardinal Wolsey, being abbot, might probably put a stop to printing here, having shewn his disapprobation of it in a convocation held in St. Paul's Chapter-house, telling the clergy that, if they did not in time suppress printing, it would be fatal to the Church. True it is there was printing here before and after, but none in his time. After about 50 years rest from printing

JOHN HERTFORD, HEREFORD, or HERFORD,

BEGAN to revive the art in this place, by printing the following* books; but finding it would not answer, removed to Aldersgate-street, London.

"+ Here begynnethe the glorious lyfe and passion of seint Albon 1534.
prothomartyr of Englande/ and also the lyfe and passion of saint Amphabel/ whiche conuerted saint Albon to the fayth of Christe." This title is over a whole length cut of St. Alban, dressed in a long robe, with a cross in his right hand, and a walking stick in his left. Before the 2d book is a cut of St. Alban on his knees, with his head off, which hangs on a tree by its hair; the blood spouting from the neck upon the king, who is standing before the body. "Here begynneth the seconde boke of the glorious Prothomartyr saynt Albon/ how he was made gouernour of the citie of Verolayme." On signature F 1, before the 3d book is a cut of St. Amphibalus tied to a pillar with only a cloth about his waist, holding a cross with both hands; a man wounding him in his right arm, another

* Such mistakes are very excusable: Mr. Bagford intending himself to compile a history of printing, though he lived not to perform it, collected in loose papers every report tending thereto. He died at Islington, 5 May 1716, and was buried in the burying-ground belonging to the Charter-house, where he was a brother.

* Of these, the first only has come to my sight, which indeed has neither printer's name nor place of printing; but as it was printed at the request of the abbot of St. Albans, and at a time so near the allowed revival of printing here, no place seemed to me more proper for it than this. Of the other five books, two only appear to have Hertford's name.

another feemingly pulling open his belly*. On fignature P, "Here begynneth the thyrd boke/ whiche telleth of the conuerfion of many of the paynims vnto the fayth. And alfo of the martyrdome of holy Amphibalus/ whiche conuerted faynt Albon to the fayth of Chrifte, whiche Amphibalus was the princes fonne of wales." The whole contains y, in fours. In feven lined ftanzas; four on a page. "¶ Here endeth the glorious lyfe and paffyon of feint Albon prothomartyr of Englande/ and alfo the lyfe and paffyon of faynt Amphybell/ whiche cōuerted faynt Albon to the fayth of Chrifte. whofe lyues were tranflated out of frenche and laten in to Englifhe/ by John Lydgate monke of Bury/ and now lately put in printy at requeft of Robert Catton, abbot of the exempte monafterye of faynt Albon. The xxvi. yere of our foueraigne lorde kyng Henry the eyght. And in the yere of our lorde God. M.D.xxxiiii." Bric. Mufeum. Quarto.

1536. "The confutacyon of the firft parte of Frythes boke, with a dyfputation before, whether it be poffyble for any heretike to know, that himfelf is one, or not. And alfo another, whether it be worf to denye directly more or leffe of the fayth, put forth by John Gwynneth, clarke. M.CCCCC.XXXVI." R. S. *(Richard Stevenage)* in a knot, within a circle. About it, "Dominus dedit, Dominus abftulit, ficut Domino placuit, ita factum eft." See the copper-plate, p. 1430. Octavo.

1537. "An introduction for to lerne to reken with the pen. and with the counters, after the true caft of arifmetyke, or awgrym, in hole nombers, and alfo in broken; newly corrected, and certayne rules and enfamples added thereunto, in the year of our lorde 1536." Contains S v. and three blank leaves; Numbers to the end. "Thus endeth the fcyence of awgrym, the wiche is newly corrected out of dyvers bokes, becaufe that the people may come to the more underftandynge and knowlege of the fayde arte, or fcyence of Awgrym. And becaufe the marchaunt men occupyenge beyonde the fee, may have the better knowlege of the beyonde fee coynes, we have fet dyuers proper rules, as of crones, ducates, and of frances, and with all other fmall money after theyr value. And alfo, of dyuers meafures both of wyne and corne. Imprented in the yere of our Lorde, MCCCCCXXXVII." W. Jones, Efq; See p. 579. Octavo.

1538. "A Godly difputation betweene Juftus and Peccator, and Senex and Juuenis: very expedient for euery man to read. Compiled by the holy man Carthufianus Dionifius, and lately tranflated into Englifh for the furtherence of them in vertue that are not learned in Latin. Imprinted at St. Albans by me Jo. Hereford, for M. Richard Steuenage." Bagford's MSS. 8°.

1538. "The rule of an honeft life, written by the holy man Martine, bifhop of Dumience, unto king Mito, king of Galitia in Spain: whereunto is added, the enchiridion of a fpiritual life." Octavo.

1538. "An epiftle againft the enemyes of poore people. Impryuted at S. Albons by me Joēs Herford, for M. Rychard Steuenage." Octavo.

OF

* This feems to allude the legend of his martyrdom taken out of the library of St. Albans, viz. having his belly opened and made to run about a ftake while all his bowels were drawn out, then thruft in again with fwords and daggers, and at laft ftoned to death. See Fox's Martyrol. Vol. I; p. 125. Edit. 1641.

OF PRINTING AT *YORK.*

PRINTING at this city was early, in reſpect to other places in this kingdom, which would incline one to conclude, they had ſome brave ſpirits among them, willing to cultivate common ſenſe. One Matthias Goes, an ingenious man at Antwerp, who printed a book entitled, " Cordiale de quatuor noviſſimis, Octavo, 1483, perhaps was the father to Hugh Goes, who ſet up the firſt preſs we know of here.

Bagford's papers mention that " At York, In the days of Hen. 7. there was one who printed a proclamation on vellum." It is pity but the date of it were known.

The Pica of the church of York, thus: " In laudem Sanctiſſime Tri- 1509.
nitatis, totiuſque Milicie celeſtis, ad honorem & decorem S. eccleſie Eboracenſis Anglicane, eiuſque devotiſſimi cleri, hoc opus, quod Pica, ſive Directorium ſacerdotum nuncupatur, vigilanti ſtudio emendatum et reviſum, impreſſum Eboraci, per me Hugonem Goes, in vico, qui appellatur Steengate, anno Domini MDIX. 18 die menſis Februarii." There is a Preface to it by Thomas Hannibal, which is thus inſcribed. Thome Hannibal legum doctoris, ac canonici Eboracenſis, in picam Eboracenſis, nuper a diſcreto viro Domino Thoma Hothyrſall, eccleſie Eboracenſis vicario chorali, reviſam & emendatam, preludium," *&c.* It is therein ſaid, Nonnulli hanc immenſam provinciam ac pergrande onus aggreſſi fuerunt, inter quos Robertus Aniſlede potiſſimum inſudavit, &c. Robertus Aniſſede erat capellanus Eccleſie S. Gregorii in magno vico Ebor. Sidney coll. libr. Octavo.

" Miſſale ad vſum celeberrime eccleſie Eboracenſis, optimis carac- 1516.
teribus recẽter Jmpreſſum, cura peruigili maximaq; lucubratione, mendis quam pluribus emendatum. Sumptibus & expenſis Johannis gachet, mercatoris librarii bene meriti, iuxta preſatam eccleſiam commorantis.

 Anno

Anno dnī decimo sexto supra millesimum et quingētessimū. Die vero quinta Februarii, completum atq; perfectum." With musical notes, and several very neat wood-cuts and blooming letters; no catch-words, nor numbering to the leaves. Neatly printed on Great Primer English, in black and red. My copy contains by signatures + in eights, viz. the common alphabet, &, and +, ending with Cautele ad missam celebrandam. W.H. Folio.

1516. "I find in a Primer intituled The Houres of our Ladie, after the vse of the church of York, printed anno 1516. a charme with this titling in red letters; To all them that afore this image of pitie deuoutlie shall saie fiue[1] Pater nosters, fiue Aues, and one Credo, pitiouslie beholding these armes of Christs passion are granted thirtie two thousand seuen hundred fiftie fiue years of pardon. It is to be thought that this pardon was granted in the time of pope Boniface the ninth; for Platina saith that the pardons were sold so cheape, that the apostolicall authoritie grew into contempt." Scot's Discovery of witchcraft, p. 234.

1516. "Whyttintoni *(Roberti)* Editio de concīnitate grāmatices et Constructione nouiter impressa Ebor. Per me Vrsyn Mylner in vrbe parrochia Sancte Helene in vico (Blaake strete) Moramtrahentem." This title is over a cut of a schoolmaster seated on a stately chair with a rod in his left hand, three scholars on a form before him. See p. 195. Contains by signatures A 8, B 4, C 8, D 4. "Explicit Whittyntoni Editio—in vico vulgariter nūcupato (blake strete) Anno domini Millesimo quingentesimo decimo sexto, die vero. xx. mensis Decembris." This colophon over a shield hanging on the bough of a tree with these arms, Parte per pale, on the dexter side a sort of windmill, on the sinister a sun (both very rudely executed) supported by a bear and an ass. Underneath is a scrole with  between "Vrsin" and "Mylner." His Majesty. Quarto.

1526. "Breviarium ad usum insignis metropolitane ecclesie Eboracensis: unacum pica diligentissime accuratissimeque recognitum et emendatum: in preclara Parrhisiensi academia: in edibus videlicet Francisci Regnault impressum; ac expensis honesti viri Joannis Gachet: in predicta Eboracensis civitate commorantis: hic suum capit exordium pro tempore hyemali. Anno nostre reparationis 1526." Octavo.

1530. "Processionale completum per totum anni circulum. Ad usum celebris ecclesie Eboracensis de novo correctum et emendatum cum collectis. Impensis Joh. Gachet, librarii Ebora. 1530." See Gough's Brit. Topography, II; p. 425, and 426. Octavo.

Thomas Rawlinson, esq; had a book with this colophon, "Feliciter finiunt festum visitationis beate Marie virginis, secundum vsum Ebor, Nouiter impressi per Ursyn. Mylner, commorantem in cimitero minsterii sancti Petri. +" Octavo.

At

[1] "If the party faile in the number, he may go whistle for a pardon."

At BEVERLEY in Yorkſhire.

GOES printed a broadſide, being a wooden cut of a man on horſeback, —— with a ſpear in his right hand, and a ſhield with the arms of France in his left. " Emprynted at Beverlay in the Hyegate, by me HEWE GOES," with his mark or rebus of a great H, and a gooſe. It was in the poſſeſſion of the late Mr. Thomas Martyn, of Norfolk.

He alſo printed a Latin grammar at LONDON, in quarto, formerly among lord Oxford's books. No date to either.

TAVISTOCK, in Devonſhire,

AN exempt monaſtery particularly famous for its lectures on the Saxon language, which uſed to be read here, that the knowledge thereof might not be quite loſt.

Below a wood-cut of the Father crowned, or as others, of Chriſt, and 1525. the emblems of the four Evangeliſts, is this title, " The Boke of comfort called in laten Boetius de Conſolatione philoſophie Tranſlated in to engleſſe tonge." On the next leaf begins, " Prefatio Tranſlatoris." Then, " Prologus." After which " Incipit liber Boetij de conſolatõne philoſophie." In Engliſh verſe: divided into five books, the running-titles are according to each of them, as " Liber primus," &c. The firſt three books, as alſo the preface and prologue, are in the octave ſtanza, the fourth and fifth in ſeven-lined ſtanzas. At the end, " Collectis in ſequentibus cuiuſlibet linee primis litteris/ non ſolum Tranſlatoris ſed & transferri procurantis/ nomina cũ cognominibus/ inueſtigare poteris. Nomen transferri procurantis, the initials whereof are " ELISABET. Cognomen, BERKELEy. Nomen tranſlatoris, JOHANNES Cognomen Tranſlatoris, WALTWNEM:* " Here endeth the boke of comfort called in latyn, Boecius de conſolatione Ph'ie Enprented in the exempt monaſtery of Taveſtok in Denſhyre. By me Dan Thomas† Rychard monke of the ſayd Monaſtery/ To the inſtant deſyre of the ryght worſhypful eſquyer Mayſter Robert Langdon. Anno d'. MDxxv. Deo Gracias." The arms of Langdon of Keverill, eſq; at the cloſe, who dwelt in the pariſh of St. Martin's, near Looe in Cornwall; ſo that Mr. Hearne is to be corrected. J. Anſtis. See Carew's Survey of Cornwall, p. 110. Sheets R 7, in eights." W.H.; Quarto.

" Here ſoloyth the confirmation of the charter, perteyninge to all the (1534) tynners wythyn the countey of Devonſhyre, with there ſtatutes alſo made

 at

* Waltowneem or Walton, a canon of Oſney; and the tranſlation was finiſhed in the year 1410. See Hearne's Robert of Glouceſter, p. 707. Alſo, Catal. Bibl. Harleiana Vol. 3. No. 6203.

† Perhaps the famous printer T. Richard, at Paris afterwards.

Crockeryntorre, by the hole assent and consent of al the sayd tynners. Yn the yere of the reygne of our sovereyne lord kynge Henry VIII. the secund yere. Here endeth the statutes of the stannary, imprented yn Tavystoke, the xx day of August, the yere of the reygne off our soveryne lord, kynge Henry the viii, the xxvi yere. God ssave the kyng.' Quarto.

Mr. Hearne in his appendix to Hemingi Chartularii Ecclesiæ Wigorniensis, Vol. II; p. 662. mentions "The long Grammar," printed at Tavistock, the account of which he had from Mr. Bagford: that is by way of enquiry after it; for Mr. Lewis in his MSS. says, The diligent and inquisitive John Bagford never could meet with it.

SOUTH-

[t] This singular book, consisting of 16 leaves, was communicated to Mr. Ames by the reverend Mr. Joseph Sandford, fellow of Baliol college. Reprinted with additions. See p. 947, and p. 1291. Nearly the same size letter with the abovementioned Boetius.

SOUTHWARK.

¶ Imprentyd at London in Southwarke by me Peter Treueris/ dwellynge in the sygne of the wodowes. In the yere of our lorde god. M.D.xxvi. the xxvii. day of July.

PETER TREVERIS,

PERHAPS of Treveris, or Triers, a city of Germany, (ſeated in an air ſo cloudy, and ſubject to rain, that it is by ſome merrily called, Cloaca planetarum) appears to be the firſt printer in this place. He printed for John Reynes and Laurence Andrewe; and ſold for William Raſtell in 1532. See p. 412 and p. 176. Mr. Wood thought he had printed a Latin grammar of Whitinton's at Oxford in 1527, as alſo other books about and before that time, but we have not met with any ſuch. See Hiſt. & Antiq. Oxon. p. 227.

1. Diſticha

1514. "1. Diſticha moralia, titulo Catonis, cum ſcholiis auctis Eraſmi Roterdami. 2. Apothegmata Graeciae ſapientum, interprete Eraſmo. 3. Eadem per Auſonium, cum ſcholiis Eraſmi. 4. Mimi Publiani, cum eiuſdem ſcholiis auctis recogniti. 5. Inſtitutum hominis Chriſtiani, carmine per eundem Eraſmum Roterdamum." With Eraſmus's epiſtle to "M. Joannes Nevius Hondiſcotanus, Liliaorum apud inclytum Lovonium Gymnaſiarcha." Bagford's MSS.

1516. "The grete herball, which giueth parſyt knowledge and vnderſtanding of all manner of herbes, and their gracyous vertues," &c. See it in 1529. Colophon, "Jmprented at London in Southwark, by me Peter Treueris, dwellynge in the ſygne of the wodows,* in the yere of our Lorde God MDXVI. the XX day of June." Printed again the 27th of July, 1526, and frequently. Folio.

1525. "The noble experyence of the vertuous handy warke of ſurgeri/ practyſyd & compyled by the mooſt experte mayſter Jherome of Bruynſwyke/ borne in Straeſborowe in Almayne/ ÿ whiche hath it fyrſt proued, and trewly founde, by his awne dayly exercyſynge. ¶ Item, there after he hath authoryſed and done it to vnderſtande thrugh the trewe ſentences of the olde doctours and mayſters very experte in the ſcyence of Surgery as Galienus/ Jpocras/ Auicenna/ Gwydo/ Haly abbas/ Lancfrancus of mylen/ Jamericus/ Rogerius/ Albucaſis/ Placētinus/ Brunus/ Gwilhelmus de ſaliceto/ & by many other mayſters whoſe names be wryten in this ſame boke. ¶ Here alſo ſhall ye fynde for to cure & hele all wounded mēbres/ and other ſwellynges. ¶ Item yf ye fynde ony names of herbes or of other thynges wherof ye haue no knowlege/ ÿ ſhall ye knowe playnly by the potecarys. ¶ Item Here ſhall you fynde alſo for to make ſalues/ plaſters/ powders/ oyles/ and drynkes for woundes. ¶ Item whoſo deſyreth of this ſcience ÿ playne knowlege let hym oftentymes rede this boke/ and than he ſhall gette perſyte vnderſtandynge of the noble ſurgery." This title over two wood-cuts of mens heads with broken ſculls and trepaning inſtruments applied to them: the ſame are uſed again in h, 3. There are ſeveral others of inſtruments, and operations. On the back of the title-page are the Arms of England and France quarterly crowned, within the compartment of boys, &c. which he uſed to his Polichronicon. Contains T, 6, in fours. "¶ Thus endeth the noble experyence and the vertuous handy worke of Surgery/ with the Antidhadario/ practyſed and compyled by the experte mayſter Jherome/ whiche boke of late was tranſlated out of the ſpeach of hye Almaynem to lowe Duche. And afterwarde into our mothers tonge of Engliſſhe/ moche neceſſary and profitable for ſurgyans/ as wel for thē that haue conynge as for thē that be lerners. For who diligently often tymes redeth ouer this preſent boke ſhal fynde therin true ſcyence and conynge. ¶ Jmprynted at London in Southwarke by Petrus Treueris. Jn the yere of our lorde god. M.D.XXV. and the vi. day of Marche." Underneath is his device. T 6, in fours. W.H. Folio.

1525. "The vertuous booke of the diſtillation of all manner of waters, of the

* Query, if not wodehouſes, or wild men.

the herbes in this present volume expressed, with the figures of the stillatories, to that noble work belonging; first made in high Almaine, by me Jerom Brunswicke."—Translated by Laurence Andrew. 26 March. Folio.

"Rob. Whitintoni De viii partibus orationis opusculum." See p. 279. Quarto. 1526.

"Polycronycon" cut on wood in large square letters, and printed in red. A medallion of the king's Head. See it in p. 414. Folio. 1527.

"The grete herball," &c. For Laurence Andrew. See p. 412. 1527.

"The grete herball/ whiche gyueth parfyt knowledge and vnderstandyng of all maner of herbes and theyr vertues whiche God hath ordeyned for our prosperous welfare and helthy for they hele and cure all maner of dyseales and sekenesses that fall or myssfortune to all maner of creatures of god created practysed by many expert and wyse maystery as Auicenna and other. &c. Also it geueth parfyte vnderstandynge of the booke lately prynted by me (Peter Treueris) named the noble experiẽce of vertuous hand warke of surgery." This title is over a wood-cut of a man, with a spade in his right hand, gathering grapes, and a woman emptying herbs and flowers out of her apron into a basket. In the foreground, a male mandrake in one corner, and a female in the other. On the next page is a preface or introduction, without any head title, name, or date. Then "The registre of the chapytres in Latyn and in Englysshe." The herbal with a cut to every plant, &c. contains C c 4, in sixes. At the end thereof, "Here after foloweth the knowledge of the dyuersytees and colours of all maner of vrynes thrugh the whych the Physycyens mynystre all maner of medycyens to the vcyll and profytable helthe of man." Then, on D d, i, begins "The exposiciõ of the wordes obscure/ and euyll knowen." At the end of which, "Here after foloweth a table very necessary and proufitable for them that desyre to fynde quyckely a remedy agaynst all maner of dyseases/ &c. Thus endeth the grete herbal with his tables which is translated out of Frensshe ĩto Englysshe." On a separate leaf is his device, with this colophon under it, "¶ Jmpryntyd at London in Southwarke by me Peter Treueris. Jn the yere of our lorde god. M.D.xxix. the xvii day of Marce." W.H. Folio. 1529.

"The secũde dyaloge in Englysshe bytwene a doctur of dyuynytye and a student in the lawes of Englande.*" In a compartment; at top, Christ standing and teaching the populace seated on the ground; at the bottom, He is giving charge to S. Peter, holding a key, the other disciples passing on. Contains Fo. cxlvii, and a table. "Thus endyth the seconde dyaloge in Englysshe &c. Jmpryntyd at London in Southwarke by Peter Treuerys Jn the yere of our lorde god M.v.C.xxx. the xxiiii. day of Nouembre." W.H. Octavo. 1530.

"The secunde dyalogue ĩ englysshe wyth new addycyons, ¶ Here after folowyth the secũde dyalogue in Englyssh bytwene a doctour of dyuynytye and a student in the lawes of Englande/ newly correctyd and Emprentyd 1531.

* The first dialogue was printed in Latin by John Rastell in 1523 and 1528. Also in English by Rob. Wyer, without date.

Emprentyd. with new *addicions. Jesus." Contains Fo. c lxvi, with a cut of the Trinity at the end, as p. 310. used afterwards by Hen. Smith. "¶ Hereafter foloweth the table, &c. Jmprynted at London in Southwarke by Peter Treueris. 1531."* W.H. Octavo.

— "¶ De Heteroclitis Nominibus. Grammaticae VVhitintonianae liber tertius." &c. as p. 165. In this book, when printed by Wynken de Word, 1533, Whittinton complains of our printer's printing his grammar in a bad manner. See a copy of verses at the beginning of that book, by Wynken de Worde, p. 186. The title and text are in Roman, the notes in black letter. On 8 leaves without running-titles or catchwords. "Impressum per me Petrum Treueris." W.H. Quarto.

— "Vocabula magistri Stanbrigi, primum iam edita, sua saltem editione.† Quarto.

— "¶ Vocabula mgrī Stābrigi sua* saltem editione edita." In a scroll over a wood-cut of a schoolmaster with a rod in his left hand, sitting behind a desk, and six scholars before it, 3 sitting and three standing. On the back, "Ad lectorem Epistola," beginning thus: "Cum de latinis vocabulis extemporale opusculū nostro noīe (clam me tamen) editū: ac multa istinc adempta mutataq; viderem (vt quamvis cursim recognitum) vt homini negocioso licuit: tunc cultis expostulo apparatu prodiret. Qui vt magiscula habeatur fidelis, legis hic nihil cādide lector quod non sit dictū prius." &c. The whole containing D, in fours is printed in black letter. "Jmprinted at London in the Southwarke by me Peter Treueris." His device, or sign, on the last page. W.H. 4°.

— "¶ Paruulorum institutio ex Stanbrigiana collectione." In a scroll, and over the same wood-cut as the foregoing article. 12 leaves, wholly black letter. "Jmprynted at london in Southwarke by my Peter Treveris." W.H. Quarto.

— "Editio Roberti Whitintoni Lichfeldiensis, grammatices magistri, et protouatis Anglie in florentissima Oxoniensi academia, nuperrime recognita. Declinationes nominum, tam Latinorum quam Graecorum patronymicorum, et barbarorum, ex Joanne Despauterio Niniuita, Petro Pontano, Prisciano Sipontino, et Ascensio, amussatim collerte, cum commentariolo interliniari, et dictionum interpretatiunculis," &c. Quarto.

— "¶ Grammatices primæ partis liber primus Roberti VV. L. L. nuperrime recognitus. De nominum generibus," &c. See p. 177. The title and text in Roman, the notes in black letter. D, in fours. "Expliciunt genera nominū reuisa recognitaq; summa cum diligentia Impressum per me—in suburbio Londoniensi vulgariter (Southwarke) nuncupato."

* These new additions were also printed separate by Tho. Berthelet. See p. 419.

† If this was really printed by P. Treveris, he must have printed very early, as it was printed by W. de Worde in 1507. See p. 148; also p. 159.

* The first edition, with a date having these words, was printed by W. de Worde in 1507; but he printed two editions before that time, viz. in 1500 and 1501, and seem to have been printed without them, and if so, are probably what the author points at in the beginning of his prefatory epistle.

cupato:" My copy wants the laſt leaf, probably cut out for the ſake of the device. W.H. Quarto.

" Grammatices prima pars Roberti Witintoni, L. L. nouiter diligenterque recenſita. Liber quintus. Verborum praeterita et ſupina. De verborum praeteritis et ſupinis, cum commento, nec non interliniari dictionum interpretatione. Eiuſdem R. Whitintoni *Tetraſtichon cum Thoma R. &c. D T R." Quarto.

" Whitintoni editio cum interpretamento Franciſci Nigri. Diomedes de accentu in pedeſtri oratione potius quam ſoluta obſeruanda." See p. 151. " Excuſſum Londinis, in officina Petri Treueris." Quarto.

" Accidētia ſtābrigiana editione nuper recognita & caſtigata lima Roberti whitintoni Lichfeldiēſis in florentiſſimo oxoniēſi academia laureati." Over the ſame cut as to the Vocabula &c. above. D, in fours, wholly black letter, " Jmprynted at London in Southwarke by Peter Treueris." W.H. Quarto.

Another edition with the title over the cut of a prieſt ſitting with a plutus before him, as deſcribed in p. 251. C 6, in fours. " Jmprynted in Southwarke by me Peter Treueris." The Rev. Dr. Lort. Quarto.

Rob. Whitintoni—de octo partibus orationis, editio. My copy wants ſignature A. See it by W. de Worde, p. 174. The text in Roman. B has ſix leaves, C 4, " Impreſſum per me Petrum Treuers." On the laſt page his device, or ſign. W.H. Quarto.

" Genera Nominum." At the end, " Expliciunt genera nominum, reviſa recognitaque ſumma cum diligentia. Impreſſum per me Petrum Treveris, in ſuburbio Londonenſi, vulgariter Southwark nuncupato," with his ſign, as commonly uſed. Quarto.

" Vulgaria Roberti Whitintoni Lichfeldienſis Laureati & de inſtitucione grāmaticulorū opuſculum, libello ſuo de cōcinnitate grāmatices accommodatum & in quatuor partes digeſtum." See it printed by W. de Worde in 1524 and in 1533. This edition is without Cum privilegio. The title, in Roman, incloſed with four pieces, ſome of which were uſed by R. Redman. On the back begins " Epiſtola ad lectorem, which is in Roman; but the reſt of the book in black letter. 48 leaves. Has no colophon, but his ſign on the laſt page. W.H. Quarto.

" ¶ The myrrour of the chyrche." Over a neat wood-cut of Jeſus Chriſt at full length, his head irradiated, clothed in a long veſt with ihs on it, and an imperial robe over it, holding in his his left hand a mund, his right hand lifted up as proclaiming judgement to the perverſe and mercy to penitents: in the upper corner on the right ſide is a half length repreſentation of the Father, and in that on the left a Dove, both encompaſſed with clouds. Under this cut, " ¶ Here foloweth a devout treatyſe cōteynynge many gooſtly medytacyons and inſtruccyons to all maner of people, neceſſary and conſortable to the edyfycacion of the ſoule and body to the loue and grace of god." There are other cuts diſperſed through the work, the chief of which was uſed by W. de Worde to

* See p. 172.

Thordinary of christen men in 1506. On the back of the title-page is the "Petycyon of R. Coplande the prynter," in four seven-lined stanzas; in the first, addressing the Holy Trinity to be his guide in this[a] business and to raise the minds of the readers to holiness, and "Suche werkes to vie/ as may purchase thy loue." This being the concluding line of each stanza. The three remaining stanzas are addressed one to each person of the trinity separately for grace and strength to his readers. On the next leaf begins a table of the contents of the 31 chapters, into which this book is divided, thus introduced "In the name of our swete lorde Jesu Chryste here begynneth ỳ artycles and poyntes of the maters whiche are touched in a sermon ỳ cometh after/ rudely edyted for to auoyde and eschue curyosyte/ that ỳ reders leue not the fruytfull sentence of within for the coryous fable of without." This seems to be a breviate of the doctrine thought necessary by the Romanists to be taught the laity, explaining, among other matters, the seven deadly sins, the seven Gospel vertues, the seven gifts of the Holy Ghost, the ten commandments, the creed, and the pater-noster. Contains F 4, in eights and fours, alternately. "Thus endeth the deuoute treatyse called the myrour of the chyrche made by St. Austyn[c] of Abyndon. Emprynted at London in Southwarke by Peter Treueris." Then, for a tail-piece, a small grotesque cut, frequently used by him to make up compartments or borders to his title-pages, viz. two apes mounted on fancy beasts, justling; the assailant armed with a pitchfork which passes through the mouth of the beast he is sitting on, so that the handle appears to have been run through its head; the defendant opposing the assault with a broom. On the last page "Lenuoy of R. Coplande the prynter," praying for a blessing to attend the reading of this book. Beneath is his device. W.H. Quarto.

—— Here after followeth a lytell treatyse against Mahumet, and his cursed secte, and fyrst followeth the introductyon. Imprinted by Peter Treverys," &c." Sixteens.

JAMES

[a] Which seems to indicate his being the translator, St. Austin of Abingdon being in the colophon announced the author; but see the following note.

[c] The ascribing this work to St. Austin of Abyndon or Abingdon, seems to be a mistake, as no such name is found in any of the biographers of our English writers. Both Bale and Pits ascribe this work to Edmund, son of Edward Rich a merchant of Abingdon in Berkshire. He was treasurer of Salisbury in 1222, and archbp. of Canterbury in 1234; but being continually thwarted by the king and Otto the popes legate, he retired first to Pontiniac in France, and from thence to Soissy, where he died, according to Godwin, 16 Nov. 1241; and within six years after his death he was canonized by Innocent IV. I have a small collection of ancient MS. tracts, the first of which is entitled, "Speculum Eccl'ie." begining thus, "Here begynnyt the sermon of Saynt Edmund of pountency that ys clepyd—the merrour of holy chyrche. In the name of our Swete lorde ih'u crist/ here begynnys the maters that bene toched in the sermon that folowyt here after boynylly endytyd for to fle that busynes that lyuyth men to serve god." Then follows the table of contents. This MS. is more concise than the printed edition: they seem to be translations by different persons. It does not appear who was the translator of the MS. Perhaps Walter Hilton, who translated the tract immediately following in this collection: R. Coplande however most probably translated the printed edition, but more paraphrastically, and inserting the quotations in Latin as well as in English.

JAMES NICHOLSON,

AS Mr. Ames had heard from Maurice Johnson, esq; began printing so early as 1526, but he could not recall the book. The first we have met with, bears this title.

"A treatyse of Justificacyon by faith only, otherwise called, The parable of the wicked Mammon, by William Tindal. Imprinted in Southwark for J. Nycholson." See p. 617. Sixteens. 1536.

"The byble, that is the holy scrypture of the old and new testamente, faythfully translated in Englysh, and newly overseне and correcte M DXXXVII. S. Paul II. Tessa: III. ¶ Pray for us, that the word of God may have fre passage, and be gloryfyed. S. Paul. Coloss. III. Let the worde of Christ dwel in you plentiouslye in al wysdome, Josue I.—Imprynted in Southwarke, in saint Thomas hospitale, by James Nycolson. Sett forth with the kynges moost gracious licence. Dedicated by M. Coverdale to the king." The Apocrypha and parallel places. This he seems to have printed again. 4°. 1537.

"The Byble, that is the oulde and newe Testamẽt faithfully Traunslated into Englissh and newly ouerseen and corrected. ✠. MDXXXVII. Josua. i. 'Let not the boke of this lawe depart out of thy mouth but exercise thyselfe therein day and night. Imprinted in South warke in St. Thomas Hospital by James Nicolsõ. Set foorth with the Kyngs most Gracious lycence." In an architective compartment with a medallion at top; the same as was used by John Wayland, p. 561. On the back, "The contentes of this boke." So that this edition, though of Coverdale's translation, was printed without his dedication to the king. The book of Hester ends on Fol. CC.XXX; on the back of which begin the apocryphal books, which end on Fol. CCC.XXVII. "The thyrd part," containing the poetic and prophetic books, ends on Fol. C.lxxix. This copy, the only one i have met with, contains only the Old Testament. Mr. J. Denyer. Quarto. 1537.

"The exposition of the fyrste, seconde, and thyrd canonical epistles of S. John, wyth a prologe before it." Maunsell p. 49. Sixteens. 1537.

"Concio quam habuit Reuerendiss. in Christo pater Hugo Latimer, epũs Vvorcestriẹ" &c. as p. 493. W.H. Octavo. 1537.

"The original and sprynge of all sectes and orders by whome, whã or were they beganne. Translated out of hye Dutch in Englissh." &c. as p. 493. On the back of folio 61, begins "The fayth of the *Indians, euen as one Mathew the embassadoure of Presteriãs dyd vtter it before Emanuel kynge of Portingale. Anno M. D. xiii," consisting of 49 articles. W.H. Octavo. 1537.

"How and whither a Christen man ought to flye the horrible plage of the pestilence. A sermon &c By Andrew Osiander." Translated by Miles Coverdale. &c. as p. 593. The title in a neat architective compartment (1537.)

* Christians in Ethiopia.

partment with a cherubic head at top, and 1537 on the fell. Colophon, "Printed in Southwarke by me—for Jan. Gough Cum priuilegio." 16°.

1537. "A cōparison betwene the Olde learnynge and the Newe Translated out of latin in Englysh by Wyliam Turner. Pryntcd in Sowthwarke by me—Anno. 1537." In the same compartment as the foregoing article. See p. 750. On the back, "The contentes---To the readers. On the next leaf begins, "Urbanus Regius to a certayne frende of his," &c. introducing the treatise, which ends on G 8. Then follows an epistle "To the Christen Reader. That thou mayest the better vnderstande the artycles of Fre wyll, Fayth, Good workes, and of Meryttes, which in this present boke be treated upon, J shall here brefely shew what God doth and hath done for vs, and what we agayne oughte to do for his sake, as they that be thankfull of the benefites receaued of hym." &c. four leaves more. W.H. Again 1538. Octavo.

1537. "The causes why the Germanes wyll not go nor consente vnto the Councell which Paul the 3. now Bp. of Rome hath called to be kept at Mantua in Italy, and to begynne the 23. daye of Maye, an. 1537." MSS. T. Baker. Octavo.

1537. "A goodly treatise of Faith, hope and Charity. Translated into English." Printed for him. MSS. T. Baker. Octavo.

1537. M. Luther's exposition of the 23 psalm, translated from the German by Miles Coverdale. Bibl. Tanneri, p. 203, &c. Sixteens.

1538. "The *newe* testament *both* Latine *and Englyshe* ech *correspondent* to the other after the vulgare texte, communely called S Jeroms. Faythfully translated by Myles Couerdale. *Anno.* M CCCC.XXXVIII. Jeremie xxiii. Js not my worde lyke a fyre sayeth the lorde, and lyke an hammer that breaketh the harde stone? *Printed* in Southwarke by James *Nicolson.* Set *forth* wyth the Kynges moost *gracious* licence." This title in black and [e]red, is in an architective compartment, with a medallion of two heads at top, the same as afterwards was used to the Manuale by Kingston and Sutton. Dedicated "¶ To the moost noble, moost gracious, and oure moost dradde soueraigne lord Kynge Henry ẏ eyghty kynge of Englāde and of Fraunce. &c. Defender of Christes true fayth, and vnder God the chefe and supreme heade of the churche of Englande, Jrelande. &c.—Youre graces humble and faythfull subiecte. Myles Couerdale.[f]---To the Reader.---*An* Aimanack *for* xviii. *yeares*;" beginning 1538, and a kalendar of the 12 months, in red and [g]black. The Latin is printed on Roman, the English on black letter. Contains Fol. 344, which should be only 342, as 167 and 168 are omitted; several leaves are misnumbered but afterwards accounted for. At the end, "A table to finde the Epistles and Gospels vsually red in ahe church after Salysbury

e What was printed in red in the original is distinguished by Italics.

f For the purport of this dedication and preface see Lewis, p. 113, &c.

g The conception of the V. Mary is printed in black, but her nativity, annunciation, purification and assumption are in red.

Salysbury vse, &c. Here followeth ŷ table—on diuerse sayntes dayes in the yeare." Among the rest, for 3 masses Christmas day, and for all the five days in commemoration of the Virgin Mary. This edition was printed in Lent; and is very scarce. W.H. Quarto.

1538. "The newe testament both in Latyne and Englyshe eche correspondente to the other after the vulgare texte, communely called S. Jeromes. Faythfullye translated by Johan Hollybushe. Anno MCCCCC.XXXVIII. —Prynted in Southwarke by—Set forth wyth the Kynges moost gracious lycence." This title, all in black, is in the same compartment as the foregoing article. My copy begins with the gospel according to St. Matthew immediately after the title-page, but Mr. Lewis's appears to have had the same prefixes as the last article; which edition he seems not to have seen, being indeed very scarce. Mr. Denyer also has a copy with them, differing a little in the orthography. The whole printed page for page, and with the same types as the foregoing. This edition has the appearance of being the same as that with Coverdale's name, with a new title-page only; but, on examination, find every sheet new composed, and both Latin and English differing in some few places. This is said to be Coverdale's translation, and indeed it differs so very little from the other, that it seems to have the same claim; but with more propriety perhaps both might rather be deemed Hollybushe's. The case, as may be gathered from Coverdale's several dedications, seems to be thus. Coverdale appears to have published, not for lucre sake, but to promote the knowledge of the Gospel; and for that purpose was very solicitous to have the Holy Scriptures made public in the mother tongue. With this intent he published th whole Bible in 1535, and set forward the forementioned edition of the New Testament in English, with the Vulgar Latin; but being abroad, committed the care of it to this Hollybush, with particular instructions, as we learn from his epistle dedicatory of a subsequent edition to Lord Cromwell, that as the New Testament he had[a] set forth in English, did so agree with the Latin, he was well content that the Latin and it should be set together, provided that the corrector should follow a true copy of the Latin, and keep the true and right English of the same, and so doing he was content to set his name to it; trusting that though he was absent, and out of the land, all would be well. It was accordingly printed in Lent, 1538. In July following, he accidentally met with a copy of it, which perusing he found disagreable to his former translation: the true copy of the Latin text not observed, neither the English correspondent thereto. This no doubt, as he expresses it, dammaged his poor name, yet the good man not only forgives, but apologizes for [i]them, as men glad to print and set forth any good thing; and seems only to have had those copies with his name [k]called in. It was dedicated

[a] Viz. in his Bible, 1535.

[i] Nicholson the printer, and Hollybushe the corrector.

[k] This in some measure accounts for the scarcity of the edition. I have met with no other copy of it.

cated however to the King, encouraged thereto' by his Majesty's so favourably accepting his former translation of the whole Bible, dedicated to him in 1535. W.H. Quarto.

Mr. Ames mentions " Another edition of the new testament the same year," &c. See it in p. 512, &c.

1538. " An exposicion vpon the songe of the blessed virgine Mary, called Magnificat. Whereunto are added, the songes of Salue regina, Benedictus, and Nunc dimittis. Translated out of Latine into Englysh, by Jhon Hollybush." Dedicated to Jhon Frederyke, duke of Saxony, &c. Folio.

1538. The same, but without printer's name. Octavo.

1538. " The summe or substaunce of the seconde Epestle of S. Paul to the Thessalonyans, by H. Bullinger; translated by R. H." Octavo.

1538. A comparison between the old learning and the new. Ath. Oxon. Vol. I; c. 156. See p. 750.

Palmer puts a book called Invectives *against cardinal Woolsey, to this printer; but he had it from Maunsell, who in p. 63, mentions it as printed at Wesel 1546 by Henry Nicolson. Yet he makes this remark, that it was common in those days to say, printed beyond sea. There were two editions; one printed about 1530, the other, temporised, 1546. See them in our General History, under those years.

—— The Bible as set forth by archbp. Cranmer. The copy before me wants the general title-page, and whatever else might have been before sig. *. i. " A table of the principal matters conteyned in the Byble, in which the Readers maye fynde, and practise many commune places." Genesis begins on Fol. 1. and the leaves are numbered in progression to the end of Job, without any title-page for a second part. Job ends on Fol. ccliij. Then, in a compartment, the same as to this printer's edition of Coverdale's Bible, 1537. " The thyrd part of the Byble contaynynge these bookes. The Psalter." &c. to the end of the prophets, on Fol. Cxxxiij. —" The volume of the bokes called Hagiographa," &c. within the same compartment; which ends on Fol. cxxiij.—" The newe Testament in Englyshe translated after the Greke," which ends on Fol. c; but this copy wants the last leaf, with whatever might have followed. The title to the N. Test. is printed in Italics, and in the same compartment as the foregoing parts. Mr. Joseph Parker, upper Thames street, near London Bridge. Quarto.

" This

1 " Consyderynge (moost gracious Soueraigne) how louyngly, how fauourably, and how tenderly your hyghnesse hath taken myne infancy and rudenesse in dedicatynge the whole bible in Englysh to your moost noble grace. And hauyng sure experience also how benygne and gracious a mynde your hyghnes doth euer beare to all them that in theyr callyng are wyllynge to do theyr best: It doth euen animate and encorage me now lykewyse to vse the same audacite towarde your grace: Neuer intendyng nor purposynge to haue ben thus bold, yf your most noble kyndnes and princely benygnite had not forced me here vnto."

* Consisting chiefly of a dialogue between two priests servants, named Watkin and Jeffraye.

"This Boke Newely Jmprynted sheweth the maner of measuryng of all maner of Lande, as well of woodlande as of Plowelande, and pastour in the Felde, and comptynge the true nombre of Acres of the same. Newely inuented and compyled by Syr Richarde Benese, Chanon of Marton Abbay besyde London." See another edition, p. 952. W.H. 4 Sixteens.

JOHN REDMAN,

PROBABLY related to Robert Redman, who died in the year 1540; however he printed for him about that time

"The Paradox of M. T. Cicero, lately translated out of the Latin tongue into Englishe by Robert Whittinton, poet laureat. Printed in Southwarke by Johan Redman for Robert Redman." See p. 397. 16°. (1540.)

He printed also Thomas a Kempis without date; said to be the first edition.* Perhaps so under that name; but it was first ascribed to John Gerson, and printed by W. de Worde in 1502, and next year by R. Pinson. Concerning the real author of The following of Christ, see Gent. Mag 1772, p. 559. It does not appear whether this was printed in Southwark, or in Pater-noster row, where he printed Octavo.

"The Genealogye of heresye. Compyled by Ponce Pantolabus.— Jmprynted at London Jn Pater noster rovve. At the signe of our Ladye of Pytye By Johan Redman, Ad imprimendum solum." The same was printed by Rob. Wyer. See p. 373. 1542.

CHRISTOPHER TRUTHALL,

SUPPOSED to be a feigned name; for in queen Mary's reign, there were several books printed under it. As,

"A confession of the most auncient, and true christē catholike olde belefe, accordyng to the ordre of the xij. articles of our cōmon Crede, set furthe in Englishe to the glory of almightye God, and to the confirmacion of Christes people in Christes Catholike olde faith. By J. O.—Imprinted in Sothewarke by Christophor Truthal. Cum priuilegio Regali. In April. 1556." The orthography of this differing so much from Mr. Ames's copy makes it probable that there were two editions of it this year. My copy begins on the back of the title-page inscribed "To the vnfayned fauourours and louers of the pure worde and Gospell of Jesus Christ, enhabiting within the cities and diocese of Couentrie and Lichfelde, and in all other places, where it hathe chaunced me to haue occupied the rowme of a Preacher: Grace," &c. Contains E, in eights, and concludes, "Youre poore seruaunt in the Lorde. Io. Olde." W.H. 16°. 1556.

"Antichrist, That is to saye: A true reporte, that Antichriste is come; wher

* Catal. Bibl. Harleian. Vol. 1; No. 1938.

wher he was borne, of his Perſone, miracles, what tooles he worketh withall, and what ſhalbe his ende: Tranſlated out of Latine into Engliſhe. By J. O. O Lorde, why haſte thou broken downe the hedge of thy vyne (in Englande) that al they, which go by, plucke of her grapes?—It is brent with fire and cut downe, &c. Pſal. 80. Imprinted in Sothwarke by Chriſtophor Truthall. Cum priuilegio Regali. 1556." In the margin at top; "Fol. 1." On the back begins "The tranſlatour to the reader;" at the end of which epiſtle, "The autors owne tytle of thys boke is thus. Antichriſt. That is to ſaye, ſyue Homilies, wherin it is proued, that the Biſhoppe of Rome is the ryght and myghtye houge Antichriſt, whom the oracles of the Prophetes, Chriſt and the Apoſtles tolde before ſhoulde come, and that we ſhoulde beware of him. Set furthe by Rodulphe Gualter of Zuirik." &c. (This ſeems to have occaſioned Mr. Ames's making two books of this.) Then, on fol. 3, begins the author's introductory epiſtle "To his deare brethrē, that preache the Goſpell of Chriſt in the Countie of zuirike, Rodulphe Gualter, grace &c.—At Zuirike the xii. daye of Decēbre. 1546." The whole, 104 leaves. W.H. Sixteens.

CANTERBURY.

—— "A goodly narration, how S. Auguſtine (the Apoſtle of England) rayſed two dead bodies at Longcomptō, collected out of diuers Authors, tranſlated by Joh. Lidgate, Monke of Bury. Pri. at S. Auſtens at Canterburie, in 4." Maunſell, p. 6. Neither printer's name nor date mentioned. Mr. Lewis, (Life of Caxton, p. 115,) ſays, "about 1525." See p. 106. Quarto.

JOHN MYCHELL, of the pariſh of St. Paul,

PRINTED many books without dates, which i take to be earlier than thoſe with; for at the death of king Henry the VIII, printers, as well as authors, took great liberties.

1549. "The pſalter or pſalmes of Dauid after the tranſlacion of the great Bible, poynted as it ſhall be ſonge in Churches. + Cum priuilegio—ſolum. 1549." Prefixed is a kalendar; and annexed, Te Deum, Benedicite, The ſong of Zacharie,—of Mary, Symeon, Quicunq; vult, The Letany and ſuffrages; and a table of the Pſalms, &c. "Prynted at Cantorbury in ſaynt Paules paryſhe by John Mychell." The Rev. Dr. Lort. Again 1550. Quarto.

1550. "A treatiſe of predeſtination and election by John Lamberd, miniſter of the church at Elam." MSS. T. Baker. Octavo.

"A breuiat

" A breuiat Cronicle contaynynge all the Kinges from Brute to this daye, and manye notable actes gathered oute of diuers Cronicles sith Wil-lyam Conquerour vnto the vere of christ a. M.v.c.li. Printed at Canter-bury in Saynt Paules parysh by John Mychell. Cum priuilegio—solum." Dedicated " To—syr Antony Auchor master of the kinges Juel house, John mychell boke Prynter wissheth helthe and prosperitie at Can-torbury. &c.---To know when the four terms begin and end.---The years from Adam unto Christ.---A table of the kings from Brute unto the conqueror." Besides; L., in eights. " Finis. Here J should haue put in the notable waies from certaine cities to Londō, but some of them be not marked truely wherefore J left them out till such tyme as J haue more knowlege in these waies. Jmprinted at Cantorbury" &c. W.H. Again 1. 5. 53. by Johan Michel, O 4, in eights. Brit. Museum. 8°. 1552.

John Proctor, in his dedication of The history of Wyat's rebellion, mentions another printed account thereof set forth at Canterbury, but not so full and particular as his. See p. 829, &c.

" Articles to be enquyred in thordinary visitacion of the most reuerende father in God, the Lorde Cardinall Pooles grace Archebyshop of Caun-terbury wythin hys Dioces of Cantorbury. Jn the yeare of our Lorde God. m.v.c.lvi+" On four leaves. My copy has only the first and last leaves. These articles are very scarce: only some of them are mentioned by Collier; to the same purport, though not in the same words. Strype mentions more of them, but with greater variation. Theirs toge-ther will not make up the compleat number of 21 touching the clergy, and 33 relating to the laity. See Eccl. Hist. Vol. II; p. 402. Eccl. Me-mor. Vol. III; p. 291. W.H. Quarto. 1556.

" Newes from Rome, concerning the blasphemous sacrifice of pa-pistical masse; with diuers other treatises very godly and profitable. De-dicated to my ryghte honourable lorde and mayster, my lorde Thomas Hawarte: Randall Hurlestone wyssheth helth in the lorde. Imprented by John Mychell for E. Chamton." Or Campton, as Mr. Ratcliffe's copy. Sixteens. —

" A short epistle to all such, as do contempne the mariage of us poor preestes." Sixteens. —

" The spirituall matrimonye betwene Chryste, and the Soul." 24°. —

" Two dyaloges wrytten in Latin by the famous clerke, D. Eras-mus of Roterdame, one called Polyphemus, or the Gospeller, the other dysposyng of thynges and names. Translated in to Englyshe by Ed-monde Becke. And prynted at Cantorbury, in saynt Paules paryshe, by Johan Mychell.+." Sixteens. —

" An exposytion in Englyshe vpon the Epistyll of saynt Paule to the Phillipiās, for the instruction of them that be unlerned in tōges: ga-thered out of holy scriptures, and of the olde catholike doctours of the churche and of the best authors that now adayes do write. By Lancelot Rydley.* of Canterbury. + —

8 H Quisquis

* Bale calls him Cantuariensis ecclesiæ prebendarius, but he seems to have mistaken Nicholas Ridley for him. Strype says he was one of the six preachers of that Cathe-dral

Quiſquis amas verum huc aderis nec mēte recedas.
Jnuenies verum ſcripta ſacrata legēs."

On the next leaf begins "The preface to the reader." By which it appears this comment was written, if not printed, ſoon after Hen. 8. had allowed the ſcriptures to be had and read in Engliſh. Contains L 4, in eights. "Prynted at Cantorbury in Saynt Paules paryſhe by John Mychell. +" W.H. Octavo.

"The confeſſyon of fayth, delyuered to the emperour Charles the Vth, by the lordes of Germany, written in Latyn by Phylyppe Melanchton, and tranſlated into Englyſhe by Robert Syngylton. ¶ The names of the lordes, John Duke of Saxonye, &c.—Finis. Thus endeth the confeſſyon of faythe." See p. 395. "Printed at Canterbury by John Mychell." Octavo.

I P S W I C H.

CARDINAL Wolſey being born, and erecting a ſchool at this place, which he founded about the year 1524, one might have expected to have heard of the ſettlement of a preſs, for the encouragement of learning, before the date of our firſt book; but you will obſerve, that he made uſe of foreign preſſes to ſerve this grammar ſchool, whatever might be the occaſion of it; as we find from an epiſtle of his, dated at Weſtminſter 1ſt September 1528, prefixed to a grammar, with this title-page. "Rudimenta grammatices, & docendi methodus, non tam ſcholae Gypswichianae, per reverend. D. Thomam cardinalem Ebor. foeliciter inſtitutae, quam omnibus aliis totius Angliae ſcolis praeſcripta. Joan. Grapheus excudebat impenſis Arnoldi Birckmanni, Antwerp 1534" The cardinal alſo vouchſafed to direct the uſe of it in a ſhort epiſtle to the maſters of his ſchool. A copy of which you have among the Collections in Fiddle's Life of Card. Wolſey, p. 130. The ſame grammar was printed the next year in Twelves, at Antwerp, by Martin Ceaſer. The Rev. Dr. Lort has an edition 1536, without printer's name, or place. See Knight's Life of Dean Colet, p. 127.

It is remarkable that three printers appear printing here in the year 1548, and not any of their performances have yet been found bearing a later date; neither do we find any other printing here within our preſcribed time. Beſides, it is not eaſy to determine which of them began printing firſt, their books being all dated the ſame year, and only one of them

dral. Life of Cranmer, p. 91. In the time of Q. Mary, Bale intimates his quitting his wife and temporizing; for which however he appears to have been ſoon ſorry, as we learn from bp. Tanner that he was deprived of his Eccleſiaſtical Benefice "ob conjugium, 15 Martii 1553." In 1560, we find him again one of the ſix preachers; but nothing more of him after this.

them mentioning the month. I hope therefore to stand excused for not following Mr. Ames's order, but placing Ant. Scoloker first, as the last book ascribed to him by Mr. Ames, without date in the margin, appears to me by the title to have been printed in 1547, and shall therefore begin with it.

ANTHONY SCOLOKER,

FROM London as supposed; but that does not appear on the face of any of his works. The book entitled "The iust reckenyng," &c. attributed to him at this place, has the appearance of being the first book he printed in England; at least that we yet know of. If so, being versed in the German, Dutch and French languages, he probably came from some of the protestant dominions of Germany either to this place, or to London; (where he appears to have been connected occasionally with W. Seres, both in the Savoy Rents, and without Aldersgate.) But then again for want of dates, we cannot say for certain, at which of these places he dwelt first; though probability indicates the former. Mr. Ames[p] indeed, imagined The chronicle concerning Sir John Oldcastle was printed by him and Seres, "about 1547;" but as it mentions expresly their "dwelling wythout Aldersgate," it is not probable that they printed there before the middle of the year 1548. The "symple instruction concernynge the Kinges Maiesties procedinges in the comunyon," annexed to "The olde Fayth of greate Brittaynge," &c. as p. 748, without date, seems to have been one of the earliest books he printed at London, which announces his living then in Savoy Rents. The Communion, printed by R. Grafton,[q] was published 8 March 1547-8; therefore The simple instruction, concerning it, cannot reasonably be supposed to have been printed till some time after. He printed other books whilst he dwelt there jointly with Seres, before they went to St. Botolph's parish without Aldersgate. For it is remarkable that the only two books we have of theirs, dated, were printed without Aldersgate, in 1548.[r] Another, though it is without date of printing, mentions its being translated in June 1548, which was printed also without Aldersgate. The whole series of his printing in England seems to have been transacted nearly, if not entirely within the year 1548.

"The iust reckenyng, or accompt of the whole nomber of the yeares, from the beginnynge of the world, vnto this presente yere of 1547. A certaine and sure declaration, that the world is at an ende, *&c.* Of the last day of iudgement, or day of dome, and howe it shal come to passe. Translated out of Germaine tonge—by Anthony Scoloker, the 6 daye of July—1547. Matthew 25. Watche therefore," &c. Mr. John Notcutt, near Ipswich. (1547.)

Sixteens.

"Certeyne

p p. 507.
q See p. 705.
r See p. 511.
s See p. 690, and p. 748.

1548. "Certeyne Preceptes/ gathered by Hulricus Zuinglius/ declaring howe the ingenious youth ought to be instructed and brought vnto Christ. Translated out of latin into Inglysh by Master Richarde Argentyne Doctour of Physyck. Imprinted at Ippeswich by Anthony Scoloker. Dwellyng in S. Nycholas Paryshe. Anno 1548. Cum priuilegio—solum." Dedicated "Vnto the ryght worshipfull Master Edwarde Grymeston/ R. Argentyne wyssheth peace &c.—From Ippeswich this xxviij of January. An. 1548.---Vnto Gerolde Meier a very good young man/ Huldrichus Zuinglius wissheth grace &c.—At Strasburch/ the Calendes of Auguste 15.32." Contains c 6, in eights. On the last page is his device as p. 748. W.H. Sixteens.

1548. "M. Luthers sermon of the Keys, and of Absolution, on John xx; 21, 22. translated by R. Argentine." Maunsell, p. 101. Octavo.

1548. "Sermons (6) of the ryght famous &d excellent clerke Master Bernardine Ochine/ borne within the famous vniuersyte of Siena in Italy/ nowe also an exyle in this lyfe/ for the faythfull testimony of Jesus Christ. Psal. cxvii. I wyll not dye but lyue and declare the workes of the Lorde. Imprinted at Ippeswych by Anthony Scoloker. Dwellyng in S. Nycholas Paryshe. Anno 1548. Cum priuilegio—solum." Dedicated "Vnto—Edward, Duke of Somerset—Protectour. His graces mooste humble Seruant Rychard Argentyne wisheth the increase of honour and grace.—At Ippeswych the xiiij daye of February. Anno. M.D.xlviij.—Anthony Scoloker vnto the Reader." The six sermons on 48 pages. Mr. John Notcutt. Sixteens.

JOHN OVERTON.

OF whom we know nothing more than may be collected from the colophon of the following book:

1548. "Illustrium maioris Britanniae scriptorum, hoc est, Angliae, Cambriae, ac Scotiae Summariū, in quasdam centurias diuisum, cum diuersitate doctrinarū atq; annorū recta supputatione per omnes aetates a Japheto sanctissimi Noah filio, ad annum Domini. M.D.XLVIII, Authore Joanne Balaeo Sudouolca." This title is over a wood-cut of Bale on his knees presenting his book to king Edward VI. seated on a throne, his tutor Cheek[a] standing by at a curtain. Beneath the cut, "Excudebatur praesens opus VVesaliae per Theodoricum Plateanum, Anno a seruatoris natiuitate, M.D.XLVIIII.[b] Pridie Calendas Augusti." The prefixes are

[a] Eccl. Memor. Vol. II; p. 146.

[b] This date M.D.XLVIIII must be a mistake, for M.D.XLVIII. by adding a I too much, as appears evidently by the ending of the fifth century; for Bale concluding this first edition of English writers with a memoir of himself, mentions his purpose speedily to return into England, "finitis his laboribus," in 1548, the 53 year of his age, Fo. 244. Now this he would not have suffered to pass, if the book was not printed at Wesel till the last day of July, 1549. Besides, in his introduction to a register of English writers, annexed to "The laboryous

are a dedication, "Longe praeclarissimo Edwardo eius appellationis sexto, Anglie, Franciæ, & Hiberniæ regi, fidei defensori, ac immediate post Christum Anglicanæ & Hibernicæ ecclesiæ capiti supremo, Joannes Baleus *&c.*---Liber ad lectorem, authore Joanne Lithodio.---Index alphabeticus.---Epigramma extemperarium, M. Henrici Bomelij.---Andr. Sadlerus Britannus, apud Bucholdianos ludimagister: ad lectorem: ad librum.---Epigramma M. Ioannis Lithodii, ad lectorem." At the end of which "Figura Ioannis Wicleui doctoris Angli," neatly cut on wood.---"M. Ioannis Mursaeus candido lectori." At the end of this a neat wood cut of Bale presenting his book to the king, standing by a desk. ---On a single leaf, a portrait of Bale half length, and under it

"Hæc est effigies docti genuina Balæi,
Quem studijs natum terra Britanna dedit.

Ætatis suae anno LIII." This edition begins with a preface on the first four centuries, which end on Fo. 109. Then, "Accedit—Centuria quinta, propter eos qui in prerelectibus exterarum intermissum sunt natione." This 5th century concludes with a memoir of himself; which ends thus, on Fo. 244, "Fugiens ab impijssimæ Romanæ Jesabelis facie, quæ hucusque sitit prophetarum sanguinem, apud Germanos in Christo fidelissimos octennio cum uxore ac liberis delitui. In patriam tandem post longum exilium pijssimi regis Edwardi sexti suffragijs liberis, anno hoc a Christo incarnatione, 1548, & ætatis meæ, lij. finitis his laboribus, et dnō fortonante reditū maturo." Thus far it may be presumed was printed at Wesel. Then follows, on Fo. 245, "Conclusio Operis peroratio," which ends on the front of Fo. 248, with this colophon, "☞ Completum erat presens Britannicorum scriptorum opus, doctrinarum per omnes ætates ecclesie, pateſaciēs discrimē, ac diuersitatē manifestans, Excusum que fuit Gippeswici in Anglia per Ioannem Ouerton, anno a Christi incarnatione, 1548. pridie calendas Augusti." On the back is a correction of the errors in some copies. Afterwards, "Additio" (the running title to the end,) viz. first a list of such English writers as were Carmelites; then another list of such writers names as he had collected for a sixth century, which concludes the volume, on Fo. 255. The whole is printed on white letter, except the w; the memoirs of authors in the largest English Roman types, and the lists of their writings in Italics: both in Roman to signature I. The blooming letters are remarkably singular. I do not find what became of them, or the printer afterward. W.H. Quarto.

JOHN

ryous Journey and serche of Johan Lelande," printed by Bale himself, at London, in 1549, he says, "Sens I returned home agayne from Germany, where as I both collected, and emprented my symple wurke, de Scriptoribus Britannicis, I have for the full correccyon and further augmentacyon of the same, perused many libraryes both in Cambridge and Oxforde." The inserting "Pridie Calendas Augusti" at Wesel and also at Ipswich; and the similarity of types throughout the whole book are very remarkable circumstances. Some copies have under the cut in the title page, "Excudebatur presens opus quo a nativitate unicæ illius pro peccatis victimæ, patri in eternum placatæ quadragesimo octavo supra millesimum & quingentesimum, pridie Calendas Augusti."

JOHN OSWEN,

PRINTED at Ipswich for some time; from thence went to Worcester, where he printed longer.

1548. "The Mynde of the Godly and excellent lerned man M. Jhon Caluyne, what a Faithfull man, whiche is instructe in the Worde of God, ought to do, dwellinge amongest the Papistes. 2. Cor. 6. What felowship hath righteousnes with vnrighteousnes? &c. Anno Domini M.D.XLVIII." In a compartment formed with odd pieces; some of them such as were used by John Tisdale. At the end, "☞ Translated* by R. G." Contains K 4, in eights. On the last leaf, "Jmprinted at Ippyswiche by me Jhon Oswen. Cum priuilegio—solum."* W.H. Sixteens.

1548. "Christopher Hegendorphine, his domesticall or household sermons, for a godly housholder to his children and famely, translated by Henry Reginald. Printed at Ipswich by John Oswen 1548." Maunsell, p. 58. 8°.

1548. "John Oecolampadius his epistle, that there ought to be no respect of personages of the poore, but all to be holpe and comforted in their necessities.—at Ipswich,—1548." Ib. p. 76. Sixteens.

1548. "+ Of the trewe auctoritie of the Churche, Compyled by the excellent learned man Philippe Melancthon, and dedicate vnto the noble Duke off Prussia, newely translated out of Latin into Englyshe. Anno M.D.XLVIII." At the end is "A godly prayer to say at thy vpryssynge, translated out of French." H, in eights. "Jmprinted at Ipswiche by me John Oswen, 1548." Sixteens.

1548. "A Brief declaration of the fained sacrament, commonly called the extreame vnction, wryten by the godly learned man M. Jhon Caluine, and translated out of the latine into Englysh by W. B. In Septembre, Anno 1548." B, in eights. "—at Ippyswich—Cum priuilegio—solum." Sixteens.

—— "Inuectiue against Drunkennes." Maunsell p. 63. Sixteens.

—— "A Declaration of the Masse." Running title; my copy wanting the title-page, which might probably have the date of printing. Contains G 4, in eights, including a table at the end, which is not found in copies of the original edition, printed by Hans Luste at Wittenberge, 1547. See it in our Gen. Hist. where the title may be seen at large. W.H. 16°.

—— "A short treatise of certayne thinges abused,
In the popish church long vsed;
But now abolyshed to our consolation
And God's word aduanced, the light of our saluation."

Written by Peter Moone, and printed at Ipswich, the beginning of K. Edward VI. See Warton's Hist. of Eng. Poetry, Vol. III; p. 319, 320. Contains 8 leaves. Quarto.

WOR-

* Mr. T. Baker has added, in his interleaved Maunsell, after this word Translated, "into English;" and before Cum priuilegio, "the 2 daye of August."

WORCESTER.

JOHN OSWEN,

LATE of Ipswich, settled here probably on a prospect of better encouragement about Christmas 1548. In the Rolls chapel, P. 1. M. 32. the sixth January, (1548-9) 2 Edward VI. is a licence for John Oswen, of the city of Worcester, and his assigns, to print, reprint, *&c.* every kind of book, or books, set forth by us, concerning the service to be used in churches, ministration of the sacraments, and instruction of our subjects of the principality of Wales, and marches thereunto belonging, *&c.* for seven years, prohibiting all other persons whatsoever from printing the same.

The New Testament. Mr. Ames MS. catalogue Quarto. 1548.

The New Testament. The late Mr. Calamy. Folio. 1548.

" Chr. Hegendorphine, his howshold sermons. Translated out of Latin by Hen. Reignalde, 1548." Maunsell, p. 100. Octavo. 1549.

" Consultory for all Christians, most godly and earnestly warning all people to beware least they beare the name of Christians in vaine. Written by H. H. Cum priuilegio Regali per septennium." Octavo. 1549.

" A Dialogue betwene the seditious anabaptist and the true christian, about obedience to magistrates," &c. See it in 1551. Octavo. 1549.

" Spirituall Matrimonie betweene Christ and his Church." Sixteens. 1549.

" A [y]message from King Edward the 6th at Richmond, the 8th of July, the 3d yeare of his reigne, concerning obedience to Religion. Imprinted the 5th day of August, anno M DXL IX. at Worcester by John Oswen. Cum privilegio—solum." Sixteens. 1549.

The Common prayer, &c. " Imprinted the 23 day of May, anno M DXL IX. They be also to sell at Shrewsburye. Cum privilegio—solum. Unbound ii shillings and two-pence; bound thre shillyngs and eyght pence." Quarto. 1549.

" The Liturgy." In a compartment, and about it is printed: " Let everye soule submyt hymself unto the auctoritie of the higher powers. For there is no power but of God. The powers that be, are ordained of God. Whosoever therfore resisteth power; resisteth the ordinance of God, *&c.* Rom. xiii." Within it are the king's arms encircled with the garter, 1549.

and

y Probably to the Lady Mary, who still used the Romish service, to press her conformity to *The Book of Common Prayer*, according to an Act of *Parliament*, which had taken place about a month before. Both Bp. Burnet, and Mr. Collier mention such a letter from the protector and *Privy Council*, doubtless in the king's name. See Hist. of Reform. Vol. II; p. 98. Eccl. Hist. Vol. II; p. 276.

and beneath, "+ The boke of the common praier and administration of the Sacramentes, and other rites and ceremonies of the church, after the use of the church of England. Wigorniae in officina Joannis Oswen. Cum privilegio—solum, anno Domino 1549. Mense Julii." The contents in xv heads. A preface. "Finis + Imprinted the xxx day of July, anno Domini MDXLIX, at Worcester by John Oswen. Cum privilegio—solum." On the back of the title-page, "The kinges maiestie, by the aduise of his moste deare Uncle the lord Protector, and other his highnes counsell, streightlye chargeth and commandeth, that no maner of person do sell this present boke vnbound, aboue the price of ii shyllinges vi pence the piece; and the same bound in paste, or in boordes, not aboue the price of four shyllyngs the piece. God save the king." This book was thought so great a rarity, that it was sold to Lord Oxford for ten pounds, at Thomas Rawlinson's sale, 1727. The late Mr. Edmund Calamy. Folio.

1550. "The new Testament of our sauiour Jesu Christe, with notes and expositions of the dark places therein. Imprinted the xii daye of January, anno Domini M.CCCCCL. at Worcester by Jhon Oswen. cum gratia & privilegio—solum." With the epistles taken out of the old testament." Also without date, 8vo. Lewis p. 191, &c. Quarto.

1550. "A short pathewaye to the ryghte and true vnderstanding of the holye and sacred Scriptures: set fourth by that most famous Clerke, Huldrich Zwinglius, and now translated out of Laten into Englyshe by John Veron, Senonois. James. i. Chap. He that wanteth wisdome, let him aske of hym that geueth, that is to say, of God, whiche gyueth vnto all men withoute reproche or castynge in the teethe, but let hym aske with faith, doubting nothynge." In a compartment as "The Mynde of—M. Jhon Caluyne, p. 1458. "The prologue to the reader," as the running title has it, inscribed "To—Sir Arthur Darcey Knight, Jhō Veron wyssheth peace and grace," &c. Contains n, in eights. "Imprinted the xxiiii. day of Maie. Anno Do. 1550. At worcester by Jhon Oswen. Cum privilegio—solum." W.H. Sixteens.

1550. "St. Ambrose of oppression: translated by John Oswen, and entituled Poore Naboth oppressed by rich Ahab. Printed by *him*, 1550." Maunsell, p. 2. It has no date of place; but as he did not stay so long at either Ipswich or London, have placed it here. Sixteens.

1550. "The godly sayings of the old auncient faithful fathers vpon the Sacrament of the bodye and bloude of Chryste. Newlye compyled and translated oute of Latin intoo Englishe. By Jhon Veron Senonoys. 1 Cor. xi. As often as ye eate of thys breade," &c. On the back begins "The names and times of ẏ holy doctors whiche we do folow in thys lyttle treatye.---To—Syr Jhon Yorke, Knight, treasurer of the Kinges Maiesties Mint in Southwarke, master of all ẏ Kinges wooddes, on this syde Trente, and Shriue of the noble citte of London, Jhon Veron wissheth healthe, *&c.*---To the christen reader," &c. At the end of The Godly sayings of the ancient doctors is "An exhortatyon to all Christians.—Written at Hackeney ẏ laste day of October, in the yeare of our

our Lord. M.D.XLVIII." Contains H, in eights. " Imprinted the xj. day of October. Anno Do. 1550. At Worceter by Jhon Oswen. They be also to sell at Shrewesburye. Cum priuilegio—solum." W.H. 16°.

" + A notable and maruailous epistle[a] of the famous Doctor Mathewe Gribalde, professor of the law in the vniuersitie of Padua: concerning the terrible iudgement of god vpon hym, that for feare of men denyeth Christ, and the knowen veritie: with a Preface[b] of Doctor Caluine. Translated out of Latin intoo English by E. A.[c] At the end, " Imprinted the xx. day of Aprill. Anno Do. 1550. At worceter by Jhon Oswen. They be also to sell at Shrewsbury. Cum priuilegio—solum." Mr. William White, Crickhoel. It was printed also by H. Denham for W. Norton, without date. W.H. Sixteens. 1550.

" Three Dialogues betweene the seditious libertine or rebell Anabaptist, and the true obedient Christian: wherein obedience to Magistrates is handled. By Hen. Bullynger, and translated out of Latin by John Veron. Printed at Worcester, in the high street, and they be also to sell at Shrewesbury." In the Bodleian. Octavo. 1551.

" Godly and most necessary Annotations in ỹ. xiij. Chapyter too the Romaynes: Set furthe by the right vigilant Pastor, Jhō Hoper, by gods calling, Busshop of Gloucestre. Anno Do. 1551. Mense Maij. Cum priuilegio—solum." In a compartment formed with odd pieces. Dedicated " To my very louynge and dere beloued felowlabourers in the worde of God, and brethrē in Christ, William Jenyns Deane of the Cathedrall church in Gloucestre, Jhon Williams, doctour of the lawe, and Chauncelour, and to the rest of all the churche appoynted there to serue the lyuinge God, with al other, Archedeacons, Officiales, Deanes, Persons, Vycars and Curates, wythin this the Kyngs Maiesties diocese of Gloucestre, grace, &c.—Jhon Gloucestre.---The Prologe." Contains E 4, in eights. " Jmprynted the. xiij. day of May. Anno. Do. 1551. At worceter by Jhō Oswen, Printer appoynted by ỹ Kinges Maiestie, for ỹ Principalitie of Wales, and Marches of ỹ same. Cum priuilegio—solum." W.H. Sixteens. 1551.

" A most sure and strong Defence of the Baptizing of Children, against the pestiferous Sect of the Anabaptists. Set forth by that famous Clerk Henry Bullinger, and now translated out of Latin into English by John Veron Senonoys. Imprinted at Worcester—1551." Eccl. Memor. Vol. II; p. 317, and p. 318. 1551.

" The most frutefull dialogues, treatynge vpon the baptisme of chyldren, very necessary to be rede of all chrystyans in these moste paryllouse tymes; by Jhon Heron.[d]" 1551.

8 I " A

[a] Dated at Padua, 27. Nov. 1548.

[b] Dated at Geneva, 5 Dec. 1549.

[c] Edward Aglionby, as appears by " An Epigram of the terryble example of one Fraunceys Spera, an Italian, of whom this boke is compiled." This Epigram is an acrostic, with " Sub his acrostichis, latet authoris nomen" under it, though he was only the translator.

[d] Of whom see Ath. Oxon. Vol. I; c. 77, &c. and Bibl. Tanneri, p. 399. Though he is said to have written several things, nothing of his, in English, has yet been handed down to us. It is therefore much to be suspected that Heron is a misprint for Veron; and this article perhaps gives the original title of the foregoing one, which seems to have been modernized.

1553. " A homilie to bee reade in the time of pestilence; and a most present remedie for the same. By bishop Hooper. Maunsell, p. 60. Quarto.

1553. Statutes, 7 Edw. VI. Colophon, "At Worcestre—, Printer appoincted by the Kinges Maiestie, for the Principalitie of Wales, and Marches of the same. Anno Domini M.D.LIII. Cum priuilegio—solum." W.H. 4 Folio.

NORWICH.

IT appears that in the year 1565, many strangers from the Low Countries came, and settled in Norwich city, masters, workmen, and servants, (and had her Maiesties letters patent to work, and make all sorts of woollen manufactures) men, women, and children, to the number of about 3925. This was encouraged by the mayor and sheriffs of this city, who waited on Thomas, duke of Norfolk, at his palace there, and got the freedom and liberty of the city granted to them. Among these strangers the art of printing was introduced by Anthony Solmpne, or Solen, in 1570, which was so well approved by the city that they presented him with his freedom. See Blomefield's Hist. of Norfolk, Vol. II; p. 210.

ANTHONY DE SOLMPNE

IS taken notice of as a printer at Norwich, in Leland's appendix to his Collectanea. part 2. vol. VI. p. 41. and in the Bodleian library among the archives. The peice is intitled thus, "Certain verses written by Thomas Brooke, gentleman, of Rolsbie, concerned with Throgmorton and others in a conspiracy in Norfolk, (Stow's annals, p. 1130. Edit. 1605. 4°.) in the time of his imprisonment, the day before his death, who suffered in Norwich the 30th of August 1570." They are thirty two verses, and at the end, " Finis quod, Thomas Brooke. Seen and allowed according to the queens maiesties iniunction. God save the quene. Imprinted at Norwich, in the parish of saynt Andrew, by Anthony de Solmpne." This is the only thing we have heard of, but time may discover others.

GREENWICH:

GREENWICH.

PRINTING at this place seems to be supposititious; however, we know only of this one book; though there are two editions of it.

" A FAITHFULL ADMONITION of a certaine true Pastor and Prophete, sent vnto the Germanes at such time as certain great princes went about to bryng Alienes into Germany, & to restore the papacy, the kingdom of Antichrist, &c. Now trãslated into English for a like admonition vnto all true Englyshe harts, wherby they may learn and know how to consider & receive the procedinges of the Englishe Magistrates and Bishops. Wyth a Preface of M. Philip Melancthon. Take hede and beware of the Leuen of the popysh Phariseis. Take heede and beware of the pestilẽt poison of the cursed Papistes. Take heede & beware in time of these godles Alienes and brutish Spaniardes, which minde to cõquer your nation, and to subuerte the whole state thereof." 1554.
It begins with " The Preface of the Translator. Eusebius Pamphilius, the Translator of thys folowyng treatise vnto the Christen Reader.---The Preface of Master Philip Melancton." Treating of the invocation of saints, " And from whence do they fetch theyr proses to proue theyr doctryne trow ye? out of noble authors J warrant you, euen out of olde barbrous Dõses. J red once in a boke of theirs, which was a boke of Moralizacions, how the Virgin Marye ought to be worshipped with offerings and gyftes. And why? Mary, for this cause: Ther was once a thefe which was one that robbed by the high way, which neuer did good al his life long, sauyng that he hapned once by chaũce to come into a Churche vpon Candlemas day: wher seyng the people offeryng mony and candels vpon the altare, he offered ther also as others dyd. After that the same thefe was taken for robbry, and hanged. Whan he was dead, the diuils wold haue had his soule to hel: But ther was a good angel, ỷ wythstode thẽ, saying vnto the diuels, whi wold ye take this man awai, seing ye haue nothing to do wyth him, nor no power ouer him? The diuils made answere agayne and saide: He hath done much euyl and mischiefe, and neuer dyd good in al his life. So thei went together before the iudgemẽt seate of god, and there the diuels accused the thefe, that he had neuer don any good. Thẽ the good angel brought forth ỷ crosse peny, together with the candle, which he had offered vpon the altar. Vpon ỷ the iugge gaue sentence, that the thefe should defend himselfe against the diuels. And ỷ angel gaue him this coũsel, that he should take the peny in the left hand, in the steade of a bukler, & the candle in the right hand in the steade of a sword, and so to fight with the Dyuels, and to strike nothing but crosse strokes at them. And so he did, and bi that means chased

8 I 2 away

away the diuels. After that, the soule came to the body agayne, and was taken from the gallowes, and the man lyued afterward very honestly. Hec ille. Who wold euer haue beleued, that they had had such strong reasons to proue theyr doctrine with, if we had not theyr bokes for wytnesses?" See p. 163, &c. At the end is "A praier to be saide of all true Christians agaynst the Pope, and al the enemies of Christ and hys Gospel." This prayer is reprinted in Morgan's Phœnix Britannicus, 4to. p. 95.

Quarto

MOULSEY, &c.

HERE might be recited the titles of great numbers of scurrilous pamplets written, printed, and dispersed on both sides, concerning ecclesiastical discipline, and never ending cavils and disputes about rites and ceremonies, in a snarling and ridiculous manner; and the public printing presses being shut against the puritans, some of them purchased a private one. If any desire to know the motions and stages of the press, which printed these books; know, it was first set up at Moulsey, near Kingston, in Surry, thence conveyed to Fawsley in Northamptonshire, thence to Norton, and afterwards to Coventry; from Coventry to Woolston in Warwickshire, and from thence to Manchester in Lancashire; discovered by Henry, earl of Darby, in the printing "More work for cooper." It might well have many errata, when itself was a pilgrim, or vagabond press. See Fuller's church history, lib. ix. page 194. It was often visited by the high commissioners messengers, who seized what books they found of theirs, &c. Strype in the life of archbishop Whitgift, p. 314, says, that Sir Richard Knightly, and sir— Wigston, who had entertained the press, together with the printer, and Humphrey Newman the disperser, were deeply fined in the star-chamber; and others put to death. See more in Camb. Annals of queen Elizabeth.

Dr. H. Sampson in his MS. papers of lives, in the account of the ministers of Coventry since the reformation, divided into decads—in decad the 5th from 1580 to 1590, has the following passage: "Another matter, that procured an ill aspect upon the town, was the printing of Martin Marprelate, junior, in it; which tho' it was done without the knowledge or approbation of any in the town, yet the place and the people was upon this mere occasion reflected on. The story was thus; Mr. Hales of White Fryers had now his house standing empty, whilst himself lived elsewhere. Mr. Knightly his cousin took that opportunity to borrow his house for a divertisement of a month or two, or other pretence

tence; which when it was granted, Mr. Knightly privately conveyed thither the printing press and letters, and in a back chamber, which is well remembered and marked to this day, the book was printed off. It cannot be denied, but that this house stands remote from neighbours, being uninhabited at that time, and that chamber, removed from the house-keepers usual residence, was well chosen for this purpose. But it was discovered afterwards, I suppose, by the printers, who being taken in Lancashire, confessed other places, where the ambulatory press had been, and the persons that employed them, sufficiently to Mr. Hales's cost. First for the fact of lending his house, though altogether ignorant of the use it should be put to, yet upon suspicion of his guilt, he was fined 15-el. and afterwards compounded with the queen, and actually paid 500l. Yet after this, the officers not having registred the composition and payment of the money, his grandson Mr. John Hales, in king James's days, was call'd on again to pay the fine; which he had certainly done, if after many days sollicitous seeking the discharge in vain he had not found it at last very accidentally among papers, that were destined to wast or burning.

" One person more about the printing this unhappy book. Amongst others that were accused for having a hand in it, Mr. ——— Throckmorton was one, and being sent for by a messenger, who in his yard meeting with a man, or rather shadow and case of a man, that was little removed from a mere natural, askt him where Mr. Throckmorton was? he answered, He is just gone into Scotland. When said the messenger? Just now said the fool. Now the fool meant only the house of office, which in the language of the servants of that house, was called Scotland, where Throckmorton then was sculking, and over heard all this discourse. The rest of the wiser servants by that time, were so well alarmed of the messenger and his errand, that they would discover nothing in particular of him. So the messenger taking it for granted, that children and fools speak true, and that he was gone indeed into Scotland, went away with this account of his message to him that sent him; by which means he escaped a troublesome journey, and had opportunity to stave off and weather out that trouble, which by a sudden surprize had unavoidably come upon him."

Waldegrave and Legate both lived in the parish of St. Alban's Woodstreet, from the same H. Sampson's papers. Dr. Williams's publick library in Redcross-street, London.

For these private printed books, &c. I must refer you to my general history, &c. annexed, not knowing how otherwise to place them, but as near as I could in order of time, from some dates, or other circumstances in the books themselves.

Many books were also privately printed on the side of the Roman Catholicks, and dispersed all over the kingdom, though not without the greatest difficulty and danger of life; and for this purpose they had a press, printers, and a secret place under ground, which was changed very often, and the young nobles with great caution distributed the books. See Ribadeneira's Scisma d'Inglaterra, Edit. 1595, under the year 1580.

WALES.

W A L E S.

ONE Thackwell is mentioned as a printer here, in a book intitled, Oh read ouer D. John Bridges &c. by Martin Marprelate, p. 23. where he ſays, "Pitifully complayning, is there any reaſon (my Lord's grace) why knaue Thackwell the printer, which printed popiſhe and trayterous welſhe bookes in wales, ſhoulde haue more fauour at your graceleſſe handes, then poore Walde-graue, who neuer printed book againſt you, that contayneth eyther treaſon or impietie.* Thackwell is at libertie to walke where he will, and permitted to make the moſt he could of his preſſe and letters: whereas Robert Walde-graue dares not ſhew his face for the blood-thirſtie deſire you haue for his life, onely for printing of bookes which toucheth the biſhops Myters. You know that Walde-graues printing preſſe and Letters were taken away: his preſſe being timber, was ſawen and hewed in pieces, the yron work battered and made vnſeruiceable, his Letters melted, with caſes and other tooles defaced (by John Woolſe, alias Machiuill, Beadle of the Stacioners, and moſt tormenting executioner of Walde-graues goods) and he himſelfe vtterly depriued for euer printing againe, hauing a wife and ſixe ſmall children. Will this monſtrous crueltie neuer bee reuenged thinke you? When Walde-graves goods was to be ſpoiled and defaced, there were ſome printers, that rather then all the goods ſhould be ſpoyled, offered money for it, towardes the reliefe of the mans wife and children, but this coulde not be obtayned and yet popiſhe Thackwell, though hee printed popiſh and trayterous bookes, may haue the fauor to make money of his preſſe and letters. And reaſon to. For Walde-graues profeſſion ouerthroweth the Popedome of Lambehith, but Thackwels popery maintayneth the ſame. And now that Walde-graue hath neither preſſe nor letters, his grace may dine and ſup the quieter.—Walde-graue hath left houſe and home, by reaſon of your vnnaturall tyrannie: hauing left behinde him a poore wife and ſixe Orphanes, without any thing to relieue them. (For the huſband, you haue bereaued both of his trade and goods) Be you aſſured that the crie of theſe will one day preuaile againſt you, vnleſſe you deſiſt from perſecuting.

"And good your grace, I do now remember myſelfe of another printer, that had preſſe and letter in a place called Charterhouſe in London (in *Anno* 1587. neere about the time of the Scottiſh Queenes death) intelligence

* And in a pamphlet called, *Hay any work for Cooper*, p. 39. thus, "Where thou ſaieſt M. Yong had onely the dealing with Thackwel the popiſh printer, without his graces priuitie, thou lieſt in thy throat: M. Yong himſelfe brought him to his grace, who ordered the matter, as is ſet downe in my Piſtle." Mr. Yong was a juſtice of peace.

gence was giuen vnto your good grace of the fame, by fome of the Stacioners of London, it was made knowen vnto you what worke was in hand, what letter the booke was on, what volume, viz. in 8vo. in halfe sheetes, what workemen wroght on the fame; namely, I. C.[1] the Earle of Arundels man and three of his feruants, with their feuerall names, what liberallitie was beftowed on thofe workemen, and by whom, &c. Your grace gaue the Stacioners the hearing of this matter, but to this daye the parties were neuer calde in Coram for it: but yet by your leaue my Lord, vpon this information vnto your honourable worfhip, the ftacioners had newes, that it was made knowne vnto the printers, what was done vnto your good grace, and prefently in fteed of the work which was in hand, there was other appointed, as they faye, authorifed by your Lordfhip. I will not faye it was your owne doing, but by your fleeue, thought is free. And my good L. (nay, you fhalbe none of my L. but M. Whitgift & you will,) are you partiall or no in all your actions tell me? yes you are? I will ftand to it? did you get a Decree in the high court of Starchamber onely for Walde-graue? If it bee in generall (& you not partiall) why fet you not that printing preffe and letters out of Charterhoufe, and deftroye them as you did Walde-graues? Why did you not apprehend the parties, why? Becaufe it was poperie at the leaft, that was printed in Charterhoufe: and that maintayneth the crowne of Canterburye? And what is more tollerable then popery? Did not your grace of late erecte a new printer contrary to the forefayd decree? One Thomas Orwine (who fometimes wrought popifh bookes in corners: namely, Jefus Pfalter, our Ladies Pfalter, &c.) with condition he fhould print no fuch feditious bookes, as Walde-graue hath done? Why, my Lorde? Walde-graue never printed any thing againft the ftate, but onely againft the vfurped ftate of your Paultripolitanfhip," &c. See bifhop Cooper's anfwer to thefe reproaches in "An admonition[2] to the people of England," p. 41, &c. But from neither of thefe authors can it be gathered in what part of Wales this Thackwell printed, or what were the titles of thofe Welch books faid to have been printed by him.

[1] John Charlewood. See p. 1093. [2] See p. 1084.

OF

OF

PRINTING

IN

SCOTLAND.

SINCE an account has been given of printing in England, i shall now proceed to offer a few hints, relating to the rise and progress of that art in Scotland, which may be of use to such, as would pursue this subject further, in that formerly antient kingdom.

The late ingenious JAMES WATSON, who with one Freebairn obtained a patent from Q. Anne for printing in Scotland, and was afterwards one of his majesty's printers there in the time of K. George the first, did in the year 1713, publish a short history of the art of printing, containing an account of its invention and progress in Europe; to which he added a preface, wherein he mentions three or four books, and as many printers of Scotland within my assigned time; that is, from the introduction of the art there, to the year 1600, which i shall take notice of in their place. He indeed supposes they had the art of printing early, from their having a constant trade with the Low Countries; from their cases and presses being all of the Dutch make, till of late years; from their manner of working, in distributing the letter on hand with the face from us, and the nick downwards; and their making ink; as the printers there do at this day; but that the books may be lost, being either lives of saints, and legendary miracles, or of devotions then in vogue, carried away by the priests, who fled beyond sea, or destroyed by the zeal of the reformers. His further accounts of the Scotch printers are later than my time.

1509. The first book i have found mentioned by any, is, A breviary of the church of Aberdeen, printed at Edinburgh 1509. thirty five years after the introduction of this art by William Caxton. The account Mr. Ames had of this, is in a letter directed to his good friend, Dr. John Mitchell, from Mr. Charles Mackey, professor of history in the university of Edinburgh.

burgh. "The art with us is as early as 1509. I imagine, though I am not certain, that I have found Mr. Ames's voucher for it. Mr. John Ker, late humanity professor here, gave into the lawyers library an old breviary in octavo, for the use of Aberdeen, but the title page, and some sheets at the end are wanting. The first page begins with the following words, which I excerpted from the book. '*In nomine sanctae et individuae Trinitatis, Patris, et Filii, et Spiritus Sancti.* Breviarium ad usum et consuetudinem percelebris ecclesiae cathedralis Aberdon. in Scotia, regnante principe nostro serenissimo Jacobo, quarto, divina favente clementia Scotorum rege illustrissimo, imperii sui anno vicessimo secundo, pro hyemali parte feliciter sumit exordium.' Now as King James the ivth succeeded upon his father's death, which happened the 11 June, 1488, the year 1509 after the 11 June, is the 22d year of his reign; and 1509 is marked with a pen on the margin of the book, opposite to "imperii sui anno vicessimo secundo."

Afterward, Mr. Ames himself had a further account of the second part of this Book, from his worthy friend Mr. Professor Ruddiman, no small encourager of his undertaking, by his many searches for him at Edinburgh, and elsewhere; and we may safely conclude, the first vol. was printed at the charge of the same person, and at Edinburgh. 1510.
"Ejusdem breviarii pars aestivalis. per reverendum in Christo patrem Wilelmum, Abirdon. episcopum, studiosius, maximisque cum laboribus collect. non solum ad ecclesiæ suæ Abirdonensis, verumetiam ad tocius ecclesiæ Scoticanæ usum percelebrem: oppido Edinburgensi impressa, jussu & impensis honorabilis viri Walteri Chapman, ejusdem oppidi mercatoris, quarto die mensis Julii, anno Domini millesimo ccccc decimo." At the end are these words: "Laus Deo, cuius gracia finis adest presenti opusculo *estivalis* partis breviarii divinorum officiorum de tempore et de sanctis: ac *Davitico psalterio* congruenter per ferias diviso: cum invitatoriis, *hymnis*, antiphonis, *capitulis*, responsoriis, horis: feriarum commemoracio penitus per anni circulum. Necnon communi sanctorum, plurimarum virginum, & matronarum cum kalendario et mobilium festorum *tabula perpetuae* cum diversorum sanctorum legendis: que antea sparsim vagabantur, & nonnullis aliis adiunctis sacerdotibus quam necessariis *per reverendum* in Christo patrem, *Wilelmum* Abirdonen. *episcopum*, studiosius maximisque cum laboribus collect. non solum ad ecclesiae suae *Abirdonen.* verum eciam ad tocius ecclesie *Scoticane* usum percelebrem. Opido Edinburgensi impressa, jussu et impensis honorabilis viri *Walteri Chepman* ejusdem opidi mercatoris, quarto die mensis Junii,[h] anno Domini millesimo ccccc decimo." On the back of this page there is a curious wooden print representing two savages at full length; their heads adorned with flowers, and they have in their hands flower stalks; their bodies are clothed with skins of wild beasts, with a girdle of flowers; and their legs bare from the ancles downwards. Betwixt these two figures stands a tree, upon which is suspended a shield Sable, with W. and C. in cypher, Argent: at the

h This probably is a misprint for Julij, as on the title-page.

bottom between two black lines are these two words, "x Walterus x chepman S." This would seem to prove that the art of printing was first introduced into Scotland from France, and probably the types &c. came from thence; for this kind of device was at that time peculiar to the French printers, and the cut agrees with Pigouchet's Salisbury and Rouen heures, except in the cypher. Gough's British Topography, Vol. II; p. 644. Both parts of this Breviary are in the Advocates' library, but want the title-pages and some leaves in the middle; the first is more defective than the second. N. B. The words in the extracts from both parts of this breviary printed here in Italic are distinguished by red ink in the original. I have throughout this article followed the extracts as they were sent to Mr. Ames, but am pretty confident, from observation, that the j was not used at that time as a letter, only as a numeral; nor v in the middle of words, unless they were in capitals. Small Octavo.

These Breviaries evince Mr. Watson's conjecture to have been well founded: however, the Scotch afterwards made use of foreign printers; as indeed did some of the early English printers occasionally, especially for law-books in the Norman French.

1521. "De Historia Gentis Scotorum Libri sex, seu Historia Maioris Britanniæ, tam Angliæ quam Scotiæ e veterum Monumentis concinnata. Parisiis; Anno 1521, apud Jodocum Badium." See Mackenzie, Vol. II; p. 344. My copy wants the title-page; but by the modern edition there appear to have been the following verses on the back page, "Ad Jacobum quintum Scotorum Regem, magni spei ac spectatæ indolis puerum. Jodocus Badius Ascensius.

"Rex Jacobe, puer fatis melioribus orte,
Cui moderanda dedit Scotica sceptra Deus:
Perlege maiorum regalia gesta tuorum,
Et libertatis protege iura tuæ."

The Preface is addressed "Spectabilissima indole & sũmis vtriusq; Maioris Britãniæ Regni natalib9 inclyto Jacobo Scotorum Regi Quinto, Joannes nomine Maior, natione Scotus, & professione Theologus academie Parisien. cũ expectata felicitate, Rege dignam obseruantiam.—E Gymnasio Montisacuti apud Parrhisios frugi & non ignobili.—Tabula rerum insignium." Besides; "Fo. CXLVI. Ex officina Ascensiana ad Idus Aprilis. MDXXI." W.H. Quarto.

1522. "Episcoporum Murthlacen. & Aberdonen. Per Hectorem Boetium Vitæ." Over a cut of the printing press having Prelũ Ascẽsianũ on the beam, and his mark at the bottom: the whole in an architective compartment, with medallions on the sides, and his mark in a shield on the sell. Dedicated "Reuerẽdo in Christo patri Gauino Dunbari Aberdonen. antistiti Hector Boeti9 Deidonen. debitã reuerẽtiã.—Vale semper felix. Ex tuo collegio Aberdonensi Pridie Calendas Septembris Anno supra sesquimillesimum vicesimo primo." The running-title throughout, is "Aberdonensium episcoporum vitae;" tho' the first four of these were bishops of Murthlac, founded by King Malcolm II. in 1010; and when

when Nactenus, the fourth bishop, had sitten 14 years there, the see was translated from thence to Aberdeen, by K. David I. in 1137. On the last printed leaf is an index of the four bishops at Murthlac, and 25 at Aberdeen; on the back thereof are verses, Dominus Gulielmus Elphinstonus Aberdonen. Episcopus & Collegii scholasticorū illic institutor ac patronus, collegium suum alloquitur.—Respondet Collegium.—Joannes Vaus in laudem huius operis & Authoris.---Impressa sunt hæc prelo Ascensiano Ad Idus Maias Anno Salutis M. D. xxii. Deo Gratias." Contains 40 leaves including the title; the last blank. Neat full bodied English Rom. No. 2. The Gothic 𝔚 used for want of a Roman one. Richard Gough, Esq. Quarto.

" SCOTORUM *Historiae a prima gentis origine, cum aliarum & rerum & gentium illustrationenon vulgari: praemissa epistola nuncupatoria, tabellisq; amplissimis, & non paenitenda Isagoge quae ab huius tergo explicabuntur diffusius.*" This over a cut of the printing press somewhat different from that to the preceding article," Episcoporum—vitae," having on its legs 15-20. Under it, *Quae omnia impressa quidem sunt Jodoci Badii Ascensii typis & opera: impensis autem Nobilis & praedocti viri Hectoris Boethii Deidonani*: a quo sunt & condita & edita." What is here in Italics was printed in red. The whole inclosed within a grotesque compartment, with a medallion at top (perhaps the author, laureated, and writing at a desk) supported by lions rampant. On the back, " Farrago operis huius, seu quæ in hoc continentur opere;" also, " In historiæ autem libris xvii." On the next leaf: The arms of Scotland suspended under a close helmet. The crest, a demi-lion in front, crowned, holding in its right paw a sword, and a lance pennanted in the left, issuing out of a ducal coronet on the helmet. The Supporters are 2 unicorns collared and chained. The motto, on 2 scrolls, " Sub mea—defensione." Beneath these arms, " P. Rosseti poetæ laureati de insignibus Scotorum regum carmen," in 29 hexameters. At the end of these, to fill up the next page, " Jodoci Badii Ascensii, Ad illustrissimū Scotorum regem Jacobum quintum, in Hectoris Boethii historiam commendatio," an octastichon. Then follow, " Ad illustrissimum Scotorum regem Jacobum quintū Hectoris Boethii Deidonani in eiusdem gentis historiam. Prefatio.—Datum Aberdonie Kalendis Aprilis, Anno ab natali Christi domini supra sesquimillesimū sexto & vigesimo.---Reverendissimo in Christo patri Jacobo a Betuun. S. Andree archiepiscopo & primati in terra Scotia, natalibus claris orto eiusdēq; regni cancellario dignissimo, Hector Boethius debita cum reuerentia felicitatem.—Ex regali collegio Aberdonēsi, ad Kalēdas Maias, Anno salutis Christiane sexto & vigesimo supra millesimū quingentesimum.---Idem ad lectorem. ---Gulielmus Gordonus illustri academiæ Aberdonensi S. P. D.---Scotorum regum catalogus, quo tempore regnarint, *&c.*---Index rerum & verborum:" *&c.*---A copious table of corrections. (1527.)

These prefixes are contained on signatures a, e, i, o, in eights, and u 10; the leaves not numbered. Then follows another title page, wholly in black, in the same compartment as before, " IN HAC IN Scotorum

torum Historiam Isagoge continentur. Tabella literaria in ea contentorum. Scotorum Regni descriptio & mores. Regum Britanniæ, quæ nunc Anglia, series. Regum Scotorum Catalogus." The printing press, as before. Under it, "Quæ impressa sunt Typis Jodoci Badii: & impensis Hectoris Boethii." These latter prefixes have most of their leaves numbered, and a fresh series of signatures, C 6, in eights. On the back of the last of these "Alexander Leo Moraviensis ecclesiæ Cantor, Scotorum nobilitati Salutem.—Ex Parrhisiorũ Academia celeberrima Ad Idus Martias, MDXXVII. ad calculum Romanorum." Then begins "Scotorum Historiæ, Lib. 1." The numbering of the leaves and signatures commencing anew, to Fo. CCCLXVIII, or Z, the 2d alphabet, in eights. Very neatly printed on full-bodied Roman types, about the size of Eng. Rom. No. 1, but the lines rather wider spaced. Many abbreviations are introduced; no semicolon used; V, or V v, supply for W; and the running-titles only on the dexter page throughout. Richard Gough, Esq. Folio.

—— "Ad Serenissimum Scotorum Regem Jacobum Quintum de suscepto Regni Regimine a Diis feliciter ominato Strena. Impressum Edinburgi apud Thomam Dauidson." In verse. There is a MS note prefixed to the copy in the library of the late James West, Esq; probably by some Scotch Antiquary, who conjectures it to have been printed about 1525, "and that it is the first essay in the art of printing executed in Scotland." How well founded so ever this latter conjecture may be, that of the date seems at present rather too early, as we have not yet met with any account of Thomas Davidson's printing, bearing a date, prior to 1536. Quarto.

1533. "Alexandri Alesii epistola contra decretum quoddam episcoporum in Scotia, quod prohibet legere Novi Testamenti libros lingua vernacula." Without printer's name or place[1]; but probably at London, if it was not sent abroad to be printed. Mackenzie mentions it printed at Strasburgh in 1542; perhaps a subsequent edition. His dispute with Cochle on the same subject was likewise printed in 1535. Most of this author's works were printed at Lipsic; and though within my proposed time, yet as they appear to have been printed there only in Latin, and after printing had recommenced in Scotland, they do not accord with my plan. They may be seen in Mackenzie's Lives and Characters of Writers of the Scots Nation, Vol. II; p. 183. Sixteens.

Mr. Ames accounted a chasm of 30 years in the history of printing in Scotland, computing them from the year 1510, when the "Breviarii pars aestivalis" was printed in Edinburgh, to the year 1540, when he supposed the Scotch Acts of Parliament (made in the reign of king James the 5th) were printed; excluding "Hectoris Boethii Scotorum historia," printed at Paris "per Jodocum Badium Ascensium;" as also "Alexandri Alesii epistola," doubting its being printed in Scotland. At present there appears

[1] The author having made his escape by night from Scotland, where he had been imprisoned three times, and was to have been tried for heresy the next day, it cannot be supposed to have been printed in that kingdom, were we even assured that they had printers there at the time.

appears a chasm of only 26 years in the history of printing in Scotland, the 30 mentioned by Mr. Ames being shortened 4 years by the intervening of the following book since his time. Probably the account of more, if not the books themselves, may be retrieved in future.

"The History and Chronicles of Scotland, compilit, and newly cor- 1536.
rectit and amendit, be the Reverend and Noble Clerk Mr. Hector Boeis, Chanon of Aberdene, translated lately by Mr. John Ballanden, Archdene of Murray and Chanon of Rosse, at Command of James the Fyfte, King of Scottis; imprentet, in Edenburgh be Thomas Davidson, dwelling fornens the Fryere-Wynde." Mackenzie, Vol. II; p. 596. Folio.

The Works of Sir David Lindsay. See Mackenzie, Vol III; p. 37 1540.
and 39, where all that author's poems publisshed before 1600 are enumerated, and said to have been several times printed, but the earliest edition he had seen was this in 1540; yet they could not be all printed at that time; particularly The tragedy of cardinal Beaton, which did not happen before 1546: besides, that list contains 6 more poems than the *Copenhagen* edition, of which an account will be given preceding the year 1560. See Pinkerton's Scottish poets, &c. Vol. I; p. civ, note * 8°.

About this time (1540) the Scotch parliament passed an Act[a] ordaining the Clerk of *the* Register, or Lord Register of Scotland, to publish the Acts of Parliament made in the reign of king James V. and to employ what printer he pleased, provided that printer had the king's special licence thereto. Mr. Thomas Ruddiman, in a letter to Mr. Ames, dated 31 January, 1744-5, among other observations relating to printing in Scotland, gave him information of the said book, saying, "By it you will see, that it is not properly a patent granted to Davidson, of being the king's printer, but only a confirmation of a licence, granted by act of parliament to sir James Foulis of Collington, then lord register of Scotland, to cause these acts to be imprinted by what printer he should think fit to choose; but so, that the said printer should have a special licence[b] from the king to the same purpose."

"The

[a] This act, No. 107, is the last of James V. and is entitled, "The Clerke of Register havand the Kingis licence suld cause imprent the actes of Parliament."

[b] "The copy of the kingis grace licence and priuilege, grantit to Thomas Dauidson prentar, for imprenting of his gracis actis of parliament.

"James be the grace of God, king of Scottis, to all and sindry, quhom it efferis. Forsamekill as it is ordanit be ws, be an act maid in plane parliament, that all our actis maid be ws be publist outthrow al our realme; and that nane our schereiffis, stewardis, balliez, prouest, and baillies of oure burrowis, suld pretend ignorance throw misknawing thairof, that our clerk of registre, and counsel, suld mak ane autentik copie of all sik actis as concernis the commoun weil of our realme, and extract the samin under his subscriptioun manuale, to be imprentit be quhat prentar it sall pleis him to cheis; providing alwayis, that the said prentar sall have our special licence thairto, as in the said act at mair lenth is contenit. We heirfore has gevyn, and grantit, and be the tenour heirof gevis and grantis our licence, to oure louit Thomas Davidson, imprentar in our burgh of Edinburgh, to imprent oure saidis actis of parliament, and dischargis all uthir imprentaris, and writtaris, within yis our realme, or without, present, and for to cum, to imprent, or writ our saidis actis of parliament, or bring thaym hame to be sauld, for the space of sex zeris nixt to cum, efter the dait of

(1541.) "The new actis and constitutionis of parliament, maid be the rych excelent prince, James the fyft king of Scottis, *1540." On the sam page are the Scots arms; above the crest, IN DEFENS, and on one sid JACOBUS, on the other side, REX 5. On the back of the title is the king privilege as note l. Then, two distichs.

"Distichum
Fama secunda ferat Jacobum ad Sydera quintum,
Quo regnante, bonum celitus omne venit.
Aliud.
Pace bonus, belloque potens, justissimus orbis,
Hoc regnum quintus Rex Jacobus habet."

It contains the acts of two parliaments, the former "begunnyn and haldin at Edinburgh the vii day of Junii, the zeir of God M D and XXXV zeris; the later begunnyn and haldin at Edinburgh, the third day of December, the zeir of God M D and XL zeirs." The last act is for printing them. At the end in one page is, "Imprentit in Edinburgh be Thomas Davidson, dwelling abone the Nether-bow, on the North side of the gait, the aucht of Februarii, the zeir of God, 1541 zeris." On the other side is a picture designed for Imago Crucifixi sedentis ad judicium.

"En ego, justiciae typus atque figura, tribunal
Hic ascendo meum; dextra assertoribus alta
Adstipulor veri, quibus haec mea lilia merces:
At si quis contra sentit, demissa sinistra
In stygios jubet ire lacus, gladioque feriri.
Edinburgi ex aedibus Thomae Davidson, regii impressoris. Cum privilegio."

The book is printed on vellum in folio, in black letter, as beautifully as any to be seen at this day.

1541. "The history and croniklis of Scotland, with the cosmography and dyscription thairof. Compilit be the noble clerk, maister Hector Boece, channon of Aberdene. Translatit laitly in our vulgar and commoun langage be maister Johne Bellenden, archedene of Murray, and channon of Ross; at the command of the richt hie, richt excellent, and noble prince James the 5th of that name, king of Scottis; and imprentit in Edinburgh be me Thomas Davidson, prenter to the kingis nobyll grace, dwellyng fornens the Frere wynd. Cum privilegio." Folio.

—— I have an edition without date, thus intitled, "Heir beginnis the hystory and Croniklis of Scotland:" and printed in red, over the arms of

of thir presentis, under the pane of confiscatioun of the samyn. Subscrivit with our hand, and gevin under our prive seill, at Edinburgh, the feat day of December, and of our regne the xxix zeir.

¶ God keip the king."

From the date of this licence it appears, that these acts of parliament were not printed till towards the end of the year 1541, and that though the frontispiece has 1540 in it, yet it would seem, that that figure had been cut before, and designed for other books, that should be printed by Davidson in that form afterwards.

* I take this to be rather the time of passing the act, than of printing it.

of Scotland, as to The new actis, &c. On the back, "The excusation of the prentar," in 5 seven-lined stanzas.—"The contentis of this buke. —The proheme of the cosmographe," in 40 nine-lined stanzas.—"Heir begynnis the Cosmographe and discription of Albion," comprised in 16 chapters, with a recapitulation.—"Tabula." A table of the contents of the history.—"Heir begynnis the names of all Scottis kyngis, sen thair realme began, &c.—The proheme of the history," in 29 octave stanzas.— "Heir after followis the history and croniklis of Scotland compilit and newly correckit be the reuerend and noble clerke maister Hector Boece channon at Aberdene. Translatit laitly be maister Johne Bellenden Archedene of Murray, channon of Ros. At the command of the richt hie, richt excellent, and noble prince James the V. of that name king of Scottis. And imprentit in Edinburgh be Thomas Dauidson dwellyng fornens the frere wynd." These prefixes on F, in sixes. The history has a fresh set of signatures, and the leaves numbered to Fo. cc.l. "Heir endis the hystory and Croniklis of Scotland, with the Cosmography and dyscription thairof. Compilit be the noble clerk maister Hector Boece channon of Aberdene. Translatit laitly in our vulgar and commoun langage, be maister Johne Bellenden Archedene of Murray. And imprentit in Edinburgh, be me Thomas Dauidson, prenter to the kyngis nobyll grace: Cum priuilegio." On the back of the last leaf is a very curious wood-cut, which I take to be the same as Mr. Ames tells us was designed for Imago crucifixi sedentis ad judicium, (see p. 1474,) but without the verses. The block is about 7 inches by 6. The Imago crucifixi is within a circle of roses, having here and there a cross interspersed; the interior part consists of 4 divisions; in the middle of the uppermost is represented God the Father crowned and irradiated, invested with an imperial robe, holding up his right hand, and a mund in his left. At his right hand is the Virgin crowned, and holding on her arm the child Jesus irradiated. At his left is an angel in a posture of adoration, with the holy dove irradiated between them. Christ Jesus crowned with thorns and nailed on the cross, at full length divides the three lower partitions in the midst. In the second division appear Moses, David, and the prophets on his right hand; the apostles and evangelists on his left. In the third, on the right, a child sitting, and holding up a sword; behind him some holy martyrs or pilgrims, the foremost of them bearing three wafers upon a book; on the left, a pope, with his ecclesiastical hierarchy. In the lower division, virgins on the right; matrons and confessors on the left. All these, except children, appear at half length. Without the circle, in the upper corner on the right, is a priest kneeling before the altar, on which is represented Christ rising from the tomb: in the opposite corner is an angel appearing to some holy person on his knees, drawing him as it were to him with four strings. At the bottom is a scene of purgatory, represented by a group of persons in flames, encompassed by rocks and mountains, in the middle; while two persons on each side, kneeling, with their beads, are supposed to be praying

praying for them. Sprigs of roses are seen as springing out of several parts of the cross. W.H. Folio.

(1543.) In the Appendix, No. IX. to George Crawfurd's lives and characters of the officers of the crown and state in Scotland, fol. 1726, is an "Act of Parliament, allowing the Reading of the Bible in the vulgar Tongue, Anno 1543, copied out of the Registers of Parliament, in the publick Archives at Edinburgh. Anent the Writing gevin in be Robert Lord Maxwell, in presens of my Lord Governour, and Lordis of Articklis, to be avisit by thaim, giff the samin be resonable or not, of the quhilk the Tenor followis. It is statute, and ordainit, that it sal be lesfull to all our Soviraine Ladyis Leiges to have the haly Writ, to wit, the New Testament and the Auld, in the Vulgar Toung, in Inglis, and Scotis, of an gude and trew Translation, and that thai sal incur na Crimes for the hefing and reding of the samen; providing always, that na Man dispute, or hald opinezeonis under the pains conteinit in the Actis of Parliament. The Lordis of Articklis beand avisit with the said Writing, finds the samin resonable, and therefore thinkis that the samin may be usit amongis all the Leiges of this Realme of our Vulgar Toung, of an gude, trew, and iust Translatioun, becaus there was na Law shewn nor producit in the contrar; and that none of our soverayne Ladyis leiges incur ony Crimes for haifing or reding of the samin, in Form as said is, nor sall be accusit therefore in Time coming, and that na Personis dispute, argou, or hold oppunionis of the samin, under the saidis Painis containit in the foresaids Actis of Parliament." This act is not printed among the laws and acts of parliament collected by Sir Thomas Murry, of Glendock, knight, from the public records of Scotland, and printed at Edinburgh, 1681. Nor, so far as i can find, was it ever observed. I never could yet hear, or be informed of any translation of the New and Old Testament, in English and Scotch. Mr. Lewis[a] says, in "1536, there was another edition of this[b] English Testament, printed in a large 4to, very probably, in Scotland;" but without assigning his reason for such a probability. On the contrary, it is intimated by James Watson, in his preface to the printers of Scotland, 1713, that the first folio English Bible was printed at Edinburgh, by Thomas Bassandyne, in the year 1576, three and thirty years after the date of this act. But what prevented their having the scripture in the vulgar tongue (as the English had for some years before) after the granting this licence, i do not know.

1546. "The Tragical Death of David Beaton, Bishoppe of St. Andrewes in Scotland, whereunto is ioyned the Martyrdom of Maister George Wyscharte, for whose sake the aforesayed Bishoppe was not longe after slayne." By Sir David Lindsay.[c] Catal. Bibl. Harleianæ, Vol. I, No. 8375. 8vo.

Scotland's

[a] Eng. Translations, p. 85.
[b] Tyndal's.
[c] His Papingo, and some other pieces, are said to have been printed at Paris. See our General History, under 1558.

Scotland's Complaint is said by Watson to have been printed in the year 1540, but that date must be a misprint if he meant what Doctor Mackenzie[s] attributes to Sir James Inglis, knight, with this title, "Scotland's Complaint against her Three Sons, the Nobility, Clergy, 1543.
and Commons, imprinted at St. Andrews in 1548;" in the first chapter of which the author laments the loss his nation sustained at the battle of Pinkie, 10 Sept. 1547.

In Catal. Bibl. Harleianæ, Vol. I, No. 8371[r], besides other books of 1549.
Scotch affairs, without name of place or printer, we find a book of a like title, but assigned to a different author, thus, "Vedderburn's Complainte of Scotlande, vyth ane Exortatione to the thre Estaits, to be vigilante in their Deffens of their Public Veil. 1549." I have made enquiry, but cannot as yet learn who possesses this Harleian copy, which seems to have had a title-page; and if so, would probably enable us to judge with more certainty who is the real author of this Complaint; for though this and the foregoing article may be different editions, they are unquestionably the same work; there being a copy of it in the British Museum, which agrees exactly with the account Mackenzie gives of it.

[s] Writers of the Scots Nation, Vol. III; p. 42 and 43.

[r] Mackenzie peremptorily ascribes it to Sir James Inglis, without the least suspicion of any other person being the author; but the Harl. Catal. as confidently attributes it to Vedderburn, or Wedderburn; for the font having now, v singly, and not doubly, is substituted for it throughout the whole book, in the Brit. Museum; which has lately been perfected, except the title-page, from another copy in the possession of Mr. G. Paton, of the custom-House, Edinburgh; to whom I am greatly indebted for his kind intelligences concerning printing in Scotland. This circumstance of the Harl. Catal. giving the author's name Vedderburn, is a presumptive evidence of that copy having a title-page, neither author's name nor date appearing in any other part.

Who this Vedderburn was, or even what was his christian name, I cannot learn. A MS. short history of the estate of the kirk of Scotland, in Mr. Paton's possession, written by an old minister (Mr. Row), mentions "Sir David Lindsayes poesies, Wedderburne's Psalmes and godlie ballads," &c. A Psalm book, &c. was published about the time of the reformation in Scotland; of which see Mackenzie, Vol. III; p. 187. A subsequent edition was printed by Andr. Hart, entitled "A Compendious Book of Godly Sangis & Ballats;" in which such as had given offence in the first edition were omitted. These are supposed to be the same psalms as are mentioned in Mr. Row's MS. short history; and the same as were censured in the 3d session of the General Assembly at Edinburgh, 1568, of which some account will be given under that year: but the author of those psalms is not there mentioned.

[t] Mr. Row was born not far from Stirling, had his education as a priest at Rome, returned to Scotland, turned protestant, and died minister of Perth: he was cotemporary with Sir David Lindsay, &c.

In the Bannatyne collection of Scotch poems by various authors, now in the Advocate's library, Edinburgh, three of them are found with the name of Wedderburn; but whether the same with the abovementioned, I cannot say, neither being distinguished by christian name or other addition. See Pinkerton's Ancient Scotish poems, II; 480, 481. Qu. When was that collection compiled?

The Deliciæ poetarum Scotorum contains a few Latin poems by one David Wedderburn; but as one of them was written in 1617, 'tis not likely he was the author of this Complaint of Scotland.

In the collection of printed ballads, late Major Pierson's, is one entitled The Complaint of Scotland, beginning, "Adew all gladnes, sports and play." Ending with "Sen now to grail is gone my deir." Contains 24 five-line stanzas; without date, printer's or author's name. A broadside.

* This at present has only a MS. title-page, written by Mr. Pinkerton.

Whoever was the author, this book is dedicated " To the excellent ande illustir Marie queen of Scotlande, the margareit ande perle of princessis." In this epistle he tells his patroness, the queen regent, the widow of K. James V. that God " of his grace hes inspirit zow to be an instrament to delyuir vs fra the captiuite of the cruel philaris, the protector of ingland,.—Ther is no prudēt man that vil iuge ŷ this pistil procedis of assentatiōe or adulatiōe, cōsiderant that ve maye see perfitlye quhou that zour grace takkis pane to duelle ī ane strayngë cūtre destitute of iustice. Ande als zour grace beād absēt fra zour only zong dochter, our nobil princes, and rychteous heretour of Scotlād: quha is presentlye veil tretit ī the gouernāce of hyr fadir of lau, the maist illustir potēt prince of the maist fertil & pacebil realme, vndir the machine of of the supreme olimp, quhar that zour grace mycht remane & duel amāg the nobil princes & princessis of France, quhilkis ar zour natiue frendis of consanguinite" &c. He then proceeds in like manner to rehearse the valiant feats of all her progenitors, concluding with the story of the poor man offering to Darius a little fair water, and the poor widow's mite in the gospel. " Nou—my esperance is sa grite, that ī beleif that zour grace vil resaue this tracteit as humainly, as kyng darius resauit the clene vattir fra the pure man of perse. this tracteit is na bettir nor as mekil vattir, bot zit my gude vil and hartly intentione ande my detful obediens, excedis the hartly intentione of the pure mā that offrit the fayr vatir to kyng darius, prayand to god to preserue zour grace in perpetual felicite." Without either subscription of name or date. Then follows the " Prolug to the redar," which begins with reciting the decrees of certain lawgivers against idleness, which may be read[t] below. The author then, to avoid being censured, as condemning himself for not being occupied in any mechanic business, says, " i vil arme

t " Amasis the feeund, quhilk vas the last kyng ande indegete of the egiptiens, (ande as diodore rehersis, he vas the fyist legislator of egipt) maid an ordinance, contrar the vice of ydilnes, that al his subiectis of egipt, var oblid vndir the pane of dede, to bring euery zeir, ther namis in vrit, to the prouest of the prouince quhar ther remanyng vas: ande ther to testife the stait of ther vacatione, ande the maneir of ther lyuing. be this politic ordinance, the egiptiens var inducit tyl adhere to vertu, ande to leyrne sciens craftis ande mecanyke occupations maist comodius ande conuenient for the public veil of egipt. Than eftir this ordinance of amasis, the Gymnosophides institut ane mair strict ordinance amang the pepil of inde: that is to say, that ane persone suld nocht be admittit to resaue his corporal refection, quhil on to the tyme, that he hed manifest realye, or ellis be certan testificatione the fruitis of his laubours, of the daye precedent. the seuerite of this strict ordinance, var augmentit, be ane edict of sesostris the grit kyng of egipt, for he statut ane ordinance til excerse his propir childer ande the zong princis ande gentil men of his court, to vse them tyl indure excesse of laubirs: he statut that nane of them suld tak their refectione, quhil thai hed gone ande ron, the tyme of fiue or sex hours: to that effect, that throucht sic excerse ther membris mycht be purgit fra corruppit humours, the quhilkis humours nocht beand degeistit, mycht be occasione to dul their spreit, ande mak ther body on abil to resist ydilnes. thir ordinances of the egiptiens, ar verray necessair to be vsit in al realmys: be rason that the maist part of the pepil, throucht ther natural fraigilite, consumis the maist part of ther dais in ydilnes," &c.

arme me vitht the vordis of publius scipio—scipio was neuer les ydil as quhē he apperit to be idil. *&c.* i vil apply thir vordis to myself. for quhou beit that the laubir vitht the pen and the studie on the speculatiōe of vertu apeir to be ydilnes, zit thai ar no ydilnes bot rather ane solitt byssynes of the body & of the spreit. ande nou sen gode hes nocht dotit me vitht speculatione of liberal sciēs nor philosophie, nor vitht strynth of my body til indure seruile subiectiōe, nor zit vitht no art nor mecanyc crast, ther for i vil help to the auansing of the public veil vitht my study & vitht my pen.—Euerye crast is necessair for the public veil, ande he that hes the gyst of traductione, compiling or teching, his faculte is as honest as crasty ande as necessair, as is to be ane marinel, ane marchant, ane cordinar,—or ony vthir crasft or sciēs.—ane man of ane crasf, suld nocht detest ane vther sort of crast, considerand that our hurt nature hes nocht dotit ane man til vse al crastis. Aristotil sais in the fyrst beuk of his politiques, that nature hes nocht maid ane man lyck gladius delphicus,—bot nature hes maid ane man abil to be ane prince, ane abil to be ane seruand, ane abil to be ane clerk, ane abil to be ane crastis man,—ande ilk ane hes sum part of vertu of diuerse degreis, ande ilk ane of thir degreis ar ordanand til help vthirs in necessite, Cicero gyuis ane exempil in his retorie, quhou that the citinaris of cartomat in ytalye, sende for an excellēt payntur, callit eracleon, thai promest to gys hym ane grit some of moneye, for to paynt ane fayr ymage of the deesse iuno. than eracleon gart al the fayr ande best lyik zong vemen of that cite cum to his presens ande thā he chesit fise of the best lyik amang them al, to be his patrone, quhen he hed contemplit & spyit the proportions & properteis of nature of thir fise ladeis he chesit the face of ane, the een of ane vthir, the handis of the thrid, the hayr of the feyrd, the armis the myddil ande the feit of the fyift,—because he culd nocht get al his patrone in ane special lady. for sche that vas pleysand of hyr face, vas nocht pleysand of hyr hayr, *&c.* for that cause—al sortis of crastis suld cōcur to gyddir, ande ilkane til help vthirs, as nature prouidit fyrst in the begynnyng. thir prolixt vordis befor rehersit, ar ane preparatiue, cōtrar the detractione, of inuysul clerkis that ar mair expert in latyne tong nor i am, quhilkis vil nocht set furtht ane gude verk tyl induce the pepil to vertu, nor zit vil correct my ignorāt error: bot rather thai ar mair prōpt to repreif ane smal ignorant salt nor to commende ane grit verteous act. bot zit no man suld decist fra ane gude purpose, quhou beit that detractione be armit vitht inuy reddy to suppedit & tyl impung ane verteo' verk: for quhat euyr he be that intendis to compile ane verk to content euerye man he suld fyrst drynk furtht the ocean see." He afterwards introduces the story of Hannibal going with Antiochus to hear the orator Phormio; who, on seeing them enter his oratory, changed the subject he was discoursing on to that of war. When he had done, Antiochus asked Hannibal how he liked his philosopher, who answered, " Nobil prince anthioc, i hes seen mony ald men tyne ther vit, bot i sau neuyr sa grit ane fule among them al, as thy' philosophour phormion,—*who* presumis

to

to teche—ane man that hes baytht speculatione ande experiēs.—be his vane consaitis that he hes studeit on bukis, he beleuis to leyrne annibal the prettik of the veyris ande the conquessingis of realmis.—O anthiocus, thy philosophour phormion sau neuyr the iunyng of ane battel, vit cruel escharmouchis in the ryding of forrais. he saw neuyr the array of men of veyr brokyn, ande twa armeis myxt amang vthirs, fechtand be fellone forse, quhar the destuxione of blude hed payntit ande collourt all the feildis, he herd neuyr the dolorus trompet sounde befor the iunyng of ane battel, nor zit he harde it neuyr sound to gar the men of veyr retere fra ane dangeir, he persauit neuyr the traison of ane party, nor the couuardeis of ane vthir party. he sau neuyr the litil nummir of them that fechtis, nor the grite nummir of them that fleis for dreddour.—Therfor it is grit folye to thy philosophour, til vndirtak to leyrn the ordiring of battellis vitht in his solitair achademya, it var mair necessair ande honest for hym, to vse his auen professione ande facolte: nor to mel vitht ony faculte that passis his knaulage. annibal said mony vthir gude purposis tyl anthiocus, anent this samyn purpose as plutarque rehersis in his apothigmatis. This exempil tendis, that al prudēt men, hes mair occasione to condamp and repreif this raggit nakyt tracteit, nor annibal hed occasione to repreif the philosophour phormion: for my dul rude brane suld nocht hef been sa temerair as to vndertak to correct the imperfectiōe of ane comont veil, because the maist part of my knaulage, is the smallest part of my ignorance: zit nochtheles i hope that vyse men vil repute my ignorāce for ane mortifeit prudens, be rason of my gude intentione that procedis fra ane affectiue ardant fauoir. that i hef euyr borne touart this affligit realme quhilk is my natiue cuntre. Nou heir i exort al philosophouris, historigraphours & oratours of our scottis natione to support & til excuse my barbir agrest termis for i thocht it nocht necessair, til hef fardit ande lardit this tracteit vitht exquisite termis, quhilkis ar nocht daly vsit, but rather i hef vsit domestic scottis langage, maist intelligibil for the vlgare pepil.*—Nou for conclusione of this prolog, i exort the (gude redar) to correct me familiarly ande be cherite, Ande til interpreit my intentione fauorablye, for doubtles the motione of the compilatione of this tracteit, procedis mair of the cōpassione that i hef of the public necessite, nor it dois of presumptione or vain gloir, thy cheretabil correctione, may be ane prouocatione to gar me studye mair attentiuelye in the nyxt verkis that i intēd to set furtht the quhilk i beleif in gode, sal be verray necessair, tyl al them that desiris to liue verteouslye indurād, the schort tyme of this oure fragil peregrinatione, & sa fayr veil." I have made larger extracts from the dedication, and especially from the preface, that the reader may see what the author says of himself, and have a specimen of the Scotch language at the time when the book was written; and though the orthography

* I have recited this last paragraph, that the orthography of it may be compared with Mackenzie's quotation of it, Vol. III; p. 41, 43. His certainly differs from the Museum copy; and yet seems to me to be too antiquated for the Scotch spelling in the Doctor's time.

graphy is not alwaies alike, yet it is moſtly ſo; and the Engliſh was not arrived at a regular method, (any more than the Scotch) though attempts for that purpoſe were afterwards made by Sir Thomas Smyth, Cheſter, Bullaker,[a] &c.

A copious account of the contents of this curious book may be ſeen in Mackenzie, III; p. 40—46. where he has alſo enumerated[b] the titles of the moſt eſteemed Scotch ſongs, or poems then in vogue; and the names of diverſe herbs with their chief qualities, but of theſe he has omitted two mentioned in this copy. Mr. Pinkerton[c] has recited the fables or ſtories, and the dances in common vſe. I ſhould alſo have tranſcribed here the names of beaſts and birds, with their ſeveral peculiar properties; the technical terms relating to a ſhip, and an engagement between two ſhips, and the muſical inſtruments, but that Mr. Pinkerton has informed us he means to reprint the whole book.

This book is very neatly printed on Rom. long primer, with marginal notes on Italics, ſuppoſed at Paris, at leaſt ſomewhere in France, the v being uſed for w throughout. Howbeit, it ſeems to have undergone great alterations from the original deſign, having evidently large interpolations, particularly 22 leaves unnumbered between leaf 31 and 32; others appear to have been cancelled. "The Complaynt" ends on the leaf numbered 143; then "Tabula" not numbered on one leaf, which would be 144; but if they had been regularly numbered, including the title-page, would have made 148 leaves. It is obſervable that the proper names moſtly begin with a ſmall letter; and that the pronoun of the firſt perſon ſingular is always printed with the ſmall i, though the font did not want the capital I.

Having thus given a faithful and impartial account of this myſterious little book, as it may be deemed in its preſent ſtate, without a title-page, i beg leave to ſubmit a few queries and remarks concerning the author and this work to the candid reader: but deſire that what is further added may be cancelled, whenever a copy of this book, with its proper title-page, containing the name of the author, comes to light.

Might not both Mackenzie and the compiler of the Harl. Catalogue tranſcribe from written title-pages, or perhaps from tradition? Is it not highly probable, conſidering the ſubject and the time, that the book ſhould be printed privately; and if the printer was in danger, was it not neceſſary for the author[d] to conceal his name? If the author's name was mentioned on the title-page, what occaſion to omit it at the end of the dedication? This copy in the Muſeum is ſo packed and cooked that it cannot reaſonably be pronounced a ſecond edition, eſpecially as the contents given by Mackenzie appear evidently to have been taken from a copy

[a] See p. 951 and 1015.
[b] He ſays in the Author's own words.
[c] Ancient Scotch Songs, &c. Vol. II; p. 543, &c.
[d] Having ſharply cenſured the three eſtates of his country: the commons for their familiarity with the Engliſh; the nobility for their pride and contentions; and eſpecially the clergy for negligence of their proper duty, luxury, and wicked lives; provoking them to bear arms, &c.

a copy of this edition, and his quotations of the songs and herbs from the interpolated leaves, though not so correctly as might have been. May not the title-page, as the book is so neatly printed, have had as neat a compartment, and so have been transposed into collections of that sort; the subject of the book, as to the main intention, becoming obsolete on the happy union of the two nations, though the book itself, as long as it can be preserved, will ever remain, in point of language, customs, &c. a curious relique of antiquity, a genuine Scotch classic. In the Brit. Museum; and Mr. G. Paton, of Edinburgh. Sixteens.

1550. A treatise concerning justification by Mr. Henry Balnaves. Edinburgh. See Mackenzie, Vol. III; p. 147. Octavo.

(1551.) In the fifth parliament of queen Mary held at Edinburgh the 1st day of Feb. 1551, No. 27 is an act[b] entitled "Prenters suld prent na thing without licence. Item, For-sa-meikle as there is diverse Prenters in this Realme, that dailie and continually prentis buikes concerning the Faith, ballattes, sanges, blasphemationes, rimes, alsweill of Kirk-men, as Temporal, and vthers Tragedies, alsweill in Latine, as in English toung, not seene, viewed, and considdered be the Superioures, as apperteinis to the defamation and sclander of the Lieges of this Realme, and to put ordour to sik inconuenientes: it is devised, statute, and ordained be the Lord Govenour, with advise of the three Estaites of Parliament: That na Prenter presume, attempt, or take vpon hande to prent ony buikes, ballattes, sanges, blasphemationes, rimes, or Tragedies, outher in Latine, or English Toung, in ony times to cum, vnto the time the samin be seene, viewed, and examined be some wise and discreit persons, depute thereto be the Ordinares quhat-sum-ever. And there after ane licence had and obteined fra our Soveraine Ladie, and the Lord Governour, for imprenting of sik buikes, vnder the paine of confiscation of all the Prenters gudes, and banishing him of the Realme for ever." The Lawes, &c. Edinb. 1597.

1551. John Hamilton, archbishop of St. Andrew's, primate of the kirk of Scotland, his catechism of date 26 January, 1551. St. Andrew's. See Watson's Preface, p. 8. Again, Quarto.

1552. "The catechisme,[c] that is to say, ane commone and catholik instructioun

[b] It is certain, from publications still extant, that, besides the degeneracy of morals among the papists, the reformed had made *too licentious* use of the press. Many of them probably had renounced the errors of popery, not so much from the convictions of conscience, as through the contempt which they had of its clergy, on account of their gross ignorance, superstition, and immorality of every kind. As poetry had been fashionable in the late reign, many wits diverted themselves by ridiculing a religion founded on such absurdities, and taught by such professors: but their compositions were too often indecent, and sometimes illiberal. Add to this, that many translations of foreign authors, and some original compositions in favour of the reformation were now common in Scotland, so that the popish clergy thought a licensing act absolutely necessary. See Guthrie's Hist. of Scotland, Vol. V; p. 372.

[c] A provincial Synod meeting at Edinburgh in January, order was taken for publishing an English Catechism, containing a short explanation of the Commandments, Belief, and Lord's Prayer; and the curates enjoyned to read a part thereof every Sunday and Holy-day to the people, when there was no sermon. This being imprinted, was sold for two pence, and therefore called by the vulgar, The two-penny Faith. Spotswood's Hist. of the Ch. of Scotland, p. 91.

tioun of the christin people in materis of our catholik faith and religioun, quhilk na gud christin man, or woman suld misknaw: set furth be ye maist reverend father in God, Johne, archbischop of sanct Androus, legatnait, and primat of ye kirk of Scotland, in his provincial counsale, haldin at Edinburgh the xxvi day of Januarie, the zeir of our lord, 1551, with the advise and counsale of the bischoippis, and uthir prelatis, with doctours of Theologie and canon law of the said realme of Scotland, present for the tyme. Prentit at sanct Androus, by the command and expensis of the maist reverend father in God, Johne, archbischop of sanct Androus, and primate of the hail kirk of Scotland, the xxix day of August, the zeir of our lord, MDLII." It has 205 leaves numbered. 4°.

Mackenzie recites the same in Octavo.

" A FAYTHfull admonition made by John Knox, vnto the professours of Gods truthe in England wherby thou mayest lerne howe God wyll haue his Churche exercised with troubles, and how he defendeth it in the same. Esaie. ix. After all this shall not the Lordes wrath ceasse, but yet shall hys hande be stretched out styll. Ibidem. Take hede that the Lorde roote thee not out bothe heade and tayle in one daye." On the back begins " The Epistle of a banyshed manne out of Leycester shire, sometyme one of the Preachers of Godes worde there, to the Christen reader" &c. This on 7 pages: besides; J 3, in eights. Concludes, " Remember me deare brethren in your dayly prayers.—Yours with sorowfull herte, John Knox. Jmprynted at *Kalykow the 20. daye of Julij. 1554. Cum gratia & priuilegio—solum." W.H. Sixteens. 1554.

" In Dominicam Orationem pia meditatio, qua, in Deum animus fidelis, mirum in modum excitatur. Authore Patricio Cocburno, Scoto." &c. Device; Hercules and Centaurs, from a small coarse engraving. " Ex typographia Johannis SCOT. In Civitate Sancti Andreæ 15 Calendas Octobris. 1555. Cum Privilegio Regali." Dedicated " Mariæ, Regni Scotorum Regenti dignissimæ, Patricius Cocburnus, &c. —Ex academia tua Andreana, 15 Calendras Octobris. Anno Domini 1555.---In oratione pia, & fideli Observanda.---Oratio Dominica." Besides; LXXXI leaves. The signatures are noted on the first leaf only of each sheet. On the last page are the errata, under which " Excudebat Joannes *Scott, 1555." Mr. G. Payton, Edinburgh. Sixteens. 1555.

" Joannis Retorfortis commentarius in lib. Aristotelis de arte metrica. Edinburgi." See Mackenzie, Vol. III; p. 144. Quarto. (1557.)

About this time the Earl of Argile and other noblemen of Scotland, having (1558.)

* This book of Knox's must have been printed abroad, and not in Scotland, for he was not then in the kingdom, nor durst have printed it there at that time. This place Kalykow, seems to be fictitious. Mr. Ruddiman. See Mackenzie, III; 136; who asserts this to have been really printed at Geneva. But as Mr. Knox dates a letter the very same day to his Mother Mrs. Elis. Bowes at Deip, there can be scarce any doubt of that being the place meant by Kalykow. See his answer to Tyrie's Letter in 1572. See other pieces of his, printed 1556; and 1558. in our General History.

* This may very probably be the same John Scott, or Skot, who printed in London. See p. 317, &c.

having petitioned the Queen Regent for reformation of the Church without effect, procured the Book of Common Prayer to be read in those parishes where they had command: of which the Clergy, complaining to the queen to as little purpose, forthwith called a provincial council at Edinburgh; where, professing to make reformation of abuses, they renewed some old popish constitutions, which they caused to be printed and affixed upon the doors of all the parish churches. See Spotswood's Hist. of the Ch. of Scotland, p. 117. In this council perhaps it was that Sir David Lindsay's works were condemned to be burnt, as Pitscotie tells us. See Pinkerton's List of Scotish poets, p. cv.

1558. "Ane compendius Tractive conforme to the Scripturis of Almychtie God, Ressoun, and Authoritie, declaring the nerrest, and only way to establyche the Conscience of ane Christiane Man, in all Matters (quhilks ar in Debate) concerning Faith and Religioun, sett forth be Maister Quintin Kennedy, Commendator of the Abbay off Crosraguell, and dedicat to his deerest and best beluiffit Nepuo Gilbert, Meister of Cassillis. In the Zeir of God, Ane thousand fyve houndreth fifty aught Zeris." Without name of printer, or place. [f]Mackenzie, III; 62. Quarto.

—— "Ane Dialog betuix Experience and ane Courteour, off the Miserabyll Estait of the warld. ☞ Compylit be Schir Dauid Lyndesay of the mont Knycht Alias Lyone Kyng of Armes. And is Deuidit in Four partis As efter Followis. And Jmprentit at the Command and Expensis of Doctor Nacabeus. Jn Copmanhouin, (*Copenhagen*.) ☞ Attour thare is bukis imprentit in France, of twa sortis the quhilkis ar verray fals as it is knawin, & wantis mekle that this Buke hes for this is Juste and trew, and nane bot this Buke. be war with thame for thay well Dissaue zow. Absit gloriari, nisi in Cruce domini nostri Jesu Christi." On the back begins "The Epistil: To the Redare." Which is not in any other edition i have yet seen. N. B. At the end of the third book are J. and S.[g] In large capital letters. The 4th and last book ends on R 1, in eights. "Finis. Quod Lyndesay, 1552." See Mackenzie's Scotch Writers, III; p. 37, 39.

"Heir followis the Tragedie of the Vmquhyle maist Reuerend Father Dauid be the Mercy of God, Cardinall Archibyschope of Sanctandrous. &c. ☞ Compylit be Schir Dauid Lyndesay of the Mont, king of armes." This head title is over a rude cut of Hercules making a stroke at a centaur, used by John Scott in 1555; under which are the first two stanzas of "The Prolog." This poem is on 8 leaves, signature S. As therefore the former poem was compleated on R 1, and dated at the end, as above observed, i am inclined to believe this of the Cardinal was

[f] He inserts likewise in his catalogue of the same author's works, "De Publico Ecclesiæ Sacrificio." And "Contra errores Germanorum in Fidei capita quatuordecem defensa contra Georgium Sophocardium." (*Wyshart*.) These, says he, according to Dempster, were printed, but no mention where, when, &c. Ibid. p. 58.

[g] I know no one to whom these initials are more applicable than to John Scott, who printed at St. Andrews, about 1555; and also printed a more compleat edition of this author's poems there in 1568.

was printed soon after, and annexed to it; and afterwards, the following pieces, which begin with a fresh set of signatures A—G, in eights. "Here followis the Testament, and Complaynt of our Souerane Lordis Papungo. Kyng James the Fyrst. Quhilk lyith sore woundit, and may not dee. Tyll euery man haue hard quhat he sayis. Quharefor gentyll redairis haist zow that he wer out of paine. Compylit be Schir Dauid Lyndesay" &c. This title is over two birds, as in conversation. "Heir followis the Dreme of Schir Dauid Lyndesay of the mont Familiar Seruitour to our Souerane Lord Kyng James the Fyst. &c." Over the same cut as to the tragedy of the Cardinal. At the end is an "Exhortatioun to the Kyngis Grace." Lastly, "Heir beginnis the Complaynt of Schir Dauid Lindesay.—Finis. Quod Lindesay to King. ☞ Gentyll redaris, J wyll aduerteis zow that thare is of thir Bukis, Jmprentit in France, The quhilkis ar verray fals. And wantis the tane half, and all wrang spelit, and left out heir ane line, and thar twa wordis. To conclude thay ar all fals as may be sene, quha lytle luke thame baith ouer, thay sall fynd my sayingis verray trew and wors nor J do say, preue and se than ze wyll geue me credence. thay ar nocht worthe ane plake." Though the title-page announces this book to have been printed at Copmanhouin, supposed to mean Copenhagen, yet it is highly probable that it was privately printed by John Scott, in Scotland, sometime after 1552, and before 1566, when it was reprinted by T. Purfoot in London. However, to bring the time of printing nearer to a point, Mr. Pinkerton has an edition of The testament and complaint of king James the Fifth's Papingo; The dreme, addrest to James V; On the death of Queen Magdalen, 1537; to which he judiciously supposes The Monarchies preceded, and other of Lindsay's Poems to have followed, "imprintit, at the command and expensis of maister Sammuel Jascuy, In Paris, 1558." 4to, black letter. Whether printed there, or at Rowen as supposed, does not affect our present purpose, as it was apparently the French edition pointed at in the title and colophon of this edition, which therefore must doubtless have been printed after 1558, as against that time there appears no exception. On the other hand the place of printing this edition is evidently fictitious, of which circumstance it would probably have stood in no need if printed after 1560, when the reformation had got good footing in Scotland. The premises therefore considered, I have placed it here. See Pinkerton's List of Scotish poets, Vol. I; p. ciii; also Vol. II; p. 542." In Lambeth Library, and the late John Baynes, Esq. Quarto.

The discipline of the Church of Scotland as it was set forth, Anno 1560. 1560.
This first book of discipline, by an edition of both "The first and second booke of discipline," printed in 1621, appears to have been thus introduced: "To the great Councell of Scotland now admitted to the Regiment, by the providence of God, and by the common consent of the Estates thereof, your Honours humble servitors and ministers of Christ Jesus within the same, wish grace, &c. From your Honours we received a charge dated at Edinburgh the 29. of April,—1560. requiring and commanding us in the name of the eternall God, as we will answer in

his presence, to commit to writing, and in a book deliver to your wisedomes our judgements touching the reformation of Religion which heretofore in this Realme (as in others) hath been utterly corrupted: upon the receit whereof (so many of us as were in this towne) did convene, and in unitie of minde doe offer unto your wisedomes these subsequents for common order and uniformitie to bee observed in this realme concerning doctrine, administration of Sacraments, election of Ministers, provision for their sustentation, Ecclesiasticall discipline, and policie of the Church;" &c. At the end of the articles, which may be seen in Abp. Spotswood's History of the Ch. of Scotland, p. 152, &c. "From Edinburgh the 20 of Maij 1560."

1561. "The Confessione of the fayht and doctrin beleued and professed by Protestantes of the Realme of Scotland exhibited to the estates of the sam in parliament and by thare publict votes authorised as a doctrin grounded vpon the infallable wourd of God. Matth. 24. And this glaid tydinges of the kingdom shalbe preached throught the hole world for a witness to all nations and then shall the end cum. Jmprinted at Edinburgh, be Robert Lekprewik. Cum priuilegio, 1561." Thus inscribed, "The estates of scotland with the inhabitantes of the same professing Christ Jesus and his holy euangell. To their naturall cuntre men, and to all others realmes and nations, professing the same Christ Jesus with them, wyshe grace mercy & peace from God the father, of our lord Jesus Christ with the spirite of righteous iudgement for, Saluation." 24 leaves, including the title. On the last leaf, "From Edinburghe, 17. Augusti, 1560. These actes and articles ar red in the face of Parliament, and ratified by the thre estatis." W.H. See p. 801. 16°.

1561. "Robert [a]Nornel Scot, man of Armes, his Mirrour of ane Christian. Printed at Edenburge by Rob. Lepreuicke. 1561." Maunsell, p. 71. 4°.

1562. "Ane answer made the [b]4th Day of Septembre, 1561, by maister Theod. de Beeza, minister of the holy Euangile, in the presence of the quene mother, the king, and quene of Navarre, &c. to the cardinal of Lorraine, in the name of the reformed churches, &c. Imprinted at Edinburgh by Robert Lekprevik.—Cum privilegio." Octavo.

(1562.) "An Exhortation to the maist excellent and gracious Sovereign, Mary Queen of Scottis, &c. To the Bishopis and utheris Pastors, and to all them of the Nobility within this her Graces Realme, for unfenzie Reformation of Doctrine and Maneris; and for obtaining of Licence, to propone in Writ to the Prichouris, certain Articulis twiching Doctrine, Ordour and Maneris, approven by them, and presented to her maist excellent Majesty, February 15th, 1562." By Ninian Winzet. See Mackenzie, Vol. III; p. 156. Octavo.

Not long after this the said Winzet, in the name of the clergy, gave in writing several challenges to John Knox, and particularly to answer for assuming to himself the office of priesthood: Mr. Knox from the pulpit

[a] Probably Norvel, or Norval. Pinkerton's List of Scotish poets, p. cxx.

[b] Rather the 14th. See Hist. of Reform. in France, Vol. I; p. 547.

pulpit exposed him as the main agent for the papists, and gave no other answer to his main question, but that he had an extraordinary call from heaven. Mr. Winzet—immediately committed to the press a treatise concerning the priesthood, which Mr. Knox being informed of, he caused seize upon the [a] printer and all the copies, and pursued the author so hotly, that he was obliged to take the occasion of a ship that was bound for Flanders, where he safely arrived, and stayed for some time at the university of Louvain, and in 1563, he caused print " The Buke of Fourscoir Three Questions, tuching Doctrine, Ordour, and Maneris," &c. Of which notice will be taken in our Gen. Hist. See Mackenzie, III, 148.

" The Confutation of the Abbote of Crosraguels Masse, set furth by Maister George Hay. Math. 15. All plantation that is not planted by my heauenly Father, shalbe rooted out: leaue them for they be blinde guides to the blinde. Cypriane. Lib. 3. Epist. 2. If in the Sacrifice which is Christe, onely Christe is to be followed, &c. Jmprinted at Edinburgh by Robert Lekpreuik, and are to be fauld at his hous at the nether Bow. Cum priuilegio 1563." On the back of the title-page is an epistle by " The Prenter to the Reader," acquainting him how hard it was for him to obtain the copy from the author, "a man shamefast of his owen nature." Likewise apologizing for his want of Greek characters, which he was forced to have supplied by manuscript, that in case of any error the author might not suffer in his reputation. So late was it before the Greek types were introduced at Edinburgh. Dated, " At our buith, the penult of July, 1563.—The Epistle dedicatorie. To the most Noble, potent, and godly Lorde James, Earle of Murray, the Author wisheth grace, mercy, peace, and increase of heauenly giftes of the Spirit of God.—At Edinburgh, the penult day of July. 1563. Your Lordshipes moste humble and obedient Seruiture, George Hay.--- To the Reader.—At Edinburgh, the 15. of Julie. 1562.---Heir followeth the Confutation—made by maister George Haye." Containing 96 leaves, including the preface to the reader, which begins on fol. 1, a. Colophon, " Jmprinted" &c. as on the title-page. On the last leaf, only 1563.

" Jte, Missa est:
Ire licet: missa hinc quo debuit ire remissa est:
Nempe ad tartareum trans phlegetonta Patrem."

Over a rude wood-cut of an angel with expanded wings holding a burning lamp in the right hand, and a square in the left. W.H. Quarto.

Collier tells us that " at a General Assembly held at Edinborough, Decemb. 25. 1564 'tis ordain'd That every Minister, Exhorter, and Reader, should have one of the Psalm-Books[b] lately printed at Edinborough, and to use the Order therein contain'd, in Prayers, Marriage, and Administration of the Sacrament." Eccl. Hist. of Great Britain, Vol. II, p. 562. (1564.)

 " The

[a] John Scot, who was imprisoned and fined.

[b] These Psalm-books were in Sternhold's metre, with the Genevan translation in the margin; and generally annexed to their service-book or Directory, in like manner as to the English common prayer books.

1565. "The Forme of prayers, &c. used in the English Church at Geneva, approved and received by the Church of Scotland. Edinburgh—by Robert Lekprevik. 1565." MS. T. Baker.

1565. "Ane brief gathering of the halie signes, sacrifices, and sacramentis. Edinburgh." See p. 804. Quarto.

1565. "Allegations against the surmised title of the queen of Scots, and the favourers of the same." See the editor's preface to The defence of Q. Mary's honour, in Anderson's Collections, Vol. I; p. ii. Quarto.

1565. *"The Actis and Constitutionis of Parliament maid be the rycht excellent princes Marie quene of Scottis." This title is over the arms of Scotland, under an open helmet crowned; the crest, a demi-lion crowned, holding in its right paw a sword, and in its left a sceptre: the arms are encompassed with a collar of the order of the Thistle, and supported by unicorns collared with ducal coronets and chained: the motto, IN DEFENS, is on a scroll, or ribbon, extended over the crest by 2 lances pennanted, one with the arms, the other with the standard of Scotland. On 2 scrolls over the heads of the supporters, MARIA—REGINA. These arms are about 8½ by 7½ inches. The block is the same as was used to "The new Actis" &c. 1541, and to the "croniklis of Scotland, p. 1474, with this difference only, that they have JACOBVS—REX, 5. in the places where this has Maria—Regina. The head title, "The Actis of the last parliament haldin in Edinburgh in the zeir of God ane thousand fyue hundreth thre score thre zeiris." These are 25 in number, with a table at the end; under which, "Thir ar the trew *copyis of the Actis of Parliament, maid be our Souerane Lady: Quene of Scottis. Extractit furth of the buikis of Parliament, at command of our Souerane Lady, be me Maister James Makgill of Rankelour nether, clerk of our said Souerane Ladyis Registre, Counsall and Rollis, vnder my Signe and subscriptioun manual. JACOBUS MAKGILL. Imprintit at Edinburgh, be Robert Lekpreuik. 1565." Black letter. W.H. Folio.

1566. "The ordour and doctrine of the general faste, appointed be the general assemblie of the kirkes of Scotland, halden at Edinburgh, the 25 day of December, 1565. Edinburgh—*R. Leprevik." Sixteens.

1566. "A sermon *preached by John Knox, minister of Christ Jesus, in the publique audience of the church of Edenbrough, within the realme of Scotland, vpon Sonday the 19 of August, 1565. For the which the said John Knoxe was inhibite preaching for *a season. 1 Tim. iv. The time is come, that men cannot abyde the sermon of veritie, nor holsome doctrine. To this is adioyned, an exortation vnto all the faithfull within the sayde realme, for the releife of such, as faythfully trauayle in the preaching of Gods word. Written by the same John Knoxe, at the commandment

* Chap. 5. 17. 23 and 25 of this edition are not printed in Skene's collection, 1597.

* Mr. T. Baker has added to this article in his interleaved copy of Maunsell, p. 49. "be H. Charteris, 1596." But that might probably be an Order for another day of public humiliation, mentioned by archbishop Spotswood in his Hist. of the Ch. of Scotland, p. 418.

* Reprinted at the end of his Hist. of the Reform. of religion in—Scotland. The text, Isaiah 26; 13—16, &c.

* Abp. Spotswood says he was inhibited preaching by the Council, and silenced for some months. Mackenzie,—for 15 or 20 days.

commandment of the ministrie aforesaid." 49 leaves, and 11 more, "Of the superintendents to the faithfull." No name of place, nor printer.* Sixteens.

"The Actis and Constitutiouns of the Realme of Scotland, maid in Parliamentis, haldin be the rycht excellent, hie and mychtie Princeis, Kingis James the first, Secund, third, Feird, Fyft, and in the tyme of Marie now Quene of Scottis, viseit, correctit, and extractit furth of the Registers be the Lordis depute be hir Maiesties special commissioun thairto. Anno Do. 1566."—This title is over the arms of Scotland, as p. 1474, but on one side "Maria," on the other "Regina." On the back, "The Quenis Grace Privilege Grantit for Imprenting of hir Maiesteis Lawis and actis of Parliamentis.—At Edinburgh the First day of Junii, the zeir of God ane thousand fyue hundreth thre scoir sax zeiris, and of our Regne the twentie four zeir." On the next leaf begins the queen's commission "for viseing, correcting and Imprenting of the Lawis, &c.—In witnes of the quhilk thing we haue causit our greit Seil be put to thir presentis, At Edinburgh the First day of Maij the zeir" &c. as to the privilege.—"The preface. Signed, "Ed. Henrison.—The tabill of the actis." At the end of the acts made in Q. Mary's reign, "Thir. xxv. actis next precedant war in the zeir of God, ane thousand fyue hundreth lxv zeris, extractit furth of the buickis of parliament, at command of our Souerane Lady, be Maister James Makgill, of Rankelour, nether Clerk of our Souerane Ladyis Registre, counsall and Rollit, vndir his signe and subscriptioun manuall. Jacobus Makgill." Afterwards is added on the last leaf, "Parliamentum excellentissimæ principis Mariæ reginæ Scottorum tentum apud Edinburgh. xxv. die Mensis Decembris An. Do. Millesimo Quingentesimo Sexagesimo Quarto, Præsentibus tribus Regni statibus. Anent the confirmatioun of fewis. Ca. i.—Extractit furth of the bukis of Parliament at command of our Soueranis Lord and Lady be me Schir James Balfoure of Pettinbreich Knycht, Clerk of their hienes Register, counsall and Rollis, vnder the Signe and Subscriptioun manuall. Signed, Jacobus Balfour." On the last page, "Heir endis the actis and Constitutiounis of the Realme of Scotland maid in Parliamentis haldin be the rycht excellent, hie, and mychtie Princis Kingis James the First, secund, Thrid, Feird, Fyft, and in the tyme of Marie now Quene of Scottis, viseit, and correctit be the Lordis depute be speciall Commissioun thairto and extractit furth of the Registers be the Clerkis of *our* Soueranis Register respectiue.. Cum priuilegio ad Decennium. Imprintit at Edinburgh be Robert Lekpreuik, the. xij. day of October the zeir of God ane thousand fyue hundreth thre scoir sax zeiris." Contains Z z. i, or Fol. Clxxxi, besides the prefixes. Folio. 1566.

"The Irish Liturgy for the Highlands of Scotland, composed by Mr. John Kerswell, or Carswell, bishop of the Isles by presentation of Q. Mary in 1566, and afterwards bishop of Argyle, was printed in the year 1566, and dedicated to the Earl of Argyle. In it is the form of prayer used by many of the Islanders at sea, after the sails are hoisted, of which a copy from the original 1566.

original may be seen in Martin's Description of the Western Isles of Scotland, p. 127, &c.[a]

1567. "Ane declaratioun of the Lordis iust quarrell." Contained in 34 seven-line stanzas. "Imprentit at Edinburgh be Robert Lekpreuik. Anno Do. 1567." Collection of Ancient Ballads, late Major Pierson's. A broadside.

1567. The form of Divine Service, commonly called Knox's Liturgy. The compiler of this Liturgy, and the time of its publick approbation is mentioned at the end in these words: "This book is thought necessary and profitable for the Church, and commanded to be printed by the general Assembly. Set furth by John Knox Minister: And sighted by us, whose Names follow, as we are appointed by the said general Assembly, 1567. John Willok. Mr. John Craig. Robert Pont. John Row. David Lindesay. Gulielmus Christisonus. James Craig, &c." Collier's Eccl. Hist. Vol. II; p. 561, 562.

—— An exact draft of the Sea-coast of Scotland, was done by Humphry Lhuyd, as appears by his letter to Abraham Ortelius, dated the 5th of April 1568. But this map we have not seen, nor any engraved work in Scotland till 1576, if that of the famous folio Bible is so, and was done there.

1568. "The warkis of the famous and vorthie knicht, schir David Lyndesay, of the mont, alias, Lyoun king of armes. Newly correctit, and vindicate from the former errouris quhair, with thay war befoir corruptit, and augmentit with sindrie warkis, quhilk was not befoir imprentit. The contentis of the buke, and quhat warkis ar augmentit, the nixt syde sall schaw. The contentis of this buke following: Ane dialogi betwix father experience, and ane courteour, of the miserabill estait of the world: deuydit in four bukis, or in four monarcheis. The testament and complaynt of our souerane lordis Papingo, king James the fyft. The dreme direct of our said souerane lord, quhairin ar contenit: The diuisioun of the eirth, The descriptioun of paradice, The descriptioun of the realme of Scotland, And the complaint of the commoun weil of Scotland. Ane exhortation to the kingis grace. The complaint vnto the kingis grace, omittit in the imprentingis of Rowen and Londoun. The Tragedie of Dauid Betoun, cardinall, and archebischop of sanct Androis. The deploratioun of the deith of quene Magdelene. Ane answer to the kingis flyting, neuer before imprintit. The complaynt and confessioun of Bagsche, ye kingis auld hound, direct to Bawtie and his companzeonis. Ane supplicatioun to the kingis grace, in contemptioun of syde taillis, and missellit facis. Kitteis confessioun. The iusting betuix James Watsone, and Johne Barbour, familiar seruitouris to king James the fyft. Newlie imprentit by Johne Scot, at the expensis of Henrie Charteris: and are to be sauld in his buith, on the north syde of the gait, aboue the throne. Cum priuilegio regali." This is the first compleat edition of Sir David Lindsay's poems. Quarto.

"Ane

[a] Mr. Toland in a copy of this book notes "Martin has set this form of prayer down very incorrectly, for though he understood Irish he could not write it; but in this place he is unpardonable, because there only needed careful transcribing."

" Ane breue descriptioun of the pest, quhairn the causis, signis, and 1568.
sum speciall preseruatioun, and cure thairof ar contenit. Set furth be maister Gilbert Skeyne, doctoure in medicine. Edinburgh, printed by Robert Lekpreuik." Octavo.

" The actis of [q]parliament of the maist hie, maist excellent, and michtie 1568.
prince, and our souerane lord, James the sext, be the grace of God king of Scottis, begun and halden at Edinburgh, the xv day of December, the zeir of God, ane thousand syue hundreth LXVII zeir, be our said souerane lordis derrest cousin and uncle, James of Murray, lord Abirnethie regent to our souerane lord his realme and leigis; togeddir with the prelatis, erlis, barronis, commissioneris of burrowis, specialie comperand in the said parliament, as the thre estatis of this realme. The said actis being oppinlie red, concludid, and votit in the said parliament, to remane as perpetual lawis to the subiectis of this realme in all tymes cuming." Then the Scotch arms. At the end, " Imprintit at Edinburgh be Robert Lekpreuik, prentar to the kingis maiestie, the vi day of April, the zeir of God, ane thousand syue hundreth thre scoir aucht zeiris." Again by John Ross, 1575. Folio.

" The copie of a letter, written by one in London to his frend, con- (1568.)
cernyng the credit of the late published detection of the doynges of the ladie Marie of Scotland." In 8 leaves. At the end of this letter is published the Scottish Act of Parliament for the restraint of the queen of Scots while she was in Scotland, from the copy of that act, printed as above. See Oldys's Catal. of Harleian pamphlets, No. 42. Reprinted verbatim in Anderson's Collections, Vol. 2; p. 261, &c. Sixteens.

Session third. In the general Assembly, anno 1568, Edinburgh. It (1568.)
was debated and found, that Thomas Bassindane, printer in Edinburgh, imprinted a buke intituled: The fall of the Romains Kirk, naming our King and soveraigne Supreame Head of the Primitive Kirk: and a Psalme buik, in the end whereof was found printed ane lewd song called, Welcome Fortunes. Ordanit that printer to call in all those books, and to sell no more of them till such time as he change the title of the one, and expunge the lewd sung out of the other: and that in time coming he print not without the licence of the supreme magistrate, and their *(the assembly)* revising such books as he shall print concerning religion, and that particularly the book concerning the Fall of the Church of Rome should be revised by Mr. Alex. Arbuthnet. See Mackenzie, III; 187.

" Ane [r]proclamation anent the tressonable conspiratouris, and tru- 1568.
blaris

[q] In this parliament was an act for " the annulling of the Actes of Parliament made against God his word, and maintenance of Idolatrie in ony times bypast." Wherein is inserted " The confession of the faith and doctrine beleeved and professed be the protestantes of Scotland, exhibited to the Estatis of the same in Parliament, and be their publick votis authorized, as a doctrine grounded vpon the infallible word of God." It consists of 26 articles, with scripture-proofs in the margin. At the end, " Thir Actis and Arrickles ar red in the face of Parliament & ratifyit be the thre Estatis, At Edinburgh the 17. day August, the zeir of God, 1560. zeiris." John Ross's Edit. 1557.

[r] This is the first proclamation we have yet met with published originally and authentically in print. Tho. Davidson had been appointed king's printer to James V. and had his licence to print the acts of parliament

blaris of the tranquillitie of the commoun welth, now laitlie aganis the kingis grace authoritie. Geuin vnder our signet, &c. At Glasgow, vii Maii.—Robert Lekpreuik, prentar to the kingis maiestie." Broadside.

1568. " An answer to a letter written by James Tyre, a Jesuit. Edinburgh, 1568." Mackenzie's Writers, III; p. 137. See it in 1572. Octavo.

1569. " The order of excommunication and public repentance, vsed in the church of Scotland, and commanded to be printed by the general assembly of the same in the mounth of June., Edinburgh, printed by Lekpreuik." Octavo.

1570. A proclamation against the rebels. Same printer. Three sides. Folio.

1570. " The cruikit liedis the blinde." A poem. Lekpreuik. Broadside.

1570. " Maddies Lamentation." A poem. Lekpreuik. Broadside.

1570. " The deploratioun of the cruel murther of James, erle of Murray, umquhile regent of Scotland: togidder with ane admonitioun to the Hammiltounis committaris thairof, and to all thair fortifiaris, mantenaris, or assistance: with ane exhortatioun to the lordis and nobilitie, keiparis and defendaris of our kingis grace maiestie." In 28 eight-line stanzas. " Lekpreuik." Broadside.

1570. " The regentis tragedie, ending with ane exhortatioun." In 17 nine-line stanzas. And " The tragedies Lenuoy," containing 6 eight-line stanzas. " Finis quod Robert Sempill." Broadside.

1570. " The exhortatioun to all plesand thingis, quhairin man can haif delyte, to withdraw thair plesure from mankynde, and to deploir the cruell morther of vmquhile my lord regentis grace." In 19 eight-line stanzas " Lekpreuik." Broadside.

1570. " The poysonit schot." In 20 eight-line, and " Lenuoy," in 4 shorter eight-line stanzas. Broadside.

1570. " The admonitioun to the lordis." In 14 eight-line stanzas. Broadside.

1570. " The spur to the lordis." In 14 eight-line stanzas. No Printer's name, but a better letter. Most of these Broadsides were in the possession of the late Martin Folkes, Esq.

1570. " The Actis and Deidis of the illuster and vailyeand Campioun Schir William Wallace, knicht of Ellerslie." This is the head, or second title. A fine copy of this book is in the Brit. Museum, except its wanting the title page. Colophon, " Imprentit at Edinburgh, be Robert Lekpreuik, at the expensis of Henrie Charteris; and ar to be sauld in his buith, on the north syde of the gait aboue the throne. Anno Do. M.D.LXX." See Pinkerton's Scotish poets, p. xci. Quarto.

" Tilnei

liament made in that reign; and though he did not stile himself printer to his majesty to them, yet he did so to the cronicles of Scotland printed the same year; but we have not found any proclamation printed by him, or any other, during the short remainder of that reign, or the whole of Q. Mary's; for though we have some copies of her proclamations handed down to us, we have no intimation of their having been printed at their first proclamation; neither indeed does there appear to have been any particular printer appointed for the State till after she had resigned the crown to her son James VI.

* It does not appear that this command for printing passed in the Gen. Assembly before June 1571. See the form of prayers &c. in 1584. The same is affirmed in an edition 1601.

"Tilnei Paraenesis ad Scotos, Geneuensis disciplinae zelotas." Printed at St. Andrews. Octavo. 1570.

"The confessioun of M. John Kelle, minister of Spott. Lekprevik." Sixteens. 1570.

"Ane tragedie in forme of ane diallog betwix honour, gude fame, and the authour heirof in ane trance.—Edinburgh. Lekpreuik." Octavo. 1570.

About the year 1570, some popish fugitives in Scotland, not content with having printed there several seditious books, sent one of them entitled "A Detection of certain practices," &c. with a letter addressed to their loving friends, Sir Thomas Littleton, and Sir Thomas Russel, the Queen's Lieutenants in the county of Worcester. From the close of which letter it appears that letters of the same sort had been dispatched to every county in England. See Biogr. Brit. I; p. 366, note F. Edit. 1747. (1570.)

"Ane admonitioun direct to the trew lordis maintenaris of iustice, and obedience to the kingis grace. M. G. B. (*Mr. George Buchanan*) Imprintit at Striuiling be Robert Lekpreuik." 16 leaves. See p. 642. Reprinted in the Harl. Miscel. Vol. III; p. 395. See Oldys's Collection of the pamphlets, No. 43. Octavo. 1571.

"To his louing brethren, whome God ones gathered in the church of Edinburgh, and now are dispersed for tryal of our faith, &c. Johne Knox. Printed at Striuiling be Robert Lekpreuik." Octavo. 1571.

Volusenus (*Wilson*) de tranquillitate animi dialogus. Edinb. Octavo. 1571.

The order of Excommunication &c. as in 1569. 1571.

"The warkis of the famous and vorthie knight Schir David Lyndesay of the mont, &c. Edinb. MDLXXI." Bibl. Tanneri; p. 495. Quarto. 1571.

"The bischoppis lyfe and testament." In 27 eight-line stanzas. And ends, "quod Sempill. Striuiling be Robert Lekpreuik." 4 leaves. Folio. 1571.

"The copie of the proclamatioun, set furth be the kingis maiestie and his counsall, for ane conuentioun of the professouris of the trew religioun within this realme, to consult and deliberate vpon the imminent dangeris and conspiraces of the papistis. Ane aduertisment to the faithfull. Ane breif extract of the articklis of the secreit contract betuix the pape, the empriour, the kingis of Hispanze, and Portugal, the dukis of Bauar, &c. Lekpreuik, sanct Androis." Broadside. 1572.

"De Maria Scotorum regina, totaque eius contra Regem coniuratione, fœdo cum Bothuelio adulterio," &c. as in our General History. —

"Histoire de Marie royne d'Escosse touchant la coniuratioun faicte contre le Roy, & l'adultere commis auec le comte de Bothwel, histoire vrayement tragique, traduicte de Latin en François, par Thomas Waltem." The Colophon, "Acheué d'imprimer à Edimbourg, ville capitalle d'Escosse, le 13 de Feurier, 1572. par moy Thomas Vvaltem." Yet after all the printer's name is fictitious, and the book was actually printed in London. Mr. Ruddiman. Sixteens. 1572.

"L'Innocence de la tresillustre, tres-chaste, & debonnaire Princesse, Madame Marie Reyne d'Escosse, contre les Calomnies publiée en France. 1572.

imprimé l'An. 1572." A translation of The treatise of Treasons against Q. Elizabeth, &c. Bodleian. Octavo.

1572. Ane Detectioun of the doingis of Marie Quene of Scottis twiching the Murther of hir Husband: And hir Conspiracie, Adulterie, and pretensit Mariage with the Erle Bothwell. And the Defence of the now Lordis Mantenaris of the Kingis Grace, Actioun and Authoritie. Translatit out of Latine, quhilk was written be M. G. B. Imprntit at Sanctandrois be [1]Robert Leckpreuik, An. Dom. MDLXXII." This is reprinted verbatim in Anderson's Collections, Vol. II; with a very instructive preface by the editor. Among other things, he gives a list of the several editions of the Detection that had occurred to him; of which this was the first, and thought to have been translated by Buchanan himself, from his own Latin copy, in the old Scottish dialect. About the same time, says he, it was printed in Latin, but the Latin is not so full as the Scots translation. Then also was printed the old [2]English translation, in the black letter also; but neither it nor the Latin copy bear place, date, nor printer's name, and are thought to have been done at London by John Day, soon after the edition at St. Andrews. 8°.

1572. "An Answer to a letter of a Iesuit named Tyrie, be Iohne Knox. Prov. xxvi. (4, 5.) Answer not a foole according to his foolishnes least thow be lyke him: answer a foole according to his foolishnes least he be wise in his owne cōseat. The contrarietie appearing at the first sight betuix thir twa sentēcis, stayit for a tyme, baith heart to meditate & hand to wryte any thing, cōtrair that blasphearnous letter. But when with better mynd, God gaue me to considder, that whoso euer opponis not him self bouldly to blasphemy & manifest leis, differis lytill fra tratouris: cloking and fostering, so far as in them ly, the treasoun of tratours, &c. To quyet therefore my owne conscience, I put hand to the pen as followeth. Imprentit at Sanctandrois be Robert Lekpreuik. Anno. Do. 1572." This answer is introduced by an address thus superscribed, "Iohne Knox The seruand of Iesus Christ, now wearie of the world, and daylie luiking for the resolution of this my earthly Tabernakle, to the faithfull, that God of his mercy sall appoint to feght after me," &c. Wherein we are told "There ar seuin yeares past, sen a scrole, send frō a Iesuite to his brother, was presented vnto me be a faithfull brother, requyring sum answer to be maid to the same: whais iust petitioun, I willing to obey, I pat my hād to the pen, althogh I fand small tyme of quyetnes: for it was immediatly efter that I was called back from

[1] He was brought from Edinburgh to St. Andrews to print for the Reformers; was under the direction and influence of the learned Mr. Andrew Melvell, and his nephew Mr. James Melvell: this latter was minister of Anstrother, and assisted in relieving the distressed situation of the famished crew of one of the Spanish armada, who for want of provisions, and being ignorant of the coast, were driven in there. He afterward printed at Striveling, or Stirling.

[2] Some of the Scotch words are indeed changed into English, but yet a great part is really Scotch, and not the English of that time. Both It and the Latin, were omitted under John Day, but will be inserted in our General History, under 1571.

from exyle, be the Kirk of Edinburgh after Davids Judgement. Amongs my other caires, I scriblit that which followis, and that in few dayis: which being finished, I repented of my laubour, and purposed fullie to haue suppressed it. Which na dout I had done, if the Devil had not steirit vp the Iesuites of purpois to trouble godlie harts, with the same argumentis which Tyrie vsis: — for suppresing of the fre progres of the Euangell of Iesus Christ, &c.—I haue added vnto this preface, a meditatioun or prayer thrawin furth my sorrowful heart & pronounced by my half dead toung, befoir I was compelled to leaue my flocke of Edinburgh, who now ar dispersed, &c.—The Prayer.—Iohne Knox with deliberat mynd to his God.—At Edinburgh the 12. of Marche. 1565." Then follows "An Answer to a Letter" &c. thus introduced, "Of leat dayis there came to our hands a Letter direct, vnto yow, right worshipfull, from Iames Tyrie, who styleth him self your hūble seruitour & brother:— Our answeres must exceid ẏ measure of a missiue: & yet, we sall auoide sa far as we can, all vnprofitabil prolixitie. But leist that any suld thinke, that we depraue, either his dytement, or argumētis, we shal insert his hole letter, from parcel, to parcell: and giue answer," &c. Tyrie's letter is dated "Paris the vj. of December:" the answer, which is concluded on E 6, "Of Edinburgh the 10. day of August Anno Do. 1568." Hereunto is annexed a letter "To his louing mother Maistres Elizabeth Bowes, troubled in spirite, &c. as it past from *his* hand at Deip the *20 of Julij. 1554." The same is prefaced by another "To the faithfull reader," concluding with "I hartly salute & take my goodnight, of all the faithfull in bothe the Realmes: earnestly desyring ẏ assistance of their prayers, that without any notable sclander to the Euangell of Iesus Christ I may end my battell. For as the worlde is wearie of me: so am I of it. Of Sanctandrois the 12. †of Julij. 1572. Iohne Knox." The whole F 5, in eights, including the title-page. Roman letter. W.H. 8°.

"Orationes De origine & dignitate Juris." By Alex. Arbuthnot. 1572.
"Edinburgh, 1572." Mackenzie, III, p. 194. Quarto.

"The taill of Rauf Coilzear, how he harbreit king Charles. Printed 1572.
at sanct Androis be R. Lekpreuik." Sixteens.

Knox's sermons at Leith before the regent. And other of his tracts 1572.
the same year. Printed at sanct Androis. Octavo.

"The lamentation of lady Scotland, compylit be hirself, speiking in 1572.
maner of an epistle in the moneth of Marche, the zeir of God, 1572.
Printed at sanct Androis by Lekpreuik." Sixteens.

"My lord Methwenis tragedie." In 24 nine-line stanzas. "Finis, 1572.
with the dytone. Quod Sempill." Then 4 lines. "Sanct Androis.
Lekpreuik." Folio.

"The lamentation of the commounis of Scotland." In 16 eight-line 1572.
stanzas. "Sanct Androis. Lekpreuik." Broadside.

 "Ane

* N.B. This is the very day on which he dates his "Faythfull admonitioun—Imprinted at Kalykow:" generally allowed to be a fictitious place; but hereby we have a clew to the real one. See p. 1483, note d.

† He died 27 Nov. following.

1572. "Ane premonitioun to the barnis of Leith." In 38 six-line stanzas. "Imprentit at sanct Androis by Robert Lekpreuik." Folio.

1573. "The exhortatioun to the lordis." In 22 eight-line stanzas. "Striuiling."

1573. "The Sege of the castel of Edinburgh. Jmprintit at Edinburgh be Robert Lekpreuik, Anno M.D.LXXIII." The description of the siege in 34 eight-line stanzas; "The Lenuoy to the Regent" in 5 nine-line stanzas; "Lanuoy to the Ambassade," in 7 like stanzas. Finis Quod †Sempill." In the British Museum. Quarto.

1573. "A trew copie of the mutuall band betuix the castell and toun of Edinburgh, contractit in the obedience of the kingis maiestie, our souerane lord: publischit, that all men may the better persaue how the laird of Grange, againis his faith, honour, and promeis, is, and hes bene, the instrument and occasioun of the present unquyetnes, and by past vastatioun of the toun, to the suppressing of the exercise of Goddis trew religioun, the hinderance of iustice and policie, and calamitie of the haill commoun wealth.—Edinburgh, Lekpreuik." Folio.

1573. "De furoribus Gallicis, horrenda & indigna Admirali; Castilionei, Nobilium atq; illustrium virorum caede scelerata, ac inaudita piorum strage, passim edita per complures Galliae civitates, *&c.* Vera & simplex Narratio, ab Ernesto Varamundo *Frisio Auctore. Edinburgi. Anno salutis humanae, 1573." In fact the book was not printed in Scotland, but probably in London.* Mr. Ruddiman. Contains CCXII pages. Brit. Museum. Quarto.

1573. "A true and plaine report of the furious outrages of Fraunce, and the horrible and shameful slaughter of Castillion the Admirall, and diuers other Noble and excellent men, and of the wicked and straunge murther of godlie persons, committed in many Cities of Fraunce, without any respect of sorte, kinde, age, or degree. By Ernest Varamund, of Freseland.—At Striveling, 1573." It is prefaced by the translator with an epistle "To the reader," giving his reason for publishing this book printed in Scotland in the English phrase and orthography. The body of the book is neatly printed in Roman and Italic characters, and is paged in the middle of the top to CXLIII. It has been supposed to be printed at London; but see the notes to the foregoing article. Harl. Misc. VII, p. 317. W.H. Octavo.

1573. "The kingis maiesties proclamatioun, beiring the verie occasioun of the present incumming of the Inglis forces, with his hienes commandement for their gude intreatment and freindly vsage. Imprintit at Edinburgh be Thomas Bassandyne. Cum privilegio regis, 13 April." Broadside.

"The

† Sempil died in 1595. Dempster. See Pinkerton's List of Scottish poets, p. cxcj.

* It has been thought this name, as the author, is fictitious, and that it was composed by Theod. Beza, as some; or Hubert Languet, as others have reported. See Oldys's Catal. of Harl. pamphlets, No. 176.

* That it was printed in London, see p. 972-3; but why not printed in Scotland also, as that kingdom was neither under Papistical nor French influence at that time!

"The warkis of the famous and worthie Knight Schir David Lyndesay of the Mont: Alias, Lyoun King of Armes. Newly correctit and vindicate from the former Errours quhairwith thay war befoir corruptit: And augmentit with sindry warkis quhilk was not befoir imprentit. ¶ The Contentis of the Buik and quhat warkis ar augmentit the nixt syde sall schaw. Viuet etiam post funera virtus. Iob vii. Militia est vita hominis super terram." Device, an anchor supported by two hands, a serpent twisted up the shank, and over the stock, like Binneman's. "Imprintit at Edinburgh be Thomas Bassandyne, dwelland at the nether Bow. M.D.LXXIJJJ. Cum Priuilegio Regis." After the contents, "Ane Adhortation of all Estatis to the reiding of thir present warkis;" in 11 octave stanzas. Then, "The Epistil Nuncupatorie of Schir Dauid Lyndesay of the Mount Knicht, on his Dialog of the miserabill Estat of the warld;" in 13 nine-line stanzas. This is omitted in the subsequent editions. 362 pages. See p. 1490. Mr. Barnarde, Hatton-street. Quarto. 1574.

"Dialogi ab Eusebio Philadelpho Cosmopolita in Gallorum et caeterarum nationum gratiam compositi, quorum primus ab ipso auctore recognitus & auctus: alter verò in lucem nunc primum editus fuit. Edinburgi ex Typographia Iacobi Iamæi. 1574." There are prefixed "Typographus lectori S.---Ordinibus, Principibus, Proceribus, Baronibus, Nobilibus, ac populo Poloniæ Eusebius,—salutem—exoptat.---Exemplar epistolæ cuiusdam nobilis ad Ducem Guisium—Rhemis. Calend. Ian. 1574.---In effigiem pacis Valesiæ Dialogismus." In hexameters. The interlocutors, Polonus and Pax Valesia subscribed, "D.S.P.R.I.A.A C.H.C.L.M.E."---Ten distichs "In Carolum IX Regem Franciæ.---Argumentum prioris dialogi." In which the interlocutors are Alethia, Philalethes, Historiographus, Politicus, and Daniel. This first dialogue, exclusive of the prefixes, contains 110 pages; at the end thereof are eleven distichs, "In Regiam perfidiam;" and seven others "In Reginam Matrem." The second dialogue has a separate title-page, having on the back thereof "Argumentum secundi Dialogi." In this there are only two disputants, Politicus and Historiographus. Contains 136 pages, including the title-page, Roman letter. W.H. The signatures are in fours, half-sheets, forming an uncommon size for the time, being that of a modern Octavo. 1574.

"Le Reveille-matin des François & de leur voissins. Composé par Eusebe Philadelphe Cosmopolite, en forme de dialogues. A Edimbourg de l'imprimerie de Jaques James, avec permission." One of these is translated from the other, but neither of them really printed at Edinburgh. Ruddiman. Octavo. 1574.

"The catechisme in two partes; the first in Scotch poetry, having a kalender before it. The second part in Latin and Scotis prose, entituled, Catechismus ecclesiae Genuensis, hoc est, formula erudiendi pueros in doctrina Christi. Authore Johanne Calvino. Ubi colloquuntur praeceptor, et discipulus, vel minister, et puer. ¶ The catechisme, or maner to teiche children the christiane religioun. Wherein the minister demandeth 1574.

mandeth the questioun, and the chylde maketh answer; made by the excellent doctour, and pastour in Christis Kirk, Johne Calvin. The first question is, Quhat is the principal and cheif end of mannis Lyfe? The chyld: To knaw God. Edinburgh. Imprinted by John Ross, for Henrie Charteris." Sixteens.

1575. "The Actis of the Parliament of the maist hie maist Excellent, and Michtie Prince, and our Souerane Lord James the sext, be the grace of God King of Scottis, begune and haldin at Edinburgh, the xv. day of december. The zeir of God ane thousand fiue hundreth lxvij. zeiris. Be our said Souerane Lordis derrest cousing and uncle James Erle of Murray, Lord Abirnethie. &c. Regent to our Souerane Lord, his Realme and liegis. Togidder with the Prelatis, Erlis, Barronis, Cōmissionaris of Burrowis, speciallie compeirand in the said Parliament, as the thre Estatis of this Realme. The saidis Actis being oppinlie red, concludit and votit in the said Parliament to remaine as perpetuall Lawis to all the subiectis of this Realme in time cumming." Device: Truth, three quarters length, irradiated, holding in her right hand an open book, "Verbum Dei," and in her left a lighted candle. On an oval enclosing the same "Vincet tandem Veritas." I, on one side, and R, on the other. Beneath: "Imprentit at Edinburgh be Iohne Ros. M.D.LXXV. Cum Priuilegio Regali." This title in a border of metal flowers. This session contains 41 acts: in the fourth is the confession of faith at large, consisting of 26 chap. or articles; and at the end of them "Thir Actis and Artickles ar red in the face of Parliament, and ratifyit be the thre Estatis. At Edinburgh the 17. day of August, the zeir of God. 1560. zeiris." Cap. xl is entitled "Anent the prenting of the Actis, maid in this present Parliament," &c. which may be seen below.[b] At the end of these acts, "Extractum de libro Actorum Parliamenti Per me—sub meis signo & subscriptione Manualibus. Jacobus makgill." Then, "The Tabill," at the end thereof "Imprentit" &c. as on the title-page. See Anderson's General preface to his Collections, p.ix. W.H. Folio.

1575. "In the Parliament of the richt excellent, richt heich, and michtie Prince, Iames the sext, &c. begune at Striuiling, the xxviij. day of August, the zeir of God ane thousand fiue hundreth thre scoir and elleuin zeiris, and in the Fyst zeir of his hienes Regne. Be his Maiesties derrest Gudschir vmquhile Mathew Erle of Lennox, Lord Dernelie. &c. Regent to his hienes, his Realme, and liegis: and thre Estatis of this Realme. And

[b] "Item, the xxix. day of December, the zeir of god 1567 zeiris, quhilk wes the last day of this Parliament, the samin being contineuit to the xj. day of Julij nixt tocum.

Our soverane Lord, with auise of my Lord Regent and thre Estatis of Parliament, hes ordanit, and ordains ye foirsaidis Actis of Parliament, to be autentickli Imprentit, as alswa ordainis ye Act of Parliament maid in our souerane Lordis vmquhile derrest Gudschiris Parliament, haldin at Edinburgh ye xij. day of Nouember, ye zeir of God 1526. zeiris, maid anent birning of housis, and utheris specifyit thereto, to be alswa Imprentit. Swa yat nane of our Souerane Lordis liegis may pretend Ignorance of the samin." Then follows the said act, "Anent the raising of fyre and birning. Cap. xlj."

And endit, and concludit vpon the seuint day of September nixt thairefter following, be vmquhile Johne Erle of Mar. Lord Erskin, &c. being Regent to his hienes, his said Realme and liegis for the time: and the said thre Estatis. The Actis and Constitutiounis following war concludit to be obseruit as Lawis in time cumming." Device: Truth, &c. as to the foregoing article. "Imprentit at Edinburgh be me Iohne Ros. M.D.LXXV. Cum Priuilegio Regali." In a border of metal flowers. Contains 13 chapters, or acts, authenticated at the end, and signed "Jacobus makgill." Then, on signature B. iij.

"In the Parliament haldin at Edinburgh the xxvi. day of Ianuar the zeir of God ane thousand, fyue hundreth, thre scoir twelf zeiris, Thir Lawis, statutes and Cōstitutiounis, ar deuysit, concludit, statute, and ordanit be the richt hie, Excellent,—James the sext,—with auise and consent of ane Nobill, and Michtie Lord, and his richt traist Cousing, James Erle of Mortoun, Lord Dalkeith, &c. Regent—and thre Estatis of this Realme, Assemblit and conuenit to that effect. Of the quhilkis Lawis and Constitutiounis the Tennouris followis." These consist of 12 Chapters authenticated as before. Then follows, on D ij,

"In the Parliament haldin at Halyruidhous the last day of Aprill, the zeir of God ane thousand, fiue hundreth, thre scoir threttene zeiris. Thir Lawis,—ar deuisit—be the richt hie, excellent,—James the sext,—with auise and consent of ane Nobil and Michtie Lord,—James Erle of Mortoun—Regent—Of the quhilkis Lawis—the Tennouris followis." These are eight in number authenticated as before, with a table of these three Parliaments at the end. The original Acts under the 4 regents being lost; the edition 1568, (see p. 1491) and these of 1575, are really valuable. W.H. Folio.

The Bible &c. Genevan translation, in English. Dedicated to King James the sixth, in Scotch. Edinburgh. Tho. Bassandine. Folio. 1576.

"Commentatorium de arte disserendi libri quatuor, Joanne Retorforti Jedburgaeo Scoto, authore. Et nunc demùm ab eodem diligenter recogniti & emendati. Edinburgi, apud Henricum Charteris. Cum priv. regali." Again 1580. Quarto. 1577.

"Jo. Leslæus Ep. Rossen. De origine, moribus & rebus gestis Scotorum. Romæ, 1578. Quarto. 1578.

"Baptistes, sive Calumnia, tragoedia, auctore Georgio Buchanano, Scoto. Edinburg. apud Hen. Charteris." Octavo. 1578.

"A request presented to the king of Spayn and the lordes of the counsel of the state, By the inhabitantes of the lovve Countreyes, protesting that they will liue according to the Gospell: the xxij. of June. 1578." Device: The tree of Charity on a shield; as sometimes used by Reynold Wolfe. "At Edinburgh, Imprintit be Leighe Mannenby. Anno Domini. 1578." C, in fours, Roman letter. At the end, by way of Postscript, "To the reader. Of late aduertisements are come ouer, that the xiiij. of this present moneth of July, the Estates assemble thēselues to deliberate vpon this request, the sequel wherof is vncertaine, for as Euripides in Iphigenia saith, Ασημάντα δὲ βροτοῖσι τὰ τῶν θεῶν, σώζει δ', οὓς φιλοῦσιν: that is, Gods doings fall out otherwise than men looke for, 1578.

and

and he saueth whom he loueth." See p. 1487. W.H. Quarto.

1578. "The seuen Seages, translated out of prose into Scottish Metre, by John Rolland. Edinb. See it in 1592. Quarto.

1579. "Vindiciæ contra tyranos: siue, de principis in populum, populique in principem, legitima potestate, Stephano Junio Bruto Celte, auctore. Edinburgi." There is reason to think it was not printed there, nor at the time. Octavo.

1579. "Ad virulentum Archibaldi Hamiltonii apostatae dialogum, de confusione Caluinianae sectae apud Scotos impiè conscriptum, orthodoxa responsio. Thoma Smetonio Scoto, auctore. In qua celebris illa quaestio de ecclesia, de vniuersalitate, successione, & Romani episcopi primatu, breuiter, dilucidè, et accuratè tractatur. Adiecta est vera historia extremae vitae et obitus eximii viri Joan. Knoxii, ecclesiae Scoticanae instauratoris fidelissimi. Edinburgi apud Joan. Rosseum pro H. Charteris. Cum priuilegio regali." 123 pages.[*] Quarto.

1579. "Heir beginnis ane treatise callit, The palice of honour, compilit be M. Gawine Dowglas, bischop of Dunkeld. Imprinted at Edinburgh by Johne Ros for Hen. Charteris." The printer in his preface to the reader shews, that besides the copie printed at London, there were copyis of this werk set furth of auld amangis our selfis" (i. e. in Scotland.) It was printed by Wm. Copland in 1553. See p. 362. For the object of this allegory, see Warton's Hist. of Eng. Poetry, II; 294; also, Pinkerton's List of Scotish poets, p. xcvi.

1579. "De iure regni apud Scotos dialogus, authore Georgio Buchanano, Scoto. Edinburgi apud Joan. Roseum pro H. Charteris." Dated Sterlini, 10 Jan. 1579. Again 1580 & 1581. Quarto.

1579. "In the Parliament haldin at Striviling the xxv. day of Julij, the zeir of God, ane thousand, fyue hundreth, thre scoir and auchtene zeiris. Thir Lawis—ar deuysit,—be the richt Excellent,—James the sext,—and thre Estatis of this Realme, as followis." Device: Truth, &c. as to the acts in 1575, but larger. "Jmprentit at Edinburgh be Johne Ros. Anno Do. 1579 Cum Priuilegio Regali." In a border. In this session are eight acts. Then,

"In the Parliament haldin and begun at Edinburgh the xx. day of October, the zeir of God, ane thousand, fyue hundreth, thre scoir and nyntene zeiris. Thir Lawis—ar deuysit—be the richt Excellent—Jame the Sext," &c. &c. In this session are 34 acts; at the end thereof "Extract furth of the buikis of our Souerane Lord's Parliament at command of his hienes vvith auise of his preuie counsall, be me Alexander Hay Clerk of the Rollis, Register, and Counsall vnder my Signe and subscriptioun manuall. Alexander hay." Here follows a table of both parliaments; as also the titles of "Actis and materis past in the same Parliament being Temporall for short space, or concerning particular parteis not Imprentit," Annexed is

"Ane

[*] Mr. Ames has inserted a paragraph after this article with a "N. B. It seems they had no Hebrew or Greek types, even at this time, nor till 1599;" but with respect to Greek types, the last article but two evinces the contrary.

" Ane Proclamatioun for publischeing of the Actis of Parliament.— Geuin vnder our Signet At Halyreuidhous the xxiij. day of Januar, and of our Regne the threttene zeir. 1579. Per Actum secreti Consilii." This on one leaf; Colophon, as on the title-page, under the same device, on another. W.H. Folio. 1579.

" The bible, for the use of Scotland, by the commissioners of the kirk. Edinburgh, printed by Alexander Arbuthnett, the king's printer, at the kirk in the field." This account from bishop Tanners MSS. Folio. 1579.

" Latinae grammatices rudimenta, in gratiam iuventutis Scoticae conscripta. Edinburgi." Octavo. 1580.

" Ane breif descriptioun of the qualiteis, and effectis of the well of the woman-hill, besyde Abirdene, anno Domini 1580." This book is contained in one sheet, and has a pretty border about the margin. Penes Mr. Hilyar. Sixteens. 1580.

" The promine, conteining the maner, place, and time of the maist illuster king James the sext, his first passing to the feildis: directit to his hienes be P.H. familiar seruitour to his maiestie. Imprinted at Edinburgh be Johne Ros, for H. Carteris. Cum priuilegio regali." 8°. 1580.

" Ane short and generall confession" &c. as p. 1135. 1580.

Commentariorum de arte disserendi, Lib. 4. &c. as p. 1499. 1580.

" Adami Blackvodæi Aduersus Georgii Buchanani dialogum de Jure Regni apud Scotos, pro regibus apologia. Pict." See Mackenzie, III; 488. Octavo. 1580.

Jo. Leslæus Episc. Rossen. De Titulo & Jure sereniss. principis Mariæ Scotorum Reginæ, quo regni Angliæ successionem sibi iustè vendicat. Rhem. 1580. Quarto. 1580.

" A short summe of the whole catechisme, wherein the Question is proponed and answered in few wordes, for the greater ease of the commoune people and children. Gathered by M. Iohne Craig, Minister of Gods Worde, to the Kings M. Iohne xvii. This is Lyfe Eternall, to knowe thee the onely verie God and whome thou hast sent Iesus Christ. Imprinted at Edinburgh, by Henrie Charteris Anno M.D.LXXXI. Cum Priuilegio Regali." On the back, " The contentes of this Booke." Dedicated, " To the Professoures of Christis Euangell at Newe Abirdene, &c.—At Edinburgh, xx of Julie. M.D.LXXXI.---To the Reader." G 6, in eights. Trinity Coll. Cambr. Octavo. 1581.

" Catechismus Latino carmine redditus, et in libros quatuor digestus, Patricii Adamsoni Scoti, poetae elegantissimi, opera atque industria." Dedicated to king James VI. Edinburgh, printed by Robert Lekprevik. Sixteens. 1581.

" An answer to the calumnies, letter, and erroneous propositions of an apostate named, Mr. John Hamilton, by Mr. William Fouler. Edinburgh." Quarto. 1581.

" Ane Declaratioun of the iust and necessar causis, mouing vs of the Nobilitie and vthers ye Kings Maiesties faithful Subiectis to repair to his Hienes presence, and to remaine with him, for resisting of the present 1582.

Dangeris appearing to Goddi's new Religion, and Professours thairof, and to his Hienes's awin Person, Estait, and Croun, and his faithful Subiectis that hes constantly continuit in his Obedience; and to seek Redres and Reformation of the Abuse and confusioun of the Common-Wealth, removing from his Maiestie the chief Authoures thairof, quhil the Treuth of the samin may be maid manifest to his Hienes's Estates, that common Consent, Redres and Remeid may be provided. Derectet from Striuiling with speciall command and licence to be prentit, Anno 1582." Octavo.

1582. "In the Parliament Haldin and begun at Edinburgh the xxiiii. Day of October, the Zeir of God, ane thousand, fyue hundreth, four scoir ane zeiris. Thir Lawis—ar deuisit—be the richt Excellent,—James the sext,—And thrie Estatis of this Realme, As followis. Imprentit at Edinburgh, be Henrie Charteris. Anno, M.D.LXXXII. Cum Priuilegio Regali." Contains 37 chap. or acts, "Extract furth of the Buikis of our Souerane Lordis Parliament, at command of his Hienes, with aduise of his Preuie Counsaill, Be me Alexander Hay, Clerk of the Rollis, Register, and Counsaill. Vnder my Signe and Subscriptioun Manuall. Alexander hay." Then tables of the acts printed and not printed. On the last page a colophon as on the title-page. W.H. Folio.

1582. "Rerum Scoticarum historia, authore Georgio Buchanano Scoto. Edimburgi apud Alexandrum Arbuthnetum, typographum regium, MDLXXXII. Cum priv. regali." W.H. Folio.

1584. A catechism, or confession of Faith by Henry Balnaves. Edinb. 8°.

1584. "THE FORME OF Prayers and administration of the Sacramentes vsed in the Eng. Church at Geneua, appointed & receiued by the Churche of Scotland. Wherevnto besides that which was in the former bookes, are also added sundrie other prayers." This title in a compartment, with a sun horned at top, terminuses on the sides, and "1584" in a tablet at bottom. On the back are "The contents* of this Booke." F f 7, in eights; the last page blank. W.H. Twenty-fours.

1584. "The temporisour, that is to say, the obseruer of time, or he that changeth with the time. Compyled in Latin by the excellent clarke, Wolfangus Musculus, and translated into French by maister Valleran Pulleyn

* "The order of excommunication, and of publike repentance, vsed in the Church of Scotland, and commanded to be printed by the generall Assemblie of the same, in the moneth of Iunii. 1571.---The confession of the Christian Faith.---The order of electing Ministers, Elders & Deacons.---The Assemblie of the Ministrie, &c.---An order for interpretation of the scriptures, & answering of doubtes, &c---A confession of our finnes vsed before the sermon.---Another vsed in the Church of Eding.---A Confes. vsed in time of extreme trouble.---A generall prayer after the sermon. &c.---Other forte of prayers to be vsed, &c.---Prayers vsed in the time of persecution, &c. and when the L. Tab. is ministred.---A thankesgiuing for our deliuerance, &c.---A prayer vsed at generall & part. assem.---The Administration of Baptisme & the Lordes Supper. -- The forme of Mariage: the visitation of the Sicke.---A prayer for the Sick & maner of burial. An order of Ecclesiasticall Discipline. The Catechisme of M. Iohn Caluin.---A brief examination of children, &c." Sundry other forms of prayers for private families, now first annexed.

Pulleyn, and out of French into English by R. P. 1555.* Imprinted at Edinburgh by Thomas Vautrollier."* Sixteens.

" The new Godly garden (*Prayers*): whereunto is ioyned Bradford against the feare of death. Printed in Edinburge 1584. by Thomas Vautrollier." Maunsell, p. 85. Sixteens. 1584.

" The essayes of a prentise in the diuine art of Poesie." Device: Anchora Spei, in an oval. " Imprinted at Edinbrugh by Thomas Vautroullier 1584. Cum Priuilegio Regali." G 1, in fours. Again 1585, containing Q sheets. See Pinkerton, p. cxix. Quarto. 1584.

Knox's History of the Church of Scotland. See p. 1074. 1584.

" A Treatise tovvching the right, title and interest asvvell of the most excellent Princesse, Marye Queene of Scotland, and the most noble Kyng Iames, her Graces sonne, to the succession of the Croune of England. And first, touching the Genealogie, or pedegrue of suche Competitors, as pretend title to the same Croune." This title in a neat compartment, having at top the arms of France and England quartered, encircled with the garter, and crowned; to which two laurels are twining up the sides, enclosing within its branches the claimed arms. At the roots, OLIVA on dexter side, and PACIS NVNCIA on the sinister; at the extremities, which terminate at top, on each side the English arms, POST LITES, on one side, and VNIO on the other. At the bottom are two men in armour joining hands, and supporting a flaming heart, over which is the word CONCORDIA. In the back ground, a camp to the right, and an encountre of horse-men to the left. There are prefixed, An address to the Emperor, Kings and Princes of Europe, which my copy wants.—" To the most excellent, and most graciouse quene Marie, and to the most noble king Iames her sonne, Quene and kyng of Scotland, his vndoubted Souereignes, Iohn Lesley, Byshop of Rosse wisheth all true felicitie.—A Preface conteyning the argument of this treatise, with the causes mouyng the Author to wryte the same.—To the nobilitie and people of England and Scotland, A Poesie made by T. V. Englishman.—A Declaration of the table following, touching the rase & progenie of suche persones as, descēding from the Princely families of Yorke and Lācastre, doe eyther Iustlye clame, or vniustlye aspire vnto the Croune of England:" &c. My copy wants this genealogical table, but I apprehend it to be the same as to the Latin edition, printed this same year at Rome, in 4°. having on the said table the portraits of Q. Mary, and K. James, at 12 years of age. The same may be seen in the Latin edition 1672. This treatise of the succession ends on the front page of fol. 61. To which is annexed, beginning on fol. 62, "An exhortation to the Englysh and Scottishe nations, that after so long warres, they wolde now at last agree, and Ioyne together in one true league of fast frendshippe and amitie." Which concludes on fol. 71; the back page blank. The whole neatly printed (1584)

8 O 2 on

* When it was printed beyond sea. See it in our Gen. History under that year. The prefatory epistle by the said R. P. to that foreign edition is addressed to " Ingland;" query if not now to Scotland?

on white letter; without printer's name, date, or place. K 4, in eights. WH. Large octavo.

1585. "A Declaratioun of the Kings maiestles intentioun and meaning toward the lait actis of parliament." Device: Anchora Spei. "Imprinted at Edinburgh, by Thomas Vautroullier. 1585. Cum priuilegio regali." C, in fours. W.H. Quarto.

Morgan in his Phœnix Britannicus, p. 493, seems to have copied from another edition "Imprinted at Edinburgh, by assignement of Thomas Vautroullier, 1585." It was printed this same year also in English, for Thomas Nelson, in 8vo. entitled, "Treason pretended against the King of Scots, by certain Lordes and Gentlemen, whose names hereafter followe. With a Declaration of the Kinges maiesties Intention to his last Acts of Parliament: which openeth fully in effect all the saide Conspiracy. Out of Skottish into English." Harl. Miscel. VII, 49.

(1585.) "An abridgement of the institution of christian religion written by M. Ihon Caluin. VVherein briefe and sound aunsvveres to the obiections of the aduersaries are set dovvne. By VVilliam Lawne minister of the word of God. Faithfullie translated out of Latine into English by Christopher Fetherstone Minister of the word of God." Device: Anchora Spei. "1. Pet. 3. 15. Be alwaies readie to aunswere euerie one that demandeth a reason of the hope which is in you, with lenitie and reuerence. Imprinted at Edinburgh by Thomas Vautrollier. 1585.[f] Cum priuilegio regali." Dedicated "To the right vertuous and godlie ladie, the ladie Judeth Pelham, &c.—From Maighfield in Sussex this xvij. of Aprill. 1586.—Christopher Fetherstone.---To the Christian Reader.---To the right worshipfull M. Richard Martin, Maister of her Maiesties mints, and Alderman of the most famous citie of London, &c. —At London the 18 of Februarie. 1583.—William Lawne.---A generall (analytical) table." Contains 398 pages, besides the prefixes; and an alphabetical table of the chief points, at the end. W.H. Octavo.

1585. "The essayes of a prentise in the diuine art of poesie. At Edinburgh, by Thomas Vautrolier. Cum privilegio regali." Containing Q[g] sheets. See it in 1584. Quarto.

1586. "An abridgement of the institution of christian religion," &c. as under 1585, but without any printer's name, having only "Printed at Edinburgh. 1586." The dedications dated as before. Contains only 306 pages, besides the prefixes, &c. the same type, but the form is somewhat wider, and has 5 lines more in a page. W.H. Octavo.

1587. The same, "Now againe corrected and in manie places augmented.—Printed at Edinburgh. 1587." Contains 358 pages, beside the prefixes, &c. dated as in 1585: the same type and form as in 1586. W.H. 8°.

"The

[f] This date must be a misprint, seeing the dedication in this and the subsequent editions are alike dated 17. April, 1586.

[g] The signatures of this edition probably had only four leaves, and those of 1584 had eight.

" The elleuenth Parliament halden at Edinburgh the xxix. day of (1587.)
Julii; the zeir of God, 1587. Be the richt excellent, richt heich, and
michtie Prince, James the Sext, be the grace of God, King of Scottes, with
advise of his Estates. *Chapter* 25. The sellers and dispersers of erroneous
buikes, suld be punished, and the buikes destroyed. " Forasmeikle as sindrie persones brings furth of vtheris Realmes divers buikes and writtes,
conteining erroneous doctrine, against the trew word of God, and Religion
professed, and be the lawes established in this Realme: Or conteining
superstitious rites and ceremonies papisticall, quhairby the people ar
greatly abused. For remeid quhairof, our soveraine lorde, and *the* three
Estates of this present Parliament, statutis and ordainis, that quhaso-euer
ony persones, suspecte of hame-bringing of the saids buikes, sall repaire,
resort, and remaine within ony Burgh, it salbe lauchfull to the Provest
and Baillies of the same Burgh, with ane Minister, to search and seeke
the saidis buikes, and being funde sik buikes as ar before declared, to
destroy them, and commit the hame-bringers to wairde, quhill they be
punished in their persones and gudes, at our soverane Lordis will. For the
quhilk this persent Act salbe sufficient commission to the saids Provest,
Ballies, and Minister: And their said searching, seeking, intromission,
and destruction of the saids buikes, salbe repute ane lauchfull deede, for
the quhilk they sall incurre na danger of spuilzie, or intrusion, or ony
thing, that may follow there-upon." Copied from Skene's Laws,
Edit. 1597.

" Martyre de la Royne d'Escosse, douairiere de France. Contenāt 1587.
le vray discours des trahisons à elle faictes à la suscitation d'Elizabet An- 1588
gloise, par lequel les mensonges, calomnies & faulses accusations dressees
contre celle tres-vertueuse, tres-Catholique, & tres illustre Princesse sont
esclarcies, & son innocence averée Auec son oraison [h]funebre prononcée
en l'Eglise nostre dame de Paris. Pretiosa in conspectu Domini mors
sanctorum eius. A Edimbourg. Chez Jean [i]Nafeild." There are
prefixed, an address " Au lecteur.---Monumentum Mariæ Scotorum
Reginæ. --Vitæ summa.---Monumentum regale.---P. C. Posuit.---Sonet.
Les vertus de Iesabel Angloise.---Aux Anglois affligez pour la religion
Cartholique.---Comparison de Londres à Rome." The narrative on
472 pages; at the end of which, " Epitaphium Elisabethæ Titheræ,
Angliæ.---Aliud." Then, " Oraison funebre de la Royne d'Escosse,
sur la subject de celle prononcée par M. de Bourges." This with the
affixes are paged afresh; though the signatures are continued. The
oration is on 50 pages.---" Epitaphium Mariæ Scotiæ Reginæ.---Epi-
taphe de la Royne d'Escosse douairiere de France.---Mariæ Stuartæ Scotorum

h As Mr. Ames copied from the edition 1587, and makes no mention of this funeral oration, perhaps it was annexed only to this edition of 1588.

i The printer's name declares itself to be fititious, and the book was really printed in France by Adam Blackwood. Mr. Ruddiman. Mackenzie asserts A. Blackwood to be the author, and that the book was printed at Antwerp. Probably the edition 1587 was printed in France, and this of 1588, at Antwerp, being the same which Mackenzie treats of. Vol. III: p. 511 and 513.

torum Reginæ Tumulus.—N. P. A.---Regale monumentum.---Sonet.---N. R. P.---Ode sur la mort de la tres-chrestienne, tres-illustre, tres-constante, & tres-vertueuse Marie Royne d'Escosse douairiere de France.—R. G. P. T.---Ode." A a 5, in twelves. W.H. Twelves

This book is reprinted in Jebb's 2d vol. of Collections, " De vita & rebus gestis Mariæ Scotor. reginæ," p. 175—378 fol. 1725, from an edition at Paris, by Cramoisy, 1644. the concluding sentences of which differ. The address " Au lecteur" is put after " Monumentum Mariæ Scotor. reginæ.---Vitæ summa. Monumentum regale." and the three copies of French verses are omitted. The 2 latin Epitaphs on " Elizabetha TITHERA" (Eliz. Tudor). " The Oraison funebre" is printed apart in Jebb II, 671. and after it the 5 Epitaphs and Sonnet, but not the Ode.

1588. " The warkis of the famous and worthie knicht, sir David Lindesay, at the command of king James the syft." With a print of justice and religion, and H. C. (Hen. Charteris). Quarto.

1588. " ANE FRVITFUL MEDITATION, conteining ane plaine and facill expositioun of ye 7. 8. 9. and 10 versis of the 20 Chapt. of the Reuelatioun, in forme of ane sermone. Set doun be the maist christiane King, and synceir professour, and cheif defender of the treuth, James the 6 King of Scottis.—Imprentit at Edinburgh be Henrie Charteris.—Cum Priuilegio Regali." This is introduced by an addresse " To the Christiane Reider.—The first of October. 1588. M. Patrik Galloway Minister of Perth.—Epigramma per tropum allusionis ad nobile Regiæ Maiestatis nomen, quod huius pij & eruditi Sermonis præcipuum argumentum complectitur. Per M. J. Malcolmum.---Vaticinij de maxime vere Christiano Scotorum Rege explicatio, & ad opus applicatio. Per eundem." The reprinted edition by John Harrison in 1603 has also " The same in English by I. St." 4°.

Printed also in French at Rochelle, in 1589.

1589. " ANE MEDITATIOVN vpon the XXV, XXVI, XXVIII, and XXIX verses of the XV chapt. of the first buke of the Chronicles of the Kingis. Set doun be the maist christiane king and sincere professour of the treuth James the sext king of Scottis. Psalm. LXXXIIII. Vers. X, XI, XII. Ane day in thy courtes is better then ane thowsand vther quhair. I had rather be ane dure keeper in the hous of my God, then to dwell in the tabernacles of wickednes. For the Lord God is the sunne and sheild to vs: the Lord will giue grace and glorie: and no gude thing will be withhald from them that walk vprichtlie. O Lord of hostes, blessed is the man yat trusteth in the. Imprentit at Edinburgh be Henrie Charteris. 1589. Cum Priuilegio Regali." Introduced " To the Christiane Reider.[a]—M. Patrik Galloway Minister

[a] Wherein, speaking of his majesty as witnessing his upright meaning in the cause of Christ,—" and that now twyse: Anes in forshawing, according to the line of the writtin word, the iust wrak that was to fall vpon the proude persequutaris of the Kirk in the hicht of their pryde, as is exponed in his Maiesties former Meditatioun vpon the 20 of ye Reuelatioun: and now agane in ane vther Meditatioun vpon the 15 of ye first buke of ye Chronicles, expressing the dewtie of the trew Kirk toward God for yair deliuerance, and ye maner of thankisgeuing that aucht to be geuin

Minister of Perthe.---Epigramma, quo videri possit inuictissimum Scotorem Regem multò maximè Christianum Dauidica stirpè esse oriundum. Per M. I. Malcolmum." - Contains B, in fours. On the last page, "His Maiesties avvn Sonnet.—Idem latinè.—Per Metellanum Cancellarium." W.H. Quarto.

De augustissimo Jacobi 6. Scotorum Regio, & Annæ Frederici 2. Danorum Regis Filiæ conjugio: 13 Calend. Septemb. 1589. in Dania celebrato: Georgio Scotiæ Mareschallo sui regis vicem obeunte. Epithalameum ad eamdem Annam, serenissimam Scotorum Reginam. Hercule Rolloco Scoto authore. Edinburgi, Excudebat Henricus Charteris." 10 leaves. Lambeth Library. Quarto. 1589.

"La Mort de la Royne d'Escosse." This book is embellished with 4 elegant wood-prints, 1. Representing the manner of the quen's receiving the messenger of her death. 2. Her passing the night in prayer with her ladies. 3. Her being led to the place of execution. 4. Her decapitation. This is not in Jebb. Octavo. 1589.

"The confession of Faith, subscriued by the Kingis Maiestie and his Houshold: togither with the copie of the band, maid touching the maintenance of the true Religion, the Kingis Maiesties person and estate. &c: seuerally to be Subscribed by all Noblemen, Barrons, gentlemen, and otheris, according to the tenor of the acte of secret Counsell, and Commissionis therein contayned, as heirafter followeth.—At Edinburgh. Printed by Robert Walde graue, Anno Dom. 1590." On the back is "The priuiledge granted to the Printer," as below.[1] The confession of faith is on 5 pages with this head-title, "Ane schort and generall confession of the trevv Christiane Faith and Religion, according to Godis worde and actis of Parliamentis, subscriued be the Kingis Maiestie 1590.

geuin to God thairfoir. Quhilk wirk so soone as it come to my handis I did diligence to communicat it to the, to be ioynit with ye former."

[1] "The Lordis of the Secreit Counsell grants and geuis licence & Priuiledge, by thir presents, to Robert Walde-graue, to Imprent, or cause to be imprentit, the Confessioun of Faith, togidder with the generall Band. maid touching the maintenance of true Religioun, the Kingis Majesties person and Estate, and withstanding of al forraine preparations and forcis, tending to the trouble thairof. As also the Acte of secreit Councell, Contenyning a Commissioun to certaine Nobill men, Barons, and vthers: for serching, seeking, apprehending, and pursute of Papists, Iesuits, Seminarie Priestis, and Excommunicate personis: with the like Commissioun to certaine Ministers of Gods word, To receive de novo, the subscriptions of all Nobill men, Barons, gentlemen, and vthers his highnes liegis, of quhatsumeuer degree, to the said generall Band. For the Imprinting of the quhilk Band, act of secret counsell, & confession forsaid, the said lords decerns, and declare, that the saide Robert sall not be callit, or accusit, criminalie, nor ciuilie, be any maner of way in time cumming. Nor incur na skaith, or danger in his person, lands, or guds. But the samin salbe countit & esteemit gud & acceptable seruice vnto his Majestie, tending to the aduancement of Gods glorie, & common weale of this realme. Exonering him be thir presents, of all paine & danger that he may incur thairthrow for euer. Discharging be their samin presents, all and sundrie Iudges and ministers of his highnes lawis, & vthers his Majesties liegis and subjects quhatsumever: Of al calling, accusing, troubling, persuing, or in anye wise proceeding against the saide Robert, for the cause foresaide, and of their offices in that part. Subscriuit be the saide Lordis, at Edinburgh, the six. day of March: the zeir of God, ane thousand fiue hundred fourescore nine zeirs."

Maiestie and his housholde, with sundrie vtheris, to the glorie of God and good example of all men. At Edinburgh the 28. day of Ianuarie: The zere of God. 1580. And the fouretene zere of his Maiesties raigne." Annexed is "The Kingis Maiesties Charge to all commissioners and ministers within this Realme.—At Halyrudhous, 1580. the 2. day of March, the 14. yere of our raigne." Then, the following running title at the head of 4 blank pages, "The subscrivers vnto the Confession of Faith." Then, "The Generall Band," on 4 pages, and 4 more for "The subscrivers vnto the Generall Band." Lastly, "The act of secreit counsaill,—Giuen vnder our signet, At Edinburgh the saxt of Marche, and of our reigne the xxiij. zeir, 1589. Per Actum secreti consilij. I. Andro." W.H. Quarto.

1590. "ΣΤΕΦΑΝΙΣΚΙΟΝ. Ad Scotæ regem, habitum in coronatione Reginæ. 17 Maij, 1590. Per Andream Meluinum. Edinburgi, Excudebat Robertus Walde-graue. Cum priuilegio Regali." 5 leaves. Lambeth Library. Quarto.

1590. "In epistolam Pauli apostoli ad Ephesios, Roberti Rolloci Scoti, ministri Jesu Christi, in ecclesia Edinburgensi, commentarius. Edinburgh Robert Walde-graue." On the back of the title page a wooden cut, of the arms of Scotland and Denmark. See Mackenzie, III; 446. 4°.

(1590.) "Sermons vpon the sacrament of the Lords supper, preached in the kirk of Edinburgh, be M. Robert Bruce, minister of Christes Evangel there; at the time of the celebration of the supper, as they were receaued from his mouth. John vi. 54, 63.—At Edinburgh, printed by Robert Waldegrave, printer to the kings maiestie. Cum privilegio regali." Without date. They are dedicated to James VI. "From Edinburgh, the 9th of December, 1590." On the back of the title page, and fronting the dedication, there is a fair distinct wooden cut of the royal arms of Scotland, empaled with those of Anne, king James VIth's Queen, she being a daughter of Frederick II. king of Denmark. The arms of Scotland has its double tressoir dimidiated, in complaisance (I suppose) to those of the queen's, being the arms of Denmark. And these are quarterly to the nombril point, leaving the base for the arms of Sclavonia. 1. Denmark. 2. Norway. 3. Sweden 4. Gothland. These four quarterings are surmounted of a cross, or banner of Denmark; and over all, a surtout surmounted of another. The first surtout is quarterly. 1. Slefwick. 2. Holstein. 3. Stormarsh. 4. Ditmarsh. The second surtout surmounting the whole is, per pale, Oldenburg, and Delmhorst. The whole atchievement is surrounded with the collar of the order of the thistle (which is not usual for an empaled coat baron and femma to be surrounded with an order of knighthood) and supported on the dexter side by the Scots unicorn, holding up the banner of the royal arms of Scotland; and on the sinister, by a Dragon, holding up the banner of Denmark. And for crest (over the imperial crown of Scotland) a lion sejant, holding a sword in his dexter paw, and the royal scepter of Scotland in his sinister. The motto, IN MY DEFENCE GOD ME DEFEND. The pages are not numbered. There are only five sermons, the three first

first of which are from 1 Cor ii. 27. and were preached February 1, 8, and 15, 1589. The two last are from 1 Cor. ii. 26, and were preached February 22, and March 2, 1589. In possession of John Michell, M. D.

"Dr. Bancrofts rashes in rayling against the church of Scotland noted, in an answer to a letter of a worthy person of England, and some reasons rendred, why the answere thereunto hath not hitherto come foorth. By I. D. a brother of the sayd church of Scotland. Walde graue." 32 pages. Sixteens. 1590.

"Schediasmata Hadriani Dammanis a Bisterfelt Gandavensis, de nuptiis regis Jacobi VI. De maris tempestate. In atheos. De reginae coronatione et introitu in Edinburgum." (Lambeth Library, 4°.) 8°. 1590.

"Gratiarum actio ob profligatam Hispanorum classem, que ecclesie Dei in vtroque Britanniae regno extremam vastitatem minata est." A poem dedicated by the author Johannes Brius, To Mr. Robert Bruce, M. in Edinburgh, in Latin elegiac verse. R. Walde-graue. 6 leaves. 16°. 1590.

"Eleuen sermons vpon the sacrament of the Lords supper, preached in the kirk of Edinburgh, be M. Robert Bruce, minister of Christes Euangel there, at the time of the celebration of the supper, as they were receaued from his mouth; meet to comfort all sik, as are troubled ather in bodie or minde. At Edinburgh by Robert Waldegraue, printer to the kingis maiestie, cum privilegio regali." The number of the sermons is set down in the page following, thus: "Six on the 38 Isaiah. Two on 76 Psalm. One on 40 Psalm. One on 2 Timothy ii. 22, &c. One on 2 Timothy ii. 15." These are dedicated by Mr. Bruce to king James VI. the 9th December, 1590. And that discourse on "2 Timothy ii. 22. preached 9th November, 1589, at the quhilk time the earl of Bothwell maid his public repentance in the kirk of Edinburgh," is dedicated to the magistrates of Edinburgh, the 6th December, 1591. Octavo. 1591.

"The Sacrifice of a Christian Soule Conteining godlie prayers and holy meditations for sundry purposes; Drawne out of the pure fountaines of the sacred Scriptures. Psal. 51. 17. The sacrifices of God are a contrite spirite: &c. Edinburgh Printed by Rob. Walde-graue, printer to the Kings Maiestie. 1591. Cum Priuilegio Regali." Dedicated "To the the honorable, noble, and potent Lorde, John, Lorde Thirlstane. great Chancelor of Scotland: And to the noble vertuous, and godly Lady, Dame Iane Flemeng, Ladie Thirlstane his wife: &c.—Your Honors most bounden R. W.---A Table of the Prayers" &c. Besides; 285 pages. W.H. Twenty-fours. 1591.

"His Maiesties poeticall exercises at vacant houres. At Edinburgh Printed by Robert Walde-graue printer to the Kings Maiestie. Cum Priuilegio Regali." This title is enclosed with odd pieces; those on the sides are emblematical, the one having over it Amor, and under it "Pacis alumnus;" the other, over it Pax, and under it "Infesta malis." These exercises consist of The Furies, translated from the French of Du Bartas, and the Lepanto, a poem of his majesty's enditing: to these 1591.

8 P are

are annexed a translation of the Lepanto into French by Du Bartas. The latter two of these have separate title-pages, though the signatures are progressive throughout, to P. 1, in fours. There are prefixed to The Furies "The author to the reader," who is told "I composed these things in my verie young and tender yeares: *&c.*—which beeing well accepted, will moue mee to hast the presenting vnto thee of my *Apocalyps, and also such nomber of the Psalmes as I haue perfited: & incourage mee to the ending of rest.---To the King of Scotland.—Henrie Constable.—Sonet To the onely Royal Poet.—M. W. Fouler. Musa Cœlo beat.---In serenissimum inuictissimumque Scotiae regem Iacobum sextum." In four Greek distichs.---"Idem Latine.—Hadr. Damman à Bistervelt Gandauensis Flander.—Aliud eiusdem.---To the Kings Maiestie of Scotland.—Henrie Loe.--The exord, or preface of the second vveek of Du Bartas.---The translators invocation." The Furies consists of 1510 lines, besides the epilogue.

"The Lepanto of Iames the sixt, King of Scotland. At Edinburgh Printed by Robert Walde-graue Printer to the Kings Maiestie. Cum priuilegio Regali." This title enclosed with odd pieces; on the sides Veritas and Castitas. Prefixed is "The authors preface to the reader." Wherein we learn that this poem was "both begun and ended in the same summer, wherein the League was published in France." It consists of 916 lines, besides the "Chorus Veneus," and "Chorus Angelorum." Affixed is a "Sonet.—I. R. S."

"La Lepanthe de Jaques vi. Roy d'Escosse, Faicte francoise par le Sieur Du Bartas. Imprimé a Edinburg par Robert Walde-graue, Imprimeur le Roy. Anno Dom. 1591. Auec Priuilege de sa Majesté." Prefixed is a preface "Au lecteur," and another "Preface du traducteur a l'autheur," in verse. W.H. Quarto.

1591. "In librum Danielis prophetae Roberti Rolloci Scoti, ministri Jesu Christi in ecclesia Edinburgensi, commentarius. Edinburgi excudebat Robertus Walde-graue, typographus regiae maiestatis." Quarto.

1591. "Propositions and principles of Diuinitie propounded and disputed in the vniuersitie of Geneua, by certaine studients of Diuinitie there, vnder M. Theod. Beza, and M. Anthonie Faius, professors of Diuinitie. Wherein is contained a Methodicall summarie, or Epitome of common places of Diuinitie. Translated out of Latine into English, to the end that the causes, both of the present dangers of that Church, and also of the troubles of those that are hardlie dealt vvith els-vvhere, may appear in the English tongue. At Edinburgh Printed by Robert Walde-graue, printer to the Kings Maiestie. Anno Dom. 1591. Cum Priuilegio Regali." This title enclosed in odd pieces, with Veritas on one side, and Castitas on the other, as the Lepanto. Dedicated "To the renouned and noble lord, the lord Nicholas earle of Ostrorog, &c.—From Geneua the tenth of the Kalends of September. 1586.—Your Honors at commandement Anthonie Faius.---To all those that wish wel vnto the Lord Iesus and his poore Church wandring here vpon earth: the Translator

* Written before he was 20 years of age.

lator wisheth" &c. Besides; 274 pages (printed 268 by mistake) and a table. The principles consist of 81 propositions, each with the name and country of i's desender. W.H. Quarto.

" A catechisme of Christian Religion, taught in the Schooles and 1591.
Churches of the Low-Countries, and dominions of the Countie Palatine: With the arguments and vse of the seueral doctrins of the same Catechisme By Jeremias Bastingius. And now authorized by the Kings Maiestie for the vse of Scotland. Whereunto is adioyned certain Praiers, both publike and priuate, for sundry purposes. Edinburg, Printed by Robert VValde-graue, printer &c. 1591. Cum priuilegio Regiæ Maiestatis." Prefixed are " The A. B. C.---The Lords prayer.---The beliefe.---The ten commandements of Almightie God.—A praier to be vsed before Catechising." At the end, Truth holding up an open book with her Right-hand, & a lighted torch in her Left; the motto, VINCET TANDEM VERITAS. See An exposition, &c. p. 1423. W.H. Sixteens.

" Certain godly and learned Treatises. Written by that worthie Mi- 1592.
nister of Christe M. Dudley Fenner; for the behoofe and edification of al those, that desire to grovv and increase in true Godlines. The titles whereof are set downe in the Page* following. Edinburgh Printed by Robert Walde-graue, Printer to the Kings Maiestie. 1592. Cum privilegio Regali." Dedicated " To the right honorable, noble, and potent Lorde James, Lord Lindsay of the Byres: &c.—Edinburgh the 24 of December. 1591. Your H. to commande in the Lord. R. W." Wherein he tells his patron, " Amongst the number of those, whome in the Lords great mercies wee inioyed, and lost for our vnthankfulnesse, M. Dudley Fenner was one, whome the Church of God in this age could haue hardliest spared; he ended his testimonie in this life, being vnder thirtie yeares of age: but yet of that growth in the knowledge of God, that fewe (if euer anie of his yeares) haue left behind them the like monuments of great knowledge and learning, in the true and sound feare of God, as hee hath done. His works both in Latine and English doe beare witnesse hereof.—Some Treatises of his being printed at sundrie times, and now rare to be gotten, I haue gathered together, and presumed to dedicate vnto your Lordshippe:" &c. Besides; 192 pages. He printed it again this same year. W.H. Octavo.

" Dudley Fenner his Catechisme. printed by Robert Walgraue." 1592.
Maunsell, p. 30. Octavo.

" The warkis of the famous and worthie knicht, sir David Lyndsay, of 1592.
the Mont, &c. now augmentit with the hystorie of the squyer, William Meldrum

* " The contents of this Booke.
1. The Order of Houshold gouernement, described out of the word of God. 2. An Interpretation vpon the Lords praier. 3. A briefe Interpretation vpon the Epistle to Philemon. 4. A short and plaine Table, orderlie disposing the principles of Religion, out of the first Table of the Law. 5. A Treatise of the whole doctrine of the Sacraments, plainlie and fully set downe and declared out of the worde of God. 6. A short and profitable Treatise of Lawfull and vnlawfull Recreations, and the right vse, and abuse of those that are lawfull."

Meldrum of the Bynnis, never foir imprentit. The testament of th said squyer, imprentit at Edinburgh be Henrie Charteris. Cum priuilegio regali." Quarto.

1592. "Onomasticon Poeticum siue Propriorum quibus in suis monumentis vsi sunt veteres poetae breuis descriptio poetica, Thoma Iacchaeo Caledonio authore." Device: Truth, &c. like that at the end of Bastingius' catechism, but larger. "Edinburgi. Excudebat Robertus VValdegraue, Typographus Regiæ Maiestatis. 1592. Cum Priuilegio Regali." Dedicated "Magnae Spei adolescenti Iacobo Hamiltonio Claudii Pasletensis Domini filio hæreditatis iure natu maximo, Thomas Iacchaeus S. D.—Ex Sylva, vulgò dicta, Orientali. Septimo Kalendas Augusti. 1592.—Hadr. Damman a Bisservelt Thomæ Iacchæo. S. D.—Edinburgi vestræ III. Kal. Sept. CIↃ. IↃ. XCII." Then sundry commendatory verses by Robert Rollock, Hercules Rolloc, Hadr. Damman, Patrick Sharp, Andrew Melvin, and Tho. Craig. The head-title, "Onomasticon Poeticum.

Quos prisci qui homines, quę mõstra hominũq; Deûmque,
Quas Vrbes, quæ Regna, quibus retulêre Poëtæ
Gentibus & Populis; Montes cum Vallibus imis:
Fontesq; Fluviosq;, Lacus, Stagna atque Paludes,
Et Maria, & Terras omnes prompto ordine paucis
Musa refer: Tu Musam audi Phœbæa iuventus."

The proper names are given in a separate column, in dictionary order; against the name of the person or place is a verse or two, and sometimes more, wherein that name is described, set in the middle of the page; and and then the poet, with the book where the assertion is confirmed, in a 3d column: thus,

"A B

Abatis.	Caucasus vates Abatis ventura profatur.	Ovid, 5. met.
Abas.	Argivum bis sextus Abas rex, Martis in armis	
	Acer, Hypermnestra Lynceoq; parentibus ortus:	Vergil, 3. æn."

Contains 150 pages. W.H. Quarto.

1592. "Heir beginnis the sevin Seages, Translatit out of Prois in Scottis Meiter, be Jhon Rolland in Dalkeith, With ane moralitie efter euerie doctouris Tale, and Siklyke estir the emprice Tale; Togidder with ane loving and lawd to every Doctour estir his awin Tale; and ane Exclamatioun and outerying vpon the Empreours Wyfe, estir hir fals contrused tale. Edinburgh, Printit be Robert Smyth, dwelland at the nether Bow. Cum privilegio regali." To which is added at the end, "And are to be sauld in his Buith at the nether Bow." Octavo.

1592. Plato's Axiochus; on the shortness and uncertainty of life. Quarto.

(1592.) "A discoverie of the vnnatural and traiterous conspiracie of Scottisch papistes against God, his kirk, their native country, the kingis maiesties persone and estate. Set downe as it was confessed ane subscribed bee M. George Ker, yet remaining in prison, and David Grahame of Fentrie, iustly

iustly executed for his treason in Edinburgh, the 15th of Februarie 1592. Whereunto are anneaed, certain intercepted letters, written by sundrie of that faction, to the same purpose. Printed and published at the speciall command of the kinges maiestie. At Edinburgh, printed by R. Walde-graue, Printer, &c. Cum privilegio Regali." 16 leaves. See Oldys's Catal. No. 146. Quarto.

" A plaine discouery of the whole Reuelation of St. Iohn: set downe in two treatises: The one searching and prouing the true interpretation thereof: The other applying the same paraphrastically and historically to the text. Set forth by Iohn Napier L. of Marchistoun younger. Whereunto are anneaed, certaine Oracles of Sibylla, agreeing with the Reuelation and other places of Scripture. Edinburgh printed by Rob. Walde graue, printer, &c. Cum privilegio regali." This title is enclosed with odd pieces, having on the sides PAX and AMOR, as to his majesty's poetical pieces, 1591. On the back is the king and queens atchievement as described in p. 1508. Under it, " In vaine are al earthlie coniunctions, vnles vve be heires together, and of one bodie, and fellovv partakers of the promises of God in Christ, by the Evangell." Dedicated " To the right excellent, high and mightie prince James the sixt, king of Scottes."--A preface " To the Godly and Christian Reader.---The book this bill sends to the Beast, Crauing amendment now in heast.---A Table of the Conclusions introductiue to the Reuelation, and proued in the first Treatise." This first treatise consists of 36 propositions, which occupy 69 pages. On p. 70 is " A table Definitive and Diuisive of the whole Revelation." The second treatise is concluded on p. 269. Then, an address " To the misliking Reader whosoever.---Hereafter followeth certaine notable prophecies—extract out of the books of Sibylla," &c. Mackenzie says, it was immediately translated into Dutch, French, Italian, and Latin; and many were persuaded of the truth of what he had advanced in his conjectures upon those visions: but how much both he and they were mistaken appears from the 14th proposition of his first book,—that the day of judgement was to happen betwixt the years 1688 and 1700. But it happened to him, as to all those who have meddled with these abstruse Mysteries, that none of them have as yet had the good fortune to open the Seals, so far as to convince any rational man, that they have been admitted to those hidden secrets of the kingdom of Heaven: and all the attempts that have been hitherto made in the explanation of this book, have only served to shew how unsuccessful their endeavours that way have proved. W.H. Quarto. 1593.

" A treatise concerning the true catholick and apostolick faith of the holy sacrifice and sacrament, ordeyned by Christ at his last supper; with a declaration of the Berengarian heresy renewed in our age; and an answer to certain sermons made by Mr. Robert Bruce, minister of Edinburgh, concerning this matter, by William Reynolde, priest at Antwerp: imprinted by Joachim Trognesius." The work is dedicated to king James VI. and contains 447 pages, with an index of 12 pages. It 1593.

is

is imagined to be printed at Edinburgh, and that Joachim Trognesius is a feigned name. Octavo.

1593. "Acts of Parliament, past sen the Coronation of the Kinges Maiestie, in furtherance of the progresse of the true and Christian Religion professed by his hienes, and al his faithful subiects, and for punishing of the aduersaries of the same, as alswa concerning prouision for the puyr and impotent, and punishing Idle vagabonds. Pri. at Edinb. by Rob. Walgraue, 1593." Maunsell, p. 1. Quarto.

1593. "The testament of Cresseid, Compylit be M. Robert Henryson Sculemaister in Dunfermeling. Imprentit at Edinburgh be Henrie Charteris. M.D.XCIII." In 58 seven-line stanzas; beginning on the back of the title-page. Then, "The Complaynt of Cresseid;" in 7 nine-line stanzas, and 21 seven-line stanzas. C 2, in fours. Brit. Museum. Quarto.

(1593.) "A parte of a register, contayninge sundrie memorable matters, written by diuers godly and learned in our time, which stande for, and desire the reformation of our church, in Discipline and Ceremonies, accordinge to the pure worde of God, and the Lawe of our Lande. Luke 19. 14. Verse 27. Verse 45. See the contentes of this book on the next leafe." It contains 42 small tracts, is without printer's name, time, or place to it; but Dr. Bancroft in his dangerous positions,* published 1593, says It appears to have been printed at Edinburgh by Robert Waldegraue. See p. 1181. Contains 554 pages besides the title and table of contents, prefixed. Very rare. W.H. Quarto.

1594. "A true reportarie of the most triumphant and royal accomplishment of the baptisme of the most excellent, right high, and mightie prince, Frederick Henry, by the grace of God prince of Scotland. Solemnized the 30th day of August, 1594."—Walde-graue.—Cum priv. regali. 4°.

1594. "The Historie of ane nobil and wailzeand Squyer, William Meldrum, umquhyle Laird of Cleische and Bynnis. Compylit be Sir Dauid Lyndesay, of the Mont, alias Lyoun King of Armes. The Testament of the said Williame Meldrum, Squyer. Compylit alswa be Sir Dauid Lyndesay. —Imprentit at Edinburgh be Henrie Charteris. Anno M.D.XCIIII. Cum Priuilegio Regali." D 4, in eights. Brit. Museum. Quarto.

Mr.

* "And now vpon better care taken by her Maiesty, that no such libels should be hereafter printed in England, (at the least without some daunger to the parties, if it may bee knowne) they have founde such fauour, as to procure their chiefe instrument, and old seruant Waldgraue, to be the King of Scots Printer, from whence their wants in that behalfe shall be fully supplyed. For hauing obtained that place, (as hee pretendeth in print) they haue published by hundreths, certaine spitefull and malicious bookes against her Maiesties most honorable priuy Counsell.—And now it seemeth, for feare that any of all their sayd Libels & rayling Pamphlets, (that haue bin written in her highnesse time) should perish, (being many of them but triobolar chartals) they haue taken vpon them to make a Register; and to Print them altogether in Scotland,—as it appeareth by a part of the sayde Register, all ready come from thence, and finished:" B. 2. p. 46. In the Wardens account of expenditures, from 15. July 1593 to 1594. is this entry; "In serch at Billingigate 3 days for books that came out of Scotland, being a Barrels and 3 firkins. Delivered to my Lordes grace. 11 sh. 8 pence." Stat. Reg. A. fo. 268.

Mr. Pinkerton thinks Sir David Lindsay's Satyre upon the three Estates of Sco land, (a dramatic piece) was printed this year. It was however printed in 1602, or 1600, at Edinburgh, in 4to. The Interludes are low, filthy, and obsceene. The grave matter of it treats of the reformation of a king, heretofore influenced by *Sensuality*, who at length harkens to the advice of *Good Counsel*, (who by *Flattery*, *Falshood* & *Deceit* had been artfully kept from his presence) and by the assistance of *King Correction* reforms the three estates; more especially the *Spirituality*. (1594.)

" Papatûs, seu depravatae religionis origo et incrementum. Summâ fide diligentiâque è gentilitatis suæ fontibus eruta: ut fere nihil sit in hoc genus cultu, quod non sit promptum ex hisce, meis reddere suis authoribus: Vt restitutæ Evangelicæ Religionis, quam profitemur, simplicitas, fucis amotis, suam aliquando integritatem apud omnes testatam faciat. Per Thomam Moresinum Aberdonanum, Doctorem Medicum. Edinburgi excudebat Robertus Walde-graue," &c. On the back is the atchievement of the king and queen as p. 1508. but without the inscription under it, as p. 1513. Dedicated " Serenissimo, invictissimo que regi Scotorum, Iacobo sexto.—Edinburgi, 5. Februarij. 1593. Vestræ Majest. addictissimus Thomas Moresinus Aberdonnus Doct. Med.--- Lectori.—Authores ex quibus ista sunt deprompta." N 3, in eights. W.H. Octavo. 1594.

" Alexander Hume Scot, his treatise of conscience, quhairin diuers secreats concerning that subiect are discouered. Printed by Rob. Walgraue. 1594." Octavo. 1594.

" —of the felicitie of the world to come, vnsauorie to the obstinate, alluring to such as are gone astray, and to the faithfull full of consolation. Printed at Edinburgh by Rob. Walgraue, 1594. Octavo.

"—Fower Discourses, of praises vnto God, to wit, 1. in praise of the mercy and goodnes of God. 2.—of his iustice. 3.—of his power. 4.—of his prouidence. Printed at Edinburghe by Rob. Walgraue. 1594." Maunsell, p. 60, &c. Octavo. 1594.

The Acts of Sir William Wallace. See it in 1570. 1594.

Roberti Rolloci in librum Danielis. Sanctandreæ. See p. 1510. Quarto. 1594.

—Analysis logica in Pauli epistolam ad Romanos. Edinb. Octavo. 1594.

Amoretti, or Sonnets. 85. Sixteens. 1595.

A preparative to marriage, &c. By H. Smith. Edinb. Walde-graue. Octavo. 1595.

" Andreae Duncani Latinae grammaticae pars prior, sive etymologia Latina, in vsum rudiorum. Edinb. excud. R. Walde-graue," &c. 8°. 1595.

" — Appendix etymologiae, ad copiam exemplorum, vnà cum indice interprete. Edinb. excud. R. Walde-graue," &c. 1495 instead of 1595. Octavo. 1595.

" A proclamation to be in a readiness to muster against the 2 Feb. 1595. Robert Walde graue, printer to the kingis majesty." Printed 2 Jan. before. 1595.

" Rudimenta

1595. "Rudimenta Pietatis." Dedicated to the earl of Rothes, and subscribed A. D. *(Andrew Duncan.)* Ten leaves. Walde-grave. Sixteens.

1595. "Sommons To Doomes-daie Sent vnto his beloued England, as a memoriall of his deepe printed Loue and Loyaltie. By Henoch Clapham. Edinburgh—Rob. Walde-graue, &c. Cum Priuilegio Regio." On the back, "Scolasticis.—H. C.—The Epistle.—Edinburgh, 1595.

Fulgura sic flammas qui terris servat iniquis
Anglorum Sater semper, vbique fiet.

Thy humble petitioner vnto God for thy good. Henoch Clapham." The text, 2 Pet. 3. vers. 10, 11. In this sermon, Napier's vain notion, that the Latter Day or end of the world is covertly[s] indicated in the Scriptures, is briefly refuted. "To answer all these things at large would require a peculiar treatise: and it is bruited that [t]one of Immanuel in Cambridge, hath publikelie there confuted the opinion." 79 pages. At the end "Sic vivamus in τῷ κόσμῳ, Vt ne simus in τῷ κόσμῳ. Amen." Again 1596. W.H. Octavo.

1596. His Sinners Sleep, wherein Christ willing her to arise: receiveth but an untoward answer. Edinb. by Rob. Walgraue. 1596. Octavo.

1596. His Briefe of the Bible, drawn first into English poesy, and then illustrated by apt annotations, together with some necessary appendices. Rob. Walgrave. 1596. Octavo.

1596. "Theses philosophicae, quarum patrocinium suscepere Adolescentes Laureae candidati, easdem propugnaturi, Aug. die 2. in aede sacra regii collegii, praeside G. R. sub horam 8 matutinam, Edinburgi. Edinb. ex officii H. Charteris." Quarto.

1596. "Vocabula Magistri Stanbrigii, ab infinitis, quibus antea scatebant, mendis repurgata; observata interim (quoad eius fieri potuit) carminis ratione, et melusculè etiam correcta, studio & industria Thomae Newtoni Cestreshyrii. Edinb. excud. R. Walde-grave," &c. Octavo.

(1596.) "De prosodia libellus, authore G. Buchanano. Edinb. excud. R. Waldegrave," &c. This book is without date, but was probably printed the same year as the former, with which it is joyned. Mr. Ruddiman. Octavo.

1596. "Officina Theologica Danielis Hofmani, professoris et doctoris Theologiae in illustri Ducis Brunsuicensium academia Julia. Eme, lege, judica. Edimburgi imprimebat Johannes Schenk." It is doubtful whether printed in Scotland. Twelves.

1596. Calvin's catechism. Printed at Edinb. by Hen. Charteris. See p. 840. Sixteens.

1596. "Forme of Prayer for the kirk of Scotland: with the Psalmes in metre. Edinb. be Hen. Charteris, 1596. Cum priuilegio Regali. 8°.

1596. "Order of Excōmunication. Edinb. be Hen. Charteris, 1596." 8°.

1596. "Quæstiones et Responsiones aliquot de Fœdere Dei: Deque Sacramento quod Fœderis Dei sigillum est. In gratiam rudiorum collectæ per Robertum

[s] See his plain discovery, &c. p. 1513. [t] "L. Chadderton, master of that colledge."

bertum Rollocum Scotum. Edinburgi, Excudebat Henricus Charteris, 1596.—Cum priv." Dedicated, "Viro bono et ſerio pio, eiuſ vrbis Edinburgi honoratiſſimo, et eiuſdem Vrbis Præfectura ſemel atque iterum functo cum laude Gulielmo Litillo.—Edinburgi 13 Calendas Martias, —Robertus Rollocus." D 3, in eights. W.H. Octavo.

"The lavves and actes of parliament, maid be king James the firſt, 1597.
and his ſucceſſours, kinges of Scotland: Viſied, collected, and extracted furth of the Regiſter. The contentes of this buik are expremed in the leaſe following." The atchievement of the king and queen as deſcribed in p. 1508. "At Edinburgh, imprented be Robert VValde-graue prenter to the Kinges Majeſtie. 15 Martii. Anno Dom. 1597." On this title-page, in MS. "Johannes Skene, qui de verborum ſignificatione ſcripſit." The firſt page of the next leaf in my copy is blank, and on the reverſe are 11 Latin diſtichs ſuſcribed "Tho. Cragius;" the ſubjects are "In libri frontiſpicium. Ad Iacobum ſextum. Ad reginam Annam. In principem Henricum. In Mariam reginam. In Iacobum quintum. Ad Iacobum quartum. Ad Iacobum tertium. In Iacobum ſecundum. In Iacobum primum. In Leonem, Scotorum inſignia." On the front of the 3d leaf is the dedication, "Sereniſſimo et inviĉtiſſimo principi, Jacobo ſexto, Dei gratia, Scotorum Regi, &c.—Johannes Skene conſecravit Dditq;" The back blank. Then, on the front of the 4th leaf. "The contentes of this buik." and on the reverſe, "The Privelege" ſor printing granted to the clerk of the regiſter for the time being as below.' All the acts are not printed herein; but there are liſts of

' "The privelege.

"JAMES Be the grace of God King of Scotles, To all and ſondrie our lieges and ſubiectes, quhom it effeiris, to quhais knawledge thir preſents ſall com, Greeting. For ſameikle, as it is ſtatute and ordaned be our umquhile darreſt gudſchir King James the Fifth, of gud memorie, That al & ſindrie the lawes and actes of Parliament, concerning the commonweil, ſuld be imprented be quhat ſum-euer Prenter it ſuld pleaſe the Clerk of Regiſter for the time to nominate and choſe. And ſua to be publiſhed to the haill ſubiectes, that nane ſuld pretend ignorance thereof, throw miſ-knawing of the ſame. And we vnderſtanding all and haill the lawes, conſtitutiones, ordinances, and actes profitable for the gouernement of our Realme, maid and ordained be the thre Eſtaites in Parliament, be vs, and umquhile our maiſt Noble Progenitors and predeceſſours Kinges of this Realme, alſweill nocht imprented of before, as imprented: to be collected & gathered in ane volume, in ſik forme and maner, as they may be eaſelie vnderſtanded be all our lieges. Therefore to haue given and granted, like as we be thir preſentes gives and grants our full power and licence, to our truſtie and welbeloved Clerk and Counſellour, M. John Skene, Clerk of our Councell, Rolles, and Regiſter; To cauſe the ſaides lawes, conſtitutiones, and actes be imprented be Robert Walde-graue, our prenter. Or be onie vther quhom it ſall pleaſe him to nominate to that effect, togidder with ane treatiſe intitulat, *De verborum ſignificatione*, & ane Chronology of the Kings of this realm, our maiſt Noble progenitors. With full power to our ſaid Clerk of our Regiſter, his aires, executors, and aſſignayes, after the imprenting thereof, to ſell & diſtribute the ſamin. And to cauſe the ſamin be ſauld and diſtribute throw-out our haill Realme, to the effect that they may com to the better knawledge of all our lieges. Dischargeand all our ſubiectes and lieges, that nane of them take vpon hand, to imprent, or cauſe imprent, ſell, or cauſe be ſauld, bye, or cauſe be bocht, within our Realme, or without the ſamin, the ſaides lawes, conſtitutiones, and actes, without the ſpeciall conſent and licence of those which are not. These are divided into 2 parts; the first occupies 162 leaves, the second 178. Then, "Ane table of the principall matters conteined in this buik, &c.---A table of all the kinges of Scotland," &c. with a folding sheet representing "The race of the Kings of Scotland, since Malcolme the second, Kenneth the thirds sonne.---Ane table of the moueable feastes for 50 zeires to cum." These affixes are not paged, and commence with a fresh set of signatures. According to the table of contents prefixed, here should follow, "The Interpretation of the termes" &c. and "Ane Catalogue of the Buikes conteinand the auld Lawes written before King James the First of gud memorie." The former of these we find in the next article, and probably the latter may be annexed to it. W.H. Folio.

1597. "De verborum significatione. The exposition of the termes and difficill wordes conteined in the foure buikes of *Regiam Majestatem*, and vthers in the actes of parliament, infeftments, and vsed in practicque in this realme; with divers rules and common places, or principalles of the lawes; collected and exponed be M. John Skene, clerke of our soveraine lordis register, council, and rolles. Edinb. printed by R. Waldegraue," &c. See the last article. Again 1599. Folio.

1597. "The Cherrie and the Slae. Compylt into Scottis meeter, be Alexander Montgomerie." A poem, describing the various passions of the human soul. "Edinburgh, printed be R. Walde-graue." In Mr. Ames, 1595 is set in the margin against this book; but, by the order in which it stands, suppose that date to be a misprint for 1597. Octavo.

1597. "Andreae Duncani studiorum puerilium clavis, miro quodam compendio ac facilitate Latinae linguae, ac poeticae rudimenta complectens. Edinb. excud. R. Walde-graue," &c. Octavo.

1597. "Certain sermons on several places of St. Paul's epistles. By Mr. Robert Rollock. Edinburgh." Mackenzie, III; 446. Octavo.

1597. "Tractatus de vocatione efficaci, que inter locos Theologie communissimos recensetur, deque locis specialioribus, qui sub vocatione comprehenduntur, &c. Authore Roberto Rolloco, Scoto. Edinburgi. Cum privilegio regio." Dedicated to King James VI. Quarto.

1597. Sir David Lindsay's works. Quarto.

1597. "The questions to be resolvit at the convention of the estaits and Generall Assemblie, appointed to be at the Burgh of Perth, the last day of Februarie

licence of our saide Clerk of Register, and his foresaides, induring the space of ten zeires, nixt after the daie and dait of this present, vnder the paine of escheitting of the samin, to our said Clerk of Register and his foresaides. And paying to him, and his foresaides, the summe of twa hundreth punds money of our Realme. To be taken vp be him and his foresaides, to their vtilitie and profite, induring the space foresaid, fra ilke ane of the contraveeners of this our privilege, inhibition, licence and discharge, als oft as it sall happen them, or onie of them, to break or contraveene the samin. Quhilk consent and licence of our said Clerk of Register, and his foresaids to the premisses, salbe verified be his awin manuall subscription, and na vtherwise, vpon onie paire or leafe of the saides imprented lawes. Subscrived with our hand, at Halyrude house, the 1. day of March. The zeir of God 1597 zeires. And of our Reigne the 31 zeire.

James R.

M. James Elphinstoun, Secretarius."

Februarie nixt to come." The arms of Scotland crowned, with I. R. on the sides, encircled with a ribbon of the order of the Thistle, having the motto, IN MY DEFENCE GOD ME DEFEND. Edinburgh Printed be Rob. VValde-graue Printer to the Kings Majestie. Anno Dom. 1597." The introduction "To the Reader" announces, "We—haue thocht comely,—To convene and assemble ane nationall counsell aswell of the ministrie as of our Estaits, and of all sorts of men of deepest learning and greatest sinceritie in Religioun, To be haldin &c. grauelie to treat—and determine (according to the word of God as the onely rule) vpon the clearing and distinguishing of the spirituall Iurisdictioun, alswell in applicatioun of doctrines as in the haill pollicie and government of the house of God. And—that all men may cum the better prepared to the saide Conventioun, being dewely forewarned and advised with the matteris that then are to be treated on. We haue thocht gude to set down certane Articles thairof in forme of questiouns as heirafter followis," &c. These questions are 55 in number, and subscribed, "James R." with a small x over the R, as p. 1518. W.H. Quarto.

"Daemonologie, in forme of a Dialogue, Diuided into three Books." 1597.
The King's arms as to the foregoing article. "Edinburgh Printed by Rob. Walde-graue—An. 1597. Cum priuilegio Regio." The preface to the Reader is subscribed, JAMES R, as p. 1518. Besides; 81 pages. Reprinted in king James's works. W.H. Quarto.

"Ane compendious booke of Godly and Spirituals sangs, collected 1597.
out of sundrie partes of the Scripture, With sundrie other Ballates, changed out of profane sanges, for avoyding of sinne, and harlotrie." Printed at Edinburgh,—1597. It was reprinted by Andr. Hart in 1601, with additions.

"In epistolam Pauli apostoli ad Thessalonicenses priorem com- 1598.
mentarius Roberti Rolloci Scoti, ministri Jesu Christi in ecclesia Edinburgensi." R. W. Also, "in posteriorem." The same size and year, "Adjecta est ejusdem authoris in epistolam Pauli apostoli ad Philemon Analysis logica." R. Walde-graue. Octavo.

"The recantation of maister Patrik Adamsone, sometime archbishop 1598.
of sanct Androwes in Scotland." No place, nor printer mentioned. 16°.

"The countesse of Pembrokes Arcadia. Written by sir Philip 1599.
Sidney, knight. Now the third time published, with sundry new additions of the same author. Edinburgh, printed by Rob. Walde-graue."* It is dedicated to his sister. Folio.

"Against sacrilege. Three sermons preached by maister Robert 1599.
Pont, an aged pastor in the kirk of God. Edinb. by R. Walde-graue." Octavo.

"Ane godly treatis, calit the first and second cumming of Christ, 1599.
with the tone of the wintersnycht; shewing breiflie of our native blindnes

* Spotswood has recited them all, very justly, though in English orthography, with here and there some peculiar Scoticisms. Hist. of the Ch. of Scotland, p. 434, &c. Collier has given them all paraphradically. Eccl. Hist. of Gr. Brit. Vol. II; 654, &c.

nes. Be James Anderson, minister of Christ his Evangell, 1595. Edinburgh be Robert Smyth, dwelling at the nether Bow." This contains 16 leaves, in seven-line stanzas. Sixteens.

1599. "Theses philosophicae, et ex iis illatae conclusiones, quas, auspice et propitio Deo, praeside Guil. Cragio, propugnaturi sunt Adolescentes magisterii candidati, è scholis Edinburgi philosophicis hac vice emittendi triginta tres, quorum nomina sequens indicabit pagina. Disputabuntur Edinburgi die Lunae 3 Kal. Augusti, a septima matutina in duodecimam, et ab hora prima pomeridiana usque ad vesperum, in aede sacra regii collegii.—Apud Henricum Charteris." Quarto.

1599. "Roberti Rolloci Scoti commentarius in Evangelium secundum Joannem.—Edinburgi." Octavo.

1599. Tusser's 500 points of good husbandry. By R. Walde-graue. Quarto.

1599. "A newe treatise of the right reckoning of yeares and ages of the World, and mens liues, and of the estate of the last decaying age thereof, this 1600 yeare of Christ, (Erroniouslie called a yeare of Jubilee) which is from the Creation, the 5548. yeare. Conteining sundrie singularities, worthie of obseruation, concerning courses of times, and revolutions of the Heauen, and reformations of Kalendars, and Prognostications: with a discourse of Prophecies and signes, preceeding the latter daye, which by manie arguments appeareth now to approch. With a godlie admonition in the end, vpon the words of the Apostle, to redeeme the time, because the dayes are evill. By M. Robert Pont, an aged Pastour in the Kirk of Scotland. The heades (8 *in number*) are set downe in certaine Propositions, in the Page following. Luke. 17. As it was in the dayes of Noe, so shall it be in the dayes of the Sonne of man. Edinburgh Printed by Rob. Walde-graue, printer to the Kings Maiestie, Anno 1599. Cum Priuilegio Regio." Dedicated "To the right reverende noble lord Alexander Seyton L. Vrquhard and Fyvie, President of the Senate of Justice, and Provest of Edinburgh, &c.—This last of October. 1599. Your L. ever ready to power in God. Robert Pont.---To the readers —Read, learne well, and try, Then judge advisedly." My copy is imperfect at the end; but seems not to want above a leaf or two, as it contains 5 leaves of the admonition. (N, in fours.) W.H. Quarto.

1599. "Vitae et mortis D. Roberti Rolloci, Scoti, narratio. Scripta per Georgium Robertsonum. Adjectis in eundem quorundam epitaphiis." With a catalogue of his works. Edinb. printed by Henry Charteris. 16°.

1599. "ΒΑΣΙΛΙΚΟΝ ΔΩΡΟΝ. Devided into three bookes. Edinburgh Printed by Rob. Walde-graue Printer *&c.* 1599." Enclosed within odd pieces, "Amor Pacis alumnus" on one side, and "Pax infelix malis" on the other. On the next leaf "The dedication of the booke. *A* Sonnet. ---The argument of the booke. *A* Sonnet.---To Henrie my dearest sonne and natural successour." The first book superscribed, "Anent a kings christian duetie towards God;" the second, "Anent a kings duetie in his office;" the third, "Anent a kings behaviour in indifferent things." X, in fours, Double pica Italic. At the end is the king's arms crowned, with

with I and R on the sides, and 6 under the crown, but without the motto, as p. 1519. W.H. Quarto.

"Gowries Conspiracie: A Discourse of the vnnaturall and vyle Conspiracie, attempted against the Kings Maiesties Person, at Sanct-Iohnstoun, vpon Twysday the Fifth of August, 1600. Edinburgh, Printed by Robert Charteris, 1600. Cum Privilegio Regio." Three sheets and a half. Harl. Miscel. III; 76. Octavo. 1600.

"An exposition of some select psalms of David, conteining great store of most excellent and comfortable doctrine, &c. Written by M. Robert Rollok, and translated out of Latin into English by C. L. from that printed at Geneva, 1599. Edinburgh, printed by R. Waldgrave." Octavo. 1600.

"Commentarius D. Roberti Rolloci, ministri ecclesiae, et rectoris academiae Edinburgensis, in epistolam Pauli ad Colossenses: Cum indice rerum, sententiarum & obseruationum dignissimarum copioso. 2 Cor. 3: 8. Omnes nos retecta facie gloriam Domini vt in speculo intuentes, &c. Edinburgi Excudebat Robertus Walde-graue, Typographus Regius. Anno Dom. 1600. Cum priuilegio Regis." Contains 181 pages besides the index, &c. Sixteens. 1600. 1600.

"Hadriani Dammanis a Bysterveldt Dn. de Fair-hill, Bartasias; qui de mundi creatione libri septem, è Gulielmi Sallustii Dn. de Bartas Septimana, poemate Francico liberius tralati, et multis in locis aucti. Edinburgi excudebat Robertus Walde-graue, Typographus Regis Anno Dom. 1600. Cum Priuilegio Regio." Dedicated "Sereniss. potentissimoq; regi Scotorum Jacobo sexto—P. P. Britanniarum principi optimo, Had. Damman—maiestati eius serenissimæ cliens devot. L.M.DD.C.Q." with another dedication "Ad illustriss. potentissimosq; Dnn. Dnn. Ordines in provinciis Geldriæ, &c. (the seven provinces only) parentes patriæ sanctissimos. Hadr. Damman.—Valete. Edinoduni Scotorum iv. ID. Februarias. ab Iesv nato, M.DC." Then, sundry commendatory verses, &c. in Greek and Latin, on 27 pages. The work 311 pages of Latin Hexameters. Brit. Mus. and W.H. Octavo. 1600.

"Theses philosophicae, quas Dei Opt. Max. ductu et auspiciis, praeside Joan. Adamsonio, ad diem IIII Non. Augusti, in aede sacra regii collegii, tueri conabimur Adolescentes 35 ex scholis Edinburgi philosophicis, hoc 1600 anno emittendi, Adamus Bruceus, &c. Excudebat Edinburgi Robertus Charteris, typographus regius." Quarto. 1600.

"Theses physicae de generatione et corruptione, quas favente Deo Opt Max. defendere conabor, sub praesidio clarissimi viri D. M. Joannis Echlini, philosophiae professoris in alma academia Sanctandreana dignissimi, Tobias Mierbekius, ad diem Aprilis, in collegio Mariano. Edinb. excud. Rob. Charteris. Cum privilegio." Quarto. 1600.

Daemonologie, &c. By King James VI. See it in 1597. Quarto. 1600.

OF

OF PRINTING IN *IRELAND.*

IRELAND was one of the last European states into which the art of printing was introduced. Mr. Ames used his best endeavours to procure from thence an account of its rise and progress in that kingdom before 1600; but all the information he received was the following

Extract of a letter from Dr. RUTTY, *of Dublin, dated June* 28, 1744, *to Dr.* WILLIAM CLARK, *of London.*

'THY commission for furnishing a catalogue of books, printed in Ireland before the year 1600, I think I have had pretty good opportunities of executing, and have accordingly made use of them. First, I had a particular acquaintance with a learned man, who has made things of this sort his particular study for many years, who is able to furnish me with but one book, which he can assure to have been printed here within that period, which is this:

1551. " The book of common prayer, and administration of the sacraments, and other rites and ceremonies of the church of England. Dubliniæ in officina Humphredi [1]Poweli. Cum privilegio ad imprimendum solum, anno Domini 1551." In black letter, a large *quarto.

Next, I had recourse to the large library of Dr. Worth, a late eminent physician here, who was exceedingly curious in collecting antient pieces, but there I found but one printed here, so early as even 1633. Lastly, on perusing the catalogue of the college library, I found within the period by thee limited, but that one individual book, as above recited. The truth is, printing is but of very late date in Ireland. Here were indeed some few authors within that period, but their works were printed abroad, as in England, France, Flanders, Italy, *&c.* Even down to 1700 very few books were printed here, but whatever was written here, was generally printed in London; even now the printing trade here consists chiefly in reprinting

[1] See p. 749. * Rather, as in Emmanuel Coll. Library, Folio.

reprinting books printed in London, and they that value their reputation, commonly send their writings to England to be printed. And this is all the satisfaction in my power to give thy friend, on this account.'

The two following books, purporting to have been printed at Waterford, are thought to have been privately printed in England, having no assurance of any press being set up so early at Waterford; besides it must have been as dangerous printing these books openly there during queen Mary's reign as in England; therefore they more properly belong to our General History: however we have given them a place here; one of them bearing the superscription; and the other having the same types, on the authority of Maunsell.

"The acquital or purgation of the moost catholyke Christen Prince Edwarde the VI. Kyng of Englande, Fraunce, and Irelande &c. and of the Churche of Englande refourmed and gouerned vnder hym, agaynst al suche as blasphemously and traitorously infame hym or the sayd Church, of heresie or sedicion. They are gone to Baal Peor, and runne awaye from the Lorde to that shamefull Idole, and are become as abominable as theyr louers. Ephraim flyeth lyke a birde, so shall theyr glorye also. Ose. 9." Dedicated "To the nobilitie and to the reste of the charitable christen laytie of Englande, John Olde wisheth grace and mercy from god the father, and from Jesus Christ the common and only saueour of the worlde, with the gifte of perfite faithe and earnest repentaunce." Contains F, in eights. Neatly printed in black letter, with the quotations in Italics, and the following colophon in Roman. "☞ Emprinted at Vvaterford the. 7. daye of Nouembre. 1555. ☞" W.H. Sixteens. 1555.

"An Epistle wrytten by John Scory the late bishope of Chichester vnto all the faythfull that be in pryson in Englande, or in any other troble for the defence of Goddes truthe: wherein he dothe, as well by the promises of mercy as also by thensamples of diuerse holy martyres, comfort, encorrage and strengthē them paciently for Christes sake to suffer the manifolde cruell and moste tyrānous persecutiōs of ẏ Antichristian tormentours: exhorting them to contynue in faythfull prayers, innocency of lyfe, pacience, and hope, that God maye the rather deliuer them, restore againe the light of his gospell to Englande, and consounde all the proude, beastly, & deuelishe enterprises of Antichristes garde, that doo imagine nothing els but ẏ subuersion of the gospell of Christ, and contynually thurste for the bloud of all true Christians. In the world ye shall haue tribulatiō: but be of good cheare, I have ouercum the worlde. John. 15. Anno 1555." Dedicated "Vnto the faythfull, and most valeaūt souldiours of the great captaine, the Lorde Jesus Christ, that be in prison in England, or any other where in banyshmēt and trouble for the defence of Goddes worde, John Scory willyngly a banished man for the same worde, wisheth from God our father, the grace, comfort, and strength of his holy Goost thorowe our only mediatour Jesus Christ." Contains B, in eights. Printed wholly in the black letter, with the marginal references in Italics, like the foregoing article. At the end, 1555.

"Apoca. 22.

"Apoca. 22. Veni Domine Jesu cito. Anno. 1555." Without printer's name, or place. See Maunsell, p. 95. W.H. Sixteens.

— A catechism translated into Irish by John Kerney,* treasurer of St. Patrick's, was printed with Irish types; and is supposed to have been the first book printed in that character. This seems to have been accomplished while his intimate friend and companion Nicholas Walsh was chancellor of St. Patrick's, who was consecrated bishop of Ossory in Feb. 1577. Though this may be the first book printed in Irish in that kingdom, yet we find an Irish liturgy printed in 1565 for the use of the Highlanders of Scotland. See p. 1489. Indeed we are not told where it was printed, nor whether it was in the Irish character, or not.

— Sir Henry Sidney ordered All the statutes enacted in Ireland from their prime institution down to his own time to be collected and published in *print. That they were printed accordingly, See Vowel's Epistle dedicatory in the following article. Sir Richard Bolton, Lord Chief Baron of Ireland, in a new edition, printed at Dublin in folio 1621, is said to have supplied several defects in the former edition; many good statutes in full force having been overlooked and omitted by Sir Henry's collectors. See the writers of Ireland, p. 327 and 337.

(1572.) "The Order and vsage of keeping of the Parlements in England, collected by Iohn Vowel alias Hooker gentleman," Thus inscribed, "To the right honorable his very good Lord Sir VVilliam fitz vvilliams, Knight, L. deputye of Ireland, Iohn Vovvel alias Hooker, vvith all humblenes and due reuerēce, vvissheth a happy successe and a prosperous gouernmēt to th'encrease of Gods honor in true Religion, the Queenes maiesties seruice in due obedience, and the administration of the publique vvelth in Iustice, Equitie and Iudgement." In which epistle after mentioning, "the good and wholsōe lawes which though with great wisdome and for the preseruation of the comon welth were deuised: yet beeing laid vp in a secret and priuat place, and nother published nor put in execution: great disorders and continual rebellions haue growen dayly therby, which great euils and inormities growing by thone, the Queenes maiestie of her goodnes and by the aduise of her prudent gouernors in this land hath for redresse caused, commaunded and willed all tholde wholsome and good lawes and Statutes of this land to be imprinted, & to be dispersed throughout all the whole land, that ignoraunce by knowledge, and disobedience by loyaltie, being banished and

* He translated, at least greatly assisted in translating, the Bible into Irish, which was extant in MS. in Sir James Ware's time. See Harris's translation of Ware, Vol. I; p. 419. Irish Writers, p. 98.

* "Whereas there were manie good lawes and statutes established in the realme, which hitherto were laid vp and shrowded in filth and cobwebs, and vtterlie vnknowne to the most part of the whole land, and euerie man ignorant in the lawes of his owne countrie, he (*Sir Henry Sidney*) caused a thorough view, and a review to be made, and then a choise of all such statutes as were most necessarie to be put in vre and execution: which being done, he caused to be put in print, to the great benefit of that whole nation." The Chronicles of Ireland, by Vowel, printed in Holinshed, 1586. p. 151.

and chafed out of this land: each man dutifully doth yeeld him felf loially to her highnes and obedient to her lawes, thefe being the only meanes and remedies to make a profperous gouernment and a happy common welth." Dated, "The third of Octobr. 1572." The author had been a burgefs in the Irifh parliament held at Dublin in January 1568-9, before Sir Henry Sidney, Lord Deputy; in which there had been great commotions for want of order and regularity: whereupon motion and requeft was made to the Speaker that fuch diforderly behaviour might be reformed, who not only promifed fo to do, but alfo praied advice and counfel for his doings therein of fuch as were acquainted with the orders of parliaments in England, which was promifed by our author, and that a book of fuch orders fhould in time be fet forth in print. He came over into England accordingly and was chofen a member for Exeter in the parliament, held at Weftminfter the 13th of Eliz. 1571. "And beeing thus placed in that honorable affembly: *(he tells his patron)* I thought it then a moste fit time for the acquittall of my faid promife, wherfore diligently I did obferue, confider and mark all maner of orders, vfages, rites, ceremonies and all other circumftāces, which either I fawe with eye, or found regeftred among the records of that affembly. And having written the fame: I did then confer with the exemplars and prefidents of tholde and auncient Parlemēts vfed in tymes paft, within the faid Realme of England, wherof I found two, the one was that, which king Edgar (or as fome fay, king Edward the cōfeffor) vfed, thother, which was in vre in the time of kīg Edward the firft. The forme afwel for antiquities fake, as alfo for a prefidēt to the good gouernemēt in tholde yeers: I haue annexed to thefe prefents, thother in fōe things agreeable, & in many things difagreeable, bothe frō the first and the laft: I haue omitted. This which now is in vre being it which is onely to be folowed and vfed." After this epiftle dedicatory, "The olde and auncient order of keeping of the Parlement in England, vfed in the time of King Edward the Confeffor." This ancient order is on 8 leaves. Then, "The order and vfage how to keep a Parlement in England in thefe dayes, colected by John Vowel alias Hooker gentleman, one of the Citizens for the Cittie of Exeter at the Parlement holden at VVeftminfter Anno Domine Elifabethæ Reginæ decimo Tertio. 1571." This on 31 pages is reprinted in his Chronicles of Ireland, inferted in Holinfhed, 1586. Annexed are "The names of all fuch perfonages as ought to appeer and be in the Parlement. In the higher [y] houfe.---What they be that ought to be In the lower [z] houfe. Contains J, in fours. On

the

y "The King. The Lord Speaker. A Proctor for the kingdome of Fraunce. A Proctor for Scotland. A Proctor for the Duchie of Aquitane. A Proctor for the Duchie of Guyen. A Proctor for the Duchie of Angewe. The Archbifhop of Canterbury,—of York. The Bifhop of London. —of Couentrie,—of Welles." (Without mention of Litchfield, or Bath.) Alfo, the reft of the bifhops. "The Duke of Norfolke. The Marques of Northampton.—of Winchefter. The Earle of Arundel." &c.

z Knights, particularifed for the feveral counties of England and Wales. Citizens, —for the cities. Barons of the five Portes. Burgeffes of towns.

the last leaf, only his achievement of arms in a larger form than that to his lives of the bishops and officers of Exeter. See p. 958. This book has neither printer's name, nor date of printing; however, the singularity of some of the types, and the repeated expressions of *this land*, &c. in the dedication, make it highly probable that it was printed in Ireland. W.H. Quarto.

1587. William Farmer wrote an Almanac for Ireland, printed in Dublin 1587, which I mention as being perhaps the earliest almanac published in, or for, that country. Quarto.

I have not found any other books printed in this kingdom within our limited time; but though authors might generally send their works to London, Paris, or Antwerp to be printed, it may very reasonably be supposed that small treatises, proclamations, ballads, &c. were printed here from time to time.

Mr. Ames mentions The Irish Common Prayer printed in the Irish character, in 1608; dedicated to sir Arthur Chichester, knight, Lord Deputy general, by William, archbishop of Tuam, 20. October, 1609. Printed by John Franckton. Folio.

When the said Franckton began printing here, or indeed elsewhere, we have not learned. I have examined, but cannot find him apprenticed to any member of the Stationers' company in London; so that probably he learned the art of printing here, and had practised it for some time before the abovementioned Common Prayer.

Mr. Ames mentions also The English statutes in force in Ireland, and several proclamations printed by him as king's printer, &c. but as they were after our prescribed time, hope to be excused in not enlarging further on them.

Very good printing has been carried on in Ireland for more than a century past.

THE

THE

GENERAL HISTORY

OF

ENGLISH PRINTING,

As well in Foreign Parts as in *ENGLAND*.

CONTAINING,

Besides several private books, and such as could not be ranged under the foregoing Printers, an account of those printed abroad by Englishmen, and other printers for them. Many books are inserted also for want of being able to ascertain the printer's name; being deficient in their respective title-pages, colophons, &c.

ALSO,

Several Orders, Acts, Proclamations, Patents, *&c.* relating thereto; for the better illustrating this subject before the year 1600.

"A BOKE of noblesse, compiled to the most high and mighty prince, king Edward the IV. for the avauncing and praeferring the commyn publique of the royames of England and France. Written to stir up the English to recover the lost lands in France, MCCCCLXXI." This from Bishop Tanner's MSS. 1471.

Among Mr. Bagford's papers, which were in the possession of the Rev. Dr. Wilkins, is this note: 'The Booke called, " Lumen Animae," ends happily, which after it had layd hid, not without great paynes, is brought to light, by characters, or letters of tin, to the praise 1482.

of almighty God, and the honour of the whole church triumphant; as also to the utility of its pious sons, being finished with the greatest diligence in the year of our Lord 1481. the next day after Litane.' But no place, printer, nor size mentioned.

In the year 1483, we do not seem to have had printers enow of our own; for, in the statutes made I. Richard 3. concerning Italians and other Foreigners, is this proviso at the conclusion of the 12th chapter, viz. "Provided always, that this act, or any parcel thereof, or any other act made, or to be made in this said parliament, shall not extend, or be in prejudice, disturbance, damage, or impediment, to any artificer, or merchant stranger, of what nation or countrey he be, or shall be of, for bringing into this realm, or selling by retail, or otherwise, any books written or printed, or for inhabiting within this said realm for the same intent, or any scrivener, alluminor, reader, or printer of such books, which he hath, or shall have to sell by way of merchandise, or for their dwelling within this said realm, for the exercise of the said occupations; this act, or any part thereof notwithstanding."

1485. "Heir eyndet dat boeck welck ghehieten is Bartholomeus vanden propriepten derdinghen inden iaer ons heren M.CCCC. ēn LXXXV optē heynlighen kersauent. Ende is gheprint en de oeck mede volyndt to Haerlem in Hollant teren godes ende om lerin ghe der menschen van mi meester Jacop Benaert ghiboren van Zerixzee." In the Bodleian library. Folio.

(1485.) The Shepherdes Kalendar. See p. 209. Note f. Quarto.

1492. "The veray trew history of the valiaūt knight Jasō How he conqueryd or wan the golden fles. by the Counsel of Medea. and of many othre victoryouse and wondresfull actis and dedys that he dyde by his prowesse and chevalrye in his tyme:." Over a cut representing Jason attacking a dragon and two bulls, before an edifice; at a distance is a ram on the declivity of a hill: This cut is introduced again on the back of signature i,iiij. This edition of Caxton's translation, with the addition of cuts, is printed on a remarkable square and fat letter. Contains n 6 in eights, without pages, running-titles, or catch-words. Colophon, "Here endyth Thystorie of the noble & vailliaūt knight Jason: & prentyd by me Gerard Leeu in the towne of Andewarpe/ In the yere of oure lord/ M.CCCC. fowre skore and twelve/ & synyshed the secunde day of Juyne". Under which is a castle. W.H. Folio.

1493. "Here ben endyd the cronycles of the reame of England, with their apperteynaunces. Emprentyd in the duchye of Braband, in the towne of Andewarpe, in the year of our lord M.CCCCXCIII. by maister Gerard de Leeue, a man of grete wysdom in all maner of kunnyng, whych now is come from lyfe unto the deth, whych is grete harme for many a poure man. On whos sowle God almyghty for his high grace have mercy." Peterborough library. Small Folio.

1494. Liber festivalis with the Quatuor Sermones. Colophon, "Finitum et completum Rothomagi Anno Domini. MCCCCLXXXXIV." Again 1495. 4°.

"Incipit

"Incipit liber qui vocatur festiualis de nouo correctus et impressus." 1495.
This title is under a representation of the pope receiving mass; and on the back is a cut of the crucifixion over Abraham offering up his son Isaac, separated by a pillar from Moses lifting up the brazen serpent; underneath is a small cut of St. George, probably for R. Pinson's sign. The Liber festivalis ends on folio cxxv with this colophon, "Finitū et completū extat hoc opusculu Jn celeberrima vrbe Parisiensi. Anno dnī M.cccc.xcv. die vero xxvi. Februarii. impensis Nicolai Comitis." My copy wants part of the table and the quatuor sermones. W.H. Quarto.

"Imagynation de Uraye noblesse." Dedicated to king Henry vii. (1496.)
"10 Jan. from the manor of Shene 1496. per Poulet."

"Lac puerorum." See Knight's Life of Dean Colet, page 133. (1497.)

"Robertus Castellēn. Apostolice sedis protonotarius. Et adhuc (1498.)
sanctissimi domini nostri pape commisarius. Tibi, &c. Datum London xxvi Feb. M cccc xcviii." A single sheet.

A similar one; but on vellum, dated Lond. 2 die Feb. 1499, The (1499.)
Rev. Dr. Lort. It is an indulgence from the pope, and appears to be Wm. Faques's Letter.

"¶ Incipit liber qui vocatur festiualis de nouo correctus & īpressus 1499.
rothom." This title is under a cut of a group of persons at prayer. Colophon, "Finitum et completum extat hoc opusculū Jn celeberrima vrbe Rothomagensi, per Magistrum Martinum Morin. Anno domini Millesimo quadringentesimo nonagesimo nono, die vero vicesima secunda mensis Junii, impensis Johannis Richardi. ¶ Non viribus aut velocitatibus aut celeritate corporum: res magne geruntur: sed Cōsilio Sentēcia et Auctoritate. ¶ Postea sequitur tabula huius libri." Then follow the "Quatuor sermones." At the end, "Jmpressum est hoc opus impensa et ere Johānis Richardi mercatoris in ciuitate Rothomagen. commorantis. Anno domini Millesimo quadringētesimo nonagesimo nono. et venale inuenies iuxta ecclesiam metropolitanā ante domum consilii." His device on a shield hung on a tree supported by a lady in robes, and an unicorn. Neatly printed in double columns. Rev. Dr. Lort. W.H. 4°.

"¶ The valuacyō of golde and syluer made ī ẏ yere m.cccclxxxxix. (1499.)
holde ī the marke vnce englice quart'trope. dewes and aes The maner for to weight wyth pēnes and graynes and here in is sett ẏ fygures of ẏ spaynyssh and Poortyngalyssh ducates whiche is now." Illustrated with representations of several coins. Contains c 6, in eights. On the last page is a cut of the V. Mary and Elizabeth, with the child Jesus as passing from the lap of one to the other's. The arms of England underneath. See p. 412. W.H. Sinteens.

"The kalendayr of the shyppars." See p. 208. This title is over 1503.
a table of contents and on the back is a cut as described in p. 280. It has neither pages, running-titles, nor catch-words. The type is very rude, though the wood-cuts are in general very neat. The following extract may serve as well for a specimen of the orthography as to shew the time

time of its being originally writen in French, viz. "Etshal serwe the sayd nūbers be for the lettars seryals. xix. zear cūpleyt: from the zear of thys present kalendar oon thowsand. iiii. hondreth. lxxxxvii. wnto the zear oon thowsand.[a] xvi. in the qwych zear shall begyn to serue the goldyn nūber et the others nombrys after the lettars seryals al in the maynayr as they be for other xix. zear. Al the remanant of the compot & of the kalendayr ys perpetwel: fors the two goldyn nombrys so shal they be. xxxviii. zear hool of the qwych zear oon thowsand. cccc.iiiixx. &. xvii. ys the fyrst.—The zear of thys present cūpot & kalēdar qwych as begown to haue cowrs the fyrst day of ianuer ys. M.cccc.iiiixx. &. [b]vii. in the qwych rynnys for the golden nombyr. xvi. The lettar domynycal a the lettar tabulayr f & ar in the first lynys of theyr fygurs & nerest the goldyn nombyr. xvi. for zear qwych ys sayd of this presant cōpot and kalendayr." Contains m, in eights. "¶ Heyr endysh the kalendar of shyppars translatyt of franch I englysh to the lowyng of almyghty god & of hys gloryows mother mary and of the holy cowrt of hywvn prentyt ī parys the xxiii day of iuyng oon thowsand. ccccc. & iii." W.H. Folio.

1503. "The traytte of the art of good lyuyng and good deyng, translatyt in Parys the xiii day of May, of Franch in Englysh, oon thowsand v hondreth and iii zears; imprentyt in Parys xxx day of the mowneth of May." With wooden cuts by Antoine Verad. Emmanuel College, Camb. Quarto.

1506. The Siege of Rhodes, translated by John Kay. See p. 100.

(1508.) "The passion of owr lord iesu christe wythe the contemplatiōs." On the back is a cut of the author presenting his book to the king; opposite, is another of our Saviour and his disciples apparently going from Bethany towards Jerusalem; on the back of which the treatise begins thus, "¶ Her begynnythe ẏ passion of dar seygneur, Jesu chryste front y resuscytaciō of lazarus and to thende translatet owt of frēche ynto englysche the yer of dar lorde. M.v.c.viij. On to the leawde of god ād of the souueraīe vyrgyne marie & of all ẏ saīctes of peradys celestyall. And at the requeste of the moste puissāt and redoubtye kynge Henry the. vij. be the grace of god bynge of englande and of frāce: the passiō of owr sauueur Jesu chryste ys translated owht of frēche yn to ēglysche with an addiciō of moralytees hystoricees examples or fygures Takyg the begynnyg of ẏ resuscitatiō of lazare. &c. It is very incorrectly printed, and has neither running-titles, catch-words, nor pages; nor name of printer, place, nor date of printing, but contains g 4, in eights. W.H. Folio.

1508. "Parabole alani cum commento. 23 Augusti." 17 leaves. Quarto.

1510. Libellus sophistarum ad vsum Cantabrigien. 7 Sept. Quarto.

—— "Vocabula magistri Stanbrigii, primum jam edita, sua saltem editione. This piece has only five leaves, imprinted for Martin Coeffin, dwelling at Exeter. "Impressum Rothomagi in officina Laurentii Hostinque et Jameti Loys, juxta Nonne forum commorantium."

"Catho,

[a] Evidently an omission of 500 years. [b] An x is certainly left out here.

"Catho, cum Commento." At the end, "Explicit tractatus verborum defectivorum. Impressus Rothomagi in officina Richardi Goupil, juxta conventum sanct. Augustin ad intersignum regulae aurae commorantis." At the expence, and for Martin Coffin, dwelling at Exeter. Quarto.

"The wonderful shape and nature of man, beastes, serpentes, fowles, fishes, and monsters." See p. 412. Folio.

"The storie *(or adventures)* of the parson of Kalenborowe." Who pretended to fly, to get off his bad wine in a hot day. With wooden cuts. One of which is his pretending to fly over the river Tonowa, as may be seen below.[a] There are no catch-words, running-titles, or pages. W.H. Quarto.

"Virgilius. ¶ This boke treateth of the lyfe of Virgilius/ and of his deth, and many maruayles/ that he dyd in his lyfe tyme by whychcrafte and nygramansy/ thorowgh the helpe of the deuyls of hell." This title is over a very ludicrous cut, repeated on signature C. 1. The back, blank: on the front of the next leaf is "¶ The prologe." Contains A, B, & D, in sixes: C, E, and F, in fours. Colophon, "¶ Thus endethe the Lyfe of Virgilius/ with many dyuers consayetes/ that he dyd/ Emprynted in the Cytie of Anwarpe, By me John Doesborcke/ dwellynge at ÿ camer porte."

"¶ The Copye of the letter folowing whiche specifyeth of the greatest

[a] "Our parson of kalenborow had wyne in his seler whiche was marred/ and because he wold haue no losse be it he practysed a wyle to be ridde of it, and caused it to be poblysshed in many Parysshes there abowt that the parson of kalenborow at a daye assigned wolde fle ouer the reuer of Tonowa frome the steppyll of his churche/ and this he proclaymed in his owne parisshe alsoy and than he caused, ij. wynges of pecockes fedders to be made/ and also he caused his noughty wynes to be brought vnder the churche steppyll where as he sholde stande for to fle ouer the reuer/ and he gaue the clerke charge of his wyne because he sholde sell it well and dere to the moste profyte. ¶ And when the day was come that the parson sholde fle, many one come theder to se the maruayle/ frome farre contrey/ and than the parson went vpon the steppyl arayed lyke an Angell redy for to fle, and there he flickered oftentymes with his wynges but he stode styll. In the mean whyle that the people stode so to beholde hym, the sonne shone hote and they had great thurste/ for the preste dyd nat fle, and he se that and beckened to them sayage ye good people my tyme is nat yet to fle/ but tary a whyle and ye shall se what I shall do/ and than the people went and dronke apace of this wyn that they se ther for to sell/ and they dronke so long that they coude gete no more wyne for money and cryed out for drynke and made great prease/ and within a lytell whyle after the clerke come to the parson and sayde sir your wyne is all solde and well payde for though there had ben more/ The parson beinge very gladde of this tydinges began to flicker with his wynges agayne/ and called with a lowde voyce vnto the peple/ saing harke, harke harke/ is their any amonge you all that euer se man haue winges or fle/ there stepped one furth and saide/ nor neuer shall be my fay. ¶ Therfor go your wayes home euery chone and say that ye haue dronke vp the parson of kalenborows euyll wynes and payd for it well and truly more than euer it cost hym/ thus ware the vilayns or paysants merueilously angry/ and in their language cursed the parson perillously/ some with a myschaunce/ and vengeaunce/ and some sayd god geue hym a hondred drouses/ for he hathe made amonge vs many a fole and yonge ape. But the parson Cared not for all theyr curses. And this subtyle dede was spred all the countre about."

greatest and meruelous visyoned batayle, that euer was sene or herde of, And also of the letter ẏ was sent frome the great Turke vnto our holy fad' ẏ pope of Rome." The former one was written by Bartholomeus de Clere ville "in ẏ castell of ville clere, in ẏ yere of our lorde M.CCCCC.XVj. in the month of Januarij." The latter, for its singularity, may be seen in the notes.[d] The whole contains 4 leaves; no signatures. Quarto.

—— "¶ Here begynneth a lyttell story, that was of a trewthe done in the lande of Gelders, of a mayde that was named Mary of Nēmegen, ẏ was the dyuels paramoure by the space of .vij. yere longe." This title over a cut of the maid, the divel, &c. Contains 20 leaves; no signatures. At the end, "¶ Al this in this boke conteyned is for a treweth and if that ye wyll nat beleue me that was the fyrst maker of this boke if that it fortune ony of you for to goo into the Lande of Flanders to a towne called Mastryche and go to the Nonry of the conuerted synners there shall ye see Emmekyns graue and also ẏ yron rynges hangyng there ouer and vndernethe wryten hyr lyuynge and also hyr pennaūce and she lyued but iij. yere after she was delyuered of ẏ rynges and so departed and went vnto the blysse euerlastyng to the whyche blysse God brynge both you and me. AMEN. + ¶ Thus endeth this lytell treatyse Jmprinted at Anwarpe by me John Duisbrowghe dwellynge besyde the camer porte." The last leaf the same as to Virgilius. Quarto.

1512. Some of Skelton's poems and Satyrs. See Hist. Eng. Poetry, II;
1512. "More knaues?" &c. Catal. Bibl. Harl. iii; N. 5926.
p. 336, note f. And Bibl. Tanner, p. 675.

1513. "Roberti Whittintoni, Lichfeldiensis, Grammatices Magistri,—de octo partibus Orationis." Hist. of Eng. Poetry. II; p. 131.

1515. "A Brief graunted by Pope Leo X. for the relief of John and Richard Busset Merchants of Avignon. To be published in all Parish churches. In

[d] "Marboryn Ramosyn sone of the grete kinge Olisornes be the grace of the great god Mahounde descended of the hye lyne captayne of Tartaryne Baron of Turkye, prince of the hebrues. Emperour of parygoone of the londes of hungary and of walaricque, of the londe of Sury vnto paradys terrestre, atcheuer of Constantynople, and of the christen londes geue knowlege vnto the grete preest of Rome that we haue vnderstande that you and your yonge kynge will warre vpon vs through the broders request of the Rodes, but we beleue nat that the great god hathe geuen your so moche power, wherfore we commande you to ouerse this letter and tourne frome your great folisshenes and cause for to sease the iiij. knyghtes of the Rodes, that is to vnderstande Amas queron, Potell, Vaophanne, and Gerson, or elles we will comme and visite you wyth. lxxj. noble kynges of ours, and wyll do wyth your temple of Rome as we haue done of our great god mahounde. Also we send worde vnto your alyed yonge kynge that we wyl stryke of his hede the best cite of his royalme. & because ye sholde knouwe that we are able ynough therto we send you here. iij. giftes the first is plate golde, the secunde is clothe of golde, the thyrde is ryche orient perles with precyous stones. and as for this tyme present, no more to you butt the great god Mahounde kepe and preserue you Wrytten in our grete cite of Chapne, in that yere. vi M. and of our reigne the. x. yere.

"Emprented in the famous cite of Andwarpe Be me John of Dousborowe."

In English. Graunted 28 Aug. 1515." No printer's name, but greatly like Pinson's smaller letter. A broad Sheet.

An Indulgence in Latin by Wm. Prior of Crutched Friars, near the Tower of London, for pardon of all Sins to those that visit that house on certain days and bestow their alms on it. London dated at their Monastery. This and the preceding article is in the collection of the Rev. Dr. Lort. A long Sheet. 1515.

"The houres of our Ladie after the vse of the Church of Yorke." See Reg. Scot's Discovery of Witchcraft, p. 234. 1516.

"Causes that be proponed and tracted in a Consultacyon of a Journey, to be made with the Tokyn of the holy Crosse/ agaynst the Infideles and Turkes, and sent to all cristen prynces, to thentent that they throughe their good counsell, and wyse examinacyon, sholde examyne, yf any thynge therin be, that out ought to be encreased, or mynyshed; or yf ought to be correctyd. This done the xii daye of Nouember." Quarto. 1517.

"This mater treateth of a merchaũtes wyfe/ that afterwarde went lyke a mã, and becam a great Lorde/ and was called Frederyke of Jennen afterwarde." Beneath, a woman in a martial equipment. Colophon, "Thus endeth this lyttell storye of lorde Frederyke/ Inprynted ĩ Anwarpe by me John Dusborowghe/ dwellynge be syde ẏ Camer porte/ in the yere of our lorde god a M.CCCCC. and XVIII." On the back of the title-page is his device; on another leaf the king's arms, and on the back thereof his device repeated. Contains 25 leaves; without numbers, signatures, or catch-words, but has many cuts. Quarto. 1518.

"Erasmi Latina versio metrica IPHIGENIÆ in Aulide. Fabric. Biblioth. Gr. Londini." See Maittaire, vol. 2, p. 339. 1519.

"Vulgaria Guil. Hermani Cæsarisburgensis. Apud urbem Londini. Ib. 2; p. 341. Quarto. 1519.

A Salisbory Missal.—"Opera magistri Petri Oliuier expensis Jacobi Cousin, Parisiis, 1519." Folio. 1519.

"The chance of the dolorous Lover." Hist. Eng. Poetry, III; p. 84. 1520.

"Of the newe landes/ and of the People founde by the Messengers of the kynge of Portyngale/ named Emanuel. Of the x dyuers nacyons crystened. Of pope Johan and his landes, and of the costely keyes and wonders Molodyes, that in that lande is." With several cuts. The end thus: "And we pray you/ that ye wyl writte us agen with the berer of this lettre, and send to us ageyn a good knyght of the generacyon of Fraunce. And we pray the kynge of Fraunce, that he wyll vs recommaunde to the myghty kyng of Englande; and also to all other kynges, the whyche dwelleth beyonde the see, tho that bee crystened; and we pray God, that he thou wyl gyue the grace of the holy goost, Amen. Written in oure holy pallays, in the byrth of my self v houndred and seuen. Emprenteth by me John of Doesborowe." Then the king's arms. It has no date; but by mentioning Emanuel king of Portugal, and exclaiming against Luther, it might be about 1521, or 1522, when king Emanuel died, and Luther was burnt in effigy. Quarto. ——

"A breif, or indulgence, granted to syr John Pyllet, &c. knight of 1521.

8 S the

the holy sepulcre at Jerusalem, comming from thence; who had been taken prisoner by the infidells, and redeemed by the Venetian merchants, at the value of two thousand ducates. To collect and receive from all the kings subjects, and pay the merchants. The sume of the whole Indulgence is vii thousand 5 hundred dayes of pardon, and God's blessing, with the kings." A broadside.

"A mery jest of the mylner of Abington, with his wife and doughter, and two poor schollers of Cambridge." Imperfect at the end. Twelves.

1524. "Psalterium cum hymnis ad usum insignis ecclesiae Sarum et Eboracens. Opusculum quidem non solum ad ecclesiasticum observandum ritum, tum et cuilibet diuino eloquio insudanti apprime commodum et necessarium. Venundantur Londonii apud Petrum Kaetz." Colophon, "—Antwerpiæ opera & industria Christopheri Ruremunden, sumptibus autem Petri Kaetz, feliciter impressum, anno virginei partus M.CCCCC.XXIIII. die vero XII mensis Novembris." Brit. Topogr. II; p. 340. Octavo.

1524. "Arte or Crafte of Rhetoricke." By Leonard Coxe. Hist. Eng. Poetry, II; p. 446.

—— "Manuale secundum usum insignis et preclare ecclesie Sarum optimis typis (ut res ipsa indicat) non sine singulari industria. Antwerpie impressum, plurimis quibus prius scatebat mendis superuacaneisque tum tersis tum sublatis.—Venundantur Londoni apud Petrum Kaetz." At the end a cypher, and under it "Christopherus Endoviensis." Brit. Topogr. II; p. 340.

1525. "Processionale ad vsum insignis ac preclare ecclesie Sarū/ nouiter ac rursus castigatū/ per excellentissimū ac vigilantissimum et reuerendissimum in Christo patrem dominū nostrū dominū episcopū de vinton. feliciter incipit. Antwerpie impressum/ per Christophorū. endouiē. impensis honesti mercatoris Petri kaetz). Anno Domini. 1525. Die vero. 6. Februarij." Device, three roses on a shield hanging on a tree supported by two lions; his mark with "Petrus KAETZ" on a ribband at the bottom. Under it, "¶ Venundantur Londonii apud Petrum kaetz." Colophon, "Processionale cum bonis notulis/ et bonis ligaturis cū stationibus picturatis infra appositis. Secundum vsum—Sarum/ noviter correctum ac rursus emendatū/ per Christophorū endouien. Antwerpie excusū. Impensis fidelissimi Petri kaetz. Anno ab incarnatione domini. 1525. Die vero. 6. Februarij." On the last page is a device, three red flower de luces in chief & the mark. C. E. on a shield hanging on a tree, on the top of which is the Virgin & child; at bottom, "Christophor, ruremūden." Underneath "¶ Venales reperiuntur Londonijs apud fidelissimum Petrum Kaetz." Contains Folios clxxv, besides another on which is the colophon and device. Rev. Dr. Lort. Quarto.

1525. "Opus nouum. Gildas Britannus monachus, cui sapientis cognomentum est inditum, de calamitate, excidio, et conquestu Britanniae, quam Angliam nunc vocant. Author vetustus à multis diu desyderatus, et nuper in gratiam D. Cutheberti Tonstalli Londinens. Formulis excusus. Polydor Vergil." Dedicated to bishop Tonstal, London. See p. 644. Octavo.

"The

" The exposicyon of saynt Augustynes rule, after the great clerke and holy saynt Hugh, called, " De sancto Victore," by the wretche of Syon, Rycharde Whytforde. London. See p. 168. Quarto. 1525.

" Jo. Wiclefi viri undiquaque piis, dialogorum libri quattuor. Quorum primus diuinitatem et ideas tractat. Secundus uniuersarum creationem complectitur. Tertius de uirtutibus, uitiisque ipsis contrariis, copiosissime loquitur. Quartus Ro. ecclesiae sacramenta, eius pestiferam dotationem, antichristi regnum, fratrum fraudulentam originem, atque eorum hypocrisim, variaque nostro aevo scitu dignissima, graphice perstringit; quae ut essent inuentu facilia, singulorum librorum, tum caput, tum capitis summam, indice praenotavimus." It has 175 leaves, in Roman letter, numbered with capital numerals, besides six, containing the prologue and index.* Quarto. 1525.

The discovery of printing contributed greatly to the revival of learning in Europe. Lord Herbert, in his life of king Henry VIII. p. 157. supposed that Cardinal Wolsey stated the effects of this new art to the pope, thus: " That his Holinesse could not be ignorant what divers effects this new invention of Printing had produced. For as it had brought in and restored Books and Learning, so together it hath been the occasion of those Sects and Schismes, which daily appeared in the World.—For this purpose, since Printing could not be put down, it were best to set up Learning against Learning; and by introducing able persons to dispute, to suspend the layity, betwixt feare and controversies. This at worst yet would make them attentive to their Superiors and Teachers."

The New Testament translated into English by William Tindal was printed about this time.[f] See Lewis, p. 72, Ch. II. and Crutwell's preface to the Bible with the various renderings, and notes by Bishop Wilson. It begins with an epistle to the reader which concludes, as below.[g] Contains 353 leaves, besides the epistle to the reader and errata; no marginal texts but what are written, and the initial letters beautifully gilt and illuminated. Sixteens. (1526.)

 After

* This very scarce book was in Mr. Ames's possession, bought at Dr. Evans's sale for 3l. 14s. There is no printer's name to it, but probably as it has the same compartment with another book of his, intituled, " Nova medicinae methodus curandi morbos, ex mathematica scientia deprompta, nunc denuo revisa et exactissime emendata. Johanne Hasfurto Virdungo, medico et astrologo doctissimo authore Haganone excusum, anno 1533." quarto, by Valentine Kob, and having the same compartment, he might be the printer.

[f] This first edition was in the possession of Mr. Ames, who bought it for 15s. out of the Harleian Library, N. 410, sold by T. Osborne, 1743. Mr. John White purchased it for 15l. 4s. 6d. at the auction of Mr. A's books, N. 1252, sold by Langford, 1760; and sold it for 21l. to Doctor Gifford, who at his decease bequeathed it, with many others, to the Baptist Museum, Bristol.

[g] " Them that are learned christenly, I beseche; for as moche as I am sure, and my conscience beareth me record, that of a pure entent singilly and faithfully I haue interpreted itt, as farre forth as God gave me the gyfte of knowledge, and understondyng; that the rudnes of the worke nowe at the fyrst tyme, offende them not; but that they consyder how that I had no man to counterfet, nether was helpe with Englysshe of eny that had interpreted the same, or soche lyke thinge in the scripture before tyme. Moreover, even very necessitie and combraunce (God is recorde) above strengthe, which I will not rehearse, lest we should seem to bost our selves, caused that many thynges are lackyng, whiche necessaryly are required

After the first edition, the Dutch printed others in 1527, 1528 or 29,[h] 1530, and 1534,[i] of which last, see p. 567. The Biogr. Brit. mentions editions in both 1528 and 1529, making five before Tindal printed his second edition.

Sometime between this edition of Tindal's New Testament, and the second in 1534, he published

—— "A compendious introduccion, prologe or preface vn to the pistle off Paul to the Romayns." This is muchhe same, except a few additions, with that published in the N. T. 1534, but, by whom, or when, this was printed, I cannot determine; the bottom part of the last leaf in my copy being cut, which possibly might have had a colophon. At the end of the introduction is "Here foloweth a treates (to fill vpp the leefe with all) of the pater noster, very necessary and profitable, wherein (yff thou marke) thou shalt perceave what prayer is and all that belongeth to prayar. The sinner prayeth the peticions of the pater noster, and God answereth by the lawe;" &c. Contains c, 6, in eights, no catch-words or pages. W.H. Octavo.

A prohibition sent out by C. Tonstall bp. of London, to the arch-deacons of his diocesse, for calling in the New Testaments translated into English, with divers other books, &c. may be seen in Fox's Martyrol. "Given under our seale the 23 of Octob. in the fifth yeare of our consecration, An. 1526."

1527. Horæ beatissimæ Virginis Mariæ in verum usum Sarum. The title is lost; at the end "Horæ b-tissimæ virginis Mariæ in verum usum Sarum quã plurimis Bibliæ historiis decoratæ, &c. Impressæ quidem Parisiis in officina industrii calcographi Nicolai Prevost Impensis vero fidelissimi Mercatoris Francisci Byrkman civis Coloniensis & apud eundem venundantur Londonii apud Cæmetrium Sancti Pauli. Anno Dnĩ 1527. die 18 Julij." 122 leaves, a very curious book, and beautifully printed with red and black ink. Rev. Dr. Lort. Large Quarto.

(1527.) "The letters, whyche Johan Ashwell Priour of Newnham Abbey besydes Bedforde, sente secretly to the byshope of Lyncolne, in the yeare of our Lord M.D.XXVII. Where in the sayde pryour accuseth George Joye

quired. Count it as a thynge not havynge his foll shape, but as it were borne afore hys tyme, even as a thing begunne rather than fynnyshed. In tīme to come (yf God have appoynted us thereunto) we will give it his full shape; and put out, yf ought be added superfluusly; and adde to, yff ought be oversene thorowe negligence; and will enfoarce to brynge to compendeousnes that, which is now translated at the lengthe; and to give lyght where it is requíred; and to seke in certan places more proper Englyshe; and with a table to expound the words, which are nott commenly used; and shewe how the scripture useth many words, which are wotherwyse understonde of the common people; and to help with a declaration where one tonge taketh nott another. And will endever oureselues, as it were to sethe it better, and to make it more apte for the weake stomakes, desyreyng them that are learned, and able, to remember their dutie, and to help thereunto, and to bestowe unto the edyfyinge of Christis body (which is the congregation of them, that beleve) those gyftes, whyche they have receaued of God for the same purpose. The grace that commeth of Christ be with them that loue him. Pray for us."

[h] In Emmanuel College, Cambridge.

[i] Printed at Antwerp by the Widow of Cristophall of Endhoven. See Lambeth list.

Joye/ that tyme beyng felow of Peter College in Cambrydge, of fower opinyons: wyth the answere of the fayde George vnto the fame opinyons. Euery man that doth euyll, hateth the lyghte: and comethe not to the lyght/ that hys dedas fhuld not be reproued. Johan. iii." Contains D 4, in eights. At the end "¶ At Strafzburge the 10. daye of June. ¶ Thys lytell boke be delyuered to Johan Afhwel Priour of Newnhā Abbey/ befydes Bedforde/ with fpede." W.H. Sixteens.

"A miraculous work, of late done at Court of Streete in Kent, pub- (1527.)
lifhed to the deuoute people of this tyme, for their fpiritual confolation; by Edward Thwaytes, gent." Lewis's MSS. penes W.H.

"A Supplicacyon for the Beggers." This is all the title; but in the ——
edition annexed to "A fupplication of the poore Commons," 1546, it is thus enlarged "The fupplication of Beggers, compyled by Symon Fyfhe. Anno M.CCCCC.XXIIII. Pfalmus xciii. Bleffed is the man, whom thou learneft (O Lord) and teach hym in thy lawe. That thou mayeft geue hym patience in tyme of aduerfitie, vntyll the pyt be digged vp for the vngodly." The whole of this firft edition is printed in Italics. Contains 8 leaves. At the end, "Domine faluum fac regem." See Wood's Athenæ, Vol. I. Col. 26. and Atkins's Glocefterfhire, p. 421. edit. 1768. W.H. Octavo.

"¶ The obedyence of a Chryften man:"[a] &c. as p. 757. Contains ——
140 leaves. No printer's name, date, or place, but appears to have been printed with

"The parable of the wicked mammō" &c. as ib. In a compartment, 1528.
fee p. 416. Contains 60 leaves. Colophon "¶ Prynted at Malborowe, in the lande of Heffe, by Hans Luft. The. viii. daye of Maye. Anno M.D.XXIII." W.H. Quarto.

I have another edition apparently printed without a title, beginning with the fame difcourfe on faith as the 4to. has on the back of the title; with the reverfe blank; then the epiftle by. "William Tyndale otherwife called hychins to the reader." Contains J, in eights. Colophon, "Printed at Malborow in the londe off heffe, by Hans luft the. viij. day of May. Anno M.D.XXVIIJ." The three laft articles of "The notes of the boke" at the end, are omitted. W.H. Octavo.

"The obediēce of a Chriften man" &c. In a compartment of dancing 1528.
women. Contains 168 leaves. Colophon "At Marlborough in the lāde of Heffe The feconde daye of October. Anno. M.CCCCC.XXVIIJ/ by me Hans luft." W.H. Again 1536.* Mr. Ames mentions a former edition "11 Dec. 1527." Octavo.

"An exhortation to the diligent ftudye of fcripture, made by Erafmus 1529.
Roterodamus. And trāflated into inglifsh. ¶ An expofition in to the feuenth chaptre of the firft piftle to the Corinthians." In the fame compartment as the former article. Contains I. in eights; the firft 8 leaves have

[a] This book is faid to have been the means of firft enlightening Queen Anne Boleyn and even Henry viii. himfelf, againft the arbitrary power of the pope, and in the event of fetting forward the reformation; See Eccl. Memor. Vol. I, p. 112, &c. Alfo Fiddes's Life of Card. Wolfey, p. 517.

have no signature. Colophon "¶ At Malborow in the londe of Hesse. M.D.XXIX. xx daye Junij. By my Hans Lust." W.H. Octavo.

1529. "¶ A pistle to the Christen reader/ ¶ The reuelation of Antichrist. ¶ Antithesis/ wherein are compared togeder Christes actes and oure holye father the Popes." In the same compartment as the preceding. On fo. ij. begins an epistle by "¶ Richarde Brightwell[1] vnto ẏ christē reader." Colophon "¶ At Malborow in the lande of Hesse/ The. xij. day of Julye/ Anno. M.CCCCC.XXIX by me Hans lust." On the last leaf is "¶ The fautes of printinge." 103 leaves. W.H. Octavo.

1530. "A compendyous Olde treatyse" &c. See p. 408. "Emprented at Marlborow in the lande of Hessen/ by me Hans Lust, in the yere of oure Lorde M.CCCCC. and XXX." Octavo.

1530. "The practyse of Prelates. ¶ Whether the Kynges grace may be seperated from hysquene/ because she was hys brothers wyfe. Marborch. In the yere of oure Lorde M.CCCCC. & XXX." Contains K, in eights. W.H. Octavo.

1530. "The Psalter of David in Englishe, purely and faithfully translated after the Text of Feline" &c. See Lewis, p. 86. Colophon "Emprynted at Argentine in the yeare of our lorde 1530 the 16 daye of January by me Francis foye ¶ praise ye the lord." 235 leaves, besides a table. Publ. Libr. Camb. Sixteens.

1530. The Pentateuch translated by William Tindal and "Emprinted at Malborow in the lande of Hesse/ by me Hans Lusty the yere of oure Lorde. M.CCCCC.XXX. the xvii dayes of Januarij." Again, 1534, both in the Baptist Museum, Bristol. Octavo.

—— "A dyalogue of one Clemente, a clerke of the convocacyon, and one Barnarde, a burges of the parlyament, dysputynge betwene them, what auctoryte the clergye have to make lawes. And howe farre, and where theyr power dothe extende." Twelves.

—— "The examinacion of Master William Thorpe preste accused of heresye before Thomas Arundell/ Archebishop of Cāturbury/ the yere of ower Lorde. M.CCCC. and seuen. ¶ The examinacion of the honorable knight syr Jhon Oldcastell Lorde Cobham, burnt bi the said Archebisshop in the fyrste yere of Kynge Henry the fyfth: ¶ Be no more ashamed to heare it/ then ye were and be/ to do it." I 4, in eights. W.H. Octavo.

—— "*Rede me and be nott wrothe*
For I saye no thynge but trothe."

I will

1 This is one of the first books printed in English against the pope. It is addressed unto the Christian reader by Richarde Brightwell, which is a fictitious name that John Fryth made use of. In a book entitled "Yet a Course at the Romyshe Fox" It is said, (*fol.* 47) "As touchynge the Reuelacyon of Antichrist, though he (Fryth) ded translate yt out of a forem tonge into Englyshe, with an Antithesis annexed vnto yt, yet was yt not of hys makynge." Catal. of Mr. Tutet's books for sale 1786, Lot 172.

* What is here inserted in Italics is printed in red.

I will ascende makynge my state so hye/
That my pompous honoure shall never dye."

Underneath in red and black is a satyrical coat of arms designed for Cardinal Wolsey's, beneath which are these lines

" O Caytyse when thou thynkest least of all/
With confusion thou shalt have a fall."

On the back of the title, the arms are described in verse.* Next is an epistle thus addressed, " To his singuler goode frende and brother in Christ Master P. G. N. O. desyreth grace and peace from God the father/ thorowe the lorde Jesus Christ." From which the following is a short abstract. " By youre last letter/ dere brother in Christ/ J perceyue/ that youre desyre was/ to haue the lytle worke which ye sent wele examined/ and diligently put into prynt. Which thynge—J coulde no lesse but fulfill and accōplysshe.—Wherfore dere brother/ yf eny mo soche—come vnto youre hondes/—sende them vnto me (yf in englonde they maye not be publisshed)" *&c.* Then, a dialogue between " The Author* of the worke," and " The Treatous," in 14 seven-lined stanzas. " Heare foloweth the lamentacion," for the loss of the mass, in 34 stanzas. " ¶ Here foloweth a brefe Dialoge betwene two prestes servaunts/ named Watkin and Jeffraye:" which is the work itself, in verse. At the end is this correction " ¶ Jn descripciō of the Armes/ for wherfor rede wherby." On the back of the last leaf,

" Christ goddis sonne/ borne of a mayden poore/
Forto save mankynd/ from heuen descended.
Pope Clemente the sonne of an whoore/
To destroye man/ from hell hath ascended."

over a bare shield for the pope's arms; beneath which,

" Jn whom is evidently comprehended.
The perfett meknes of oure saveoure Christ/
And tyranny of the murtherer Antichrist."

Contains

* " Of the prowde Cardinall this is the shelde
Borne vp betwene two angels off Sathan.
The sixe bloudd'y axes in a bare felde
Sheweth the cruelte of the red man/
Whiche hathe devoured the beautifull swan.
Mortall enemy vnto the whyte Lion,
Carter of Yorcke/ the vyle bouchers sonne.

" The sixe bulles heddes in a felde blacke
Betokeneth hys stordy furiousnes
Wherfore the godly lyght to put abacke
He bryngeth in hys devillisshe darknes.
The ban dog in the middes doth expresse
The mastif Curre bred in Ypswitch towne
Gnawynge with his teth a kynges crowne.

" The cloubbe signifieth playne hys tiranny
Covered over with a Cardinals hatt
Wherin shalbe fulfilled the prophecy
Aryse vp Jacke and put on thy salatt
For the tyme is come of bagge and walatt
The temporall chevalry thus throwen downe
Wherfor prest take hede and beware thy crowne."

* John Anstis Esq. in a letter to Fiddes takes Skelton to be the author. He is said indeed in some of his writings to have reflected on the cardinal, but he died 21 June 1529. about the time of the publication of this. Besides, bishop Barlow in his forced recantation acknowledges for his, " The treatise of the Burial of the Mass." See Eccl. Memor. Vol. III; p. 153.

ᵖ At Strasbourgh, as appears in the work.

Contains i, in eights, without paging, running-titles, or catch-words The paper-mark is the brazen serpent twisted about the trunk of a cross resting on a bull's head. W.H. See it somewhat altered under 1546. 8°.

(1531.) "The Praier and Complaynte of the Ploweman vnto Christe: Written not long after the yere of oure Lorde A Thousande and thre hundred." See Harl. Miscel. vol. vi. p. 84, &c. Octavo.

1531. The primer of Salisbury. Paris "per Franciscum Regnault commorantem in vico Sancti Jacobi, juxta templum Maturinorum ad signum elephantis. Anno Domini M.CCCCCXXXI. die decima Junii." Octavo.

1531. Isaiah, translated by Geo. Joy. Printed at Strasburg by Balthassar Beckeneth. 2. May. Baptist Museum, Bristol. Octavo.

1533. "An answer, that by no manner of law, it may be lawfull for the most noble king of England, king Henry VIII. to be divorsed." Printed at Luneburgh. Quarto.

1533. "The Mystik sweet Rosary of the faythful soule: garnished rownde aboute, as it were with fresshe fragraunt flowers, according to the trewthe of the Gospel: with systye pagens of the whole lyfe and passion of our lorde Jesu Cryst, with certain placis of the holy scripture corresponding euery pagen:—vnto eche place is added a deuoute prayer. Also vnto euery sayynge or facte of Cryst, ther is correspondent a fayer picture: that the inwarde mynde might sauour the thinge that the vtwarde eye beholdeth. Printed in Anwerpe at Martyne Emprowers. M.D. & xxxiij." Octavo.

1533. A book made by John Frith prisoner in the tower &c. See p. 689. Colophon "¶ Jmprintid at Monster, Anno. 1533 By me. Conrade Willems." Contains L, in eights. W.H. wanting title. Again 1546 & 1547, without the Printer's name or place. Octavo.

—— "¶ A disputacion of Purgatorye made by Jhon Frith whiche is deuided in to thre bokes. ¶ The fyrst boke is an answere vnto Rastell/ which goeth aboute to proue purgatorye by naturall Phylosophye. ¶ The seconde boke answereth vnto Sir Thomas More, which laboureth to proue purgatorye by Scripture. ¶ The thyrde boke maketh answere vnto my lorde of Rochestre which moost leaneth vnto the doctoures. ¶ Beware lest any man come and spoyle you thorow phylosophye and deceytfull vanite/ thorow the tradicions of men/ and ordinacions after the worlde/ and not after Chryst. Collos. ii." It is introduced with an epistle by "¶ Jhon Frith vnto the Chrysten Reader." Contains L, in eights. No date, place, or printer's name to this and the subsequent article. Octavo.

—— "An other boke against Rastel named the subsedye or bulwark to his fyrst boke, made by John Frithe presoner in the Tower. ¶ Awake thou that slepest and stonde vppe from dethe/ and Chryste shall geue the lyght. Ephesiãs. v." Contains C, in eights. W.H. Octavo.

1533. "The Souper of the Lorde: wher vnto, that thou mayst be the better prepared and suerlyer enstructed: haue here firste the declaracion of the later

later parte of the . 6 . ca. of S. Johã, beginninge at the letter C. the fowerth lyne before the crosse, at these wordis: Verely vere. &c. wheryn incidently M. Moris letter agenst Johan Frythe is confuted." Contains fo. 32. Colophon "Jmprinted at Nornburg by Niclas twonson. 5. April. An. 1533." W.H. It was reprinted with a preface by R. Crowley. See p. 762. Octavo.

In the 25th of Henry viii, we find the following act, "concerning printers and binders of bookes. Ca. xv." 1533.

"Whereas by the provision of a statute made in the first year of the reign of king Richard the third, (See p. 1528) it was provided in the same act, that all strangers repairing into this realm, might lawfully bring into the said realm, printed and written books, to sell at their liberty and pleasure. By force of which provision there hath come into this realm, sithen the making of the same, a marvelous number of printed books, and daily doth; and the cause of making of the same provision seemeth to be, for that there were but few books, and few printers, within this realm at that time, which could well exercise and occupy the said science and craft of printing; nevertheless, sithen the making of the said provision, many of this realm, being the kings natural subjects, have given themselves so dilegently to learn and exercise the said craft of printing, that at this day there be within this realm a great number of cunning and expert in the said science or craft of printing, as able to exercise the said craft in all points, as any stranger in any other realm or country. And furthermore, where there be a great number of the king's subjects within this realm, which live by the craft and mystery of binding of books, and that there be a great multitude well expert in the same, yet all this notwithstanding there are divers persons, that bring from beyond the sea great plenty of printed books, not only in the Latin tonge, but also in our maternal English tonge, some bound in boards, some in leather, and some in parchment, and them sell by retail, whereby many of the king's subjects, being binders of books, and having no other faculty, wherewith to get their living, be destitute of work, and like to be undone, except some reformation be herein had. Be it therefore enacted by the king our sovereigne lord, the lords spiritual and temporal, and the commons in this present parliament assembled, and by authority of the same, that the said proviso, made the first year of the said king Richard the third, that from the feast of the nativity of our Lord God next coming, shall be void and of none effect.

¶ And further, be it enacted by the authority aforesaid, that no persons, resiant, or inhabitant, within this realm, after the said feast of Christmas next comming, shal buy to sell again, any printed books, brought from any parts out of the king's obeysance, ready bound in boards, leather, or parchment, upon pain to lose and forfeit for every book bound out of the said king's obeysance, and brought into this realm, and bought by any person or persons within the same to sell again contrary to this act, 6s. 8d.

¶ And be it further enacted, by the authority aforesaid, that no person or persons, inhabitant, or resiant, within this realm, after the said feast of Christmas, shall buy within this realm, of any stranger born out of the king's obedience, other then of denizens, any manner of printed books, brought from any the parts beyond the sea, except only by engross, and not by retail, upon pain of forfeiture of 6s. 8d. for every book so bought by retail, contrary to the form and effect of this estatute. The said forfeitures to be always levied of the buyers of any such books contrary to this act, the one half of the said forfeitures to be to the use of our sovereign lord the king, and the other moiety to be to the party, that will seize, or sue for the same in any of the king's courts, to be by bill, plaint, or information, werein the defendent shall not be admitted to wage his law, nor no protection, ne essoin shall be unto him allowed.

¶ Provided always, and be it enacted by the authority before said, that if any of the said printers, or sellers of printed books, inhabited within this realm, at any time hereafter, happen in such wise to enhance, or encrease the prices of any such printed books in sale or binding, at too high and unreasonable prices, in such wise as complaint be made there of unto the king's highness, or unto the lord chancellor, lord treasurer, or any of the chief justices of the one bench, or the other, that then the same lord chancellor, lord treasurer, and two chief justices, or two of any of them, shall have power and authority to enquire thereof, as well by the oaths of twelve honest and discreet persons, as otherwise by due examination by their discression. And after the same enhauncing and encreasing of the said prices of the said books, and binding, shall be so found by the said twelve men, or otherwise, by examination of the said lord chancellor, lord treasurer, and justices, or two of them; that then the same lord chancellor, lord treasurer, and justices, or two of them at the least, from time to come, shall have power and authority to reform and redress such inhauncing of the prices of printed books from time to time by their discressions, and to limit prices as well of the books, as for the binding of them. And over that, the offender or offenders thereof being convict by examination of the same lord chancellor, lord treasurer, or two justices, or two of them, or otherwise, shall lose and forfeit for every book by them sold, whereof the price shall be enhanced for the book, or binding thereof, 3*s.* 4*d.* the one half thereof shall be to the kings highness, and the other half to the parties greived, that will complain upon the same, in manner and form before rehearsed."

(1534.) "Pronostication, by Gaspar, late of Antwerpe, calcled upon the meridyan of the same citie, for the yere of our lorde God, M.CCCCCXXXIIII."

1534. The New Testament, translated by Tindal, and corrected by George Joy. See Lewis, p. 79 and 80 (F 8).

1534. "¶ The newe Testament, ¶ Imprinted at Anwerp by Marten Emperowr. M.D.xxxxiiij." In a compartment; at bottom in a shield the initials M. K. Prefixed is an epistle of W.T. to the Reader." At the end, after "The Revelacion Of S, John." which has several wooden cuts, are, "The Pistles of the Olde Testament." and a table to "fynde the

the Epistles and the Gospels/ after the vse of Salsbury."* W.H. Octavo.

"¶ The newe Testament ¶ Anno M.D.xxxiiii." In a compartment, at top Jesus preaching on the mount as Mat. v. On the right side, Moses with the two tables. On the left, the brazen serpent. At the bottom, a shield with G. H. At the end, the epistles, &c. of the old Testament and a table. The late Benjamin Ibbot, Esq. Octavo. 1534.

"The newe Testament diligently corrected and printed in the yeare of oure Lord M.cccc & xxxiiii. in November." This seems to be the same with 1534.

"The New Testament dylygently corrected and compared wyth the Greke by Willyam Tyndale: and fynyshed in the yere of oure Lorde God a M.D.xxxiiii. in the moneth of Nouember." Lewis, p. 89. Sixteens. 1534.

"An Apology made by Geo. Joye, to satisfye, if it may be W. Tyndale, to pourge & defend himself agaynst so many sclanderause Lies feigned upon him in Tyndale's uncharitable & unsober Pistle, so well worthye to be prefixed for the Reader to induce him into the understanding of his New Testament, diligently corrected and printed in the Yeare of our Lord 1534, in November." See Biog. Brit. Vol. VI. p. 3956. Note k. Lewis, p. 83. Rev. Dr. Lort. Again 1535. Public Library, Cambridge. Octavo. 1534.

"The subuersion of Moris faulse foundation; whereupon he sweteth to set faste and shoue vnder his shamles shoris, to vnderproppe the popis chirch, made by George Joye. More is become a vayn lyar in his owne resening and argumentis; and his folysshe harte is blynded. Where he beleued to haue done most wysely, there hath be shewed himself a starke foole, Rom. i. *Moros* in Greke is *stultus* in Latyn, a fool in Englyshe. Vivit Dominus, cuius inuicta veritas manet in eternum. At Emdon by Jacob Aurik." 41 leaves.* Octavo. 1534.

"Jeremy the Prophete/ translated into Englisshe: by George Joye: some tyme felowe of Peter College In Camebridge. ¶ The songe of Moses is added in the ende/ to magnifye our Lorde for the fall of our Pharao/ the Bisshop of Rome. ¶ Anno M.D. and xxxiiii. in the monethe of Maye." After the title is "The Preface." and "¶ The fawtes escaped in the prindinge" Contains P, in eights. Public Libr. Camb. W.H. The Catl. Bibl. Harl. Vol I, No. 419, mentions an edition 1533. Octavo. 1534.

David's Psalter diligently and faithfully translated by Geo. Joye, with brief Arguments before every Psalme declaringe the effect therof. At the end "Thus endeth the text of the Psalmes translated oute of Latyne by Geo. Joy, the yere of oure Lorde M.D.xxxiiii. the monethe of Auguste." Then follows an alphabetical table to find the psalmes at the end of which is "Martyne Emperour. 1534." The Latin from which Joy translated, is said to be Friar Felix's of the order of Heremites of St. Austin. Pub. Libr. Camb. Octavo. 1534.

"¶ *Thys prymer of salysbury* vse is set out a long without any serchyng 1534.
wyth many prayers and goodly pyctures in the kalēder in the matyns off

* What is here inserted in Italics is printed in red.

our lady in the houres *of the crosse* in the vij psalmes and in the *dyryge* wyth the. xv. oos and the confessionall. newly emprynted *in Paris* wythin the howse of *Thylman kerver* at the expenses off *Jhon growte bokeseller* in London dwellyng wythyn the blak freers next the chyrche doore. *And be new corrected.*" Kerver's sign and name. "M.D.XXXIIIY." At the end is "*The contentes of this boke.*" at the conclusion of which is "¶ *Catalogus codicum* a. b. c. d. e. f. g. h. i. k. l. m. n. o. p. q. r. s. t. v. x. y. z. A. B. C. D. E. F. G. *Omnes sunt quaterni.*" On the back is this colophon "¶ *Expliciunt hore* beatissime virginis Marie secundum vsum Sarum totalit' ad longum: cum or'onibus btē Brigitte, ac mlts alijs or'onib'. *Impresse Parisiis per* honestā matronā yolandā bōhōme, viduā defuncti spectabilis viri *Thielmanni kerver*, sub signo vnicornis in vico scti Jacobi. *Impensis* qdē honesti viri ioānis *growte* librarij Lōdon. cōmorantis. in domo predicatorum. *Anno dni.* M.D.XXXIIIJ." On the last leaf is a cut of our Saviour on the cross, and underneath "Adoramus te christe et benedicimus tibi quia per sanctam crucem tuam redemisti mundum." On the back, Kerver's sign and name "M.D.XXXIIIJ." Annexed is "¶ *An innocatyon gloryouse named the psalter of Jhesus.*" over the same cut of our Saviour crucified. At the end, Kerver's sign and name "M.D.XXXIIIJ." Contains 16 leaves. There are many very neat cuts in form of medallions." W.H.

1534. The Pentateuch, &c. as p. 1538.

1534. "Joannis Coleti theologi, olim decani divi Pauli, una cum quibusdam G. Lilii gramatices rudimentis." In this book are the following orders: "The mayster shall reherse these articles to them, that offer their chyldren, on this wyse here followinge. If your child can rede and wryte Latin and Englisshe sufficiently, so that he be able to rede and wryte his own lessons, than he shall be admitted into the schole for a scholar. If your child after reasonable season proved to be found here unapte, and unable to learning, than ye warned thereof, shall take him away, that he occupye not here rowme in vayn. If he be apt to learn, ye shall be content that he continue here till he have sume compytent literature. If he be absent six days, in that mean season ye shew not cause resonable (resonable cause is al onely sekenes) then this rowme to be voide, without he be admitted again, and pay IIIId. Also, after cause shewed, if he continue so absent tyll the week of admission in the next quarter, and then he shew not the continuance of hys sekenes, than hys rowme to be voyde, and he none of the schole, tyll he be admitted agayne, and pay IIIId. for wryting of his name. Also, yf he fal thryse into absence, he shall be admitted no more. Your childe shall on Childermas day wayte upon the bishop at Pouwls, and offer there. Also, ye shall find him wax in wynter. Also, ye shall fynde him convenient bokes to his lerning. If the offerer be content with these articles, than let his childe be admitted." See p. 190. Quarto.

1535. THE BIBLE. This is the first edition of the whole bible in english. It is dedicated to Hen. viii. by Miles Coverdale the translator; which may

may be ſeen in Annals of the Reformation, Vol. II. Appendix No. xxii. It has ſome wooden cuts interſperſed. The firſt part of the old teſtament viz. the five books of Moſes, contains Fo. xc. Then is inſerted a map of the promiſed land. " The ſeconde parte of the olde Teſtament" from " The boke of Joſua." to " The boke of Heſter" contains Fo. cxx. From " The boke of Job" to " The ende of Salomons Balettes" are Fo. lij. " All the Prophetes in Engliſhe" contain Fo. cij. The " Apocripha" contains Fo. lxxxi. " The new Teſtament" contains Fo. cxiij. At the end, " Prynted in the yeare of oure LORDE M.D.XXX.V. and fyniſhed the fourth daye of October." The contents of the chapters are all ſet before their ſeveral books. See Lewis, p. 91, &c.. Mr. Dayer. W.H. There were 2 editions, but with little variation. Folio.

" ¶ A Paraphraſis/ vpon all the Pſalmes of Dauid/ made by Johannes Campẽſis, reader of the Hebrue lecture/ In the vniuerſite of Louane/ and trãſlated oute of Latyne into Englyſhe. 1535." In a compartment with C. E. at bottom. On the back is a cut of David and Bathſheba. Then, an epiſtle " Vnto the Reader." After the pſalmes is " The table of the Pſalmes/ after the olde tranſlacyon.—¶ Here foloweth the boke of Solomon called Eccleſiaſtes." This is a tranſlation of that mentioned in p. 423. Contains B, in eights. W.H. Twenty-fours. 1535.

" A dialogue betwene pope Julius (who died 1503) and ſaint Peter at heauen gate—where the pope is replyed. Imprinted at the beginning. Tranſlated into Engliſh. Printed at London. Cum priv. reg." See p. 486. Quarto. 1535.

" Storys and propheſis out of the holy ſcriptur/ garnyſchede with faire ymages/ and with deuoute praeirs/ and thanckgeuings vnto God. With grete diligence ourſien and aprouued by the inquiſitor of the Chriſten ſaithe/ maeſter Nycholas Coppyn/ de Montibus/ Deane of ſaincte Peters/ and Chãceler of the vniuerſitie of Louen. Anno M.CCCCC.XXXV." In a compartment, at the top of which is repreſented Pharoah and his hoſt drowning in the Red Sea, while the Iſraelites are ſafe got over; and a little farther, the raining of manna from heaven. On one ſide Moſes receiving the tables and on the other breaking them at the ſight of the golden calf, which is in one corner at bottom and the brazen ſerpent in the other. Contains x, in eights. On the back of the laſt leaf is " ¶ I have foughten a good batayle/ I haue ended the courſe/ I haue kepte the beleaſe." over a cut of St. Paul reſting one foot on a ſtone with the cutter's mark.  and this label on a ſcroll, " Bene naufragium feci." On one ſide of which is " ¶ Oure ſuffringe here is lyght and tranſitorios/ after the rehearſinge of Paul." On the other " Oure worckynge in the heauenly ſituacion a croune of ioye without faylinge." And underneath, " ¶ This boke is prentyd in Andwarpe vpon the Lombardes walle/ ouer agaynſt the golden hande By my Symon Cowke. Anno xxxvi." Mr. W. Collins, and W.H. Octavo. 1535.

Biſhop Gardiner's Oration De vera obedientia, with Bonner's preface. " Printed at Hamburgh, in Latine In officina F. Rhous." See it under 1553. Octavo. 1536.

" A

1536. " A compendious letter, which Jhon Pomerane, curate of the congregation of Wittenberge, ſent to the faithſull chriſten congregation in England." Octavo.

1536. " A tretiſe of juſtification by faith only, by William Tindale." 8°.

1536. The prymer, &c. with S. Heroms's pſalter, Latin and Engliſh. Colophon " Imprinted in *Rouen* the yere of our Lorde 1536." W.H. 4°.

1536. A Declaration, called the Biſhop's Book, probably becauſe ſigned by the 2 Archbiſhops and 19 other Biſhops. However, care muſt be taken not to confound this with the Inſtitution of a Chriſtian Man, which alſo is often cited by the name of The Biſhops Book. This is a declaration againſt the papal ſupremacy, written on occaſion of Cardinal Pole's book of eccleſiaſtical union.*

1536. " The newe Teſtament yet once agayne corrected by willyam Tindale: whereunto is added a neceſſarye Table: wherin eaſily and lightelye may be foūde any ſtorye contayned in the foure Euangeliſtes and in the Actes of the Apoſtles.

" The Goſpell of { S. Mathew, S. Marke, S. Luke, S. John.

" The Actes of the Apoſtles.

" Jeſus ſayd Mark xvj. Go ye into all the worlde/ and preache the glad tydynges to all creatures/ he that beleueth and is baptiſed/ ſhall be ſaued. Prynted in the yeare of oure Lorde God. M. D. and xxxvi."

Tindale's preface is prefixed, at the end of which is " The office of all eſtates," and at the bottom of the ſame page is " A prayer to be ſayd dayly," which may be ſeen under the " Hore" &c. p. 467. The Epiſtles have a ſeparate title before Tindale's " prologe vpon the Epiſtle— to the Romayns." This ſeems to have been annexed ſince the teſtament was worked off, ſeeing the ſignature and paging at the firſt chapter of the Epiſtle to the Romans proceed orderly from the Acts of the Apoſtles. It has ſeveral neat wood-cuts indented like that printed by, or for, John Gowghe. See p. 492. Indeed there are only a few orthographical differences between them. The moſt material one, and by which they may be diſtinguiſhed, is the engraver's mark to the cuts of St. Pauls that to Gowghe's being ſomewhat like a mole; this as p. 1545. At the end is a table to find the epiſtles and goſpels after the uſe of Saliſbury. Mr. Denyer, Chelſea. Large octavo.

1536. " The newe Teſtament newlye corrected M.D.XXXVJ." In a ſmall compartment. Prefixed is a calendar; an epiſtle by " ☞ ¶ Willyam Tindale vnto the Chriſten reader." and " An exhortacion to the diligent ſtudye of ſcripture/ made by Eraſmus Rot." Annexed are " The Pyſtles of the Olde Teſtament." and " The Table." The Reuelacion alone has cuts. W.H. Octavo.

" A

* See Lord Herbert's Hen. viii p. 390, &c. Alſo Strype's Memor. of Abp. Cranmer, p. 58.

"The summe of christianitie gatheryd out almoste of al placis of scripture, by that noble and famouse clerke, Francis Lambert of Auynyon. And translatyd, and put in to prynte in Englyshe, by Tristram Revel, the yere of our lorde 1536." It begins with, "An epistle of the translator to the most vertuouse quene Anne." Then, "The epistle of the author." The whole is contained in 385 paradoxes * Octavo. 1536.

"A sermond made before the Kynge hys Hyghnes at Rychemunte upon Good Fryday, the yere of our Lorde M.CCCCC.XXXVI by Johan Longland Byshope of Lincoln, upon Psalm. 129." Quarto. (1536.)

"¶ The Byble," &c. as p. 511. Folio. 1537.

"Of the auctorite of the word of god agaynst the bisshop of london, wherein are conteyned certen disputacyons had in the parlement howse betwene the bisshops, abowt the nomber of the sacraments, and other things, very necessary to be known; made by Alexander Alane Scot, and sent to the duke of Saxon." The author says, the Lord Crumwel took him with him to the parliament house 1537. where he had a part in the debates. It contains 46 leaves, without name of place, printer, or date. Octavo. (1537.)

"The prophete Jonas, with an introduction before, teachinge to understande him, and the right vse also of all the scripture, and why it was written, and what is therein to be sought, and shewing, wherewith the scripture is locked up, that he which readeth it, cannot understond it, though he studie therin never so much: and agayne, with what keyes it is so opened, that the reader can be stopped out with no sotilte, or false doctrine of man, from the true sense and vnderstondynge therof." 8°. ——

John Traverse, a native of Ireland, a secular priest and Dr. of Divinity, about the year 1537 or 1538, published a book in Defence of the Pope's supremacy, and in contempt of the statute, 28th Hen. VIII. cap. 13. For which he was indicted and punished according to Law. See The Writers of Ireland, p. 93. ——

"¶ Here begynneth the Pystles and Gospels: of euery Sonday and holy daye in the yere," a cut of St. Paul "1538." On the back of this title is a cut of St. John. Contains Fo. lxvij. besides a table of four more. Colophon "Jmprinted at Paris The vere of our lorde, M.D.XXXVIIJ." Annexed is "¶ *Thys prymer in Englyshe* and in *Laten* is newly trāslated after the Laten texte. ¶ *The contentes of thys boke.*— On the back is "An almanacke for xx, yeres" beginning at "M.D.XXXVI." "*The preface and maner to lyue well, &c. Compyled by mayster Johan quentin doctour in dyuinyte at Parys: translated out of frenche in the englysshe by Robert Copland prynter at London.*" Contains Fo. clxxxviij. Colophon "*Jmprynted* in *Parys* the yere of our *Lorde* 1538." Annexed is "¶ *An exposityon* after the manner of a cōtēplacyō vpon the. lj. *Psalme* called *Miserere mei De*°, whiche *Hierom of Ferrarye* made at the later ende of hys dayes," also "¶ *A meditacyon* of the same 1538.

* The Italic type distinguishes what is printed in red.

same Jerom vpon the *Psalme of* Jn the *Dne* speraui, whiche preuentyd by death he coulde nat synyshe." Contains h 4, in eights. b ij & b iiij are printed S ij & S iiij. Colophon "Jmprynted in *Pays* the yere of our Lorde 1538." The two first treatises have many wooden cuts. W.H. 8°.

1538. "The Romaunt of the Rose." See Warton's Hist. of Eng. Poetry, Vol. I. p. 369.

(1538.) "A treatyse made by Johan Lambert vnto kynge Henry the. viij. concernynge hys opynyon in the sacramẽt of the aultre as they call it, or supper of the lorde as the scripture nameth it. Anno do. 1538." A cut of Hope standing on the stone of Faith, looking at the crucifix in the clouds. Underneath is "The waye of the ryghteouse is iudged to be vtter destructyon, but they are in rest. And though they suffer payne before mẽ, Yet is their hope full of immortalyte. Sapi. 3." It begins with an addresss by "Johan Bale to the christen reader." At the end thus "Though Johan Lambert wrote sumwhat more concernynge thys matter to the kynge. Yet came there no more to my hãdes in the vncorrected, yea rather corrupted coppye whych I receyued. Jn the yeare of our lorde a M.D.XXXVIIJ. was thys seruant of God brẽt ĩ Smythfelde at London, by the only vyolence of the spirituall mynysters of Antichrist, in october." Contains Fo. 32.* W.H. Sixteens.

1538. "A Tragedie or Enterlude, manyfestyng the chefe promyses of God." &c. See p. 1094. Dodsley's Old Plays, Vol. I. p. 1. Octavo.

(1538.) "A brefe Comedy or Enterlude of Iohan Baptystes preachynge in the wyldernesse, openynge the craftye assaultes of the hypocrytes, with the gloryouse Baptyme of the Lorde Jesus Christ Compyled by Iohan Bale, Anno M.D.XXXVIII.—Luce. iii. Interlocutores. Pater Cœlestis, Ioannes Baptista, Publicanus, Pharisæus, Iesus Christus, Turba uulgaris, Miles armatus, Saducæus; Baleus prolocutor." Harl. Miscel. Vol. I. p. 97, &c. Octavo.

(1538.) "A brefe comedy, or enterlude, concernynge the temptacyon of our Lorde and Sauer Jesus Christ, by Sathan in the desart. Compyled by Johan Bale, Anno. M.D.XXXVIII. Interlocutores: Jesus Christus, Angelus primus, Satan tentator, Angelus alter; Baleus prolocutor." In a compartment representing the fall of Adam. Octavo.

A Comedy concernynge thre lawes of nature Moses and Christ," &c. See p. 930. Annexed is "A songe vpon Benedictus Compyled by Johan Bale." beginning on the back of a fine wooden cut designed for the author. At the end "Thus endeth thys Comedy concernynge thre lawes, of Nature, Moses, and Christ, corrupted by the Sodomytes] Pharisees, and Papystes most wycked. Compyled by Johan Bale. Anno M.D.XXXVIII, and lately inprented per Nicolaum Bamburgensem." Contains G 4, in eights. See Warton, Vol. III; p. 78. W.H. Octavo.

1538. "The Kernell of St. Augustin's Confessions." Bibl. Monast. Fleetwood. No. 416. Octavo.

1538. "A Commentary vpon the second Epistle to the Thessalonians." &c. Maunsell, p. 35. Octavo.

Search

"Search the Scriptures." in a label over a tablet containing "The 1538.
new Teſtament," then follows "faithfully tranſlated and newly corrected by Myles Couerdale, with a true concordance in the Margent/ and many neceſſary Annotacyons. after the Chapters/ declaryng ſundry harde places contayned in the Texte. Prynted in the yeare of oure Lorde M.CCCCC.XXXVIII. Set forth by the Kynges Licence." This title is in red and black. Then, An Almanac for 18 years and Calendar, in red and black.—An epiſtle to the reader, with a beautiful red initial.— "Prologe vnto the new Teſtament." At the end of the goſpels is a blank page: "*The Actes of the Apoſtles*"[*] in an ornamental tablet ſupported on each ſide by a cherub, begins on a freſh ſet of ſignatures, "*The Goſpell of St. John.*" ending on y, in eights. "*The Epiſtle of the Apoſtle* Saynt Paul to the Romaynes." begins on I iij,[†] and the cut is different and larger than that to the two epiſtles to the Corinthians, the epiſtle to the Epheſians, and the firſt epiſtle to Timothy, which may alſo be diſtinguiſhed by his holding two keys and a book in his right hand, and a ſword in his left, from the other epiſtles of St. Paul, where he has only a ſword in his right hand, and ſomewhat ſmaller: the ſecond to the Theſſalonians and the ſecond to Timothy, (both which have at the beginning in the tablet as above, by miſtake, "*The j. Epiſtle of the Apoſtle*") and Philemon, have no cut at all; as alſo the epiſtles of St. Peter, ſecond and third of St. John and St. Jude; 1. St. John and St. James have a ſmall one. "*The Apocalipſis or Reuelacion*" in a tablet without cherubs, the ſame as before St. John's goſpel, has many large neat cuts; then "*The ende of the new Teſtament.*" over "*Here foloweth the Epiſtles*" in a tablet with the cherubs, under which "of the olde Teſtament/ which are red in the church after the vſe of Saliſbury/ vpon certayne dayes of the yeare." Then follows "¶ *The Table wherein ye* ſhall fynde the Epiſtles and the Goſpels/ after the vſe of Saliſbury." The initial letters and running-titles are all in red; the whole printed within red lines. The contents of the chapters are all ſet before their reſpective books, as to Coverdale's Bible, 1535. The late Mr. Bayntun. W.H. Sixteens.

The new teſtament. Printed by Mathew Cromer at Antwerp. 1538.
Baptiſt Muſeum, Briſtol. Octavo.

The new teſtament. Prefixed is "*The Kalender,*" in red and black.— 1539.
"*The Prologe* vpon the new Teſtament."—Under a cut of St. Matthew, "*A Prologe of ſaynt Matthew.*"[‡] At the firſt chapter of St. John's goſpel (which the running-title by miſtake calls the xvi.) is indented a ſquare encloſing a circle with לא תשא את־שם־יהוה אלהיך לשוא about the circumference, and יהוה in larger letters withinſide. The circular label is taken from Exod. xx; 7. Thou ſhalt not take the name of the Lord thy God in vain. Each corner of the ſquare is ſupplied with a cherub. The Hebrew characters are rather uncouth

[*] The Italic type is to notify the red, which I have not been able to do throughout, my copy being imperfect.

[†] There are two ſignatures with this letter, I; the former has only four, the latter eight leaves; upon which the epiſtle to the Romans begins.

[‡] The Italic is to diſtinguiſh the red.

..., and without the proper spaces; but by the help of my good friend and neighbour the Reverend Mr. Woisley, the text was decyphered. The Acts of the Apostles end on B b, in eights. "The Prologe of the Epystle of St. Paul to the Romayns." and "The Summe of the Scrypture." occupy 16 separate leaves. At the end, "The Epistles of olde Testamente.---Faules escaped in the pryntynge.---The Table." Colophon "¶ At Antwerpe/ by Matthew Crom. M.D.XXXIX." Contains v, in eights, reckoning from "The Epistle of the Apostle saynt Paul to the Romayns." which begins on signature a. There are many small cuts to the Gospels: The cut of St. Matthew, by having the prologe under it, is rather less than those prefixed to the other 3 Evangelists, which with that of the descent of the Holy Spirit before "The actes of the Apostles/" of St. Paul before his epistle to the Romans; of St. Peter before his first epistle; of St. James before his epistle, and those in "The Apocalipsys" take up whole sides. W.H., wanting title-page and part of the calendar. Octavo.

1539. "An Epitome of the Psalmes," &c. as p. 407.

1539. The New Testament by Richard Taverner. See p. 543. &c. After the calendar is "¶ A Table for the foure Euangelystes: wherein you maye lyghtlye fynde any story conteyned in them. and specyally/ yf ye shall note that by the syde of euery Chapyter, standeth these capytall letters. A. B. C. D. and the fyrst story that I resyte to be in the Chapyter standeth vppermost, and the seconde farther into the Chapyter, and so the thyrde, that the last standeth lowest, and the fyrst hyghest, and by notynge of this ordre, you shall lyghtely fynde anye story conteyned in them, & fyrst I begyn with Mathew. Saynt Mathew. The generacyon of Jesu Chryste. The byrthe of Chryste. How the wyse men came from the East to worshyp Chryste, whose starre they had sene. Howe Herode enquyred of the wyse men the tyme of the starre. Howe Joseph fledde with the chylde and his mother into Egypte. How Herode commaunded all the chyldren to be slayne that were vnder two yere olde. Howe Joseph after the death of Herode, was called out of Egypte into Israell," &c. with the chapters in the margin, to the end of the Acts: The table continues no further. Then the names of the books in the new testament. Saint Luke's Prologue, ch. 1. 1—4, is omitted. W.H. Quarto.

De Bibliis in vulgari edendis ex supervisione Domini de Crumwell, anno Domini 1539. 31 Hen. 8. M. 15.

"HENRY the eight, *&c.* To all and singular prynters, and sellers of books, within this our realme, and to all other officers, ministers, and subjects, theise oure letters heryng or seyng, gretyng. We late you witt that beyng desirous to have our people at tymes conveynent geue themselfes to the atteynyng of the knowlege of Goddes worde, wherby they shall the better honour hym, and observe and kepe his commaundements, and also do their duties the better to us, beyng their prince and soveraigne ſoverainge lord; and conſideryng, that as this our zeal and deſire cannot by any meane take ſo good affecte, as by the grauntyng to theym the free and lyberall uſe of the bible in oure owne maternall Engliſh tonge, ſo onles it be forſeen, that the ſame paſſe at the begynnyng by one tranſlation to be peruſed and conſiderid, the frailtie of menne is ſuche, that the diverſitie thereof maye brede and brynge forthe manyfolde inconvenyences, as when wilfull and hedy folkes ſhall conferre uppon the diverſitie of the ſaid tranſlations: we have therefore appoynted oure right truſty and welbeloved counſellour, lorde Crumwell, keper of our pryvye ſeale, to take for us, and in our name, ſpeciall care and charge, that no manner of perſone, or perſones, within this our realme, ſhall enterprize, attempte, or ſete in hand, to print any Bible in the Engliſh tonge, of any maner of volume, duryn the ſpace of fyve yeres next enſuyng after the date hereof, but only all ſuche, as ſhall be deputed, aſſigned, and admytted by the ſaid lord Crumwell. Willyng and commanding all maires, ſhireſes, bailyffes, conſtables, and all other oure officers, miniſters, and ſubjectes, to be aydyng to oure ſaid counſailour, in the execution of this oure pleaſure, and to be conformable in the accompliſhment of the ſame, as ſhall apperteigne. In witnes whereof, &c. Witnes our ſelf at Weſtminſter, the fourteenth day of Novembre. Per ipſum regem."

"Littelton Tenures neuly imprinted. In the yere of our Lord God M.ccccc.xxxix." Encloſed within 4 odd pieces. Contains Fo. 155, and the table; but my copy wants the laſt leaf, which probably has a colophon, declaring the printer's name. W.H. Thirty-twos. 1539.

"Certayne other iniunctions ſet forth by the authoritie of the kyng, againſt Engliſhe bookes, ſectes, &c.* 1539.

"Firſt, that none without ſpecial licence of the king, tranſporte, or bring from outwarde parties into Englande, any manner of Engliſhe bookes, neyther yet ſell, geue, vtter, or publiſhe any ſuche, upon payne to forſeyte all their goodes and cattelles, and their bodyes to be impriſoned, ſo long as it ſhal pleaſe the kyngs maieſtie.

"Item, That none ſhal print, or bring ouer any Engliſhe bookes with annotations or prologues, unles ſuch bookes before be examined by the kinges priuie Counſayle, or others appoynted by his highneſſe, and yet not to put therto thoſe wordes: Cum priuilegio Regali, without addyng, Ad imprimendum ſolum: neither yet to print it, without the kinges priuilege be printed therewith in the Engliſhe tongue, that al men may read it. Neither ſhal they printe any tranſlated booke, without the plaine name of the tranſlatour be in it, or els the printer to be made the tranſlatour, and to ſuffer the fine and puniſhment thereof at the kinges pleaſure.

"Item, That none of the occupation of Printyng ſhall within the Realme, print, vtter, ſell, or cauſe to be publiſhed any Engliſhe bookes of Scripture, unleſſe the ſame be firſte viewed, examined, and admitted by

* From Fox's Acts and Monuments, p. 1108. edit. 1576.

the kings highnesse, or one of his priuie Counsaile, or one Bishop within the Realme, whose name shall therein be expressed, vppon paine of the kinges most high displeasure, the losse of their goodes and cattels, and prisonment, so long as it shall please the king." &c.

——— " The enquirie and verdite of the quest panneld of the death of Richard Hune, who was found hanged in Lolars tower." Sixteens.

——— " The Lordes flaile handled by the bishops powre thresher, Thomas Solme [to drive the reader to the confession of the one Christ, &c.] Basil, by Theophilus Emtos." Octavo.

1541. " The rescuing of the Romish fox. Imprinted have at Winchester, 1545. Nones Martii. By me Hans Hitprike." See it under 1545. 16°.

1541. " The old fayth, an euydent probation out of the holy scripture, that the christen fayth (which is the right true old vndoubted faith) hath endured sens the begynnynge of the world. Herein hast thou also a shorte summe of the whole Byble/ and a probation, that all vertuous men haue pleased God, and were saued thorow the Christen faith 1541. By Myles Coverdale." Again 1547. Sixteens.

1541. " A frutefull treatis of Baptyme and the Lordis Souper/ of the vse and effect of them/ of the worthey and vnworthy receyuers of the Souper/ necessary to be knowne of all christen men/ which yerely receyue the Sacrament." Contains D, in eights. Colophon " At Grunning. M.D.XLJ. Apryle xxvij." W.H. Sixteens.

1541. " The Christian state of Matrimony" &c. By Miles Coverdale. See p. 497. Octavo.

1542. A new work, &c. See p. 727. Octavo.

1542. " A Godly consultation vnto the brethren and companyons of the Christen religyon. By what meanes the cruell power of the Turkes/ bothe may/ and ought for to be repelled of the Christen people/ Theodore Bibliander beinge the Author. Thow shalt also fynde here (most gentle Reader) of the reasons wherwyth a firme and sure concorde and peace in the Churche/ and the Christen publyke weale may be constytuted/ and of the fyrst begynnynge and incresacementes of the Turkes domynyon/ and also of the superstytyous and damnable lawe of the Mahumetanes/ and of other certen thynges moste worthy truly to be red and consydered. The horse is prepared agaynste the daye of batayle/ but the Lorde alone gyueth the victorye. Prouerb. xxi." Addressed " To hys moste derely beloued bretherne the faythfull worshyppers of oure Lorde Jesus Christe/ Theodore Bibliander wyssheth grace and peace from God the father.— Fare you well/ frō Zurik 1542." Contains V, in eights. At the end, " Thus endeth the consultacion of Theodorus Bibliander translated owte of Latine in to Englysshe and printed at Basill by Radulphe Bonifante in this troblouse tyme ragynge with warre and batayle by all the partes of Christendome/ the yere of ower Lorde. M.D.XLIJ. Men. of Auguste." W.H. Sixteens.

1542. " The assize of bread, newly corrected and enlarged, according to the raising and falling of the price of wheate in the market; togither with

with fundrie good and needful orders, commanded to be kept in making all kinds of bread, that are appointed to be fold in all places whatfoeuer; whereunto are added, fundrie other good ordinances, for bakers, brewers, inhulders, vintners, butchers, and victulers: and alfo other affizes in weights and meafure, to be obferued and kept, agreeing with the anneaed ftatutes of this realme: leading greatly to the general commonwealth of the fame. Lond. 1542." Gough's Brit. Topography, Vol. I; p. 6.9. See p. 376. Quarto.

"The prymer in Englyffhe and Laten, after the vfe of Sarum, fet out at length, with many goodly prayers, with the epyftles and gofpel throuut the hoole yeare." Cum privilegio. Octavo. 1542.

"The lamentation of a chriftian againft the cittie of London, made by Roderigo Mors. Printed at Jericho in the land of promife." Octavo. 1542.

"The Maydens Dreme." See Warton's Eng. Poetry III; p. 84. 1542.

"Declaration, conteyning the juft Caufes and Confyderations of the prefent Warre with the Scottis, wherein alfo appeareth the trewe and right Title, that the Kinges Royal Majefty hath to the Souerayntie of Scotlande." Harl. Cat. III; 4955. Quarto. 1542.

Of the auctorite of the word of god agaynft the bifshop of london/ wherein are conteyned certen difputacyons had in the parlament howfe betwene the bifshops abowt the nomber of the facramẽts and other things, very neceffary to be known/ made by Alexāder Alane Scot* and fent to the duke of Saxon. There is nothing hydden that fhal not be opened and come to lyght. Math. x." Contains F 6, in eights. W.H. Sixteens. (1542.)

"Liber viarum Dei." This book in Latin and Englifh, begins thus, "Hic eft liber viarum dei," &c. "This is the boke of the wais of God, whiche was fhewed from the angell of God Almighti, moft high, vnto Elizabeth, the hand mayden of Chrifte, and of the lyuinge God, in the fyft yeare of the vifitacion of her. In the which yere the fpirite of our Lord hathe vifited her, to the health of all theim, whyche perceyue, and take the fatherlye monicions, or warnynges of our Lord God, with a thankful bleffynge and benediction. And it was in the yeare of our Lordes incarnation, a thoufande, a hundred fyfte and fixe."* Octavo. —

"The actes of the difputation in the cowncell of the empyre, holden at Regenfpurg: that is to fay, all the artycles concerning the chriften relygion, both agreed and not agreed vpon, euen as they were propowned of the emperour vnto the nobles of the empire, to be judged, delebered, and debated, &c. Tranflated owt of Latyne into Englifh, by Mylys Couerdale." In this book are the names of all the ftates, which are called Proteftants.* Octavo. —

"A

* See George Mackenzie's Lives of the Scotch Writers. Edin. 1711. Vol. II; p. 144—183. Where our author is called Alasse or Alesius. The book is faid to be printed at Lipfie, 1542. In the catalogue of his works at the end of his life, which are all in Latin.

—— " A book of Ydrography, made by John Rotz, a Frenchman born, servant to king Henry VIII, anno Domini 1542." It contains all the sea coasts, &c. of the world, curiously delineated in 18 large skins of parchment. Query, if ever printed by R. Wolfe, who had the patent. Bishop Tanner's MSS.

1543. " The huntyng and fyndyng out of the Romishe fox whiche more then seuen yeares hath bene hyd among the bisshoppes of Englond after that the Kynges Hyghnes had commãded hym to be dryuen out of hys realme. Foxes haue holes and byrdes of the ayer haue nestes/ but the son of man hath not Where he may rest hys hede in. Whosoeuer happeneth upon thys book/ if he loue god beter then man/ et the Kynges hyghnes better then the bysshoppes fals hypocrisy let hym gyue it to the Kyng/ that he may rede it before the bysshopes condemn it. M.D.XLIII." Dedicated " To the most excellent prince Kyng Henry the eight Kyng of England Frãce & of Jrland supreme gouerner in earth of thes hys realmes willm Wraghton Wissheth helthe prosperite of bothe body and soul.—From basil the first day of may. Anno domini 1543." Contains F 4, in eights. On the back of the last leaf under " The fawtes of thys book." is this colophon, " Jmprynted at Basyl the year of owr lord 1543 the 14 of September. W.H. Sixteens.

1543. " Yet a course at the Romyshe foxe. ☞ A dysclosynge or openynge of the Manne of synne, Cõtayned in the late Declaratyon of the Popes olde faythe made by Edmonde Boner bysshopp of London: wherby wyllyam Tolwyn was than newlye professed at paules crosse openlye into Antichristes Romyshe relygyon agayne by a newe solempne othe of obedyence, notwythstãdinge the othe made to hys prynce afore to the contrarye. ¶ An alphabetycall dyrectorye or Table also in the ende therof, to the spedye fyndynge out of the pryncypall matters therin contayned. Compyled by Johan Harrison. 2 Thes. 2. Before the lordes commynge schall the manne of synne be opened. Esa. 11. wyth the breathe of hys mouthe schall the lorde slee that wycked one." It begins with " A preface to the Christen Reader." contained in 10 leaves. On signature L iij is this colophon " ¶ Thus endeth the Manne of synne wyth hys Dysclosynge, collected by Johã harrysõ *(Bale)* in the yeare frõ Christes incarnacyõ. M.D.xlij. ãd imprented at Zurik by Olyuer Jacobson Anno Domini. 1543. the x. daye of Decẽbre." On the back, " Fawtes through neglygence of the Prynter." Then, " An alphabetycall dyrectorye or Table" &c. Contains P 4, in eights. W.H. 16°.

1543. " ¶ The Rekening and declaraciõ of the faith and beleif of Huldrik Zwingly," &c. See p. 711. W.H. Octavo.

1543. " ¶ George Joye confuteth/ Vvinchesters false Articles." Contains 24 leaves. At the end " ☞ Alexander Macedonis sentence is this seyinge. J muste nedes haate that Gardiner and herbe seller whiche plucketh vp his herbes by the rootes. The axe therfor is bẽte to his roote saithe John Bapt. He is cut downe and caste into the fyer/ except

except he repēt. Printed at Wesill in Chiese lande the yere of owr lorde M.D.xliij. in the Monethe of June." W.H. Sixteens.

"Our sabiour Jesus Christ hath not overcharged his Chirche with many 1543.
ceremonies. The Lorde shall knit vp his mynde in fewe wordes for our rightwise makynge euen by faith onely to be iustified. Esaye. x. M.D.X.LIIJ: in Febru." Contains C, 6, in eights. At the end "At Zijrik." W.H. Octavo.

"Primasii* Vticensis, in Affrica Justinopoli civitate episcopi, Com- 1544.
mentariorum libri quinque in Apocalypsin Joannis Euangelistae, ante mille annos ab autore conscripti, nuncque primum aediti. Robertus Winter, (*an Englishman*) Basileae. 1544."

"The epistle exhortatorye of an Englyshe Christiane vnto his 1544.
derelye beloued contreye of Englande, against the pompouse popyshe bysshoppes therof, as yet the true members of theyr fylthye father the great Antichrist of Rome. Made by Henrye Stalbrydge. ☞ As I haue compyled this treatyse in the zele of God and my Prince against the tyrāt of Rome and his secret mayntenerss so ys yt my desyre that his grace maye haue yt as a frute of my Christen obedience. And I doubt yt not, but some godlye manne louynge his grace better then that wycked Pope, wyll faythfullye delyuer it vnto him, the slaughtes of theyr false generation consydered. Praye (gentyll reader) that yt maye fynde grace in his syght. Deale with Babylon as she hath deserued, for she hath set vp herselfe against the Lorde, and against the holye one of Israel. Hiere. L." In Fo. 14. after having shewn the cruelty of the clergy to great numbers of persons he had named, with the burning of the New Testament by Somers and sixteen others, in Cheap, at London, he says thus: "Speciallye wode Whynchester, lewde London, lurkynge Lyncolne, dreamynge Durham, yorke without wytt, chatterynge Chychestre, smylynge Salysburye, fleryng fryer wattes, and that double-faced trayter Wilson, namyng it (*the Testament*,) full of errours and verye yll translated." &c. On the back of Fo. 28. "☞ Written from Basyle a cyte of the Heluecyanes by me Henrye Stalbrydge in the yeare from Christes incarnacion. 1544. and the fyrst daye of August." Then "☞ An Appendyce Joyned to the foreseyd Epistle." and concludes at the end of "A brefe table." with "Set youre selues at large, and beare not the straungers yoke with vnbeleuers. ij. Cor. vi." Contains D, in eights. W.H. Sixteens.

I have another edition without any date with the title, as follows:

"The Epistel Exhortatorye of an Jnglyshe Chrystian vnto his derely beloved coutrey of Jngland, agaynst the pompouse popysh Bisshops therof, as yet the true membres of theyre fylthye Father the great Antychryst of Reme. Made by Henrye Stalbrydge. (*Bale*) ¶ Hieremie. L. ℔ Deale wyth babylon" &c. On the back of the title is "As J haue

* This Antiq. M.S. cost Walter Clavel, esq. 26l. 17s. 6d. was bought at Mr. Ames's sale of books, Lot 1350, for 10 Guineas, by Mr. Tutet, at whose sale, Lot 511, it sold for 4l.

haue compyled thys treatise" &c. as inserted in the title of the foregoing article. On the back of Fo. 15. is "Specially wode Winchester/ lewde London/ &c. On the back of Fo. 31. before the "appendyce" and "brefe table" is "¶ Written from Basle a citie of the Heluecyans by me Henry Stalbridge Finis." Contains E 4, in eights. W.H. 16°.

1544. "A supplycacion to our moste soueraigne lorde Kynge Henry the eyght, Kynge of England of Fraunce and of Jrelande/ & moste ernest defender of Christes gospell/ supreme heade vnder God here in erthe/ next & Immedyatly of his churches of Englande/ and Jrelande. (☞) Matthei. ix. The harweste is greate but the laborers are fewe. Wherfore praye the lorde of the harweste to sende forthe laborers into his harweste." Contains D 6, in eights. Colophon "Emprynted In the yeare of our lorde. M.CCCCC.xliij. in the moneth of Decembre." W.H. Sixteens.

1544. "A SVPPLICATION TO OVR MOSTE Soueraigne Lorde Kyng Henry the eight, king of England, of Fraunce, and of Jreland, and moste earnest defender of Christes Gospell, supreme head and immediately of his Churches of England and Jreland. ¶ Nowe newly imprinted and set forth for the speciall vse thereof, that may be made in our time. Mathew. ix. The haruest is great," &c. Contains D 2, in eights. Colophon "Imprinted in the yeare of our Lord. M.CCCCC.xliiij. in the month of December." W.H. Octavo.

1544. "A brefe Chronycle concernynge the Examinacyon and death of the blessed martyr of Christ syr Johan Oldecastell the lorde Cobham/ collected togyther by Johan Bale." &c. See p. 704. Octavo.

1544. "A present consolacion for the sufferers of persecucion for ryghtwysenes." In September. By George Joy. Octavo.

—— "A proper dyaloge, betwene a gentillman and an husbandman, eche complaynenge to other theyr myserable calamyte, through the ambicion of the clergye." Begins, "An A, B, C. to the spiritualte." In verse. 8°.

—— "Two notable sermons at Paul's crosse, one November 16, 1544, by William Chedsey, vice president of Corpus Christi college, Oxon. The other by —— Scot of Cambridge, both allowed by bishop Bonner." Octavo.

—— "A confutacion of that treatise/ which one John Standish made agaynst the protestacion of D. Barnes in the yeare. M.D.XL. Wherin/ the holy scriptures (peruerted and wrested in his sayd treatise) are restored to their owne true vnderstonding agayne by Myles Couerdale. Iacobi iij. Nolite gloriari/ & mendaces esse aduersus ueritatem." Addressed "To all them that either reade or heare gods holy worde/ and geue ouer them selues to lyue vnfaynedly according to the same/" &c. beginning thus "The seuenth daye of Decembre/ was delyuered vnto me a certayne treatyse/ composed by one John Standish Felow of Whittington college in londō (so is the tytle of it) and prynted by Robert Redeman/ Anno M.D.XL.iij. Nonas Octobris." See p. 397 and 404. Contains O 7, in eights. On the last leaf "Jacobi. iij. Yf ye haue a bytter Zele/

Zele/ and there be contencions in youre hartes/ make no boast/ nether be lyars against the trueth." The back blank. In a very gothic type. W.H. Octavo.

" The rescuynge of the Romishe fox otherwyse called the examination of the hunter deuised by steuen gardiner. The seconde course of the hunter at the romishe fox & hys aduocate, & sworne patrone steuen gardiner doctor & defender of the popis canonlaw and hys ungodly ceremonies. Rede in the last lefe the xij articles of Bisshop Steuens neuu popish *credo*." On the back is the cut of a fox holding a pastoral staff, &c. under it are these wordes " The bannisshed fox of Rome speakethe.[1] Dedicated " To the most victorious and triumphant Prince, Kynge Henry the eyght, kyng of Englond, France, & Irelande, Supreme Gouernour in earth, of thes hys realmes next vnder God, Vuillyam Wraghton, Vuisseth prosperite of bothe body & soule." Then, " The Rescuer of the Romishe Fox and hys whelpes, agaynst the hunter & hys houndes." Contains n, in eights. On the back of the last leaf " The fautes of thys book." Underneath is this colophon " Jmprynted haue at winchester Anno Domini 1545. 4. nonas Martij. By me Hanse hit prik." W.H. Octavo. 1545.

" The Huntyng of the Romysshe Vuolfe, made by Vuilliam Turner doctour of Phisik. Take hede of false Prophetes," &c. On the back is an address " To the ryght honourable yonge Lordes and worchipfull yonge gentylmen, of Summersetshyre, &c. and to the yonge gentylmen of all other shyres in Englande and Jrelande, Wyllyam Turner doctour of Phisyck, wyssheth, a parfyt knowlege of Goddes worde, and grace of almyghtye God to lyue therafter.——The Romysshe Foxe, latelye returned into Englande agayne speaketh.* Then, a dialogue between " The Foster." and " The Hunter." Contains f 4, in eights. W.H. Octavo.

" The dysclosyng of the Canon of ẏ popysh Masse, with a sermon annexed vnto it, of ẏ famous Clerke of worthy memorye. D. Marten Luther. Apocal. xviii. Come away from hyr my people, that ye be not partakers in her synnes, ẏ ye receiue not of her plages. All honour, ——

[1] " My son steuen gardiner with wepyng teares
Hath cut away the toppes of myn eares
But the rest of my body abydeth hole still
With alle my ceremonyes euen at my will
I trust my eares shal grow agayn
When all the gospellers ar o es slayn.
Whiche steuen my son both sterck and stout
Doth now right craftily go about
If he can bryng thys matter to pass
He schal be Cardnal as fisher was."

* Gardiner my sonne whych wyth wepyng teares.
Cut oute awaye quyte the toppes of myne eares,
Hath taken for me, of late suche payne:
That they are growen and healed agayne.
The reste of my bodye is whole and sounde:
And bryngeth the Gospellers all to grounde.
My doughter Masse he hath quickened agayne.
And putteth her enemyes to great payne.
My Constitucions, Decretales & Decrees:
Are taken no more for fables and lyes.
But are had in suche pryce, and store:
As euer they were had in before.
Because syr Steuen both stercke and stoute:
Hath brought these matters so well aboute.
My doughter Masse shalbe hys wyfe,
Wyth whome I wyll gyue hym for terme of lyfe:
Power in England to do what he lyst,
And to kyll them al that do him resyst."

prayse and glorye be geuen onely to God." The epistle "To the Reader" begins thus, "From the beginyg or at ẏ fyrst entraunce after the creaciō good christē reader God in hīselfe," &c. Contains C, in eights. At the end, "Jmprynted haue at al Papistes. By me Hans hitprycke." The pages are misplaced, especially in the form of signature B. W.H. Octavo.

— "A PORE HELPE.

Begins, "Will none in al this land, Step forth and take in hand,
The Bukler and defence of mother holy kyrke,
And weapon to dryue hence al that against her wircke." 8°.

See Strype's Eccl. Memor. Vol. 2. p. 55.

1554. "The exposicion of Daniel the prophete gathered oute of Philip Melanchton/ Johan Ecolampadius/ Chonrade Pellicane & out of Johan Draconite. &c. By George Joye. A prophecye diligently to be noted of al Emperowrs & kinges in these laste dayes. And nowe ye kinges get ye vnderstanding & knowlege/ be ye taught and lerned in Gods worde/ ye iuges of the erthe. Psal. 2. Serue ye the lorde in feare/ kisse ye the sonne (and not images) lest he be wrathe and ye perisshe from the way/ for shortely shall his anger be kindled. But then blessed be thei all that truste vnto him. 1545. Jn Auguste." Dedicated "☞ Vnto the most cleare Prince/ lorde Maurice Duke of Saxone/ Lantgraue of Turinge and Marchis of Misne; Philip Melanchton whissheth helthe.—Jn the Calends of January. 1545. translated.---The argument or mater contained in Daniel the Prophete by Philip Melanchton.---A brife supputacion of the Ages and yeris of the worlde." Contains 244 leaves. At the end, "Emprinted at Geneue. 1545. G. J." W.H. Again 1550. Octavo.

— "The Lamētacyon of a Christen Agaynst the Cytye of London, for some certayne greate vyces vsed therin. Psal. lxx. Let them be abasshed and ashamed, that seke after my sowle. let them be put to flyght and shame that wyll me euyl. In the yeare of our Lorde M.D.XLV." Contains D 4, in eights. Colophon "Prynted at Nurenbergh in the yeare of our Lorde. M.DXLV. in the laste of Nouembre." W.H. Sixteens.

1545. "A mysterye of inyquyte contayned within the heretycall Genealogye of Ponce Pantolabus/ is here both dysclosed & confuted By Johan Bale. An. M.D.xlii. Marke in the capytall letters of this boke/ the. A. B. C. with the name of the Author. J wyll shewe the (sayth ẏ Angell to Johan) the mysterye of the greate whore/ & of ẏ Beast that beareth her. Apoca. 17." Within a Compartment. "☞ Emprynted at Geneua. By Mychael Wode. 1545." On the back of the title is "The Preface." Then, "the Table." Contains M, in eights. W.H. See p. 373, &c. Sixteens.

1545." A shorte Recapitulacion or abrigement of Erasmus Enchiridion, brefely comprehendinge the summe and contentes therof. Very necessary to to be rede of all trew Christen men. Drawne out by M. Couerdale Anno. 1545. Timo. ij. Suffer afflitions, as goode and feathfull sowdyars of Jesu Christ. ii. Iob vij. Syeng the lyffe of man, ys but A battell or werfare apon the erathe." Contains E 4, in eights. Colophon "Imprinted at Ausborch by Adam Anonimus In the moneth of May. Anno. 1545." W.H. Sixteens.

"The defence of a certayne poore Christen man: Who els shuld haue bene condemned by the Popes lawe. Written in the hye Allmaynes tonge by a right excellent and noble Prynce/ and trāslated into Englishe by Myles Couerdale." Colophon "Printed at Nurenbergh/ And translated owt of douche into Englishe by Myles Couerdale/ in the yeare of our Lorde M.D.XLV. in the laste of Octobre." Contains E, in eights. W.H. Sixteens. 1545.

"Mr. Robert Legats catechisme betweene man and wife, what the holy catholicke church is; and betweene truth, and the unlearned man." At Wessel. 1545.

"The primer, set foroth by the kynges maiestie (*Hen.* 8.) and his clergie, to be taught, lerned, and read; and none other to be used throughout all his dominions." See p. 520, and 542. Quarto. 1545.

"A supplication of the poore Commons. Prouerbes. xxi. Chapiter. Whoso stoppeth his eare at the criynge of the poore/ he shall crye hym selfe/ and shall not be heard. Wherunto is added the Supplication of Beggers." See p. 1537. The supplication of the poore commons concludes on signature c 6, thus; "Your moste faythfull and obeysaunt subiectes: the pore commones of the royalme of Englande. Anno M.CCCCC.XLVI." Contains d, in eights. W.H. Sixteens. 1546.

"Wycklyffes wycket: whyche he made in Kynge Rycards days the second in the yere of our lorde God M.CCC.XLV. Jhon the vi. chapiter. I am the liuynge bread which came downe from heauen:" &c. It begins with "A verye brefe diffinition of these wordes, Hoc est corpus meum." To which is added on the back of signature B 3, "The testament of maister wylliam Tracie esquier, expounded by Wylliam Tyndall. Wherin thou shalt perceyue with what charite the chaunceller of worceter Burned when he toke vp the deade carcas and made asshes of it after it was buried. M.D.XXXV. To the reader.—The Testament hit selfe." Contains c 3, in eights. At the end "Here endeth the Exposicion of wyllyam Tyndall. Jmpryntd at Norenburch, 1546." W.H. Sixteens. 1546.

"A boke, made by John Fryth prysoner in the Tower of London, answerynge vnto M. Mores letter, which he wrote agaynst the fyrste lytle treatyse that John Fryth made concernynge the Sacramente of the body and bloode of Christ: vnto whiche boke are added in the ende the artycles of hys examynacyon before the Byshoppes of London, Wynchester and Lyncolne, in Paules churche at London, for whyche John Fryth was condempned and after brente in Smythfelde wythout Newgate, the fourth daye of July. Anno. 1533. Now newly reuysed corrected & prynted. Jn the Yeare of our Lorde. 1546. the last daye of 1546.

8 W 2 June.

June. Deade men shall ryse agayne." It begins with "The Preface." Contains 108 leaves. At the end, "Be wyse as Serpentes, and innocent as Dooues." W.H. See p. 1540. Sixteens.

1546. "The refutation of the byshop of Winchesters derke declaration of his false articles, once before confuted by George Joye. Be not deceiued by this bysshops false bokes. Heare now the tother parte, and iudge truly of the trueth. For the veritie wyll haue the victorye." 192 leaves.* Sixteens.

1546. "The true hystorie of the Christen departynge of the reuerēde mā, D. Martyne Luther, collected by Justus Jonas, Michael Celius, and Joannes Aurifaber whych were therat, & translated into Englysh by Johan Bale. Arma Ducis Saxoniæ.—I hearde a voyce from heauen (sayth S. Johan) whych sayd thus vnto me. Blessed are the dead whych depart in the lorde. For they from hens forth shall rest from their labours. Apoca. xiiij." Contains fol. 21. "Thus endeth the oracyō or processe rehearced off Philippe Melanchton at the buryall of the Reuerende man, Doctor Martyne Luther. Translated by Johan Bale. Anno M.D.LXVI."* W.H. Octavo.

1546. "Burying of the Mass." in verse. It begins with a preface "To all thē that loue Goddes worde vnfaynedly L. R. wyssheth grace and peace from God the Father, through our Lorde Jesus Christ." A short abstract from which is given below.[7] Then, a dialogue between "The Authoure of the boke," and "The Boke." in 14 seven-lined stanzas. "Here foloweth the Lamentacion of A ranke Papist concernynge the death of the Masse." in 44 similar stanzas. "Here foloweth a breife Dialogue betwene two Prestes seruauntes, named Watkyn and Jeffraye, reasonynge vpō their Masters Lamētacyon." Colophon "Prynted at Wesell in the yeare of our Lorde 1546 in the last of June. By Henry Nycolson." On the back of the last leaf, over the triple crown and cross-keys,

"Christ Goddes sonne, borne of a mayden poore,
For to saue mankynde from heaven descended:
Popes commonly the sonnes of an whoore,
To destroye man, from hell hath ascended."

Beneath,

* This date M.D.LXVI. I think most evidently be a typographical error for M.D.XLVI; being only a misplacing of the numericals L and X. There could be no occasion for it to have been printed abroad in 1566; besides, Bale died in 1563.

[7] "Ryght gentle Brethern and Fryndes in the Lorde, as I was syttynge at the table vpon Easter daye last past, a certayne fryade of myne delyuered me this lytle treatise, desyrynge me to peruse & reade it: whych thynge whan J had ones done, J consulted with me frynde shewynge hym that J thought it good to set it forth in Print.—This boke was prynted in the Cardynal his tyme (*See p.* 1536.) whiche whan he harde that it was done, caused a certayne man whome J coulde name if J lusted to bye them all vppe.—

This lytle treatyse though he hath lyen longe hydden by the space of xvi. or xvij. yeares, now as a sparcle of Truthe (by the prouysyon of God) at the last he doth appeare, and wyll declare vnto the wyde worlde as well the abhomynations of them (which our most dreade Soueraygne Lorde hath suppressed and put downe for their desertes) as of those whiche do yet remayne vnsuppressed, not lesse worthy (all thynges consydered) than their Brethren the Monkes and Fryres, whiche are gone before them." &c.

Beneath,

" Jn whome is evydently comprehended.
The perfecte mekenes of oure savyoure Christ,
And tyranny of the murtherer Antichrist."

Contains H, in eights. It has running-titles and catch-words, but no paging. W H.4 wanting title. See a former edit. p. 1538-9. Octavo.

" Dowfal of Antichristes mas." See Warton, vol. III; p. 145. 1546.

John Bale's English Votaries, the first part. See p. 772. " Printed at Wesel Jn the Yeare of our Lorde God. 1546." Octavo. 1546.

" The first examinacion of the worthye servaunt of God mastres Anne Askew the yõger doughter of Sir Wyllyam Askewe knyght of lyncolneshyre, latelye martyred in Smithfelde, by the Romysh popes vpholders. The censure or iudgemēt of Johan Bale therupon, after the sacred Scriptures and Chronycles." On folio 42 is " The conclusyon." a kind of epistle to the reader. Colophon " Thus endeth the first examynacyon of Anne Askewe, latelye done to deathe by the Romysh popes malycyouse remnaunt, and now canonysed in the precyouse bloude of the lorde Jesus Christ. Jmprented at Marpurg in the lande of Hessen, in Novembre, Anno 1546." Then follows (after folio 46) " The voyce of Anne Askewe out of the 54. Psalme of David, called. Deus in nomine tuo," and " A table compendyouse of thys first boke." W.H.4 Sixteens. 1546.

" The lattre examinacion of the worthye servaunt of God mastres Anne Askewe the yõger doughter of Sir Wyllyam Askewe knyght of Lyncolne shyre, latelye martyred in Smithfelde by the wycked Synagoge of Antichrist. The censure or iudgemēt of Johan Bale therupon, after the sacred Scriptures and Chronycles." Prefixed is a long preface. On fol. 63 is " The Balade whych Anne Askewe made and sange whan she was in Newgate." Then " The conclusyon." Colophon " Thus endeth the lattre conflict of Anne Askewe, latelye done to death by the Romysh popes malycyouse remnaunt, & now canonysed in the precyouse bloude of the lorde Jesus Christ. Imprented at Marpurg in the lande of Hessen, 16, die Januarii, anno 1.5.4.7." Then, " A table compendyouse of thys lattre boke."—God save the kynge. Contains fol. 71.* W.H. Sixteens. 1547.

" The epistle of the famous and great Clerke Philip Melancton made vnto oure late Souereygne Lorde Kynge Henry the eight, for the reuokinge and abolishing of the six articles set forth and enacted by the craftie meanes and procurement of certeyne of our prelates of the clergie, newly trāslated out of laten into Englishe by I. C. The truth wyll haue the victorie." Colophon " Printed at Weesell. 1547. the. 18. of Maye." Contains B, in eights. W.H. Sixteens. 1547.

" A Declaracion of Christe and of his offyce compylyd by Johan Hoper, Anno 1547. Matth. 7. Hic est filius meus dilectus, in quo mihi bene cōplacuit, ipsum audite." Dedicated " To the moost noble an victorious prince Edwarde Duke of Somerset: Erle of Hertforthe: viscount beaue Champe: Lord Semer: Gouerner of the person of the Kynges 1547.

Kynges Maiestie: and Protector of all his Realmes his leaue tenant generall of all his Armyes, boothe by land and by sea. Treasurer and Erle Marshall of Inglöd. Gouerner of the illes of Guernsey and Jersey and Knyght of the moost Noble order of the garter Johann Hoper wyshythe grace and peace withe long and gracious lief in the lyuyng God throwghe Christ Jesus oure only sauiour.—Tiguri 6. decembris. 1547. Youre gracis moost humble Oratour." Contains M v, in eights, & on a separate leaf this colophon "Pryntyd in Zurych by Augustyne Fries Anno M.D.XLVII." The Roman & Black letters are intermixed even in the same words. W.H. See p. 1343. Octave.

1547. "An Answer vnto my lord of wynchesters booke intytlyd a detection of the deuyls Sophistrye, wherwith he robbith the vnlernyd people of the trew byleef in the moost blessyd sacrament of the aulter made by Johann Hoper. Psalm 119. Vestigia mea dirige in uerbo tuo domine, & non dominabitur mei ulla iniquitas, Prynted in Zurych by Agustyne Fries. Anno M.D.XLVII." It begins with "Johan Hoper wyshythe grace and the yefftes of the holy Gooste unto my lord of wynchester.—Tiguri 9. Septembris M.D.XLVII. Johannes Hoperus Anglus, uoluntate ac legibus." Contains X, in fours. Roman & black letter intermixed. W.H. Quarto.

1547. "The olde fayth/ an euident probation out of the holy scripture/ that the christen fayth (whiche is the right, true, old and vndoubted fayth) hath endured sens the beginnyng of the worlde. Herein hast thou also a short summe of the whole Byble, and a probaciory that al vertuous men haue pleased God, and were saued through the Christen fayth. 1547. Myles Couerdale." It begins with an epistle "To the reader." Contains H, in eights. W.H. Sixteens.

1547. "An ansvver to the deuillish detection of Stephane Gardiner, Bisshoppe of Wynchester, published to the intent that such as be desirous of the truth should not be seduced by hys errours, nor the blind & obstinate excused by ignorance. Compiled by A. G. Judicum. vi.—Anno. 1547. the. 24. of January: Jn the viii. leafe i. page and xiiii. line: for siame mne, reade same mine." It begins with an epistle "To the Reader." Contains Fol. ccx. beside "The Table" on six more; on the back of the last is a cut of St. John. W.H. Octavo.

1547. "A BRIFE AND FAYTHFULL declaration of the true fayth of Christ, made by certeyne men susspected of heresye in these articles[a] folowyng. ¶ i. Thessalonians. v. ☞ Quench not the spirite, despise not the prophecziynges, but proue all thynges, and kepe that, that is good. ¶ Esaye. v. ☞ Wo be vnto them that call good euyll, and euyl good, whyche make darknesse lyght, and light darknesse ☞.☜ ¶ Anno M.D.XLVII. Per me I. B." (Q. *John Bale?*) B, in eights. W.H. Sixteens.

"Recantations

[a] These articles are not mentioned on the title-page, but collected from the treatise are the following: The apostles creed, with an exposition; Baptism; The Lord's Supper; The Christian kingdom; The weapons of the Christian warfare; and matrimony.

"Recantations of Mr. Harcocke, priest, made at Halsworth and Bonghay in Suffolk, 1547." Octavo.

"A declaration of the Masse, the fruite therof, the cause and the meane, wherfore and howe it ought to be maynteyned. Newly perused and augmented by the first author therof. Maister Anthony Marcort at Geneue. John vi. ☞ J am the breade of lyfe, whoso cometh to me shall haue no hunger. And who that beleueth in me shall neuer haue thurste. Trāslated newly out of French into Englishe. Anno M.D.XLVII. 1547.

☞ Reade me firste from toppe to too
And afterward iudge me a friende or a foe.
If you iudge me or J be tryed
You shalbe blamed when you are spied."

On the back of this title is an epistle by "Cephas Geranius to the reader." Then "The preface of the authour." Contains D, in eights. Colophon "MDXLVII. Printed at Wittenberge by Hans Luste." W.H. Octavo.

"The com-Plaint of Roderyck Mors, sometime a gray-Fryre, vnto the parlamenthouse of Englande his naturall countrye. For the redresse of certeyne wicked lawes, euill customes & cruell decrees. A table whereof thou shalt finde in the nexte leafe. Psalme LIIIJ.—Imprinted at Geneue in Sauoye by Myghell boys." Contains O, in fours. Black letter. W.H. I have two other editions; as follows. Sixteens. ——

"The cōPlaint of Roderyck Mors/ som tyme a gray Fryre, vnto the parlament house of Jngland hys naturall countrey/ For the redresse of certein wycked lawes/ evell custumēs ād cruell decrees. A table wherof thou shalt finde in the next leafe. Psalme. liiij.—Imprinted at Geneve in Savoye by Myghell boys." Contains H, in eights. Black letter. W.H. Sixteens. ——

"THE COMPLAYNT OF RODERYK MORS, somtyme a grayfryre, vnto the parliament howse of Ingland his natural cuntry: For the redresse of certen wicked lawes, euel customs ād cruel decreys. A table &c.—Psalme. liiij." At the end "Imprinted at Sauoy per Franciscum de Turona." Contains H, in eights. Mostly in Italics, except the capitals, which are in Roman, or blooming letters. W.H Sixteens. ——

"A ballet, declaringe the fal of the whore of Babylone, intytuled, Tye thy mare Tom-boye, with other, and thereunto annexed a prologe to the reders. Apocalyps 18." Ends, "quod Wyllyam Kith." Octavo. ——

"The lamentacyon of a Christē agaīst the Citye of London," &c. See p. 1558. "Jmprīted ī ẏ yere of our Lord m.d.xlviii." Contains f 6, in eights. W.H. Sixteens.

"Of vnwritten verities." Begins, "In the day of Pentecoste." 8°. 1548.

"A declaration of the power of Gods worde, concerning the holy supper of the Lord, confuting all Lyers and fals teachers, which mayntayne theyr maskynge Masse inuented agaynst the woorde of God, and the Kynges Maiesties must godly proceedynge compyled Anno M.D.XLVIII. 1548.

M.DXLVIII. By John Mardeley clerc of the Kings Maiesties mynte called Suffolke house." Octavo.

1548. "The Lamentable and wofull complaynte of my Lady Masse, by her alone, earely in a morenynge preparynge her selse towardes her Father the Sodomite, and great Symon Magus of Rome, made the yeare after the death of the moste famous and Inuyncible Kynge of Israell Iesus Christe 1.5.4.8. Prayse the euerlastynge, For that thou hast receauyd Distrybute accordynly, for so is his wyll." Contains 8 leaves. At the end "quod Henry Johnes." Octavo.

1548. "The coniectures of the end of the Worlde by Andrew Oseander, translated by George Joye, with many things by him added. Foxe unbounde." Octavo.

1548. "A Godly Medytacyon of the christen sowle, concerninge a love towardes God and hys Christe, compyled in frenche by Ladye Margarete quene of Nauerre, aptelie translated into Englisch by the ryght vertuouse lady Elyzabeth doughter to our late souerayne Kynge Henry the viii." This title over a cut of the princess Elizabeth kneeling, offering her book to our Saviour, and receiving his blessing "Inclita filia, serenissimi olim Anglorum Regis Henrici octaui Elizabetha, tam Græce quam latine fœliciter in Christo erudita. The Epystle dedycatory To the right vertuouse and christenly lerned yonge lady Elizabeth, the noble doughter of our late souerayne kynge Henry the viij.— Your bounde oratour Johan Bale." After the meditation, "The xiij Psalme of Dauid, called, Dixit insipiens, touched afore of my lady Elizabeth." In English verse; at the end of which is the same cut as on the title-page. Contains 43 leaves. "Jmprented in the yeare of our lorde 1548. in AprylI." See p. 955 and 963. Octavo.

"A Letter sent to Master A. B. from the most godly and learned Preacher. I. B. (*John Bradford.*) In which is set forth the authoritie of Parentes vpon their children, for gyuing of correction vnto them. With an addition of a Sermon of Repentance annexed thereunto. (*My copy has it not.*) Anno Domini. 1548." Contains 9 leaves. W.H. Octavo.

1548. John Rogers's Translation of Philip Melancthon, waying and considering of the Interim. London. Harl. cat. Vol. I. 2922. Octavo.

1548. "Gratulatio Buceri ad Ecclesiam Anglicanam." See Strype's Eccl. memor. II; 146. Quarto.

—— "Wickliesses wicket. Faythfully ouerseene and corrected after the originall and first copie. The lack wherof was cause of innumerable and shamfull erroures in the other edicion. As shall easyly appeare to them, that lyste to conferre the one wyth the other. Hereunto is added an epistle to the reader. With the protestacion of Jhon Lassels, late burned in Smythfelde; and the Testament of Wyllyam Tracie, esquire, expounded by Willyam Tyndall, and Jhon Frythe. Ouersene by M. C." Octavo.

—— "Two bokes of the noble doctor and B. S. Augustine, thone entiteled of the predestinacion of saintes; thother of perseueranee vnto thende:

thende: wherunto are annexed the determinacions of two auncient generall councelles, confermyng the doctrine taught in theſe bokes, by S. Auguſtine: all faythfully tranſlated out of Laten into Englyſhe, by John Scory, the late B. of Chicheſter, very neceſſary for al tymes, but namely for oures, wherin the papiſtes and anabaptiſtes haue reuiued agayne the wycked opinions of the Pelagians, that extolled mans wyll and merites agaynſt the fre grace of Chriſte."* See p. 755. Octavo.

A book called, PHILOXENVS in English. At the end of the firſt book: "Londini in aedibus Richardi Taverneri. Cum priv. ſolum." Octavo. ——

"The olde Faythe of great Brittaygne and the new learnyng." ——

"A Dyalogue or Diſputacion bytwene a Gentylman and a Preſt concernyng the Supper of the Lorde." 14 leaves. Octavo. ——

"A Short deſcription of Antichriſt vnto the nobilitie of Englande, and to all my brethren and countreymen borne and dwelling therin, with a warning to ſee to, that they be not deceaued by the hypocriſe and crafty conueyance of the Clergie. John. 10. He that is of God heareth the word of God." Octavo. ——

"A dialoge or communication of two perſons, deuyſed and ſet forthe In the laten tonge, by the noble and famoſe clarke Deſiderius Eraſmus, intituled the pylgremage of pure deuotyon. Newly tranſlated into Engliſhe." Octavo. ——

"A goodly dialogue and dyſputacion betwene Pyers Plowemã and a popish Preeſt cõcernynge the Supper of the Lorde: no leſſe frutefull then neceſſary to be noted of all Chriſten mẽ ſpecially, conſidering the great controuerſies and varyaũces had therein nowe in oure tyme. 1 Corinth. 1." God hath choſen the weake thinges of the wourlde, &c. 8 leaves. W.H. Mr. Ames had a MS. title, differing greatly from this in orthography. Sixteens. ——

"A Declaration of the ten holy cõmaundementes of allmygthye God, wroten Exo. 20. Deu. 5. Collectyd out of the ſcripture Canonicall, by Joanne Hopper. Cum̃ and ſe: Joan. 1. Anno M.D.XLVIII.* It concludes with an apology for the errors of the preſs, and contains O 7, in eights. It is paged in the middle with Roman numerals. W.H. 8°. (1549.)

"The Images of the Old Teſtament, lately expreſſed, ſet forthe in Ynglishe & Frenche, vuith a playne and brief expoſition. Printed at Lyons by Johan Frellon, the yere of our lord God. 1549." The cuts, which are very neat wooden ones, and in number 96, were deſigned by Hans Holbein. Quarto. 1549.

"The laboryouſe Journey and ſerche of Johan Leylande, for Englandes Antiquitees, geuen of hym as a newe yeares gyfte to Kynge Henry the viij. in the xxxvij. yeare of his Reygne, with declaracyons enlarged: by Johan Bale. ij. Macha. ij. He that begynneth to wryte a ſtorye, for the fyrſte, muſte wyth hys vnderſtandynge gather the matter togyther 1549.

* This date muſt be concluded upon as a miſprint, eſpecially as the epiſtle "Vnto the Chryſtiane Reader," is dated "5 Nouembris Anno M.D.XLIX." in this, as well as in two other editions. See p. 709 and 714.

togyther, set hys wordes in ordre, and dylygently feke out on euery parte. To be folde in Fletestrete at the signe of the Croune next vnto the whyte Fryears gate." Dedicated "To the most vertuouse, myghtie, and excellent Prynce, Edward the. vi. by the grace of God kynge of Englande, Fraunce, and Irelande, Defender of the faythe, and in earth vndre Christe, of the Churches of the sayde Englande, and Irelande the supreme head, your most humble subiecte Johan Bale wyssheth all honour healthe and felycyte.---Johñ Bale to the Reader." Contains H 7, in eights. Colophon "Emprented at London by 'Johan Bale. Anno. M.D.XLIX." W.H. Sixteens.

1549. "A confession of the synner after the sacred Scriptures. Collected by John Bale." Octavo.

1549. "A vocabularye in six Languages." Printed at Nurenberg. Octavo.

—— A symple instruction concerning the Kinges maiesties proceedings in the Communion. Octavo.

—— Jovis, 2 Jan. 1549. A bill to avoid, and burn diuers papistic books, and books of prophecies. See journals of the House of Commons.

"¶ An Acte for the abolishing and putting away of diuers bookes and Images."

Whereas the king's most excellent majesty hath of late set forth & established by authority of parliament, an uniform, quiet, and godly order of common and open prayer, in a book entitled, "The booke of commõ praier, and administracion of the Sacramentes, and other rytes and ceremonies after the church of England," to be used and observed in the said church of England, agreable to the order of the primitive church, much more comfortable unto his loving subjects than other diversity of service, as heretofore of long time hath been used, being in the said book ordained nothing to be read, but the very pure word of God, or which is evidently grounded upon the same. And in the other, things corrupt, untrue, vain, and superstitious, and as it were, a preparation to superstition; which, for that they be not called in, but permitted to remain undefaced, do not only give occasion to such perverse persons, as do impugn the order and godly meaning of the king's said book of common prayer, to continue in their old accustomed superstitious service, but also minister great occasion to diversity of opinions, rites, ceremonies, and services. Be it therefore enacted, by the king our sovereign lord, the lords spiritual and temporal, and the commons, in this present parliament assembled, that all books called, "Antiphoners, Missales, Grailes, Processionalles, Manueles, Legẽdes, Pies, Portuasses, Primers, in Latine or Englishe, Couchers, Journalles, Ordinalles," or other books, or writings whatsoever heretofore used for service of the church, written, or printed in the Englishe or Latine tongue, other than such, as shall be set forth by the king's majesty, shall be by authority of this present act clearly and utterly &

' See The Life of Bale annexed to that of Leland, &c. 8°. 1772.

utterly abolished, extinguished, and forbidden for ever, to be used or kept in this realm, or elsewhere, within any the king's dominions.

And be it further enacted by the authority aforesaid, that if any person or persons of what degree, estate, or condition soever, he, she, or they be, bodies politick or corporate, that now have, or hereafter shall have, in his, her, or their custody, any of the books, or writings, of the sorts aforesaid, or any images of stone, timber, alabaster, or earth, graved, carved, or painted, which heretofore have been taken out of any church or chappel, or yet stand in any church or chappel, and do not before the last day of June next ensuing, deface and destroy, or cause to be defaced, or destroyed, the same images, and every of them, and deliver, or cause to be deliverrd, all and every the same books to the mayor, bayliff, constable, or churchwardens of the town, where such books then shall be, to be by them delivered over openly within three months next following after the said delivery to the archbishop, bishop, chancellor, or commissary of the same diocese, to the intent the said archbishop, bishop, chancellor, or commissary, and every of them, cause them immediately after either to be openly burnt, or otherwise defaced and destroyed, shall for every such book, or books, willingly retained in his, her, or their hands, or custody, within this realm, or elsewhere, within any the king's dominions, and not delivered, as is aforesaid, after the said last day of June, and be thereof lawfully convict, forfeit and lose to the king our sovereign lord, for the first offence, ten shillings, and for the second offence shall forfeit and lose (being thereof lawfully convict) four pounds; and for the third offence shall suffer imprisonment at the king's will.

And be it further enacted by the authority aforesaid, that if any mayors, bayliffs, constables, or churchwardens, do not within three months after receipt of the same books, deliver, or cause to be delivered, such books, so by them received, to the archbishop, bishop, chancellor, or commissary of their diocese; and if the said archbishop, bishops, chancellor, or commissaries, do not within forty days after the receipt of such books, burn, deface and destroy, or cause to be burned, defaced, or destroyed, the same books, and every of them; that then they, and every of them so offending, shall lose, and forfeit to our sovereign lord the king, being thereof lawfully convicted, fourty pounds; the one half of all which forfeitures shall be to any of the king's subjects, that will sue for the same in any of the king's courts of record, by bill, plaint, action of debt, or information; in which action no essoign, protection, wager of law, or other delay, shall be allowed.

And for better execution of the said act, be it enacted by the authority aforesaid, that as well justices of assise in their circuits, as justices of peace within the limits of their commission, in the general sessions, shall have full power and authority to enquire of the offences aforesaid, and to hear and determine the same in such form, as they may do in other such like cases.

 Provided

Provided always, that this act, or any thing therein contained, shall not extend to any image, or picture, set, or graven upon any tomb in any church, chapel, or churchyard, only for a monument of any king, prince, nobleman, or other dead person, which hath not been commonly reputed and taken for a saint, but that all such pictures, and images, may stand and continue in like manner, and form, as if this act had never been had, nor made; any thing in this act to the contrary in any wise notwithstanding.

Provided also, and be it enacted by the authority aforesaid, that any person or persons may use, keep, have, and retain any primers in the English or Latine tongue, set forth by the late king of famous memory, king Henry the eighth, so that the sentences of invocation, or prayer to saints in the same primers, be blotted, or clearly put out of the same; any thing in this act to the contrary notwithstanding.

Repealed 1 of Mary, cap. 2. but see 1 of Jac. cap. 25. which repeals 1 of Mary, cap. 2. Hence may be observed the names of old church books; how the loss of many pieces of antiquity came; and the blotting of the word pope in old books.

1550. "¶ The hystory writtone by Thucidides," &c. as p. 560. W.H. Folio.

1550. "The whole Bible" &c. as p. 568. Dedicated "Vnto the moost victorious Prince & our moost gracious soueraigne lorde, kynge Edwarde the sixte, kynge of Englonde, Fraunce and of Irlonde &c. Defendour of the Fayth and vnder God the chefe and supreme heade of the Church of Englonde.---Myles Couerdale, to the Christen Reader." Then a calendar in red and black. Before "The fyrst boke of Moses called Genesis" is a wooden cut, representing the formation of Eve from Adam's rib. In the Lambeth List it is mentioned as printed at London for Andrew Hester: and in Skipton's travels among Churchill's collection, Vol. 6, p. 462, Edition 1746—"printed at Zurich by Christopher Forshower 16th August 1550." But see Lewis, p. 182 and 191. W.H. Quarto.

1550. "Miles Huggard his treatise of three weddings." Maunsell, p. 60. Quarto.

1550. "A short catechisme, or a briefe and godly bringinge up of Youth," &c. Octavo.

1550. "A homelye of the Resurrection of Christe by John Brentius, translated by Thomas Sampson." Octavo.

1550. "Historia Martyrum Angliæ." Catal. Bibl. Harleianæ. iij. 6844. 4°.

1550. "A Confutation to the answer of a wicked ballad." Warton's Eng. Poetry. III. p. 197. note i. See p. 618. Octavo.

1550. "Injunctions given in the Visitacion of Nicholas Bishop of London." See Hist. of the Reformation, Vol. II: Records, No. 52. p. 187.

1550. Confession of the Christian Faith in 100 Articles. See p. 1081; also Ath. Oxon. Vol. I. Col. 93. Octavo.

1550. "A little Booke set forth by Paynel (*Thomas*) containing remarkable Sentences

Sentences taken out of the Holy Scriptures, suitable to the Christian on all occasions." Dedicated to the Lady Mary's Grace.

" Diatribe de hominis Justificatione, contra Pet. Martyrem. Lovain. 1550." Octavo. 1550.

" Defensio cælebatûs sacerdotum, contra P. Mart. Octavo. 1550.

" Confutatio quorundam articulorum de votis monasticis Pet. Martyris Itali." These two last being printed at Lovain in one volume, are very full of faults by the negligence of the printer, and the absence of the author. Both reprinted at Paris more correct, as follows. 1550.

" Defensio Sacri Episcoporum & Sacerdotum Cælibatûs contra impias & indoctas Petri Martyris Vermilii nugas & calumnias, quæ ille Oxonii in Anglia duobus retro annis in Sacerdotalium nuptiarum Assertionem temere effutavit," &c. These treatises against P. Martyr are by Hen. Smith, D. D. See Strype's Eccl. Memor. II; 40. Also Ath. Oxon. I; 143. 1550.

" Here begynneth a booke called the fal of the Romish Church, wyth all the abhominations, wherby euery man may know and perceiue the diuersity of it, betwene the prymatiue church, of the which our soueryne Lorde and King is the supreme head, and the malignant Church asunder." Contains c 7, in eights. W.H. Octavo. —

Another edition; without date, or Printer's name. Also, —

" A Dyalogue or Disputation bytwene a Gentylman and a Prest, concerning the Supper of the Lord." This seems to have been reprinted by R. Waldegrave, in 1581. Octavo. —

" A Table of the principall matters contained in the Bible, in which the reader may find and practise many common places." Sixteens. —

Nicolas Udal, a noted author, had a patent granted him the 4th of Edward vi. to print the works of Peter Martyr, entitled, Tractatus de Eucharistâ; (See p. 751.) and the English Bible, either in great or less volume, for seven years. *Query.*

" Pro Laurentio Torrentino, super Pandectis imprimendis.

Rex omnibus, ad quos, &c. salutem. Cum Laurentius Torrentinus Germanus, ab illustrissimo viro Domino Cosmo, Florentiae duce (sicut accepimus) conductus ad imprimendum complures libros ex iis, quorum exemplaria recondita sunt in celebri Florentiae bibliotheca, nobis exponi et supplicari fecerit, ut, quoniam ipse sub prelo habet praeclarum opus Digestorum seu Pandectarum juris civilis Romanorum, accuratè desumptum ad verbum, ex archetypo, quod per multa secula Pisis, deinde Florentiae, conservatum extitit, quod etiam plurimi docti homines illud ipsum esse crediderunt, quo usus olim fit Justinianus imperator, eorum voluminum conficiendorum author, magnosque sumptus ad illorum utilitatem, qui jurisprudentiae studiosi sunt, fecit in nova hac editione adornanda, quae a vetustissimi exemplaris illius fide et auethoritate nusquam discrepat, id quod nullus hactenus librorum excusor praestitit, hac de causa benignè providere velimus, nè aliorum avaritiâ et fraudi- Rymer, Vol. xv. 5 Edw. VI. 1551.

fit,

sit, hoc illi privilegium facilè concessimus, pro ea voluntate, qua præditi sumus erga omnes, qui bonarum literarum studiis aliquam utilitatem et commodum afferunt. Propterea jubemus, nè quis Anglus, vel Alienigena, usquam in nostro imperio et ditione libros Digestorum seu Pandectarum juris civilis Romanorum ad Laurentii Torrentini editionis, quam diximus, exemplum et emendationem conformatos, intra septenne ab hoc die inchoatum, imprimat quibuscumque characteribus, aut voluminum magnitudine, vel alibi a quolibet impressos venales habeat, absque illius Laurentii assensu et permissione, etiam si fortè additis quibusdam annotationibus vel explicationibus editi forent. Si quis verò contra hoc nostrum jussum facere ausus fuerit, volumus eum libros ejusmodi omnes amittere, et Laurentium Torrentinum illos sibi hàc nostrâ concessione acquisitos et adjudicatos repetere jure posse; quorumcumque hominum privilegiis quibuscumque non obstantibus. In cujus rei, &c. Teste rege apud Westm. 18 April. 1551." I have not met with any printing of his in England. See Eccl. Memor. II; p. 317.

1551. Alciat's Emblems. Lugduni 1551. Octavo.

1551. "Dr. Thomas Raynalde his declaration of the vertues of a lately invented oyle, called for the worthines thereof, the Oyle Imperiall, with the manner how the same is to be vsed against innumerable diseases. Printed at Venice by Jo. Griphius." Octavo.

1551. Sir John Check's "Epitaphium in Anton. Denneium. Lond. 1551." See Warton, III; 46, note e. Quarto.

1551. J. Fox's tables of grammar. Subscribed by eight lords of the council. Broadside.

1551. The Book of Common prayer in Latin by Alex. Alesius, Scotchman. Lipsiæ. Quarto.

1551. "¶ An explicatiō and assertion of the true Catholique fayth, touchyng the moost blessed Sacrament of the aulter with confutacion of a booke written agaynst the same. Made by Steuen Byshop of Wynchester, and exhibited by his owne hande for his defence to the Kynges maiesties Commissioners at Lambeth. 1551." On the back of this title are "Certayne faultes escaped in the prentyng. The rest thou mast gētle reader easely correcte thy selfe." Then follows "The preface." Contains besides 152 leaves. W.H. Sixteens.

1551. "A Prymer of Salisbury, printed at Rouen, 1551." Hearne's preface to Robert of Gloucester's Chronicle, p. xix. Octavo.

—— "A dialoge or communication of two persons, deuysed and set forthe in the latē tonge, by the noble and famouse clarke Desiderius Erasmus intituled the pylgremage of pure deuotion. Newly trāslated into Englishe." This title is in a curious border of birds & flowers on a black ground. The epistle "To the reader" is somewhat more than 10 pages; the pilgrimage contains 42 leaves. Mr. William White. 16°.

—— "The Psalmes of David translated into English metre by T. Sternhold, sir Thomas Wyat, and William Hunnis, with certain chapters of of the Proverbs, and select Psalms by John Hall. Dedicated to King Edward vi." From bishop Tanner's MSS.

" Brevis & dilucida de Sacramentis Ecclesiæ Christi, Tractatio. In qua & Fons ipse & Ratio totius Sacramentariæ nostri Temporis Controversiæ, paucis exponitur, Naturaque ac Vis Sacramentorum compendio & perspicuè explicatur: Per Joannem A Lasco, Baronem Poloniæ, Superintendentem Ecclesiæ Peregrinorum Londini, Anno 1552." Eccl. Memor. II; 374. Octavo. 1552.

Wilson's "Collection of " Epitaphia" on Charles and Henry Brandon. Printed at London. Warton, III; 432, note c. 1552.

" Marten Micron, minister of the Dutch Church in London, his short and faithfull instruction for the edifyeng & comfort of the symple christians, which intende worthely to receyue the holy Supper of the Lorde. Dated 8 Dec. 1552. Translated out of Dutch into Englyshe by T. C." (1550.)

" Bart. Greene his admonition to all Gentlemen professing the Gospell, (by life slandering the same) to repentance & amendment of life." 8°. ——

" The debate betwyn Churchyard and Camell." Beginning with a preface thus: ——

" Draw nere gentill reader, and harken to me,
Her slondes David Dicar dremynge as you see;
He sleapethe, and wakes not, but dremethe on still.
To scanne what he dremeth, eche mañ hath a will."

Ends with " Camellies crosse rowe," but has the names of several poets about that time. It contains 28 leaves. Quarto.

" Two bokes of the noble doctor and B. S. Augustine;" &c. I make no doubt of these being the same two books as mentioned above in p. 1564-5. In the original they are two books; but the translation may rather be deemed one book in 2 parts. It appears that Mr. Ames had in his possession a printed copy of it, and probably through forgetfulness of having given it before (a circumstance not to be wondered at) has here repeated it literatim, except in the word Chichester, here printed Chicester, which perhaps may be only a typographical error, with the following addition, " Gal. ii. Read fyrst, and then juge, who haue preached the true catholyke doctrine of the churche of Christ, we, or our aduersaries."[a] Another translation by Nich. Lesse. See p. 755. Octavo.

" Catechismus brevis Christianae Disciplinæ" &c. as p. 602 " Tiguri apud Andream Gesnerum F. Anno Domini, M.D.LIII." Octavo. 1553.

" Defensio verae et catholicae doctrinae de sacramento corporis & sanguinis Christi Seruatoris nostri, & quorundam in hac causa errorum confutatio, verbo sanctissimo Domini nixa atq; fundata, & consensu antiquissimorum Ecclesiæ scriptorum firmata, à Reuerendiss. in Christo Patre ac Domino D. Thoma Crannero Archiepiscopo Cantuariensi, Primate Totius Angliæ & Metropolitano, scripta. Jesus Christus. Joannis, 6. Spiritus est qui viuificat, caro non prodest quicquam. M.D.LIII." 1553.

Dedicated

[a] See Ath. Oxon. I; 179.

Dedicated "Illustrissimo ac Nobilissimo Principi Eduardo Sexto, Angliæ, Franciæ & Hiberniæ Regi, fidei defensori, & in terris secundum Christum Ecclesiæ Anglicanæ & Hiberniæ capiti supremo, Thomas Cantuariensis Archiepiscopus.—Lambethæ, Idibus Martijs. M.D.LIII.---Prooemium ad lectorem." Besides, 118 leaves. W.H. Octavo.

—— "Soon after the English fled from the Roman Tyranny exercised in England, a learned and excellent letter of the Lady (late queen) Jane written to the Apostate Harding, her father's chaplain, was printed in English in Strasburgh: This I make little doubt Aylmer, formerly her Tutor, (*afterward Bishop of London*) was the publisher of, and perhaps the bringer of it along with him from England." Strype's Life of bp. Aylmer, p. 11.

1553. John Bradford's Sermon on Repentance, with an epistle prefixed, dated July 1553. W.H. Sixteens.

1553. "The true and liuely historyke purtreatures of the vvoll bible. At Lyons, by Jean Fournes. M.D.LIII." The late M. C. Tutet. Octavo.

1553. "The Communication betwene my Lord Chauncelor and iudge Hales," being among other iudges to take his oth in VVestminster hall. Anno M.D.LIII. vi. of October." 4 leaves. W.H. Sixteens.

1553. "A godly psalm of Mary queen, which brought vs comfort all,
Thro God whom we of deuty praise that give her foes a fall."
With psalm-tunes in 4 parts. By Richard Beearde, parson of St. Mary-hill in London. See Warton, III, p. 319.

—— "A Treatise wherein is declared the pernitious opinions of those obstinate people of Kent: by James Cancellar." Octavo.

1553. "AN Admonishion to the Bishoppes of VVinchester, London and others, &c. Ecclesia. v. Make no tariyng to turne vnto the Lord, and put not of from daie to daie, for sodenly shall his wrath come, & in the time of vengeance he shall distroye the. From Roane by Michael wood, Anno M.D.LIII. the first of October." This treatise begins on the back of the title-page. 15 pages. W.H. Sixteens.

1553. Beza's Admonition to the Parliament. Roan, 1553. Octavo.

1553. "VVHETHER Christian faith maye be kepte secret in the heart, without confession therof openly to the worlde as occasion shal serue. Also what hurt cometh by thē that haue receiued the Gospell, to be presēt at the Masse, vnto the simple vnlearned. iii. Regum. xviii. Howe long halte ye on bothe the sides? If the Lord be God, thē walk after him: but if Baal be he, thē follow him. Mathew vi chapter. No man can serue two masters: &c. Luke xvi chapi. That which is high among men is an abhominatiō before god. From Roane Anno M.D.LIII. the iii of October." 8 leaves. W.H. Sixteens.

1553. "Certaine homilies of . m. Joan. Calvine, conteining profitable and necessarie admonitiō for this time, with an Apologie of Robert Horn. Imprīted at Rome, before the castle of S. Angel, at the signe of S. Peter. Anno M.D.LIIJ." H 3, in eights. W.H. Sixteens.

"De

"De Vera Obediencia.[h] An Oration made in Latine by the ryghte Reuerend father in God Stephan B. of Winchestre, nowe lord Chaūcellour of england, with the preface of Edmunde Boner, somtime Archedeacō of Leicestre, and the kinges maiesties embassadour in Denmarke, & sithence B. of London, touchinge true Obedience. Printed at Hamburgh in Latine, In officina Frācisci Rhodi. Mense Ja. M.D.xxxvi. And nowe translated into english and printed by Michal wood: with the Preface and conclusion of the traunslatour. From Roane xxvi. of Octobre, M.D.liii. In Readinge marke the notes in the margine. A double mynded man is inconstāt in al his waies. Jac. i." k 4, in eights. At the end, "God saue the quene." W.H. Sixteens. 1553.

"The vocacyon[i] of Johā Bale &c. as p. 741. Over a cut, which has under it this explanation, "The English Christiā/ The Jrishe Papist. God hath deliuered me from the snare of the hunter/ & frō ẏ noysome pestilēce. Psal. xcj. Jf J must nedes reioyce J wil reioice of myne infirmytees. ij. Cor. xj." After this title is "The preface." being an address by "Johan Bale to ẏ folowers of Christes Gospell." At the end of which is a representation of Truth with a book in her right hand, labelled VERBV DEI, & a torch in her left hand; over her is this inscription "VERITAS DOMINI, Manet in aeternum. Psalm. 116." and under her "Novit Dominvs viam iustorum, & iter impiorum peribit. Psalm I." In fol. 24. Bale says, "On the xx daye of August, (1553) was the ladye marye with vs at kylkenny proclamed Quene of Englande/ &c. with the greatest solempnyte that 1553.

8 Y

[h] Another edition was printed this year, with the contents on the back of the title-page; H 4, in eights. See p. 741.

[i] Concerning which he tells us in his preface, "J was put to it against my wille/ by a most christien kynge/ and of his oane mere motion only/ without sute of frendes/ mede/ labour, expensis/ or any other sinistre meane els." And in his narrative gives the particulars, viz. "Vpon the 15 daye of August—1552. beynge the the first daye of my deliueraunce/ as God wolde/ from a mortall ague/ which had holde me longe afore. Jn reioyce that hys Maiestie was come in progresse to Southampton/ whiche was 5 myle from my personage of Bysshoppes stocke, within the same countye. J toke my horse about 10 of the clocke/ for very weaknesse scant able to syt hym/ & so came thyder. Betwixt 2 and 3 of the clocke that same daye/ J drew towardes the place where as his Maiestie was/ and stode in the open strete ryght against the gallerye. Anon my frinde/ Juhan Silpot a gentylman/ & one of his preuie chambre/ called vnto him a mere of his companyons/ which in mouing their heades towardes me/ shewed me most frindely countenaunces. By one of these 3. the Kynge hauynge informacion that J was there in the strete/ he marueled therof/ for so much as it had bene tolde hym a lytle afore/ that J was bothe dead & buried. With that hys grace came to the wyndowe/ and earnestly behelde me a poore weake creature/ as though he had had vpon me so symple a subiect/ an earnest regarde/ or rather a very fatherly care. Jn the same very instaunt as J haue bene sens that time credibly infourmed/ his grace called vnto him/ the lordes of his most honourable counsell/ so manie as were than present/ willinge them to appoint me to the bisshoprick of Ossorie in Jrelande. Whervnto they all agreably consentinge/ commaunded the letters of my first callinge therunto/ by and by to be written and sent me.—From Southampton the xvj daye of August, 1552. Your louinge frendes. W. Winchestre J. Bedforde. H. Suffolke. W. Northampton. T. Darcy. T. Cheiny/ Johan Gate. W. Cecill."

that there could be deuysed/ of processions/ musters and disgysinges/ all the noble captaynes and gentilmē there about beinge present.—The yonge men in the forenone played a Tragedye of Gods promises in the olde lawe at the market crosse/ with organe plainges and songes very aptely. In the afternone agayne they played a Commedie of sanct Johan Baptistes preachinges/ of Christes baptisynge and of his tēpracion in the wildernesse/ to the small contentacion of the prestes and other papistes there."[i] W.H. Octavo.

—— A brife and faithful declaration of the true faith of Christ, &c. as p. 1562. was reprinted in Q. Mary's time.

1554. "Vera Expositio Disputationis institutæ mandato D. Mariae reginae Angl. Franc. & Hibern. &c. in Synodo Ecclesiastica, Londini in Comitijs regni ad 18 Octob. Anno 1553. His accessit Reuerendiss. in Christo patris ac Domini, D. Archiepiscopi Cantuariens. epistola apologetica ex Anglico autographo latina facta. Et Precatio ad deum quam Rex Eduuard. vi. habuit cum ageret animam. 1. Joan. 4. Probate spiritus, an ex deo sint. S. D. S. M. 1554." A preface signed V. Pollanus. At the end, "Lecta pub. Londini in uico mercatorum ab amico qui clam autographum surripuerat 5 Septemb. Anno Dom. 1553.—Impressum Romae coram castro S. Angeli ad signum S. Petri. Anno 1554." d, in eights. W.H. Sixteens.

(1554.) "The trew report of the dysputacyon had and begōne in the conuocacyō hows at london among the clargye there assembled the xviij daye of October in the yeare of our lord M.D.LJJJJ.[k] (1553) i. Johan. iiij. Proue euery spyryt whether thei be of god or no." This is a translation from the foregoing article, omitting the prayer of K. Edw. vi. and Abp. Cranmer's Apology. Prefixed, is an epistle "To the Chrysten reader."[l] E 5, in eights. "Jmprinted at Basil by Alexander Edmonds." John Philpot, archdeacon of Winchester, one of the disputants, who for certain expressions there uttered, which were deemed heresy, was burnt in Smithfield, 18 Dec. 1555, acknowledged this book to be "of his own penning and setting forth." See Fox's Acts and Monum. III, p. 591. Edit. 1641. Probably the Latin original; and perhaps this translation also, which his friends might send abroad to be printed. W.H. Sixteens.

1554. "Vinc. Lerinensis [m]boke against certain hereticks in the time of Theodosius, then emperour: which book was written about 1124 yeres

[k] Evidently a typographical error.

[l] In which we read "And as by readyng and weyng the reasons and answers of thys dysputacion J dowt not but thow shalt be suffyciently confyrmed in the truth of the artycles therein reasoned and debated/ euen so in a lytle treatyse of the treue sacryfyce of a christen man which by gods grace shall shortly be set forthe thow shalt be instructed what to iudge off other artycles as of the masse/of altarys/of the innocacyon of sayntys and such lyke."

[m] This seems to be the same with The way home to Christ and Truth, &c. mentioned by Mr. Strype, Eccl. Memor. III; 171. ascribing the translation thereof to John Proctor; which was printed by R. Caley. See p. 630.

yeres past, and now translated out of Latin into English. 12 June." See other editions under 1559 and 1563. Quarto.

" The Resurrection of the Masse, with the wonderfull vertues of the same, set forth for the comfort of all Catholickes, by Hugh Hillarie Printed at Stralburge. 1554." Maunsell, p. 72. Octavo. 1554.

" A confession & declaraciō of praiers added ther-vnto/ by Jhon Knox/ minister of christes most sacred Euangely/ vpon the death of that moste verteous and most famous king Edward the vi. kynge of England/ Fraunce and Ireland/ in whiche confession/ the sayde Ihon doth accuse no lesse his owne offences/ then the offences of others/ to be the cause of the awaye takinge/ of that moste godly prince/ nowe raininge with Christ whyle we abyde plagues for our vnthākfulnesse. Imprinted in Rome, before the castell of s. Aungel, at the signe of sainct Peter: In the moneth of July in the yeare of our Lorde 1554."—An alphabetical table, at the end of which is Singleton's mark, or rebus. See p. 741. Octavo. 1554.

" A letter to the trew professors of Christes Gospell, inhabitinge in the Parishe off Allhallowis/ in Bredstrete in London/ made by Thomas Sampson/ sometyme their Pastore. 2. Cor. 6. We as helpers therfore exhorte you/ that ye receaue not the grace of God in vayne. Jmprynted at Strasburgh in Elsas/ at—the golde Bibell/ Jn the moneth of Auguste. —1554." B 6, in eights. W.H. Sixteens. 1554.

" The Huntyng of the Romyshe Vuolse, made by Vuylliam Turner doctour of Physik. Take hede of false Prophetes/ whyche come vnto you in Shepes clothyng/ but wythin/ are rauenyng Wolues. +" On the back begins the dedication " To the ryght honourable yonge Lordes and worchipful yonge gentylmen/ of Summersetshyre, of Wylshyre, of Harforshyre, of Dorsetshyre, of Sussex, of Kent, of Essex, of Northfolke, of Southfolke, of Lincolneshyre, of Yorkshyre, of Northumberland, of Westmorland, of Cumberland, and to the yonge gentylmen of all other shyres in Englande and Jrelande, Wyllyam Turner—wysheth a parfyt knowlege of Goddes worde, and grace of almyghtye God to lyue therafter." Then, " The Romyshe Foxe/ latelye returned into Englande agayne speaketh,—" Gardiner my Sonne, &c. as p. 1557, note *; where this book was prematurely entered, having evidently been printed in the reign of Q. Mary, who is mentioned as living at the close of the book. It has no head-title properly, only " The " Foster," which is the name of the first speaker: the whole trea-

8 Y 2 tise

* In which. " But now the same Romyshe Foxe, whych youre fathers with no smale ieopardye, &c. droue out of thys realme, is commed in agayne and yet vseth all hys olde prankes, and hys [illegible] whyche was a Foxe when he was dryuen into the Tower, is nowe chaunged into a greuous Wolfe.—J haue founde out these wolues—so dysgysed, that a man that were—would haue thought that they had ben men, and not onely men, but honest men, and no Wolues. J haue in thys my boke shewed you where they be, & who they be.—As for thys my lytle boke, J dedicate it vnto you, desyryng you to defende me and it agaynst these wolues, which without doute wyl rend my boke in peces, and me to, yf they can catch me."

tise being a dialogue between a Foster, a Hunter, and a Dean, as in a subsequent edition, about 1561. Contains F 4, in eights. W.H. Sixteens.

1554. "Exetasis testimoniorum, quæ Martinus Bucerus ex Sanctis Patribus, non Sancte edidit, ut patrocinetur opinioni de caelibatus dono, quam sine dono Spiritus contra Ecclesiam defendit orthodoxam. Steph. Winton. Episcopo, Angliæ cancellario Authore. Lovanii prostant apud Johannem Waen Scotum, Bibliop. Jurat Anno 1554." Quarto.

1554. A Declaration of Edm. Bonner's Articles, &c. See p. 767. "Printed at Basil in Swisserland, A. D. 1554."

1554. "Joh. Venæus his Oration pronounced at Paris before the whole body of the Vniuersitie of Paris, 1537, in defence of the Sacrament of the Aultare, with a presace taken out of Tonstals booke of that argument, translated by John Bullingham, 1554." Maunsell, p. 118. 8°.

1554. "The Vngodlinesse of the Hethnicke Goddes, or the Downfall of Diana of the Ephesians, by J. D. an exile for the word, late a minister in London, M.D.LIV." In verse. See Hist. of Eng. Poetry, III, 314.

1554. "A compendious treatise in metre, declaring the first original of sacrifice and of building churches and aultars, and of the first receiving the christen faith here in England. Printed at London, 1554." Dedicated to George Wharton, Esq. Ibid. p. 319. Quarto.

1554. "An Epistle of the Ladye Jane, a righte vertuous woman, to a learned man of late falne from the Truth of Gods most holy Word, for Fear of the Worlde: Reade it to thy consolacion. Whereunto is added the communication that she had with Master Feckenham, vpon her Faith, and belefe of the Sacraments. Also, another epistle whiche she wrote to her Sister: with the words she spake vpon the scaffold before she suffered." Harl. Misc. III; 109.

1554. "An Admonition or vvarning that the faithful Christiãs in London, Newcastel, Barwycke & others, may auoide Gods vengeaũce both in thys life and in the life to come. Compyled by the Seruaunt of God John Knokes." A cut of Truth, poor woman, handcuffed and fastened in the stocks, with a halter about her neck, held by Tyrranye, on the one hand; while Crueltye with a cornered cap is threatening her with a rod, on the other. Beneath the cut, "The Persecuted speaketh.

"J fear not for death, nor passe not for bands:
  Only in God put J my whole trust,
For God wil requyre my blod at your hands,
  And this J know, that once dye J must,
Only for Christ, my lyfe if J gyue:
  Death is no death, but a meane for to lyue."

Under these verses in ancient writing "John Frythe boke Red and send yt agayne." E, in eights. "From Wittonburge by Nicholas Dorcastor. Anno M.D.Liiii. the viii of May. Cum priuilegio ad imprimendum solum." W.H. Sixteens.

"A

" A Soveraigne Cordial for a Chriſtian Conſcience. 1554.

Content thi ſelfe with pacience,
With Chriſt to bear the cros of paine,
which can and wil the recõpence
A thouſand fold with ioyes againe.
Let nothĩg cauſe thi hart to quail,
Laũch out thi bote, hoiſe vp the ſail,
Put from the ſhore.
And be thou ſure thou ſhalt atain
Vnto the port that ſhall remayne,
For euermore.

From Roane the xi day of May Anno Domi. M.D.L.iiii." B 3, in eights. W.H. Sixteens.

" The humble and vnfained conſeſſion of the beleſe of certain poore banished men, grounded vpon the holy ſcriptures of God, and vpon the articles of that vndefyled and onlye vndoubted true chriſtian faith, which the holy catholicke (that is to ſay, vniuerſal) churche of Chriſt profeſſeth, ſpecially concerning, not only the worde of God, and the miniſterye of the ſame, but alſo the church and ſacraments thereof. Which we ſend mooſt humbly vnto the lordes of England, and all the commons of the ſame." At the end, " From Wittonburge, by Nicholas Dorcaſter,* M.D.LIIII, the xiiii[b] of May." Without paging, and contains 33 leaves. The running-title, " The conſeſſion of the baniſhed miniſters." Sixteens. 1554.

" The Doctrine of the Maſſe booke, cõcerning the making of holye Water, Salt, Breade, Candles, Aſhes, Fyre, Inſence, Paſcal, Paſcal Lãbe, Egges, and Herbes, the Marying Rynge, the Pilgrimes Wallet, Staffe, & Croſſe, truly tranſlated into Englyſhe, Anno Domi. M.D.LIIII. the xx of May. From Wyttonburge by Nicholas Dorcaſter. Lord increaſe our Faith." C, in eights. W.H. Sixteens. 1554.

" A letter of K. Philip and Q. Mary, 1 & 2 reg. to the lord mayor (*Thomas White*), with his precipe to the ſeueral wards, for putting in execution the laws againſt the inhabitants for not putting out lanterns and candles, 1554." Two ſheets paſted lengthwiſe. Gough's Brit. Topography, I, 684. 1554.

" A conſortable Epiſtle/ too Goddes ſaythſull people in Englande/ wherein is declared the cauſe of taking awaye the true Chriſten religion from them/ & howe it maye be recouered and obtained agayne/ newly made by Thomas Becon. Abacuk 1. Thoughe the lorde tarye/ yet wayte thou for hym/ for he will vndoubtedly come/ yea/ and that oute of hande. Imprynted at Straſburgh in Elſas, at—the goldẽ Bibal, in the moneth of Auguſt—M.D.LIIII." Octavo. 1554.

" Supplication

* " Borceſter" in Mr. T. Baker's interleaved Maunſell, p. 36.

b " xxiii." Ibidem.

1554. " Supplication to God for reftoring his holy word to the Church of England, printed at Strafburgh, 1554." Maunfell, p. 112. 8°.

About this time feveral perfons were imprifoned for having and felling certain books fent into England by the preachers that fled into Germany, &c. Fox, Vol. III, p. 105. Edit. 1641.

An Act paffed in parliament this year, that whofoever fhould write, cypher or print any thing againft the king or queen, or that move fedition or rebellion, for the firft offence to have their right-hand cut off, and for the next offence, lofs of goods, and perpetual imprifonment.

1554. " An excellent and a right learned meditacion, compiled in two prayers, moft frutefull and neceffary to be vfed and faid of all true Englifhmen, in thefe daungerous daies of affliction, for the comfort and better ftay of the chriften confcience, bewailing the deferved plagues of England. Prynted at Roane, by an Englyfh fcolers copie, by Micheal Wodde, 3 day of Januarye." Sixteens.

1554. " The champion of the Church. To the nobles of England. Printed at Roane, by an Englyfh fcolers copie, by Micheal Wodde, the 3 January." Sixteens.

1554. " A dialogue of familiar talk between two neighbours, concerning the chiefeft ceremonies, that were by the mighty power of Gods moft holy word fuppreffed in England, and now for our vnworthinefs fet vp again by the bifhops. Interlocut. Olyuer, profeffor of the gofpel, and Nicholas Rofe, led in blynd fuperftition. Roan, by Michael Wodde, 20 February." Sixteens.

1554. " Commentarii rerum in ecclefia geftarum, maximarumque per totam Europam perfecutionum, à Vuicleui temporibus ad hanc ufque, aetatem, defcriptio. Liber primus. Autore Joanne Foxo, Anglo. Hiis in calce acceflerunt Aphorifmi Joannis Uuicleui, cum collectaneis quibufdam Reginaldi Pecoki, epifcopi Ciceftrenfis. Item, ΟΠΙΣΤΟΓΡΑΦΙΑ quaedam ad Oxonienfes. Argentorati excudebat Vuendelinus Rihelius, anno 1554." pages 212.

—— " An Expofition vppon the fyxt Pfalme of Dauid, &c. by John Knox." To which is annexed " A comfortable Epiftle fente to the afflicted Church of Chrift, Exhorting them to bear hys Croffe, &c. I. K." See p. 1118. Twenty-fours.

1554. " Manuale ad vfum per celebris ecclefie Sarifburienfis. Londini recenter impreffū, necnō multis mendis terfum atq; emēdatum. Londini.—1554." In the fame compartment as that printed this year by John Kingfton and Hen. Sutton. See p. 833. It is afcribed to Wayland by miftake. See p. 561, &c. where it is more particularly defcribed. This was Mr. Tho. Baker's book, who has written in it " This book being printed in Cardinal Pole's time, and before the Council of Trent was up, is probably the laft of its kind, at leaft in England." W.H. Quarto.

1554. " Manuale ad vfum infignis ecclefie Sarifburienfis, continens ecclefie facramenta, & modum adminiftrandi ea: cum multis aliis commoditatibus

tatibus que in ceteris desiderantur. 1554. Venale habetur Rothomagi apud Robertum Valentinum calcographum in atrio bibliopolarum cathedralis ecclesie moram degentem." Gough's Brit. Topogr. II, p. 353.

" Horæ beatissime virginis Marie secundum vsum Sarum tot liter ad longum: cum orationibus beate Brigitte cum multis aliis orationibus. Impresse per Johannem le Prest pro Robertum Valentinum commorantem bibliopola in porticu ecclesie beate Marie." With wood cuts by Jehan Mallart. The late Mr. Tho. Martin, whose book this was, had another, 1555, the cuts by R. V. Ibid, p. 354. 1554.

" A short description of Antichrist vnto the Nobilitie of Englande, and to all my brethren and contreymen borne and dwelling therin, with a warnynge to see to, that they be not deceaued by the hypocrisie and crafty conueyaunce of the Clergie. Ioh. 10. He that is of God heareth the worde of God." On the back is a short prayer for trust in God. On the last leaf, fol. 43, is a table of contents. ——

" This prymer of Salisbury vse is set out a long without ony serchyng, with many prayers, & goodly pyctures in the Kalender, in the matins of our lady, in the houres of the crosse, in thes vii psalmes, and in the dyryge. And be newly enprynted at Rouen, 1555." Colophon: " Expliciunt hore beatissime virginis Marie, &c. Impresse per Johannem le Prest, impensis honestissimi viri Roberti Valentini suam officinam tenentis in porticu bibliopolarum iuxta edem beate Marie." Valentine's device at the beginning and end. Octavo. 1555.

" This prymer of Sarysbury vse is set out along without ony serchyng, vvith many prayers, & goodly pyctures in the matyns of our lady. And benewly imprynted at Rouen." The device: A bird standing with expanded wings as just going to mount, over which is R. V. on a shield hanging on a tree, and supported by 2 unicorns: At the bottom, Robert Valentin. " Venundantur Rothomagi apud Robertū Valentinū in porticu bibliopolarum, prope edem beate Marie. M.D.Lv." The cuts are small, indented, and without any monogram. V, in eights. " Expliciūt hore beatissime virginis Marie secundum vsum Sacrum' totaliter ad longum cum orationibus beate Brigitte, ac multis aliis deuotis orationibus. Impresse, Rothomagi. Anno domini millesimo quingētesimo quinquagesimo quinto. Sarum." To this is annexed, 1555.

" Here begynneth the Pystels and Gospels, of euery Sonday, and holy Daye in the yere." The same device as to the Prymer. " Venales habentur Rothomagi, in officina Florenti Valentini bibliopole illius ciuitatis, prope templum beate Marie virginis. M.D.Lv." K 4, in eights. " Imprynted at Rouen, by Jhon prest, for Roberte Valentin, dwellynge, be our Lady churche. W.H. Sixteens. 1555.

" Here after foloweth the Prymer in Englysshe and in Latin, sette out alonge, after the vse of Sarum. In edibus Roberti Valentini." With cuts: Rothomagi at the end. Sixteens. 1555.

" Here after followeth the prymer in English and in Latyn, sette out along after the vse of Sarum." With fine wood-cuts. At the end: " Impressum 1555.

[q] These have R. V. on them. [r] Perhaps for Sarum.

"Impressum Rothomagi impensis honesti viri Roberti Valentini, bibliopolarum porticulo moram tenentis." Octavo.

1555. "Manuale ad vsum insignis ecclesie Sarisburiensis—1555. Venale habetur Rothomagi apud Robertum Valentinum calcographum in atrio bibliopolarum cathedralis ecclesie moram degentem." Colophon, as in 1554. Richard Gough, Esq; Quarto.

1555. "Portiforium seu breviarium ad vsum ecclesie Sarisburiensis castigatum suppletum marginalibus quotationibus adornatum, ac nunc primum ad verissimum ordinalis exemplar in suum ordinem a peritissimis viris redactum. Pars estivalis (Pars hyemalis)" Device: an elephant, and M. B. "Parisiis apud viduam Francisci Regnault, in vico Sancti Jacobi, ad signum elephantis. 1555." At the end, it is said to be printed by "Magdalen Boursette, vidua Francisci Regnault." Richard Gough, Esq.

1555. "Missale ad vsum insignis ecclesie Sarisburiensis, nunc recens typis elegantioribus exaratum, historijs nouis, varijs ac proprijs insignitum: & a mendis, quam plurimis (quibus passim scatebat) omni diligentia nuper emendatum." Device: The arms of France and England quartered, crowned and supported by angels; the rose, with I. H. S. in the centre, crowned.

"Hæc rosa virtutis, de cœlo missa sereno.
Æternum florens: regia sceptra tenet."

Under these, St. George and the dragon. "Parisijs Apud Guilielmum Merlin in ponte Telonearum, ad Hominis syluestris signum, e regione horologij Palatij. 1555." Printed in black and red, with many neat cuts, some with this monogram and one with N. R. Colophon: "Missale secundum consuetudinem ac ritum insignis ecclesie Sarisburiensis nuper exacte, accurateq; elaboratum et emendatum, varijs etiam ac nouis atq; proprijs insignitum historijs, et id genus additamentis multipharium locupletatum, in honorem dei optimi, maximi, ac benedicte dei genitricis semperq; virginis Marie atq; ceterorum beatorum, spirituumq; celestium feliciter Finit. Impressum Parisijs typis Joannis Amazeur typographi pro Guilielmo Merlin super pontē nummulariorum, ad syluestris Hominis signum commorante." Then, "Index chartarum." Under which is the printer's device, a swan supporting a crosier, in a compartment with this motto, "In hoc signo vinces." W. H. Folio.

1555. "Processionale ad vsum insignis ac preclare ecclesie Sarum, nouiter ac rursus castigatum & emendatum. Impensis honesti viri Roberti Valentini Rothomagi impressum 1555. Venale habetur" &c. as his Manuale. At the end, "Finit processionale secundum vsum Sarum. Rothomagi impressum in officina Ricardi* Hamilionis impensis Roberti Valentini. Anno salutis humane millesimo ccccc.LV. xviii. die mensis Octobris." Richard Gough, Esq; Quarto.

1555. "A Treatise of the Cohabitacyon of the faithfull with the vnfaithfull.

By

* Sir John Hawkins refers to a Sarum missal printed by Richard Hamilln 1555. Hist. of Music. Vol. v. 4.

(By *Peter Martir*) Whereunto is added. A Sermon made of the confessing of Christe and his gospell/ and of the denyinge of the same. Anno M.D.LV. Apocal. 18. Come awaye from her my peple/" &c. On the back, " Jn this furst treatise theys' thinges ar contayned." The sermon begins on fol. 66, with this head-title " A Sermon of the true confessinge of Christe/ and the truithe of the gospell: and of the foule denyinge of the same/ made in the conuocacion of the clergie at Zurich the 28 daye of Januarie in the yeare of our lorde 1555. By H. B." L 6, in eights. W.H. Octavo.

" A nevv booke of spirituall Physik for dyuerse diseases of the nobilitie and gentlemen of Englande, made by William Turner doctor of Physik. Prouer. 12. The waye of the folyshe man semeth ryght in hys owne eyes, but he that is wyse wyll heare counsell. 1555.

" Ad nobilem Britannum.

Viuere si cupias multos feliciter annos
Et post hanc vitam regna videre Dei:
Pharmaca quæ grata Turnerus mēte propinat
In mentem penitus sume, q; tutus eris.

Anno 1555. 10. Calen. Martij." Dedicated " To the ryght honorable Dukes & Erles, the Duke of Northfolke, the Duke of Suthfolke, the Erle of Arundale, the Erle of Derbi, the Erle of Shrosbery, the Erle of Huntyngton, the Erle of Combrelande, the Erle of Westmerlande, the Erle of Penbrook, and the Erle of Warwik William Turner Physician wysheth persyt knowlege in Godes holy worde and grace to lyue accordyng vnto the same.—To the reader. Ys thou be mynded, (gētle reder) to rede thys booke here folowynge with pleasure and profyt: amend these fautes folowynge as J shall teache thee. Rede in the fyrst lefe and al thorowe the booke cuntre & not countre.— Jn the xxvi (*xxxvi.*) lefe rede Wolseys house and not Wolsey hys house." ---The contentes of thys' booke." N, in eights; the last leaf blank.

¹ " 1. The question of Cohabitation. 2. Christians maye not be present at popishe masses and superslicions. 3. The masse is a prophanacion of the lordes supper. 4. The dutie of princes is to mayntain pure Religion amonge ther subiectes/ and what inferior Rulars must do when they be commaunded contrarie by their superiors. 5. A confutacion of the reasons which ar made to proue the cohabitacion lawfull. 6. How the Iues ar to be handeled of christians. 7. The papistes ar heretikes."

² " In the fyrst parte of thys boke the author sheweth who be noble and gentlemen: and howe many workes and properties belonge vnto a noble or gentleman, and wherein hys office chefelye standeth: whyche he proueth is to maynteyne, defende, and obserue the wrytten worde of God, and the true worshippyng of hym according to the same, & sheweth that neither faire buylded and trimmed houses, nor yet ryche apparell, dauncyng, lutynge, dycyng nor cardyng, haukyng nor hunting are the chefe tokens, offices or duties of noble and gentlemen. Jn the seconde parte he proueth great diseases to be in the true nobilite and gentlemen, whyche letteth them to do theyr offices and duties. Jn the thyrde parte he nameth the diseases that are in the nobilite to be these, the hole Palsey, the Dropsey, the Romyshe pockes, and the Lepre: and sheweth the nature of the diseases, the daunger of them, and telleth the remedies for euery of the diseases accordyngly. And in the ende of the boke is added the prayer of Daniel conteyned in the ix. Chapter of hys prophecie."

"Jmprented at Rome by the vaticane churche, by Marcus Antonius Constantius. Otherwyse called, thraso miles gloriosus." Thus to be corrected by the forementioned table "Jmprented—by the vatican Chyrche agaynst Marcus—thraso or gloriosus Pape miles." W.H. 16°.

(1555.) "A godlye medytacion, composed by the faithfull and constant seruant of God J. B. (*John Bradford*) preacher who lately was burnt in Smithfield." Perhaps the same with

"Jo. Bradford his godly meditations which he vsed being in prison, entituled his Beades." Maunsell, p. 84. See p. 690. Sixteens.

1555. "A mirrour of loue, which such light doth giue
That all men may learn, how to loue and liue
Compiled by Miles Hogard, seruant to the queens highness." Dedicated to the queen. "Mense Maii." See Hist. of Eng. Poetry, II, p. 459, note k. See p. 377. In the Pub. Libr. Cambridge. Quarto.

(1555.) "A supplicacyō to the queenes maiestie." &c. as p. 793. Herein are introduced Bonner's prologue to Gardiner's De vera obedientia, as p. 1573; and an extract from Tunstal's sermon before K. Hen. 8. as p. 434. The author dates this supplication, 26 Jan. 1555, and adds a postscript. The date of printing at the end M.D.L. is evidently a mistake. W.H. Octavo.

(1555.) "The Copye of a letter sent by John Bradford to the right honorable lordes the Erles of Arundel, Darbie, Shrewsbury & Penbroke, declarīg the nature of spaniardes, and discouering the most detestable treasons, whiche they haue pretended moste falselye againste our moste noble kyngdome of Englande. VVherunto is added a tragical blast of the papisticall trōpet for mayntenaunce of the Popes kingdome in Englande, by T. E. If ye beleue the trueth, ye saue your liues &c." This is introduced by "A preface to the faythfull reader." At the end of which, "A man once warned is twise armed." Both this title-page and preface seem to have been prefixed after the the book was printed; for after this is another title-page, without mentioning The tragical blast &c. and a preface signed "Thy louinge frende Iohn Bradeforte." My copy contains G 5, in eights, but suppose it wants two or three leaves at the end, perhaps with a colophon, or at least a date. I have given it a place here, as it mentions "A supplicacion to the queenes maiestie," and treats chiefly of the same matter. The author John Bradford, or Bradeforte tells us in C 1, that in king Edward's time he serued sir William Skipewithe in Lincolnshire, and writes as from abroad; therefore can by no means be taken for that Godly Martyr who was burnt in Smithfield in July this year, neither is he or his case so much as hinted at. W.H. Sixteens.

1555. "A Warnyng for Englande/ Conteynyng the horrible practises of the Kyng of Spayne/ in the Kyngdome of Naples/ and the miseries wherunto that noble Realme is brought. Wherby all Englishe men may vnderstand the plage that shall light vpō them/ yf the Kyng of Spayn obteyne the

the Dominion in Englande. ☞ Beware of I had wist. +" 8 leaves. At end, "An. D. 1555." W.H. Sixteens

"AN EPISTLE wrytten by John Scory the late bishope of Chichester vnto all the faythfull that be in pryson in Englande, or in any other troble for the defence of Goddes truthe: wherin he dothe as well by the promises of mercy as also by thensamples of diuerse holy martyres, comfort, encourage & strengthē them paciently for Christes sake to suffer the manifolde cruell and moste tyrānous persecutiōs of ẏ Antichristian tormentours: exhorting them to contynue in faythfull prayers, innocency of lyfe, patience, and hope, that God maye the rather deliuer them, restore agayne the light of his gospell to Englande, and confounde all the proude, beastly, & deuelishe enterprises of Antichristes garde, that doo imagine nothing els but ẏ subuersion of the gospell of Christ, and contynually thruste for the bloud of all true Christians. In the world ye shall haue tribulaciō: &c. Anno 1555." Inscribed "Vnto the faythfull, and most valeant souldiours of the great captaine, the Lorde Jesus Christ, that be in prison &c. John Scory willyngly a banished man for the same worde, wissheth" &c. B, in eights. W.H. Sixteens. 1555.

"The Temporisour (that is to saye: the obseruer of tyme, or he that chaungeth with the tyme,) Compyled in Latyn by the excellent Clarke Wolfangus Musculus, and translated into Frenche by Mayster Valleran Pulleyn. And oute of Frenche into Inglishe by R. P. 1555. iij. Regum. xviij. How long will ye halt on both sydes, yf the Lord be God, folowe him: but yf Baal be he, then go after him. Enprinted Anno Domini. 1555. In the moneth of Julij." Prefixed is an epistle by R. P. (Probably Rob. Pownell) in which he says "for the tender loue that I beare vnto my natiue country,—I haue taken vpō me to reduce into our natyue tounge (according to my promyse in my former translated Boke) this worthye worke that latelye happened into my handes,—Compiled in iiij. Dialoges," &c. The last dialogue ends on G 8. Annexed is "An excellent admonicion and resolucion of the godlye and famous learned man Celius secundus Curio. Dedicated vnto all faythful Christians to the ende, they (beyng warned) may auoyde al superstitious and erronious papisticall seruices. Translated out of Frenche into English by R. P." The signatures continued to H 7, in eights. W.H. Sixteens. 1555.

"An Apologie or defence agaynst the calumnacion of certayne men, which preferring wylfull wyll and carnal reason before the playn trueth of Gods gospel, (do sclaundre those men, which for the better seruinge of God with a more pure conscience, according to his holy word) haue abandoned theyr liuinges and vocacion, abydinge as exyles in poore estate oute of theyr natyue coūtrye. Exodi. xxxiij. O Lord let our hartes euermore ioye in thy testimonies, folowe not the multitude to doe euyll. Psalm lxxiij. Lyke as a man waketh there remayneth nothing of his slepe, (how pleasaunt soeuer it was to the 1555.

the ſleper) So ſhall there be nothing left of theyr Goddes. Where through they thought thẽſelues happy in this worlde. But thou (O Lord) ſhalt rather make euẽ theyr pictures to be abhorred of euery man in the Cytie. ¶ 1555." The head-title: "The mercy and fauour of God oure heauenly father, purchaſed to vs by the merites of our Sauiour Chriſte. Communicated to us by his holy ſpirite. J. T. wiſheth to the gentle Reader." The author herein apologizes for having ſent over his wife and children into Flanders, intending to follow them, preferring a voluntary exile to temporizing. 11 leaves. At the end, "Imprinted in the yeare of our Lorde 1555. The xxi. daye of Julij." W.H. Sixteens.

1555. "The accompt, rekenyng and confeſsion of the faith of Huldrik Zwinglius, byſhop of Zuryk the chief towne of Heluetia, ſent vnto Charles fyfte nowe Emperoure of Rome, holdynge a counſel wyth the mooſt noble Princes, Eſtates, and learned men of Germany aſſembled together at Auſburgh 1530, in the moneth of July. Tranſlated out of Latyn by Thomas Cotsford. And imprinted at Geneua. In April 1555." See p. 711. Prefixed are a table of the contents, and of the "Fautes eſcaped.---To all hys faythfull brethren and ſyſters other willyngly fled or tyrannouſly exyled out of Englande for Chriſtes Goſpel ſake, Thomas Cotſforde wyſheth" &c. Hereunto are anneaed "The copy of an Epiſtle wrytten from Copynhauen in Denmarke vnto an Englyſhe Marchaunt dwellyng at Wyncheſtre in Englande.---An Epiſtle vvritten to a good Lady, for the comfort of a frende of hers, wherin the Nouations erroure now reuiued by the Anabaptiſtes is confuted, and the ſynne agaynſte the holy Goſte playnly declared.---The prayer of Daniel turned into metre and applied vnto our tyme. Daniel ix." W.H. Sixteens.

1555. "An Anatomie, that is to ſay, a parting in peces of the Maſſe, which diſcouereth the horrible errours, and infinite abuſes vnknowne to the people, aſwell of the Maſſe as of the Maſſe booke. with a ſermon of the Sacrament, which declareth whether Chriſt be bodily in the ſacrament or not, by Anthony de Adamo. Printed 1555." Maunſell, p. 72. Again 1556. Octavo.

1555. "A brief declaracion of the Lordes Supper, written by the ſyngular learned man, and moſt conſtaunt Martir of Jeſus Chriſt, Nicholas Ridley Biſhop of London priſoner in Oxforde, a litel before he ſuffred deathe for the true teſtimonie of Chriſt. Roma. 8. For thy ſake are we killed all daye long, &c. Anno 1555." The preface "To the Reader" is on the back. E 7, in eights. W.H. Sixteens.

"A proclamation by the King and Queen.

An. Dom. 1555. "Whereas dyuers books, filled both with hereſye, ſedition, and treaſon, haue of late, and be dayly brought into this realme, out of forreigne countrys, and places beyond the ſeas, and ſome alſo couertly printed within this realme, and caſt abroade in ſundry partes thereof, whereby not only God is diſhonoured, but alſo an encouragement geuen

to

to disobey lawful princes and gouernours; the king and queens maiesties, for redress thereof, doth by this thyr present proclaymation declare and publysh to all theyr subiectes, that whosoeuer shall, after the proclaymation hereof, be found to haue any of the sayd wicked and seditious bookes, or fyndyng them, do not forthwith burne the same, without shewing or readyng the same to any other person, shall in that case bee reputed and taken for a rebell, and shall without delaye be executed for that offence, according to thorder of martiall law. Geuen at oure manor of sainct Jamesis, the sixt day of June." John Cawood, printer.

"A proclamation.

"Whereas by the statute made in the secunde yeare of kinge Henrye the fourthe, concerning the repressynge of heresies, their is ordeyned, and prouyded, of greate punyshment, not only for the authors, makers, and wryters of books, conteynynge wycked doctryne, and erronious and heretycall opynions, contrarye to the catholyque faythe, and determynation of the holye churche, and lykewyse for the fautours and supporters, but also for suche, as shall haue, or keape any suche books or wrytings, and not make delyuery of them to the ordenarye of the dyoces, or his mynisters, withyn a certeyne tyme lymytted in the sayd statute, as by the sayde statute more att large it dothe apprare: whych acte, or statute, being by aucthorytie of perlyament, of late reuyued, was also openly proclaymed to thyntente the subiects of the realme vpon suche proclamatyon, should the rather eschue the daunger and penaltie of the sayde statute, and as yet neuerthelefs in moste partes of the realme, the same ys neglected and lytle regarded: An. Dom. 1555.

The kynge and quene, our soueraigne lorde and lady, therefore moste entirely and earnestlye tenderynge the preseruation and saulfty, as well of the soules as of the bodyes, landes, and substaunce, of all their good louynge subiectes, and others, and myndynge to root oute and extinguishe al false doctryne and heresyes, and other occasyons of scismes, dyuisyons, and sects, that come by the same heresies, and false doctryne, straightly charge and command, that no person or persons of what estate, degree, or condytion soeuer he or they be, from hencefourthe presume to bringe, or conuey, or cause to be broughte and conueyed, into this realme anye bookes, wrytinges, or workes hereafter mentyoned: that ys to saye, any booke, or bookes, wrytinges, or workes, made, or sett fourthe by, or in the name of Martyn Luther; or any booke, or bookes, wrytings, or woorks, made or sette forthe by, or in the name of Oecolampadyus, Suinglius, John Caluyn, Pomerane, John Alasco, Bullynger, Bucer, Melancthon, Barnardinus Ochinus, Erasmus Sarcerius, Peter Martyr, Hughe Latymer, Roberte Barnes, otherwyse called Freere Barnes, John Bale, otherwise called Freere Bale, Justus Jonas, John Hoper, Miles Couerdale, William Tyndale, Thomas Cranmer, late archebysshop of Canterburye, Wylliam Turner, Theodore Basyll, otherwyse called, Thomas Beacon, John Frythe Roye; and the booke commonly called, Halles

Halles cronycles; or any of them in the Latyn tonge, Duche tonge, Englissh tonge, Italyan tonge, or French tonge; or any other lyke booke, paper, wrytinge, or wourke, made, prynted, or sett forth by any other persone, or persons, conteynynge false doctryne, contrarye, and agaynste the catholyque faythe, and the doctryne of the catholyque churche.

And also, that no persone, or persons, presume to wryte, prynte, vtter, sell, reade, or keape, or cause to be wrytten, prynted, vttered, rede, or kepte, any of the sayde bookes, papers, works, or wrytings, or any booke, or books, wrytten, or prynted in the Latten, or Englyshe tonge, concernynge the common seruice and mynistratyon, sett forthe in Englyshe, to be vsed in the churches of this realme, in the tyme of kinge Edward the vi. commonly called, the communyon booke, or books of common seruice, and orderynge of mynisters, otherwyse called, the booke sette forthe by the aucthorytie of parlyament for common prayer, and admynistration of the sacraments, to be vsed in the mother tonge, wythin the churche of Englande, but shall wythin the space of fystene dayes nexte after the publicatyon of this proclamatyon, brynge, or delyuer, or cause the sayde bookes, wrytings, and works, and euerye of them remayneinge in their custodies, and kepinge, to be broughte, and delyuered to thordinarye of the dioces, where suche books, works, or wrytings be, or remayne, to his chauncelloure, or commyssaryes, without fraude, colour, or deceipte, at the sayde ordinaries will and disposition to be burnte, or otherwyse to be vsyde, or orderyd by the said ordenaries, as by the cannons, and spirituall lawes it is in that case lymyted, and apoynted, vpon payne that euerye offendor contrary to this proclamatyon, shall incurre the daunger and penalties conteyned in the sayde statute, and as they will auoide their maiestyes highe indignatyon and displeasure, and further awnswer att thire uttermost periles.

And their maiesties by this proclamatyon geuethe full power and aucthorytie to all byshops, and ordynaryes, and all iustices of peace, mayors, sheriffes, baylyffes of cyties, and townes corporate, and other hedde offycers within this realme, and the domynions theirof, and expresselye commaundeth and willethe the same, and euerye of them, that they, and euerye of theim, within their seueral lymyts and iurisdictions, shall, in the defaulte and neglygence of the saide subiects, after the sayd fystene dayes expyred, enquyer, and serche owte the sayde bookes, wrytings, and works, and for this purpose enter into the howse, or howses, closettes, and secrete places of euery person of whatsoeuer degre, beinge negligente in this behalf, and suspected to kepe anye suche booke, wrytinge, or workes, contrary to this proclamation.

And that the saide iustices, mayors, sheryffs, baylyffs, and other hede officers aboue specified, and euery of them, within their sayde lymytes and iurisdictions, fyndinge anye of the sayde subiectes negligent, and faultie in this behalfe, shall commytte euerye suche offendour to warde,

theire

theire to remayne withoute bayle, or maynepryse, tyll the same offendour, or offendours, haue receauid suche punyshment, as the said statute dothe lymitte and appoynte in this behalfe. Geuen vnder our signes manuell, at oure Honoure of Hampton courte, the xiiith daye of June, the fyrste and seconde yeres of our reignes.

God saue the kinge and the quene." See p. 791.

"AN APOLOGIE FVLLY AVNSVVERINGE by Scriptures and aunceant Doctors a blasphemose Book gatherid by D. Steph. Gardiner/ of late Lord Chauncelar/ D. Smyth of Oxford/ Pighius/ and other Papists/ as by ther booke appeareth and of late set furth vnder the name of Thomas Martin Doctor of the Ciuile lawes (as of himself he saieth) againſt the godly marriadge of priests. Wherin dyuers other matters which the Papists defend be so confutid/ that in Martyns ouerthrow they may see there own impudency and confusion. By Iohn Ponet Doctor of diuinitie and Busshop of Winchester. Newly [*]correctid and amendid. The author desireth that the reader will content himself with this first book vntill he may haue leasure[w] to set furth the next/ wiche shalbe by Gods grace shortly. Yt is a hard thing for the to spurn against the prick. Act. 9." On the back begin "The contents of the first book of this Apologie." 7 chapters.---" The booke to the papists." In a stanza of 6 lines. "The books frind to the booke." In 6 lines more.---" The preface to the Christian reader." At the end is a list of above 50 heretics, with the year in which they flourished. M 3, in eights. On the last page, "From the Tyrannie of the bushop of Rome and all his detestable enormities/ from all false doctrine and Heresies/ from hardnes of hart and contempt of thy word and commandmēt: good lord deliver vs/ Amen. The end of the first bok of answer to Martin and other of that hereticall sect. 1556." W.H. Octavo. 1556.

"Reformatio Angliæ, ex Decretis Reg. Poli cardinalis." Strype's Life of archbp. Cranmer, p. 368. 1556.

"An Anatomi—aswell of the Mass as of the Mass Boke, very profitable, yea most necessary for al Christian people. 1556. With a Sermon of the Sacrament &c. By Chrystes humble Seruant Anthoni de Adamo. A.D. 1556." In 4 parts. To which is added "A sermon of the sacrament of Thankes geuing" &c. In all 264 leaves, and 2 of the faults. See p. 1583. 1556.

"The copie of a letter, sent to the ladye Mary dowagire, regent of Scotland, by John Knox, in the year 1556. Here is also a notable sermon, made by the sayde John Knox, wherein is euidentlye proued that the masse is, and alwayes hath ben, abhominable before God, and idolatrye (1556.)

[*] A. Wood intimates its having been printed in 1555. Ath. Oxon. I, 218. Martin's book was printed in May 1554. See p. 830.

[w] Dr. Ponet on the reestablishment of popery fled into Germany, where he began this treatise, and just lived to correct this edition; for he died soon after, and was buried at Strasburg, 11 Apr. as Godwin, 11 Aug. as Bale, 1556. But though he was prevented by death from making a full answer as he intended, yet it was fully answered in the beginning of Q. Elizabeth's reign, by an anonymous author, said to be Mat. Parker, afterwards Archbishop of Canterbury. See p. 848.

idolatrye. Scrutamini scripturas." See the letter with additions in 1558. Both are annexed to his Hist. of the reformation of the Church of Scotland, Edit. 1644. Octavo.

(1556.) "A prayer to God for his afflicted church in Englande. By Wm. Samueli." It seems to have been wholly in metre. See Crowley's Apologie, fol. 2, 3. The same author abridged the Old Testam. into Sternhold's metre. See p. 700.

1556. "A copye of a very fyne and wyttye letter, sent from the right reuerende Lewys Lippomanus, bishop of Berona in Italie, and late legate in Polone, from the most holy and blessed father pope Paul iv. and from his most holy sea of Rome. Translated out of the Italien language, by Michael Throckmerton, curtigiane of Rome, 23 July MDLVI. It is dedicated "To the most reuerend Reynold, cardinal Pole, legate à latere, archebishop of Canterbury, portionare of Winchestre, &c. metropolitane and primate, of al England." One sheet. - Sixteens.

1556. "A litell dialogue off the consolator, comfortynge the churche in hyr afflictions, taken out off the 129 psalme. Composed in Frenche by M. Peter du Val. and translated in Englyche by Robert Pownoll. Mens Junii 14." Sixteens.

1556. "The copy of certain lettres sent to the Quene, and also to doctour Martin, and doctour Storye, by the most reuerende father in God, Thomas Cranmer, Archebishop of Cantorburye, from prison in Oxeforde: who (after long and most greuous strayt emprisoning, and cruell handlyng) most constantly and willingly suffred Martirdome ther, for the true testimonie of Christ, in Marche. Psal. 119. I spake of thy testimonies: (O Lorde) euen before Kynges, and was not confounded." On the back begins an epistle from the editor "To the reader." B, in eights. W.H. Sixteens.

1556. "The Examination[a] of the constant Martyr of Christ, John Philpot," &c. as p. 844. "Reade fyrst, and then iudge. VVhen the vvaters arose, the floudde bet vpon this house, and could not moue it: for it vvas builded upon a rock. Luc. 6. And the rocke vvas Christe. 1 Corinth. 10." O, in eights. W.H. Sixteens.

1556. "Certein godly, learned, and comfortable conferences, betwene the two Reuerende Fathers, and holye martyrs of Christe, D. Nicholas Rydley, late Byshoppe of London, and M. Hughe Latymer, sometyme bisshop of Worcester, during the tyme of theyr empryfonmentes. Psal. 116. Ryght deare in the sighte of the Lorde is the death of his saintes. 1556." On the back begins the editor's epistle "To the reader." At the end, "A cõclusion to the Reader.—J.O." *(John Olde.)* F 4, in eights. W.H. Sixteens.

I have another [r]edition, the editor's epistle beginning on the second leaf;

[a] Mr. Ames has annexed to this book Philpot's Apology for spitting upon an Arian, but that is a separate book, and printed by Hen. Sutton, 1559. These are sometimes bound together. The colophon of the Apology is on a separate leaf, which probably Mr. Ames's copy wanted. See it in p. 845.

[r] The form of this edition is about half an inch longer, and an inch broader than the former one; also, the leaves of this are numbered, but my copy wants all after 63, or H 7, in eights.

leaf; without the concluſion by J. O. but has annexed, " A treatiſe agaīſt the errours of tranſubſtantiation/ made by the fornamed Reuerend father Nic. Rydley Byſhop of London/ in the time of his emprisonmente." The ſame as " A brief declaracion of the Lordes Supper," &c. See p. 1584. W.H. Octavo.

" Bleſſed Ciprian Martir, his ſermon of Mortalitie, or the willing forſaking of this life. 2. his exhortation to Martirdome. 3. an exhortation to keep and endure the faith of Chriſt, &c. tranſlated by John Scory exile. Print. 1556. Maunſell, p. 34. Octavo. 1556.

" The forme of Prayers* and miniſtration of the Sacraments, &c. vſed in the Engliſhe Congregation at Geneva, and approued by the famous and godly learned man Iohn Caluin. Printed at Geneva by Jo. Creſpin, 1556." Printed alſo in Latin. Sixteens. 1556.

" A ſhorte treatiſe in metre vpon the cxxix Pſalm." Quarto. 1556.

" A treatiſe of the union of the Church, written to Card. Pole, by Dr. John Standiſh. Lond. 1556." Ath. Oxon. I. 98. 1556.

John Frith's Diſputation againſt Purgatory. Sixteens. 1556.

Beza's Treaſure of Truth, tranſlated by M. Wittingham, was printed at Geneva, in the time of Q. Mary, which was before Beza had enlarged, and more orderly methodized it. See Stockwood's dedication of his tranſlation of it to Sir John Pelham. See p. 1107.

" The Pathway to the towre of Perfection." By M. Hoggard. Quarto. 1556.

" Portiſorium ſeu breviarium ad inſignis Sariſburienſis eccleſiæ vſum, nuper ſumma diligentia emendatum. pars æſtivalis (& hyemalis.") His device as to Miſſale p. 1580. Pariſiis apud Gulielmum Merlin, in ponte teloneorum ad ſylveſtris hominis ſignum. 1556." Richard Gough, Eſq; Folio. 1556.

" Portiſorium ſeu breviarium ad vſum eccleſiæ Sariſburienſis caſtigatum, ſuppletum, marginalibus quotationibus adornatum, ac nunc primum ad veriſſimum ordinalis exemplar in ſuum ordinem a peritiſſimis viris redactum. Pariſiis apud Gulielmum Merlin, in ponte teloneorum 1556." The 2d volume, or Pars eſtivalis, is dated 1557. The colophon of both ſays they were printed by John de Blanc for Merlin. Octavo. 1556.

Portiſorium, &c. as the foregoing article. " Rothomagi apud Robertum Florentinum & Florentinum auum eius." Dr. Rawlinſon's in the Bodleian library. Octavo.

" Hereafter foloweth the primer in Engliſhe and in Latin, ſette out alonge after the vſe of Sarum, in edibus Florent. Valentini, 1556." In the title Sarum, at the end Rothomagi. Mr. Keyſer Mole. Octavo. 1556.

THE " STATIONERS, or TEXT-WRITERS, who wrote and ſold all

 ſorts

* This book was uſed by the Diſſenters in England, an. 1567. See Part of a Regiſter, p. 25; printed in Scotland by R. Waldegrave, 4to. 1593.

ſorts of books then in uſe, namely, A, B, C, or Abſies, with the Pater noſter, Ave, Creed, Graces," &c. dwelt about Pater noſter row. "Alſo turners of beades, and they were called, Pater noſter makers, as I read in a record of one Robert Nikke, pater noſter maker, and citizen, in the reign of Henry IV. and ſo of other." Stow's Survey of London, edit. 1598. p. 273. &c. They were of great antiquity, even before the art of PRINTING was invented; yet hitherto we have not been able to find their priviledge, or charter, though ſeveral of the old printers are ſaid to be of the ſtationers' company, nor had they any authority with relation to printed books, as a company, till the following charter was granted them in 1556; wherein may be obſerved the names of ſeveral of our ancient printers, which we hope will be acceptable to ſome readers.

The CHARTER granted to the company of STATIONERS on the 4th day of May anno MDLVI, and in the third and fourth of Philip and Mary, being a true copy of the original record remaining in the chapel of the rolls. Examined, and tranſlated from the original Latin copy, by Mr. Henry Rook, clerk of the rolls.

"The king and queen to all thoſe to whom theſe, preſents ſhall come, greeting.

I. Know ye, that we conſidering, and manifeſtly perceiving, that ſeveral ſeditious and heretical books, both in verſe and proſe, are daily publiſhed, ſtamped, and printed, by divers ſcandalous, ſchiſmatical, and heretical perſons, not only exciting our ſubjects and liegemen to ſedition and diſobedience againſt us, our crown, and dignity, but alſo to the renewal and propagating very great and deteſtable hereſies againſt, the faith and ſound catholick doctrine of holy mother the church; and being willing to provide a proper remedy in this caſe:

II. We of our own ſpecial favour, certain knowledge, and mere motion, do will, give, and grant, for ourſelves, our heirs, and ſucceſſors of the above mentioned queen, to our beloved and faithful liegemen,

(The maſter)
1 Thomas Dockwray
(The keepers or wardens)
2 John Cawood
3 Henry Coke
(The freemen, or commonalty)
4 William Bunham
5 Richard Waye
6 Simon Coſton
7 Reynold Wolf
8 James Hollyland
9 Stephen Keval
10 John Turk
11 Nicholas Taberner
12 Michael Ubley, als Mic. Lobley
13 John Jaques
14 William Ryddall
15 John Hudſon
16 John Walley
17 Thomas Duxwell
18 Anthony Smith
19 William Powell
20 Richard Jugge
21 William Serreys, or Seres
22 Robert Holder
23 Thomas Purfoo
24 John Rogers
25 William Steward

26 Richard

26 Richard Patchet
27 Nicholas Borman
28 Roger Ireland
29 Richard Crosse
30 Thomas Powell
31 Anthony Croste
32 Richard Hyll
33 Alen Gamlyn
34 Henry Norten
35 Richard Lant
36 Henry Luttell
37 Andrew Hertes
38 Thomas Devell
39 John Case
40 William Hill
41 Richard Richardson
42 Giles Hucke
43 John Kynge
44 John Fairbarne
45 John Hyll
46 Peter Frenche
47 Richard Harrison
48 Humphry Powell
49 John Clerke
50 William Copland
51 William Marten
52 Edward Sutton
53 Thomas Parker
54 John Bonham
55 John Gough
56 John Daye
57 John Whitney
58 Simon Spylman
59 William Baldwyn
60 William Coke
61 John Kewell
62 Robert Broke
63 Thomas Sawyer
64 Charles Walley
65 Thomas Patenson
66 Thomas Mershe
67 Richard Tottell
68 Ralph Tyer
69 John Burtoste
70 William Griffith
71 Edward Broune
72 Nicholas Clifton
73 Richard Harvey
74 James Gunwell
75 Edward Cator
76 John Kele
77 Thomas Bylton
78 Thomas Maskall
79 William Norton
80 William Pycheryng
81 Richard Baldwyn
82 Richard Grene
83 Thomas Beyden
84 Robert Badborne
85 John Alday
86 Robert Blyth
87 George Brodehead
88 Hugh Cotisforth
89 Richard Wallis
90 Thomas Gee
91 Richard Kevell, junior
92 John Shereman
93 Thomas Skeroll
94 Owen ap Roger
95 John Tysdale
96 Adam Croke, and
97 John Fox,

freemen of the mystery, or art of a stationer, of our city of London, and suburbs thereof, that from henceforth they may be indeed, fact, and name, one body, of itself for ever, and one society corporated for ever, with one master, and two keepers, or wardens, in the society of the same mystery, or art of a stationer of the city aforesaid, and that they may enjoy a perpetual succession.

III. And further, we of our own special favour, certain knowledge, and mere motion, do by these presents, ordain, erect, make, and constitute, the foresaid THOMAS DOCKWRAY, the master of the same mystery,

 or

or art of a ftationer of the forefaid city, for one year next enfuing; and the forefaid JOHN CAWOOD, and HENRY COKE, the keepers, or wardens of the fame myftery, or art of a ftationer of the forefaid city, for one year next enfuing; and we by thefe prefents do make, create, and conftitute, the forefaid William Bonham, Richard Way, Simon Cofton, Reynold Wolfe, &c. and the forefaid perfons, the commonalty of the fame myftery, or art of a ftationer of the city aforefaid.

IV. And further, we ordain, create, erect, make, and conftitute, by thefe prefents, the forefaid mafter, and keepers, or wardens, and commonalty, one body, in deed and name of themfelves for ever, and one fociety for ever, corporate, with one mafter, and two keepers, or wardens, and the commonalty of the fame myftery, or art of a ftationer of the city of London aforefaid. And we do incorporate the fame mafter, keepers, or wardens, and commonalty, and by thefe prefents we do really and fully will, grant, create, erect, ordain, make, declare, and conftitute, the faid mafter, and keepers, or wardens, and commonalty, a body corporate, to continue for ever, by the name of the mafter, and keepers, or wardens, and communalty of the miftery, or art of a ftationer of the city of London; and that the fame mafter, and keepers, or wardens, and commonalty, may, from henceforward, have a perpetual fucceffion; and that the fame mafter, and keepers, or wardens, and commonalty, and their fucceffors for ever may be ftiled, entituled, and called, by the name of the mafter, and keepers, or wardens, and commonalty of the myftery, or art of a ftationer of the city of London; and that they may be able to plead, and to be impleaded, to anfwer, and be anfwered, by that name in all and fingular matters, fuits, and plaints, actions, demands, and caufes, before any of our judges and juftices whomfoever, in any courts, or places whatfoever: and that they may have a common feal to ferve, and to be ufed for their affairs and bufinefs; and for the fealing of all and fingular their deeds and writings, any wife touching, or concerning their affairs and bufinefs.

V. And that the fame mafter, and keepers, or wardens, and commonalty, and their fucceffors, may from time to time, make, and ordain, and eftablifh for the good, and well-ordering, and governing of the freemen of the forefaid art, or myftery, and of the forefaid fociety, ordinances, provifions, and laws, as often as they fhall fee proper and convenient.

VI. Provided, that thofe ordinances, provifions, and laws be in no wife repugnant, or contrary to the laws and ftatutes of this our kingdom of England, or in prejudice to the common-weal of our fame kingdom.

VII. And that the fame, and their fucceffors for ever, are enabled, and may, lawfully, and fafely, without moleftation or difturbance of us, or the heirs, or fucceffors of our forefaid queen, or of any other perfon, hold, as often as they pleafe, lawfull, and honeft meetings of themfelves, for the enacting fuch laws, and ordinances, and tranfacting other bufinefs for

for the benefit of the same mystery, or art, and of the same society, and for other lawful causes in the manner aforesaid.

VIII. And that the foresaid master, and keepers, or wardens, and the commonalty of the same mystery, or art of a stationer of the foresaid city, and their successors, or the greater part of them, being assembled lawfully, and in a convenient place, may yearly for ever, or oftner, or seldomer, at such times and places within the said city, as they shall think fit, chuse from amongst themselves, and make one master, and two keepers, or wardens of the same mystery, or art of a stationer of the foresaid city, to rule, govern, and supervise the foresaid mystery and society, and all the men of the same mystery, and their business; and to remove and displace the former master, and the former keepers, or wardens, out of those offices, as they shall see best.

IX. And that if, and as often as it shall happen in any election, that the master, and keepers, or wardens, and the foresaid commonalty, are equal in votes, one part against another in such an election, that then, and so often, the master of the foresaid mystery, if there shall be then any master, or the upper keeper, or warden of that mystery, if there shall then be no master, may have two votes in such elections.

X. And that the master, and keepers, or wardens, and commonalty of the foresaid mystery, and their successors for the time being, shall be deemed fit and able persons in law, as well to give, grant, and to let their lands and tenements, possessions, goods, and chattels, as to purchase, possess, take, and receive for themselves, and their successors, lands, tenements, possessions, goods, chattles, and inheritances to be had, enjoyed, and possessed, by themselves, and their successors, for ever, the statute against putting lands and tenements in mortmain, or any other statute, act, or ordinance to the contrary notwithstanding.

XI. Provided that the said lands, tenements, and inheritances so to be purchased, and to be possessed by them, be within our said city of London, or suburbs, or the liberties of the same city; and so that they do not in any wise exceed the yearly value of twenty pounds, of lawful money of England.

XII. Moreover we will, grant, ordain, and constitute for ourselves, and the successors of our foresaid queen, that no person within this our kingdom of England, or dominions thereof, either by himself, or by his journeymen, servants, or by any other person, shall practise, or exercise the art or mystery of printing, or stamping any book, or any thing to be sold, or to be bargained for within this our kingdom of England, or the dominions thereof, unless the same person is, or shall be, one of the society of the foresaid mystery, or art of a stationer of the city aforesaid, at the time of his foresaid printing, or stamping; or has for that purpose obtained our licence, or the licence of the heirs, and successors of our foresaid queen.

XIII. Moreover we will, grant, ordain, and constitute for ourselves, the

the heirs and successors of our said queen, to the foresaid master, keepers, or wardens, and the commonalty of the mystery, or art of a stationer of the foresaid city of London, and to their successors for ever, that the foresaid master, and keepers, or wardens, and their successors, for the time being, shall very lawfully as well search, as often as they please, any place, shop, house, chamber, or building of any stamper, printer, binder, or seller of any manner of books within our kingdom of England, or dominions thereof, concerning, or for any books, or things printed, stamped, or to be printed, or stamped, as seize, take away, have, burn, or convert to the proper use of the said society, all, and singular those books, and those things, which are, or shall be printed, or stamped contrary to the form of any statute, act, or proclamation, made, or to be made.

XIV. And that, if any person shall practise, or exercise the foresaid art, or mystery, contrary to the form above described, or shall disturb, refuse, or hinder the foresaid master, and keepers, or wardens for the time being, or any one of them for the time being, to make the foresaid search, or to seize, take away, or burn the foresaid books, or things, which are, or any one of which has been printed, or stamped, or are to be printed, or stamped, contrary to the form of any statute, act, or proclamation, that then the foresaid master, or keepers, or wardens for the time being, shall imprison, or send to goal, or either of them shall imprison, or send to goal, every such person so practising, or exercising the foresaid art, or mystery, contrary to the form aforesaid, or so that, as aforesaid, the disturber, refuser, or hinderer, shall there remain without bail, or mainprize, for the space of three months; and that the same person so practising the art, or mystery aforesaid contrary to the said form, or so that, as aforesaid, the disturber, refuser, or hinderer, shall pay, or cause to be paid, for every such practising or exercising as aforesaid, contrary to the said form, and for every such disturbance, let, or hindrance, one hundred shillings of lawful money of England, one moiety thereof to us, our heirs, and successors of the foresaid queen, and the other moiety thereof to the foresaid master, keepers, or wardens, and commonalty, &c. In witness whereof the king and queen at Westminster, May 4.

"By writ of privy seal," &c.

1555. "A Shorte Treatise of politique power, and of the true Obedience which subiectes owe to kynges and other ciuile Gouernours, with an Exhortacion to all true naturall Englishe men, Compyled by D. I. P. B. R. VV.* (*Dr. John Ponet, bishop of Rochester; afterwards of Winchester.* 1556.) Psal. 118. It is better to trust in the Lorde than to trust in Princes." On the back is a short epistle "To the gentil reader." M 4, in eights. W.H. Octavo.

"A

* It was reprinted in 1639, and again in 1642. Its contents may be seen in Oldys's Catal. of pamphlets in the Harleian library, No. 409.

" A trewe mirrovr or glase wherin we may beholde the wofull state of thys our Realme of Englande, set forth betwene Eusebius and Theophilus. Matthewe. 12. Omne regnum in se diuisum desolabitur. Imprinted Anno Domi. M.D.L.VI." The running title " A Dialogue Betwene Euse. and Theo." This, printed on a singular type, Long Primer, ends on the back of C ii, in eights. On the next page, in two line great primer, " Dominus michi adiutor nõ timebo quid faciat mihi homo. ¶ P. N. ¶" On the back begins " The Lordes prayer." in stanzas of 6 lines. W.H. Sixteens. 1556.

An exposition of the 6 psalm. See p. 1118. Sixteens. 1556.

" Theod. Beza his briefe declaration of the chiefe points of Christian religion, set forth in a table of predestination, printed at Geneua by Jo. Riuery. 1556." Maunsell, p. 9. See p. 884. Sixteens. 1556.

" Anth. Gilbie his Treatise of election and reprobation with certain answeres to the obiections of the aduersaries of this doctrine. Printed at Geneua by James Poulain and Ilen. Houdouin. 1556." Ib. p. 54. See p. 884. Sixteens. 1556.

Calvin's Catechism translated for the use of the English. Geneva, printed by John Crespin. Octavo. 1556.

" The Nevve Testament of our Lord Jesus Christ. Conferred diligently with the Greke, and best approued translations. VVith the arguments aswel before the chapters, as for euery Boke, & Epistle, also diuersities of readings, and most proffitable annotations of all hard places: whereunto is added a copious Table." Device: Time bringing truth to light. With this motto up and down the sides, " God by Tyme restoreth Truth, And maketh her victorious. At Geneva Printed By Conrad Badius. M.D.LVII." On the back is " The ordre of the Bookes," &c. Then, " The epistle declaring that Christ is the end of the Lawe, By John Caluin.--To the reader mercie and peace through Christ our Sauiour.---The argument of the Gospel, writ by the foure Euangelists." The New Testament occupies 430 leaves. The tables annexed end on folio 455. " Printed—this x. of June." This first edition of the Geneva translation is very neatly printed on Roman and Italic types, and is the first English New Testament divided into verses. See Lewis, p. 207—210. W.H. Sixteens. 1557.

" Defensio verae et catholicae doctrinae de sacramento, &c. as p. 1571. 1557.

" An Exposition of a parte of S. Johannes Gospel made in sondrie (6) readinges in the English Congregation at Wesel by Bartho. Traherõ* and now published against the wicked enterprizes of new sterte vp Arians in Englande. He that beleueth in me, beleueth not in me, but in him that sent me. And he that seeth me, seeth him that sent me. Jhon. 12. Imprinted. Anno. 1557." Addressed thus, " + To my most dere sister Elisabeth P.—Commende me to him, whom lawes permitte you to love,—Your Bro. Bartho. Traheron." K, in eights. In Roman letter, supplied with the German w, h, and sh. W.H. Again 1558. Sixteens. 1557.

" An

* Library keeper to king Edw. VI. See Rymer, Tom. 15, p. 351.

1557. "An Expositiō of the. 4. Chap. of. S. Joans Reuelation. made by Bar. Traheron in sondrie Readinges before his countre men in Germanie. Where in the prouidēce of God is treated, with an aunswer made to the obiections of a gentle aduersarie. Jmprinted Anno 1557." Addressed "To master Ro. Parker/ and maistres Anne his godlie wife/ exiles for Christes cause/" &c. In 3 readings or lectures. To which is added "An exposition of these wordes (Leade vs not in to tentation) made by Bar. Traheron, lōge before these former lectures, & now added hereto, that you maie know, that he neuer saide nor thought that god is the autor of sinne, as some most falsly, and vngodly would haue men to weene."* At the end, no place, but Anno 1558." W.H. Sixteens.

1557. "The Order of the Hospitalls* of K. Henry the viijth and K. Edward the vjth, viz. St. Bartholomew's. Christ's. Bridewell. St. Thomas's. By the Maior, Cominaltie, and Citizens of London, Gouernours of the Possessions, Reuenues and Goods of the sayd Hospitalls, 1557." Reprinted in the old character and size at the expence of secretary Pepys. Gough's Brit. Topogr. Vol. I; p. 639. W.H. Sixteens.

1557. "An answer to a certain godly mānes letters/ desiring his frendes iudgement/ whether it be laufull for a christian man to be present at the popishe Masse/ and other superstitious churche seruice. 1557. 3 Re. 18. Wherfore halte ye on bothe sydes? If the Lorde be God/ folowe hym/ and if Baal be/ than folowe hym." In this small tract of 8 leaves we learn that D. Petre Martyr was the author of the "Treatise of the Cohabitacyon of the faithfull with the vnfaithfull." See p. 1580. Also, that D. Ponet late bishop of wynchestre/ was reported to be the author of another tract, wherein "Hill and Petresone with other such like disse-lders ād haltīg heretiks of these later dais" are reproued. W.H. 16°.

1557. "The Boke named The gouernour deuised by sir Thomas Elyot Knyght. Londini, An. M.D.LVII." In a compartment with a cherub's head on each jamb, used by John Tisdale in 1561, and by Tho. Marshe in 1565. This edition is without any printer's name. W.H. Sixteens.

1557. "Missale ad vsum insignis ecclesie Sarisburiensis," &c. as p. 629.

1557. "Officium beatissime virginis Marie in vsum Sarum. Lond. 1557." Latin and English. Harl. Catal. Octavo.

1558. "The First Blast of the Trumpet against the monstruous regiment of women. Veritas temporis filia. M.D.LVIII." At the head of the preface, "The Kingdome apperteineth to our God." At the head of the treatise, "The first blast to awake women degenerate." Contains 56 leaves, neatly printed on Small Pica Rom. types. See an account of this and the following article in Strype's Annals of the Reformation, Vol. I; p. 120, &c. W.H. Octavo.

"How

* It was reprinted by Hen. Bynneman for Hum. Toye, in 1573. See p. 935, 1116, and 1270.

* Maunsell mentions "Orders of St. Thomas's Hospitall." Probably they were printed for each hospital separately, with some variation proper to each.

Some of Sir David Lindſay's poems. " Heir followis the teſ- 1558.
tament and complaynt of our ſouuerane lordis papingo. Kyng James the Fyſt. *&c.* Compylit be the ſaid* Schir Dauid Lyndeſay of the Mont, Knycht Alias Lyoun Kyng of Armes." The author's portrait, whole length, with the arms of Scotland on the breaſt of his ſurcoat. Under it, " And imprentit at the command, and expenſes of maiſter Sammuel Jaſcuy, Jn Paris. 1558." This is concluded on the front page of F 3, on the back thereof the portrait, as on the title-page. With the foregoing is bound " The Dreme" &c. as p. 1485; but the copy before me wants the title-page of it, with perhaps the following pieces. It begins on A 2, with the epiſtle to the king.---" And exhortatioun to the Kyngis grace.---The deploratioun of the deyth of Quene Magdalene." Concluded on the back page of G 2, in fours, with the author's portrait as before. The ſignatures, which are all in Gothic capitals, are ſet to the firſt page only. Mr. Pinkerton. Quarto.

" An anſwere made by Bar. Traheron to a priuie papiſt, which 1558.
crepte into the Engliſh congregation of chriſtian exiles, vnder the viſor of a fauorer of the goſpel, but at length bewraied himſelf to be one of the popes aſſes, thorough his flouche ears, and than became a laughing ſtocke to al the companie, whom he had amaſed before with his maſke," &c. Sixteens.

" An abridgment, bref abſtract, or ſhort ſume of theſe bookes following, taken out of the bible, and ſet into Starnolds meter, by me William Samuell, miniſter of Chriſts chirche (1 Gen. 2 Exod. *&c.* to the 4th book of kinges incluſiue.)

" Such faltes as you herein ſhall find,
I pray you be content;
And do the ſame with will and mynd,
That was then our intent.
The printers were outlandiſh men,
The faltes they be the more;
Which are eſcaped now and then,
But hereof are no ſtore." See p. 700. Sixteens.

" How ſuperior powers oght to be obeyd of their ſubiects: and wherin 1558.
they may lawfully by Gods worde be diſobeyed and reſiſted. Wherin alſo is declared the cauſe of all this preſent miſerie in England, and the onely way to remedy the ſame. By Chriſtopher Goodman." Device: an anchor ſupported by two hands, a ſerpent twiſted about the ſhank and the ſtock, with I. C. at the bottom of the ſhank. Under it, " The Lord hath broght vpon them a nation from a farre contrey, an impudent nation, and of a ſtrange langage. Baruch 4. Deut. 28. Printed at Geneua by John Criſpin. M.D.LVIII." Prefixed are an introductory epiſtle by " VVilliam VVhitingham to all them that loue to knowe the trueth and

* Hence it is evident ſome other of his poems had preceded this: biſhop Tanner informs us it was his Monarch, Bibl. p. 495.

felowe it:---The preface," by the author. At the head of the treatise, originally a sermon, "Peter and John answered vnto thē, and said: Whether it be right in the sight of God to obey you rather thē God, iudge you. Act. 4." The running title, "How to obey or disobey." It is divided into 15 chapters, and ends on p. 234. "From Geneua, this first of Januarie. M.D.LVIII." Then, "William Kethe to the Reader," in 19 stanzas of 4 lines. On the last page, "Geue not thy glorie to an other: neither that whiche is profitable for thee, to a strange nation. Baruch. 4." Then, a cut of the pythagorean Y, from the top of the broadside of which a youth is tumbling down; over the top of the narrow side is a laurel crown, Pythagoras standing under it and pointing up to it; this motto up and down the sides, "The way to life is (*is*) streicte, and fewe finde it. Mat. 7." Beneath, "Imprinted at Geneua by John Crespin the first of Ianuarie. Anno D. M.D.LVIII." W.H. See Strype's Annals, Vol. I; p. 122, &c. Sixteens.

——— "A Confutatiō of vnwrittē verities, both bi the holye scriptures and moste auncient autors, and also probable argumentis, and pithy reasons, with plaine aunswers to al (or at the least) to the moste part and strongest argumentes, which the aduersaries of gods truth, either haue, or can bryng forth for the prose and defence of the same vnwritten vanities, verities as they woulde haue them called: made by Thomas Cranmer, late Archebishop of Cantorburie, Martyr of god, and burned at Oxford for the defēce of the trewe doctrine of our sauiour Christ, translated and set forth, by E. P. ¶ The contentes whereof, thou shalte finde in the next side (*leaf*) folowinge." After which is a copious preface, and at the end thereof "The boke to the Reader," in 4 stanzas of 8 short lines. The whole, O 7, in eights. Towards the conclusion are related sundry stories of visions, and pretended miracles, as the holy maid of Lemster, Elizabeth Barton the holy maid of Courtop-street in Kent, &c. On the last page is a table of "Faultes escaped in the pryntynge." After which is a blank leaf, so that it evidently had no colophon. See p. 612, and 999. W.H. Sixteens.

1558. "The copie of a lettre deliuered to the ladie Marie, Regent of Scotland, frome Iohn Knox minister of Goddes worde, in the yeare of our Lord 1556, and nowe augmented and explaned by the Author in the yeare of our Lord 1558." Device: two arches, one narrow, the other broad; over the narrow one is a crown of laurel, over the broad one flames of fire; with this motto about them, "Enter in at the strait gate: for wide is the gate, and brode is the waye, that leadeth to destruction, Matth. 7." Beneath, "Printed at Geneva, By James Poullain, and Antonie Rebul. M.D.LVIII." 28 leaves. W.H. 16°.

1558. "The appellation of Iohn Knoxe from the cruell and most iniust sentence pronounced against him by the false bishoppes and clergie of Scotland, with his supplication and exhortation to the nobilitie, estates, and cōmunalitie of the same realme. Printed at Geneva, M.D.LVIII. The appellation is addressed "To the nobilitie and estates of Scotlād" only;

only; the epistle, "To his beloved brethren the communaltie of Scotland" annexed, begins on folio 47, and concludes on fo. 59. "Be witnesse to my appellation.—From Geneua The 14. of July, 1558. Your brother to commaunde in godlines Iohn Knoxe." On the back of which leaf begins "An Admonition to England and Scotland to call them to repentance, written by Antoni Gilby," which ends on folio 77. On the back thereof "Iohn Knoxe to the reader." Then, "Psalme of David xciii, turned into metre by W. Kethe." The whole on 80 leaves. See Oldys's Catal. of pamphlets, &c. No. 73. W.H. 16°.

"A Declaration of the triumphant mariage of the twa maist nobill Prince and Princesse Francis de Valoys and Mary Stuart by the grace of God King and Quene of Scotland, and Dolphine and Dolphines of France." Printed at Paris, 1558. Octavo. 1558.

"A warning to England to Repent, and to turn to God from Idolatrie and Poperie, by the terrible example of Calice, giuen the 7. of March. Anno Dom. 1558. by Benthalmay Outis. Prin. Anno 1558." Maunsell, p. 90. Octavo. 1558.

"An Admonition to England and Scotland to call them to repentance. By Anth. Gilbie. Imprinted at Geneua by John Crispine, 1558." See Stapleton's Counterblast, &c. fo. 23, a. 1558.

"A Lamentation of England, with an addition of Calis. Prin. 1558." Maunsell, p. 65. Octavo. 1558.

"A sparke of friendship, and warm good will; with a poem concerning the commodity of sondry sciences; especially concerning paper, and a mill, lately set vp neer Dartford by a high German, called Mr. Spilman,[†] ieweller to the queenes maiesty." Dedicated to sir Walter Raleigh. Begins, "enforced by affection that, &c. where friendship finds good grownd to grow upon.—London. 1558."—Again 1588. Quarto. 1558.

"The Primer in Englysh after Salysburie vse: sette out at lengthe with manye Godlie prayers: Newlye Imprinted this presente yere. Anno domini M.D.LVJ.JJ. Cum priuilegio—solum." This title is printed in red and black: not only one line in red and the next in black, whereby some of the words are part in one colour and the rest in the other, but the date has M.D.LVJ. in red and JJ. in black, in the same line. My copy is imperfect at the end, where perhaps was a colophon with the printer's name; probably J. Wayland, who had a patent. W.H. 16°. 1558.

"Mich. Nostrodamus his prognostication for the year 1559 With the predictions and presages of euery Moneth. Antwerpiæ." See p. 844. Octavo. (1558.)

"An Harborovve for faithfull and trevve subiectes, agaynst the late blowne Blaste, concerninge the Gouernemēt of VVemen, wherin be confuted all soch reasons as a straunger of late made in that behalfe, with a breife 1559.

[†] Mr. John Spilman had a patent to make paper. However this was not the first paper made in England. See p. 200.

breife exhortation to Obedience Anno M.D.lix. Prouerbes. 32. (29—31.) Many daughters there be that gather riches together: but thou goest aboue them all. &c. At Strasborowe the 26. of Aprill." Dedicated, "To—Francis Earle of Bedford one of the Quenes Maiesties priuie Counsell, and the Lord Robert Duddeley, master of her highnes horsse, and knight of—the Garter." R 3, in fours; Rom. Letter. On the last page the device: A right hand extended out of a cloud, &c. as p. 645. See Strype's Life of Bp. Aylmer, p. 16, and 224. W.H. Quarto.

1559. "The copie of his (*John Knox's*) epistle sent vnto Newcastle, & Barwick. Also a briefe exhortation to Englande for the sperdy embracing of Christes Gospell, heretofore by the tyranny of Mary suppressed. Prin. at Geneua. 1559." Maunsell, p. 65. With a catalogue of Martyrs. See p. 741. Sixteens.

"The Boke of Psalmes" &c. as p. 800.

1559. "The complaynt of veritie, made by John Bradford. An exhortation of Mathewe Rogers vnto his children. The complaynt of Raufe Allerton and others, being prisoners in Lollers Tower, and wryten with their blood, how God was their comforte. A songe of Caine and Abell. The saieng of maister Houper, that he wrote the night before he suffered, vppon a wall with a cole, in the newe Inn at Gloceter, and his saying at his deathe." As Maunsell has this with some variation, there seem to have been two editions of it this year. Octavo.

(1559.) "The Golden Treatise of the auncient and learned Father Vincentius Lirinensis. For the antiquitie and vniuersalitie, of the Catholicke Religion: against the prophane nouelties of all Heresies: Newly translated into English by A. P. Verie profitable for all such as desire, in these dangerous times, to imbrace the true Gospell of Iesus Christ, and to remain free from all infectiō of false doctrine, as in the preface more at large is declared. + With Priuiledge." The preface is superscribed "To the Christian Reader zelous of truth, and desirous of Saluation: A. P. wisheth the knowledge of the one in this life, and the fruition of the other in the life to come." Herein we learn that the original was written three years after the general council of Ephesus. H 6, in eights; white letter. W.H. See it translated by N. Winzet, 1563. Sixteens.

1559. "Cœnæ Dominicæ et Missæ Papisticæ comparatio. Authore Tho. Becon." Bibl. Bodleiana. Octavo.

Queen ELIZABETH confirmed the STATIONERS' charter in these words, "We ratifying and allowing the foresaid letters, and all, and every thing contained therein, do, as much as in us lies, accept and approve them for ourselves, our heirs, and successors, and do ratify and confirm them to our beloved Reynold Wolfe, now the master of the foresaid mystery, or art of a stationer, and Michael Lobley, and Thomas Duxwell, the keepers, or wardens of the same mystery, and to their successors, in such manner, as the foresaid recited charter and letters do reasonably in themselves testify. In witness whereof, &c.

The

The queen at Westminster, on the tenth day of November, and in the first year of our reign." 1559.[*]

In the injunctions given by the queen's majesty, anno Domini 1559. No. 51. against heretical and seditious books, the wardens and company of stationers were especially to be obedient, thus: " Item, because there is a great abuse in the Printers of bokes, which for couetousnes cheefly regard not what they print, so they may haue gaine, whereby ariseth great disorder by publication of vnfruitefull, vaine, and infamous bookes and papers; the Queenes Maiestie straitlie chargeth and commaundeth, that no maner of person shal print any maner of booke or paper, of what sort, nature, or in what language soeuer it be, except the same bee firste licensed by her Maiestie, by expresse wordes in writing, or by six of her priuie counsell: or be perused and licensed by the Archbishops of Canterburie, and Yorke, the Bishop of London, the Chauncelors of both Vniuersities, the bishop being Ordinarie, and the Archdeacon also of the place, where any such shalbe printed, or by two of thẽ, wherof the Ordinarie of the place to be alwaies one. And that the names of such, as shall allow the same, to bee added in the end of euery such worke, for a testimonie of the allowaunce therof. And because many pamphelets, playes, and ballads, be oftentimes printed, wherein regarde woulde be had, that nothing therein should be either hereticall, seditious, or vnseemely for Christian eares: her Maiestie likewise commaundeth, that no manner of person shal enterprise to print any such, except the same be to him licensed by suche her Maiesties commissioners, or three of them, as be appointed in the citie of London, to heare and determine diuers causes Ecclesiasticall, tending to the executiõ of certayn statutes, made the last parliament for vniformity of order in religion. And if any shal sell or vtter any maner of bokes, or papers, being not licensed, as is abouesayde: that the same party shalbe punished by order of the sayd Commissioners, as to the quality of the fault shalbe thought meete. And touching all other books of matters of religion, or pollicie, or gouernaunce, that hath bene printed, eyther on this side the Seas, or on the other side, bicause the diuersity of them is great, and that there needeth good consideratiõ to be had of the particularities therof, her Maiestie referreth the prohibition or permission thereof, to the order, which her said Commissioners within the City of London shall take & notifie. According to the which, her Maiestie straitly commaundeth all manner her subiects, and specially the wardens and company of Stationers, to be obedient.

Prouided that these orders doe not extende to any prophane authours, and works in any language that hath bin heretofore commonly receiued or allowed in any the vniuersities, or schooles, but the same may be printed and vsed, as by good order they were accustomed."

" Rerum in Ecclesia gestarum, quæ postremis et periculosis his temporibus 1559.

[*] Translated from the Latin by Mr. Henry Rock, clerk of the rolls, 10th Decem. 1741.

poribus evenerunt, maximarumq; per Europam persecutionum, ac Sanctorum Dei martyrum, caeterarumq; rerum si quae insignioris exempli sint, degesti per Regna & nationes Commentarii Pars Prima. In qua primum de rebus per Angliam et Scotiam gestis, atque in primis de horrenda, sub Maria nuper Regina, persecutione, narratio continetur. Authore Joanne Foxo, Anglo. Basileae per Nicolaum Brylingerum et Joannem Oporinum." At the end, "Anno M.D.LIX. mense Augusto." Folio.

1559. "De religionis conservatione et reformatione vera; déque primatu regum et magistratuum, & obedientia illis ut summis in terra Christi vicariis, praestanda, liber. Laurentio Humfredo authore." Basil per Operinum. Octavo.

—— A Latin Common Prayer: the first of Q. Elizabeth. See p. 605.

1560. "Disticha in Novum Testamentum memoriae iuuandae caussa, conscripta à Joan. Schepreuo Oxonienss, nuper opera." Octavo.

—— The Common prayer turned into French, by a chaplain of the bishop of Ely, as soon as the first liturgy was settled. See p. 766.

1560. "An answer to a great Nomber of blasphemous cauillations written by an Anabaptist, &c. And Confuted by John Knox, &c. Wherein the Author discouereth the craft and falshode of that sect, that the godly, knowing that error, may be confirmed in the trueth by the euident Word of God." Device, as p. 1597. Beneath; "Prov. XXX. There is a generatiō that are pure in their owne cōceit, and yet are not washed from their filthines. Printed by John Crespin. M.D.LX." Rom. Letter. 445 pages. See p. 1106. Sixteens.

1560. "The summarie of certaine Reasons, which haue moued Quene Elizabeth to procede in Reformations of her base and course Monies, and to reduce them to their Values, in Sorte, as they may be turned to fine Monies. Appointed to be declared by her Maiestie, by Order of her Proclamation, in her Citie of London.—Given under the Queenes Maiesties Signet at her Honour of Hampton Court, the 29th of September, the second year of her Maiesties Reign, M.D.LX." With Stamps of the base testons at the end. 6 pages. See Harl. Miscel. VIII; p. 67. Octavo.

1560. "The life and damnable heresie of Dauid George, a very blasphemer of our Messias Iesu Christ, translated out of latine. Printed at Basill by Conrad Meuse. 1560." Maunsell, p. 68. Quarto.

1560. "The New Testament of our Lord Jesus Christ," &c. This is the 2d edition of the Genevan version, with short marginal notes. See Lewis, p. 210, &c. Lambeth Library. Sixteens.

1560. "The Bible" &c. as p. 800, et seq. Printed at Geneva. Quarto.

1560. Beza's Admonition to the Parliament. English. Octavo.

"England repent, Bishops relent, Return, while you haue space:
Time is at Hand, for Truth to stande, If you haue any Grace." &c.

1560. "The Defence of Women, especially English women against a book intituled the School-house of women. By Edw. More." See p. 375. Dedicated

Dedicated "To Master William Page, secretary to his neighbour and patron sir Edward Hoby of Bisham abbey." See Hist. of Eng. Poetry, Vol. III, p. 320. Quarto.

"The Account of the Furniture of the Inthronization of W. Warham Archbishop of Canterbury; with the Entertainment of the Emperor Charles V. Henry VIII. Cardinal Wolsey, and many of the Nobility, &c. by the said Archbishop: Also, the Bills of Fare for the several Days. Imprinted on a Paper Roll above three Yards long. London, 1560. 1561." See the Brit. Librarian, p. 349. Also, Somner's Antiq. of Canterbury, revised and enlarged by Nicholas Battely, M.A. edit. 1703. Appendix, p. 21, &c. 1560.

A plan of London, cut on wood, and printed on six sheets and two half sheets, measuring 6 feet 3 inches by 2 feet 4 inches. It was re-engraved by Geo. Vertue in 1748 on pewter, with this inscription "Civitas Londinum, 1560," and printed on 6 sheets: these were purchased, and republished by the Society of Antiquaries, 1776. See an account of this and several other plans of London in Gough's Brit. Topography, Vol. I, p. 745, &c. (1560.)

JOHN BODELEIGH, one of the English refugees at Geneva, had a patent[b] granted him for the imprinting bibles of the Geneva version in the English tongue, though none have yet been met with in consequence thereof, unless perhaps the following. ——

The Bible and Holy Scriptures contained in the Old and New Testament, &c. See p. 800, &c. My copy wants the general title and table of the principal things contained in the Bible. It is dedicated to Q. Elizabeth the same as in Rowland Hall's edition 1560; but now dated "From Geneua, 10. April. 1561." Likewise, the epistle to the bretheren of England, &c. The leaves are numbered progressively from the title to the end of the Apocrypha, 432. Fff 4, in sixes. 1561.

"The

[b] "ELIZABETH by the grace of God, &c. To all manner of printers, bookesellers, and other officers, mynisters, and subjectes, greeting. We do you to understand, that of our grace especiall, we have graunted, and given pryveledge and licence, and by these presents, for us, our heirs, and successors, do grant, and give pryveledge, and lycence, unto our well-beloved subject, John Bodeleigh, and to his assignes, for the terme of seven yeres next ensuynge the date hereof, to imprinte, or cause to be imprinted, the Englysh byble, with annotations faythfully translated and fynyshed in this present yere of our Lord God, a thousand, fyve hundred, and threscore, and dedicated to us: streightlie forbydding and commanding by these presents, all, and singuler our subjectes, as well printers and bookesellers, as other persons within our realmes and domynions, whatsoever they be, in anie manner of wise to imprynte, or cause to be imprinted, anie of the foresaid Englishe bibles, that the said John Bodeleigh shall by thauthoritye of this our licence, imprinte, or cause to be imprinted, or any part of them, but onlie the said John Bodeleigh, and his assignes, upon pain of our high indignation and displeasure; and that every offender therein shall forfayt to our use fortie shillings, of lawfull money of England, for every such bible, or bibles, at any time so printed, contrary to the true meaninge of this our licence, and priviledge over and besides all such booke, or bookes so printed, to be forfayeted to whomsoever shall susteyne the charge, and sue the said forfayture in our behalf. In wytnesse whereof, &c. 8 Jan. 1561."

1561. " The Newe Testament of our Lord Iesus Christ. Conferred diligently vvith the Greke, and best approued translacions in diuers languages. This is the message vvhiche vve haue heard of him, and declare vnto you, that God is the light, and in him is no darknes. (1.) Iohn 1. ver. 5." Device: A branch with 7 lamps; the same as used to Exod. 25. Up and down the sides, " No man lighteth a Candle for to put it vnder a Bushell, But vpon the Candlestike." Beneath, " If vve vvalke in the light as he is in the light, vve haue felovvship one vvith another, and the blood of Iesus Christ clenseth vs from all sinne. (1.) Iohn 1. Vers. 7. Printed at Geneua. M.D.LXI." On the back is a table of " The order of the yeres from Pauls conuersion, shevving the time of hys peregrination, and of hys Epistles vvritten to the Churches." The New Testament ends on folio 111. Then, " A brief table of the interpretation of the propre names," &c.---A table of the principal things that are conteined in the Bible." This title is at the foot of the first table; but the table, and whatever followed it is wanting, and I know not where to get intelligence from any other copy. The whole printed on Rom. Let. See Lewis, p. 233, &c. W.H. Folio.

1561. " The forme of Prayers and ministration of the Sacramentes, &c. vsed in the Englishe Congregation at Geneua: and approued, by the famous and Godly learned man M. Iohn Caluin. 1 Corinth. III. No man can laye any other foundation, then that which is layde, euen Christ Iesus. 1561." On the back are " The contentes' of the Booke." Then, a preface addressed " To our bretheren in England, and els where, whiche loue Iesus Christ vnfeynedly," &c. 84 leaves; to which are annexed 8 more, containing prayers, graces, &c. Neatly printed in Long Primer Roman, No. 1. The Psalms of David in metre, the 11th article of the contents, are not inserted in the order here described, nor does it appear they were designed so to be; for the order of Eccl. Discipline is concluded on fol. 35; and fol. 36 is the title-page of " The catechisme of (or) maner to teache chyldren the Christian Religion. —1561." Whereby it seems designed to be sold separate; as probably the Psalms might also. W.H. Sixteens.

1561. " In Symbolum Apostolicum Comment. Lond. 1561." By Patrick Cockburn. Mackenzie, Writers of the Scots Nation, III; p. 56.

1561. " Examples of vertue and vice," &c. See p. 767.

1561. Tully's Tusculane Questions translated by Mr. John Dolman of the Middle

' " 1. The Confession of the Christian faith. 2. The order of electynge Ministers, Elders, and Deacons. 3. The assemblie of the Ministrie, euery Thursdaye. 4. An order for the interpretation of the Scriptures and answering of doubtes, obserued euery mondaye. 5. A confession of our sinnes vsed before the sermon, and framed to our state and time. 6. Another confession for all states and tymes. 7. A generall prayer after the sermon, for the whole estat of Christes Churche. 8. The ministration of Baptisme, and the Lordes Supper. 9. The forme of Mariage, the Visitation of the sicke, and the Maner of Buriall. 10. An order of Ecclesiasticall Discipline. 11. Psalmes of David in metre. 12. The Catechisme. 13. A brief examination of children, before they be admitted to the Lordes table, &c."

Middle Temple, and dedicated to John Jewel bishop of Salisbury. Printed 1561. Hist. of Eng. Poetry, Vol. III; p. 215.

Hercules furens, a tragedy by Seneca, translated by Jasper Heywood. Ibid. p. 386. 1561.

"A most excellent and perfecte homish Apothecarye or homely physick booke for all the greses and diseases of the bodye. Translated out of the Almaine speche into English, by Jhon Hollybush." Device: A hen standing before a tree, in a very heavy compartment, with Arnold Birckman on a tablet at bottom: the engraver's initials W.K. on the dexter side. Beneath; "Jmprinted at Collen by Arnold Birckman, Jn the yeare of our Lord M.D.LXJ." Contains H 3, in sixes. W.H. Folio. 1561.

"The Hunting of the Fox and the Wolfe, because they make hauocke of the sheepe of Christ Jesus." This title is over a cut of a Romish bishop with a wolf's head mitred, devouring a lamb hung up by its heels: under it "¶ Take heede of false prophetes, which come vnto you in sheepes clothing, but within are rauening wolues." On the back, "An Admonition to colde [h]preachers."

This tract is the very same as that published in Q. Mary's time under the title of "The Huntyng of the Romysh Vuolfe," &c. as p. 1575; but now reprinted with a new title-page, as above, and this head-title, "A Dialogue betweene the Foster,[l] the Hunter,[m] and the Deane." It is introduced with an address by an anonymous author[n] "To al my faithful Brethren in Christ Jesu, and to all other that labour to weede out the weedes of popetie. Peace in the Lord Jesu be with you," &c. In which he very zealously excites them, "that by no subtelty as the Apostle warneth, they shoulde be corrupted from the simplicity of Christe:—My good fathers and deare Brethren who are first called to ẏ battel to strive for Gods glory and the edificatiō of his people, againste the Romish reliques and rags of Antichriste, J doubt not but that you wil courageouslye and constātly in Christ, rap at these rages of Gods enemies, and that you will by this occasiō race vp many as great enormities, that we al know and labour to race out al the dregs and remnāts of transformed poperie, that are crept into England, by to much lenitie of

[h] "If preaching fayle, as it doeth begin,
The people must quayle, and die in their sin:
And if it decrease,, Gods curse is at hand
To destroy vs, our peace,, our soules & our land.
Therfore let's be mending, Gods plag's to prevent
For after our ending,, 'tis to late to repent.
Take heed then to preching,, gods word to imbrace
And turne to take warning,, lest God you deface."

[l] A burgess in Q. Mary's parliament.

[m] Who had been a burgess 5 years in K. Edward's parliaments.

[n] So far as one may be allowed to guess at the author by the style, &c. I am inclined to believe this address was written by John Knox, who for magnanimity, courage and zeal for God's glory was at least equal to any of our reformers. This surmise is in some measure supported by the cut of Truth, &c. at the end of this tract; the same as prefixed to that author's "Admonition or warning" &c. as p. 1576, except only the name of *Sutleti* being here given to the figure there inscribed *Crueltye*.

thẽ that wilbe named the Lords of the clergie." &c. This seems to have been set forth not long after the Act of Uniformity; certainly however before the death of Bonner (1569) who it is expresly said " remaineth and is fedde as papistes say, for theyr sakes," &c. Contains E 4, in eights. W.H. Octavo.

1562. " The Bible in English. Printed at Rouen, at the cost of Richard Carmardon." Bibl. Harleianæ, Vol. I; No. 172. See it in 1566. Folio.

1562. " The history of that whiche hath happened sens the Departure of the House of Guise and others from S. Germanes." Sixteens.

1562. " Refutatio luculenta crassæ et exitiosæ hæresis Johannis Calvini & Christop. Carlili Angli, qua astruunt Christum non descendisse ad inferos alios, quam ad infernum infimum." By Dr. Richard Smith. Ath. Oxon I; 144. See p. 1191.

1562. " A Dialogue agaynst the Tyrannye of the Papistes. Translated out of Latin into Englyshe by E. C. 17. Septembris. 1562. VV. S." This ends on C 5, the three remaining leaves blank. On D 1 begins " A Prayer. Surge Deus, Dextra, seruos attolle cadentes, &c. VV. S." In Sternhold's metre: 3 leaves, another blank. Then, on E 1, and E 2. " A Copye of the Aunswere of the noble and worthye Prynce, the Counte Palatyne, made to Mounseur Doysell, the Frenche Kynges Embassadoure.—Dated at Heydelberge. 3. August, 1562 VV. Sc." W.H. Sixteens.

1562. " The Treaty of Thassociation, made by the Prince of Condee, together wyth the Princes, Knithes of the order, Lords which be entred, or hereafter shal entre into the said Association for to mainteine the honour of God, the quiet of the Realme of Fraunce, and the state and Lybertie of the Kyng, &c. Anno 1562." Octavo.

1562. " The seconde parte of Vuilliam Turners herball, wherein are conteyned the names of herbes in Greke, Latin, Duche, Frenche, and in the apothecaries Latin, and sometyme in Italiane, wyth the vertues of the same herbes, wyth diuerse confutationes of no small errours, that men of no small learning haue committed in the intreatinge of herbes of late yeares. Here vnto is ioyned also, a booke of the bath of Baeth in Englãnd, and of the vertues of the same, wyth diuerse other bathes, moste holsum and effectual, both in Almany and Englande.* Set furth by William Turner, doctor of physik. Printed at Collen by Arnold Birckman. Cum gratia et privilegio, reg. majest." Again 1568. Folio.

1562. A bill was brought in, 22 Feb. 1562-3, that the book of service in the church shall be in the Welch tongue in Wales. On the 2d Reading, 4 March, That the Bible also shall be in the Welch tongue. Read the
1563. 3d time and passed, 27 March, 1563. See Journals of the house of commons.

1563. By whose order the bible, and book of common prayer, shall be translated into the Welch tongue.

" The

* This seems to have had a distinct title-page, so as to sell separate on occasion.

5 Eliz. cap. 28. The bible, and book of common prayer, translated into the Welch tongue.

" The bishops of Hereford, saint David's, Asaph, Bangor, and Landaff, and their successors, shall take such order amongst themselves for the soules health of the flocks, committed to their charge, within Wales, that the whole bible, containing the New Testament, and the Old, with the book of Common Prayer, and administration of the sacraments, as it is now used within the realm in English, to be truly and exactly translated into the British or Welch tongue. 2. And that the same so translated, being by them viewed, perused, and allowed, be imprinted to such number at the least, that one of every sort may be had for every cathedral, collegiate, and parish church, and chappel of ease, in such places, and countrys, of every the said diocesses, where that tongue is commonly spoken or used, before the first day of March, *anno Domini* 1566. 3. And that from that day forth, the whole divine service shall be used and said by the curates and ministers, throughout all the said diocesses, where the Welch tongue is commonly used, in the said British, or Welch tongue, in such manner and form, as is now used in the English tongue, and differing nothing in any order or form from the English book. 4. For the which books so imprinted, the parishioners of every the said parishes shall pay the one half or moiety, and the said parson and vicar of every of the said parishes (where both be) or else the one of them, where there is but one, shall pay the other half or moiety. 5. The prices of which books shall be appointed and rated by the same bishops, and their successors, or by three of them at the least. 6. The which things, if the said bishops, or their successors, neglect to do, then every one of them shall forfeit to the queen's majesty, her heirs, and successors, the sum of xl. l. to be levied of their goods and chattels.

A bible, and book of common prayer, in English, shall be in every church in Wales.

" II. And one book containing the bible, and one other book of common prayer, in the English tongue, shall be brought, and had in every church throughout Wales, in which the bible, and book of common prayer in Welch is to be had by force of this act (if there be none already) before the first day of of March, one thousand five hundred sixty six. 2. And the same books to remain in such convenient places within the said churches, that such as understand them, may resort at all convenient times to read and peruse the same; and also such, as do not understand the said language, may, by conferring both tongues together, the sooner attain to the knowledge of the English tongue; any thing in this act to the contrary notwithstanding."

" This Booke is called the Treasure of Gladnesse: and seemeth, by the Copie, beeing a verie little Manuell, and written in velam, to be made about CC yeeres past at the least. Wherby it appeareth how God in olde time, and not of late onely, hath beene truely confessed and honored. The Copie hereof, is for the antiquitie of it, preserued, and to be seene in the Printers Hall. Sette foorth and allowed according to the Queenes Iniunctions. Jmprinted, Anno 1563." Again 1601. Rev. Dr. Lort. 1563.

Sixteens.

" Vincentius

(1563.) "Vincentius Lyrinensis of the Natioun of Gallis, for the Antiquity and Vniversality of the Catholic Fayth againis the prophane Nouatio of all Heresies." Translated by Ninian Winzet, and dedicated to Mary queen of Scotland from Antwerp, 1563. See Mackenzie, Vol. III; p. 156. Another translation by A. P. about 1559. See p. 1600. 8°.

1563. "The Buke of Fourscore three Questions, touching Doctrine, Ordour, and Maneris proponit to the Prechoris of the Protestantis in Scotland, by the Catholicks of the inferiour Order of the Clergy and Laitmen, thair cruellie afflictit and dispersit, be Persuasioun of the saids intrusit Prechiouris, set furth be Ninian Winzet, a Catholick Priest, at the desayre of the faythful afflictit Breithsen, and deliuerit to John Knox, the xxth of Februar or yairby in the Zere of the blessit Birth of our Saviour 1563. Antwerp, ex officina Ægidii Diest MDLXIII, XIII Octob. cum gratia & priuilegio." Mackenzie, Vol. III; p. 148, and 156. 8°.

1564. "A Dialogue both Pleasaunte and Pietifull," &c. See p. 838 and 839.

1564. "A pleasant dialogue betwene the Cap and the Head." Sixteens.

1564. "An Ansvvere to Maister Ivelles chalenge, by Doctor Harding. 1 Cor. 14. An à vobis verbum Dei processit? aut in vos solos peruenit. Hath the word of God proceded from you? Or hath it come among you only?" Device: Over an ancient city is a winged heart, and over that an open book, encompassed with this motto, Cor rectum inquirit scientiam; the whole in a rich compartment. "Imprinted in Louaine by Iohn Bogard at the Golden Bible, with priuilege. Anno 1564." On the back is Bogard's privilege for the sole printing for 6 years from 15 Sept. 1563: "Datum Bruxellæ." Prefixed are, An epistle "To the reader.—Louaine: 14. of June: 1563. Thom. Harding.---A collection of certaine places out of Maister Iuelles bookes, &c.---The wordes of M. Juelles challenge.---The preface to M. Iuell."---A table of ecclesiastical writers "within syx hundred yeres after Christ:—for the most part, such as be in this treatise alledged." The Answer beginning on fol. 9, is concluded on fol. 193. Then, A table. W.H. Quarto.

1564. "A confutation of a sermon, pronoũced by M. Iuell, at Paules crosse, the second Sondaie before Easter (which Catholikes doe call Passion Sondaie) Anno Dñi. M.D.LX. By John Rastell M. of Art, and student in diuinitie. Miror quòd tam citò &c. I maruell that yow be so sone carried awaie from hym which called yow vnto the grace of Christ, in to an other Gospel. Τὰ ἀρχαῖα κρατείτω. Mores antiqui obtineant. Lett old customes preuaile. Imprinted at Antwerp by Ægidius Diest. 21 Nouemb. 1564. Cum priuilegio," &c. On the back is Rastell's privilege for the sole printing it by such printers as he pleases, forbidding all others; "Datum Bruxellæ, xvij. Nouemb. 1564." The preface to the Reader is dated "At Louaine. Nouemb. 20." The treatise contains 159 leaves, and then concludes with "A challenge[a] agaynst the Protestantes;" after which is "A table of the cheefest matters." W.H. Octavo.

"A

[a] This was reprinted separate the following year.

"A treatyse of the crosse gathered out of the Scriptures, Councells, and auncient Fathers of the primitiue church, by Iohn Martiall Bachiler of Lavve and studient in Diuinitie. Multi ambulant &c. For many vvalke of whome" &c. (Phil. 3; 18.) Device: a husbandman sowing seed. Motto: Spes alit agricolas. "Imprinted at Antwerp by Iohn Latius at the signe of the Rape, with Priuilage. Anno 1564." Dedicated to queen Elizabeth, and with a preface prefixed, contains 169 pages, and then a table. Lambeth Library. Octavo. 1564.

Monas Hieroglyphica, dedicated to the Emperor Maximilian, by John Dee. 1564.

"The Copy of a challenge taken out of the confutation of Mr. Jewells Sermon. Antw. 1565." Ath. Oxon. I; 306. Octavo. 1565.

"The apologie of Fridericus Staphilus counseller to the late emperour Ferdinandus, &c. Intreating Of the true and right vnderstanding of holy Scripture. Of the translation of the Bible in to the vulgar tongue. Of disagreement in Doctrine amonge protestants. Translated out of Latin into English by Thomas Stapleton, Student in Diuinitie. Also a discourse of the Translatour vppon the doctrine of the protestants vvhich he trieth by the three first founders and fathers thereof, Martin Luther, Philip Melanchthon, and especially Iohn Caluin. Matth. 24. Videte ne quis vos seducat. Take hede that no man deceaue you. Matth. 7. Ex fructibus eorum cognoscetis eos. Ye shal knovve them by their frutes." The Sower, or husbandman, sowing seed; with this motto, Spes alit agricolas. "Imprinted at Antwerp by Iohn Latius, at the signe of the Rape, with priuilege, Anno 1565." On the back is a copy of Stapleton's privilege for the sole printing and publishing this book: "Datum Bruxellæ, 17. Nouembris, Anno 1564.—The preface of the translatour.—At Louvain the 12. of Nouember, 1564.---To the right reuerend father in God, prince and lorde, his singular good lorde, the Lorde Martin Bishop of Eystat,—Writen on Christmas eue, in the ende of the yeare, 1560. To your most reuerend highnes the most affectioned Fridericus Staphylus Counseller to the Emperoures Maiestie, &c.---To the Christian Reader." These prefixes occupy more than 31 leaves; the treatise begins on the back of folio 32, the leaves being numbered from the title-page; the whole 254 leaves, and a table of contents. W.H. Quarto. 1565.

"An ansvvere to Maister Juelles challenge, by Doctor Harding, augmented vvith certaine quotations and additions." &c. as p. 1608. Device: An angel standing, with an open book in his right hand and a sithe in his left, between the word SCAVTA MINI. "Jmprinted in Antwerpe, At the golden Angel by William Sylvius the Kinges Maiesties printer. M.D.LXV. VVith priuilege. On the back is the copy of a privilege to Dr. Harding to employ such allowed printer as he pleases in these hereditary dominions, "Darum Bruxellæ, 15 Januarij, Anno 1563." On the next leaf, "The correctour to the reader.—About halfe a yere past coming into M. D. Hardinges chambre, (which to his frēdes is neuer shutte) 1565.

ſhutte) and there findinge a booke newly quoted, and with ſome annotations augmēted with his owne hande: vpon affiance of his frendſhip, I was bold in his abſence, as for a time to take it with me, and according to the ſame to note myne owne booke, not mynding as then euer to ſet it in print, but to vſe it to my priuate inſtruction. And the ſame now hath ſerued the printer for his copie.—If faultes be founde in the print, they are myne and the printers: the authour therewith is not touched. Who doubtles had he taken the ouerſight of it himſelfe, would haue done better:" &c. The whole G g, in eights. W.H. Octavo.

1565. "A Replie againſt an anſwer (falſlie intitled) in the Defence of the Truth, made by John Raſtell, M. of Art, and ſtudent in diuinitie. 3 Eſd. 3. Forte eſt vinum &c. Wyne ys ſtrong &c. Imprinted at Antwerp by Ægidius Dieſt, x Martij, Anno M.D.LXV. Cum privilegio." An epiſtle "To the reader." Beſides, 206 leaves. Lambeth Library. Octavo.

1565. "An epiſtle of the Reuerend father in God Hieronimus Oſorius Biſhop of Arcoburge in Portugale, to the moſt excellent Princeſſe Elizabeth—Quene of England, Fraunce and Ireland. &c. Tranſlated oute of Latten into Engliſhe by Richard Shacklock M. of Arte and ſtudent of the Ciuill Lavves in Louaine." The Sower, as p. 1609. "Imprinted at Antwerp by Iohn Latius Anno 1565." On the back are a ſeven-lined ſtanzas by "The Tranſlatour." Then, an epiſtle "To the reader.—Farewell from Antwerp. xiiij. of March. R. S." The running-title, "A Pearle for a Prynce." At the end is a threatening[a] epiſtle "To M. Doctor Haddon."—From Antwerp the 27. of Marche." K, in eights. W.H. Sixteens.

1565. "A Defenſe and Declaration of the Catholike Churchies doctrine touching Purgatory, and prayers for the ſoules departed, by William Allen Maſter of Arte and ſtudent in Diuinitye. Mortuo ne prohibeas gratiam. Eccleſ. 7. Hinder not the departed of grace and fauoure." The Sower, as p. 1609. "Imprinted at Antwerp by Iohn Latius, with Priuilege. Anno 1565." On the back is the copy of a privilege, or licenſe, to Wm. Allen to employ ſuch allowed printers as he pleaſes, &c. "Datum Bruxellæ, 14 Martij Anno 1564. Stilo Brabantiæ." On the next leaf begins an apologetical epiſtle "To the Reader.—At Antwerp

[a] "—If you wil not ceaſſe, I aſſure you, you ſhall ſtyrre vp ſo many aduerſaries agaynſt you, that whereas you be M. of the Requeſt, and for that cauſe, ought allway to be at leaſure to heare petitions, when ſuetors come to you, you ſhal be ſayne to make them anſwer: I pray you, troble me not, I muſt go anſwer Oſorius of Portugall, I muſt anſwer Hoſius in Polonia, ſuche a man in ſuch a countrie, &c. And if you wyll not make them ſuche an anſwer, yet your brayne ſhall be buſied with ſo many bookes and letters, from ſo many places of youre betters, that your mynde ſhall not be vpon youre charge. So that either you ſhall be put out of youre offyce for negligence, or elles ſent from the Court to Cambridge for pitye, that you may haue more leaſure to anſwer youre aduerſaries, Whiche thing I think you wolde not wyllingly choſe:" &c.

Antwerp the Second of May, 1565."---A table of faults corrected. The 8th leaf has only a small vignette. On folio 9 begins "The preface, wher in be noted two fortes of Hæretikes: thone pretending vertue thother openly professing vice. And that our tyme is more troubled by this second sort." &c. The defense of purgatory begins on the back of folio 21, and concludes on folio 122. "The seconde booke intreating of the prayers, and other ordinary reliefe, that the Church of Christ procureth for the soules departed," begins, with a preface, on folio 123, and ends on folio 289.---"The argumentes of euery Chapiter." &c. O o 7, in eights. W.H. Octavo.

"A confutation of a Booke intituled An Apologie of the Church of England, by Thomas Harding Doctor of Diuinitie. 2 Timoth. 3. Quemadmodum Iannes & Mambres &c. As Iannes and Mambres withstode Moyses, euen so do these felowes also withstand the truth, men of corrupt mynde, and castawayes as concerning the faith; but they shall not preuaile any further: for their folishnes shall be open vnto all men, as theirs was." The Sower, as p. 1609. "Imprinted at Antwerpe, by Ihon Laet, with Priuilege. 1565." On the back; the Queen's arms as to the next article. Dedicated "To the right mighty and excellent princesse Elizabeth—Quene of England, &c. Defender of the faith.—Your maiesties faithfull subiect and bounden oratour Thomas Harding.---To the reader."---Copy of the priuilege, "Datum Bruxellæ, 12 Aprilis, Anno 1565." Besides, 351 leaves, a table of the special matters, and one of faults escaped in printing. The whole neatly printed on white letter. W H. Quarto. 1565.

"The History of the Church of Englande. Compiled by Venerable Bede, Englishman. Translated out of Latin into English by Thomas Stapleton Student in Diuinitie. You being sometimes straungers and enemies in vnderstanding &c. He hath now reconciled in the body of his fleshe through death &c. If yet ye continuew grounded and stedfast in the Faith, &c. Colos. 1." The Sower, as p. 1609. Imprinted at Antwerp by John Laet, at the signe of the Rape: with Priuilege. Anno 1565." Dedicated by T. Stapleton "To the right excellent and most gratiouse princesse, Elizabeth,—Quene of England, &c. Defendour of the Faith." Whose arms crowned and gartered, with "God saue the Quene" under them, are on the back of the title-page.---"Differences betwene the primitive Faithe of England continevved almost these thousand yeres, and the late pretensed faith of protestants: gathered out of *this* History"---The privilege or diploma, to Stapleton, for 4 years. "Bruxellæ, 20 and 23 Iunij, 1565.—The preface* to the reader.—At Louvain. The 12. of June, 1565.—The life of S. Bede: written by Trithemius.---To the right honorable king Ceolulphe, Beda the seruaunt of Christe and Priest." The history begins 1565.

* Signature A. and the numbering the leaves, begin on the third leaf of this preface.

begins on folio 13, and ends on fol. 191. Then, "A table of the special matters.---Faultes escaped in Printing." CCC, in fours. W.H. Quarto.

1565. "A most excellent treatise of the begynnyng of heresyes in oure tyme, compyled by the Reuerend Father in God Stanislaus Hosius Byshop of Wormes in Prussia. To the moste renomed Prynce Lorde Sigismund myghtie Kyng of Poole, greate Duke of Luten and Russia, Lorde and Heyre of all Prussia, Masouia, Samogitia &c. Translated out of Laten in to Englyshe by Richard Shacklock M. of Arte, and student of the Ciuil lawes, and intituled by hym: The hatchet of heresies. Haereses ad suam originem reuocasse est refutasse.

Of hereses to shewe the spryng,
Is them unto an end to bryng.

Imprinted at Antwerp by Æg. Diest, Anno 1565, the 10 of August. Cum Privilegio." On the front of the next leaf is a cut of the tree of heresies, having at the root thereof, Raylings; on the trunk, Rebellion; on the branches, Blodshed; on the leaves, Lyes; and on the fruit, Atheisme. On the dexter side is Sathan issuing out of a pit in flames, with a whip in his left hand; over him, Insigne falsitatis, an escutcheon with a monkey holding a weather cock. On the other side, bishop Hosius, in his pontificals, holding up an ax in his right hand, as cutting down the tree already notched, and a book, De origine heresium, in his left; over him Insigne veritatis, an escutcheon with a crucifix. On the back of the title-page begin some explanatory verses by the translator, which are concluded on the back of the cut. It is dedicated "To the moste excellent and gratious Prynceсse Elyzabeth by the grace of God Quene of England, &c.—Youre graces faythfull and obedient subiect Richard Shacklock.—The translatoure vpon the holy wryter Hosius:" in 3 seven-lined stanzas.---"To the moste redoubted and moste Christian Prince, his renomed Lorde, Lorde Sigismund, by the grace of God Kyng of Poole, great Duke of Luten, Lorde and Heyre of Russia, Prussia, Masouia, Samogitia, &c. his gratiouse Lorde: Stanislaus Hosius Byshop of Wormes, proffereth his lowly seruice.—Oute of my castell of Heilsbergk, in the Ides of Octobre. M.DLVII.—Michael Scrinius Dantiscanus Prussiæ, Lectori:" a Tetrastichon.---"The Translatoure his paraphrase vpon those verses." The treatise is on 95 leaves. At the end, "Oratio R. Shacklocki pro regina, regno, et toto Christianismo:" in hexameters.---"A Table of the cheyfeist matters conteyned in this Booke.---Faultes escaped in some copies.---An admonition to the fault fynder." W.H. Sixteens.

1565. "A fortresse of the faith First planted amonge vs englishmen, and continued hither to in the vniuersal Church of Christ. The faith of which time Protestants call Papistry. By Thomas Stapleton Student in Diuinitie. Melius erat illis &c. 2 Pet. 2. It were better for them neuer to knowe the waie of righteousnesse, then after the acknowledging thereof to reuoke backe from the holy commaundement deliuered vnto

vnto them." The Sower, as p. 1609. "Imprinted at Antwerpe, by Jhon Laet, with priuilege, 1565." On the back is Stapleton's privilege for 4 years: Bruxellæ, 20 & 23 Junij, Anno 1565. Then, "To the deceived protestants of England, Thomas Stapleton wisheth Grace, Humilitie, and Vnderstanding.—In Antwerpe, 17. Octobris, 1565." S s, in fours. W.H. Quarto.

"The supper of our Lord set foorth in six Bookes, according to the truth of the gospell, and the faith of the Catholike Churche. By Nicolas Saunder Doctor of Diuinitie. The contents of euery Booke are to be seen in the side following. MAN HV? What is this? The figure. Exo. 16. This is the bread which our Lord hath geuen you to eate. The Prophecie. Prouerb. 9. Come, eate my bread, and drink the wine which J haue mixed for you. The promise. Joan. 6. The bread which J wil geue, is my flesh for the life of the world. The performance. Mat. 26. Luce 22. Take, eate, this is my body which is geuen for you. The belefe of the Churche, Hilar. de Trin. 8. Both our Lord hath professed, and we beleue it to be fleshe in dede. The custome of heretikes. Tertul. de Resur. car. The contrarie part reyseth vp trouble by pretense of figures. Louanii. Anno Domini 1565." On the back are the heads of the six books. Then a dedication "To the Body and Blood of our Sauiour Jesus Christ vnder the foormes of bread and wyne all honour, praise and thanks be geuen for euer.---The preface to the Christian Reader," beginning on fol. 1. This preface bears relation chiefly to the first book; each of the six books having a separate preface, and table of contents. The 6th book ends on fol. 328, with this notice "Hereunto is added the seuenth booke, conteining a confutation of the fifth article of M. Iuels Reply against D. Harding, concerning the reall presence of Christes body in the supper of our Lorde." This 7th book, with a preface, and table of contents also, concludes on fol. 425; at the end, "Approbatio septimi libri.—Lauanij, 20.—Decemb. 1565." This is printed on black letter, though they printed so neat here and at Antwerp about this time on the white letters. W.H. Quarto. 1565.

"Responsio venerabilium sacerdotum, Henrici Joliffi et Roberti Jonson, sub protestatione facta, ad illos articulos Joannis Hoperi, episcopi Vigorniae nomen gerentis, in quibus à catholica fide dissentiebat. &c. Chr. Plantin." Octavo. 1565.

"The tragical history of two English lovers," &c. See p. 814. 1565.

"Certaine Tables set furth by the right Reverend father in God William Bushopp of Rurimunde in Ghelderland: where in is detected, and made manifest the doting, dangerous doctrine, and haynouse heresyes of the rashe rablement of heretikes: translated into Englishe by Lewys Euans, And by hym intituled, The betraing of the beastlines of heretykes. 1565.

"Reade and judge, let selfe will walke:
Peruse the booke, before thowe talke.

 "Imprinted

"Imprinted at Antwerpe by Ægidius Dieſt, with Priuilege, 1565." The dedication thus ſuperſcribed, "To Maiſter Grindal, Lewys Evans wiſheth perfecte healthe." No catch words, folios, or pages. E 5, in eights. At the end, under a ſmall cut of the crucifixion,

"Suche men as hate the Croſſe of Chriſt,
Are mates become of Antichriſt."

Sir John Fenn. Sixteens.

1565. "The Declaration of ſuche Scruples and ſtaies of Conſcience touchinge the Othe of Supremacy as M. Iohn Fakenham, by writinge did deliuer vnto the L. Biſhop of Wincheſter, with his Reſolutions made thereupon. Imprinted &c.* 1556." See p. 939.

1565. "Cooper's Chronicle" &c. as p. 465, &c. "Anno 1565, the firſt day of Auguſte." Without printer's name. W.H. Quarto.

1565. "Allegations againſt the ſurmiſed title of the Q. of Scots, and the fauourers of the ſame. Pr. 7 Dec. 1565." T. Baker's interleaved Maunſell, p. 91.; but ſee Stranguage's Hiſt. of Mary, Q. of Scotland, p. 15; Alſo; Biogr. Brit. Vol. I. p. 366. Quarto.

1565. Renatus Benedictus concerning compoſing diſcords in religion, tranſlated by Ninian Winzet. Paris, 1565. Octavo.

1565. "A brieue Admonition vnto the nowe made Miniſters of Englande: Wherein is ſhewed ſome of the fruite of this theyr late framed fayth: Made by Lewys Euans ſtudent in Louain, 24 Aug. 1565. Ioan. 8. Vos ex patre Diabolo eſtis, et deſideriis patris veſtri vultis obſequi. Ye are of your father the deuyll, and the luſtes of your father yowe wyll doe. Antverpiæ typis Æ. Dieſt, M.D.LXV." On the back is a cut of the 3 croſſes, the Virgin and St. John ſtanding between them. Underneath,

"The heretikes indeuoure is, by al the meanes they may,
The memorie of Chriſt his death, to doe and put away:
And therefore his Croſſe, and how he dyd dye
To take out of ſight, all ſhameles they trye.
But thowe that art Chriſtian, of Chriſt his death ſee
The paſſion here printed, as picture to thee. L. E."

B, in eights; neat Rom. Letter. W.H. Sixteens.

—— "A Dietary; being Ordinances for the Prices of Victuals and Diet of the Clergy: For the preventing of Dearths." See Strype's Life of Abp. Parker, p. 191.

1566. "The Bible In Englyſhe of The largeſt volume, that is to ſaye: the contentes of all the holye Scripture, booth of the oulde and newe Teſtament According to the tranſlation apoynted by the Queenes Maieſties Iniunctions to be read in all churches vvith in her Maieſties Realme. At Rouen. At the coſte and charges of Richard Carmarden. Cum Priuilegio. 1566." This title, in black and red, is within a compartment: at top, "יהוה. ΘΕΟΣ. DEVS. GOD." ſurrounded with rays

* A miſtake, probably for 1565, the preface being dated 12 Feb. 1565; beſides, the oath of ſupremacy was not appointed till the firſt year of Q. Elizabeth's reign. 1558-9.

rays of glory, from which issue 2 labels; one with " These are the lavves vvhich thou shalt sett before them. Exod. xxi. Chapter." On the other, " This is my dear son in vvhome I delyte, heare hym. Matth. the xvii Chapter." On the dexter side stands Moses, holding the two tables, with this label, " Thease are the ordynaunces and lavves vvhiche ye shall obserue and doe. Deutero. xii. Chapter." On the opposite is Jesus Christ, with this label, " Come vnto mee al ye that labour and ar ladē and I vvil eais you. Math. xi." Under them, on a tablet from side to side, " The Lavve vvas Geuē by Moses, But Grace and Truth Cam bi Iesus Christ. Iohn 1." At the bottom; the queen robed sitting on a throne of state; underneath, " Elizabetha Regina." On her right hand sits Faith with the queen's arms, crowned and gartered, beside her; on the other hand, Hope, with her anchor. The labels are printed in red. For the prefixes, &c. See Lewis's Hist. of the Eng. Translations of the Bible, p. 214, &c. But his copy seems to have had the same compartment for the title of the New Testament as for the second, third, and fourth books, or divisions, of the Old Testament and Apocrypha; whereas mine has the same compartment as the general title, above described, but the labels printed in black. W.H. Folio.

" The Fortresse of Fathers, ernestlie defending the puritie of Religion, and Ceremonies, by the trew expositiō of certaine places of Scripture: against such as wold bring in an Abuse of Idol stouff, and of thinges indifferent, and do appoinct th'austhority of Princes and Prelates larger then the trueth is. Translated out of Latine into English for there sakes that vnderstand no Latine by I. B. Actes, ix. Saul, Saul why persecutest thou me. &c. M.D.LXVI." On the back are " The Names of the Fathers in this fortresse.---The places whereon those fathers in this Fortresse do stand.---To all such as vnfainedly hate (in the zeale of a Godly loue) all monumentes, and remnauntes of Idolatrie. The translator wisheth perseueraunce into thend, through Christ Iesus.---Certaine conclusions" &c. Contains E 1, in eights, neat Rom. Letter. W.H. Sixteens. 1566.

" An ansvvere for the tyme, to the examination put in print, vvithout the authours name, pretending to mayntayne the apparrell prescribed against the declaration of the mynisters of London. Phillip. III. As many as be perfect, let vs be thus mynded, but if you be othervvise mynded, god shall reuele euen the same to you. M.D.LXVI." Contains 153 pages, and a folding table after p. 18; also, an additional paragraph to come in at p. 23, after these words " to render our reasones." The first 16 pages are not numbered. W.H. Sixteens. 1566.

" A brief discourse against the outwarde apparell and Ministring garmentes of the popishe church." My copy has " by Mr. Cowley in London," in MS. " psalme 31. I haue hated all those, that holde superstitious vanities. 1566." On the back, and the next page " The Booke to the Reader," in verse. The head title, " A declaration of the 1566.

 doings

doings of those Ministers of Gods worde and Sacraments, in the Citie of London, which haue refused to weare the outwarde apparell, and Ministring garmentes of the Popes church." The running title, "The vnfolding of the Popes Attyre." At the end, "A godly prayer, agreable to the tyme and occasion." C, in eights. W.H. Again 1578. 16°.

—— Bound up with my copy of the forgoing article are these anonymous epistles, without printer's name, place or date; yet as they all treat of the same subject, suppose they were printed abowt the same time. The first two have the following inscription on a separate leaf: "To my louynge brethren that is troublyd abowt the popishe aparrell, two short and comfortable Epistels. Be ye constant: for the Lorde shall fyght for yow, yours in Christ." In MS. "Gylbyes Epistell." C, in fours.—The next is with this head title, "To my faythfull Brethren now afflycted, & to all those that vnfaynedly loue the Lorde Jesus, the Lorde guyde vs with his holy spret, that we maye always serue hym bothe in body and mynde in all synceryte to oure lyues ende." Over this, in MS. "Wyttynghams Epistell." A, in eights.—The remaining one is introduced with a short address "To the Reader" only, without any other superscription; but has annexed "An answere to a question, that was mouyd, whi the godly men wold not weare a surples." This is without any MS. ascription. C, in fours. W.H. Sixteens.

1566. "The iudgement of the Reuerend Father Master Henry Bullinger/ Pastor of the church of Zurich, in certeyne matters of religion, beinge in controuersy in many countreys euen wher as the Gospel is taught. Matth. xviij. Wo be to the worlde because of offences, &c. Titus j. Take not hede to Jewish fables, &c. 1566." On the back, "The names of the matters that are intreated of, in this booke." They are extracts from his decades of sermons. C, in eights. W.H. See p. 697. Sixteens.

1566. "The mynd and exposition of that excellente learned man Martyn Bucer/ vppon these wordes of S. Matthew: Woo be to the worlde bycause of offences. Matth. xviij. Faythfully translated in to Englishe, by a faythfull brother, with certayne obiections* and answeres to the same. Mathew 15. Euery plante that my heauenly Father hathe not planted, shall be pluckt vp by the rotes. Printed at Embden. 1566." On the back is an address "To the godlie Reader." D, in fours. W.H. Sixteens.

1566. "A treatise intitled, Beware of M. Iewel. By Iohn Rastel Master of Arte and Student of Diuinitie. Math. 7. Beware of false Prophets, which come vnto you in the cotes of sheepe, but inwardlye are Rauening wolues. &c." Device: A tree, at the top of which is a nest of young birds gaping for food, an open hand extended from the clouds feeding them; other birds about on the wing; the printer's initials I. F. beside the trunk of the tree; about the whole, "Respicite volatilia coeli, et

* Concerning the apparel of priests and ministers.

et pullos corvorum." Beneath: "Antverpiae Ex officina Ioannis *Fouleri. M.D.LXVI." It is introduced with an epiſtle "To the Indifferent Reader. —At Antwerpe the 10 of May."---Raſtell's privilege, "Datum Bruxellæ, 8 Martij,—1565." Beſides: Fol. 130. W.H. Oclavo.

"The Parliament of Chryſte auouching and declaring the enacted and receaued trueth of the preſence of his bodie and bloode in the bleſſed Sacrament, and of other articles concerning the ſame, impugned in a wicked ſermon by M. Iuell. Collected and ſeth furth by Thomas Heſkyns Doctour of dyuinitie. Wherin the reader ſhall ſynde all the ſcriptures alleaged oute of the newe Teſtament, touching the B. Sacrament, and ſome of the olde Teſtament, plainlie and truely expounded by a nombre of holie learned Fathers and Doctours. Eccleſiaſt. viii. Non te pretereat narratio ſeniorum, &c. Go not from the doctryne of the elders, for they haue learned of their fathers. For of them thowe ſhalt learn vnderſtanding, ſo that thowe maiſt make anſwer in tyme of nede. Auguſt. Lib. 1. de moribus. cap. xxv. Audite doctos &c. Heare ye the learned men of the catholique churche with as quiet a mynde, and with ſoche deſyre as I haue heard yowe." Device: an angel as p. 1609. "Imprinted in Antvverpe, At the Angell by VVilliam Silvius prynter to the Kynges Maieſtie. M.D.LXVI. VVith Priuilege." On the back, "The names of ſoche authours alleaged in this booke of the Parliament of Chryſte, placed as yt were in two houſes, that ys to wite, ſoche as were before a thouſand years or verie neer, in the higher houſe, ſoche as were ſince, in the lower houſe. 1566.

"Ieſus Chriſtus.

Apoſt. & Euangeliſt.	Apoſt. & Euangeliſt.
Ioannes.	Mattheus.
Marcus.	Lucas.
Paulus.	Andreas.
Latines of the higher houſe.	Grecians of the higher houſe.
Clemens.	Martialis.
Alexander.	Abdias.
Sixtus, &c.	Anacletus. &c
Latines of the lower houſe.	Grecians of the lower houſe.
Beda.	Damaſcenus.
Haymo.	Theophilactus.
Remigius. &c.	Oecumenius." &c.

On

* An Engliſhman, who dwelt at Antwerp, Lovain, and other places abroad; "and was ſo learned that he might paſ. for another Henry Stephens, being very well ſkilled in the Latin and Greek tongues; a good poet, orator, and divine. He wrote an abridgement of Aquinas's ſums, and tranſlated Oſorius into Engliſh; but being a zealous papiſt, he could not brook the reformation of religion made in England by king Edward VI. and queen Elizabeth, ſo conveyed himſelf and his preſs over to Antwerp, where he proved very ſerviceable to the church of Rome, in putting out their pamphlets, which they *cauſed to be* printed and ſent over into England. He died at Namur, *anno* 1579, and lies buried in the church there." See Magna Britannia, vol. IV; p. 751.

On the next leaf is a very neat wood-cut, the size of the page, with this title over it, "The Parliament of Christe vpon the matter of the B. Sacrament." The cut consists of nine parts or divisions; that in the middle is a parallelogram, 5 inches ½ by 3½, at the top of which is Jesus Christ sitting on a rainbow, with outstretched arms, two angels bearing a pyx with the Sacrament before him; in the upper corners are the hieroglyphics of the 4 evangelists; about the pyx appear in 2 circles the heads of the fathers of the higher and lower house, variously dignified, some with triads, mitres, &c. others bareheaded. The rest of the divisions are in the following forms, viz. Three on each side in circles, one at top and another at bottom in ovals; these are all numbered, beginning at the lower part of the dexter side, proceeding to the top, and down on the other, each with a tablet announcing its purport, &c. 1. The Israelites gathering manna: On the tablet, "Figured. Exod. 16." 2. The prophet Malachi: "Prophecied. Malach. 1." 3. Christ with his disciples: "Promised. Joan. 6." 4. The last supper: "Instituted. Math. 26." 5. A priest at the altar, elevating the host: "Practized. Jac. in Miss." 6. A priest putting the pyx into the tabernacle: "Reserued. Clem. epist. 2." 7. A priest administring the wafer: "Continued. 1 Cor. 11." 8. One praying on his knees; "Adored." On the back is the author's privilege: "Datum Bruxellæ, 7 Julij, 1565." Then, "To M. Io. Iuell Thomas Heskins wisheth grace and restitucion of faith.—The prologue to the gentle reader." Besides: cccc leaves. Neat Roman Letter. W.H. Folio.

1566. "The supper of the Lord" &c. as in 1565. "With a confutation of such false doctrine as the Apologie of the Churche of England, M. Nowel's chalenge, or M. Iuels Replie haue vttered, touching the reall presence of Christe in the Sacrament. MAN HV? &c. Louanii—1566." On the back are Mr. Saunder's privilege, or permission to have the book printed, "Datum Bruxellæ, 22 Decembris, Anno Christi 1565;" and, "Approbatio sex priorum librorum.—Louanij, 7 August.—1565." Dedicated as before. Besides: 425 leaves. W.H. Quarto.

1566. "A returne of vntruthes vpon M. Iewels Replie." By Tho. Stapleton. Ath. Oxon. Vol. 1; c.

1566. "AN ORATION Against the Vnlawfull Insurrections of the Protestantes of our time, vnder pretence to Refourme Religion. Made and pronounced in Latin, in the Schole of Artes at Louaine, the xiiij. of December. Anno 1565. By Peter Frarin of Andwerp, M. of Arte, and Bacheler of both lawes. And now translated into English, with the aduise of the Author." Fouler's device as p. 1616. Antverpiæ, Ex officina Ioannis Fouleri. M.D.LXVI." On the next leaf are sentences from the Ep. of Jude, and Prov. 16. in Latin and English. On the back, "The Extracte of the Priuilege" to P. Frarin. "Bruxellæ, 14 Martij,—1565. stilo Brabantiæ." Then, "The Translatour to the Gentle Reader.—From Andwerp, Maij 9, Anno 1566. Jhon Fouler." The oration is concluded, with a certificate of approbation, on K 3; then

then follows "The table of this booke set out not by order of Alphabet or nūbre, but by expresse figure, to the eye & sight of the Christian Reader, and of him also ẏ cannot reade." In verse, with many cuts. The whole contains L, in eights. W.H. Octavo.

"A Reioindre to Mr. Jewels Replie. By perusing wherof the discrete and diligent Reader may easily see, the Answer to parte of his insolent Chalenge iustified, and his Obiections against the Masse, whereat the Priest sometime receiueth the holy Mysteries without present companie to receiue with him, for that cause by Luthers Schoole called Priuate Masse, clearely confuted. By Thomas Harding Doctor of Diuinitie. Prouerb. 25. Nubes & ventus, &c. Like as is a cloude, and winde, and no raine folowing: so is a man, that craketh much, and performeth not his promises." Device: A tree, as p. 1616. Beneath: "Antverpiae. Ex officina Ioannis Fouleri. Anno M.D.LXVI." On the back is the author's privilege, "Datum Bruxellæ, 20 Maij, 1566." Then, "To the reader.—To M. Iewel." Which concludes thus, "At Antwerpe Jn the ende of August, 1566. Jn which time your brethren of this low Countrie, professours of that ye cal the Gospel, haue geuen euident testimonie to the worlde, with what Spirite they be lead by their spoiling and robbing Churches and religious houses, by destroying of Libraries, by threatning to fyer the places where they be resisted, and with other wicked outrages: through occasion whereof this Treatise could not be printed neither so spedily, nor so exactly as in quiet times it might haue ben. Thomas Harding.—Faultes escaped in printing.—Other faultes that may be espied should haue ben corrected, had not the troubles here begonne forced vs to make an end. Antuerpiæ. vlt. Augusti, 1566." Besides: 315 leaves, and "A table of the chiefe matters." W.H. Quarto. 1566.

"The third book, declaring by examples out of ancient councels, fathers, and later writers, that it is time to beware of M. Jewel. By John Rastel, master of art and student in diuinitie. Antwerpiae, ex officina Joannis Fouleri." Octavo. 1566.

"A replie to M. Calfhills blasphemous answer, made against the treatise of the crosse, by John Martiall, bachiler of lawe, and studient in diuinitie. Imprinted at Louaine, by John Bogard, at the golden Bible, with the kinges maiesties priuilege." It begins with "A request to maister Grindal, and other superintendents of the newe church of England." 227 leaves. See p. 925. Quarto. 1566.

A pleasant dialogue between a Soldier of Berwick and an English chaplain. See it in 1581. Octavo. 1566.

"John Knoxe his sermon on Esay 26, 13—21. preached in the publique audience of the church of Edenborough, 19 Aug. 1565: for which he was inhibited preaching for a season. Printed 1566." 8°. 1566.

Metromachia, sive Ludus geometricus, &c. Burton's Leicestershire, p. 182. See p. 1070. Quarto. 1566.

"A President for a Prince, wherin is to be seene by the testimonie of 1566.

of auncient writers, the dutie of the Kings, Princes and gouernours. Collected by Anthony Rush Doctor in diuinitie. Printed 1566." 4°.

1566. "The excellent history of Theseus and Ariadne." Hist. of Eng. Poetry, Vol. III; p. 420. Octavo.

1566. "Testimonies for the real presence of Christes body and blood in the blessed Sacramēt of the aultar set foorth at large, & faithfully translated, out of six auncient fathers which lyued far within the first six hundred yeres, together with certain notes, declaring the force of those testimonies, and detecting sometimes the Sacramentaries false dealing, as more plainly appeareth in the other syde of this leaf. By Robert Pointz student in Diuinitie. Athanas. ad Epist. contra Hæret. Si veltis filij patrum esse, *&c.* If ye will be children of the Fathers, you must not dissent from those thinges which the Fathers themselues haue written. Lovanii, Apud Ioannem Foulerum. M.D.LXVI." On the back are "The summes of the (xij) Chapters." Then an epistle "To the Reader:—Robert Pointz.---Faultes escaped in printing."—Extracts from Basil the great, and Augustin.---Privilege to the author: "Datum Bruxellæ, 20 Augusti. Anno 1565." Besides: 200 leaves. W.H. Sixteens.

Strype's Life of Archbishop Parker, p. 221, &c.

Ordinances decreed by the court of star-chamber, and high commission court, for the reformation of divers disorders in printing and uttering of books, dated from the Star-chamber, June 29, 1566.

I. That no person should print, or cause to be printed, or bring, or procure to be brought, into the realm printed, any book against the force and meaning of any ordinance, prohibition, or commandment, contained or to be contained, in any the statutes or laws of this realm, or in any injunctions, letters, patents, or ordinances, past, or set forth, or to be past or set forth by the queen's grant, commission, or authority.

II. That whosoever should offend against the said ordinances, should forfeit all such books and copies; and from thenceforth should never use, or exercise, or take benefit by any using or exercising the feat of printing; and to sustain three months imprisonment without bail or mainprize.

III. That no person should sell, or put to sale, bind, stitch, or sow, any such books, or copies, upon pain to forfeit all such books and copies, and for every book 20 s.

IV. That all books so forfeited, should be brought into stationers'-hall, and there one moiety of the money forfeited to be reserved to the queen's use, and the other moiety to be delivered to him, or them, that should first seize the books, or make complaint thereof to the warden of the said company; and all the books so to be forfeited, to be destroyed, or made waste paper.

V. That it should be lawful for the wardens of the company for the time being, or any two of the said company thereto deputed by the said wardens, as well in any ports, or other suspected places, to open and view

view all packs, dryfats, maunds, and other things, wherein books or paper shall be contained, brought into this realm, and make search in all workhouses, shops, warehouses, and other places of printers, booksellers, and such as bring books into the realm to be sold, or where they have reasonable cause of suspicion. And all books to be found against the said ordinances, to seize and carry to the hall, to the uses abovesaid; and to bring the persons offending before the queen's commissioners in causes ecclesiastical.

VI. Every stationer, printer, bookseller, merchant, using any trade of book-printing, binding, selling, or bringing into the realm, should before the commissioners, or before any other persons, thereto to be assigned by the queen's privy council, enter into several recognizances of reasonable sums of money to her majesty, with sureties, or without, as to the commissioners should be thought expedient, that he should truly observe all the said ordinances, well and truly yield and pay all such forfeitures, and in no point be resisting, but in all things aiding to the said wardens, and their deputies, for the true execution of the premises.

And this was thus subscribed; "Upon the consideration before expressed, and upon the motion of the commissioners, we of the privy council have agreed this to be observed, and kept, upon the pains therein contained. At the Star-chamber, the 29 June, *anno* 1566, and the eighth year of the queen's majesties reign.

N. Bacon, C. S.	Winchester,	R. Leicester,	E. Clynton.
E. Rogers,	F. Knollys,	Ambr. Cave,	W. Cecyl."

To which the commissioners for ecclesiastical causes also underwrit. "We underwrit think these ordinances meet and necessary to be decreed, and observed:

Matthue Cantuar.	Ambr Cave.	Tho. Yale.
Edm. London.	David Lewis.	Rob. Weston.
		T. Huycke."

A printed copy is among the Proclamations of the Society of Antiquaries, London. Vol. VII; p. 32. Folio.

"Dialogi sex, contra summi pontificatûs, monasticæ vitæ, sanctorum, sacrarum imaginum, oppugnatores & pseudo-Martyres." By 1566.
Nicholas Harpsfield, but published under the name of Alan Cope, lest danger should befal the author, being in prison. Yet lest truth should be concealed, and friend defraud friend of his due praise, he caused these capital letters to be set at the end of his book. "A. H. L. N. H. E. V. E. A. C." Hereby mystically meaning, Auctor Hujus Libri Nicholaus Harpesfeldus. Edidit Verò Eum Alanus Copus." See Fuller's Ch. Hist. B. 12, p. 143. "Antw. 1566." Ath. Oxon. I; 214. Quarto.

"Of the Expresse Worde of God. A Shorte but a most Excellent 1567.
Treatyse and very necessary for this tyme. Written in Latin, by the right Reuerend Lerned, and vertuous Father Stanislaus Hosius, Bishop or Warmis, Cardinal of the Holy Apostolyke See of Rome, and one of

 the

the Presidents in the late General Councel holden at Trent. Newly translated into English. Beholde I come to these Prophetes &c. Jerem. 23. Hilarius, lib. 2. de Trinitate. Of vnderstanding not of Scripture ryseth hæresy: And the meaning not the vvorde is blamed. Imprinted in Louayne by John Bogard at—the golden Bible: with Priuilege. An. 1567." Contains fo. 113, and a table. Lambeth Libr. Octavo.

1567. "A Treatise Of the Images of Christ, and of his Saints: and that it is vnlawfull to breake them, and lauful to honour them. With a Confutation of such false doctrine as M. Iewel hath vttered in his Replie, concerning that matter. Made by Nicolas Sander, Doctour of Diuinitie. Ecclesiastici 45. Τὸ μνημόσυνον &c. Memoria Dilecti &c. ☞ The Remembrance &c. Lovanii, Apud Ioannem Foulerum. 1567." Prefixed: "The preface, conteining a Brief Declaration, which is the true Churche of Christ." 192 pages, and a table. Lambeth Library. Octavo.

1567. "A Briefe Shew of false VVares packt together in the named Apology of the Church of England by John Rastell M. of Art, and student of Diuinitie.—He that leaneth to lies feedeth the winds: and the self same foloweth the fleying of birdes." Fouler's device as p. 1616. Lovanii, apud Joannem Foulerum. 1567." An Imprimatur on the back of the title-page. An epistle "To the Reader," prefixed. Contains fo. 140. Lambeth Libr. Octavo.

1567. "The Rocke of the Churche, Wherein the Primacy of S. Peter and of his Successours the Bishops of Rome is proued out of Gods Worde. By Nicolas Sander D. of diuinity. The eternal Rock of the vniuersal Church. Christ was the rock, an other foundatiō no man is hable is (to) put. 1 Cor. 3 and 10. The temporal Rock of the militant Church. Thou art Peter, and vppon this Rocke I wil build my Church. Math. 10. The continuance of the temporal Rocke. In the Church of Rome the primacy of the Apostolike chaire hath alwaies florished. August. in Epist. 162. Recken euen from the very seate of Peter: and in that rew of Fathers, consyder, who succeded the other. That is the rock which the proud gates of hel doe not ouercome. In Psal. cōt. part. Don. Tom. 7. Lovanii, apud Joannem Foulerum. Anno D. 1567." On the back is the author's privilege: "Datum Bruxellis, 27 Febr. 1566." Addressed "To the right Worshipfull M. Doctor Parker bearing the name of the Archbisshop of Canterbury, and to al other protestants in the realme of England, Nicolas Sander wissheth perfect faith and charity in our Lord, declaring in this Preface, that the Catholiks (whom they cal Papists) doe passe the Protestants in al manner of Signes or Marks of Christes true Church." This occupies 59 pages. ---The heads of "The (18) Chapiters.---The Rocke of the Church," on 566 pages. Then, "A brief some of the chief points of this treatise.---Faultes escaped in the printing." On the back of which is Fouler's device, as p. 1616. W.H. Sixteens.

1567. "A treatise made in defence of the lauful power and authoritie of Priesthod to remitte sinnes: Of the peoples ductie for confession of their

their ſinnes to Gods miniſters: And of the Churches meaning concerning Indulgences, commonlie called Pope's Pardõs. By William Allen M. of Arte, and Student in Diuinitie. Iude 1. Væ illis qui perierunt in contradictione Core. Wo be vnto them that periſhed in the diſobedience and contradictiõ of Cores. Lovanii, Apud Ioannem Foulerum, Anno D. 1567." An addreſs "To the Chriſtian Reader.---Faultes in the printing."---The privilege, "Datum Bruxellis, 26 April, 1567. ---The Preface, conteininge a iuſte complaint of the diſobediẽce that now is towardes the ſpiritual gouernours, and of the pitiful lacke of ſuche neceſſarie reliefe of our ſoules, as by them wee ſhoulde haue, with the argument of the treatiſe folowinge." Beſides: 412 pages, and an index to the whole. Neat white letter. W.H. Sixteens.

"A Counterblaſt to M. Hornes vayne blaſte againſt M. Fekenham. Wherein is ſet forthe: A ful reply to M. Hornes Anſwer, and to euery part thereof made, againſt the Declaration of my L. Abbat of Weſtminſter, M. Fekenham, touching the Othe of Supremacy. By peruſing vvhereof ſhall appeare, beſides the holy Scriptures, as it vvere a Chronicle of the Continual Practiſe of Chriſtes Churche in al ages and Countries, frõ the time of Conſtantin the Great, vntil our daies: Prouing the Popes and Biſhops Supremacy in Eccleſiaſtical cauſes: and Diſprouing the Princes Supremacy in the ſame cauſes. By Thomas Stapleton Student in Diuinitie. Athanaſ. in Epiſt. ad ſolita. vitã agentes. p. 459. When was it heard from the creation of the worlde, that the Iudgement of the Churche ſhould take his authoritie from the Emperour? Or when was that taken for any iudgement? Ambr. lib. 5. epiſt. 32. In good ſooth, if we call to minde either the whole courſe of Holy Scripture, or the practiſe of the auncient times paſſed, who is it that can deny, but that in matter of faith, in matter, I ſaie of faith, Biſhops are wont to iudge ouer Chriſtian Emperours, not emperours ouer Biſhops. Lovanii, Apud Joannem Foulerum. An. 1567. Cum Priuil." A copy of which is on the back: "Datum Bruxellis, 27 Maij,—1567." Prefaced "To M. Robert Horne, Thomas Stapleton wiſheth Grace from God, and true repentance of al Hereſies.—Vale et Reſipice. Thomas Stapleton. Τὸ ἀληθὲς ὡς ἀληθῶς ἀληθές.—The Preface to the reader.—In Louaine, the laſt of September, An. 1567.---An Aduertiſement to the Lerned Reader.—Vale. Ὠφέλιμα προθύμως τὰ δίκαια." Beſides: 542 leaves, an index, errata, and Approbation. Herein Mr. Horne's book is wholly quoted by its diviſions, as alſo part of M. Fekenham's. Neatly printed on white letter. W.H. Quarto. 1567.

"A (*ſecond*) Reioindre to M. Iewels Replie againſt the Sacrifice of the Maſſe. In which the doctrine of the Anſwere to the xvij. Article of his Chalenge is defended, and further proued, and al that his Replie conteineth againſt the Sacrifice, is clearely confuted, and diſproued. By Thomas Harding Doctor of Diuinitie. Luke 22. Doo this in my Remembrance. Irenæus lib. 4. Cap. 32. Chriſte (at his laſt Supper) 1567.

 taught

taught the new Oblation of the new Testament, which the Churche, receiuing it of the Apostles, offereth vp vnto God through the whole worlde." Fouler's device, as p. 1616. Lovanii. Apud Ioannem Foulerum, Anno 1567. Cum Privilegio." Which privilege to the author is on the back, " Datum Bruxellis, Callend. Septemb. Anno 1567." Then, an epistle " To M. Jewell.---The Preface to the Catholike Reader touching the Sacrifice of the Masse." 42 leaves told over; very incorrectly numbered. The Reioindre on 262 leaves, and has an alphabetical table, or index, at the end. Neat white letter. W.H. 4°.

1567. " A Breffe Instruction and manner howe to kepe Merchantes Bokes of accomptes. After the order of Debitor and Creditor, as well for proper accompts, partable, Factory and other &c. Very needfull to be knowen, and vsed of all men, in the feattes of merchandize. Now of late newly set forthe, and practisyd, by Johan Weddington Cyttizen of London. M.D.LXVII. The treweth sekeith corners. Prentyd in Andwarpe, by Peter van Keerberghen dwelling by owre lady Charche, at the signe of the golden Sonne. Cum gratia & Privilegio." Folio.

—— " A Discourse of the late Troubles that happened in Scotland, between the noble and mighty Princess Mary, by the Grace of God Queen of Scotland, and her Husband Henry the King, with others, Earles, Lords, Barons, Gentlemen, Free-holders, Merchants and Craftsmen. By Patrick Lord Ruthven. Printed at London." Mackenzie, Vol. III; p. 69—75.

1568. " A Detection of sundrie foule errours, lies, sclaunders, corruptions, and other false dealinges, touching Doctrine, and other matters, vttered and practized by M. Iewel, in a Booke lately by him set foorth entituled, A Defence of the Apologie. &c. By Thomas Harding Doctor of Diuinitie. Psalm. 4. Filij hominum, vsquequo graui corde? vt quid diligitis vanitatem, et quæritis Mendacium? O ye sonnes of menne, how long wil ye be dul harted? what meane ye thus to be in loue with Vanitie, and to seeke after Lying?" Fouler's device as p. 1616. " Lovanii, Apud Ioannem Foulerum, Anno 1568. Cum Privilegio." Which privilege to the author is on the back, " Datum Bruxellis, 24 Maii, Anno 1568." Then, " The preface to the reader." Besides: 417 leaves, and an index. Neat white letter. W.H. Again 1569. 4°.

1568. " A learned and very eloquent Treatie, written in Latin by the famouse man Hieronymous Osorius Bishop of Sylua in Portugal, wherein he confuteth a certayne Aunswere made by M. Walter Haddon against the Epistle of the said Bishoppe vnto the Queenes Maiestie. Translated into English by Iohn Fen student of Diuinitie in the Vniuersitie of Louen. Lovanii, Apud Ioannem Foulerum, Anno 1568. Cum Gratia et Priuilegio." Dedicated " To the Catholike Reader.—From Louen, the fyrst of Nouember,—1568, Jhon Fen." Besides: 284 leaves; on the last, the Approbation of the book, with Fouler's device on the back. Neat white letter. W.H. Sixteens.

1568. The Bible &c. Geneva translation. Printed by John Crispin. Quarto.

" Com-

"Commẽtarioli Britannicę descriptionis fragmentum." By Hum. Lhuyd, and dedicated to Abr. Ortelius. Printed at Colone. See p. 1040. See it again in 1572. Octavo. 1568.

A treatise of usury. Printed by John Fouler. Octavo. 1568.

"The first and seconde partes of the Herbal of William Turner Doctor in Phisick, lately oversene/ corrected and enlarged with the Thirde parte/ lately gathered/ and nowe set oute with the names of the herbes/ in Greke/ Latin/ English/ Duche/ Frenche/ and in the Apothecaries and Herbaries Latin/ with the properties/ degrees/ and natural places of the same. Here vnto is ioyned also a Booke of the bath of Baeth in England/ and of the vertues of the same with diuerse other bathes/ moste holsom and effectuall/ both in Almanye and England/ set furth by William Turner Doctor in Phisik. God saue the Quene." The queen's arms crowned and gartered, in a compartment. "Jmprinted at Collen by Arnold Birckman/ Jn the yeare of our Lorde M D.LXVIII. Cum Gratia et Priuilegio Reg. Maiest." Dedicated "To the most noble and learned Princesse in all kindes of good lerninge/ Quene Elizabeth/ &c. William Turner—wissheth continual helth of both bodye and soule/ and daylye encrease of the knowledge of Goddes holy worde/ with grace to lyue and rule Goddes people according to the same.—From my house at London in the crossed Fryers the 5 daye of March 1568.---The Table of the names of herbes." Besides: 223 pages. "The seconde parte—wherein are conteyned the names of herbes in Greke/—the Apothecaries Latin, and sometyme in Jtaliane/ with the vertues of the same herbes with diuerse confutationes of no small errours/ that men of no small learning haue committed in the intreating of herbes of late yeares." &c. as aboue. "The table." Besides: 171 leaves, and "The fautes &c. needfull to be corrected." &c. "The thirde parte—wherein are conteined the herbes/ trees/ rootes and fruytes/ whereof is no mention made of Dioscorides/ Galene/ Plinye/ and other olde Authores." &c. as in the title-pages of the former parts. Dedicated "To the right worshipfull Felowship and Companye of Surgiones of the citye of London chefely/ and to all other that practyse Surgery within England/—At Welles 1564. The 24 day of June.--- Of the degrees of herbes," &c. Besides: 91 pages. "A Booke of the natures and properties/ as well of the bathes in England as of other bathes in Germanye and Jtalye/ very necessarye for all syke persones that cannot be healed without the helpe of natural bathes/ lately ouersene and enlarged by William Turner Doctor in Physick." &c. as in the other title-pages. "The Preface of the Author vnto his welbeloued neighboures of bath/ Bristow/ Wellis/ Winsam and Charde.—From Basil the x. Martij,—1557.—An addition vnto the Booke of Bathes," with tables of authors, baths, and sicknesses which may be healed by these baths. Besides: 17 leaves. W.H. Folio. 1568.

A letter from James Tayre (Jesuit) to his brother in Scotland. Paris, 5819. Octavo. 1568.

"A

1569. " A Commemoration or Dirge of Bastarde Edmonde Boner," &c. See p. 889.

—— " A discourse touching the pretended match betwene the Duke of Norfolke and the Queene of Scottes." This head-title is on signature A ij, and the book seems to have had no other; it consists of 6 printed leaves, having besides the 1st and the 8th (evidently of the same paper) blank. Anderson, in his [r]preface to The defence of Q. Mary's honour, attributes this to " one Sampson a preacher," but my copy has in ancient MS. " Don by M. Norton, the first thing that ever he did, 1570." This writer however, must have been mistaken in his date, if Anderson[s] is right in saying " The chief design of publishing at London the first edition of the Defence of Q. Mary's honour, seems to have been to answer and wipe off the Aspersions cast upon her in the Discourse, concerning the intended match between her and Norfolk," &c. Printed in 1569; an account of which you have in the succeeding article. This whole Discourse, &c. is reprinted in Anderson's Collections, Vol. I; p. 21, &c. agreeing exactly with the original. W.H. Octavo.

1569. " A Defence of the honour of the right highe, mightie, and noble princesse Marie, quene of Scotland, and dowager of France: with a declaration, as well of her right, title and intereste to the succession of the crown of Englande, as that the regiment of women ys conformable to the lawe of God and nature. Imprinted at London in Fletestrete, agains the blacke bell, by Eusebius Dicaeophile." Thus, Mr. Ames; to which we may add, from Secretary Cecil's letter to Sir Henry Norris, Q. Elizabeth's ambassador in France, after Fletestrete, " at the Signe of Justice Royall," and after Dicaeophile, " Anno Dom. 1569." The whole repeated at the end of the book, with this addition, " And are to be sold in Pauls Churche Yearde at the Signes of Tyme and Truthe, by the Brasen Serpent in the Shopes of Ptoleme, and Nicephore Lycosthenes Brethren Germanes." See Anderson's preface to a copy of the subsequent edition of this book, in 1571. Collections, Vol. I; p. 55, &c. Octavo.

1569. " Calendar Historical. Wherein is contained an easie declaration of the golden nombre. Of the Epacte. Of the indiction Romaine. Also of the Cycle of the sunne, and the cause why it was inuented." The device, a serpent twisted on an anchor stock, with I. C. between the flukes. " Printed By John Crispin. M.D.LXIX." In a flourished border.

1569. De Summo Pontifice Christi in Terris Vicario eiusque officio et potestate autore Reginando Polo. Lovanii apud Joannem Foulerum Anglum. 1569." Rev. Dr. Lort. Octavo.

1569. " A treatie of Justification. Founde emong the writinges of Cardinal Pole of blessed memorie, remaining in the custodie of M. Henrie Pyning, Chamberlaine and General Receiuer to the said Cardinal, late deceased in Louaine. Item, certaine Translations touching the said matter

r Collections, Vol. I. p. iii. s Ibid. p. xiii.

matter of Iustification, the titles whereof, see in the page folowing. Prouerb. 4. Ne declines &c. Turne not aside to the right hand, nor to the lefte." Fouler's device as p. 1616. " Lovanii, Apud Ioannem Foulerum, Anno 1569. Cum priuilegio." On the back, " Beside the Treatie of Iustification, in this Volume are comprised these Translations. First, The Sixte Session of the Generall Councell of Trent, whiche is of Iustification, with the Canons of the same Session. Item, a Treatie of S. Augustine that famouse Doctour, by him entituled: Of Faith and VVorkes. Item, a Sermon of S. Chrysostome, Of Praying vnto God. Item, a Sermon of S. Basil, of Fasting. Item, certaine Sermons of S. Leo the Great, of the same Argument. Last of al, a notable Sermon of S. Cyprian that blessed Martyr, Of Almes deedes. All newly translated into English." Then, " The Preface to the Reader." My copy ends with the 33 canons of the Sixth Session of the Council of Trent. fol. 98. W.H. Quarto.

" The History of Nastagio and Traversari translated out of Italian into English by C. T." perhaps Chr. Tye. Printed at London. Hist. of Eng. Poetry, Vol. III; p. 194. 1569.

" The Children of the Chapel stript and whipt." Among bishop Tanner's books at Oxford. Ibid. p. 288. 1569.

A collection of short comic stories in prose, " sett forth by maister Richard Edwardes mayster of her maiesties reuels." Ibid, p. 293. 1570.

" Harmonia sive Catena Dialectica in Porphyrianas constitutiones:" a commentary on Porphyry's Isagoge. London, 1570." By Richard Stanihurst. Ibid. p. 401, note w. Again 1579. Folio. 1570.

" The Bible, translated according to the Ebrue and Greke, 2 Vol. At Geneva." Bibl. Bodleiana. Quarto. 1570.

The same. Lambeth List. Folio. 1570.

" A treatise of the holy sacrifice of the altar, called the masse. In which by the word of God, and testimonies of the apostles, and primitiue church, it is prooued, that our sauiour Jesus Christ did institute the masse, and the apostles did celebrate the same. Translated out of Italian into English, by Thomas Butler, doctor of the canon and civil lawes." Sixteens. 1570.

" A Treatise concerning the defence of the honour of the right high, mightie and noble princesse, Marie Queene of Scotland, and Douager of France, with a Declaration, as wel of her Right, Title, and Interest, to the Succession of the Croune of England: as that the Regiment of women is conformable to the lawe of God and Nature. Made by Morgan Philippes, Bachelar of Diuinitie, An. 1570. Leodii. Apud Gualterum Morberium. 1571." Each part seems to have had a distinct title-page, signatures, and numbers to the leaves peculiar to itself, so as to sell separate occasionally. Next after the general title-page is an epistle " To the Reader," respecting chiefly the first and second parts; which, as well as The defence of Q. Mary's honour, may be seen in Anderson's Collections, vol. 1. The running title, " The first Booke A Defense of her Honour." 50 leaves, besides the prefatory epistle. 1571.

" A

1571. "A Treatiſe touching the Right, Title, and Intereſt of the mightie and noble Princeſſe Marie, Queene of Scotland to the ſucceſſion of the Croune of England. Made by Morgan Philippes,—aſſiſted vvith the aduiſe of Antonie Broune Knight, one of the Iuſtices of the Common Place. An. 1567. Leodii. Apud Gualterum Morberium. 1571." The running title, "The ſeconde Booke touching the ſucceſſion." 67 leaves.

1571. "A Treatiſe VVherin is declared, that the Regiment of Women is conformable to the lawe of God and Nature." Head title: my copy wanting the diſtinct title-pages of this, and the firſt book. The running title, "The third Booke For the Regiment of Women." 30 leaves, and the Errata for the ſecond and third books. W.H. Octavo.

1571. "The choſen eloquent oration of M. T. Cicero for the poet Archias, ſelected from his orations, and now firſt publiſhed in Engliſh." See Hiſt. of Eng. Poetry, Vol. III; p. 431.

(1571.) A Letter ſuperſcribed, "Salutem in Chriſto," concerning the ſecond commitment of the duke of Norfolk to the tower. Dated "At London the xiij. of October, 1571. Your louing brother in Lawe. R. G." My copy has in ancient MS. "Thought to be don by William Cecill, 1571." On 7 pages. See "A treatiſe of the Treaſons againſt Q. Elizabeth" &c. in 1572. Alſo, Annals of the Reformation, Vol. II; p. 136. Appendix, N° XIV. W.H. Octavo.

1571. "A patent to Raffe *Bowes, and Thomas Beddingfield Eſquiers to import Playing Cards into this kingdom for 12 years and diſpoſe of them in large or ſmall quantities, notwithſtanding any Act, &c. formerly made. 13 June.—the 13th of our reign." MS. J. Ames.

1571. "A brief anſwer to a ſhort trifling treatiſe of late ſet forth in the Britaine tongue. Written by one Clinnock at Rome, and printed at Millain, and lately ſpread ſecretly abroad in Wales." Dedicated to the earl of Leiceſter. Biſhop Tanner aſcribes this to Lewis Evans. Bibl. Tanneri, p. 270.

1571. "A copie of a letter lately ſent by a gentleman, ſtudent in the lawes of the realme, to a friend of his, concerning D. Story." It treats of his Treaſons, Confeſſion and Execution. 4 June. 12 leaves. Harleian Miſcellany, Vol. 8; p. 583. Sixteens.

"Hiſtoriæ

* This Raffe or Ralph Bowes had allowed unto him by the Stationers' Company, 18 Octob. 1588. "The whole ſute of Mouldes belonging to the olde foorme of plaieinge cardes, commonly called the Frenche Cardes with the Jew Ciſan dozen, and all other thinges thereunto belonging. Item, The newe addic'on of the whole ſute of newe mouldes belonging to the olde and newe forme of playeing cards, commonly called the Frenche Cards, with the Jew Ciſan dozen, and all other thinges thereunto belonginge." Alſo, 8 January following, was allowed unto him, by the ſaid company, to be printed, "The wholle ſute of carved mouldes in woode or caſte in mettall, belonging to the ould foorme of playing Cardes, commonlye called the Frenche Carde, with the Jew Ciſan, dozen, and all other thinges thereunto belonging.—Likewiſe—The newe addic'on," &c. Alſo, 11 January, 1590-1. "Ent'red for him to print theſe markes folowing, which are to bynd up Cardes in, viz. A dozen m'ke. Item, A Siniam m'ke. Item, A Jew m'ke."

"Historiæ Evangelicæ veritas; Seu singularia vitæ Domini Jesu Christi, eo ordine quo gesta fuerunt recensita, & ipsis quatuor Evangelistarum verbis contexta, &c. Lov. 1572." By Alan Cope. See Ath. Oxon. I, 198. 1572.

"Commentarioli Britãnicae descriptionis fragmentum. Auctore Humfredo Lhuyd Denbyghiense, Cambro Britanno. Coloniae Agrippinae, apud Joannem Birkmannum." Before, 1568. Octavo. 1572.

"De Maria Scotorum Regina, totaque eius contra Regem coniuratione, fœdo cum Bothuelio adulterio, nefaria in maritum crudelitate & rabie, horrendo insuper & deterrimo eiusdem parricidio: plena, & tragica planè Historia." To which is added in MS. "Authore Georgio Bucchannano Scoto, 1572-3." The bottom part of the title-page of my copy has been cut off. The first thirty pages, printed with roman letter, assert an history of the facts: the remainder of the book, printed with Italics, is argumentative, having this title at the head thereof, "Actio contra Mariam Scotorum Reginam in qua ream & consciam esse eamhuius parricidij, necessarijs argumentis euincitur." And my copy has this note on the margin, in the same hand as that on the title page, "Istas actiones scripsit Thomas Smythus à secretis Dominæ nostræ Reginæ Elizabethæ, sicut fama est: vel Thomas Willsonus a supplicum libellis, quod mihi magis placet." On p. 101 begin "Literæ Reginæ Scot. ad comitem Bothuelium scriptæ," with this note on the margin in the same hand-writing as the foregoing, "Thomas Wilsonus creditur has literas e Gallico transtulisse eũ autem gallicam phrasim vix credo intelligere: Thomas vero Smith hoc optime potuit præstare eo quod legat' Parisijs diu est commoratus." Indeed these letters ought to have been published in the language in which they were written. Here are only three letters, and then a short conclusion under the head of "Catastrophe huius Tragœdiæ." The whole on 122 pages, exclusive of the title-page. Without date, place, or printer's name. This, as also The Detection, are supposed to have been printed by John Day. W.H. Octavo. ——

"ANE DETECTIOVN of the duinges of Marie Quene of Scottes, touchand the murder of hir husband, and hir conspiracie, adulterie, and pretensed mariage with the Erle Bothwell. And ane defence of the trew Lordis, mainteineris of the Kingis graces [a]actioun and authaoritie. Translated out of the Latine quhilke was written by G. B." The narrative begins on signature A ij. The first blooming letter Q, of 5 lines, has a rose in the centre with two buds issuing out at the upper corners. That in my copy has the part of the outer circle of the Q to the right broken off. This translation contains more letters and papers, including the queen's sonnet entire in French and English, than the Latin copy above recited. The whole γ 4, half sheets; the last leaf blank, as is the last page of the foregoing leaf. No colophon, though room more than sufficient: no date, place, or printer's name; but supposed, as the Latin copy, to have been printed by John Day. Bibl. Ratcliff. ——

9 E Lot

[a] The omission of this *a* is a good criterion to distinguish this edition by.

Lot 1245 gives it as dated 1568, but it was only in MS. W.H Octavo

1572. "A treatise of the treasons against Q. Elizabeth, and the Croune of England, diuided into two partes: whereof, The first parte answereth certaine Treasons pretended, that neuer were intended: And the second, discouereth greater Treasons committed, that are by few perceiued: as more largely appeareth in the Page folowing. Imprinted in the Moneth of Ianuarie, and in the Yeare of our Lord M.D.LXXII." On the other side, "The argument of this treatise diuided into two Partes.[a]" Then, "The Preface[b] to the English Reader.---Allusio ad præsentem Angliæ conditionem, ex Æneid, Lib. 2." in 15 Hexameters. The first part undertakes to answer the abovementioned letter, signed R.G, paragraph by paragraph, and occupies 82 leaves. The author in the second part, in order to counteract the influence which the foresaid letter seems to have had on the generality of peoples minds, by a master-piece of policy, accuses the two[c] persons, whom he charges with the whole government of the nation's affairs, principally of abusing both the queen and the people by plotting the destruction, not only of the Scotish queen and her son, but of queen Elizabeth herself, with a design to settle the Suffolk family on the throne.[d] Continued to Fo. 174. W.H. Octavo.

An

[a] "The first confuteth the false accusations, and sklanderous Infamies, printed in certeine nameless and infamous Libelles against the Q. Maiestie of Scotland, Heire apparent to the Crowne of England: and against Thomas Duke of Norfolke, Earle Marshall of the same Realme: and defendeth the Honour and Loialtie of the said Princes.

"The seconde Parte (which beginneth Fol. 83.) detecteth sundry deepe and hidden Treasons, of long time practised and daily contriued against the Honour, Dignitie, safetie & state of Queene Elizabeth, her Roialtie, her Crowne, and all the Blood Roial of England, by a few base and ingrate persons, that haue bene called to credit by her; and remoueth the plausible visards, wherewith they couer their Coniurations. It laieth open also, the dangerous state that the said Q. and Realme doth stand in, if those Confederates and their Conspiracies be not preuented in time."

[b] Herein the author professes himself to be a stranger; to have lived in this country above 30 years; that this treatise was written in vindication of Mary Q. of Scots, and the duke of Norfolk, or as a countermine against the letter superscribed "Salutem in Christo, dated 13 Octob. 1571,—R. G." abovementioned, assigning the cause of the duke of Norfolk's second commitment to the Tower, viz. His secretly practising to have married the Scotish queen, even after both their renunciations and promises to the contrary. Two persons only are charged as the authors of all the innovations and evils complained of throughout the whole book, chiefly in the second part; one of them evidently was Sir William Cecil, characterised under the name of Sinon the Grecian imposter, the other probably Lord Keeper Bacon. The author presupposed this treatise would not be suffered to be seen and sold freely, as the other (R. G's) had been; but apologises for writing it, that in case he should not say somewhat, "adventure to tye this bel about the Cattes necke," he could not excuse himself of some participation with the accusers of the innocent, meaning the queen of Scots, and the duke of Norfolk.

[c] Sir William Cecil, lately created Lord Burghley, and appointed Lord Treasurer; and Sir Nicholas Bacon, Lord Keeper of the Great Seal. See note d.

[d] The good Lord Burghley, says Strype, was so moved at his slander, that he uttered these words, "God amend his spirit and confound his malice." &c. And—by way of protestation of the integrity and faithfulness of both their services, "God send this Estate no worse meaning servants in

al

An Admonition to the Parliament *(of England)*. " This Admonition, *Mr. Strype tells us*, had by this time been printed and reprinted privately no less than four times; in such a vogue it was, notwithstanding the diligence of the bishops to suppress it. The last time, which was this year, it came forth with additions." From this the following description is taken. It has no regular title-page, but is introduced by an epistle " To the godly Readers, Grace, and peace from God. &c." beginning thus, " Two treatises yee haue heere ensuing" &c. This on little more than 2 pages. Then this head-title, " An admonition to the Parliament." This is the first of the two treatises, and contains 12 pages. The next is " A view of Popish abuses yet remayning in the Englishe Church, for the which Godly Ministers haue refused to subscribe." Which occupies 19 pages; on the last of these begins an epistle " To the Christian Reader, *&c.* We haue thoughte good in this latter end of our booke, for sundry consyderations to certify you (beloued brethrē) of the reasons that haue moued vs, who are the authors of these treatises to kepe back our names, and also to suppresse the name of the Printer of them, because" &c. On 3 pages. Then, a preface, without any superscription, to the 2 following letters dated 1572. The first letter " To the reuerend Father in Christ, D. J. P. *(Dr. John Parkhurst)* the most vigilant B. of N. (*Bishop of Norwich*) and his louing Father.— Fare you well; at Tigurin, the 11 of September, Anno 1566. Rodolphe Gualter, Minister of the Churche of God at Tigurin.—To the Reuerend father in Christ E. G. (*Edmund Grindal*) Bishop of L. (*London*) T. B. wisheth grace and health from the Lord.—Geneue, v. Cal. Jul. M.D.lxvj. Yours most assured in the Lord Theodore Beza, minister of the word in the Church of Geneue." Then by way of epilogue to this first [a]admonition. 1572.

" England repent, Bishops relent, returne while you haue space,
Time is at hand, by truth to stand, if you haue any grace.
Joyne now in one, that Christ alone, by scepter of his word:
May beare the stroke: least you prouoke his heavy hand and sword."

 This

at Respects, than we two have been. Who indeed have not spared Labour nor Care to serve our Queen and Country. And if we had not, we might truly avow, neither our Queen nor Country had enjoyed that common Repose that it hath done." He wrote to the English ambassador in France, where the book is said to have been printed, desiring him to make enquiry who was the author; adding, that if by means of the printer it might be found out, he would bestow a reward upon the discovery. But that if it could not, then he wished that some means might be used, as of himself, to the Queen Mother, that the Print might be destroyed. Mr. Strype supposes this treatise to have been written by some French rancorous person having his instructions from some crafty rebellious papist of England. See Annals of the Reformation, Vol. II; p. 178, &c. Mr. Camden says, " so far was the queen from giving credit to these accusations, that by public proclamation she declared them to be improbable, false, and mere slanders; maliciously forged by the professed enemies of the true religion and their country,—that by their wicked and secret practices they might deprive the realm of its faithful counsellors. Wherefore she charged all men to give no credit to the said libels, but to slight and burn them, unless they would undergo the penalty to be inflicted upon the encouragers of sedition." Hist. of Q. Eliz. p. 192.

[a] See Whitgift's Answer to it, p. 934-5.

This first Admonition &c. contains D 4, in eights. Mr. Neal acquaints us it was presented to the House by the authors themselves, Mr. Field and Mr. Wilcox, for which they were committed to Newgate, October 2. This occasioned the drawing up

(1572.) "A second Admonition to the Parliament" by Mr. Cartwright. See Neal's Hist. of the Puritans, Vol I, p. 285. "Jeremie 26. 11—15. Then spake the Priestes," &c.—To the godly readers Grace and peace from God &c." Besides: 64 pages. W.H. both. Octavo.

(1572.) Soon after these 2 Admonitions came forth three other pamphlets as they are called, being but one indeed, consisting of a preface introducing two epistolary exhortations. The preface is superscribed "Grace and peace from God. &c." Beginning. "Such hath alwayes (deare brethren) bene the corrupt nature of the wicked and vngodlye of thys world/ that as yet they could neuer away with suche/ as would either but simply tell them of/ or frankly and freely reproue them for/ theyr manifest synnes and vngodlinesse.—What other cause there shuld be why those two treatises/ that were lately written and imprinted/ in ye last Parliament tyme/ iustly crauing a redresse and Reformation of many abuses and corruptions/ yet in the english church remayning/ shuld of so many be misliked/ and ye authors thereof so cruelly entreated/ &c. —From my chamber at London/ this 30. of September/ in Anno 1572. —An Exhortation to the Byshops to deale Brotherly with theyr Brethren.—An Exhortation to the bishops and their clergie to answer a little booke that came forthe the last Parliament/ and to other Brethren to iudge of it by Gods worde/ vntill they see it aunsweared/ and not to be caryed away with any respect of man." 12 leaves. See Strype's Life of Abp. Parker, p. 347, &c.—Abp. Whitgift, p. 27, &c. Neal's Hist. of the Puritans, Vol. I, p. 285, &c. W.H. Octavo.

"Certaine Articles, collected and taken (as it is thought) by the Byshops out of a little boke entituled an Admonition to the Parliament/ wyth an Answere to the same. Containing a confirmation of the sayde Booke in shorte notes. Esay 5. 20. Woe be vnto them that speake good of euill/ &c. The Prynter to the Reader.

Thys worke is fynished thankes be to God/
And he only will keepe vs from the searchers rod.
And though master Day and Toy watch and warde
We hope the liuing God is our sauegarde.
Let them seeke/ loke/ and doe now what they can/
It is but inuentions/ and pollicies of man.
But you wil maruel where it was finished/
And you shal know (perchance) when domes day is ended.
Imprinted we know where/ and whan/
Judge you the place and you can. J. T. J. S."

On the back, "To the Prelacie." in 7 four-lined stanzas. B, in fours, half sheets. Said to have been privately printed at Wandsor, (*Wandsworth.*) near London. MSS. Lewis. W.H. Octavo.

"The

"The offer and order giuen forth by sir Thomas Smyth" &c. See 1572.
p. 972.

"A treatice to receaue the blessed body of our lord sacramentally and 1572.
virtually bothe, made in the yeare of our Lorde 1534, by syr Thomas More knyghte, whyle he was prysoner in the towre of London. With, Certein deuout and vertuouse instruccions, meditacions, and prayers, made and collected by him at the same time. Lovaine,—John Fouler, 1572." This title collected from Sir Thomas More's Works, and partly from MS. Mr. Tho. Baker. Quarto.

"Thesaurus linguae Romanæ" &c. See p. 937. 1573.

"The Copie of a Letter written by one in London to his Friend,
concernyng the Credit of the late published Detection of the Doynges of the Ladie Mary of Scotland." See Anderson's Collections, Vol. II; p. 261.

"The Refutation of an Answer made be Schir John Knox, to an Letter 1573.
sent be James Tayre to his umquhile Brother: Set forth be James Tayre. Parisiis apud Thomam Brumenium, in clauso Brunello, sub signo Olivæ. 1573." Mackenzie, III; p. 432. See p. 1492, and 1625. Octavo.

"A Dialogue of Cumfort against Tribulation, made by the right Ver- 1573.
tuous, Wise and learned man, Sir Thomas More, sometime L. Chanceller of England, which he wrote in the Tower of London, An. 1534. and entituled thus: A Dialogue of Cumfort against Tribulation, made by an Hungarian[b] in Latin, and translated out of Latin into French, and out of French into English. Now newly set foorth, with many places restored and corrected by conference of sundrie copies. Non desis plorantibus in consolatione. Eccli. 7. Antverpiae, Apud Iohannem Foulerum, Anglum. M.D.LXXIII." His device is on the back. Dedicated "To the—Ladie Jane Duchesse of Feria.—From Antwarp, the last of September. An. 1573.—John Fouler.—To the Reader."--- The author's portrait on a separate leaf; about the frame, "Thomas Morus Anglus Anno Ætatis 50." On the opposite page, "Johan. Fouleri Brissoliensis in D. Th. Mori effigiem, Hexastichon. --The same in English Meter." Besides; 216 leaves, and a table of contents. See p. 808. W.H. Sixteens.

"A new Enterlude No less Wittie, than Pleasant, entituled New 1573
Custom. Devised of late, and for diverse Causes nowe set forthe. Never before this tyme imprinted. MDLXXIII." See it, Dodsley's Old Plays, Vol I.

"The Fall and evil Success of Rebellion." A poem by Wilfrid 1573.
Holme

[b] In this book, under the person of Hungarians are meant Roman Catholicks, and the danger threatened was from (what they call) Heresie, as explained by the author of Sir Tho. More's Life; and, no doubt by the Great Turk he thought the king was meant, though he does not say it; and so probably Sir Thomas meant it: and had the book then appeared, it would have been interpreted a libel. See Life, 8°. edit. 1626, p. 235, 334, &c. In some sort I take the book to be another Utopia, describing a tyrannical government, and cruel as this was. MS. T. Baker.

Holme of Huntington in Yorkshire. A dialogue between England and the author on the commotions raised in the northern counties on account of the reformation in 1537, under Cromwell's administration. Hist. of Eng. Poetry, Vol. III; p. 83.

1573. "Ludicra, seu Epigrammata Juvenillia." By John Parkhurst,[i] bishop of Norwich. See Annals of the Reformation, Vol. II; p. 232. Quarto.

—— "A Replye to an answere made of M. Dr. VVhitegifte, againste the Admonition to the Parliament. By T. C. Isaie. 62. ver. 1. For Syons sake, J will not holde my tonge/ and for Jerusalems sake/ J will not rest/ vntill the righteousness therof/ break forthe as the lighte/ and the saluation thereof/ be as a burning lampe. Ver. 6. &. 7. Ye that are the Lordes remembrancers/ keepe not silence/ and geue hym no rest/ vntill he repayre/ and set vp Jerusalem the prayse of the world." On the back is an address[k] from "The Printer to the Reader." By which this appears to be a second edition. Superscribed "To the Church of England, and all those that loue the Trueth in it, T. C. wisheth mercy" &c. Contains 224 pages, the numbers placed in the middle of the page; and has prefixed "A short Table of the princypall poyntes/" &c. Printed very close, yet distinct, in Long Primer Black. W.H. Quarto.

Francis Flower, a gentleman, though no member of the company of stationers, had privilege of printing the grammar, and other things; and had farmed it out to some[l] of the company for 100l. by the year. Which 100l. was raised in the enhancing of the prices above the accustomed order. (From Strype's survey.) His patent bearing date 16 Eliz. 15 Dec. 1573, is as follows: "Francisco Flower generoso, officium typographi, ac bibliopolae nostri, haeredum, et successorum nostrorum, in Latino, Graeco, Hebraicoque sermone, ac officium impressoris, seu excusoris, in praedict. Latino, *&c.* verumtamen omnes & singulos libros grammaticos, Græcos sive Latinos, quamvis Anglico sermone quomodolibet intermixtos. Nec non omnes mappas, *&c.* pro vita. Quod officium Edwardus sextus, 19 April, anno regni sui secundo, concessit Reginaldo Wolfe defuncto, cum 26s. 8d." (From Mr. Thomas Baker.) Some of the books have only 'By the assigns of Francis

[i] His Epigrammata Seria were published in 1560. Hist. of Eng. Poetry, Vol. III; p. 432, note c.

[k] It begins "Some perhaps will maruel at the newe impression of thys booke/ and so muche the more will they wonder/ because they shall see/ that with great confidence & boldnes (notwythstanding our most gracious Princes late proclamation/ procured rather by the Byshops/ then willingly sought for by her maiestie/ whose mildnes is suche/ that she were easyer led to yelde to the proclamation of the highest/ then drawne to proclaime any thing against hym/" &c. Subscribed J. S. This seems to be the edition printed about 1589 I have not seen the first edition.

[l] Most probably his assigns were the persons whose rebusses compose the compartment for the title-pages of his books, from which the middle of our frontispiece was copied; and that Vautrollier was employed by them as their printer and publisher.

Francis Flower,' without naming the person, as, The construction of the English accidence, by John Stockwood, schoolmaster of Tunbridge, quarto, 1590. I have seen books of his so late as 1595.*

" A Briefe Treatise of diuerse plaine and sure wayes to finde out 1574.
the truthe in this doubtful and dangerous time of Heresie: conteyning sundry worthy Motiues vnto the Catholike faith, or considerations to moue a man to beleue the Catholikes and not the Heretikes. Sette out by Richard Bristow Priest Licentiat in Diuinitie. Antwerpiae, Apud Iohannem Foulerum Anglum, M.D.LXXIIII. Cum Privilegio." Lambeth Library. Again 1599. Sixteens.

" Ecclesiasticae Disciplinae et Anglicanæ Ecclesiæ ab illa aberra- 1574.
tionis, plena è verbo Dei, & dilucida explicatio. Rupellae, excudebat Adamus de Monte. 1574." Prefixed is an epistle 'Pio Lectori Gratiam et Pacem à Deo Patre & Domino nostro Iesu Christo.—Quarto nonas Februarii anno salutis humanæ." Besides: 148 leaves; on the last, " Errata quae lectorem remorari possent corrigantur." Bodleian Library and W.H. Sixteens.

" A full and plaine declaration of Ecclesiasticall Discipline owt off 1574.
the word off God and off the declininge off the churche off England from the same. Jmprinted M.D.LXXIIII." A translation of the foregoing article, as well of the preface* as of the treatise. 193 pages besides the preface. W.H. Quarto.

" A Catechisme, together with a Treatise concerning the Ceremonies of 1574.
the Church. By Laurence Vaux, B. D." Bibl. Bodleianæ. See it in 1575. Octavo.

" Certayne Newes of the —ayde," &c. See p. 1065.

" Middleborow. A briefe rehersall of the accorde—, that the cap- 1574.
taynes, burgises, and armie of Middleborow, and Armew, haue made in yelding themselues to the right high and excellent prince, the lord William, prince of Orange, *&c.* ¶ With a lamentable discourse of the calamities, *&c.* sustayned, before they yelded vp the said townes. Translated out of the Dutch coppy. Printed at Dordrecht." See p. 1040. Sixteens.

" The life off the 70 Archbishopp off Canterbury, presentlye Sittinge; Englished and to be added to the 69 lately Sett forth in Latin. This numbre off seventy is so compleat a number, as it is great pitie ther shold be one more: but that as Augustin was the first, so Mathew might be the last. Jmprinted, M.D.LXXIIII." There is a sheet folded up

* Neal says " It was drawn up in Latin by Mr. Travers, and printed at Geneva about the year 1574, but since that time had been diligently reviewed corrected and perfected by Mr. Cartwright, and other learned ministers at their Synods. It was translated into English this year, with a preface by Mr. Cartwright, and designed to be published for more general use; but as it was printing at Cambridge it was seized at the press. The archbishop advised that all the copies should be burnt as factious and seditious, but one was found in Mr. Cartwright's Study after his death, and reprinted in the year 1644." Hist. of the Puritans, Vol. I; p. 449. Archbp. Parker was very solicitous to have this book of Discipline well answered, but met with some difficulty in accomplishing his desire. Strype's Life of Abp. Parker, p. 480.

up in the book, with the names and fees of the then set of bishops. See Ath. Oxon. Vol. I; col. 688, &c. Hearne assigns the Latin copy to John Josselin, chaplain to the archbishop. F 4, in eights, the last leaf blank. W.H. Sixteens.

1574. "The blasing of bawdrye, daily procured by Beldame B. principal broker of all iniquitie, by R. C. citizen of London." See p. 1040. Sixteens.

1574. "The Prophetie of the Spirit of Loue. Set-fourth by H. N:* And by Him perused a-new/ and more distinctlie declared. Translated out of Base-almayne into English." Device: יהוה encircled with rays of glory, about which, "Coronæ assimilabo Judicium meum. 4 Esd. 5." A corded circle enclosing the whole. Beneath; "Beholde/ J will sende myne Angell or Messenger/ which shall prepare the Wey or make plaine the Path before Mee. Hee shall turne the Heart of the Fathers/ to the Children: and the Heart of the Childrē to the Fathers/ that J come not/ and vtterlie smyte or destroy the Earth/ wyth the Cursse. Malach. 3, a. 4, a. Math. 11, b. 17, b. Mar. 1, a. Luc. 1, b. Anno 1574." On the back, over an emblematical device of the victory of the Lamb over Death, Sin, and Sathan, described on a heart, is, "Nowe goeth the Judgment over the Worlde: Now becometh the Prince of this worlde cast-out. Iohn. 12." Under it, "Now is the Saluation/ the Power/ and the Kingdom/ becom our Gods: and the Might his Christes. Apo. 12." The whole on 40 leaves: on the last is another emblematical device described on a heart also; Hand in hand holding up 3 lilies on one stem, with L.* T. on a tablet. Over this device, "Charitas extorsit." And under it,

"Our Heart/ is the Minde of God most high.
Our Beeinge amiable/ as the sweete Lillie.
Our Faithfulnes/ Loue/ and Trueth vpright/
Js Gods Light/ Life/ and Cleernes bright." W.H. Octavo.

1574. "A Publishing of the Peace vpon Earth/ and of the gratious Tyme and acceptable Yeare of the Lorde/ which is now in the last tyme; out of the Peace of Jesu Christ/ and out of his holie Spirit of Loue: published by H. N. on the Earth. Wherwith all Men that make Warre or Battaile one against another/ together with all Wyse and Scripture-learned which contende and dispute against each-other are exhorted vnto Peace and warned of the great Woe and Miserie/ which shall come vpon them all/ if-so-be that they geue them not to Peace. Translated out of Base-almayne into English." The circular device as to the last article. "O/ how louelie are the Feete of the Messenger which proclaymeth

* Henry Nichols, or Nicholas, a Dutchman of Leyden; who though the reputed Father of the sect, called the Family of Love, was not the founder thereof, but one David George, Anabaptist, of Delpht in Holland. See Deering's Nottingham, p. 46, 47. Strange things are reported of him when a child of 8 and 9 years of age, in the Mirabilia opera Dei. published by Tobias, a Fellow Elder with the said H. N. in the Houshold of Love.

* For "Love. Truth," as appears by subsequent editions.

claymeth Peace/ preacheth Good-tydinges/ and publisheth the Saluation. Esa. 52, b. Nah. 2, a. Rom. 10, c. J will make fruitfull Lyppes/ which shall preach Peace/ Peace/ both vnto them that are farre-of/ and vnto them that are neere-by/ sayth the Lorde. Esa. 57, d. Luk. 2, b. Ephe. 2, b. Anno 1574." On the back are the same device and texts as to the last article. 8 leaves. At the end, "Take it to heart. H. N." W.H. Octavo.

"TERRA PACIS. A true Testification of the spirituall Lande of Peace; which is the spirituall Lande of Promyse, and the Holy Citie of Peace or the heauenly Jerusalem; and of the Holy and spirituall People that dwell therin; as also of the Walking in the Spirit/ which leadeth therunto. Set-foorth by H. N: and by Him newly perused and more-playnly declared. Translated out of Base-almayne." The circular device. "Depart out of thy Lande, and from thy Kindred, and out of thy Fathers Hovvse: and trauayle into a Lande that I vvil shevve thee, Gen. 12, a. Act. 7, a. I vvil leade thee on the right Path, that the Course vvhen thou goest, be not paynfull vnto thee: and that thou stumble not vvhen thou runnest. Take the informacion to heart: leaue it not: keepe it: For it is thy Lyfe. Go not in the Path of the Vngodly: and vvalke not in the VVay of the VVicked: Leaue the same, and go not therin: Depart therfrom, and pas by it. Pro. 4, b." On the back is the emblem of the Lamb's victory, designed much like that to the two foregoing articles, in the general, yet improved in this; where Sin is represented not only by a mund, as before, but by a great monster swallowing the mund; and instead of being described on a heart is now within a square. The texts are the same. Contains 82 leaves, including title and preface. On the last page is an improved device of the Hand in hand, &c. at the end of the Prophetie of the Spirit of Love; the heart being now encompassed with rays of light, issuing out of bright clouds interspersed with cherubic heads, surrounding also the words יהוה and EMMANVEL, which are over the heart; and instead of the tablet with L. T. is a scroll about the wrist of each hand; one with "Loue," the other with "Trueth." W.H. Octavo.

"Revelatio Dei. The Reuelation of God/ and his great Propheatie: which God now; in the last Daye: hath shewed vnto his Elect. Set fourth by H N, and by him perused anew and more distinctlie declared. Translated out of Base-almayne." The circular device. "O all yee People that dwell on Earth, Looke now to-it, that the same com not ouer you/ which is spoken-of in the Propheates: Beholde yee Dispisers/ and wonder, and perish. For I doo a Worke, in your tymes/ which yee shall not beleeue/ when anyone shall tell it vnto you. Abac. 1, a. Act. 13, e." On the back are the same texts, and cut of the Lamb's victory; and has at the end the same device of Love and Truth as to the last article. Contains 55 leaves, including title and preface. W.H: Octavo.

"EVANGELIVM REGNI. A Joyfull Message of the Kingdom/ published

lished by the holie Spirit of the Loue of Jesu Christ, and sent-fourth vnto all the Nations of People; which loue the Truth in Iesu Christ. Set-fourth by H N, and by him perused a-new and more-distinctlie declared. Translated out of Base-almayne." The circular device. "O, Hovv louelie are the Feete of the Messengers vvhich publish the Peace, Preach Good-tydinges, and evangelize the Saluation. Esa. 52. b. &c. The Euangelie of the Kingdom shall be preached in all the VVorld, for a VVitnes vnto all People: and then shall the ende com. Math. 24, b. I savve an Angell flye thorovve the middest of Heauen, hauing an Euerlasting Euangelie, to publish vnto them vvhich sit and dvvell upon the Earth. namelie, vnto all Heathen, Generations, and People. Apoca. 14, a." The back blank. Contains 100 leaves, including title and preface. At the end, "Sent from the Spirit-of-Loue; through Loue-to-concorde, and through Loue-to-life, into all Landes, ouer the vniuersall VVorlde. Charitas extorsit per H N." W.H. 8°.

— "PROVERBIA H N. The Prouerbes of H N. Which Hee *(in the Dayes of his Olde-age; hath set-fourth as Similitudes and mysticall Sayinges. Translated out of Base-almayne." The circular device. "I will open my Mouth in Prouerbes or Similitudes, and declare-fourth the Actes which haue ben don of olde. Psal. 78, a. To the Children of Loue and the vpright Disciples of Iesu Christ; it is geeuen to vnderstand the Misterie of the heauenly Kingdom: But to Such as are therwithout; it is not geeuen. For-that-cause; all thinges chaunce vnto them in Similitudes and Prouerbes. Math 13, b. Mark 4, b. Luk, 8, b." On 46 leaves, including the title. At the end, "Take it to heart: and reuolue well these Prouerbes of the godlie VVisdom. Charitas extorsit per H N." The paper-mark, A serpent twisted about a cross, resting on a buffalo's head, with R under it. W.H. Octavo.

— "DICTA H N. Documentall Sentences: euen-as those-same were spoken-fourth by H N, and writen-vp out of the Woordes of his Mouth. And are by him perused, and more distinctlie declared. Translated out of Base-almayne." The circular device "God hath graunted mee to speake wiselie, and to consider a-right; of the Thinges which he hath gratiouslie geuen mee. Sap. 7. The mouth of the Righteous; is exercised in Wisdom, and his Toung speaketh the Iudgement. Psal. 37. Hys Lippes shall not speake the thing that is vnright, nor his Tounge vtter-fourth any Deceipt. Job. 27." On 47 leaves; the last page blank. W.H. Octavo.

— "EPISTOLÆ H N. The Principall Epistles of H N; which he hath set-foorth through the holy Spirit of Loue. and written and sent them (most-cheefly; vnto the Louers of ŷ Trueth and his Acquaintance. And are by him newly perused, and more playnly declared. Translated out of Base-almaine." The circular device. "All Scripture geeuen by the Inspiration of God; is profitable to teache, to Rebuke, to Amendment, and to Information in Righteousnes, for that the Man of God may be

* The inverted semicolon used in these Family of Love books denotes a parenthesis.

be perfect, prepared to all good vvorkes. 2. Tim. 3. No prophecie in the Scripture, cometh-to-pas by priuate Interpretation. For ther vvas yet neuer any Prophecie brought forth out of manly VVill: but as the holy Men of God haue spoken it, being mooued by the holy Gost. 2 Pet. 1." On the back is the emblem of the Lamb's victory, improved as p. 1638. This copy contains 20 epistles, which are more than i have met with elsewhere; however there is no more certainty of the 20th being the last than of the 6th, 12th, 15th, or 18th, supposing the subsequent epistles were not here present, or known; each of those having the device of Love and Truth, hand in hand, at the end, as well as the twentieth. They are all paged progressively to p. 418, exclusive of the preface, and table of contents prefixed. Probably several, if not all, these epistles had been published separate. I have the Eleventh, and have seen the First printed singly. Also the first four of them were reprinted in 1648. Indeed most of this author's pieces were reprinted about that time. W.H. Octavo.

" INTRODVCTIO. An Jntroduction to the holy Vnderstanding of the Glasse of Righteousnes. Wherin are vttered many notable Admonitions and Exhortations to the Good-life. also sundry discreet Warnings to beware of Destruction. and of wrong-conceiuing, and misunderstanding or censuring any Sentences. Sett-forth by H N, and by him perused a-new, and expressed more playnly." The circular device. " Whoso is wise, hee will be counselled, to thend he may vnderstand the Parables, and their Interpretations. also the Doctrine of the Wise and their dark Sayings. Pro. 1. Hee will be guyded in the straite Path [to the holy Vnderstanding] that: when he goeth, the Way be not tedious vnto him, and when he runneth, that he do not stumble. Pro. 4." The emblem of the Lamb's victory, of the improved design, from copper-plate, facing the title-page. This book seems to have been printed at different presses; the numbers of the leaves frequently recommencing; yet the signatures are regular by the letters, and all in eights, except N and Q, each of which has ten leaves. The first division, containing the first 7 chapters, has 40 leaves, the last blank. The 2d, containing Chap. 8—13, has 40 leaves, the last blank, also. The 3d, Chap. 14—17, on 26 leaves. The 4th, Chap. 18—21, on 18 leaves. The last, Chap. 22—25, on 20 leaves. At the end, " Take it to Heart.

Loue ye the Vertue feruently// Giue God his Honour due:
Delight therin continually// Thatt is his Doctrine true.

Charitas extorsit per H N." On a separate leaf, the device of Love and Truth, &c. now printed from copper-plate, very neatly engraved. W.H. [1]Quarto.

" A Figure of the True and spiritual Tabernacle, According to the inward

[1] See p. 855, note w.

inward Temple or House of God in the Spirit. Whereunto is added the Eight Vertues or Godlynesses. Set forth by H: N. and by him perused, and more evidently declared. The Temple of God was opened in heaven, and the Ark of his Testament was seen in his Temple. Apoca. 12. Behold the Tabernacle of God is with men, and he shall dwell with them: and they shall be his people: And he God himself with them, shall be their God. Apo. 21. 1 Cor. 3. 2 Cor. 6." With emblematical cuts. I have not seen the original edition, but have copied this title from that reprinted in 1655.

" COMOEDIA. A worke in Ryme/ contayning an Enterlude of Myndes/ witnessing the Mans Fall from God and Christ. Set-forth by H N, and by him newly perused and amended. Translated out of the Base almayne into English." The circular device. " My Heart indighteth a good Matter/ I tel-foorth vnto the King/ what I haue made. My Toung is the Penne of a redy Wryter. Psal. 45." On the back is an emblematical cut of Charity, &c. with this motto, " Charitas vincit omnia." Over it, " God is the Loue: and whoso abideth in the Loue/ hee abideth in God, and God in him. 1 Iohn 4, b." Under it, " My Babes/ let vs not loue in Woordes, nor with the Toung: but with the Deede and with the Trueth. 1 Iohn 3, b." Then, " The Preface To the good-willing Reader (whose Heart and Thoughts/ loueth Spirit and Lyfe) be Health and Saluation."---The Names and Attyre of the Parsonages[1] of thissame Playe." The Enterlude is divided into 17 chapters,

[1] " How the Parsonages (wherof there are Fifteene; That is to saye, Longing-for-comfort, Good-information, Ioye, Loue, Reasonablenes, Obedience, Trueth, Knowledge, Searcher, Playne-and-iust Cogitations, Good-thinking, Vnregarding, Lamentation, and Vnderstanding) shall stande in their Order and bee attyred.

" First-of all, Two Parsonages: The first named, Longing-for-comfort: apparelled like a comon plaine Man. The second, Good-information, like a Priest or learned man: Who do handle or plaie the Prologue and the Conclusion. Secondly, Fower Parsonages, which stand in the kingdom, in fower parts; namely, The Ioye (a Woman Parsonage) with a sweet Instrument-of-musick in her hande, as a Lute or such-like: The Loue (a Woman Personage; in her hande, a Paxe: The Reasonablenes (a Man Parsonage; in his hande a Compas: The Obedience (a Man Parsonage, like Moyses; hauing the Tables with the Lawe, in his Hande. Thirdly, Two Parsonages (which stand in the middest of the Kingdom) namely, The Trueth (a Man Parsonage, like an High-Priest or Christ; haueing in his Hande, an Image of the Sunne: And the Knowledg (a Woman Parsonage, very gorgiously and pleasantly decked; haueing in her Hande, a small Twigg with flourishing Leaues theron/ two Roles one vppon an-other: vppon the vpper-most Role, a Mans Heart figured: therby written High-Mynde: vppon the vndermost Role, a Deaths-headd: ther-by written, In-dying-to-dye. Fourthly, Tree Personages, which also bee in the middest of the Kingdom/ gooing and walkinge, namely, the Searcher (a Man Personage, clothed like a Serpent, beneath the knees, with a flyding Tayle comming out behynde; hauing in his Hande, an Image of a Serpent: thervppon written Subtiltee. Playne-and-iust (a Man Parsonage; And the Cogitacions (a Woman Personage) who haue each other by the Hande, Playnly clothed with Linnenwerde: vppon the Mans Garment written/ Simplenes: vppon the Womans, Faythfulnes. Fifthly, Fower Personages, without the Kingdom, that is to saye/ Good-thinking, and vnregarding (the Myndes of the Playe) Men Personages: Good-thinking, attyred before/ like an Hippocrate: and behind and downe to his Feete; like a Deuill.

ters, with Scripture references in the margin; also into 4 Pausas: The first at the end of the 1st Chap. or prologue; the 2d Pausa at the end of the 4th Chap. with this remark, "Heer is the Kingdom shutt: and before vppon the Doore, a Cherubin or Angel sett/ with a fyry Sword: vpon the Sword ? in a Role is written; Feare of Heart: and vppon the Angel, Accusacion." The 3d Pausa is at the end of the 5th Chap. The 4th Pausa is at the end of the 14th Chap. At the end of the 7th Chap. is this remark, or stage direction, "Heere do these fower Parsonages take each other by the handle and daunce: and from with-in, or out from above, one singeth this Song ensuing, before: and then ! in dauncing-maner; these fower Parsonages sing it after him: or els Vnregardith singeth it first, or before." Then follows the Song in 8 six-lined stanzas, being the whole of the 8th Chap. having this remark at the end of it, "Heere do the fower Parsonages sit them downe, and eate and drink." Then follows the Conclusion, consisting of the 15th, 16th, and 17th Chapters. At the end is the same device as at the end of The Prophetie, &c. p. 1636. The whole on 32 leaves. Octavo.

"FIDELITAS. A Distinct Declaratiō of the Requiring of the Lorde and of the godlie Testimonies of the holie Spirit of the Loue of Jesu Christ. Set-fourth by Fidelitas, a Fellowe-elder with H N. in the Familie of the Loue. Translated out of Base-almayne." The circular device. "Beholde I set before your eyes this-daye, the Blessinge & the Cursinge. The Blessinge/ if yee obey the Commaundementes of ẏ Lord your God, which I cōmaund or giue you this-daye. The Cursinge/ if yee obey not—but turne you out of ẏ Waye which I this-day will you vnto, or set-fourth before you. Deu. 11; 30." On the back is the same device, &c. as on the back of the title-page to Terra Pacis, p. 1637. Also, the same device of Love and Truth at the end of this, as at the end of that. Concludes with "Charitas extorsit per Fidelitas." C, in eights. Octavo.

"A good and fruitfull Exhortation vnto the Familie of Loue/ and vnto all those that are assembled ther-vnto. and rest goodwillinge to the Loue of God/ and to ẏ Loue of their Neighbour/ hauing a Lust to accomplish all Righteousnes: how they shall traine and foster them vp amonge each other/ in the Woorde and Seruice of Loue. grow-vpp to Elders in the holy and godlie Vnderstandinge of the gratious Woorde. and in the obedience of his Requiringe. Testified and set-fourth by Elidad/ a Fellow-elder with the Elder H: N, in the Famelie of the Loue of Iesu Christ. Translated out of Base-almayne." The circular device. "Let vs with each-other take good-heede to ourselues/ with stirringe-vpp to the Loue: and not forsake our Assemblinge, like as Certen doo: But exhort one-another of vs: and that somuch-the-more, as yee see that the Daye approcheth. Heb. 10, c." On the back is the emblematical cut of Charity as to Comœdia. Here is added to the

texts

Deuill. Vnregarding, before/ like a Light-myndded-one, and behind and down to his Frete/ like a Deuill: or bothy altogether like Deuills. Lamentation and Vnderstanding, Men Personages, appareled like two substanciall Citesans."

texts under it, " The right Father geeue you Power (according to the Riches of his Glorie; to be strong through his Spirit) in the inwarde Man: and Christ to dwell (through the Beleef) in your Heartes, and so to be rooted and grounded in you, through the Loue. Ephe. 3, b." On the last page " Loue" and " Trueth," Hand in hand, as p. 1638. A, in eights. Octavo.

—— " Mirabilia opera Dei: Certaine wonderfull Works of God which hapned to H. N. euen from his youth: and how the God of Heaven hath united himself with him, and raised up his gracious Word in him, and how he hath chosen and sent him to be a Minister of his gracious Word. Published by Tobias a Fellow Elder with H. N. in the Houshold of Love." The circular device, which appears to have been constantly used to all the early editions of this Family's publications. " Translated out of Base Almain. Now come hither and behold the works of the Lord, Ps. 46, 66. Know ye that the Lord leadeth his Saints wonderfully, Ps. 4, a. And take heed that ye do not despise the worke of the Lord, lest there come upon you that which is said in the Prophets. Behold, ye despisers and wonder and perish, for I do a work, in your days, which you will in no wise believe though a man declare it unto you, Hab. 1, a. Acts 13, b." Facing this title-page is the device of the Lamb's victory, &c. as p. 1638. now printed from copper-plate. Contains 137 pages, exclusive of the preface; and has on the back of the last leaf the device of Love and Truth, as p. 1638. from copper-plate also. W.H. Quarto.

—— " The First Exhortation of H. N. to his Children, and to the Family of Love. By him newly Perused, and more distinctly declared. Likewise H. N. upon the Beatitudes, and the Seven Deadly Sins. Translated out of Base-Almayne into English. Take mine Instruction to heart, and learn Wisdome and holy understanding: &c. Prov. 3. 17." This title is taken from a reprinted edition, 1656; as likewise the following.

—— " An Apology for the Service of Love, and the People that own it, commonly called the Family of Love. Being a plain, but groundly Discourse, about the Right and True Christian Religion: Set forth Dialogue-wise between the Citizen, the Countreyman, and an Exile: as the same was presented to the High Court of Parliament, in the time of Queen Elizabeth; and penned by one of her Majesties menial servants, who was in no small esteem with Her for his known wisdom and godliness. With another short confession of their Faith, made by the same people. And finally some Notes and Collections, gathered by a private hand out of H. N. upon, or concerning the eight Beatitudes." This latter with a separate title-page, as follows:

1575. " A Brief Rehersal of the Belief of the Good-willing in England, which are named the Family of Love, with the Confession of their upright Christian Religion against the false accusation of their against-Speakers. Set forth Anno 1575. Condemn no man before thou knowest the matter, know it first and than rebuke. Give no judgement

ment before thou hast heard the Cause, and let men first tell out their Tales. Eccl. 11. London, Printed—1656." See Strype's Annals, Vol. II; p. 375, &c. Neal's Hist. of the Puritans, Vol. I; p. 339, &c. W.H. Sixteens.

These pieces of the Family of Love without date are placed here together, having been probably printed about this time. The author of The Displaying—the Family of Love, &c. as p. 1057, in a list of the books of H.N. which he had seen, mentions, besides some of those above recited, the following, of which i have no other intelligence, viz. "The second exhortation of H.N.—A dialogue between the father and the son." This perhaps might be printed separate; but is introduced in the first exhortation.---"The declaration of the mass." A book with this title was printed by Hans Luft in 1547, in which Anth. Martort is announced to be the author. See p. 1563.—"The new and heavenly Jerusalem." He mentions also by hear-say, Two books intitled, "The glass of righteousness." See p. 1640; and a book called "The holy lamb."

The extract and effect of the queen's majesty's letters patents, to Thomas Tallis, and William Birde, for the printing of Musick.

"Elisabeth by the grace of God, quene of Englande, Fraunce, and Ireland, defender of the faith, &c. To all printers, bokesellers, and other officers, ministers, and subiects, greting. Know ye, that we for the especiall effection, and good will, that we haue and beare to the science of Musick, and for the aduancement thereof, by our letters patents, dated the xxii of January, in the xvii yere of our raigne, have graunted full priviledge and licence vnto our welbeloued seruantes, Thomas Tallis, and William Birde, gent. of our chappell, and to the ouerlyuer of them, and to the assignes of them, and of the suruiuer of them, for xxi yeares next ensuing, to imprint any, and so many, as they will, of set songe, or songes in partes, either in English, Latine, French, Italian, or other tongues, that may serue for musicke, either in churche or chamber, or otherwise to be either plaid, or soonge. And that they may rule, and cause to be ruled, by impression any paper to serue for printing, or pricking, of any songe or songes, and may sell and vtter any printed bokes, or papers of any songe, or songes, or any bookes, or quieres of such ruled paper imprinted. Also we straightly by the same forbid all printers, bookesellers, subiects, and strangers, other then as is aforesaid, to do any the premisses, or to bring, or cause to be brought, of any forren realmes into any our dominions, any songe, or songes, made and printed in any forren countrie, to sell, or put to sale, vppon paine of our high displeasure; and the offender in any of the premisses, for euery time to forfet to vs, our heires, and successors, fortie shillings, and to the said Thomas Tallis, and William Birde, or to their assignes, and to the assignes of the suruiuer of them, all, and euery the said bokes, papers, songe, or songes. We haue also by the same willed and commaunded our printers, maisters, and wardens of the misterie of stacioners, to 1574-5.

assist

assist the said Thomas Tallis, and William Birde, and their assignes, for the dewe executing of the premisses."*

—— " An Examination of Mr. Dr. Whitgifts censure, conteined in two tables set before his book entitled The Defense of the Aunswere to the Admonition," See p. 935. Publ. Libr. Cambr. Sixteens.

1575. " A catechisme, or a christian doctrine, necessarie for children and ignorant people, briefly compiled and set forth by Laurence Vaux, bacheler of diuinitie. With an instruction, newly added, of the laudable ceremonies vsed in the catholike churche. Antwerpe." Sixteens.

1575. " A Brieff discours off the troubles begonne at Franckford in Germany Anno Domini 1554. Abowte the booke off common prayer and Ceremonies/ and continued by the Englishe men theyre/ to thende off Q. Maries Raigne/ in the which discours/ the gentle reader shall see the very originall and beginninge off all the contention that hathe byn/ and what was the cause off the same. Marc. 4. For there is nothinge hid that shall not be opened, neither is there a secreat but that it shall come to light/ yff anie man haue eares to heare/ let him heare. M.D.LXXV." Prefixed is " The Preface To the Christian readers/ grace/ mercy/ and peace in Christ Jesu our Lorde." This begins on page I; and on page V begins " The Historie." The pages are all marked with numeral letters on the middle of the page, to p. ccxv, on the back of which is a correction of faults. W.H. Quarto.

1575. " A map of the city of Bristowe, by George Hoefnagle." A sheet.

1575. " An Engraved Mapp of STONHING by R. F. 1575." In the Museum of the Society of Antiquaries, London. Supposed to be the first of the kind in England.

—— " D. O. M. S. The Life and Death of Sir Thomas Moore Lord high Chancellour of England. Written by M. T. M. and dedicated to the Queens Most gracious Maiestie." No date. Said to have been published by a grandson of Sir Thomas, abroad. Quarto.

1575. " A true and perfect order to distil Oyles out of all manner of Spices, seedes, rootes and Gummes, with their perfect taste smel and sauour. printed 1575." Maunsell, P. II. p. 8. Octavo.

1575. Thomæ Drantæ Angli, Advordingamii Præsul." Dedicated " Edm. Grindall, archiep. Cant.--Ejus Carminum sylva.—reginæ." Bibliotheca Tanneri, p. 233. Quarto.

1575. " The Examination and Confession of a notorious witch named Mother Arnold, alias Whitecote, alias Glastonbury, at the Assise of Burntwood in July 1574: who was hanged for Witchcraft at Barking." MSS. T. Baker.

1575. " The Protestation of the most high and mightie Prince Frauncis Duke of Allenson," &c. Sixteens.

1575. " Certain deuout and godley petitions commonly called Jesus Psalter." Antwerp, J. Fouler. With I H S, or what is called the Jesuits arms, surrounded with cherubs, on the title-page. Sixteens.

1575. " The second replie of Thomas Cartwright: agaynst Maister Doctor Whitgiftes second answer/ touching the Churche Discipline. Isay. 62, vers. 1.

verſ. 1.—Ibid. vers. 6, & 7." &c. as to his Reply,—againſt the Admonition. p. 1634. "Imprinted M.D.LXXV." It has prefixed, an epiſtle "To the Churche off England," &c. and another "To the Reader.---The faultes most neceſſary to be corrected.---Other faultes which may ſomewhat ſtay the Reader.---The anſwer vnto the doctors præface: &c.---Anſwer to his two Tables," (or Notes.) Beſides: DCLXVI, (printed only DLXVI) pages, numbered with numeral letters, in the middle; alſo a table, and a note. Every 5 lines are numbered with Arabic figures on the inner margin. The ſame types as "The troubles at Franckford." W.H. Quarto.

"A MERVAYLOVS diſcourſe vpon the lyſe, deeds, and behauiour of Katherine de Medicis, Queene Mother: wherin are diſplayed the meanes vvhich ſhe hath practiſed to atteyne vnto the vſurping of the Kingedome of France, and to the bringing of the eſtate of the ſame vnto vtter ruine and deſtruction. At Heydelberge, 1575." Contains 196 pages, white letter. W.H. Sixteens. 1575.

"A ſhort catechiſm for the vſe of ſome in St. Pulcres pariſh." 1575.

"A NOTABLE Diſcourſe, plainelye and troely diſcuſſing, who are the right Miniſters of the Catholike Church: written againſt Calvine and his Diſciples, By one Maſter Iohn de Albine, called De Seres, Archedeacon of Toloſa in Fraunce. With an Offer made by a Catholike to a learned Proteſtant, wherein ſhall appere the difference betwixte the open knowen Church of the Catholikes, from the hid vnknowen Congregation of the Proteſtantes. Duaci. Per Iohannem Bellerum. 1575." It is introduced by a copious preface to the Reader. The running title, "A notable diſcourſe Againſt hereſies." This on 98 leaves, numbered. The Offer &c. annexed has freſh ſignatures, and the leaves are not numbered. C, in eights, the laſt leaf blank. W.H. See an anſwer to this book, p. 1404. Sixteens. 1575.

"An examination of M. doctor Whitgiftes cenſures. Contained in two tables ſet before his booke, entituled: The defence of the anſwere to the admonition," &c. 53 pages. See p. 935. Sixteens. 1575.

"A LETTER: Whearin, part of the entertainment vntoo the Queenz Maieſty, at Killingwoorth Caſtl, in Warwik Sheer in the Soomerz Progreſſ 1575. iz ſignified: from a freend officer attendant in the Coourt, vnto hiz freend a Citizen, and Merchaunt of London. 1575.

DE REGINA NOSTRA ILLUSTRISSIMA.
Dum laniata ruāt vicina ab Regna tumultu:
Læta ſuos inter genealibus ILLA diebus,
(Gratia Dijs) fruitur: Rūpantur & ilia Codro."

Inſcribed, "Vnto my good freend Maſter Humfrey Martin, Mercer." The author, who in p. 44 calls himſelf Laneham, in deſcribing the ſports and ſhews, repreſented for the queen's diverſion and entertainment, introduces one Capt. Cox, and ſo, in p. 34, &c. gives a liſt of the romantic and humorous books and ballads in that

 age.

age.' Concludes thus: "Well noow thus fare ye hartily well yfeith, if with wishĩg it coold haue been, ye had haa a buk or too this foomer, but we shall cum neerer shortly, & then shall we merily meet & grace a God in the mean time commed me I beseek yo: vntoo my good freends, almost most of thẽ yoor neighbors. Master Alderman Pullison, a speciall freende of mine: and in ony wise too my good old freend Master Smith Custumer, by that same token. Set my hors vp too the rak, & then lets haue a cup of Sak: He kneez the token well ynough, & wil laugh, I holde ye a grote. Too Master Thorowgood: And too my mery companion (a Mercer ye wot az we be) Master Denham, Mio fratello in Christo. he iz woont too summon me by the name of Ro. La. of the coounty *of* Nosingham Gentlman, A good companiõ I foyth. Well onez again fare ye hartely well. From the Coourt. At the Citee of Worceter, the xx. of August, 1575. Yor countreeman, companion, & freend assuredly: Mercer, Merchantauenturer, and Clark of the Councel chamber door, and also keeper of the same. El Prencipe negro. Par me R. L. Gent. Mercer.

De Maiestate Regia Benigno.

Cedant arma togæ concedat laurea lingua,
Iactanter Cicero, ad iustius illud habe:
Cedãt arma togæ, vigil et toga cedat honori
Omnia concedat Imperioq; suo.
Deo Opt. Max. Gratiæ."

Contains

* —" captin Cox an od man I promis yoo: by profession a Mason, and that right skilfull, very cunning in fens, and hardy az Gawin, for his tonsword hangs at his tabls eend: great ouersight hath he in matters of storie: For as for king Arthurs book, Huon of Burdeaus, The foour suns of Aymon, Beoys of Hampton, The squyre of lo degree, The knight of courtesy, and the Lady Faguell, Frederik of Gene, Syr Eglamoour, Sir Tryamoour, Syr Lamwell, Syr Isenbras, Syr Gawyn, Oliuer of the Castl, Lucres and Eurialus, Virgils life, The castl of Ladiez, The wido Edyth, the King & the Tanner, Frier Rous, Howleglas, Gargantua, Robin-hood, Adambel, Clim of the clough & William of cloudesley, The Churl & the Burd, The seauen wise Masters, The wife lapt in a Morels skin, The sak full of nuez, The seargeaunt that became a Fryar, Skogan, Collyn cloout, The Fryar & the boy, Elynor Rumming, and the Nutbrooun maid, with many moe then I rehearz heere: I beleeue he haue them all at his fingers endz. Then in Philosophy both morall & naturall, I think he be az naturally ouerseen: beside poetrie and Astronomie, and oother hid sciencez, as I may gesse by the omberty of his books: whearof part az I remember, the Shepherds kalender, The Ship of Fools, Daniels dreams, the booke of Fortune, Stans puer ad mensam, the hy wey to the Spitlhouse, Iulian of Brainfords testament, the Castle of Loue, the bouget of Demaunds, the hundred Mery talez, the book of Riddels, the Seauen sorowz of wemen, the prooud wiues Pater noster, the Chapman of a peniwoorth of Wit: Beside his auncient playz, Yooth & charitee, Hikskorner, Nugize, Impacient poouerty, and heerwith doctor Boords breuiary of health. What shoold I rehearz heer, what a bunch of ballets & songs all auncient: Az Broom broom on hil. So wo iz me begon, troly lo. Ouer a whinny Meg. Hey ding a ding. Booy last vpon a greene. My bony on gaue me a bek By a bank az I lay: and a hundred more he hath fair wrapt vp in parchment and bound with a whipcord. And az for Allmanaks of antiquitee, (a point for Ephemerides) I weene hee can sheaw from Iasper Laet of Antwarpy vnto Nostradam of Frauns, and thens vnto oor Iohn Securis of Salsbury. To stay ye no longer heerin, I dare saye hee hath az fair a library for theez sciencez, & as many goodly monuments both in prose & poetry, & at afternoons can talk az much without book, az ony Inholder betwixt Brainford and Bagshot, what degree soeuer he be." &c.

Contains 87 pages. See Dugdale's Warwickshire, p. 166. In his Majesty's possession. Sixteens.

"Practises touching the state of France, discouered by an Italian, a gentleman of Florence.—Printed 1575." Brit. Museum. Sixteens. 1575.

"A farewel sermon preached at Pauls cross by Edwin Sandys, sometime bishop of London, lately promoted to the archbishopric of York." See Strype's Life of bp. Aylmer, p. 25; also the enumeration of printed books, at the end. Text, 2 Cor. 13, 11. See p. 1061, and 1195. 1576.

"An epistle for the godly and christian bringing up of christian mennes children, or youth. Written in Latin by that famous learned clark, M. Coelius Secundus Curio, to his friend Fuluio Perregrino Morato, and englished by W. L. P. of saint Swithens by London stone, 28 June." Sixteens. 1576.

"Tvvo Sermons Preached by the reuerend father in God the Bishop* of Chichester, the first at Paules Crosse on Sunday beeing the fourth day of March. And the second at VVestminster." The rest of the title-page of my copy is torn off, which very probably contained the printer's name, and the date. See these sermons printed in 1584, p. 1203. The second sermon, as appears by its head title, was preached before the queen "the third Sunday in Lent last past, 1576." G 2, in eights. W. H. Sixteens. (1576.)

"A legendarie, conteining an ample discourse of the life and behauiour of Charles, Cardinal of Lorraine, and of his brethren of the house of Guise. Written in French by Francis de L'Isle. Imprinted. 1577." N 2, in eights; neat white letter. W.H. Octavo. 1577.

"The rest of the second replie of Thomas Cartvvright: agaynst Master Doctor Vuhitgifts second ansvuer, touching the Church discipline. Isay lxij, vers. j. For Syons sake, &c. Ibid. vers. 6. & 7. Ye that are the Lords Remembrancers," &c. See p. 1634. "Imprinted M.D.LXXVII." Prefixed is an epistle by Mr. Cartwright "To the Reader;" to which is annexed "An ansvver to the residvw of the surmises: as they are comprehended in the D. tvuo tables." Besides; 265 pages, white letter; but both the Roman and Great Primer Italic fonts wanted the w, which is supplied by vu, vv; except the Small Pica Italic font, which had a w, and was occasionally used to the Roman Text. At the end is a table of the principal pointes, &c. W.H. 4°. 1577.

Kendal's Flowres of Epigrammes; with a recommendatory poem, in English by Abr. Fleming. Sixteens. 1577.

Bucer's English Works were printed at Basil. Folio. 1577.

Sir Thomas More's Latin Works, translated into English, and printed at Lovain. Bodleian. (1577.)

"The Events of Comets or blazing Stars made vpon the sight of the Comet† Pagania, which appeared in Nov. and Decem. 1577. London

9 G 2

* Richard Curteis, or Courtesse, who succeeded bishop Barlow in that see, 1570. Ath. Oxon. I; 697.

† Pogonia. Maunsell, II; 24.

don 1577." Writers of Ireland, p. 327. "By John Vowell, alias Hoker, of the Citty of Exeter, Gentleman. Printed at London for the sayd John Hoker." Maunsell, II; 24. Octavo.

(1577.) "The Iudgement of that reuerend and godly lerned man, M. Lambert Danæus, touching certaine points now in controuersie, contained in his preface before his commentary vpon the first Epistle to Timothie, written in Latine, and dedicated by him to the Prince of Orange. But novv translated into Englishe for the behofe and comfort of all those, who (not vnderstanding the Latine tongue) are desirous to know the trueth in those points." At the end, "Geneva, the calends of August. 1577." English Roman, 12 leaves. W.H. Quarto.

1578. "A warning to take heed of Fowlers Psalter (sent lately from Lovain) giuen by same Thomas Sampson. Dated at Lecester, 10 Oct. 1577." See p. 1068, and 1147. Sixteens.

1578. "A Nievve Herball, or Historie of Plantes: wherin is contayned the vvhole discourse and perfect description of all sortes of Herbes and Plantes: their diuers & sundry kindes: their straunge Figures, Natures, Operations and Vertues: and that not onely of those whiche are here growyng in this our Countrie of Englande, but of all others also of forrayne Realmes, commonly vsed in Physicke. First set foorth in the Doutche or Almaigne tongue, by that learned D. Rembert Dodoens, Physition to the Emperour: And nowe first translated out of French into English, by Henry Lyte Esquyer. At London by my Gerard Dewes, dwelling in Pawles Churchyarde at the signe of the Swanne. 1578." This title is in a neat wood-cut compartment, seemingly designed for this work. At the top is a handsome flower-pot, and on the one side of it Flora, on the other Pomona, are sitting on the ground, each with her proper cornucopiæ; in the corners, Apollo and Æsculapius. On the sides, Gentius and Mithridates; Arthemisia and Lysimachus. At the bottom, the garden of Eden; wherein Adam is represented gathering fruit from one of the trees in the back ground: in the fore part, Eve is plucking an apple with one hand off the tree in the middle of the garden, and presenting one to Adam, lying on the ground, with her other: the serpent's head is discovered in the tree. At the other end of the garden Hercules is slaying the dragon, fabled to guard the Hesperian gardens: a label along the bottom of the whole, with HESPERIDVM HORTI, having P at one end and B at the other, which probably are the graver's initials; and on the scroll enclosing the garden A, perhaps the monogram of the designer. On the back, "Allusio ad Insignia Gentilitia Henrici Leiti Armigeri Somersetensis, Angli.

"Tortilis hic lituus, niueusq; Olor, arguit in te
Leite animum niueum, pictus (*pectus*) & intrepidum."

Over his paternal coat of arms; a chevron between 3 swans, the colours not noted, the crest a swan with expanded wings, standing on an antique trumpet: the motto on a scrol, LÆTITIA ET SPE IMMORTALITATIS. At one end of the scrol, "1578." Beneath,

"Lyke

"Lyke as the Swanne doth chaunt his tunes in signe of ioyfull mynde,
So Lyte by learning shewes himselfe to Prince and Countrie Kynde."

This translation appears to have been made from the author's second edition, and is dedicated "To the most High, Noble and Renowvned Princesse, our most dread redoubted Soueraigne Lady Elizabeth,—Queene of Englande, &c.—From my poore house at Lytescarie within your Maiesties Countie of Somerset, the first day of Januarie, M.D.LXXVIIJ.—Henry Lyte.—To the friendly and indifferent Reader." It has also prefixed sundry commendatory verses both in Latin and English, superscribed "VV. B. Thomas Nevvtonus Cestreshyrus. VV. Clovves. T.N. Iohannis Hardingi—Duodecasticon." Then, a very neat portrait, half length, "Remberti Dodonæi æta. XXXV. Virtute ambi.---R. Dodonæi Mechliniensis medici, in secundam commentariorum suorum de stirpium Historia, editionem, ad studiosos Medicinæ Candidatos, Prefatio.--R. D. de recognitione suurum commentariorum ad lectores epistola cum imaginum eius parte altera olim edita.—-Appendix:" containing sundry extracts from Pliny, &c. The work is divided into six[x] parts; each plant &c. having its respective figure. Contains 779 pages, besides the prefixes, and four[z] tables at the end. On the back of the last leaf is the printer's emblematical device: Jupiter in the clouds, holding in his left hand a roll, it may be presumed of decrees, and in his right hand a thunder bolt, seemingly about to hurl at an eagle ready to fly away with a hare, on which it has fixed its talons. The eagle as seeing its danger, with elevated head and open beak, seems to be apologizing for the transaction. Under the said device, "Jmprinted[y] at Antwerpe, by Hen. Loe Bookeprinter, and are to be solde at London in Powles Churchyarde, by Gerard [a]Dewes." W.H. Folio.

About this time encouragement was given to the art of engraving, and rolling-press work. Abram Ortelius mentions in his Geography several ingenious Englishmen, as one Anthony Jenkenson 1562, Robert Leeth, a man skilful in taking the plot of a country, sent over to take one of Ulster 1567, and Humphry Lhuyd 1568.[b] Strype in his life

[x] 1. Treateth of herbs, weeds, &c. 2. of flowers, seeds, &c. 3. of medicinal roots, &c. 4. of corn, grain, &c. 5. of herbs, roots, and fruits used for diet. 6. of trees, shrubs, &c.

[z] 1. The Latin names of the plants, &c. used by the ancients. 2.—by the moderns. 3. The English names. 4. Of their nature, virtues, dangers, &c.

[y] The p in the word Jmprinted had been omitted; and Jmp, to match the other letters, printed on a slip, is pasted over the Jm, in my copy.

[a] See p. 921; also, p. 1015 and p. 1016.

[b] The said Ortelius, in the catalogue of authors from whose works he compiled his Atlas, prefixed to the edition 1575, has this article "Humfredus Lhuyd, Angliæ Regni Tabulam (descripsit); Item Cambriæ Corographiam; Hoc nostro Theatro hoc anno 1563, publicatus." The said maps are inserted in this edition 1575: that of England bearing his name, and dated 1573; Wales without either name or date. The map of Scotland the same; but it is attributed to him in the index. In the said catalogue, "Thomas Geminus Hispaniæ tabulam, Londini;" but the map of Spain, in this edition, affords no intimation of Geminus's name.

life of archbishop Parker, p. 541, says thus: And now we are speaking of his servants and dependents, we may well mention his sculptores, or engravers, excellent in their art; whereof one was a foreigner, named Hogenbergh, and another was called Lyne. He employed them much in genealogies, wherein indeed a noble part of antient history consisteth. In Ruckholts (in the parish of Low Lewton in Essex) the mansion house of the family of the Hickeses, baronets (whose ancestor was secretary to the lord treasurer Burghley) there sometime was a large genealogy of the kings of England, from the conquest, well drawn, down to queen Elizabeth, and printed, with all the line of France, and of England, under these two titles, Linea Valesiorum, and Linea Angliae; and at the bottom the workmaster's name set, viz. Remigius Hogenbergius, servus D. Matt. Abp. Cant. sculpsit, 1574. Such another genealogical historical map there was entituled, Regnum Britanniae tandem plene in heptarchiam reductum à Saxonibus, expulsis Britannis, anno 686. Also on one side of it is ingraven a map inticuled, Angliae Heptarchia. (See R. Newbury.) It is done in wood, but very plain and well; to which the name is set, viz. Richardus Lyne, servus D. Matth. Archiep. Cant. sculpsit, 1574. In this map are described the seven kingdoms in seven columns, and the dioceses and countries contained in each kingdom. And in this table of genealogy is a threefold scheme; first, a scheme of the British kings, their names, and the years when they began to reign; secondly, another of the Norman dukes to William the conqueror, and the years when they began; and a third scheme of the Norman kings, beginning at William the conqueror, with the yeare and day of the month of their respective reigns, to queen Elizabeth, then reigning. So that here was represented a complete history of England, succinctly under one view. See p. 978, note t. Also a Map of England, and its several counties, were surveyed and engraved by the persons under named which now go by the name of Saxton's maps; for his encouragement, while doing, a [b]patent was obtained by Thomas Sekeford, esq. his great master and patron.

Counties

b "Nona pars patentium de anno regni reginae Elizabethe decimo nono, m. 20.

Dr Con' Christ. baxton.

"ELIZABETH by the grace of God, &c. to all manner of printers, bookesellers, and other oure officers, ministers, and subiects gretinge. Whereas Christopher Saxton, servaunte to our trustie and welbeloued Thomas Sekeford, esquier, master of requestes vnto vs, hathe already (at the greate coste, expenses, and charges of his saide master) trauyled throughe the greatteste parte of this oure realme of England, and hathe to the greate pleasure and commoditie of vs, and our louinge subiectes, vppon the perfecte viewe of a greate nomber of the seuerall counties, and sheires of our saide realme, drawen oute, and sett forthe, diuerse trewe and pleasaunte mappes, chartes, or platts of the same counties, together withe the citties, townes, villages, and ryuers, thereín conteyned, verie diligentlye and exactlie donne: and entendithe, yf God graunte hym lief, further to trauell therein, throughoute all the resídue of oure saide realme, and so from tyme to tyme to cause the same platts, and discriptions, to be well and fayre ingrauen in plates of copper, and to be after imprinted and stamped out of the same, as well to the commoditie of oure subiectes, as to all other, that shall haue pleasure to see and peruse the same: We lett youe witte, that for the better incourageinge of the saide Christopher, to proceede in this his so proffitable and beneficiall an enterprize to all

Counties names.	By whom.	
Oxfordshire		
Bucks		1574.
Berkshire	Cornelius Hogius	
Norfolk	Reinegius Hogenbergius	
Devonshire		
Dorsetshire		
Southampton		
Kent	Hogenbergius	
Southsex		1575.
Surry		
Middlesex		
Sommersetshire		
Suffolk	Leonard Terwoort, Antwerp	
	Durham	

manner of persons, of oure especiall grace, certen knowledge, and mere mocyon, we haue geuen, and graunted, and by theise presents do geue and graunte, priuiledge and lycence vnto the saide Christopher Saxton, and to the assigne, and assignes of hym, that he the said Christopher Saxton, and the assigne, and assignes of hym onelye, and none other, for, and duringe the space of tenne yeres nexte ensewinge the date of this oure lycence, shall and may by himselfe, his assigne, and assignes, factors, and deputyes, imprynte, and sett fourthe, or cause to be imprynted, and sett fourthe, any, and as manye suche mappes, chartts, and platts of this oure realme of Englande and Wales, or of anye countye, or other parte thereof, by hym allreadie, or hereafter to be sett fourthe, as to hym and to his saide deputye, and deputyes, shall seme mete and conueniente, and shall and maye sell, or vtter, or cause to be solde, or vttered, any suche imprinted mappes, chartts, or platts, as aforesaid. And further, we do by theis presentes streightlye forbydde, prohibite, and commaunde, all and singuler other parson, and parsons, as well printers and bookesellers, as all and euerye others whatsoeuer, beinge either oure subiectes, or straungers (other then the saide Christopher Saxton, and the assigne, and assignes of hym, or such other, as by the said Christopher, his executors, or assignes, shalbe appoynted) that they, nor any of them, duringe the saide terme of tenne yeres, in any manner of wyse, shall imprynte, or cause to be imprynted, drawen, paynted, or sett fourthe, any manner mappe, charte, or platte, as aforesaide, but onelye the saide Christopher Saxton, or the assigne, or assignes, seruaunts, or seruaunts, deputyes, or factors of hym the saide Christopher Saxton: nor shall bringe in, or cause to be broughte, from the partes beyounde the seas, into, or withein oure realmes, or domynyons, nor in the same shall sell, vtter, or put to sale, or otherwise dispose anye of the saide mappes, chartes, or plattes of anye oure realmes, or domynyons, or anye partes, or parcelles, of the same, made, or imprynted, in anie forreyne countrie, vppon payne of oure heighe indignacion and displeasure: and that euerye offender doinge contrarye to theffecte, and true meaninge of thies presentes, shall for euerye such offence, forfeicte to thuse of vs, oure heires, and successours, the somme of tenne poundes, of lawfull monye of Englande, and shall also moreouer forfeicte to the saide Christopher Saxton, and to th'assigne, and assignes of hym, all, and euerye suche mappes, chartts, and plattes, as shalbe imprynted, solde, or vttered, contrarie to the trewe entente and meaninge of thies presentes: willinge therefore, and commaundynge, as well the maister and wardens of the misterye of Stacyoners, in oure citye of London, as also all other oure officers, ministers, and subiectes, as they will auoyde oure displeasure and indignacion, that they, and euerye of them, at all tymes, when nede shall requier, duringe the saide terme, doe ayde and assiste the saide Christopher Saxton, and the assigne, and assignes of hym, and euerye of them, in the due exercyseinge and execucion of thies oure presente lycence and priuiledge, withe effecte accordinge to the true meanynge of the same, althoughe expresse mencion, &c. In witnes whereof, &c. Witnes oure selfe at Goramburie, the twoe and twentie daye of Julye, in the nineteenthe yere of our reigne. (1577.)

Per ipsam Reginam," &c.

	Counties names.	By whom.
1576.	Durham	
	Westmorland	Augustine Ryther, Anglus,[a]
	Cumberland	
	Cornwall	Leonard Terwoot
	Wilton	Hogenbergius
	Essex	
	Northampton	
1576.	Bedford	
	Cambridge	
	Huntington	
	Rutland	
	Warwickshire	Leonard Terwoort
	Lincoln	Remegius Hogenbergius
	Nottingham	
1577.	Worcestershire	
	York	Augustine Ryther
	Lancaster	Remegius Hogenbergius
	Chester	Franc. Scaterius
	Salop	Remegius Hogenbergius
	Hereford	
	Gloster	Saxton and Ryther
	Monmouthshire	Christopher Saxton
	Denbigh	Remegius Hogenbergius
	Flint	
	Harford	Ch. Saxton and Nic. Reynold
	Stafford	Franc. Scaterius
	Derby	
1578.	Glamorgan	
	Radnor	
	Breknok	Christopher Saxton
	Cardigan	
	Caermarden	
	Pembroke	
	Mongomery	Remegius Hogenbergius
	Mona } insulæ	
	Anglesey } insulæ	
	Carnarven	
	Scotland	William Bourough at Rome
1579.	Angl.	Augustine Ryther.
	Northumberland	
	Wales and Denbyshire.	

Cum priv.

" A

[a] Engraver, who did some of the maps of the Spanish invasion 1588, kept a shop a little way from Leadenhall, near the sign of the Tower, and got the discourse of Petruccio Ubaldino translated into English; all of which he dedicated to the lord admiral Howard 1590. See p. 1212. Harl. Miscellany, I, 115.

" A briefe discourse against the outward apparell" &c. as p. 1615. 1578.

Catechismus, sive Prima Institutio pietatis Christianæ, Græcè Latinè. By Alex. Nowell, see p. 611-2. Probably printed by the widow of Reynold Wolfe, see p. 613. 1578.

" A summe of the Guisian Ambassage to the Bishop of Rome." 16°. 1579.

A panegyric on baldness: translated from the Greek of Synesius by Abr. Fleming. At the end is his Fable of Hermes. Hist. of Eng. Poetry, III, 404. 1579.

" A Reproofe, spoken and geeuen-fourth by Abia Nazarenus, against all false Christians, seducing Ypocrites, and Enemies of the Trueth and Loue. Wher-withall their false Deuices, Punnishments and Condemnation: together with the Conuertion from their Abhominations: and their Preseruation in the Godlynes, is figured-fourth before their Eyes. Translated out of Nether-saxon." The circular device as p. 1636. " Like as Iannes and Iambres vvithstood Moses, euen so do These (namely, the Enemies of H. N. and of the Loue of Christ) also resist the Trueth. 2. Timo. 3. c. They slaunder that vvhich they knovv not, and vvhat they knovve naturallie, therin do they, like as Beastes vvhich are vvithout reason; destroy themselues. 2. Pet. 2. c. Iude 1. c. VVoe vnto them, for they go in the VVay of Cain. Gen. 4. Iudæ. 1. c. And for Lukers sake, they fall into the Errour of Balaam. Num. 24. Iudæ. 1. c. They perrish or vanish avvay in the Vprour of Chore. Leuit. 10. And are vvith their straunge Fire, like as Nadab and Abihu, consumed or brought to nothing by the Lordes Fire. Num. 16. Iudæ. 1. c. Imprinted in the Yeare of our Lorde, M.D.LXXIX." Contains 8 leaves. At the end, " Take it effectuallie to heart. Charitas extorsit per Abia." W.H. Octavo. 1579.

" The Garden of Health, Conteyning the sundry rare and hidden vertues and properties of all kindes of Simples and Plants, together with the maner how they are to be vsed and applyed in medicine for the health of mans body, against diuers diseases and infirmities most common amongst men. Gathered by the long experience and industrie of William Langham, Practicioner in Phisicke. Imprinted at London. 1579." Contains 702 pages besides an epistle " To the Reader," and " A Table of all the Simples" &c. prefixed; and " A Table conteining the effects of all the simples, set downe in this booke, by the order of the Alphabet." W.H. See p. 728. Quarto. 1579.

" Harmonia seu Catena Dialectica in Porphirium." By Richard Stanihurst. Writers of Ireland, p. 98. See p. 1627. Folio. 1579.

" A very godly and fruitfull sermon of maister Giulio of Milane, touching the Lordes supper, being the XLIIII, which he wrote. Translated out of Italian, and dedicated to the worshipful maistresse Anne Carow." See p. 727. Sixteens. 1579.

A homily of the Lord's supper, to be used in the diocese of Lincoln. Quarto. 1580.

1580. "A ful and plaine declaration of Ecclesiastical Discipline out of the vvord of God, and of the declining of the Church of England from the same." Metal flowers set in the form of a cross. "At Geneua. M.D.LXXX." Contains 202 pages, neatly printed on Small Pica Roman, No. 2; with an epistle addressed "To the godly reader," in Brevier Roman. It was published in Latin, 1574. See p. 1635. See Neal's Hist. of the Puritans, I; 449. W.H. Octavo.

1580. "A brief discours contayning certayne reasons, why catholiques refuse to goe to church. Written by a learned and vertuous man, to a frend of his in England, and dedicated by J. H. (*John Howlet, al's. Persons*) to the queenes most excellent maiestie. Imprinted at Doway by John Lyon. With privelege." Ath. Oxon. I; col. 357. Contains 70 leaves. See p. 1204; also the answer to it, p. 1120-21. 8°.

1580. The first three [a]books of Ovid's Tristia were translated into English by Tho. Churchyard, and dedicated to sir Christopher Hutton. Printed at London 1580. See Hist. of Eng. Poetry, III; 422, note r. I find "Ovid de tristibus In english" among the copies which had been the property of Tho. Marshe deceased, by the consent of one Edw. Marsh assigned over to Tho. Orwin 23 June 1591, and licensed to him by the Master and Wardens of the Stationers' Company. See p. 847. But I have not met with any account by whom it was printed; either in part, or the whole. Bodleian. Quarto.

(1580.) "The Judgment of a most reuerend and learned Man from beyond seas concerning a threefold[b] order of Bishops, &c. translated from Beza, "De triplici episcopatu," as was thought by John Field." See Strype's Annals, II; 629, &c. also "A Survay of the pretended Holy Discipline," p. 124. Without date of time, or place.

1580. "The services of Sir William Drury, Lord Justice of Ireland in 1578 and 1579, was published by Thomas Churchyard. London 1580." Additions to the Writers of Ireland, p. 363. Quarto.

1581. "An aduertisement and defence for Trueth against her Backbiters, and specially against the whispering Fauourers, and Colourers of Campions, and the rest of his confederats treasons. 1581. God saue the Queene." Four leaves; the last page blank. At the end, "God saue the Queene, long to reign in his honour." W.H. See p. 1081. 4°.

1581. "A very proper treatise, wherein is briefly set forth the art of limning, which teacheth the order in drawing and tracing of letters, vinets, flowers, armes, and imagery, and the maner how to make sundry sises, or grounds, to lay gold and silver uppon," &c. Rev. Dr. Lort. 8°.

1581. "THE DISPVTATION CONCERNING THE CONTROVERSIT HEADDIS of Religion, haldin in the Realme of Scotland, the zeir of God ane thousand, fyue hundreth fourscoir zeiris. Betuix. The prætendit Ministeris of the deformed kirk in Scotland. And Nicol Burne Professor of philosophie in S. Leonardis college, in the Citie of Sanctandrois, brocht vp

[a] Licensed to Tho. East, in July, 1577. [b] Of God, of men, and of the Devil.

vp in his tender eage in the peruersit sect of the Caluinistis, and nou be ane special grace of God, ane membre of the halie Catholik kirk. Dedicat To his Souerane the kingis M. of Scotland, King Iames the Saxt. Nisi conuersi fueritis, &c. Vnles ze be converted, God vil drau his suord: he hes bendit his bovv, and preparit it. Psalm. 7. Imprented at Parise the first day of October. 1581." On the back are quotations in Latin and Scotch from Mark 10 (29, 30.) and Mat. 10. (32, 33.) The dedication is superscribed "To the maist nobil, potent, and gratious king of Scotland king Iames the saxt.—At Parise the. 24. day of Iulij. 1581. Zour M. Maist humil, faythful subiect, and daylie Oratour Nicol Burne.—To the christian reidar." Contains 190 *leaves besides the prefixes; and, at the end, a table of "The materis of controversie quhilk ar intreated in this conference;" 41 in number. Then, 2 quotations in Latin and Scotch from I. Cor. 3. (18, 19.) and Psal. 83. (84, 10.) Colophon, "Imprentit at Pareis, the first day of October, The zeir of God, 1581." On the last leaf a flourish, by way of ornament. W.H. Octavo.

"A Treatise of Daunces. Wherein it is shewed that they are as it were accessaries and dependantes, (or thinges annexed) vnto whoredome: where also by the way is proued, that Plaies are ioyned and knit together in a ranke with them, printed 1581." Maunsell, p. 42. Octavo. 1581.

A Collection of Italian Proverbs, by Ch. Marbury. Quarto. 1581.

"A Brief Censure vppon two bookes Written (*by W. Charke and M. Hanmer*) in Answere to M. Edmonde Campions offer of disputation. Deuter. capit. 5. ver. 5. Yow feared the fyre, and therfore you ascended not vp the mountayne." I. H. S. decorated in an irradiated oval. "Imprinted at Doway by Iohn Lyon. 1581. With Privilege." 84 pages. Ascribed to Rob. Parsons. Ath. Oxon. I; 358. To this Censure W. Charke made a reply. See p. 1081. Sixteens. 1581.

"Rationes decem oblati certaminis in causa fidei redditæ Academicis Angliæ." Printed privately in the house of one Stonor a Cath. Gent. living near to Henley in Oxfordshire, an. 1581: afterwards publicly beyond the Seas. These reasons were very learnedly answered by Will. Whittaker of Cambridge, and replied upon by John Durey a Scot; which Durey was answered by Dr. Laur. Humphrey. See Ath. Oxon. I; 208. 1581.

"Davids Sling against Great Goliah." Sixteens. 1581.

"An apologie and true declaration of the institution and endeuours of the tvvo English Colleges, the one in Rome, the other novv resident in Rhemes: against certaine sinister informations giuen vp against the same. 1 Pet. 3. (15, 16, 17.) Sanctifie our Lord Christ in your hartes, &c. Printed at Mounts in Henault. 1581." On the back, 1581.

* On fo. 103. &c. is introduced an epigram of Beza's, with a libidinous translation.

" The contents[f] of this Apologie. The running title, " An Apologie of the English Seminaries." Contains 122 leaves, neatly printed on Roman types. At the end, " Your louing felovv and seruant in Christ Iesus. William Allen." W.H. Octavo.

1581. " Ane catholik and facile traictise, drauin out of the halie scripturs, treulie exponit be the aunciēt doctores, to confirme the real and corporell præsence of chrystis pretious bodie and blude in the sacrament of the alter. Dedicat. to his souuerane Marie the quenes maiestie of scotland. Be Iohne Hamilton student in theologie, and regent in philosophie to the maist excellent and catholik prince Charles of Bourbon in the royal college of Nauarre. Imprentit at Paris the first of April. 1581." On the back are these 3 texts of Scripture in Scotch, S. John 6. (53.) Heb. 13. (10.) Daniel 12. (11, 12.) This treatise, having for its running title " Of ye Lordis Supper," is concluded on fo. 116, or by signatures, P 4, in eights. Hereunto are annexed " Certain orthodox and Catholik cōclusiones, vith thair probationes, (24.) quhilk Iohne Hamilton regēt in ye Royall college of Nauarre, in name of ye Catholikis proponis to ye ministeris in ye deformit Kirk in Scotlād. To be disputit before the Kingis Maiestie ād his honorable coūsall.--- Certaine quaestionis (13) to the quhilkis ve desyre the ministeris mak resolute ansuer at yair Nixt generall assemblie, and send the same imprentit to vs with diligence: vtheruyse Ve protest yat yair prętēdit religiō is altogidder antichristian, and repugnant to God & his halie kirk." These are dedicated, " To the richt noble, verteous, and michtie Prince Iames the Saxt King of Scotland.—Vritten at Pareis in the Royall college of Nauarre the 20. of Aprile 1581. Zour maiestis maist humbill Subiect & daylie orator I. Hamilton." The signatures continued to V, in eights. The whole on neat white letter. W.H. 16°.

1581. " The Apologie or Defence of the most noble Prince William, by the grace of God, Prince of Orange, Countie of Nassau, of Catzenellenboghen, Dietz, Vianden, &c. Burgmaister of Antwerp, & Vicoūt of Bezanson, Baron of Breda, Diest, Grimberg, of Arlay, Nozeroy, &c. Lord of Castel-bellin, &c. Lieuetenant general in the low Coūtries, and Gouernour of Brabant, Holland, Zealande, Vtrecht and Frise, & Admiral, &c. Against the Proclamation and Edict, published by the King of Spaine, by which he proscribeth the saide Lorde Prince, whereby shall appeare the sclaunders and false accusations, conteined in the said Proscription, which is annexed to the end of this Apologie. Presented to my Lords the Estates generall of the lowe Countrie.—Printed in

[f] " The preface of the authors intention herein. Chap. 1. The reason of our absence and liuing out of our natiue Countrie. 2. Of our resorting sometimes to the citie and court of Rome. 3. The meaning and purpose of the institution of the Seminaries. 4. That we liue not in them against the lawes of God and our Countrie: with a dutiful exhortation to the Queenes Maiestie. 5. That the Students therof be not trained vp in erroneous doctrine. 6. Of Priests and Jesuites, and for what cause they are sent into England. 7. An admonition and comfort to the afflicted Catholikes."

in French and in all other languages. At Delft. 1581." Prefixed are "A copie of the Letters which—the Prince of Orange sent vnto the Kings and Potentates of Christendome—At Delft in Holland. the iiii. day of Februarie 1581.—A declaration made by—the Prince of Orange to my Lordes the Estates Generall of the lowe Countries.—Presented, &c. to my Lordes the Deputies of the Estates generall, and of the Prouinces vnited together, being assembled in the towne of Delft, the xiij. of December. 1580.—The answere of—the Estates generall, made to the former declaration.—Delft, the xvij. day of December. In the yeare of our Lorde, 1580." R, in fours. W.H. Quarto.

I have another edition this year, printed page for page. Quarto. 1581.

"A PLEASAVNT DIALOGVE, Betweene a Souldior of Barwicke, and an English Chaplaine. Wherein are largely handled & laide open, such reasons as are brought in for maintenaunce of popishe Traditions in our Eng. Church. Also is collected, as in a short table, 120. particular corruptions yet remaining in our saide Church, with sundrie other matters, necessarie to be knowen of all persons. Together with a letter of the same author, placed before this booke in vvay of a Preface. 2 Cor. 6. v. 15. What cōcord hath Christ with Belial? 1581." The preface is addressed "To my Reuerent Fathers and Brethren in Christ, Master Couerdale, Mai. Turner, M. Whittingham, M. Sampson, M. Doctor Humphrey, M. Leauer, M. Crowley, and others that labour to roote out the weedes of Poperie."—A. G. (*Ant. Gilby*)—Miles Monopodios the Souldiour, to his Capitayne Cornelius Theophilus.—From London, The x of May, 1566." Then, this other title more explanatory, "A pleasaunt Dialogue conteining a large discourse betweene a Souldier of Barwick, and an English Chaplain, who of a late souldier, was made a Parson, and had gotton a pluralitie of Benefices, and yet had but one eye, and no learning: but he was priestly apparailed in al points, and stoutely maintained his popish attire, by thi authoritie of a booke, lately written against London Ministers. This Dialogue was written almost seuen yeares ago, but because there was hope of reformation soone after, therefore it was of charitie by the writer suppressed. But now that no hope remayneth, it is thought good that the follie of the persecutors bee made knowne vnto all, that will see it, or read it. The Speakers. Miles Monopodios the Souldior, lame of one foote. Sir Bernarde Blynkarde, a formall Priest, and a Lords Chaplaine." N 4, in eights. The last 2 leaves contain "A Prayer for the Faythefull." See Strype's Annals, I; 480. W.H. Octavo. 1581.

"A Discouerie of I. Nicols minister, misreported a Iesuite, latelye recanted in the Tower of London. Wherin besides the declaration of the man, is contayned a ful answere to his recantation, with a confutation of his slaunders, and proofe of the contraries, in the Pope, Cardinals, Clergie, Studentes, and priuate men of Rome. There is also added a reproofe of an oration and sermon falsley pretended by the sayd Nicols to be made in Rome, and presented to the Pope in his Consistorye. (1581.)

fiflorye. Wherto is annexed a late information from Rome touching the autētical copie of Nicols recantation." Device: I H S decorated in an oval irradiated, with these texts of Scripture up and down the sides. "God hathe exalted him, and giuen him a name which is aboue all names. Philippenf. 2. ver. 9. There is no other name vnder heauen geuen vnto men, wherin we must be saued. Act. 4. ver. 12." Under it, "A lyeing witnes shall haue an yuel ende. Pro. 21. An non ex hæc odiosa impudentia, pullulabis mox impœnitentia, mater desperationis? Bern. Ser. 42. in Can." This book is ascribed to Rob. Parsons, the Jesuit, Ath. Oxon. I, 358. Contains M 9, in eights. W.H. Sixteens.

1581. Joan Crispini Lexicon Græco Latinum. Lond. 1581. Quarto.

—— "A true reporte of the death and martyrdome of M. Campion, jesuite and preiste, and M. Sherwin, and M. Bryan, preists, at Tiborne, the first of December 1581. Observed and written by a catholike preist, which was present therat. Whereunto is annexed certayne verses, made by sundrie persons." See the Appendix to Hearne's Textus Roffensis, p. 406. Sixteens.

1582. "The Nevv Testament of Iesus Christ, translated faithfully into English, out of the authentical Latin, according to the best corrected copies of the same, diligently conferred vvith the Greeke and other editions in diuers languages: Vvith Arguments of bookes and chapters, Annotations, and other necessarie helpes, for the better vnderstanding of the text, and specially for the discouerie of the Corruptions of diuers late translations, and for cleering the Controuersies in religion, of these daies: In the English College of Rhemes. Psal. 118. Da mihi intellectum, &c. That is, Giue me vnderstanding, and I vvil searche thy lavv, and vvil keepe it vvith my vvhole hart. S. Aug. tract. 2. in Epist. Ioan. Omnia quæ leguntur in Scripturis sanctis, &c. That is, Al things that are readde in holy Scriptures, vve must heare vvith great attention, to our instruction and saluation: but those things specially must be commended to memorie, vvhich make most against Heretikes: vvhose deceites cease not to circumuent and beguile al the vveaker sort and the more negligent persons.[1] Printed at Rhemes by Iohn Fogny. 1582. Cum Priuilegio." See Lewis, p. 277—285. Neat white letter. W.H. Quarto.

1582. "A discouerie of the manifold corruptions of the holy scriptures by the Heretikes of our daies, specially the English Sectaries, and of their foule dealing herein, by partial and false translations to the aduantage of

[1] The authors of this translation, which was made for the use of the English papists, are said to have been William Allyn, who was afterwards a cardinal, Greg. Martin, and Richard Bristow: the annotations were written by Tho. Worthington. A. Wood is silent as to Allyn, but says Greg. Martin "was the chief man that translated the New Testament, printed at Rheimes, 1582;" and that R. Bristow "collected, and for the most part wrote Annotations on the New Testament, translated into English at Rheimes." Ath. Oxon. I, 211-2.

of their herefies, in their English Bibles, vsed and authorised since the time of Schisme. By Gregory Martin, one of the readers of diuinitie in the English college of Rhemes. 2 Cor. 2. (17.) Non sumus sicut plurimi, &c. That is, VVe are not as very many, adulterating the word of God, but of sinceritie, & as of God, before God, in Christ vve speake. Printed at Rhemes, By John Fogny. 1582." Prefixed are "The preface conteining fiue sundrie abuses or corruptions of holy Scriptures, common to al Heretikes, & agreing specially to these of our times: with many other necessarie aduertisements to the reader.---The arguments of euery chapter," &c. Besides, 322 pages, and 2 tables at the end; one of typographical errors, the other, "A brief table to direct the reader to such places as this booke prouerh to be corrupted in diuers translations of the English Bibles: by order of the bookes, chapters, & verses of the same. Vvith some other corrupted by Beza & others, in their Latin translations." Neatly printed in white letter, with the quotations cited in the text given in their original languages in the margins. W.H. Octavo.

"A Booke which sheweth the life and manners of all true Christians, and howe vnlike they are vnto Turkes and Papistes, and Heathen folke. Also the pointes and partes of all diuinitie, that is of the reuealed will and worde of God, are declared by their seuerall Definitions, and Diuisions in order as followeth. Robert [h]Brovvne." The Middleburgh arms. "Middleburgh, Jmprinted by Richarde Painter. 1582." This begins on the back of the title-page, and contains O, in fours; the last page blank. W.H. Quarto. 1582.

Mr. Neal[i] mentions, as a prefix to the foregoing article, "A Treatise of Reformation without tarrying for any; and of the Wickedness of those Preachers who will not reform themselves, and their Charge, because they will tarry till the Magistrate command and compel them."[k] Mr. Ames annexes this to the last article as a part of its title-page: and if so, there either must have been another edition this year; or, which i am rather inclined to believe, The treatise of Reformation &c. was printed after this had been published, and then prefixed to it with a fresh title-page.

"A Treatise upon the 23d chapter of St. Matthew, both for an order of studying and handling the Scriptures, and also for avoiding the Popish disorders, and ungodly communion of all false Christians, and especially of wicked preachers and hirelings." This also is ascribed to Robert Brown —

[h] He was of an ancient and honorable family in Rutlandshire, whose grandfather Francis Browne had a charter granted by K. Hen. VIII, in 1526, and confirmed by Parliament, 'Giving him leave to put on his cap, in the presence of the King or his heirs, or any Lord Spirituall in the land, and not to put it off but for his owne ease, and pleasure.' The patent may be seen in Fuller's Worthies: Rutlandshire, p. 353. See a very particular relation of Robert Browne, the author, and his writings, in Biogr. Brit. II; 984, &c.

[i] Hist. of the Puritans, I; 375.

[k] "By me, Robert Brown" is added in the Biogr. Brit. II; 987.

Brown in the Biogr. Brit. II; 987. In this piece we are told he exclaims against the abuse of Tongues in preaching,—Hebrew, Greek, or Latin, in sermons: also against the use of logick and rhetorick, tropes, figures, *&c.* Against disorderly preaching at Paul's Cross in London, or before the queen, bishops, or noblemen: and against parish preachers, and hired lecturers. Quarto.

1582. Melchior Kling his learned Readings upon the 4 books of Institutions of Law by the Emperor Justinian. Imprinted at Leydon, 1582; and dedicated to Christian king of Denmark.

1582. "A Defence of the Censure gyuen vpon tvvo bookes of william Charke and Meredith Hanmer mynysters whiche they wrote against M. Edmond Campian preest, of the Societie of Iesus, and against his offer of disputation. Taken in hand since the deathe of the sayd M. Campian, and broken of agayne before it could be ended, vpon the causes sett downe in an epistle to M. Charke in the begynninge. Sap. 3. The sovvles of the iust are in the hande of God, and the torment of deathe shall not touche them: *&c.* An. 1582. Cum Priuilegio." On the back, "The corrector of the prynt vnto the gentle reader. To the ende this page shoulde not goe emptye, I haue presumed (vvithout the Authours knovvlege) to put downe for yonge scholers the true declynynge[1] of a Novvne Heretike: vvhereof vve haue more experience in these dayes than olde Grammarians hadde." &c. Prefixed, are, an epistle by "The setter[m] forth of this booke vnto VVilliam Charke, Minister.—The ansvvere to the *(M. Chark's)* preface touchinge discerninge of the Spirites. *(Triall of spirites.)*—The contentes of the former epistle and ansvvere." The censure is given entire in paragraphs, printed in Italics; the defence of each follows, printed in Roman. 173 pages besides the prefixes, and "A breefe table of the principall matters, &c. at the end. See an answer to this Defence of the Censure in p. 1416. W.H. Octavo.

1582. "Of Prayer and Meditation. Wherein are conteyned fovvertien deuoute Meditations for the seuen daies of the weeke, bothe for the morninges, and eueninges. And in them is treyted of the consideration of the principall holie Mysteries of our faithe. Written firste in the Spanishe tongue by the famous Religious father, F. Lewis de Granada, Prouinciall of the holie order of preachers in the Prouince of Portugall." A copper-plate cut of Christ Jesus, crowned with thorns, bearing his cross, followed by monks and friars of various orders bearing crosses

[1] "Singulariter Nominatiuo *Superbus.* Genitiuo *Temerarij.* Datiuo *Mendaci.* Accusatiuo *Pertinacem.* Vocatiuo *Seditiose.* Ablatiuo *Athea, vel Libertino.* Pluraliter: Hij & hæ *Impudentes,* per omnes casus. In English thus. The singuler number, An Heretike. In the nominatiue or first case (to beginne withall) he is *Prowde.* In the Genetiue case he groweth *Malepert.* In the Datyue case he becometh *a Lyar.* In the Accusatiue case he waxethe *Obstinate.* In the Vocatiue or preaching case he is *Seditious.* In the Ablatiue or endinge case hee proveth an Atheist, or els *a Lybertine.* The plurall number. In bothe genders, *Impudent,* throughowte all cases."

[m] Robert Parsons, a jesuit. See Ath Oxon. I; 358.

crosses also. Under which is engraved " Si quis vult post me venire, &c. luc. 9. vers. 23. Qui dicit se in ipso manere, debet sicut ille ambulauit, et ipse ambulare. 1. Iohan. 2. verse 6." Then, in letter-press, " Imprinted at Paris by Thomas Brumeau, at the signe of the Oliue. Anno Domini. M.D.LXXXII.." The translator's dedicatory epistle is thus addressed " To the righte honorable and worshipfull of the fower principall howses of the Cowerte in London, professinge the studie of the Common Lawes of our Realme, Richarde Hopkins wishethe dewe cōsideration of the holye mysteries of the Christian Religion.—From Paris, vpon the holie festiuall daie of Pentecoste. In the yeare of our Lorde. 1582.—An aduertisemente by the translatour to the Learned Reader." Wherein he says, " I doe folowe the edition in the Spanishe tongue printed at Andwarpe by Christopher Plantine,—1572." Then, " An exhortation to the Christian Reader, made by—Bernarde de Fresneda Bishoppe of Cuenca, one of the priuie Councell of Estate to the mightie Kinge Phillippe of Spayne, &c. And his Ghostly Father, to read this booke with good attention," &c. Besides, 331 leaves, neatly printed on Roman types, and adorned with several copper-plate cuts, neatly engraved. W.H. Octavo.

" Fruite of faith, containing all the praiers of the holy fathers, Patriarches, Prophetes, Iudges, Kinges, renowmed men and women, in the olde testament and new, by Richard Tauerner." Sixteens. 1582.

" A Briefe Historie of the glorious Martyrdom of 12 Reuerend Priests, executed within these twelue Monthes for Confession and defence of the Catholike faith. but vnder the false pretence of Treason. with a note of sundrie things that besel them in their life & Imprisonment: and a Preface declaring their Innocencie. Printed an: 1582." Octavo. 1582.

A plan of Nonesuch house, by George Hoefnagle. The late Mr. Tutet. Folio. 1582.

" A refutation of sundry reprehensions, cavils, and false sleightes, by which M. Whitaker laboureth to deface the late English translation, and catholick annotations of the new Testament, and the booke of Discouery of heretical corruptions. By William Rainolds, Student of Diuinitie in the English Colledge at Rhemes. 2. Timoth. 3. v. 8, 9. As Iannes and Mambres resisted Moyses, &c. Veni & vide. come and see. Iohn I. v. 46. Printed at Paris the yere 1583." Contains 561 pages, besides a preface of 91 pages, and " A table of the chapters" prefixed; and " A general (*alphabetical*) table of the principal thinges" &c. at the end. Whitaker published an answer to this, printed by Thomas at Cambridge, 1585; also at London the same year. W.H. 8°. 1583.

" A true report of the late apprehension and imprisonnement of Iohn Nicols Minister, at Roan, and his confession and answers made in the time of his durance there. Whereunto is added the satisfaction of certaine, that of feare or frailtie haue latly fallen in England. Printed at Rhemes, By Iohn Fogny. 1583." Contains 34 leaves, besides 1583.

a preface prefixed; and "An admonition to the reader.—The first of June 1583," at the end. W.H. Sixteens.

1583. "A treatyse of Christian Peregrination, written by M. Gregory Martin Licentiate, and late reader of diuinitie in the Englishe Coledge at Remes. VVhereunto is adioined certen Epistles vvritten by him to sundrye his frendes: the copies vvhereof vvere since his decease founde amonge his vvrytinges. Novv especially published for the benefite of those, that either erre in religion of simplicitie, or folovv the vvorlde of frayltie. Anno Domini 1583." On the back, "The contentes* of this booke." The peregrination occupies E 1, in eights, with a blank leaf following: the letters are on 42 leaves, without signatures or numbers. The whole neatly printed on white letter. W.H. Sixteens.

1583. "Oratio ad Pontifices Londini in Æde Paulinâ. An. Dom. 1553. 17. (7) Id. Apr. per Nic. Grimoaldum. Impressum 1583. Londini."

1583. "Rob. Payn his Hill-mans Table, which sheweth how to make Ponds to continue water in high and drie grounde, of what nature soeuer. Also the Vale-mans Table, shewing how to draine moores, and all other wette grounds, and to lay them drie for euer. Also how to measure any rouse ground, wood or water, that you cannot come into. &c. Prin. 1583." Maunsell, part II; p. 20.

1583. "A pithie and earnest Exhortation concerning the Estate of Christiandome," &c. Dedicated "To all Christian Kings, &c. by a Germaine Gentleman. Antwerpe, 1583." Chiefly political. Octavo.

1583. The Mirrour of Mirth, by R. D. 1583. Quarto.

1583. A treatise upon the 1st verse of the 122 Psalm: stirring up unto a careful labouring for the true Church government, by R.* Harrison. Printed 1583.

1583. Three forms of catechisms, containing the most principal points of Religion, by R.* Harrison. Octavo.

1583. "The tenth daie of December through negligence of vndiscreet persons, brewing in the towne of Nantwich,—the fire being carelesslie left, tooke hold (as should seeme) vpon some straw, or such light matter, and so burst foorth to the roofes of the house, and in short time so increased,—till it had consumed aboue 200 houses, besides brewhouses, barnes, stables, &c. as more at large appeared by a particular booke printed of that matter." Holinshed's Chron. III; 1356.

1583. A Christian Directory or exercise guiding Men to eternal Saluation, commonly called the Resolution. Reprinted

1584. By a catholic gentleman living at Roan in Normandy, full of errors, but in sense the same. See Ath. Oxon. I; 358.

A

* "1. A briefe preface. (The Printer's, signed R. V.) 2. A treatise of Pilgrimage and Relicks. 3. A letter sent to M. N. a maried priest. 4. A letter sent to his Sisters, married to protestants, &c. 5. A letter sent to M. D. Whyte then warden of newe colledge in Oxford," &c.

* Perhaps Richard Harrison, a country schoolmaster, and assistant to Robert Brown, the first separatist from the Church of England.

A Booke of Christian Exercise appertaining to Resolution, &c. By Edm. Bunny. See it in 1585. 1584.

"An Abstract, of certain Acts of parliament: of certaine of her Maiesties Iniunctions: of certaine Canons, Constitutions, and Synodalles prouinciall: established and in force, for the peaceable gouernment of the Church, within her Maiesties Dominions and Countries, for the most part heretofore vnknowen and vnpractized. Codex de Epis. & Cler. l. Nulli licere. Neyther let them feare to be called and suspected pickthankes, seeing their faythfulnesse, and diligent trauell carrieth with it, as well praise, as honestie and godly zeale; hauing published the trueth to the eares of all men, and brought it to the open light. Prover. 31. 8. Open thy mouth for the dumbe in the cause of all the children of destruction." The several abstracts here exhibited are to shew that "A learned Ministerie is commanded by the Lawe. 2. Dispensations for many benefices *are* vnlawfull. 3. Excommunication, by one alone forbidden. 4. Civil gouernment vnlavvfull in ecclesiastical persons. 5. Vnlavvfull to ordaine a Minister without a Title. 6. The manner of Archbishops, bishops, and Archdeacons visitations, and what procurations are due for the same. 7. Fees for Letters of Orders vnlavvfull." Concluding with certain Interrogatories. Contains 266 pages, beside a short epistle "To the Christian Reader." Without date or printer's name. See "An answer to the two first" &c. p. 958. W.H. Quarto.

"The Artes of Logike and Rethorike, plainlie set foorth in the English tounge, easie to be learned and practised: togither vvith examples for the practise of the same for Methode, in the gouernement of the familie, prescribed in the word of God: And for the whole in the resolution or opening of certayne partes of Scripture, according to the same." By Dudley Fenner. See p. 1511. The device: a printing press, having at top "Prelum," at bottom "R. Schilders; about it, "☞ In the sweat of the face, shalt thou eate the bread. Gen. 3. 19." Under all, "1584." Neither the pages nor leaves of this book are numbered. It has two sets of signatures; the first containing a preface "To the Christian Reader.---The Arte of Logike, *&c.*---The Arte of Rethorike," &c. These occupy E 3, in fours, and have a blank leaf following. The second set contains "The order of housholde, described methodicallie out of the worde of God, with the contrarie abuses founde in the vvorlde.---The resolution and interpretation of the Lordes prayer, out of Mat. 6. 9, and Luke 11, 2.---The Epistle to Philemon." These take up D, in fours. W.H. Quarto. 1584.

"Tho. Drant his 3 Sermons at the Spittel, the 1. on Canticles 5. vers. 17. and 6. ver. 1. The 2. on Genesis 2. vers. 25.[p] The 3. on Ecclesiastes 11. vers. 1, 2, 3. Printed 1584." Maunsell, p. 99. 8°. 1584.

 "The

[p] "They were both naked, Adam and Eve, and blushed not." Preached before the Court at Windsor, 8 Jan. 1569. See p. 647-8.

1584. "The Contempte of the World, and the Vanitie thereof, written by the reuerent F. Diego de Stella of the order of S. Fr. deuided into three bookes, And of late translated out of Italian into Englishe, vvith conuenient tables in the ende of the booke." This title over a neat wood-cut of IHS, with this motto "Vocabis nomen eius Iesvs." Under it, "In nomine Iesu omne genu flectatur. Philip. 2." Beneath all, "Anno domini. 1584." On the back is a cut of the shepherd's adoration, with 8 Latin rhiming verses; 4 over, and 4 under it. Addressed "To my Deare and Louing countrewomen and sisters in Christ assembled together to serue God, vnder the holie order of S. Briget in the towne of Rone in Fraunce." Contains besides, fo. 269, and tables. On the last page is a cut of the Virgin Mary and our Saviour; under it, "Iesu fili Dauid miserere mei. O mater Dei memento me." with 8 Latin rhiming verses, as before. Lambeth Libr. Octavo.

—— "A true, sincere, and modest defence of English catholiques, that suffer for their Faith both at home and abrode: against a false, seditious, and slaunderous Libel intituled; The execution of justice in England. VVherin is declared, hovv vnjustlie the Protestants doe charge Catholiques vvith treason; hovv vntrulie they deny their persecution for Religion; and hovv deceitfullie they seeke to abuse strangers about the cause, greatnes, and maner of their sufferinges, vvith divers other matters, perteining to this purpose. Psal. 62. Vt obstruatur os loquentium iniqua. That the mouth may be stopped of such as speake vniustlie. Psal. 49. Os tuum abundauit malitia, & lingua tua concinnabat dolos. Thy mouth hath abounded in malice, and thy tongue hath coninglie framed lies." Contains 218 pages, besides the preface prefixed; and the contents of the nine chapters, into which this treatise is divided, and "the faultes" corrected. The running title, "An answere to the libel of English iustice." See p. 1082. It is without date, printer's, or author's name. Mr. Ames's copy had written on the top of the title by Topclift's hand, 'A false, seditious, and immodest offence, set out by English traitors abroad, and some at home, groaning for the gallows, vnder shadow and colour off A true,' *&c.* [The title repeated] At the end, 'To be redd and used for the queen majesty's service.' In another hand it is said to be written by cardinal Allen.* A. Wood ascribes it to him without hesitation. Ath. Oxon. I; 271. Will. Parry also on a scruple of conscience, about killing Q. Elizabeth, whether it might be warranted in the opinion of some learned divines, confessed that this book had "taken hard hold" in him, and feared it would also in others, "if not prevented by more gracious handling of the quiet and obedient Catholique subiects." Which book being sent him out of France, "it redoubled, *says he*, my former conceites: Euery word in it was a warrant to a prepared mind: It taught that Kings may be excommunicated, depriued" &c. See Parry's

* "Dr. Allaine, *says he*, I desired, Persons I refused."

Parry's confession in "A true and plaine declaration" &c. as p. 1083. Also, Strype's Annals, III; 481. This book was answered by Dr. Tho. Bilson in "The true difference betweene Christian subiection and vnchristian rebellion," &c. printed at Oxford, 1585. W.H. Octavo.

"That such Papists as of late times haue been executed, were by a Statute of Edward III. Lawfully executed as Traitors. A Treatice." This was occasioned by a popish book then lately set forth, entitled 'Historia martyrum in Anglia.' Strype's Annals, III; 266. The whole is reprinted in the Appendix, p. 104. This seems to be the little book mentioned in The Scholar of Cambridge's letter of State, and there entitled "A defence of the publique iustyce done of late in Englande, vppon dyuers Pryestes and other Papystes for treason," and made the ground of the confabulation in that book. (1584.)

"The copie of a leter vvryten by a Master of Arte of Cambrige to his friend in London, concerning some talke past of late betvven tvvo vvorshipful and graue men, about the present state, and some procedinges of the Erle of Leycester, and his friendes in England. Conceyued, spoken and publyshed vvyth most earnest protestation of al duetyful good vvyl and affection, tovvardes her most excellent Ma. and the Realm, for vvhose good onely it is made common to many. Iob. Cap. 20. Vers. 27. Reuelabunt coeli Iniquitatem eius, & terra consurget aduersus eum. The heauens shal reueile the vvicked mans iniquitie, and the earth shal stand vp to beare vvitnes agaynst hym. Anno M.D.LXXXIIII." This is inserted in the Ath. Oxon. I; 360, among the works of Rob. Persons or Parsons, presumed on the affirmation of Dr. Tho. James that he was the author, yet Persons himself saith in his preface to the Warn-word to Sir Francis Hastings Wast-word, that he did not write 'Leicester's Common-wealth.* It contains 199 pages, including "The epistle directorie to M. G. M. in Gratious Street in London." and "The preface of the Conference." At the end, "A godlie and profitable meditation taken out of the 20. Chapter of the Booke of Iob," both in Latin and English. Neatly printed on White letter. The running title, "A letter of State Of a Scholar of Cambrige." W.H. 8°. 1584.

"A discouerie of the treasons practised and attempted against the Queenes Maiestie and the Realme, by Francis Throckemorton, who was for the same arraigned and condemned In Guyld Hall, in the Citie of London, the one and twentie day of May last past.† 1584." A square flourish used sometimes by Chr. Barker. C, in fours, besides an epistle by 1584.

* This assertion seems to be equivocal; for, though the book might soon after its publication have the nick-name of Leicester's Common-wealth, being a bitter invective against him, it did not appear in print under that title till 1641, when it was reprinted in 4°. See the preface to the life of Robert Earl of Leicester, 8°. 1727, the author of which appears to have seen only the last edition, 1641.

† This narration has in part been copied both by Hollingshead and Camden, yet not without the omission of several useful and necessary particulars to illustrate this part of the English history. See Harl. Misc. III; 181. The same remark will stand good with respect to most other temporary publications; later authors being frequently unacquainted with them.

by the printer "To the Reader," and "A letter sent from a Gentleman of Lions Inne to his friend concerning Francis Throckemorton," &c. Neatly printed on White letter. W.H. Another edition this year, Richard Gough, Esq. Quarto.

1584. "A true Report of the lamentable death of William of Nassawe, Prince of Orange; who was trayterouslie slayne with a dagge, in his owne courte, by Balthazar Serack, a Burgonian, the first of July, 1584. Herein is expressed the mutherers confession, and in what manner he was executed, vpon the tenth of the same month: whose death was not of sufficient sharpnes for such a caytife, and yet too sowre for any Christian. Printed at Middleborowgh, by Derick van Respeawe, Anno 1584." Contains 8 pages. See it in the Harl. Misc. III; 194, &c. Octavo.

1584. "Of prayer and meditation, &c. By F. Lewis de Granada. Rouen, 1584." See p. 1660.

(1584.) "A Treatise tovvching the right—of—Marye Queene of Scotland," &c. as p. 1503.

1584. "The Forme of Prayers and administration of the Sacramentes vsed in the Eng. Church at Geneua, approued & receiued by the Churche of Scotland." &c. as p. 1502. See p. 1604.

1585. "An Oration or Funerall Sermon vttered at Roome, at the buriall of the holy Father Gregorie the 13. who departed in Iesus Christ the 11. of Aprill. 1585. Conteyning his maners, life, deedes, and last wordes at his death concerning the affayres of this present time. Together with the lamentations of the Cardinalles and whole Clergie. Faithfully translated out of the French Copie, printed at Paris for Peter Iobert, dwelling in Harpestreate. 1585. with the Kings Priuiledge. Otherwise to be intituled: A Sermon full of Papisticall adulation and matter sufficient to procure the wise and vertuous minded to contemne such grosse and palpable blindnesse, and all persons to laugh at their absurde and erronious follies. Imprinted, Anno 1585." Prefixed are, an epistle "To the Courteous and Christian Reader.—Robert Greene.—In Papam Theodori Bezæ Carmen.—In eundem." 23 pages. W.H. Sixteens.

1585. "A true description, out of the Word of God, of the Visible Church." 4 leaves. Again 1589. Quarto.

1585. "The explanation of the true and lavvfull right and tytle of the moste excellent prince, Anthonie the first of that name, King of Portugall, concerning his warres, against Phillip King of Castile, and against his Subiectes, and adherentes, for the recouerie of his kingdome. Together vvith a briefe historie of all that hath passed about that matter, vntill the yeare of our Lord. 1583. Translated into English and conferred with the French and Latine Copies. By the commaundement and order of the Superiors. At Leyden In the Printing house of Christopher Plantyn. 1585." On the back is "The order of the Priuiledge. Maurice Erle of Nassawe, &c.—Giuen at Delft the 15. of Ianuarie. 1585. Ad Meetkerke. In the absence of my Lord the Earle, by the order

order of the counsellers of estate abouesaide. I. van Langen." 54 pages, and "A Pedigree or table of Genealogie," &c. W.H. Quarto.

"A Booke of Christian exercise appertaining to Resolution, that is 1585. shewing how that we should resolue our selues to become Christians indeed: by R. P. Perused, and accompanied with a Treatise tending to Pacification: By Edmund Bunny. Heb. 13. 8. Iesus yesterday, and to day, and the same for euer. Imprinted. 1585." Dedicated "To— his very good Lorde and Patron, Edvvin, by the prouidence of God Archbishop of Yorke, &c.---The preface to the reader.—At bolton-Percy, in the ancienty or liberties of Yorke, the 9. of July, 1584.--- The contents." Besides; 343 pages. Then, with a separate title-page, "A treatise tending to Pacification: By laboring those that are our aduersaries in the cause of Religion, to receiue the Gospel, and to ioyne with vs in profession thereof. By Edmund Bunny. Hosea 3. 45. The children of Israel shall sit a great while without King," &c. On the back is "A Table declaring the effect and method of this Treatise." 96 pages, white letter. W.H. Octavo.

"A Christian Directorie guiding men to their Saluation. Deuided into three bookes. The first vvherof apperteining to Resolution, is only 1585. conteined in this volume, deuided into tvvo partes, and set forth novv againe vvith many corrections, and additions by th'Author himself, vvith reprofe of the corrupt and falsified edition of the same booke lately published by M. Edm. Buny. There is added also a methode for the vse of al; with two tables, and a preface to the Reader, which is necessarie to be reade. Psal. 4. v. 3. Filij hominum vt quid diligitis vanitatem. You children of men why loue you vanitie. Luc. 1. v. 22. Porrò vnum est necessarium. But one thing is necessarie. Anno 1585. Augusti. 30." FFf 4, in eights; white letter. W.H. Octavo.

"A discourse of the Medicine called Mithridate, declaring the first 1585. beginning, the temperamene, the noble vertues, and true vse of the same. Prin. 1585." Maunsell, II; 16. Octavo.

"An Advertisement from a French Gentleman, touching the intention 1585. and meaning which those of the house of Guise haue in their late leuying of forces and Armes in the Realme of France: Written as an answere to a certain Declaration published in the name of the Cardinal of Burbon. Anno 1585. June." Contains 66 pages; to which is annexed "A Declaration of the causes that haue mooued the Cardinal of Burbon, the Princes, Peeres, Gentlemen, Townes & Comminalities Catholike of this Realme of France, to oppose themselues to those which by all meanes do seeke to subuert the Catholike Religion and the Estate." This, on 12 pages more. At the end, "Giuen at Shalons the of March, 1585. Signed, Charles Cardinal of Bourbon." W.H. Sixteens.

"A Summe of the Guisan Ambassage to the Bishop of Rome." 16°. ——

"A lamentable complaint of the Commonalty, by way of Sup- 1585. plication to the High Court of Parliament, for a learned Ministry. In Anno.

Anno. 1585." On the back is a short 'epistle "To the reader." The head-title, "The cry and complaint of the Commonality of this Lande," &c. This is one of the tracts for printing which Rob. Waldegraue was kept prisoner in the White-lion 20 weeks, as asserted by M. Marprelate in Hay any worke for Cooper, p. 42. F 3, in eights. W.H. 8°.

(1586.) Books delivered up by the richer printers to the company, for the reliefe of the poor, from a manuscript endorsed: "Decrees of the lords in the starre chamber, touching printers, stationers, &c. 23 Junii, Eliz. xxviii. 1585. (1586.) Orders for them sent to archbishop Whitgift."

"Whereas sundrie decrees and ordinances, have upon grave advise and deliberation, been made and published for the repressing of such great enormities and abuses, as of late (most men in tyme past) haue bene commonlye used and practised by diverse contemptuouse and disorderly persons, professing the arte or misterie of printing, and selling of books; and yet notwithstanding the said abuses and enormities are nothing abated, but (as it is found by experience) doe rather dayly more and more increase, to the willfull and manifest breach and contempt of the saide ordinances and decrees, to the great displeasure and offence of the queen's moste excellent majestie; by reason whereof sundrie intolerable offences, troubles, and disturbances, have happened, as well in the churche, as in the civile government of the state and commonweale of this realme, which seem to haue growen, because the paynes and penalties, conteyned and sett downe in the same ordinances and decrees, haue beene too light and small for the correction and punishment of so grievouse and heynouse offences, and so the offenders, and malefactors in that behalfe, haue not beene so severely punished, as the qualitie of their offences hath deserved: her majestie therefore of her moste godlie and graciouse disposicion, being carefull, that speedie and due reformacion he had of the abuses and disorders aforesaid, and that all persons using or professing the arte, trade, or mysterie of printing, or selling of books, should from henceforth be ruled and directed therein by some certeyn and knowen rules, or ordinances, which should be inviolablie kept and observed, and the breakers, and offenders of the same, to be severely and sharplie punished, and corrected, hathe straytly charged and required the most reverend father in God, the archbishopp of Canterburie, and the right honourable the lordes, and others of her majesties

' "Because our desire was, that this our complaint should be communicated to every one of the honorable of parliament, and finding no other waies to performe the same: we desired that it might be done by the way of printing. And we pray, that this our request may be made knowne to her maiesty, who in all the ciuill causes appertaining to this present life, is a myror of mercy, so we trust that her bowelles of pitty and compassion will abound and excede in this matter, that concerneth the saluation of the soules of her louing subiectes, and and that as she is the head and cheefest, so wee trust that her hand will be most forward in this sacrifice and service of the lorde, which he requireth for all the benefites that he hath most plentifully powred vppon her maiesty, and vppon vs by her maiesties gratious gouernment."

majesties privie council, to see her majesties said most gracious and godly intention, and purpose, to be dulie and effectuallie executed and accomplished. Whereupon the said moste reverend father, and the whole present sitting in this honorable cowrte, this xxiii day of June, in the xxviii yeare of her majesties reigne, upon grave and mature deliberation, hath ordeyned and decreed, that the ordinances and constitutions, rules and articles, hereafter following, shall, from henceforth, by all persons be dulie and inviolablie kept and observed, according to the tenor, purporte, and true intent, and meaning of the same, as they tender her majesties high displeasure, and as they wyll aunswere to the contrarie at their uttermoste perill. Videlicet.

" *In primis*, That every printer, and other person, or persons whatsoever, which at this tyme present hath erected, or sett vp, or hereafter shall erect, set up, keepe, maynteyn, or have anye printing presse, rowle, or other instrument, for imprinting of books, chartes, ballades, portraycetures, paper called, damask-paper, or any suche matters, or things whatsoever, shall bring a true note, or certificate of the sayde presses, or other printing instruments allreadie erected, within tenne dayes next coming, after the publication hereof; and of the saide presses, or other printing instruments hereafter to be erected, or set up, from tyme to tyme, within tenn dayes next after the erecting, or setting up thereof, unto the master, and wardeins, of the companie of stacioners, of the cittie of London, for the tyme being; upon payne, that every person fayling, or offending herein, shall have all, and everye the saide presses, and other instruments, utterlye defaced, and made vnserviceable for imprinting for ever; and shall allso suffer twelve moneths imprisonment without bayle or maynprise.

2. " *Item*, That no printer of bookes, nor any other person, or persons whatsoever, shall sett up, keepe, or mayntein, any presse or presses, or any other instrument, or instruments, for imprinting of bookes, ballades, chartes, pourtraictures, or any other thing, or things whatsoever, but onelye in the cittie of London, or the suburbs thereof (except one presse in the universitie of Cambridge, and one other presse in the universitie of Oxforde, and no more) and that no person shall hereafter erect, sett up, or maynteyne in any secrett, or obscure corner, or place, any suche presse, or instrument before expressed; but that the same shalbe in suche open place, or places, in his, or their howsse, or howses, as the wardeins of the saide companie of stationers, for the tyme being, or suche other person, or persons, as by the saide wardeins, shalbe thereunto appoynted, may from tyme to tyme have readie accesse unto, to search for, and viewe the same; and that no printer, or other person, or persons, shal, at any tyme hereafter withstande, or make resistance to, or in any suche view or search nor denye, or keepe secrett any suche presse, or other instrument, for imprinting, upon payne, that every person offending in any thing contrarie to this article, shall haue all the saide presses, and other printing instruments, defaced, and made unserviceable for imprinting for ever; and

and shall allso suffer imprisonment one whole year, without bayle, or maynprise, and to be disabled forever to keepe any printing presse, or other instrument for printing, or to be master of any printing-howsse, or to have any benefite thereby, other then onelye to worke as a journey man for wages.

3. " *Item*, That no printer, nor other person, or persons whatsoever, that hath sett up anye presse, or instrument, for imprinting within sixe moneths last past, shall hereafter use, or occupie the same, nor any person, or persons, shall hereafter erect, or sett up any presse, or other instrument of printing, till the excessive multitude of printers, havinge presses allreadie sett up, be abated, diminished, and by death giving over, or otherwise brought to so small a number of masters, or owners of printing-howses, being of abilitie and good behaviour, as the archbishop of Canterburie and bishopp of London, for the tyme being, shall thereupon think it requisite, and convenient, for the good service of the realme, to have some more presses, or instruments for printing erected, and sett up: and that when, and as often as the saide archbishopp and bishop, for the tyme being, shall so think it requisite, and convenient, and shall signifie the same to the said master, and wardeins, of the saide companie of stacioners, for the tyme being; that then, and so often, the saide master, and wardeins, shall (within convenient tyme after) call the assistants of the saide companie before them, and shall make choice of one, or more (as by the opinion of the saide archbishopp and bishopp, for the tyme being, need shall require) of suche persons being free stacioners, as for theyr skill, abilitie, and good behaviour, shall be thought by the saide master, wardeins, and assistants, or the more parte of them, meet to haue the charge, and government of a presse, or printing-howsse; and that within 14 dayes next after suche election, and choice, the saide master, wardeins, and fower other at the least of the assistants of the saide companie, shall present before the highe commissioners in causes ecclesiastical, or sixe or more of them, whereof the saide archbishopp, or bishopp, to be one, to allowe, and admitt everie suche person so chosen and presented, to be master and governoure of a presse, and printing-howsse, according to the same election and presentment, upon payne that everie person offending contrarie to th' intent of this article, shall haue his presse, and instruments for printing, defaced, and made unserviceable, and allso suffer imprisonment by the space of one whole yeare, without bayle, or maynprise. Provided allwayes, that this article, or any thing therein conteyned, shall not extend to the office of the queenes majesties printer for the service of the realme; but that the saide office, and officer, shalbe, and continue at the pleasure and disposicion of her majestie, her heires, and successors, at all tymes, upon the death of her highnes printer, or otherwise.

4. " *Item*, That no person, or persons, shall imprint, or cause to be imprinted, or suffer by any meanes to his knowledge, his presse, letters, or other instruments, to be occupied in printing of any booke, worke, coppie

coppie, matter, or thing whatsoever, except the same booke, worke, copie, matter, or any other thing, hath bene heretofore allowed, or hereafter shalbe allowed, before the imprinting thereof, according to th' order appoynted by the queenes majesties injunctions, and be first seene and perused by the archbishopp of Canterburie, and bishopp of London, for the tyme being, or one of them (the queens majesties printer for some speciall service by her majestie, or by some of her highnes privie counsell thereunto appoynted; and suche as are, or shalbe priviledged to print the bookes of the common lawe of this realme, for suche of the same books, as shalbe allowed of by the two cheefe justices, and cheefe barons, for the tyme being, or any two of them, onelye excepted) nor shall imprint, or cause to be imprinted, any booke, worke, or coppie, against the forme, and meaning of any restraynte, or ordinaunce conteyned, or to be conteyned, in any statute, or lawes of this realme, or in any injunction made, or sett forthe by her majestie, or her highnes privie counsell, or againste the true intent and meaning of any letters patents, commissions, or prohibicions, under the great seale of Englande; or contrarie to any allowed ordinaunce, sett downe for the good governaunce of the company of stacioners, within the citie of London; upon payne to have all suche presses, letters, and instruments, as in or aboute the imprinting of any suche bookes, or copies, shalbe imployed, or used, to be defaced, and made unserviceable for imprinting for ever; and upon payne allso, that everye offender, and offenders, contrarie to this present article, or ordinaunce, shalbe disabled (after any suche offence) to use, or exercise, or take benefite by using, or exercising of the arte, or feate of imprinting; and shall moreover susteyne sixe moneths imprisonment without bayle, or maynprize.

5. " *Item*, That everie suche person, as shall sell, utter, or put to sale wittingly, bynde, stitch, or sowe; or wittinglie cause to be solde, uttered, put to sale, bounde, stitched, or sowed, any bookes, or copies whatsoever, printed contrarie to th' intent and true meaning of any ordinaunce or article aforesaide, shall suffer three moneths imprisonment for his, or their offence.

6. " *Item*, That it shalbe lawfull for the wardeins of the saide companye, for the tyme being, or any two of the saide companie thereto deputed, by the saide wardeins, to make searche in all work-howses, shopps, ware-howses of printers, booke-sellers, booke-bynders, or where they shall have reasonable cause of suspition; and all bookes, copies, matters, and things printed, or to be printed, contrarie to th' intent and meaning of these present ordinances, to seaze and take to her majesties use, and the same to carrie into the stacioners hall in London; and the partie, or parties offending in printing, selling, uttering, bynding, stitching, or sowing any such bookes, copies, matters, or things, to arrest, bring, and present before the saide highe commissioners in causes ecclesiasticall, or some three, or more of them, whereof the saide archbishop of Canterburie, or bishopp of London, for the tyme being, to be one.

7. " *Item*, That it shalbe lawfull to and for the aforesaide wardeins, for the tyme being, or any two of them appoynted, without lett, or interruption of any person, or persons whatsoever, to enter into any howsse, work-howsse, ware-howsse, shopp, or other place, or places; and to seaze, take, and carrie away all presses, letters, and other printing instruments, sett up, used, or imployed, contrarie to the true meaning hereof, to be defaced, and made unserviceable, as aforesaide; and that the saide wardeins shall, so often as need shall require, call the assistants of their saide companie, or the more parte of them, into their saide hall, and there take order for the defacing, burning, breaking, and destroying of all the saide letters, presses, and other printing instruments aforesaide; and thereupon shall cause all suche printing presses, or other printing instruments, to be defaced, melted, sawed in peeces, broken, or battered, at the smythes forge, or otherwise to be made unserviceable; and the stuffe of the same so defaced, shall redelyver to the owners thereof agayne, within three moneths next after the taking, or seazing thereof, as aforesayde.

8. " *Item*, That for th' avoyding of the excessive numbers of printers within this realme, it shall not be lawfull for any person, or persons, being free of the companie of stacioners, or usinge the trade or mysterie of printing, booke-selling, or booke-bynding, to have, take, and keepe hereafter at one tyme, any greater number of apprentizes, then shalbe hereafter expressed; that is to say, every person that hath beene, or shalbe master, or upper wardein of the company, whereof he is free, to keepe three apprentizes at one tyme, and not above; and every person that is, or shall be under wardein, or of the liverie of the companie whereof he is free, to keepe two apprentizes, and not above; and every person that is, or shalbe of the yeomanrie of the companie, whereof he is, or shalbe free, to keepe one apprentize (if he himselfe be not a journey man,) and not above. Provided allwayes, that this ordinaunce shall not extend to the queenes majesties printer for the tyme being, for the service of her majestie, and the realme, but that he be at libertie to keepe and have apprentizes, to the number of sixe at any one tyme.

9. " *Item*, That none of the printers in Cambridge, or Oxford, for the tyme being, shalbe suffred to have any more apprentizes, then one at one tyme at the moste. But it is, and shalbe lawfull, to, and for the saide printers, and either of them, and their successors, to have, and use the help of anye journey man, beeing free men of the cittie of London, without contradiction; any lawe, statute, or commaundement, contrarie to the meaning and due execution of these ordinaunces, or any of them, in any wise notwithstanding."

Many of the richer stationers, who had some licences from the queen, granting them a propriety in the printing some copies, exclusively to all others, yielded divers of these copies to the company, for the benefit and relief of the poorer members thereof. A particular list of these books follows.

1583. "Books yeilded into the hands and dispositions of the master, wardeins, and

and aſſiſtants of the myſterie of the STATIONERS of London, for the reliefe of the poore of the ſaid companie, according to the diſcretion of the maſter, wardein, and aſſiſtants, or the more parte of them. 8 Jan.

Mr. BARKER, her majeſties printer, hath yeilded unto the ſaide diſpoſition and purpoſe, theſe bookes following, viz.

The firſt and ſecond volume of homilies.

The whole ſtatutes at large, with the preamble, as they are now extant.

The paraphraſis of Eraſmus upon the epiſtles and goſpells, appoynted to be read in churches.

Articles of religion agreed upon 1562, for the miniſters.

The queenes injunctions, and articles, to be enquired of through the whole realme.

The profitt and benefite of the two moſte vendible volumes of the New Teſtament, in Engliſh, commonlie called, Mr. Cheekes tranſlation; that is, in the volume called, Octavo, with annotations as they be now; and in the volume called, Decimo ſexto, of the ſame tranſlation without notes, in the Brevier Engliſh letter onely.

Provided, that Mr. Barker himſelfe print the ſayde Teſtaments at the loweſt value, by the direction of the maſter and wardeins of the company of ſtationers, for the tyme being. Provided allwayes, that Mr. Barker do reteyn ſome ſmall number of theſe for diverſe ſervices, in her majeſties cowrtes, or elſſewhere: and laſtlye, that nothing, that he yeeldeth unto by meanes aforeſaide, be prejudiciall to her majeſties high prerogative, or to any that ſhall ſucceed in the office of her majeſties printer.

Mr. TOTTELL, printer of the lawe books, hath yeilded unto the diſpoſition and purpoſe aforeſaide, theſe bookes following, viz.

Tullie's offices in Engliſh and Latin.

Morall philoſophie.

Romea and Julietta.

Quintus Curtius, in Engliſh.

Mr. Dr. Wilſon upon uſurie.

Two Engliſh lovers.

Songes and ſonnetts of th' earle of Surrey.

Mr. WATKINS, now wardein, hath yeilded to the diſpoſition and purpoſe aforeſaide, this that followeth, viz.

The broad almanack; that is to ſay, the ſame to be printed on one ſyde of a ſheet, to be ſett on walls, as uſuallie it hath bene.

Mr. JOHN DAYE, printer, hath yeilded to the diſpoſition and purpoſe aforeſaide, theſe bookes following, viz.

Calvin upon Daniell
Pilgrimage of princes
The jewell of joye
Principles of religion, by Becon
Derings ſermons in the tower
Practice of prelates
Image of nature and grace
Reliques of Rome
Hawes his examinations
Calvin's ſermons upon Ezechias
Pomander of prayers, in octavo
Governance of vertue, in octavo

Coſ-

Cosmographicall glasse
All the prayer books, which Henry Denham had from Mr. Day
Peter Martyr on the Judges
Peter Martyr on the Romanes
Poore man's librarie
Tindall's, Frythe's, and Barnes's workes
Becon's whole workes
Bullinger upon the Apocalips
Letters of the martyres
Calvin's catechisme, in sixteens
Image of God
Governance of vertue, in sixteens
Ascham's schole-master
Ascham's affaires of Germanie
Saxon lawes
Canons in English
Vita & mors Juelli
Articuli religionis
Epistola Gildae
Sylogisticon
Drant in ecclesiasten
Forrest of histories
A dialogue of Mercurie, and the English souldier
Astronomers game.

Mr. Newberye, wardein, and Henrie Denham, assignes to execute the privilege, which belonged to Henr. Bynneman, deceased, have yielded to the disposicion and purpose aforesayde, these bookes following, viz.

The breife chronicle in the volume, or sise, called, Decimo sexto. Provided allwayes, that all addicions, which hereafter shalbe putt to the same, and any other chronicle, that shalbe sett forthe in the same, or lyke volume or size, shalbe printed, and set forthe in the lyke breefe order, and forme, that the saide boke in decimo sexto, allreadie extant, is of. And all controversies, that may arise towching the saide booke, or addition, or alteration of, or to the same, or towching any other chronicle, that shall come forthe in this volume, or size, are submitted, and alwayes shalbe submitted, and referred to the ordering and determination of the master, wardeins, and assistants for the tyme being, or the more part of them.

Item, all these bookes and copies following, or so manye of them, as shall be fownd to have belonged to the saide Henrye Bynnemen, viz.

QUARTO.

Musculus common places
Cornelius Agrippa of the vanitie of sciences.
Digges his Stratiatitos
Arte of shooting in great ordinance.

OCTAVO.

The Spaniards lyfe
Booke of gardening
Colloquia Erasmi
Exercitatio linguae Latinae
Confabulationes Hessii
Justini historia
Virgilii opera
Sententiae pueriles
Psalmi Roffensis.

Mr. Newberye, now wardein, in his owne right, and of his owne copies, doth yeild to the disposition and purpose aforesaide, as follows, viz.

Bullinger's decades, now readie to print. Allwayes provided, that the printers of it shall give certeyn leaves, that he lacketh.

Mr. Cooper's postill, when Mr. Newbery hath solde those of the former

mer impression, which he hath in his hands, being under an hundreth bookes. And then he will procure the quires to enlarge it.

Panoplie of epistles, when he hath solde those he hath of the former impression.

Chronicle of ten emperours of Grecia, when he hath solde those he hath.

Galateo of good manners. }
Life of serving men. } Now ready to print.
Googe's songs and sonnetts. }

Perambulation of Kent, allmoste readie to print.

Item, The saide Henrye Denham hath yielded these bookes following:

Pasquin in a traunce	Schole of vertue
The hoppe gardein	Gardiner's laborynth
Ovid's metamorphosis	Demosthene's orations
The courtier	Two or three of Seneca his tragedies."
Cesar's commentaries in English	*Most of these books have the Stationers' arms on the compartment of the title-page.*
Ovid's epistles	
Image of idlenesse	
Flower of frendshipp	

" A defence of the reasons of the counter-poyson, for maintenaunce of the eldership, against an aunswere made to them by doctor Copequot in a publike sermon at Pawles Crosse, vpon psal. lxxxiv. *Anno* 1584. Wherein also according to his demaund is prooued Syllogistically for the learned, and plainelie for all men, the perpetuitie of the Elders office in the Church." See it in " Part of a Register, contayninge sundrie memorable matters," &c. as p. 506, &c. Sixteens. 1586.

" A choice of Emblemes and other Deuises, For the moste parte gathered out of sundrie writers, Englished and Moralized. And diuers newly deuised, by Geffrey Whitney. A worke adorned with varietie of matter, both pleasant and profitable: wherein those that please, maye finde to fit their fancies: Bicause herein, by the office of the eie, and the eare, the minde maye reape dooble delighte throughe holsome preceptes, shadowed with pleasant deuises: both fit for the vertuous, to their incoraging: and for the wicked, for their admonishing and amendment. To the Reader. 1586.

Peruse with heede, then frendlie iudge, and blaming rash refraine:
So maist thou reade vnto thy good, and shalt requite my paine."

Device: A hand extended from the clouds, with a pair of compasses describing a circle on a plain tablet, with this motto on a scroll, LABORE ET CONSTANTIA. " Jmprinted at Leyden, In the house of Christopher Plantyn, by Francis Raphelengius. M.D.LXXXVI." On the back is the Earl of Leicester's achievement, with 16 coats of arms, to whom it is dedicated: " To—my singuler good Lorde and Maister Robert Earle of Leycester, Baron of Denbighe, Knight of the moste noble orders of the garter, and of saincte Michael, Maister of her Ma.ties horse, one of her Highnes moste honorable priuie Counsaile, and Lorde Lieutenant and Captaine Generall

nerall of her Ma.ties forces in the lowe countries.—At London the xxviii. of Nouember, Anno M.D.LXXXV. Your Honours humble and faithfull seruant Geffrey Whitney.---To the Reader. Vvhen I had finished this my collection of Emblemes (gentle Reader) and presented the same in writinge vnto my Lorde, presentlie before his Honour passed the seas into the lowe countries I was after, earnestlie required by somme that perused the same, to haue it imprinted:—wherefore, licence being obtained for the publishing thereof, I offer it heare (good Reader) to thy viewe, in the same sort as I presented it before. Onlie this excepte: That I haue now in diuerse places quoted in the margent some sentences in Latin, & such verses as I thoughte did beste fit the seuerall matters I wratte of. And also haue written somme of the Emblemes to certaine of my frendes, to whome either in dutie or frendship, I am diuers waies bounde: which both weare wantinge in my firste edition, and nowe added herevnto," &c.—At Leyden in Hollande, the IIII. of Maye. M.D.LXXXVI. G. Whitney." Then, some commendatory verses in Latin and English. This book is divided into two parts. The emblems, or devices, neatly cut on wood, with their expositions, &c. of the first part occupy 103 pages. The second part, which has a distinct title-page, with the earl of Leicester's crest gartered, proceeds to page 230, on which is "Conclusio operis, Ad Illustrissimum Heroëm D. Robertum Dudlæum, Comitem Leicesteriæ,—Dominum meum vnicè colendum." The motto of this last emblem is "Tempus omnia terminat." W.H. Quarto.

1586. "Wheras sondry bookes are from tyme to tyme set furth in the partes beyond the seas, by such as are addicted to the errors of poperie, yet in many respects expedient to be hadd by some of the learned of this realme, conteyning also oftentymes matter in them against the state of this land, and sclanderouse vnto it, and therefore no fit bookes to passe through euery mans hands freely: In consideration whereof I haue tolerated Ascanius de Renialme, marchant bookseller, to bring into this realme from the partes beyond the seas, some fewe copies of euery suche sortes of bookes, vpon this condition onely, that any of them bee not shewed nor dispersed abroad, but first brought to mee, or some others of her maiesties priuiee councile, that so they may be deliuered, or directed to be deliuered furth vnto suche persons onely, as by vs, or some of vs, shall be thought most meete men (vpon good considerations and purposes) to haue the reading and perusall of them. Yeouen at Lambehith, the day of Octobre, 1586, anno regine Elizabethe, &c. xxviii." Endorsed, "Ascanios lycense to bring over popish bookes, granted by archbishop Whitgift, xiv." See Neal's Hist. of the Puritans, I, 481.

1586. The lives of the archbishops of Canterbury, written by Francis Thin, or Thynn, Esq; (taken chiefly from archbishop Parker's book "De antiquitate Britannicæ Ecclesiæ," &c. as p. 653) which Mr. Strype says was set forth this year, (1586.) It may be seen in the castrations of Hollinshed's Chronicles, p. 1435, &c.

1586. "A Letter sent by a learned Phisition to his freind, wherein are detected

tected the manifold errors, vsed hetherto of the Apothecaries in preparing their compositions, as Sirropes, Condites, Conserues, Pills, Potions, Electuaries, Losinges, &c. wherin also the reader shall finde a farre better manner how to preserue and correct the same, &c. written by *Anonymous*. 1586." Maunsell, II; 15.

"A booke of the forme of common prayers, administration of the Sacraments, &c. agreable to Gods worde, and the vse of the reformed Churches. The contentes of this Booke are conteyned in the page following. 1. Corint. 3. 11. No man can lay any other foundation then that which is layde, euen Christ Iesus. 1586." This form of common prayers is founded on that of Geneva, but has very considerable variations, additions, and omissions; probably made by the Brownists who settled at Middleburgh. By what denomination soever it was framed, there is in the "Prayer for the whole state of Christes Church," a very pious zealous clause for Q. Elizabeth and her council, which as the book is very scarce i have transcribed below.* It concludes, after describing the order of their ecclesiastical discipline, with a profession "of the civill magistrates †authoritie in causes of the Church.—Middleburgh, By Richard Schilders, Printer to the States of Zealande. 1586. Cum priuilegio." This appears to be the Form of prayer exhibited by the Puritans to the Parliament three times. See Strype's Life of Abp. Whitgift, p. 257; Neal's Hist. of the Puritans, p. 480. W.H. Again 1587. Octavo. 1586.

"A Request of all true Christians to the Honourable House of Parliament." Neal's Hist. of the Puritans, p. 480. (1586.)

* "Moreouer, because the hartes of rulers are in thine handes, we beseech thee to directe and gouerne the hartes of all Kinges, Princes, and Magistrates, to whom thou hast committed the sword: especiallie, ô Lorde, according to our bounden duetie, we beseeche thee to maintaine & increase the prosperous estate of our most noble Queene ELIZABETH: Whom as thou hast placed ouer vs in thy great mercie, and preserued her by thy mightie power; so wee beseeche thee, o Lorde, by the same mercie, to multiplie on her the excellent giftes of the holy Spirite: And by the same power as thou hast alwayes preserued her so to preserue her still. And as thou hast discouered the vnnatural treasons and wicked practises, so to discouer them still: that as for all other thy singular graces, so also for this great mercy both Prince and people may reioyce and magnifie thy great Name. Also we pray thee for her Maiesties right Honorable Councell, that thy good Spirite may furnishe euerie one of them with wisedome & strength, & other excellent giftes, fitte for their callinge. Furthermore, we pray thee for all other Magistrates, & for the whole Realme,——that they may in such sorte execute their office, that thy Religion may be purelie maintained, manners reformed, and sinne punished, according to the precise rule of thine Holie Worde."

† "Besides this Discipline of the Churche, we professe that Almightie God hath placed the Souueraine Magistrate in the highest authoritie vpon earth, next vnder him, within their Dominions, ouer al persons and causes, as well Ecclesiasticall as ciuill, to see and commande the ordering of them, as by his most holy Word he hath appointed. Therefore if any thing shal be otherwise done by negligence, contempte or any other cause, we acknowledge that by such authoritie they not only may, but also ought to enforce euery one aswell of the Ministrie and other charge in the Church, as those which are of the ciuill estate, to walke in their callinge as by the worde of God they are taught to doo; and to punish transgressors by the ciuil power committed vnto any such Magistrate, with temporall punishment in bodie, libertie, or goods, as the qualitie and condition of the offence in iustice shall require."

(1586.) "A petition made to the Conuocation house in the yeare 1586. by the godly Ministers, tending to reconciliation, and translated into English." Reprinted in A parte of a register, &c. p. 323. I have not met with the original edition.

1586. "The honourable reputation of a souldier. VVith a Morall Report of the Vertues, Offices and (by abuse) the disgrace of his Profession. Drawen out of the Lives, Documents, and Disciplines of the most renowned Romaine, Grecian, and other famous Martialists. By George Whetstone, Gent." The same in Dutch, with this addition; "Ende nu, ter liefden den Liefhebberen, beyde des Vaderlants ende dezer talen, verduytscht ende by een ghevoecht, door I. Walraven." Device: an angel as p. 1609; standing between the following sentence. "Hier volcht noch d' sche Pronunciatie." Beneath: "Tot Leyden, By Jan Paedts Jacobszoon, ende Jan Bouwenszoon. Anno M.D.Lxxxvi. Men vintse te coop by Thomas Basson Boeckvercoper, woonende tot Leyden opte breede-straet, by de Blauwe steen. Met Privilegie van zes Iaren." On the back is the Earl of Leicester's privilege, in Dutch, dated 14 Aug. 1586. Contains 103 pages, including the title page, with several prefixes in Dutch, Latin, and English, in prose and verse, to p. 25. On page 73 is a distinct title-page, viz. "English pronounciation: Or a short Introduction and Waye to English speache, very fitte for all those that intende to learne the same.

To the diligent Schooler.

Beare loue and labour in your mynde,
Than, what you seeke you shall it fynde:
For Love vanquisht, and Labour shall
What first was sowre, sweete make with all."

The same in Dutch. "Anno M.D.LXXXVI." W.H. Again 1587. 4°.

1586. Raptus Helenæ, a poem by Caluthus, was paraphrased in Latin verse by Thomas Watson, the writer of sonnets. Quarto.

1587. The same was translated into English rhyme by Chr. Marloe. See Hist. of Eng. Poetry, III; 433.

—— "The examinations of Henry Barrow, John Grenewood & John Penrie," &c. Mr. Ames has entred this book as printed in 1586, after The Harleian Miscellany, Vol. IV; p. 326, &c. where it is said, "Printed 1586." But Penrie's examination was not till the 10th of April 1593. The book indeed has no date of printing, but surely it was not printed before that time; shall therefore defer giving any further account of it to that year.

—— "William Farmer his Almanacke & Prognostication for the year 1587." Octavo.

1587. "John Fecknam, D.D. late abbot of Westminster, his* commentarie on the Canticles." Mr. Ames supposed it to have been printed at Middleburgh. Octavo.

"The

* None of our biographers, however, mention even his writing such a book.

" THE SONG OF SONGS, that is the most excellent song which was Solomons, translated out of the Hebrue into Englishe meeter, with as little libertie in departing from the wordes, as any plaine translation in prose can vse: and interpreted by a short commentarie. Colos. 3. 17. Let the vvorde of Christ dvvel in you richlie, &c. Middleburgh, Imprinted by Richard Schilders, Printer to the States of Zealande. Cum priuilegio. 1587." Dedicated " To the right worshipfull companie of the Marchant aduenturers.—I satisfie my self the better in this purpose of dedication, when I cōsider two thinges, which are adioined to this my poor labor: the one, that it promiseth a further & larger argumēt of my loue towardes you, in finishing after the same manner, the lamētations of Ieremie, and all other Psalmes, scatteringlie inserted in the Scriptures, if it be iudged profitable thus to goe forwarde: the other, that it seemeth to bee prepared for your dailie & ordinarie vse.—The Lorde direct your VV. with his spirit, perfect his good worke begun in you: blesse your good labours, so that you may still remaine an ornamēt to God his church, our most *Souueraine, and our cōmon wealth. Your VV. to commande in all thinges agreeable with my calling, Dudley Fenner." The said Fenner appears to have been the sole author of the commentary, and only of the latter part of the metre, as we gather from the preface " To the Christian Reader.---Of the certayne and vndoubted authoritie of the holy and most excellent soung of Solomon." Contains F 2, in eights. W.H. Octavo. 1587.

" Master Dudley Fenners defence of the godly Ministers against D. Bridges slaunders: with a true report of the ill dealings of the Bishops against them. Written a moneth before his death. Anno 1587." A parte of a register, &c. p. 387. (1587.)

" Hereafter ensueth the ancient seueral customes of the seuerall Mannors of Stebunhuth and Hackney, within the County of Middlesex, which were perused, viewed & approued by the Lorde of the saide Mannors, & by all the Copihold Tennants of the said seuerall Mannors, many yeeres past, and which Customes bee nowe againe newlie and fullie considered off, ratified, allowed and approued, by the right Honorable, Henry Lorde Wentworth, Lord of the saide seuerall Mannors, as in the seueral Articles & agreements hereafter following are expressed, the tenth of November. 1587. And in the 29. yeere of the raigne of our Soueraigne Ladie Elizabeth, by the grace of God Queene of England." &c. Contains 62 articles.* Quarto. 1587.

" The lamentation of Amyntas for the death of Phillis.* London, 1587." By Abr. Fraunce. Hist. of Eng. Poetry, III; 405, note o. It was printed again 1588 by John Charlewood. George Steevens Esq. Quarto. 1587.

" Certain deuises and shewes presented to her maiestie by the gentlemen 1587.

* This omission of the adjective is in the original.

* There is a Latin poem on the same subject at the end of " The third part of the countesse of Pembrokes Yuychurch," by the same author. See p. 1111.

tlemen of Grayes-inne, at her highnesse court at Greenwich, the 28th daye of Februarie, in the 30th year of her maiesties most happy reigne. Lond. 1587." Gough's British Topography, I; 672. Quarto.

1587. "Admonitio ad Orbis Terræ Principes, qui se suosque salvos volunt." Lond. 1587. Catal. Bibl. Harleianæ, III; No. 6899. Quarto.

1588. "Sir Philip Sidney's funeral procession to St. Paul's 1587, drawn and invented by Tho. Lant, gent. servant to the said hon. knight, and graven on copper by Theod. de Brij in the city of London, 1587. Lat. and Eng. Dated at the end." Gough's Brit. Topogr. I; 613.

1588. Feb. 13. "A proclamation against certaine seditious and schismatical bookes and libels," &c. was published, shewing, that they were slanderous to the state, and to the ecclesiastical government, established by law, *&c.* That they should immediately be brought in and distroyed, and that no author, printer, or disperser, should dare to offend herein, under pain of her majesties displeasure, and being prosecuted with severity. It may be seen among the records annexed to Strype's Life of Abp. Whitgift, p. 127. See more concerning libels, &c. in the Cotton library. Broadside.

1588. "A discourse of 3 kyndes of Pepper in common vse, and certaine speciall Medicines made of the same, tending to the preseruation of health. Prin. 1588." Octavo.

1588. "Jesuitarum Pont. Rom. Emissarios falso et frustra negare Papam Joan. VIII. fuisse Mulierem." Catal. Bibl. Harl. III; 6911. Quarto.

—— "The state of the Church of Englande laide open in a conference betweene Diotrephes a Byshopp, Tertullus a Papiste, Demetrius an vsurer, Pandochus an Inne-keeper, and Paule a preacher of the worde of God. Psal. 122. 6. Pray for the peace of Hierusalem, &c. Revel. 14. 9. 10. And the third Angel folowed them, saying with a loud voice, if any man worship the beast and his image," &c. Contains I 2, in eights. W.H. Sixteens.

1588. "The holy Bull, And Crusado of Rome:" &c. as p. 1173. was printed by Richard Schilders, printer to the States of Sealand.

1588. "An admonition to the nobility and people of England and Ireland concerninge the present vvares made for the execution of his Holines Sentence, by the highe and mightie King Catholike of Spaine. By *(Will. Allyn)* the cardinal of Englande." The cardinal's arms, surmounted with the Hat, supported by two angels hovering on the wing, one holding a crosier, the other a naked sword. "A°. M.D.LXXXVIII." The admonition is thus superscribed, "Gulielmus miseratione Diuina S. R. E. Tituli San[ti] Martini in Montibus Cardinalis Presbiter de Anglia nuncupatus, Cunctis Regnorum Angliæ et Hiberniæ Proceribus populis et personis, omnibusq; Christi fidelibus salutem in Domino sempiternam." Though the superscription is in Latin, the admonition is written wholly in English, and dated at the end, "From my lodginge in the Palace of S. Peter in Rome this 28. of Aprill. 1588. [a]The Cardinall."

[a] This book, together with a great number of A Declaration of the sentence of pope Sixtus the 5th—grounded on the said pope's Crusaido, (whereby he gave plenary indulgence

dinall." Contains 60 pages, including the title, neatly printed on white letter; paged with numerals in the middle. W.H. Octavo.

" A Spark of Friendship and warm good-will, that shews the Effect of true Affection and unfolds the Finenes of this World. Whereunto is ioined the Commodity of sundry Matters rehearsed in the same. With a Description and Commendation of a Paper-Mill, now of late set up (near the Town of Dartford) by an High German, called Mr. Spilman, Jeweller to the Queens most excellent Maiesty, written by Thomas Churchyard, Gent." Harl. Miscel. III; 249. See it before in 1558. 1588.

" THE MARINERS MIRROVR, Wherin may playnly be seen the courses, heights, distances, depths, soundings, flouds and ebs, risings of lands, rocks, sands and shoalds, with th'entrings of the Harbouroughs, Havens and Ports of the greatest part of Europe: their seueral traficks and commodities: Together w.th the Rules and instrumēts of Navigation. First made & set fourth in diuers exact Sea Charts, by that famous Nauigator Luke Wagenar of Enchuisen And now fitted with necessarie additions for the use of Englishmen by Anthony Ashley. Heerin also may be understood the exploits lately atchiued by the right Honorable the L. Admiral of Englād with her Ma.ties Nauie, and some former seruices don by that worthy Knight Sir Fra. Drake." This title is in a very suitable compartment, engraved by Theod. de Bry. On the next leaf is the achievement of Sir Christopher Hatton, with an hexastichon of Latin verses under it, very neatly engraved on copper also, to whom this book is dedicated:—" From the court at S. James. 20. Octob. 1588.---The authors admonition to the reader."—From Finchusen, 1586.—Operis commendatio.---The same in English in prayse of the vvoork." Prefixed to the charts are several tables, schemes, and directions pertaining to the art of navigation. The first part contains 22 charts, all engraved on copper, with a description to each in letter-press. (1588.)

" THE SECOND PART OF the MARINERS MIRROVR, conteining in diuers perfect plots & sea charts boeth the Northern and Eastern Navigation, viz. From the Streights between Dover and Callis, the coastes of England, Scotland, Norway, Emden, Yutland, &c. with all the sounds of Denmark. & the Baltick sea unto Wiburgh and the Narue. With their particular descriptions, trafiks and commodities." This title

indulgence and pardon of all sins to all that gave their helping hand to deprive Q. Elizabeth of her kingdom.) were printed at Antwerp, in order to be dispersed in England, when the Spaniard should arrive there, to stir up all the English papists to take up arms against the queen. However, upon the overthrow of the Great Armada, certain Roman Catholics procured the whole impression to be burned, saving some few that had been sent abroad beforehand to friends, &c. See Ath. Oxon. I; 271, &c. and Camden's Elizabeth, p. 409.

* Wherein we learn that the First part (of the Dutch edition) was published in 1583, and dedicated to the prince of Orange; and that a copy thereof (in 1585) was presented at the queen's Council Table by the Lord Admiral of England, and esteemed worthy to be translated and printed; and shortly after the Second part was printed and published.

title, like that of the first part, is engraved in a very elegant architective compartment, no doubt by T. de Bry, though his name is not set to it. This part contains 23 charts. The names of the engravers, viz. A. Ryther 1587, Jodocus Hondius, Joannes Rutlinger, and Theod. de Bry 1588, appear on several of the plates, especially those of the first part; but most of them are without any name, chiefly in the second part. No mention is made where or by whom this book was printed; it is however well executed, and on very stout paper fit for charts. W H. Royal folio.

1588. "A DEFENCE OF THE ECCLESIASTICAL Discipline ordayned of God to be vsed in his Church. Against a Replie of Maister Bridges, to a briefe and plain Declaration of it, which was printed An. 1584. Which replie he termeth, A Defence of the gouernment established in the Church of Englande, for Ecclesiastical matters. Iob. 31. 35. 36. 37. The booke that myne aduersarie shall write against me, I will beare it vpon my shoulder, *&c.* 1 Tim. 6. 13. 14. 15. 16. I charge thee in the sight of God,—that thou keepe these commaundements without spot, *&c.* 1588." This is introduced with a short prefatory epistle "Vnto the Christian Reader." Contains 228 pages, neatly printed on white letter. W.H. Quarto.

1588. "An humble petition of the Communalitie to their nost (*most*) renowned and gracious Soueraigne, the Lady Elizabeth, by the grace of God, Queene of England, France and Ireland, defender of the faith, &c. Also the lamentable complaint of the communalitie, by way of Supplication to the high court of Parliament, for a learned ministrie, renued and augmented. A petition made to the Conuocation house, 1586. by the godly ministers tending to reconciliation, and translated into English. John 21. ver. 15. 16. 17. Iesus said to Simon Peter, Simon the sonne of Iona, louest thou me more then these? *&c.* 1588." On the back is the same epistle "To the Reader," as to The lamentable complaint in 1585. This is a reprinted edition of these three tracts which had been printed separately before. P 6, in eights. W.H. Sixteens.

1588. "A viewe of some part of such publike wants & disorders as are in the seruice of God, within her Maiesties countrie of VVales, togither vvith an humble Petition vnto this high Court of Parliament for their speedy redresse. Wherein is shevved, not only the necessitie of reforming the state of religion among that people, but also the onely way, in regarde of substaunce, to bring that reformation to passe." A prefatory epistle "To all those that faythfully loue the lord Iesus, and vnfainedly desire the flowrishing estate of Sion, together vvith the vtter razing of vvhatsoeuer obscureth the perfect beutie thereof: & namely, to such of my brethren and countrimen, as the Lord hath enlightened with true knowledge," &c. The head-title repeats the former part of the title-page with the addition of "Anno 1588." The running-title, "A Supplication vnto the high court of Parliament." Contains 83 pages;

 subscribed

subscribed at the end, " By him that hath bounde himselfe continually to pray for your Hh. and worships. Iohn Penri." W.H. Octavo.

" An exhortation vnto the gouernours, and people of hir Maiesties countrie of Wales, to labour earnestly to haue the preaching of the Gospell planted among them. There is in the ende something that was not in the former impression. Psal. 137. 5, 6. If I shall forget thee, O Ierusalem, let my right hande forget her selfe, *&c.* 2 Cor. 1. 13. For wee write no other thing vnto you, than what you reade or that you acknowledge, *&c.* 1 Cor. 5. 13, 14. For, whether we be out of our wit, we are it vnto God, *&c.* 1588." Addressed " To the right honorable the Earle of Pembroke, Lorde President of VVales, &c. The rest of the gouernours there, and to all the gentlemen, Ministers and people my brethren, the inhabitants of Wales," &c. Subscribed on p. 45, " Your poore countrey-man, who in all dutifull good will, hath wholy dedicated him selfe to doe you good in the Lorde. Iohn Penri." On the next page follow the additions mentioned in the title-page, which end on p. 65,[d] with a short Postscript " To the reader," as below.' W.H. Sixteens. 1588.

" A Defence of that which hath bin written in the questions of the ignorant ministerie and the communicating with them. By John Penri." 63 pages.[e] Sixteens. 1588.

" The whole doctrine of the sacramentes, plainlie and fullie set downe, and declared out of the word of God. Written by maister Dudley Fenner, and now published for the church of God. Imprinted at Middelborg by R. Schilders." Octavo. 1588.

" Oh read ouer D. John Bridges/ for it is a worthy work: Or an epitome of the fyrste Booke/ of that right worshipfull volume/ written against the Puritanes/ in the defence of the noble cleargie/ by as worshipfull a prieste/ John Bridges/ Presbyter/ Priest or elder/ doctor of diuillitie/ and Deane of Sarum. Wherein the arguments of the puritans are wisely preuented/ that when they come to answere M. Doctor, they must needes say something that hath bene spoken. Compiled for the behoofe and overthrow of the Parsons/ Fyckers/ and Curraten/ that have lernt their Catechismes/ and are past grace: By the reverend and worthie Martin Marprelate gentleman/ and dedicated to the Confocationhouse. The Epitome is not yet published/ but it shall be when the Bishops are at conuenient leysure to view the same. In the mean time/ let them be content with this learned Epistle. Printed oversea/ in Europe/ within two furlongs of a Bounsing Priest/ at the cost and charges of M. Marprelate/ gentleman." The running-title throughout is " An Epistle to the terrible Priests of the Confocation house." Contains 54 pages, is full of personal reflections, ———

[d] Mr. Ames made the contents 71 pages, but that was by means of some old MS. verses annexed, at the end of the book.

[e] " I have read Master D. Somes booke, the reasons he vseth in the questions of the dumbe ministrie, and communicating with them, I had answered (as you may see in this booke) before he had written. The man I reuerence, as a godly & a learned man. The weaknes of his reasons, shalbe shewed at large Godwilling."

flections, and ends thus: "Giuen at my Castle between two wales/ neither foure dayes from penilesse benche/ nor yet at the West ende of Shrofftide: but the foureteenth yeare at the least/ of the age of Charing-crosse/ within a yeare of Midsommer/ betweene twelue and twelue of the clocke. Anno pontificatus vestri Quinto, and I hope ultimo of all Englishe Popes. By your learned and worthie brother, Martin Marprelate."* W.H. Quarto.

1588. "Triumphalia de victoriis Elizabethæ Anglorum, &c. Quarto.

"A demonstration of the trueth of that Discipline which Christ hath prescribed in his worde for the gouernment of his Church, in all times and places, vntill the end of the world. Wherein are gathered into a plain forme of reasoning, the proofs thereof out of the Scriptures, the euidence of it by the light of reason rightlie ruled, and the testimonies that haue been giuen thereunto, by the course of the Church certaine hundreths of yeares after the Apostles time: and the generall consent of the Churches rightly reformed in these latter times: according as they are alleadged and maintained, in those seuerall bookes that haue been written concerning the same. Math. 21. 38. The husbandmen said among themselues, this is the heire, come let vs kill him, and let vs take his inheritance. Luke 19. 27. Those mine enemies vvhich vvould not that I should raigne ouer them, bring hither, and slea them before me." Addressed "To the supposed Gouernors of the Church of England, the Archbishops, Lord Bishops, Archdeacons and the rest of that order.---To the Reader.---A Table of Discipline, the particular heads whereof, are handled in the seuerall Chapters," &c. Annexed to "A parte of a register," &c. but fresh paged, and with fresh signatures. Most of the things that are here expressed are acknowledged in the preface to haue been gathered out of the books that had been published. Contains 86 pages; white letter. Written by John Udall, for which he was tryed and condemned to be hanged; but died broken-hearted in the White Lion prison, just as a pardon had been procured for him, in 1592. See Strype's Annals, IV; 21, &c. Oldys's Life of Sir Walter Ralegh, p. LVII, &c. Also, A Remonstrance: &c. as p. 915. W.H. Quarto.

Mr. Ames mentions an edition of the same under 1589. Twelves.

"Oh read ouer D. John Bridges/" &c. as p. 1683: "By the reverend and worthie Martin Marprelat gentleman/ and dedicated by a second Epistle to the Terrible Priests. In this Epitome/ the foresaide Fickers/ &c. are very insufficiently furnished/ with notable inabilitie of most vincible reasons/ to answere the cauill of the puritanes. And lest M. Doctor should thinke that no man can write without fence but his selfe/ the fenceles titles of the seueral pages/ and the handling of the matter throughout the Epitome/ shewe plainely/ that beetleheaded ignoraunce/ must not liue and die with him alone. Printed on the other hand of some of the Priests." It is prefaced with an epistle superscribed "Martin Marprelate gentleman/ primate/ and Metropolitane of al the Martins in England.

England. To all the Cleargie masters wheresoeuer, sayth as followeth." From which you may see some extracts [f]below. The head-title, " The Epitome of the first booke, of this worthye volume, written by my brother Sarum, Deane John. Sic fœliciter incipit." With this running-title over it, " A very portable booke, a horse may cary it if he be not too weake." Every page hath its peculiar running-title, indicating the chief matter contained therein. Contains G 1, in fours. W.H. Quarto.

A True Description—of the Visible Church. See p. 1666. 1589.

" A short and true discourse for satisfying all those who not knowing the truth, speake indiscreetly of hir most excellent Maiestie, of the Lord Willughby Gouernour of hir Maiesties succours in the vnited Prouinces of the Low countries, and of all the English nation: by occasion of a strange placcat of the 17. of April 1589. the new stile, put foorth by certaine particular persons (as is said) vnder the name of the Generall States of those vnited Prouinces. By which discourse, euery one is praied and required to speak well and Honorably of th'actions of those Estates generall 1589.

[f] It begins, " Why my cleargie masters is it then so with your terriblenes? May not a poore gentleman signifie his good will vnto you by a Letter, but presently you must put your selues to the paines and charges of calling foure Bishops together, John Canterburie, John London, Thomas Winchester, William of Lincolne: and posting ouer citie and countrie for poore Martin? Why, his meaning in writing vnto you, was not that you should take the paines to seeke for him. Did you thinke that he did not know where he was himselfe? Or did you thinke him to haue bene cleane lost, that you sought so diligently for him? I thanke you brethren, I can be well though you do not send to knowe how I do. My mind towards you, you shal from time to time vnderstand by my pistles. As now, where you must know, that I thinke not wel of your dealing with my worship, and those that haue had of my bookes in their custodie. Ile make you rue that dealing of yours, vnlesse you leaue it.—If you dare aunswere my reasons, let me see it done. Otherwise I trow, my friends and I smnes will see you deposed.

" The Puritans are angrie with me, I meane the puritane preachers. And why? Because I am to open. Because I iest, I iested, because I dele against a worshipful iester. D. Bridges, whose writings and sermons tend to no other ende, then to make men laugh. I did thinke that Martin shoulde not haue beene blamed of the puritans for telling trueth openly.——Because you will do this, I will tell the Bishops how they shall deale with you. Let them say that the hotest of you hath made Martin, and that the rest of you were consenting thereunto: and so go to our magistrates and say, by such and such, of our puritans, haue vnder the name of Martin written against your lawes: and so call you in, and put you to your othes whether you made Martin or no. By this meanes M. Wiggington, or such as will refuse to take an othe against the lawe of the land, will presently be founde to haue made Martin by the bishops, because he cannot be gotten to sweare that he made him not: And here is a deuice to fynde a hole in the coat of some of you puritanes. In like sort, to fynde the Printer, put euery man to his othe, and fynd meanes that Schilders of Middleborough shalbe sworne to; so that if any refuse to sweare, then he may be thought to be the printer.

" For the rest that will needs haue my bookes, and cannot keepe them close: I care not how the Bishops deale with such open felowes. And bishops, I woulde I could make this year 1588. to be the wonderful yeare, by remoouing you all out of England.——There was the Demonstration of Discipline, published together with mine Epistle: which is a booke, wherein you are challenged by the puritans, to aduenture your Bishopp-ricks against their liues in disputation: You haue gotten a good excuse to be deaff at that challenge, vnder cooler of seeking for Martin: Your dealing therein is, but to holde my dishe, while I spill my pottage.——

" Eyther from countrie or Court,
M. Martin Marprelate, will do you hurt." &c.

generall lawfully assembled. Together with An Extraict of the autentique euidences and prooses for the chiefe poincts of this discourse, whereunto they are directed by respectiue quotation of page and Line. 1589." It is introduced with a short epistle by "Peregrin, Lord Willughby, Beck, Eresby, &c. Lieutenant, Gouernor, and Capteine general of hir Maiesties succours in th'united prouinces of the Low countries, to the courteous Reader." The head title, "A short discourse touching the siege before Gertrudenbergh, and the towne lost by reason thereof." Contains 51 pages, Roman letter. W.H. Quarto.

1589. "TH'APPELLATION OF IOHN PENRI, vnto the Highe court of Parliament, from the bad and injurious dealing of th'Archb. of Canterb. and other of his colleagues of the high commission: Wherin the complainant, humbly submitting himselfe and his cause vnto the determination of this honorable assembly: craueth nothing els, but either release from trouble and persecution, or just tryall. Psalm 35. 19. 20, &c. Let not them O Lord, that are mine enemies vniustly reioyce ouer me: &c. Ierem. 20. 21. The Lord is with me as a mightie Gyant, &c. Anno Dom. 1589." Superscribed, "To the right Honorable, th'assembly of the High court of Parliament, Iohn Penri wisheth the direction of Gods spirite, in all their consultations, that they may behaue themselues in the setting forward of Gods glorie, and the good of the weale publique: (as in the day, wherein the sonne of God, Christe Iesus, shall in flaming fire, render euerlasting perdition, to those that obeye not the Gospell) they may bee found blameles in his sight. March 7." Contains 52 pages; neat Roman letter. In this, as indeed in most of the tracts relating to the Puritanical controversy, there are several anecdotes of the affairs and persons of those times.* W.H. Sixteens.

—— "M. Some laid open in his coulers VVherein the indifferent reader may easily see, hovve vvretchedly and loosely he hath handeled the cause against M. Penri. Done by an Oxford man, to his friend in Cambridge. Prouerb. 30. 32. If thou hast bene foolishe in lifting vp thy selfe, and hast thought maliciously, laye now thy hande vpon thy mouth. For Proud, haughtie and scornefull is his name, that worketh wrath in his arroganeie. Prov. 21. 24." It is introduced with an anonymous epistle "To the Reader," beginning thus, "Hauing this lying by me, vvithout any purpose to publish it as yet, I vvas aduertized of the taking avvay* of M. Penries book by the Pursiuant. Whereupon I resolued (though

* "—— on the 29. of Ianuary last. (1589) At which time one Richard Walton hauing a commission from the Archb. and others,—to apprehend all those whome he should any waies suspect, and to commit them at his discretion vnto the next Gaul or prison, vntil further order should be taken with them, came into the place of mine aboad at Northampton, ransacked my study, and tooke away with him all such printed books and written papers as he himselfe thought good, what they were as yet I cannot justly tel. ——At his departure he charged the Maior of the towne, who then attended vpon him, to apprehend me as a traitor, giuing out that he had found in my study both printed bookes and also writings, which conteined treason in them. Whereas the

(though it shoulde be of some offence to my friende) not to closet it vp any longer, lest th'aduersary shoulde too much triumph & insult. Euen as it came vnto my hands, so haue I giuen it his pasport, vvithout any addition or alteration of mine: onely the Title I confesse is mine owne, the rest is my Oxford friends, vvho if he be thought in his pleasant veine anye thing too snappish, the reader is to vvey vvith vvhat kind of aduersary he deales:" &c. Besides, 124 pages. At the end, I. G. perhaps John Greenwood. W.H. Octavo.

" A Summons for sleepers: wherein most grieuous and notorious offenders are cited to bring forth true frutes of repentance, before the daye of the Lord now at hand. Hereunto is annexed a patterne for pastors, deciphering briefly the duties pertaining to that function, by Leonard Wright." Quarto. 1589.

" A Dialogue vvherin is plainly laide open the tyrannicall dealing of L. bishopps against Gods children: with certaine points of doctrine, vvherein they approoue themselues (according to D. Bridges his judgement) to be truely Bishops of the Diuell. Mallach. 2. 7, 8, 9. The Priests lippes should preserue knowledge, and they should seeke the law at his mouth: for he is the messenger of the Lorde of hostes. But ye are gone out of the way:" &c.[h] D 4, in fours, very neatly printed in white letter. It appears not to have been printed till after bishop Cooper's Admonition to the people of England. See p. 1084. W.H. Sixteens. ——

The same, dated 1589. Quarto. 1589.

" The Coblers book, which denies the church of England to be a true church, and charges her with maintaining idolatry under the name of decency, in the habits, fonts, baptism by women, gang-days, saints eves, bishoping of children, organs, wafer-cakes, &c." See life of Whitgift, p. 296. Perhaps written by Cliffe an honest Cobler dwelling at Battel-bridge, as in p. 39 of 'Hay any worke for Cooper'; Or, Newman the cobler, as in 'The reproof of Martin Junior,' p. the 2d. ——

" The lamentable complaint of the commonalty," &c. as p. 1667. 1589.

LAURENCE KELLAM a printer abroad printed many books, and is called 'Sworn printer to the English college at Doway.' Among others probably some of the puritanical tracts, especially such of them as were reprinted about this time. 1589.

" The vnlawfull practises of Prelates against Godly Ministers, the Maintainers of the Discipline of God." Contains D 3, in eights, the last page blank; neat English Roman, No. 2. W.H. Octavo. ——

the bookes and writings of greatest disgrace (even in the sight of his master) which he could there finde, were one printed coppy of the demonstration of discipline, and an answere vnto master D. Some in writing, both which he caried away with him." Appellation of John Penri, p. 6, 7.

[h] Reprinted in the time of Parliament, Anno Dom. 1640, with this addition on the title-page, 'Published, by the worthy Gentleman Dr. Martin Mar-Prelat, Doctor in all the Faculties, Primate and Metropolitan.' 4°. Which edition has moreover A prayer prefixed; and at the end, 'The description of a Puritan,' in verse.

[i] This is one of the tracts for the printing of which R. Walde-grave was kept prisoner 20 weeks in the White Lion, as asserted

—— The first and second Admonitions to the Parliament; together with Certain articles collected out of the first. &c. See p. 1632.

—— "A replye to an answere made of M. doctor Whitgifte agaynste the admonition of the parliament, by T. C." Quarto.

—— "A certayne Tragedie wrytten fyrst in Italian by F. N. B. entituled. Freewyl,[k] and translated into Englishe by Henry Cheeke." In a neat border of metal flowers. Dedicated "To the ryght honorable and vertuous Lady, the Lady Cheynie of Toddington." Whose shield, charged with 19 coats of arms, is on the back of the title-page.---"The Translator to the Reader." This tragedy, as it is termed, though apparently never designed for the stage, consists of five acts, divided into scenes, and is a most severe allegorical satire against the popish monarchy, and all it's mysteries of iniquity, relating their origin from time to time. It has neither the printer's name, date, nor place of printing; but seems to have been written about the time when the Netherlanders began to deliver themselves from the dominion of Spain, that affair being mentioned as a piece of news. The tragedy concludes with the tyrant Freewyl being destroyed by Lady Grace justifying. Contains, besides the dedication and preface, 211 pages, and a list of "Faultes escaped in the printing." W.H. Quarto.

—— "A discours of the present troobles in Fraunce, and miseries of this tyme, compyled by Peter Ronsard gentilman." Octavo.

—— "Hay any worke for Cooper: Or a briefe Pistle directed by waye of an hublication to the reverende Byshopps, counselling them, if they will needs be barrelled vp, for feare of smelling in the nostrels of her Maiestie & the State, that they would vse the aduise of reuerend Martin, for the prouiding of their Cooper. Because reuerend T. C. (by which misticall letters, is vnderstood, eyther the bounsing parson of Eastmeane, or Tom Coakes his Chaplaine) *hath shewed himselfe in his late Admonition to the people of England*[l] to bee an vnskilfull and beceytfull tubtrimmer. Wherein worthy Martin quits himselfe like a man I warrant you in the modest defence of his selfe and his learned Pistles, and makes the Coopers hoopes to flye off, and the Bishops Tubs to leake out

ferted in 'Hay any worke for Cooper,' p. 41. It was first printed in 1589. See Life of Whitgift, p. 121, &c. Again about this time; and afterwards in 'A parte of a register,' p. 380, &c. 'The Judgement of a most reverend and learned man,' &c. as p. 1654; and 'The lamentable complaint' &c. as above, are other tracts mentioned by Marprelat for which he was also imprisoned.

[k] Herein personated a king, and reported "that his maiestie was borne in earthly paradise, in the time of Adam and Eue, where his byrth was no lesse maruey-lous then the byrth of Adam and Eue. For as Adam dyd spryng of the earth without father or mother: and as Eue dyd procede of Adam without mother, so lykewise kyng Freewyl was born of two mothers, without a father: that is to say, of Lady Reason, and Lady VVyll, and of the one he was named Free: albeit since that tyme the people confoundyng these two names togeather haue made them one, and called hym Freewyl." Act I; Scene 3.

[l] What is printed in Italics was omitted in the title-page, but here supplied from the "Fauts escaped" at the end.

out of all crye. Penned and compiled by Martin the Metropolitane. Printed in Europe, not farre from some of the Bounsing Priestes." Prefixed is an epistle superscribed "A man of worship, to the men of worship, that is, Martin Marprelate gentleman, Primate, & Metropolitane of all the Martins wheresoeuer. To the John of al the sir Johns, and to the rest of the terrible priests: saith haue among you once again my cleargie masters." Contains besides 48 pages. Concludes with "Martin the Metropolitane to John the Metropolitane sayth, Nemo confidat nimium secundis. Martin to his troubled sonnes sayth, Nemo desper et meliora lapsus. Anglia Martinis disce savere tuis." W.H. Again in 1590 at Coventry. The late Dr. Marshall Mountague Merrick had them both. Quarto.

"A Whip for an Ape: or Martin displaied. ——

Ordo Sacerdotum fatuo turbatur ab omni,
Labitur & passim Religionis honos."

Begins: "Since reason (Martin) cannot stay thy pen,
We'll see what rime will doo: haue at thee then."

In 26 six-line stanzas; on 4 leaves, the last page blank. Quarto.

"Mar-Martine, ——

I know not why a trueth in rhime set out
Maie not as wel mar Martine and his mates,
As shamelesse lies in prose books cast about
Mar priests, & prelates, and subvert whole states.
For where truth builds, and lying overthroes,
One truth in rime, is worth ten lies in prose."

This consists of different epitaphs, or satirical verses of various metres. The last,

"If Martin dy by hangmans hands as he deserves no lesse,
This Epitaph must be engravde, his maners to expresse.
Here hangs knaue Martine, a traitrous Libeler he was,
Enemie pretended, but in hart a friend to the Papa,
Now made meat to the birdes that about his carkas are hagling
Learne by his example yee route of Puritan Asses,
Not to resist the doings of our most gratious Hester,
Martine is hanged, the Master of al Hypocritical hangbies."

Four leaves; printed on Italic types. Quarto.

"Asinus Onustus. The Asse overladen. To his loving and deare (1589.) Mistresse, Elizabeth the blessed queene of England." This book was reprinted in 1642 with this additional anecdote, "This book was deliuered to Queene Eliz: being at None-Such Iul. 27. Anno 1589." The preface, superscribed "The effect of the Booke, and the Asses intent, to the Reader." Begins, "The poore Asse to his Mistresse complaines of three injuries: That he is Despised; that he is Overladen; That his Provender is taken from him. This Asse is the Ministery and Clergie of England, compared to an Asse for strength, and for patience, & clemencie, &c." I have not seen the original edition.

"THESES MARTINIANAE: That is, Certaine demonstrative Conclusions, (1589.) sette

ſette downe and collected (as it ſhould ſeeme) by that famous and renowmed Clarke, the reuerend Martin Marprelate the great: ſeruing as a maniſeſt and ſufficient confutation of al that euer the Colledge of Catercaps with their whole band of Clergie-prieſts, haue, or canbring for the defence of their ambitious and Antichriſtian Prelacie. Publiſhed and ſet foorth as an after-birth of the noble Gentleman himſelfe, by a prety ſtripling of his, Martin Iunior, and dedicated by him to his good neame and nuncka, Maiſter Iohn Kankerbury: Hovv the yongman came by them, the Reader ſhall vnderſtande ſufficiently in the Epilogue. In the meane time, vvhoſoeuer can bring mee acquainted vvith my father, Ile bee bounde hee shall not looſe his labour. Printed by the aſsignes of Martin Iunior, without any priuiledge of the Catercaps." On the back, " Martin Iunior ſonne vnto the renowmed and worthy Martin Marprelate the Great, to the[a] Reader." The introduction; or, as the preface calls it, the ſmall thing before the Theſes, begins thus, " I ſee my doings and my courſe miſliked of many both the good and the bad, though alſo I haue favourers of both ſortes. The Biſhops, and their traine, though they ſtumble at the cauſe, yet eſpecially miſlike my maner of writing. Thoſe whom fooliſhly men call Puritanes like of the matter I haue handled, but the forme they cannot brooke. So that herein I haue them both for mine aduerſaries. But nowe what if I ſhoulde take the courſe in certeine Theſes or concluſions, without inueighing againſt either perſon or cauſe? might I not then hope my doings woulde be altogether approoued by the one, and not ſo greatly ſcorned at by the other?" &c. The Theſes are 110 in number, and he was going on " That our prelates. Heere the father leſte his writings vnperfite, and thus perfitely beginnes the ſonne." Then follows Martin junior's epilogue prefaced with a ſhort[b] epiſtle " To the worſhipfull his very good neame, Maiſter Iohn Canturburie." The epilogue begins thus, " Many flim flam tales goe abroad of him, but of certaintie nothing can be heard, in as much as he keepeth him ſelfe ſecrete from all his ſonnes. Some think that hee is euen nowe employed in your buſineſſe; and I thinke ſo too, my reaſon is, quoth Robert Some, becauſe it was for your ſakes and good

[a] " Thou ſhalt receiue (good Reader) before I ſet downe vnto thee anie thing of mine owne, certeyne of thoſe thinges of my fathers doings which I found among his vnperfect papers: I haue not changed any thing in them, detracted any thing from them, nor added vnto them aught of mine owne, but as I found them, ſo I haue deliuered them vnto thee. Mine owne meaning thou ſhalt vnderſtand at the latter ende in my Epilogue, to my nunckle Canterburie. This ſmall thing that followeth before his Theſes, is alſo his owne. I haue ſet downe the ſpeach as I found it, though vnperfect. One thing I am ſory for, that the ſpeach pretendeth the old man to be ſomething diſcouraged in his courſes."

[b] " After my harty commendations—The cauſe of my vvriting vnto you at this inſtant, is to let you vnderſtand, firſt, that I vvas ſomevvhat merry at the making heereof, being indeed ſory, together vvith others of my brethren that vvee cannot heare from our good father, Maiſter Martin Marprelate, that good & learned diſcourſing brother of yours,—. Moreouer I do you to vvete, that you ſhal receiue by this bearer, certaine vnperfect vvritings of my fathers, praying your prelacie, if you can ſend mee, or any of my brethren any vvord of him, that you vvould returne vs an anſvvere vvith ſpeede."

good, that hee first fell a studying the Arte of Pistle making: Others giue out, that in the seruice of his countrey, and her Maiesties, he died, or was in gret däger at the Groine. And those others (ka mine voka Bridges) haue seene motiues inducing them to be of this minde: Some there are also, who feare that you haue him in your handes. Howsoeuer it be somewhat is not well, that hee is silent all this while. We his sonnes must needes be disquieted, seeing wee can neither knowe where our father is, nor yet heare from him. If we could but heere by some Pistle, though it were but of 20 sheetes of paper, that he is well, we would not then be so inquisitiue of him. But now that he hath bin so long time tongue-tied these foure or fiue moneths, we must needes enquire of the matter." &c. I shall add a few more extracts from this very scarce tract, serving to throw some light on the contemporary publications, &c. " If you demaund of mee, where I founde this, the trueth is, it was taken vp (together with certaine other papers) besides a bush, where it had droped from some body passing by that way. I hope my fathers worship will not be offended with me, for publishing of it, being not so perfit as questionlesse he would haue had it.—A thirtie or fortie of the first Conclusions are alreadie shewed in Hai any work for the Cooper, and therefore they neede no further proofe then the reading ouer that woorthie Treatise, whence they seeme to haue beene collected. The rest I hope shall be shewed in More worke for the Cooper.—Wherefore, reuerend father, if you bee as yet on your feete, &c. Feare none of these beastes, these pursuvants, these Mar-Martins, these stage-players, &c. The reporte abroad goeth, that you are drawen drie, and can say no more. They are fooles that so thinke, I say, Let these Conclusions be iudge, &c. There bee that affirme, the rimers and stage players, to haue cleare putte you out of countenaunce, that you dare not againe shew your face.—Concerning Mar-martin, if he be a Londoner, or an vniuersitie man, tenne to one but you shall see him, one of these odde dayes, carted out of the towne for his honestie of life. &c. I can not bee induced to thinke, that hee hath had his bringing vp at any other trade, then in carryeng long Meg of Westminsters hand-basket, and in attending vppon some other of his auntes, at her appointment while shee liued. After her death, it may be he hath beene promoted vnto the seruice of some laundresse in a bishoppes house, where in hope to bee preferred by his good lordes, he hath vndertaken to mar-rimes in publishing bawdery, and filthinesse, for the defence of these honest bishops. The stage-players, poore seelie hunger-starued wretches, they haue not so much as an honest calling to liue in the common-wealth: &c. But heere by the way, Iohn Canturbury, take an odde advice of your poore nephew, and that is this, First, in regard of youre selfe, play not the tyrant as you doe, in Gods Church; &c. My second and last aduise is this in a word. Suffer no more of these haggling and profane pamphlets to be published against Martin, and in defence of thy hierarchie. Otherwise thou shalt but commend thy follie and ignorance vnto the world

to

to be notorious. Mar-martin, Leonard Wright, Fregneuile Dick, Bancroft, Tom Blan. o Bedford, Kemp, serue thee for no other vse, but to worke thy ruine, and to bewray their owne shame, and miserable ignorance.—I did all of a good meaning, to saue my fathers papers: and it would haue pitied your heart to see, how the poore papers were raine and weather-beaten, euen truely in such a sort, as they coulde scant bee read to bee printed. There was neuer a drie threede in them.—Farewell, good nuncle, and pay this bearer for the cariage. Iuly 22. 1589. With as great speede as I might. Your worships nephew MARTIN IVNIOR." B, in eights; neat Long primer Roman. W.H. 16°.

1589. "The Copy of a Letter lately written by a Spanishe Gentleman to his Friend in England, in Refutation of sundry Calumnies, there falsly bruited and spred emong the People." Octavo.

—— "Marre Mar-Martin; or Marre Martins medling in a manner misliked." In verse. Quarto.

1589. "A Countercuffe giuen to Martin Iunior: by the venturous, hardie, and renowned Pasquill of Englande, Caualiero. Not of olde Martins making, which newlie knighted the Saints in Heauen, with rise vppe Sir Peter and Sir Paule; But lately dubd for his seruice at home in the defence of his Countrey, and for the cleane breaking of his staffe vpon Martins face. Printed between the skye and the grounde, wythin a myle of an Oake, and not manie Fields off, from the vnpriuiledged Presse of the Ass-ignes of Martin Junior. Anno Dom. 1589." Both head, and running title, "Pasquill of England to Martin Junior." Accept a few extracts from this short tract. "Pasquill hath vndertaken to write a verie famous worke, Entituled, The Owles Almanack, wherein the night labours, and birth of your Religion is set downe, &c. Pasquill hath posted very dilligentlie ouer all the Realme to gather sume fruitfull Volum of The Lives of the Saints, which Maugre your fiue hundred fauorites shall be printed.—Pasquill is gone ouer sea to commit it to the Presse.—Pasquill is readie to pull your Feathers. You shall haue a Glosse and a Commentarie vppon your Epilogue, with certaine Hayes, Iigges, Rimes, Roundelayes, and Madigrals, seruing for Epitaphes to your fathers Hearse, to make the worlde laughe out the long Winters nights, which verie shortlie will steale vppon vs.—I bid your Mastership far-well till Michaelmas Tearme, commending your worshippe to the line and the leading of your owne spirite. From Grauesende Barge the eyght of August, the first and last yeere of Martinisme,—To come to the close, in Rime or in Prose, In spight of thy nose, Thine for these seauen yeeres: Pasquill of Englande." If this be the same (as i apprehend it to be) with that Mr. Collier calls The Counter-Scuffle, he attributes it to Tho. Nash as the author. Eccles. Hist. II, 6?6. But query. Contains only 4 leaves, including the title-page. W.H. 4°.

—— "The iust censure and reproofe of Martin Iunior. Wherein the rash and vndiscreete headines of the foolish youth is sharply mette with, and the boy hath his lesson taught him, I warrant you, by his reuerend and elder

elder brother, Martin Senior, sonne and heire vnto the renowmed Martin Mar-prelate the Great. Where also, least the springall shold be vtterly discouraged in his good meaning, you shall finde, that hee is not bereaued of his due commendations." This piece introduces, in the 2d and a few following pages, the archbishop as giving instructions to find out the authors and publishers of these libels, thus: "Haue you beene carefull of vs and our places, to find vs out the presse and letters, wherewith these seditious Martins are printed? Or, haue you diligently soght me out Walde-graue the Printer, Newman the Cobler, Sharpe the booke-binder of Northampton, and that seditious Welch man Penry, who you shall see will prooue the Author of all these libelles? I thanke you Maister (*Anthony*) Munday, you are a good Gentleman of your worde. Ah thou Iudas, thou that hast alreadie betrayed the Papistes, I thinke meanest to betray vs also, Diddest thou not assure me, without all doubt, that thou wouldest bring mee in, Penry, Newman, Walde-graue, letters, and all before Saint Andrewes day last. And nowe thou seest we are as farre to seeke for them, as euer we were.—Bring vs whomesoeuer you suspect, your warrants shall serue you to doe it. And if you can finde vs eyther young or olde Martin, Penry, or Walde-graue, so that you bring the presse, he shall haue fortie poundes for his labour,—his charges and all borne cleare.—Let a six or seuen of you, or your substitutes that stay heere in London, watch mee Paules Churchyard, especially haue an eie to Boyles shop at the Rose. &c. Let three or foure more of you or your substitutes be euery day at the Blacke Friers, Lincolnes inne, White-chappell, Paules chaine, as often as Charke, Gardiner, Egerton, or Cooper do preach.—Haue a watch at all common innes, &c. We will direct our warrants so, that you may search all packes at your discresion. We will take order also, that the Court may be watched who disperse or reade these libelles there.—Haue an eie also vnto all the Puritanes houses in London, especially my L. Maiors, Alderman Martins, and the Preachers houses.—As for you that goe into the countrey, I woulde haue ye especially go into Northampton and Warwicke shires,—Others must goe into Essex, Suffolke and Norfolke.—There is Moore, there is Aline, there is Knewstub, there is Wright, with many others, all very seditious men, &c. Goe me to Deuonshire, and to the North partes, where my Lords grace of Yorke will direct his warrants by you, to seeke this traitour Martin. For I will haue him, or else I wil no longer be archbishop of Canturburie. Hee die at the Groine, as they saie? Naie, heele be hanged ere heele die there. He is in some corner of England, lurking and doing mischiefe.—Spare no charges. Get him, and see what weele do for you. For if we were not in hope to come by him throgh your means,—we woulde make friendes to haue him proclamed a traitour, and haue it fellonie if wee coulde, for anie manne to reade his writings." Thus ends this imaginary oration. Martin senior then reproves his young brother thus: "Loe, sir boy, haue you not spunne a faire threed for your fathers ease and quietnesse, and for the quietnesse of your brethren ?" &c. Brother Martin, I will schoole you in a pointe or two for your learning, in these things wherein I finde your Epilogue to be vnperfite. First then, I trow, I woulde haue had some other manner of accusations against our Puritans for their slackenes, then wherwith you haue charged them, as presently I will declare." He then sets forth his Protest against the bishops in eleven articles; and mentions several curious anecdotes relating to this Puritanical controversy, in his further reproof of Martin Junior. At length "Lo yongman, do not you deserue stripes,—But yet I would haue born withall, if thou haddest taken a little paines in ryming with Mar-Martin, that the cater-caps may knowe, howe the meanest of my fathers sonnes is able to answeare them, both at blunt and sharpe. And for thy further instruction against an other time, heere* is a sample for thee of that, which in such cases thou art to performe, if I or my father should set thee a worke. Or else thou mightest haue requited him in this †Epitaph :" The beginning of which may be seen below. He concludes with "The reason whie wee must not knowe our father is, that I feare least some of vs shoulde fall into Iohn Canturburie his hand, and then heele threaten vs with the racke unlesse wee bewray all we knowe. And what get we then by our knowledge ? For I had rather be ignorant of Thatle do me good, then know Thatle hurt me, ka M. Martin Senior. Farewell boy, and learne to reuerence thy elder brother." Contains D, in fours, neat Long Primer Roman. W.H. Sixteens.

1589. "MARTINS Months minde, that is, A certaine report, and true description of the Death, aud Funeralls of olde Martin Marreprelate, the great makebate of England, and father of the factious. Contayning the cause of his death, the manner of his buriall, and the right copies both of his Will, and of such Epitaphs, as by sundrie of his dearest friends, and other of his well willers, were framed for him.

"Martin the Ape, the dronke, and the madde,
The three Martins are, whose workes we haue had.
If Martin the fourth come, after Martins so euill,
No man, nor beast comes, but Martin the deuill.

1589."

* "The first rising, generation, and originall of Mar-Martin.

From Sarum came a goses egge,
with specks and spots bepatched,
A priest of Lambeth coucht thereon :
thus was Mar-Martin hatched.
Whence hath Mar-Martin all his wit,
but from that egge of Sarum ?
The rest comes all from great Sir John,
who rings vs all this larum.

What can the Cockatrice hatch vp,
but serpent like himselfe ?
What sees the Ape within the glasse,
but a deformed Elfe ?
Then must Mar Martin haue some smell
Of forge or else of fire.
A sotte in wit, a beast in minde :
for so was damme and sire."

† If that Mar-Martin die the death, that to the dog is due,
Vpon his Tomb engraue this verse, and you shal find it true :
He lies endiched here that from the ladder toppe
Did once beblesse the people than, but first he kist the rope.
Come neere, quoth he, take heede by me, I loued to lie by ryming.
Tis just you see, and doth agree, that now I die by climing :" &c.

1589." Prefixed are, "The Epistle Dedicatorie to Pasquine of England." In which he says "Herein I haue made them but a little merie, as they doo vs, and bobde them with their owne [q]bable which I knowe must please them (for they are very pleasurable Gentlemen as their father was.) In the next which shall be verie shortly (which I terme The suing of Martin Senior his liuerie) wee shall giue them a Cuffe shall make their eares tingle: but in the third which shall be Martins models, (for he is in the building vaine as his father was) containing the mischiefes of Martinisme both to the Church and state; we shall reach them a rappe, as they will neuer clawe of, except they scratt off the skinne from the verie bones.—In the meane space (Pasquine remember your [r]promise. It growes fast towards Ianuarie: it were time your Almanacke were out.—no maruell that they haue been so firie heretofore that haue chosen a Saltpeterman for their foreman, and a gunnepowder house for their printing shop.—And so longing to heare from you, as you shall from me againe (God willing) verie shortlie I bid you farewell Your fast friend and fellowe in Armes Mar-phoreus.—To the discreet and indifferent Reader." In which epistle we haue described The four forms of old Martin's school: 1. Admonishers.[s] 2. Pistlers.[t] 3. Barbarians.[u] 4. Seditious.[w] "Thus haue I shewed thee (gentle Reader) a short sight of Martins schoole, the degrees of his sonnes, the summe of his lessons, and the drift, both of the master and schollers: *&c.* These fellows, haue heretofore been answered to their chiefest matters—by men of the best sorte—both grauelie and learnedly. But as the Ape the more sagelie you looke on him, the more he grinneth; and the foole, the more substanciallie you reason with him, the lesse he vnderstandeth:—It is therefore thought the best way—to answere the fooles, according to their foolishnes.—For what face soeuer they set on the matter, these ligges and Rimes, haue nipt the father in the head & kild him cleane, seeing that hee is ouertaken in his owne foolerie. And this hath made the yong youthes his sonnes, to chafe and fret aboue measure, especiallie with the Plaiers,—whom sauing their liueries (for indeede they are hir Maiesties men, and these not so much as hir good subiects) they call Rogues for playing their enterludes, and Asses for trauelling all daie for a pennie; not remembering that both they & their Father, playing the fooles without any liuerie, are roges indeed by the lawes of this land; and that for nothing, now two yeares together; are the veriest Asses of all the rest.—These iests, that now we deale withal, are partlie the old mans monuments, but especiallie the elder sonnes censure, and the yongers

[q] See Mr. Waldron's Appendix to The Sad Shepherd, a fragment written by Ben. Jonson, p. 154, &c.

[r] In the Countercuffe, to write The Owles almanack.

[s] The 1st, and 2d Admonition to the Parliament. See p. 1631, &c.

[t] The Epistle, and Epitome of Martin Marprelate. See p. 1683. and p. 1684.

[u] Brown, Barrow, and Greenwood."

[w] Theses Martinianae by Martin Junior; and The last censure and reproof of Martin junior by Martin Senior. See p. 1689, and p. 1691.

Theses. The first occasion indeed grew of this latter, &c. VVhat he omitted J haue supplied; touching the cause of his death, and manner of his buriall; for that J would be lothe so memorable matters, should be buried with him (which is but an Jntroduction to other matters that shortlie shall followe, and fit somewhat nearer them; &c. To conclude; marke Martins life and his proceedings; and thou wilt saie, his death, and funeralls were answerable vnto it.—Farewell, And if thou wilt fare well indeede: Beware of Martin." Head title, "A true report of the death and buriall of Martin Mar-prelate. Incipit fœliciter. Good newes to England. Old Martin the Marre-all is dead and buried.—You long (I know) to heare the cause, and manner of his death," &c. After reciting the sundry reports of his death, the true (*fictitious*) manner thereof is thus related, "After that old Martin, hauing taken a most desperate cause in hand, as the troubling of the Church,—and being therefore sundrie waies verie curstlie handled;—but especially that his labours being so great, tooke none effect,—and that euerie stage Plaier made a iest of him,—yea his owne familiars disdained to acknowledge him,—began at the length to droope.—And so hauing taken his bedde, he sent for his Phisitions, who perceiued that he was past cure, and therefore wisht him to set his worldlie affairs in order, &c. Martin fetching a deepe sigh: An withall, calling his sonnes, said to them, Oh my sonnes: I see my doings, and my course misliked of many, both the good, and the bad.—I had thought that my works sauced with those iests would haue had both speedier accesse to the greater States, and better successe with the common people, &c. But sure I was deceiued: The one are wise, and like of no such fooleries: and the other now wearie of our stale mirth, that for a penie may haue far better by oddes at the Theater and Curtaine, &c. Three things were my bane: my fooleries, my ribaldrie, and my blasphemie.—Be quiet at home; we haue troubles enough abroad. It is no time now to play the fooles: &c. And so I wil end: for these are the things that haue ended me. And therewithal, lifting vp himselfe on his pillowe, he commanded the elder Martin to goe into his studie, and to fetch his *Will,—bound fast with

* The bequests therein are comprised in 12 sarcastic jesting articles, as; "Imprimis, I giue and bequeath to Martin Senior, my eldest sonne, and Martin Iunior, my younger sonne, ioyntlie al my knauerie, &c. 2 Item, all my foolerie—to my good friend Lanam; and his consort of whom I first had it: &c. 3 Item, my scolding and rayling—to my deare Sister, Dame Law, and to her good gossips,—& to their heires female for euer. 6 Item,—to Greenwood, Browne, and Barrow, my good friends, my parrock of ground, lying on the North side of London, and abutting vppon three high waies, wherevpon standeth a Cottage, built triangle wise, with the appurtenances; onlie for the terme of their liues; reseruing the reuersion thereof to my two sonnes, &c. 11—I giue and bequeath my affections to Bridewell; my senses to Bedlem; my conditions to Newgate, &c. 12 The rest of all my good and Chattels, &c. to my two Martins, whom ioyntly I make my executors, and I appoint my especiall good friends Prichard and Pennie to bee mine ouerseers; & to each of them an Advowson: To the former of small Wittam, and to the other of little Brainford, now in the possession of Pag. (*Paget*) and Wig. (*Wigginton*) for he hath a Pluralitie; &c. Witnesses P. T. B. E. M. F. G. K. Copia vera."

with an hempen ſtring: which he commanded to be read in their hearing; &c. This being done; it was not halfe an houre, but he began to ſaint: and turning about on his left ſide, hee belked twice: and as my friend Paſquin reporteth verie truelie, the third time he belked out his breath. The Phiſitians, would needs haue him cut vp, where they found a wonderfull corrupt carcaſſe. His Heart great, yet hollowe, &c.—And this is the very truth of Old Martins death, which if the young Martins, or any Martiniſt of them all denie; I caſt him here my Mitten vpon the quarrell." Then follow "The true Copie of ſuch Epitaphs as were made by old Martins ſauorites, and others for him." Others "framed by ſome ſiends of them that are yet vnknowne, but wiſh to be better acquainted with them.—Finis Qd. Marphoreus." Afterwards, "The concluſion to the two young Martins.—And ſo (gentle Martin) much good doo it you: you ſee your faire for this time, and you are hartelie welcome. Take this in good partie, the next courſe ſhall be prouided for your owne tooth, and glutt you better. Farewell Paſquin, and diſpatch." Contains H, in fours, neat White letter. W.H. Quarto.

"Expeditionis Hiſpanorum in Angliam vera Deſcriptio, anno 1588.(1589.) Roberto Adamo authore." Accompanied with 11 maps; Auguſtinus Ryther ſculpſit. The queen's arms on the laſt map. See the tranſlation, p. 1212, to which theſe maps were alſo annexed. Quarto.

"Ha' ye any more work for the Cooper." In printing of which the preſs was diſcovered and ſeized at Mancheſter in Lancaſhire, with ſeveral pamphlets unfiniſhed as: "Epiſto (Epiſco) Maſtrix, Paradoxes, Dialogues, Miſcellanea, Variae lectiones, Martin's dream, the lives and doings of Engliſh Popes, Itinerarium or Viſitations, Lambethiſmes." The laſt two of theſe were imperfect, but to compleat the Itinerarium, the author threatens to ſurvey all the clergy of England, and note their intolerable pranks; and for his Lambethiſins, he would have a Martin at Lambeth. Other books were publiſhed of the ſame nature, as "A Demonſtration of diſcipline, &c. See p. 1684. The Counter-poiſon, &c. See p. 1142. Quarto.

"The Protestatyon of Martin Marprelat Wherin not with ſtanding the ſurprizing of the printer, he maketh it known vnto the world that he feareth, neither proud prieſt, Antichriſtian pope, tiranous prellate, nor godleſſe catercap: but defiethe all the race of them by theſe preſents and offereth conditionally, as is farthere expreſſed hearin by open diſputation to apear in the defence of his cauſ againſt them and theirs Which chaleng if they dare not maintaine aginſt him: then doth he alſoe publiſhe that he never meaneth by the aſſiſtaunce of god to leaue the aſſayling of them and theire generation vntill they be vtterly extinguiſed out of our church Publiſhed by the worthie gentleman D. martin [y]marprelat D. in all the faculties primat and metropolitan." Head title,

[y] Collier attributes the Libels written under this name of Mar-prelate to a junto of 4 perſons, whoſe names in the margin are, Penri, Throgmorton, Eudale (Udal) and Fenner. Eccl. Hiſt. II; 606.

Head title, "The Proteſtacion of Martin the great." Begins, "Thou canſt not lightly be ignoraunt good reader of that wich hath lately fallen vnto ſome things of mine, wich were to be printed, or in printing: the preſſe, leteres, workmen and all, apprepended and caried, as malefactors before the magiſtrat, whoſe authoritie I reverence, &c. Theſe events I confes doe ſtrike me, and giue me iuſte cauſe to enter more narrowly into my ſelfe to ſee whethere I bee at peace with god or no: but vtterlye to diſcouredg me from myne enterprize, a greater matterre then that coms to, I hope ſhall never be able. The ſtate of the pour men that are taken, I do bewayle, not becaus thye can hurte mee, for I aſſure thee they knowe not whoe I am, but in aſmuhc as I feare the tiranny of our wicked priſtes," &c. In p. 10. "Nowe becauſe they woulde gladly know Martin, I wil here ſet them down a waye, whereby they maye not onely know him, but (that which is more delightfull vnto them; they may quench their thirſt with his blood if they wil:) prouided that they bee able to make their cauſe good againſte him by the worde of God." He thereupon enters his proteſtation, "—perſonally to apear, and there to make my ſelfe knowen in open diſputation, vpon the danger, not onlie of my libertie but alſo of my life, to maintaine—in any Scholaſtical manner,—the cauſe of the church goverment, which is now in controverſie betwixt me and our prelats: ſo that I may have this condicion following inviolably kept & obſerued, vz. That for apearing, or for anye thinge that I haue eyther publiſhed in this cauſe, I be not delt with, or moleſted, except thei overthrow me by the worde of God, &c. Provided alſo, that if any of the Puritanes wil ioyn with me, & venture their liues in the cauſe, it may be lawfull for them to come in freely—in diſputation." In p. 14, &c. "I am blamed of many in this myne attempt, not onely for throwing my ſelfe into great daunger; but alſo for the vtter vndoing of my wife and children. I do thanke thē with all my hearte, for their care ouer thoſe poore ſoules, and commend their ſecreſie and wiſdome, that in knowing my wife and my childrē, they haue by ſhewing their vnmeaſurable loue towards them, diſcoured me. You ſee what it is when wiſe men haue the handling of a matter.—Will you beleeue me then if I tel you the truth?—I neuer had wife nor childe in all my life: not that I neuer meane to haue anye; for it may be,—I may be maried, & that ere it be long." In p. 24 he begins an abſtract of his More work for the Cooper, which had been lately ſeized, together with the preſs, &c. which continues to the end. "Now I haſtē to other matters, where it may be, good Reader, thou wilt aſke what was in that Piſtle of mine? To tel thee true, I ſigh to remember the loſſe of it, it was ſo prettie, and ſo witty. &c. Firſte then, there was ſet downe for thy learninge; the true, proper, and naturall definition, or rather deſcription of Martiniſme, to this effect. That to be a right Martiniſte indeede, is to bee neither Browniſte, Cooperiſte, Lambethiſt, Schiſmatike, Papiſt, atheiſt, traytor nor yet L. byſhop; but one that is at defyaunce with all men;—ſo far forth as he is an enimy to God and her Maiestie.—Then among al the rimers and stage plaiers, which my LL. of the cleargy had suborned against me, I remember Mar-Martin, Iohn a Cant. his hobbie-horse, was to his reproche, newly put out of the Morris, take it how He will; with a flat discharge for euer shaking his shins about a May-pole againe while he liued. Here-abouts I placed D. Vnderhil and D. Wood of Alsolne colledge, to be chaplaines vnto a certain chaste Ficker—, called sir Iames King, of Herford-shire; and some-where it was I so sliued Dick Bancroft ouer the shulders, as his chaplainship is neuer able to recouer his credite, if that Pistle of mine be once published.—After this, I had a fling at these puritanes, concerning whome, my desire is, that wherein I am faltie, ye puritanes would set me downe the particulars.—with these & such like points with an honourable mention of all noble souldiors; a complaint of the losse of my papers, and the miserie of sea iournies I ended my Pistle, being the first Tome of more warke for the Cooper. And here also I end this my protestation. Desiring thee (good reader) according vnto thy place, to be carefull of the reliefe and deliuerance of the distressed printers. In requitall whereof, if thou canst but learne the day of my marriage—thou shalt be better welcome vnto me, then the best Lord Catercap of them all, and so tell them from me when thou wilt.—Yet heare me a word afore thou goest, an thou be a goodfellow, commend me to George Bullen Deane of Liechfield, by these 4 [1]tokens." Contains D, in fours, or 32 pages (printed 23 by mistake) Indeed the frequent omission and misplacing of some letters, and others remaining upside-down, besides the numerous neglects of stops, evince the haste in which this tract was published. Good Roman types. W.H. Sixteens.

Martin's Minerals is reckoned among Mar-prelat's pieces; as also, ——

His Epistle sent from Scotland. See Collier's Eccl. Hist. II; 606. ——

The writers on the church side came not behind their adversaries in buffoonry and ridicule, as appears by the pamphlets printed about this time.

" THE Returne of the renowned Caualiero Pasquill of England, from 1589.
the other side the seas, and his meeting with Marsorius at London vpon the Royall Exchange. VVhere they encounter with a little houshold talke of Martin and Martinisme, discouering the scabbe that is bredde in England: and conferring together about the speedie dispersing of the golden Legende of the liues of the Saints." Device, A hand holding a caduceus, as described in p. 552, omitting BAL-WIN. " If my breath be so hote that I burne my mouth, suppose I was Printed by Pepper Allie. Anno Dom. 1589." The head title, " Pasquils returne to England." The running-title, " Pasquill and Marsorius." In this dialogue between Pasquill and Marsorius, the latter says "—I wonder

[1] " 1 The wind is south, the wind is south: 2 that he lately taught in Couentree, that men might fal from grace 3 that taking himselfe with a fault in the same sermon, he said, there I lyed, there I lyed 4 being another time in the pulpit, hearing his dogg cry, he out with this text; whie how now hoe, can you not let my dogg alone there; come Springe, come Spring."

wonder how I missed you? Pasq. Neuer maruaile at that, I haue learned to maske it; while some of Martins good freendes stood watching for me at Lambith bridge, I came to an Anker in Sandwich Hauen. But of fellowship tell me, howe hath my Countercuffe beene intreated? Marf. It requireth a Summers day and a Winters night to tell you all. It was verie welcome to the Court, thankfullie receiued in both Vniuersities, the Citties of the Land doe giue you good speeches, as for the Countrey, after the plainest manner, with hart and good will they are ready to greet you with a Cake and a cup of Ale in euery Parrish, &c. P.—When I came to England,—the first newes I heard—was, of a Martinist a Broker, the—which with a face of Religion, hauing gotten other mens goods into his hands, was but newe run away and left his wife to the charitie of the Parrish. With this tidings, I grew verie inquisitiue to know what Martin was? A knaue quoth one; a theefe quoth another; he teacheth the Courte a Religion to robbe the Church. And some of the Cittie that fauour him, apt Schollers to take such an easie lesson, begin to practise theyr cunning upon their neighbors.—M. Take heede what you say, it is a common report that the faction of Martinisme hath mightie freendes. P. Thats a bragge Marforius, yet if there be anie such, I shall find them in the end, and against the next Parliament, I will picke out a time to pepper them. Though they were as high as the maste, as sure as the tackling, as profitable as the fraught, and necessarie as the sayles, when the shippe is in danger, ouerboorde with all. What meaning soeuer some men haue in it, I am assured, that it can neither stand with policie nor with Religion, to nourish anie faction in ciuill matters, much lesse in matters belonging to the Church.—A faction in a Kingdome may wel be compared to a spark of fire, it catcheth hold at the first in some obscure corner,—where it lyeth couert a little time, but by little and little it gathers strength, till it reare it selfe vp to great houses, Pallaces & Princes Courts, and at last it rageth and ouerruns whole Citties & Countries, without quenching, before they be vtterly ouerthrowne.—I thinke before I end, Signor Pasquill of Englande, wyll prooue the man, that must sette a gagge in the mouth of Martin the great, and cut vp an Anatomie of all his knauerie. Me thought Vetus Comoedia beganne to pricke him at London in the right vaine, when shee brought foorth Diuinitie wyth a scratcht face, holding of her hart as if she were sicke, because Martin would haue forced her, but myssing of his purpose, he left the print of his nayles vppon her cheekes, and poysoned her with a vomit which he ministred vnto her, to make her cast vppe her dignities and promotions.—M. Inough Caueliero, the Clock strikes eleuen, and the Marchants come in to the Exchange apace, I think it were best to talke no longer here. And seeing Martins matters begin to be whust, it were good in my iudgment to suppresse your volume of The liues of the Saints.—Seeing you will forwards with the works you haue taken in hand, giue me some direction for the priuie dispersing them when they come out. P. I would haue thee principally,

pally, to drop ſome of thē down at Penrie the Welch-mans haunt. M. Where is that? P. Tut, I perceive you know nothing. At the ſign of the ſiluer ſorke and the toſted cheeſe, *&c.* M. You ſaid in the ende of your Countercuffe, that you would ſend vs a Commentarie vpon Martin Iunior, I forgot till now to aſke you what is become of that? P. I fell that night into a traunce, wherein mee thought I ſaw a very golden wit performe that matter, with ſo keene a tooth, and ſuch a pleaſant grace, that I gaue ouer to him, and farthered The liues of the Saints, as much as my leyſure would giue me leaue.—But who commeth yonder Marſorius, can you tell me? M. By her gate & her Garland I knowe her well, it is Vetus Comœdia.—this is ſhe that called in a counſell of Phiſitians about Martin, and found by the ſharpnes of his humour, when they had opened the vaine that feedes his head, that hee would ſpit out his lunges within a yere. And I promiſe you ſhe prophecied very truly of him, you may ſee by the Books that he ſet forth laſt, that his ſtrength is ſpent. P. I haue a tale to tell her in her eare, of the ſlye practiſe that was vſed in reſtraining of her. In the meane ſeaſon Marſorius, I take my leaue of thee, charging thee vpon all our old acquaintance, and vppon my bleſſing, to ſet vp this bill at London ſtone. Let it be doone ſollemnly with Drom and Trumpet, and looke you aduance my collours on the top of the ſteeple right ouer againſt it, that euery one of my Souldiers may keepe his quarter. PASQVILS PROTESTATION VPPON LONDON STONE.—Dated 20. Octobris. Anno Millimo, Quillimo, Trillimo, Per me venturous Paſquill the Caualiero. M.—Is there any thing els you would haue me doe? P. Yes, if I thought you were at leyſure, you haue been very buſie I perceiue about Martins death, & though he liue yet, it may be you prophecie of his end. Yeſter-night late, olde Martins Proteſtation in Octauo was brought vnto mee, I ſee by the volume, hee languiſheth euery day more and more, the pride of his fleſh is ſo much faine, that you may tell euery bone in hys body now. I pray thee—ſend this Piſtle to Martin by the next Poſte. *Caualiero Paſquill of England, to Martin the great, wiſheth more wit and learning, and a better minde.* May it pleaſe your Maſterdom to vnderſtand, that by the laſt Butterflie you ſent abroad,—you brag you have giuen M. D. Bancroft ſuch a ſliue ouer the ſhoulders, as the credite of his Chaplenſhip ſhall not recouer. Though the learning and honeſtie of the man doe very-much credit him, with all that are eyther learned or honeſt themſelues, yet ſeeing you come to his Chaplinſhip, I cannot forbeare you, but tell you plaine, that half a looke of his honourable Maiſter, ſhall giue hime more credit in England in one day, then Martin or all his crew ſhal be able to robbe him of while the world ſtands, though they ſwell at him with enuie like a neſt of ſoule Toades, till their bodies ſplyt, and poure out theyr bowels vppon the earth. I have many other things to lay to your charge, which I purpoſe to wink at, vntill your Dialogue be ended, but then Syr, becauſe you tell me you are yet vnmaried, I will take downe your breeches for altogether. *Caualiero Paſquill.*" Thus

 endeth

endeth this treatise, containing D, in fours, neat White Letter. Collier a[illegible]s this to Tho Nash, Eccl. Hist. II, 606. But, query. Whoever [illegible] author of this, appears to have been the author also of the Countercuffe. W.H· Quarto.

" Pappe with an hatchet. Alias, A figge for my God sonne. Or Cracke me this nut, Or A Countrie cuffe, that is a sound boxe of the eare, for the idiot Martin to hold his peace, seeing the patch will take no warning. VVritten by one that dares call a dog, a dog, and made to preuent Martins dog daies. Imprinted by Iohn Anoke, and Iohn Astile, for the Bayliue of Withernam, cum priuilegio perennitatis, and are to bee sold at the signe of the crab tree cudgell in thwackcoate lane. A sentence. Martin hangs fit for my mowing." This is introduced with an epistle, " To the Father and the two Sonnes, Huffe, Ruffe, and Snuffe, the three tame ruffians of the Church, which take pepper in the nose, because they cannot marre Prelates grating." A few extracts from which may be seen * below. Then, a prefatory epistle " To the indifferent Reader," beginning thus, " It is high time to search in what corner of the Church the fire is kindled, being crept so far, as that with the verie smoke the consciences of diuers are smothered. It is found that certaine Martins, if no miscreants in religion (which wee may suspect) yet without doubt malecōtents (which wee ought to feare) haue throwen fire, not into the Church porch, but into the Chauncell, and though not able by learning & iudgement to displace a Sexton, yet seek to remooue Bishops.—If they be answered by the grauitie of learned Prelates, they presentlie reply with railings; which argueth their intent to be as farre frō the truth of deuotion, as their writings from mildnes of spirit." &c.—He saith he is a Courtier, I thinke no Courtier so peruerse, that seeing the streight rule of the Church, would go about to bend it. It may be he is some Iester about the Court, and of that I meruaile because I know all the fooles there, and yet cannot gesse at him. What euer

* " I am sure you looke for more worke, you shall haue wood enough to cleave, make your tongue the wedge, and your head the beetle, Ile make such a splinter runne into your wits, as shal make them rankle till you become fooles. Nay, if you shoot bookes like fooles bolts, Ile be so bold as to make your judgements quiuer with my thunderbolts. If you meane to gather clowdes in the Common-wealth, to threaten tempests, for your flakes of snowe weele pay you with stones of hayle; &c. VVe care not for a Scottish mist, though it wet vs to the skin, you shall be sure your cocks-combs shall not be mist, but pearst to the skuls. I professe rayling, and think it is as good a cudgell for a Martin, as a stone for a dogge, or a whippe for an Ape, or poyson for a rat.—Who would currie an Asse with an Iuorie combe? giue the beast thistles for prouender. I doo but yet angle with a silken flye, to see whether Martins will nibble; and if I see that, why then I haue wormes for the nonce, and will giue them line enough like a trowte, till they swallow both hooke and line, and then Martin beware your gilles, for Ile make you daunce at the poles end.—Rip vp my life, discipher my name, fill thy answer as full of lies as of lines, swel like a toade, hisse like an adder, bite like a dog, and chatter like a monkey, my pen is prepared and my minde; and if you chaunce to finde any worse words than you brought, let them be put in your dads dictionarie. And so farewell, and be hanged, and I pray God ye fare no worse. Yours at an howres warning

Double V."

euer he be, if his conſcience be pind to his cognizance, I will account him more politicke than religious, and more dangerous for ciuill broyles, than the Spaniard for an open warre." &c. The head and running titles are "Pappe with an hatchet." It begins, "Good morrow, goodman Martin, good morrow: will ye anie muſique this morning? What ſalt aſleepe? Nay faith, Ile cramp thee till I wake thee. *O whoſe tat?* Nay geſſe olde knaue and odd knaue: for Ile neur leaue pulling till I haue thee out of thy bed into the ſtreete; and then all ſhall ſee who thou art, and thou know what I am.—Ye like not Biſhops rochet, when all your fathers handkerchers were made of his ſweete harts ſmocke.—Now you put me in minde of the matter, there is a booke cōming out of a hundred merrie tales, and the petigree of Martin, fetcht from the burning of Sodome, his armes ſhalbe ſet on his hearſe, for we are prouiding his funerall, and for the winter nights the tales ſhall be told ſecundum vſum Sarum: the Dean of Saliſburie can tell twentie.—In the hundred merrie tales, the places, the witneſſes and all ſhall be put downe to the proofe, *&c.*——The babie comes in with Nunka, Neame and Dad: (Pappe with an hatchet for ſuch a puppie) giue the infant a bibbe, he all to beſlauers his mother tongue, if he driuell ſo at the mouth and noſe, weele haue him wipte with a hempen wiſpe. Hui?—If Martin will fight Citie fight, wee challenge him at all weapons, from the taylors bodkin to the watchmans browne bil. If a field may be pitcht we are readie: if they ſcratch, we will bring cattes: if ſcolde, we will bring women: if multiplie wordes, we will bring fooles: if they floute, we will bring quippes: if diſpute the matter, we will bring ſchollers: if they buffet, we will bring fiſts.—Nay, we will bring Bull to hang them. —Martins conſcience hath a periwig; therefore to good men he is more ſower than wig: a Lemman will make his conſcience curd like a Poſſet.—When children play with their meate, tis a ſigne their bellies are full, & it muſt be taken from them; but if they tread it vnder their feete, they ought to be ierkt. The Goſpell hath made us wantons, wee dallie with Ceremonies, diſpute of circumſtances, not remembering that the Papiſts haue been making roddes for vs theſe thirtie yeares; *&c.*—Sed heus tu, dic ſodes, will they not be diſcouraged for the common players? Would thoſe Comedies might be allowed to be plaid that are pend, and then I am ſure he would be decyphered, and ſo perhaps diſcouraged. He ſhall not bee brought in as whilom he was, and yet verie well, with a cocks combe, an apes face, a wolfes bellie, cats clawes, &c. but in a cap'de cloake, *&c.*—Would it not bee a fine Tragedie, when Mardocheus ſhall play a Biſhoppe in a Play, and Martin Hamman, and that he that ſeekes to pull downe thoſe that are ſet in authoritie aboue him, ſhould he be hoyſted vpon a tree aboue all other." In the margin againſt this article. "*If it be ſhewed at Paules, it will coſt you foure pence: at the Theater two pence: at Sainct Thomas a Watrings nothing.* —If thou refuſe learning and ſtick to libelling; if nothing come out of thoſe lauiſh lips, but taunts not without bitterneſſe, yet without wit: rayling not without ſpite, yet without cauſe, then giue me thy hand, thou

thou and I will trie it out at the cucking-ſtoole. Ile make thee forget Biſhops Engliſh, and weep Iriſh;—Ile make him pull his powting croſcloth ouer his beetle browes for melanchollie, and then my next booke ſhall be Martin in his mubble ſubbles. Here I was writing Finis and Funis, and determined to lay it by, till I might ſee more knauerie ſilde in: within a while appeared olde Martin with a wit worn into the ſocket, twingling and pinking like the ſnuffe of a candle; quantum mutatus ab illo, how vnlike the knaue hee was before, not for malice but for ſharpneſſe. The hogſhead was euen come to the hauncing, and nothing could be drawne from him but dregs: yet the emptie caſke ſounds lowder than when it was ful; and proteſts more in his waining, than he could performe in his waxing. I drew neare the ſillie ſoule, whom I found quiuering in two ſheets of proteſtation paper. O how meager and leane hee lookt, ſo creaſt falne, that his combe hung down to his bill, and had I not been ſure it was the picture of enuie I ſhould haue ſworne it had been the image of death, ſo like the verie Anatomie of miſchieſe, that one might ſee through all the ribbes of his conſcience.—Tis not a peniworth of proteſtation that can buy thy pardon, nor al worth a penie that thou proclaimeſt.—After Martin had racked ouer his proteſtation with a ladies pace, hee runnes ouer his fooleries with a knaues gallop, ripping vp the ſouterlie ſeames of his Epiſtle, botching in ſuch frize ieſtes vppon fuſtion earneſt, that one ſeeing all ſortes of his ſhreddes, would think he had robd a taylors ſhop boord; and then hee concludes all dogedlie, with Doctor Bullens dogge Spring,—Hee ſliues one, has a fling at another, a long tale of his talboothe, of a vulnerall ſermon, and of a fooles head in ſouce.—Martin writes merely, becauſe (hee ſaies) people are carried away ſooner with ieſt than earneſt. I, but Martin neuer put Religion in a fooles coate; there is great oddes betweene a Goſpeller and a Libeller.—Paſquil is comming out with the liues of the Saints. Beware my Comment, tis odds the margent ſhall be as full as the text. —Martin, this is my laſt ſtraine for this ſleech of mirth. I began with God morrowe, and bid you God night. I muſt tune my fiddle, and fetch ſome more rozen, that it maie ſqueake out Martins Matachine. Finis. Candidiſsimi Lectores, peto terminum ad libellandum. Lectores. Aſsignamus in proximum." Contains E 3, in fours. Tho. Naſh is generally allowed to be the author of this. See Collier's Ecc. Hiſt. II; 606. Ath. Oxon. I; 260. Catal. Bibl. Bodl. II; 147. To him alſo Mr. Collier aſcribes Paſquil and Marforio, (The returne of the—Caualiero Paſquill of England) and The Counter-Scuffle (Countercuffe); but they evidently appear to have been written by a different author, whoever that might be. John Lylie, Lylye, or Lylly, is ſaid to have been the author of ſome of the tracts againſt Marprelate. Ath. Oxon. I; 206. Bibl. Tanneri, p. 493, for which the latter ſeems to quote the Preface to Mr. Thomas Watſon's paſſionate century of Love, by the omiſſion of a period point after the word Marprelate: Lyly's letter to Mr. Watſon being only complimentary, as I am informed by my good friend George Steevens, Eſq. who poſſeſſes that very ſcarce book. W. H. 4°.

"An

"An Almond for a Parrat, or Cutbert Curry-knaues Almes. Fit for the knaue Martin, and the rest of those impudent Beggers, that cannot be content to stay their stomakes with a Benefice, but they will needes breake their fastes with our Bishops. Rimarum sum plenus. Therefore beware (gentle Reader) you catch not the hicket with laughing. Imprinted at a Place, not farre from a Place, by the Assignes of Signior Some-body, and are to be sold at his shoppe in Trouble-knaue Street, at the signe of the Standish." This is introduced with an epistle dedicatory "To that most Comicall and conceited Caualeire Monsieur du Kempe, Iestmonger and Vice-gerent generall to the Ghost of Dicke Tarlton. His louing brother Cutbert Curry-knaue sendeth Greeting." This epistle concludes with a very remarkable piece of intelligence, if true, which may be seen [b] below. Both head and running titles, "An Almond for a Parrat." Begins, "Welcome Mayster Martin from the dead, and much good ioy may you haue of your stage like resurrection.—May neither Scriptures nor Fathers goe for paiment with you, but still you will bee reducing vs to the president of the persecuted Church, and so confounde the discipline of warre and peace? If you will needes make vs the apes of all the extremities, why doe you not vrge the vse of that communitie wherein Ananias and Saphira were vnfaithfull. Perswade Noble men and Gentlemen to sell their landes, and laie the money at your feet, &c.—You think we know not how pretily your Printers were shrouded vnder the name of salt-petermen, so that who but Hudgkins, Tomlins & Sims, at the vndermining of a house, and vndoing of poore men, by diggyng vp their floars, and breaking down their wals. No, no, we neuer

[b] "—coming from Venice the last Summer, and taking Bergamo in my waye homeward to England, it was my happe soiourning there some four or fiue dayes, to light in felowship with that famous Francatip' Harlicken, who perceiuing me to be an Englishman by my habit and speech, asked me many particulars, of the order and maner of our playes, &c. As we were thus discoursing, I herd such ringing of belles, such singing, such shouting, as though Rhodes had been recouered, or the Turke quite driuen out of Christendome, therewithal I might behold an hundreth bonefires together, tables spred in the open streetes, and banquets brought in of all handes. Demaunding the reason of him that was next me, he told me the newes was there (thankes be to God,) that there was a famous Schismatike one Martin newe sprung vp in England, who by his bookes, libels, and writings, had brought that to passe, which neither the Pope by his Seminaries, Philip by his power, nor all the holy Leagues by their vnderhand practises and policies could at any time effect: for whereas they liued at vnitie before, and might by no meanes be drawne vnto discord, hee hath inuented such quiddities to set them together by the eares, that now the temporalitie is redie to plucke out the throtes of the Clergie, & subiects to withdraw their allegeance from their Soueraigne: so that in short time, it is hoped they will be vp in armes one against another, whiles we aduantaged by this domesticall enuy, may inuade them vnawares, when they shall not be able to resist. I sory to heare of these triumphes, could not rest till I had related these tidings to my country men. If thou hast them at the second hand, (fellow Kempe) impute it to the intercepting of my papers, that I haue stayed for a good winde, euer since the beginning of winter: Now they are arriued, make much of them, and with the credit of thy clownery protect thy Cutbert from Carpers. Thine in the way of brotherhood,

Cutbert Curry-knaue."

neuer heard how orderly they pretended the printing of Accidences, when my L. of Darbies men came to see what they were doing, &c.— Where haue you liued my brethren, that you haue not heard of that learned Presbiter, that talking how Adam fell by eating of the Apple, discourst thus: Adam eate the Apple and gaue it to his wife, whereby is to be noted that the man eate and the woman eate, the man eate, but how, a snap and away: the woman eat, but how, she laide her thumbe on the stalke, and her finger on the coare and bitte it ouerthwart, in whych byting it ouerthwart, she broke all the commaundements, insomuch that vnder ten greene spots the ten commandements in euery Apple are comprised: and besides that corrupted her fiue senses. From whence wee may gather this obseruation that a woman alwaies eates an Apple ouerthwart.—If the dogge Martin barke againe, Ile hold him tugge for two or three courses, and then beware my blacke booke you were best, for I haue not halfe emboweld my register.—thou art like to heare of me by the next Carrier. And so bon nute to your Noddishippe.— Yours to command as your owne for two or three cudgellings at all times. Cutbert ' Curriknaue the yonger.". Contains F, in fours, Black letter; the last leaf blank. W.H. Quarto.

—— " Plaine Percevall the Peace-maker of England sweetly endeuoring with his blunt persuasions to botch vp a Reconciliation between Marton and Mar-tother. Compiled by lawfull art, that is to say, without witch craft, or sorcery: and referred specially to the Meridian and pole Artichoke of Nomans Land: but may serue generally without any great error, for more Countries than Ile speak of. Quis furor aut hos, Aut hos, arma sequi ferrúmque lacessere iussit." Seaton's rebus as described p. 1228. " Printed in Broad-streete at the signe of the Packstaffe." Superscribed " To the new vpstart Martin, and the misbegotten heires of his body: his ouerthwart neighbors, Mar-Martin, Mar-Mar-Martin, and so foorth following, the Traulila-lilismus as far as Will Solnes fluttering pronunciation may stumble ouer at a breath: To all Whip Iohns, and Whip Iackes; not forgetting the Caualiero Pasquill, or the Cooke Ruffian, that drest a dish of Martins diet, Marforius and all Cutting Hufsnufs, Roisters and the residew of light fingered younkers, which make euery word a blow, and euery booke a bobbe: Perceuall the Peace-Maker of England wisheth grace to the one party of the other Parish: and peace stitched up in a Gaberdine without pleat or wrinkle, to the other party of this Parish.—Yours if you like mee: mine owne if you strike me. P. P. P." Page 24. " This worke being finished, and red ouer by the heads of the parish, they called a vestry, wherin they concluded to write euery man some verses in the cōmendation of the Author, bicause it was a custome greatly taken vp in the Vniuersitie of late." These occupy 3 pages, and are subscribed " A. N. Carter, G. A. Sheepheard,

' Wood says, " A certain Oxford Scholar, vnder the name of Cuthbert Curry-Knave, in his book called ' An Almond for a Parrot,' &c. doth most egregiously run Martin down." Ath. Oxon. I, 160.

Sheepheard, goodman Bl. farmar, George Cobler, N. G. Botcher, H. D. Schollard maker for fault of a better." On the last leaf, "Faults escaped." Contains E 2, in fours. Mr. Ames says 26 pages, by which he must mean, besides the title-page, dedication, and the errata." Quarto.

"A briefe discovery of the vntruthes and slanders (against the true gouernment of the Church of Christ) contained in a Sermon, preached the [a]8. of Februarie 1588, by Dr. Bancroft, and since that time, set forth in Print with additions by the said Authour. This short ansvver may serve for the clearing of the truth, vntill a larger confutation of the Sermon be published. 1. Per. 2. 1. 2. 3. But there were false Prophetes also among the people." &c. This is introduced with a preface superscribed "To the godlie indifferent Reader, judgement to discerne, and zeale to embrace the truth." Towards the conclusion we read, "The deuill indeede hath within this twelmoneth, shewed himselfe to bee grieuously wounded in their [e] persons, because he hath raged so mightily, as these 32 [f] yeares his furie was neuer seene so great against the truth as at this present. That vile and scurrilous [g] pamphlet, lately suffered to come abroad by their priuity (if not allowance) and in their defence doth euidently shew, that sathan feeleth the power and sway which he was wont to bear by virtue of the hierarchie, to be greatly weakned. And because he feareth that his time vnder their gouernment cannot be long, therefore he meaneth now to infect the air at once, with all his contagions. The strength which they get by such leud and filthie stuffe, & the discredit which thereby they worke either vnto the cause, or the men and women whome they suffer to bee so vnworthilie traduced, is noe other than it were to bee wished (that seeing they will needs be filthy) they would publish such another booke euery day: That then it might appeare indeede whose sonnes they are. And this is all the confutation that I thinke, so godles & leud a scrole to deserue.—Fare well." Besides: 56 pages, numbered with Arabic figures in the middle of the pages. Neat White letter. W.H. 4°. (1590)

"A SERMON PREACHED In the Cathedrall Church in Norwich, the xxi. day of December, 1589, by W. Burton, Minister of the word of God there. And published for the satisfying of some which took offence thereat. Iob. 27. 5. God forbid that I should iustifie them, vntill I die, I will neuer take away mine innocencie from my selfe." This is introduced with an epistle "To the [h] Reader." The text, "Ieremie 3. verse 14. O ye disobedient children, turne againe saith the Lord: For I am your Lord." The passages which seem to have given offence in (1590)

[a] A mistake for the 9th. The 8th this year, 1588-9, was Saturday, and Thursday the year before. See Royal Astronomer, p. 183.

[e] The bishops and their vpholders.

[f] As Q. Elizabeth came to the crown 17. Nov. 1558, this shews the treatise to have been written about 1590.

[g] "An almond for a Parrot." In the margin.

[h] Wherein he is informed that "this Sermon hath been taken so vnkindly, as that the author thereof is for it accounted an enemy to Cæsar, is turned out of liuing, interdicted of his ministery for a sabboth of yeares

in this sermon are the following passages. "And if this rule[1] vvere obserued among those, to vvhome the censures of the church be committed, I doe not doubt but that more good, should be done, then now is done. But when men shall perceiue that all their citations, admonitions, suspensions, excommunications, and other censures whatsoeuer doe not proceede from a hatred of sinne, nor a conscience and care to amend their brethren, but either of a stomack to reuenge their ovvne quarrels, or else from a couetous affection, to mayntaine their ovvne gaines: alas, vvho vvill greatly care for them? &c.—When the Pharisies could not abide the doctrine of Christes disciples, they found quickly a iust defence of their quarrel. They doe that on the sabboth day which is not lawfull.—Our Pharisies also haue taken vp the same accusation against vs.—And first to begin vvithal, they crie out vpon him rebell, he vvil not vveare the surplice euery sunday & holy day, which he must doe whether hee hath any or no: And is not this a sufficient cause to deny the minister of his maintenance? Againe, they say we will not reade all seruice at all times, and therfore (whether the law dispense vvith him or no if he preach) we haue found sufficiēt cause to deny him his duetie. Again, they say vve vvil not read euery Collect, say gloria patri at the end of euery Psalme, nor make a leg at the name of Iesus: and is not this a sufficient cause to denie him his duetie? Again, they say we are angry vvhen vvomen of their good deuotion doe take upon them the ministers office, and reade prayers publiquely to a congregation, and yet, say they, we haue no reason for it: for vvil you haue a woman lie in a vvhole moneth, and come to church for so little as the Queenes booke doeth allow her? &c. Againe, they say vve vvil not bury the dead, vvhich vve ought to doe if it bee brought to the graue, vvhether vve knovv of it or no: &c. Againe, they say vve vvil not visite the sick of the plague, & although vve offer to doe it vvith consent of the vvhole, and so as it may not be preiudiciall to our publique ministerie: &c. Againe they say vve vvil not reade seruice euery day forenoone and afternoone, to the vvalles and the vvindows, to the stoules and the stones: &c. Again, they say vvee vvill not bid Imber dayes, according to their Almanacke, a booke of great

yeeres, and by a publique acte, disabled from all kinde of scholasticall function throughout the whole land: &c.—As for the sermon it selfe, hee protesteth (as in the sight of God) that it is faithfully translated from the pulpit to the pen, sauing that some pointes hee hath now more enlarged then hee could then for want of time, but as for these things whereof he was accused, and which were taken so greeuously, they be set downe euen as they were vttered, so nigh as he could, word for worde, without adding or detracting, without changing or altering, perswading himselfe, that there is nothing to be gotten by licking himselfe whole, as it is thought some would haue done; and therefore leauing them to God which woulde make the worlde beleeue that the hares eares be hornes, calling good euil, and euill good, groping for the light at noone day: he also committeth himselfe and his cause, this sermon and the euent thereof, vnto the God of heauen and earth, that iudgeth all hearts, and wil iudge all people in equitie and trueth."

[1] "That in all our reprehensions and admonitions we must seeke the good (or amendment) of our brother, and the glorie of God."

great authoritie and very autenticall, for it shewes vs this yeare what vve shal haue the next: &c? Item, they say vve sing psalmes in time of the communion, vvhich vvere foysted in by the Geneua puritans: &c? Againe, they say vvee preach against Papists, Atheists, Vsurers, Drunkards, Swearers, Lords of misrule, abuse of apparrel, gaming, & vvorking on the sabboth day, and such like commẽdable and common exercises of good neighborhood: &c.? Item, they say vve preach so plainly, & stand so long, that they fal either to napping, or els to prating vvhẽ vve begin, & commonly they leaue vvhen vve ende: &c? Lastly, if they should pay the minister his dutie, the loane of so much money vvere lost, vvhich in many yeares vvould amount to some round summe: and are not all these, or any of these, sufficient causes thinke you, to handle Gods pore ministers and seruãts as you haue heard before?—Well, vve haue not yet foũd the true cause, for vve haue been all this vvhile among the eares of corne, and therefore the vvrit must be returned with non est inuenta: but we wil haue another ad melius inquirendum, to make a nevve search. What are vve sharpe in reproouing their sinne? No, we dare not say to Herod, thou must not haue thy brothers vvise. Wee dare not say that a right papist is a ranke traytor, least vve shoulde be tolde that vvhen vve are in our priuiledged places vve prate vvhat we list, as once I vvas told. We dare not say that the magistrates are breakers of the Sabboth day, if they suffer it to be broken, least vve shoulde be called coram nobis for it, and hear of it againe 2. yeares after in the pulpit. And to meddle vvith any abuses or corruptions of the church is auribus canem vellere, to pul a dog by the eares, & to put our hands into a hornets nest.—And knovve you of Norwich, vvhose hearts runne after couetousness, vvho sitte and heare the preacher for a fashion, vvhich goe home & iest at him your bellyes full, vvhich censure him at your pleasure, &c.—And this is certain, vsurie is growen so strong, that it hath sinewes and bones like a man, and walketh vp and dovvn the streetes like a seruingman, like a gentleman, like a marchantman, I hope no man may iustly say like an Alderman, God forbid. But this I am sure of, it vvalketh so stoutly, that it taketh the vvall of all honestie & religiõ." Explaining the nature of repentance by turning again from sin to holiness, "There is a turning in outvvarde action, and affection.—So we in many things may turn—as from idolatrie to the gospel, from ignorance to knowledge, & in many thinges more. Some thinges are yet vvanting which the church should haue (if shee had her right) as namely a learned ministerie throughout the land, and that holy and auncient discipline vvhich was in the primitiue church: but as yet we cannot haue them, and therefore seeing in outward action wee cannot haue them, we haue them in affection: that is, vvee pray for them, we would gladly haue them if we might lawfully come by thẽ, and this vvee may doe by the lawe: for the booke of common prayer saith so in plain words, 'There was a godly discipline in the primitiue church, which is to be wished, and much to be wished that it might be restored again.' And here witnes with me I pray you that I speake not against the state, because I speake according to the Queenes booke, vvhich is established by the vvhole state, and therefore also vvhen occasion serueth it must bee taught, and yet vvith great vvisdome and discretion: for shall it be prayed for, and shal vvee not preach for it also that it may be much vvished for?—There is no desire of that vvhich is not knovven. And in affecting that vvhich is vvanting, vvee must bevvare that impatient rashnesse dravve not our affections beyonde the bonds of charitie and modestie, least we forget to be thankful for that vvee haue alreadie: and so for our impatiencie on the one side, and our ingratitude on the other side, vve be revvarded in the ende vvith the losse of all. If thus innocently yet vvisely vve hold a golden mean, vve shal geue no occasion iustly to feare the shedding of bloud, except by some butcherly Machiuel, vvho belike hauing lost his penknife, knew not how to make his pen but with a hatchet. You knowe my meaning, and so much for turniug againe." Contains, besides the epistle prefixed, A 8, B—K in fours. W. H. 16°.

1590. "Progymnasmata aliquot poemata. By John Brunswerd. Lond. 1590." Hist. of Eng. Poetry, III; 392, note k. Quarto.

1550. 'A Prayer used in the Queens Majesties House and Chapel, for the Prosperity of the French King and his Nobility; assailed by a Multitude of notorious Rebells, that are supported and waged by great Forces of Forreigners, August 21. 1590.' You may see it printed in Strype's Annals, IV; 41.

1590. The wedding garment. A sermon by Hen. Smith. See p. 1162.

1590. "A collection of certaine sclaunderous Articles gyuen out by the Bisshops against such faithful Christians as they now vniustly deteyne in their prisons togeather with the answeare of the saide Prisoners therunto. Also the some of certaine conferences had in the Fleete according to the Bisshops bloudie[1] Mandate with two Prisoners there. 1590."

This

[1] "To owre Louing freinds, Mr. Archdeacon Mullins, Mr. Doctor Andros, Mr. Conon, and Mr. Hutchinson, and the rest of the preachers, in & about London, vvithin named.

"After owre harty Commendations; I the Bisshop of London, haue receined order from my Lords grace of Canterburye vvith the aduice of both the cheiffe Justices, that conference should be presently had vvith these Sectaries, vvhiche do forsake ovvr Church, and be for the same commytted prysoners: for that it is intended, if by ovvr good & learned persvvasions, they vvill not be reduced to conforme themselues to their dutifull obedyence, that they shalbe proceeded vvith all according to the course of the common lavve: Therfore, these are to vvill & requyre you, & euery of you vvhose names are mentioned in the shedule hereunto ancxed, in her Maᵗⁱᵉ. name, by vertue of her high commission, for causes ecclesiasticall to vs and others directed; That vvise euery vveeke (at the least) you do repayre to those persons & prysoners, vvhose names are in this ticket set doune, and that you seeke by all learned & discrete demeanoure you may to reduce them from their errors: And for that eyther their conformitye, or disobedyence, may be more manifest, vvhen they shall com vnto theire trial; Therfore vve requyre you to set dovvne in vvriting the particuler dayes, of your going to confer vvith them, & lykevvise your censure vvhat it is of them, as that if occasion doe serue to vse it, you vvillbe sverne vnto; &c. And so vve byd you Farevvell: the 25. of Februar, e

This treatise is introduced with an anonymous epistle thus superscribed, " Grace to the reader with wisdome from aboue, to discerne the truth, & to walke in the same aright." Beginning, " These copies of the BBs articles & the awnsweres therunto, as also of these late conferences had in the Fleet, being come vnto my hands, I thought no lesse then my dutie to impart vnto thee, & publish to the view of all men : 1. that : the true cawses of these controuersies : 2. the BBs dealing with Christs poor seruants : 3. and cheifly the truth yt self might the sooner be brought to light & appeare." &c. These articles are the tenets or opinions of Hen. Barrow, John Greenwood, and their associates, to which they have here given their answer, or explained in their own way. The conferences here set forth are four. The first was on the 9th day of the 3d month, betwixt Mr. Archdeacon Hutchinson and John Greenwood in the Fleet. The second was between the same persons, on the 17th day. The third on the 18th day of the same month, betwixt Mr. Hutchinson and Dr. Androes on the one part, and Hen. Barrow on the other. A fourth was betwixt Mr. Hutchinson and Dr. Androes on the one part, and John Greenwood and Henry Barrow on the other part; the 13th of the 4th month. These conferences produced no good effect; for at the conclusion thereof Barrow refused to join with the church, whereupon he was desired to set down his reasons: he accordingly set down four, and subscribed his name. Greenwood refused to subscribe to them, or any other. After the said conferences are another set of answers to 12 other articles, with this head title, " A breif answeare to certayne sclaunderous Articles & vngodlie calumniations sparced abrode by the BBs & theire adherēts against diuerse faithfull & true Christians her Maiesties loyall and louing Subiectes to cullour theire owne vngodly & tyrannicall dealing with them, & to bring them into hatred both with Prince and people." At the end, " Expect theyr other Conferences with all possible speed." G, in fours; on the last leaf, only " Faults escaped in printing." W.H. Quarto.

" A collection of certain letters and conferences, lately passed betwixt certain preachers, and two prisoners in the Fleet." This, like the 1590.
foregoing article, is introduced with an anonymous epistle " To the Reader." Begining thus, " Considering the reformist Preachers are now become the BBs. trustie actors in their most conning & cruell enterprises, who erewhile would make the world beleeue that they neither pleaded for the BBs. tooke their ministrie from them, submitted it vnto them, or subscribed vnto their proceedings, nor would euer oppose against the

9 P 2

Februarye 1589. Your Louing freinds John Laud. John Herbert. Edw. Stanhope. Rich. Cosen.

" We haue sent you herewithall a note of some part of their errors, wherby those preachers that are associat vnto you may the better consider how to deale in conference with them.

" A briefe of the positions holden by the newe sectorie of recusants." These are 12 in number; then follows the list or schedule referred to in the mandate of the names of the divines who were appointed to confer, with the names of the several prisoners each was to attend, specifying in what prisons they were severally confined.

the truth or anie part therof, much lesse be at the commaundement of of their LLs. the BBs. to persecute Christs afflicted, or be partakers in their innocent bloud-shedding; againe that they pitied the ignorance of those that went to far, & charitablie sought to reduce them.—For the conferences, the truth of them thou maist perceiue in certaine Letters which passed betwixt them, &c.—And to make the matter more euident I haue at the latter end anexed certeine Arguments, giuen their cheif Teachers lõg agoe to haue answered by writing, the which they haue (as these Prisoners report) closely put vp, and with an euill conscience spoken euill in their Pulpits, instead of consent and repentance." &c. Then, on fol. or rather page 1, begins "The summe of the Conference betwixt Mr. Thomas [h] Sperin & me Henry Barrovv vpon the 14 of the third Moneth in the Fleet, as nere as my ill memorie could carie away." On p. 16 begins "The summe of a Conference had betwene Mr. Sperin & Mr. Egerton of th'one side: And Henry Barrovv & Iohn Greenvvood of th'other side in their Chamber where they were kept close Prisoners in the Fleet, vpon the 20. of the 3. Moneth 1590." On p. 31 begin the copies of several letters bettween Mr. Egerton, and the said two prisoners. Then, on p. 48 begins, "The summe of a confused conference had the 3 of the 4 Moneth, betwixt Mr. Sperin & Mr. Cooper, Iohn Greenvvood & Henry Barrovv in the Fleet." Lastly, on p. 67, begin the arguments as mentioned in the prefatory epistle: at the end, "These arguments were more than a yeare & an halfe since deliuered to Mr. Cartvvright, Mr. Travers, Mr. Charke and Mr. Floyde which still remaine vpon them vnanswered." Contains K 2, in fours, or 72 pages besides the preface; the last page blank. P. 57 being numbered twice, makes the difference between this and Mr. Ames's account. My copy wants the title leaf. White letter. WH. Quarto.

1590. "A treatise wherein is manifestlie proved, that reformation and those that sincerely fauor the same, are vnjustly charged to be enemies, vnto hir Maiestie, and the state. Written both for the clearing of those that stande in that cause: and the stopping of the sclaunderous mouthes of all the enemies thereof. Zephaniah 3. 18. 19. After a certaine time wil I gather the afflicted, that were of thee, and them that beare the reproch for it: &c. 1590." Prefixed is an epistle "To all those that sincerelie loue the Lorde Iesus, and seeke the flourishing estate of his Kingdome: and namelie, to the brethren throughout Englande, VVales, & Ireland: Iohn [i] Penri wisheth knowledge, zeale and pacience, with al other necessarie graces in Christ Iesus to bee multiplied." At the end of this epistle is

[h] This Mr. Sperio appears, in the course of this conference, to have been Rector of St. Mary Magdelen, Milk-street. This will supply Newcourt's Repertorium with an incumbent of whom he had no account.

[i] Mr. Ames has "By Mr. Penri," as if inserted on the title-page, and takes no notice of the date, even in the margin; so that it has the appearance of a different edition. Mr. Strype mentions an edition 1588. See Life of Whitgift, p. 346.

is an [*] advertisement "To the reader," which may be seen below. The head title, "Reformation no enemie to her Maiestie and the State." Contains I 2, in fours, besides the epistle prefixed. W.H. Quarto.

"The First parte of Pasquils Apologie. Wherin he renders a reason to his friendes of his long silence: and gallops the fielde with the Treatise of Reformation lately written by a fugitiue Iohn Penrie." Device, A hand and Caduceus, as p. 1699. "Printed where I was, and where I will bee readie by the helpe of God and my Muse, to send you the May-game of Martinisme for an intermedium, betweene the first and the seconde part of the Apologie. Anno Dom. 1590." In MS. 'July 2. Being an answer to Penrie's treatise of Reformation, wrote by Tho. Nash. Coll. Jo. Cantab.' T. Baker's Maunsell, p. 79. It has neither prefix, nor appendage. Contains E 1, in fours. In his Majesty's library. Quarto. 1590.

"A brief discoverie of the false church. As is the mother such the daughter is. By Henry Barrowe." 263 pages. See Neal's Hist. of the Puritans, I; 553. Reprinted in 1707. Quarto. 1590.

"An answere to George Giffords Pretended Defence of Read Praiers and deuised Litourgies with his vngodlie cauils and wicked sclanders comprised in the first parte of his last vnchristian & reprochfull booke entituled A Short Treatise against the Donatists of England. By Iohn Greenwood Christs Poore Afflicted prisoner in the Fleet for the truth of gospell. 1590." Prefixed is "The preface to the Reader," at the head of which is this text, "1 Cor. 2. 11, 12, 13. VVhat man knoweth the thinges of a man if not the Spirit of man vvhich is in himself:" &c. F, in fours. Neat White letter. See p. 1229. W.H. Quarto. 1590.

The same in Black letter, with additions. W.H. Quarto. 1590.

"Pet. Ramus his Geometrie, translated by Tho. Hood, Mathemat. Lecturer in the Cittie of London. Pri. for the sayd Tho. Hood 1590." Maunsell, II; 22. Octavo. 1590.

"A relation of certain Martyrs in England." Translated from the English into Spanish by Rob. Parsons the jesuit, who probably was the author also. "Madrid, 1590." Ath. Oxon. I; 362. Octavo. 1590.

"The dangerous adventure of Richard Ferris and others who undertooke to rowe from Tower wharfe to Bristowe in a small wherry-boate Lond. 1590." Hist. of Eng. Poetry, III; 214, note o. Quarto. 1590.

The construction of the English accidence, by John Stockwood, schoolmaster 1590.

[*] "M. D. Haldon deliuered in Parliament a Latine booke concerning church discipline, written in the dayes of king Ed. 6. by M. Crammer, & Sir John Check knight &c. This book was committed by the hoose to be translated vnto the said M. Haddon, M. George Bromely, M. Norton, &c. If thou canst good reader help me, or any other that labour in the cause vnto the said book: I hope (though I never saw it,) that in so doing thou shalt doe good service vnto the Lord and his church." In the margin "Anno 12, or 13 Elizab." I have examined the printed Journal of the House of Commons, but do not find any intimation of such a transaction. No parliament sat the 12 of Elizabeth. This however seems to allude to a book printed by John Day, in 1571, entitled 'Reformatio Legum Ecclesiasticarum,' &c. as p. 651. See Biogr. Brit. IV; 2460, note I.

schoolmaster of Tunbridge. 1590. By the assigns of Francis Flower. 4°.

1590. "A briefe and true report of the new found land of Virginia, of the commodities, and of the nature and manners of the naturall inhabitants. Discouered by the English Colony there seated by Sir Richard Greinuile Knight In the yeere 1585. Which remained Vnder the gouernement of twelue monethes, At the speciall charge and direction of the Honourable Sir Walter Raleigh Knight, lord Warden of the stanneries Who therein hath beene fauoured and authorised by her Maiestie and her letters patents: This fore booke Is made in English By Thomas Hariot seruant to the abouenamed Sir Walter, a member of the Colony, and there employed in discouering. Cum gratia et privilegio cæs. Ma^tis speciali." This title is but indifferently engraved on a copper-plate of a proper size to print in the very neat compartment engraved by Theodore de Bry for the Latin edition, which makes the first part of a History of America published at Frankfort in ix parts, at times, from the year 1590 to 1602. In a tablet at bottom, "Francoforti ad Moenum typis Ioannis Wecheli, sumtibus vero Theodori de Bry Anno CIↃ IↃ XC. Venales reperiuntur in officina Sigismundi Feirabendii." The same as to the Latin edition. Dedicated "To the right worthie and honourable Sir Walter Ralegh, Knight, seneschal of the duchies of Cornewall and Exeter, and L. Warden of the stannaries in Deuon and Cornewall, T. B. wisheth true felicitie." This inscription over an achievement of Sir VValter's arms, in 16 coats, with 3 crests; the motto 'Amore et Virtute.' This dedication, dated "—from Francksort the first of Apprill 1590," is printed in the broken English, in which no doubt it was written; seeing Hariot's preface and translation are in good English for the time. The preface is addressed "To the adventurers, favorers, and vvelvvillers of the enterprise for the inhabitting and planting in Virginia." The treatise is divided into three parts. "The first part of marchantable commodities. The second part, of suche commodities as Virginia is knowne to yeelde for victuall &c. The third and last part, of such other thinges as is behoofull for those which shall plant and inhabit to know of; with a description of the nature and manners of the people of the countrey." This 3d book is concluded on p. 33. "Thus —I take my leaue of you, this moneth of Februarii, 1588." Hereunto are annexed, with a separate title-page, and a fresh set of signatures,

"The true pictures and fashions of the people in that parte of America novv called Virginia, discowred by English men sent thither in the years of our Lorde 1585, att the speciall charge and direction of the Honourable Sir Walter Ralegh Knight Lord Warden of the stannaries in the duchies of Corenwal and Oxford who therin hath bynne fauored and auctorised by her Maiestie and her letters patents. Translated out Latin into English by Richard Hackluit. Diligentlye collected & draowne by Ihon White who was sent thiter speciallye and for the same purpose by the said Sir Walter Ralegh the year abouesaid 1585. and also the year 1588. now cutt in copper and first published by Theodore de Bry att

att his wone chardges." Then, "The table of all the pictures contained in this Booke of Virginia." XXIII in number, besides a very curious one of Adam and Eve, each taking of the fruit from the forbidden tree: the upper parts of the Serpent's body are of an human form; with dragon's wings. 'Iodocus a winghe in. Theodore de Bry fe.' This faces a prefatory epistle "To the gentle Reader," by de Bry, as may be gathered from the [a] contents. Plate I. A chart of the coast of Virginia, has on it the queen's arms crowned and gartered; and on a tablet "Autore Ioanne With Sculptore Theodore de Bry, Qui et excud." Most of the plates have on them T. B. Some have G. Veen. A few without any name or initials discernible. To these are annexed also with a separate title-page,

"Som picture, of the Pictes which in the olde tyme dyd habite one part of the great Bretainne. The painter of whom I haue had the first of the Inhabitans of Virginia, giue my allso thees 5 Figures fallowinge, fownd as hy did assured my in a oolld English cronicle, the which I wold well sett to the ende of thees first Figures, for to showe how that the Inhabitants of the great Britannie haue bin in times past as sauuage as those of Virginia." All these five plates have De Bry's initials, and fronting each of them is an explanation thereof; and at the end "A table of the principall thinges that are contained in this Historie, after the order of the Alphabet." This table refers wholly to the History of Virginia translated by Tho. Hariot; its signatures F 3, 4, are in regular succession after the Pictures, which evinces these being one entire publication. Neat White letter. W.H. Folio.

"A Petition directed to her most excellent Maiestie, wherein is deliuered, 1. A meane howe to compound the ciuill dissention in the Church of England. 2. A proofe that they who write for Reformation do not offend against the stat. of 23 Eliz. c. 2. and thereforetill matters bee compounded, deserue more fauour. Open thy mouth for the dumbe in the causes of the children appointed to death. Prov. 31. 8. I believe and therefore haue I answered, For Sions sake I will not ceasse and for Ierusalems

[a] "—Consideringe, Therfore that yt was a thinge worthie of admiration, I was verye willinge to offer vnto you the true Pictures of those peeple wich by the helfe of Maister Richard Hakluyt of Oxford Minister of Gods Word, who first Incouraged me to publish the Worke, I creaued, out of the veery original of Maister Ihon White an Englisch paynter, who was sent into the contrye by the queenes Maiestye, onlye to draw the description of the place lyuelye to describe the shapes of the Inhabitants, their apparell, manners of Liuinge, and fashions, att the speciall Charges of the worthy knighte, Sir Walter Raleigh, who bestowed me Small Sume of monnye in the serche and discouerie of that countye, From te yeere, 1584 to the ende. of The yeare 1588." —I creaued them at London, an broughe Them hither to Franckfurt, wher I and my sonnes haue taken earnest paynes in grauinge the pictures ther of in Copper, seeing yt is a matter of noe small importance.—Finallye I hartlye Request thee, that yf any seeke to Conterfaict thes my bookes, (for in this dayes many are so malicious that they seeke to gayne by other men labours) thow wouldest giue no credit vnto suche conterfaited Drawghte. For dyuers secret markes lye hiddin in my pictures which wil breede Confusion vnless they bee well obserued."

Ierusalems sake I will not holde my tong. Esa. 62. 1. Hereunto is annexed: Some opinions of such as sue for Reformation: by which it may appeare howe vniustlie they are slaundered by Bishops, &c. p. 53. Togather with the Authours Epistle to the Reader, p. 58. Also, Certayne Articles wherein is discouered the negligence of the Bishops, their Officials, Fauourers and Followers, in performance of sundrie Ecclesiastical Statutes, Lawes and Ordinances Royal and Episcopal, published for the gouuernment of the Church of Englande, p. 60. Lastlie: Certayne Questions, or Interrogatories drawen by a fauourer of Reformation, wherein he desireth to be resolued by the Prelates, p. 74." L 2, in fours; the last page blank. See p. 1086. W.H. Quarto.

(1591.) " A plaine refutation of M. Giffards booke entitled, A short treatise gainst the Donatistes of England." See p. 1229. " Wherein is discouered 1 The forgery of the vvhole Ministerie, 2 The confusion, 3 False vvorship, 4 And Antichristian disorder, Of these Parish assemblies, called the Church of England. Here also is prefixed a summe of the causes of our separation, & of our purposes in practise, vvhich M. giffard hath tvvise sought to confute, and hath novv tvvise receiued ansvver, By Henry Barrovve. Here is furder inserted a brief refutation of Mr. Giff. supposed consimilitude betvvixt the Donatistes & vs. VVherin is shevved hovv his Arguments haue bē and may be by the Papists more iustly retorted against himself & the prese̅t estate of their Church. By Io. Greenwood. Here are also annexed a fevv obseruations of M. Giff. his last Reply, not printed heretofore: as the other aforesaid vvere in the yeare 1591." See p. 1262. Dedicated " To the right honorable Pere and graue Counsellor Sr. William Cecill, Knight of the most noble order, Baron of Burleigh, Lord high Treasurer of England, &c.—Henry Barrovve & Iohn Greenvvood for the testimony of the Gospel in close prison. ---An aduertisement * to the Reader."---The preface, superscribed " VVisdome to the Reader from the Father of lightes, to discerne of these times, and to iudge of themselves what is right." Besides: 260 pages.* W.H. Quarto.

(1591.) " Newes out of France for the Gentlemen of England. A stratagem most ventrously attempted, and valiantly atchived by the French King the 27 day of July, 1591. Wherein is desciphered, what Trust his Royal Majestie reposeth on the Valour of the English, and their dutifull service unto Him at all Assayes. Newes also touching Sixteen ships taken nigh the Haven of Deepe, and the Discomfiture of the Popes Forces transported into France, towards the Aide of the Leaguers, both concurring on the 28 of July last past. With a Report of the Princely Meeting and Honorable Conjoyning of the whole Power of the French King, the first Day of this present Moneth of August, consisting of English, German,

* " Good Reader, the treatises here insuing (being some vvhile since intercepted) are novv republished for thy good, together vvith a fevv obseruations of M. Giff. his last Reply, not printed heretofore. &c. 1606." H. Barrow and J. Greenwood were executed 6 April, 1593.

German, and his own People. Printed for John Kid." The author subscribes himself to his epistle, G. B. M. of Arte. Here is mentioned a gallant action successfully performed under the said king, by a brave British commander, Sir Roger Williams, near the town of Noyan. In 10 leaves, Black letter. Oldys's Catal. of Pamphlets, &c. N° 392. See p. 1165. Quarto.

"A triple Almanack and Prognostication for the year MDXCI." By John Dee. Catal. Bibl. Bodl. I; 350. Quarto. ——

"The beginning of Heliodorus's Ethiopics translated into English hexameters by Abraham Fraunce. Lond. 1591." See Hist. of English Poetry, III; 405, note o. Octavo. 1591.

The assize of bread, &c. as p. 1552. Again 1592; and frequently. 4°. 1591.

"A profitable and necessarie discourse for the meeting with the bad garbelling of spices used in these daies; and against combination of the workmen of that office, contrary unto common good. Composed by divers grocers of London, wherein are handled such principall matters as followeth in the table before this book, 1591." Inscribed to Sir William Webbe knt. lord mayor of London; and to the right worshipfull the aldermen of the same citie, his brethren; by the retailors grocers." See the contents in Gough's Brit. Topogr. I; 932. Quarto. 1591.

"Matth. Sutlivii de Presbiterio ejusque nova in Ecclesia Christiana Politeia.". Catal. Bibl. Harleianæ, III; 6830. Quarto. 1591.

"Elizabethae Reginae Angliae Edictum, promulg. Lond. Nov. 29. 1591." Oldys's Life of Sir Walter Ralegh, p. laix, note b. 1591.

"Edw. Gennings Priest, his life and death crowned with Martyrdome at London the x. day of nov. 1591. Printed at St. Omars by Charles Boscard, 1591." T. Baker's Maunsell, p. 53. Quarto. 1591.

"A breefe aunswere of Iosephus Quercetanus Armeniacus, Doctor of Phisick, to the exposition of Iacobus Aubertus Vindonis, concerning the original, and causes of Mettalles. Set foorth against Chimists. Another[a] exquisite and plaine Treatise of the same Josephus, concerning the Spagericall preparations, and vse of minerall, animall, and vegitable Medicines. Whereunto is added divers rare secretes, not heeretofore knowne of many. By Iohn Hester, practicioner in the Spagericall Arte." His mark, composed of all the letters of his name, on a shield. "At London, Printed Anno Dom. 1591." Dedicated "To the Right worshipfull Ma. Robert Carey Esquire.—Iohn Hester.--- To the gentle Reader." In which he announces himself to be the translator. R 2, in fours. At the end, "These are to bee solde by Iohn Hester, dwelling at Pooles wharfe at the signe of the Stillitorie. 1591." Then, two alphabetical tables; one for each part of this book. W.H. Octavo. 1591.

"A hundred and fourtene experiments and cures of the famous Phisition Philippus Aureolus Theophrastus Paracelsus, Translated out of the Germane tongue into Latine. Whereunto is added certaine excellent and profitable ——

[a] This has a separate title-page, with his mark somewhat different, and sprigs of laurel up the sides.

profitable workes by B. G. a Portis Aquitano. Also certaine secretes of Isack Hollandus concerning the Vegetall and Animall worke. Also the Spagerick Antidotarie for Gunshot of Iosephus Quirsitanus. Collected by I. H." On the back, "A briefe declaration of those things which are contained in this Treatise." Dedicated "To the right worshipfull Walter Ralegh Esquier.[a]—I. Hester.---An Apologeticall Preface of Master Barnard G. Londrada A Portu Aquitanus vnto the Booke of experiments of Paracelsus, wherein is prooued that sicke bodies stuffed and filled with the seeds of diseases, can hardly be cured without Metalline Medicines: contrarie to the writinges of some which denie that mettals (after what sort or manner so euer they be prepared) may profite or helpe the nature of man.--B. G. Londrada &c. vnto the gentle reader, health." H 2, in eights; See p. 1290. Neat White letter. W.H. Octavo

— "The Mariners Mirrour," &c. See p. 1681. Frequently reprinted.

— An epistle "To the most high and mightie prince Elizabeth, by the grace of God, Queene of Englande, Fraunce, and Irelande, defender of the fayth &c.—Your Maiesties most humble Subiect, Hugh Broughton." On 5 pages, very neat Italic types. This epistle dedicatory, exactly as it is here set or composed, was printed with "Sundry workes defending the certayntie of the holy Chronicle," &c. See p. 1265. But that had on the back of the last leaf "The argument of the Bookes folowing;" whereas this has the beginning of "An Epistle sent vnto the Archb. of C. and D. Elmer then B. of London, chosen vmpires touching the D. that read against the Concent of Scripture, and the author of that Concent.—London, Nou. 4. 1591." Roman types. Both these epistles together occupy only 4 leaves. W.H. Quarto.

A grant for Richard Wrighte to print the History of Cornelius Tacitus.

Rymer, vol. XVI. p. 96. 33 Eliz. p. 17. m. 1. 1591. "ELIZABETH by the grace of God, &c. To all manner of printers, booksellars, and all other our officers, mynisters, and subjects, greeting. Know ye that we, for certen considerations us thereunto especially movinge, of our especiall grace, certain knowledge, and mere motion, have licenced and privileged, and by these presents, for us, our heyres, and successors, doe graunte and give licence and priviledge unto our lovinge subject, Richarde Wrighte of Oxford, and his assignes onlie, duringe the naturall lyfe of the said Richarde Wright, to imprint, or cause to be imprinted, the Hystorie of Cornelius Tacitus, translated into Englishe, straightlie inhibitinge and forbidding all and everye other person or persons whatsoever, as well our subjects as strangers, that they, or any of them, duringe the tyme of this our licence and grante, do not presume in any wise to print, or cause to be printed, within our domynyons, the said historie so translated, or any part thereof, or any other booke or books of the said author, whiche shall be fyrste printed by the sayde Richarde Wrighte, or his assignes. And yf it happen anye of the foresaid books, or

[a] He was knighted between Decemb. 1584, and Febr. 1585. Oldys's Life of him, p. xxv.

or anye parte or parcell of anye, to be imprinted out of our domynyons, that then yt shall not be lawfull for any person or persons whatsoever to transporte, bringe in, sell, utter, bynde, sowe, stiche, or cause to be transported, brought in, soulde, uttered, bounde, sowed, or stiched, anye of the books so imprinted, or any percell thereof, duryng the time aforesaid, upon payne of our highe indignation, and that every offender contrarie to the effect and meaninge of these presents, shall forfeyt to the use of us, our heires and successors, the said books, and fortie shillings of lawfull money of Englande, for every such booke or books, or any part of them, so printed, or to be printed, brought in, soulde, uttered, or put to sale, stiched, sowed or bounde, contrarie to the entente and meanynge of this our present licence and priviledge; further auctorisinge the said Richarde Wrighte, and his assignes, with one or more of our officers with him, as to him or them shall be thought meete, from tyme to tyme to enter the workhouses, shopes, warehouses, and dwellings of every printer, bookseller, or other person whatsoever, whom he or they shall suspecte to offend in the premises, and the same to searche, and yf it be founde or proved, that any such booke or books, or any part of them, be so printed, brought in, soulde, uttered, or put to sale, sowed, stiched, or bounde, contrarie to the entente of this our graunte, the same to take and seaze, and in his or their custodye to keepe to the use of us, and our successors. Willinge therefore and commaundinge, as well the master and wardens of the mysterie of the stacyoners in our cyttye of London, for the tyme beyng, as also all other our officers, mynysters, and subjects, as they tender our favour and pleasure, and will avoyd our displeasure and indignation for the contrary, that they and everye of them, at all tymes, when need shall requyre, to ayde and assyste the sayd Richarde Wright, and his assignes, in the due excercysinge and execution of this our present licence and priviledge with effect, accordinge the true meanyng of the same. For that expresse mention, &c. In wytnesse whereof, &c. Witnesse our self at Westminster, xxvth day of May." *Per breve de privato sigillo.*

"A declaration of the true causes of the great troubles, presupposed to be intended against the realme of England. VVherein the indifferent reader shall manifestly perceaue, by whome, & by what meanes, the realme is broughte into these pretended perills. Seene and allowed. Anno, M.D.LXXXXII." This is introduced with an address "To the indifferent reader.—Colen the 26. of Marche 1592.---Of the fained happinesse of England." Verses on "The vaunt of the pretended Gospel. The boast of continual peace. The present feare of troubles." Mr. Baker remarked to Mr. Ames, that this book is a very dangerous libel against the queen and government, but more particularly against the lord Burghley, and his second son, sir Robert Cecil. It was looked upon to be so dangerous a peice, as to receive an answer from Bacon (afterwards lord Verulam,) printed at large in Resuscitatio, under this title; 'Certain observations upon a libell, published this present year' 1592, intituled as above, in about fifty pages, in folio, very well worth reading, being 1592.

 a good

a good antidote against the poyson contained in this book. The libel, I presume, was printed abroad, containing too much treason to be published in England. And yet the print is English.

The author, who is thought to be Parsons the Jesuit by his stile, and affection to the Spanish monarchy, has in page 75, &c. mentioned certain * books, as an abuse of the multitude. Contains 77 pages, including the title-page. Neat White letter. W.H. Octavo.

1592. "An Advertisement written to a secretarie of my L. Treasurers of Ingland, by an Inglishe Intelligencer as he passed throughe Germanie towardes Italie. Concerninge Another booke newly written in Latin, and published in diuerse languages and countreyes, against her Maiesties late proclamation, for searche and apprehension of Seminary priestes, and their receauers. Also Of a letter vvritten by the L. Treasurer in defence of his gentrie, and nobility, intercepted, published, and answered by the papistes. Anno Domini, 1592." Prefixed is "The epistle of advise," according to its running title, "To my loving good frind N. secretary to the right honorable the L. Treasurer of Inglande.—from Augusta this last of August 1592." Then, "The extract and abreviation of the booke of Ihon Philopatris against her Maiesties proclamation," The running title "An extract of an answer to a late proclamation." See Oldys's Life of Sir W. Ralegh, p. lxix. note b. Contains C 10, in eights. W.H. Octavo.

1592. "Strange Newes Of the intercepting certaine letters, and a Conuoy of Verses, as they were going Priuilie to victuall the Low Countries. Vnda

* "Of these sortes of libells, many do declare great numbers of French, & Flemish victories, which are so famous, that sundry of them were neuer knowne, nor heard of in all the world, but only in England.

"Others are of obscure and trifling matters, except such as that of the happy conquest of the suburbes of Paris, &c. *Printed by ww. Blackwall.*

"Others tell of visions in the ayre, which are enterpreted to presage detriment to those of the league. *Printed by Nelson,* 1590.

"Sometymes they are of prophesied victories before they happen, and appointed tymes of the death of Princes, as that the duke of Parma should die at martinmas 1590. *Printed by VVolf,* 1590.

"Some are of triumphs of victories, before they be obtayned, and when the Earle of Essex was to go with his forces into Normandie. *Printed by Allde,* 1591.

"Some haue bene set forthe to make losses seeme victories, as the discourse of the Portugall voyage, and the loss of the Reuenge. *Printed 1589. And by Ponsonby,* 1591.

"And whereas there was one Capilla, and others of his company, executed for Heresy, and Apostasie, at Validolid in Spaine 30 yeares past: the manner of his execution is in an English libell newly set foorth, and said to be for the profession of the Gospell, and to be donne but of late. *Printed by Nelson,* 1591.

"In like sort is very particularly set downe, the glorious & constant martirdome of an Englishman (not long since) in the towne of Dunkerck, whose torments endured fowre dayes: & yet there was neuer any such man, nor any such matter herd of in the said towne, as the inhabitants will witnesse. *Printed at London,* 1590.

"So was it published, that the King of Spaine (whome the libeller calleth the Arch-tyrant of the world) was dead. *Printed by Purfoot,* 1591.

"And another libell that came foorthe of late intituled 'A fig for the Spaniard,' contradicteth that lie, with another as manifest an vntruth, and saith, that Phillip of Spaine is not dead, but lieth bedred. *Printed by VVolf,* 1591." What is here printed in Italics was set in the margin.

Vnda impellitur vnda. By Tho. Nashe Gentleman. Printed 1592." Inscribed "To the most copious Carminist of our time, and famous persecutor of Priscian, his verie friend Maister Apis lapis: Tho: Nashe wisheth new strings to his old tawnie Purse, and all honorable increase of acquaintance in the Cellar.—-Thine intirely, Tho. Nashe.--- To the Gentlemen Readers." M 2, in fours. See p. 1271. Quarto.

"Delia; conteyning certayne Sonnets with the Complaint of Rosamond." Catal. Bibl. Harleianæ, III; N° 5945. Quarto. 1592.

"A Feast full of Cheere, Where Griefes are all on Heape; 1592.
Where Sollace is full deere, And Sorrows are good cheape."
Ibidem,* N° 5946. Quarto.

"The Seamans Triumph, declaring the honourable actions of such (1592.) gentlemen, captains, &c. as were at the taking of the great carack lately brought to Dartmouth, with her burthen and commodities: also the manner of the fight with and burning of another at the Isle of Flowers of the burthen of 900 ton, written for truth to a Gentleman† of great worship in London." Quarto.

"Iohn Speed his Genealogies of the Bible, Faithfully gathered and printed in a large Table. 1592." Maunsell, p. 110. 1592.

"The Mirrour of Mirth and pleasant Conceits." Quarto. 1592.

"A Relation of the King of Spaines receiving in Vallindolid, and in the English College of the same Towne in August past of this yere, 1591. Wrytten by an Inglish Priest of the same College, to a Gentleman and his wyf in Flaunders, latelie fled out of England for Profession of the Catholique Religion. Anno M.D.XCII." Octavo. 1592.

An epistle "To the worshypfull and learned, the Vicechauncelour, and others the gouernours of learning-houses in the Vniuersitie of Oxforde." B, in fours, neat White Letter. W.H. Quarto. ——

Some time after that to the Vicechancellor, another epistle was published, addressed "To the most high and mighty Prince Elizabeth, &c. as p. 1718, subscribed "Your Majesties Subject, Hugh Broughton." I have not met with the original publication of this, but find it in his works printed in folio, 1662, p. (161.) ——

"A briefe note of the benefits, that grow to this realme by the obseruation of fish-daies; with a reason and cause, wherefore the law in that behalf made is ordained. Very necessarie to be placed in the houses of all men, especially common victualers." Ends, "Seen and allowed by the most honourable privie councell, in the yere of our lord God 1593, the 20 of March. At London, printed for Henry Gesson and Francis Coules." A broadside. 1593.

"Greens news, both from Heaven and Hell, prohibited the first for writing 1593.

*These and several more poetical and other books mentioned in this catalogue, very probably, have the printer's name, though not inserted; the compiler naming only the very ancient printers.

†"This gentleman, though his name is not prefixed to the dedication, was Sir Walter Ralegh, as may plainly appear to those who have read it, and are acquainted with the history of this action." Oldys's Life of Sir W. Ralegh, p. 189, note c.

writing of books, and banished out of the last displaying of conny-catchers. Commended to the presse by B. R. (*Perhaps Barnaby Rich,*) Londoner." This was licensed to John Oxenbridge and Tho. Adams, and probably printed by or for them. See p. 1369. Quarto.

1593. "Acta in comitiis parliamentaribus, Londini die 2 Apr. 1593, tam contra catholicos, quam puritanos collecta, et in sermonem Latinum traducta, per Johannem Dodritium, Londini commorantem." Sixteens.

1593. מַפְתֵּחַ לְשׁוֹן הַקֹּדֶשׁ That is the key of the Holy tongue: Wherein is conteineid, first the Hebrue Grammar (in a manner) woord for woord out of P. Martinius. Secondly, A practize upon the first, the twentie fift, and the syxtie eyght Psalmes, according to the rules of the same Grammar. Thirdly, A short Dictionary conteining the Hebrue woords that are found in the Bible with their proper significations. All Englished for the benefit of those that (being ignoraunt in the Latin) are desirous to learn the holy tongue; By Iohn Udall." Device, A hand extended from the clouds with a pair of compasses, encircled with this motto, LABORE ET CONSTANTIA, "Imprinted at Leyden, By Francis Raphelengius, clↃ. IↃ. XCIII." On the back, "Proverb. 1. 7." in Hebrew and English. On the next leaf is "A Table containing the principall heades of the Hebrue Grammar," The grammar on 104 pages; the dictionary, 174; the practise, 98. Then a table of "Faultes obserued in the Grammar after the dead (*death*) of the author," &c. W.H. 8°.

1593. "A Treatise Conteyning the true Catholike and Apostolike Faith of the Holy Sacrifice and Sacrament ordeyned by Christ at his last Supper: With a declaration of the Berengarian heresie renewed in our age: and an Answere to certain Sermons made by M. Robert Bruce Minister of Edinburgh concerning this matter. By William Reynolde Priest. Ioan. 6. 51.—At Anvverp, Imprinted by Ioachim Trognesius. M.D.XCIII." Dedicated "To the right Excellent and Mightie Prince Iames the Sixt, By the Grace of God King of Scotland." Then, a table of 32 chapters, &c. At the end of which is "A note for the Reader. Whereas M. Bruces Sermons are printed without any figures to distinguish ether page or leaf, which no booke lightly omitteth:—to the end of his booke, which is p. 296." Contains 447 pages, and a table at the end. Lambeth Library. Sixteens.

1593. "SPECVLVM BRITANNIAE. The first parte. An historicall, & chorographicall discription of Middlesex. Wherin are also alphabeticallie sett downe, the names of the cyties, townes, parishes, hamletes, howses of name &c. With direction spedilie to finde anie place desired in the mappe & the distance betweene place and place without compasses. Cum Privilegio." On a tablet below, "By the travaile and view of Iohn Norden.

* The industrious Mr. Norden fixed on this title, intending to have described all the counties in England in like manner; but we find none of them besides Hartfordshire and Cornwall ever published. Ant. Wood says the former was printed about the same time as Middlesex; the latter does not appear to have been printed before 1728. He made surveys of several other counties; the particulars thereof may be seen in Gough's Brit. Topogr. in the several pages annexed to his name in the indexes, and some memoirs of him, in Vol. 1; page 256.

Norden. Anno 1593." In a very neat compartment, with the queen's arms at top, a nobleman on one side, and a citizen with his livery gown on the other: the whole engraved on copper-plate. At bottom, Pieter vanden Keere sculp. 1593." On the next leaf "To the high and most mighty Empres Elizabeth, by the Divine Providence, Queene of England, Fraunce, and Ireland, powerful protector of the Faith and vndouted Religion of the MESSIAH, the most comfortable nursing mother of the Israel of GOD, in the British Isles. Her highnes loyall subiect Iohn Norden, in all humilitie, consecrateth his Speculum Britanniæ." On the back of this leaf is an achievement of the queen's arms, quartered with others of her royal predecessors, &c. crowned and gartered, with her motto 'Semper eadem,' on a ribbon at bottom; neatly engraved on copper-plate. Dedicated "To—Sir William Cecill knight,—Lord high Treasurer of England, *&c.*—Io. Norden.---To the consideration of the honorable, wise, and learned.---Aduertisements touching the vse of this labor.—Io. Nordeni vale, ad primam partem sui Speculi Britanniae." Contains besides, 54 pages, on neat White Letter, Brevier; and three maps from copper-plates, viz. Middlesex, London, and Westminster. Arms of the principal persons interred cut on wood are indented. Several commendatory verses on the last two leaves. He had the queen's patent for printing this work. W.H. Quarto.

Ant. Wood says 'A Chorographical description of Hertfordshire was printed much about the same time,' viz. as Middlesex. Probably in 1596, when his Preparative was published; under which year I shall accordingly place it.

"IDEA: The Shepherd's Garland, fashioned in nine Eglogs; with Rowland's Sacrifice to the Nine Muses. Dedicated to Mr. Robert Dudley: By M. Drayton, 1593." Biogr. Brit. p. 1745, note D. See Percy's Reliques of Ancient Eng. Poetry, I; 306, &c. Quarto. 1593.

"The famous Chronicle of King Edward the first, surnamed Longshankes, with his returne from the Holy Land. Also the Life of Lleuellen Rebell in Wales. Lastly the sinking of Queene Elinor, who sunk at Charing Crosse, and rose again at Potter's hith, now named Queenhith." An historical* play by Geo. Peele. Quarto. 1593.

"The Examinations of Henry Barrowe, John Greenwood and John Penrie, (1593.)

* The latter part of this play seems to have been taken from an old ballad, entitled 'A warning piece to England against Pride and Wickedness: Being the fall of Queen Elenor, Wife to Edward the First, King of England; who for her Pride, by God's Judgments, sunk into the Ground at Charing-Cross and rose at Queen Hithe.' It is the 13th in a collection of Old Ballads, with introductions historical, critical, &c. in 3 vol. 12mo. the 3d edit. 1727. The compiler, in his introduction to this, shews the inconsistency of this being designed to blacken so illustrious a character as that of Eleanor, queen of K. Edw. I; but concludes it to be rather an ironical satire upon Mary I, who married Philip K. of Spain. Her being swallowed up, he supposes to be a threat of the poet's, that unless she amended, vengeance would overtake her; and that he fixed on the said Eleanor, that people might see, though it was said, it could not be meant of her, for which he gives sufficient reasons. Indeed no queen ever bore a more exalted character, unless it be her present majesty. Moreover it is to be remembered, that Charing Cross was not erected till after her death, and in memory of her; as were many other crosses in the kingdom; of which Waltham cross, though piteously neglected, exhibits an original specimen.

Penrie/ before the high commissioners/ and Lordes of the Counsel. Penned by the prisoners themselues before their[*] deathes. Ther is nothing couered/ that shal not be reuiled: neither hid/ that shal not be knowen. Luke 12. 2. For euery worke God himself wil bring Vnto iudgement/ with euery secret thing whither good or euil. Eccles. 2. 14." On the back is a preface by the anonymous publisher, wherein he says, " and though they haue spilt the blood of those men/ which vexed them so sore/ yet can they not bereaue the world of their testimonie/ which by word and writing they have left behinde them." The first examination is of " Henry Barrowe the 19. of Nouember[†] 1586:—being the Lords day." The next, " the 27. of Nouember/ 8 daies after." A third, " the 24 of March." A fourth, " the 18 (or perhaps the 28) day of the 3 month/" or March. " The answers of John Grenewood" are inserted without any date. " The examination of John Penrie/—the 10 of the fourth moneth April 1593." Though this treatise evidently was not printed till after the deaths of these persons, it appears to have been printed in great hast as soon after as possible; signature B especially having not only a bad register, but the pages thereof misplaced in the form: this fault is however amended in the Harleian Miscellany, vol. IV. p. 326, &c. where the whole is reprinted. D, in fours. W.H. Quarto.

1593. " H. Jacob his defence of the Churches and Ministry of England against the Brownists. Printed by Richard Schilders at Middleburgh 1593." Quarto.

1593. " Nevves from Spayne and Holland conteyning An information of Inglish affayres in Spayne vvith a conferrence made theruppon in Amsterdame of Holland. VVritten by a Gentleman trauelinor borne in the low countryes, and brought vp from a child in Ingland, vnto a Gentleman his frend and Oste in London. Anno, M.D.XCIII." Prefixed is a short epistle " To the indifferent and discrete reader." The treatise is superscribed " To the right woorshipful M. N. my good oste and deare frend abiding in Gracious streat in London." This treatise consists of two parts, or epistles; the first from Sivil, in which are given large extracts from a sermon preached before the cardinal archbish. of that city, on the 29 Dec. the feast day for St. Thomas of Canterbury, by a scholar of the English seminary lately established there. The sermon was in Latin, but the writer has annexed a translation of the extracts. Another of those English scholars made a sermon on the same occasion in Spanish, " to giue the people a reason of so many Inglish mens coming forth of Ingland," &c. The author then describes a drawing, set up in the said English college, of the two persecutions by the two king Henries of England (Hen. II, and Hen. VIII.)—" Further doth ther not come to my remembrance, any other newes, except I should tel you of the sundry

[*] A plain indication that this book was not printed till after their deaths. See p. 1678. Barrow and Greenwood were executed at Tyburn on the 6th of April 1593; and Penry at St. Thomas Waterings, 29 May following. See Neal's Hist. of the Puritans, I; 555—567.

[†] This probably induced the compiler of the Harleian Miscellany to insert ' Printed 1586.'

ſundry bookes that I haue ſeene here printed of late, in diuers countries againſt the laſt proclamation publiſhed in Ingland, the 29 of Nouember the yeare paſt of 91. agaynſt Catholiques *&c.* And laſt of al here hath come forth a booke in Spaniſh vvritten by one father Pedro Ribadeneyra, and this booke conteyneth the ſtorye of Ingliſh affayres from the yeare eightie and eight euen vnto this year 93. And in this ſaid ſtory he layeth forth alſo the ſaid proclamation at large, and an explanation of the ſame, *&c.* Moreuuer, two new ſtatutes made about religion in your laſt parliament ended the 10 of Aprill this preſent yeare, *&c.* by which tvvo ſtatutes, as alſo by the ſundry bookes ſet out by authority at this very tyme agaynſt the puritans, *&c.* this writer (*Ribadeneyra*) concludeth that neuer common welth vvas in more dangerous plight." &c. This firſt letter is concluded on fo. 21. On the back thereof begins " The ſecond parte of this letter, conteyning certaine conſiderations of State upon the former relation." Being the ſubſtance of a conference at an ordinary in Amſterdam by divers perſons, of the different nations of Europe, concerning the political ſtate of England, or " vvhether the preſent gouerment of Ingliſh affayres, ſetting aſide al regard of partiality to religion: vvere in it ſelfe and according to reaſon, experience and law of pollicy, to be accounted vviſe and prudent, and conſequently vvhether ſuch as chiefly managed the ſame, and namely lord Burley, were in truth a vviſe mã or no:" &c. The event has anſwered this queſtion. This letter concludes with a bare nomination of " the preſent pretenders to the crowne after the Queene that now is," &c. promiſing hereafter a further diſcourſe concerning the [a] ſucceſſion. " Amſterdam in Holland this firſt of September 1593." Neat White letter. W.H. Octavo.

" Green's Mamilla; with verſes prefixed by R[d]. Stapylton." Hiſt. of Eng. Poetry, III; 402. 1593.

" A Defence of the holy Genealogies: whoſe ignorance hath greatly hurt the Iewes, and hindered Chriſtianitie." On 4 leaves. Maunſel adds, " ſeruing for an inſtruction for the vſe of the Genealogie ſet forth by Iohn Speed." My copy has, adjoined to this, ——

" A direction to finde all thoſe names expreſſed in that large Table of Genealogies of Scripture, lately gathered by I. S.[b] Whereof the firſt number ſerueth for the ſide margentes, and the later anſwerable to the higheſt ſygures." D 3, in fours; the laſt page blank. W.H. Quarto. ——

" A conference about the next ſucceſſion to the crowne of Ingland, divided into two partes, vvhereof the firſt conteyneth the diſcourſe of a ciuill Lavvyer, hovv and in vvhat manner propinquity of blood is to be preferred. And the ſecond the ſpeech of a Temporall Lavvyer, about the particular titles of all ſuch as do or may pretende vvithin Ingland or vvithout, to the next ſucceſſion. VVhere vnto is alſo added a new & perfect arbor or genealogie of the diſcents of all the kinges and princes 1594.

9 R of

[a] Hence it appears very evident that this treatiſe; the copie of a letter, &c. as p. 1665; and A conference about the next ſucceſſion &c. 1594. are the productions of the ſame pen.

[b] See p. 1781.

of Ingland, from the conquest vnto this day, whereby each mans pretence is made more plaine. Directed to the right honorable the earle of Essex of her Maiesties priuy councell, & of the noble order of the Garter. Published by R.[a] Doleman. Imprinted at N. with Licence. M.D.XCIIII." On the back is "The summe of bothe partes more in particuler." The epistle dedicatorie is dated "from my chamber in Amsterdame this last of December 1593.[b] Your honours most affectionate R. Doleman.—The contents of the first parte,—of the second booke.---The preface, conteyning the occasion of this treatis, with the subiect, purpose, and partes thereof." Wherein is detailed the subject matter of the conference at Amsterdam, in April & May last as intimated in the second part of the letter, entitled 'Nevves from Spayne' &c. as p. 1724. The first part, divided into 9 chap. occupies 220 pages. Then, "The preface to the second parte." Besides: 267 pages; paged afresh, but the signatures are continued from the first part, throughout. The types and vignettes are evidently the same as the Newes from Spayne &c. W.H. 8°.

1594. "Writing tables with a kalender for xxiiii yeares, with sundry necessarye rules. Made at London by Fraunces Adams, stationer or bookbinder, dwellinge in Distaffe lane, neare Olde Fishstreete, at the signe of the Aqua vite still, and are there to be sold anno domini 1594." It opens as a musick book. In it he says, "Printing was found out at Mentz 1459, and first brought to London by William Caxton, mercer." Sixteens.

1594. "Arraignment of the whole Society of Jesuites in France, holden in the Court of Parliament in Paris, in July 1594" Quarto.

1594. "The Execution of D. Lopez, Phisitian, Stephen Ferrara, Manuel Lewis, &c. 1594." Quarto.

1594. "The Defence of Iob Throkmorton against the slaunders of Maister Sutcliffe, taken out of a Copye of his owne hande as it was written to an honorable Personage. Prouerbes 20. 6. The taulke of th'vngodly is how they may lay waite for bloud: But the mouth of the righteous will deliuer. *Ch.* 29. 20. Seest thou a man that is hastie to speak vnadvisedly? There is more hope of a foole then of him. *Ch.* 30. 14. There is a generation whose teeth are as swords, & their iawes as kniues to deuoure the poore and afflicted from th'earth. 1594." E, in fours. W.H. 4°.

—— A petition directed to her most excellent majestie, &c. as p. 1715.

1595. "A treatise Of the Ministery of the Church of England. Wherein is handled this question, Whether it be to be separated from, or joyned vnto. Which is discussed in two letters, the one written for it, the other against

[a] See Ath. Oxon. I; 358, &c. My copy has in MS. after Doleman, 'but believed to be penned by Cardinal Allen, Sir Francis Englefield & Father Parsons.' Wood has the initial for Doleman's Christian name N. as to subsequent publications under the name of Doleman. 'Of this Nic. Doleman, says he, who was a grave Priest, and of a mild disposition, you may read in a Book entit. A relation of a Faction began at Wisbich,' &c.

[b] This date refutes a notion prevalent in Wood's time, that so soon as this book peeped forth, which was accounted a most heinous and scandalous thing, the parliament enacted, 35 Eliz. that whosoever should be found to have it in his house should be guilty of high treason; for that parliament was dissolved 10 Apr. 1593, near 9 months before the presumed publication of this book. See Ath. Oxon. I; 359.

against it. Whereunto is annexed, after the preface, A brief declaration of the ordinary officers of the Church of Christ, And a few positions. Also in the end of the treatise, Some notes touching the Lordes prayer. Seven questions. A table of some principal thinges conteyned in this treatise. Trie all thinges: keep that vvhich is good. 1 Thes. 5. 21. If (the prophets) had stood in my counsell: &c. Ierem. 23. 22. Lord who hath beleeved our report? &c. Esa. 53. 1. Ioh. 12. 38. Rom. 10. 16." Contains 143 pages, besides 4 leaves, with the preface, &c. prefixed. The date in p. 137. W.H. Quarto.

"An Epistle in the Person of Christ to the Faithfull soule, written first by that learned Lanspergius, and after translated into English by one of no small fame, whose good example of sufferance & liuing hath and wilbe a memoriall vnto his countrie and posteritie for euer." This title over a neat wood-cut of Christ preaching to a multitude. "Imprinted at Antwerpe. 1595." On signature A 4, over a cut of the crucifixion, "A Dialogue betwixt a Christian and Christ hanging on the Crosse. Written into Latine by Marcus Marulus, and Translated into English." The dialogue in verse. Then, a table. At the end are two hymns: the first in the octave stanza to each letter of the alphabet; the other of all creatures to the Creator. 310 pages. Lambeth Libr. Octavo. 1595.

"Propositions and principles of Diuinitie, propounded and disputed in the Vniuersitie of Geneva, by certaine students of Diuinitie there, vnder M. Theod. Beza, and M. Anthonie Faius, Professors of Diuinitie. Wherein is contained, a Methodicall summarie, or Epitome of the common places of Diuinitie: translated out of Latine into English. Newlie corrected with sundrie Additions. Imprinted 1595." Dedicated "To the renowned and noble Lord, the lord Nicholas, earle of Ostromg, &c. —from Geneua the tenth of the Kalends of September, 1586. Your Honors at commandement Anthonie Faius.--To all those that wish well vnto the Lord Iesus, and his poore Church wandring heere vpon Earth: the Translator wisheth the powerfull assistance of Gods spirit, while they are heere, and the speedy inioying of their sure though deferred hope.— The table and order of the Principles," &c. Besides: 400 pages. Neat White letter. W.H. Octavo. 1595.

"Cornucopiæ, or divers Secrets: Wherein is contained the rare Secrets of Man, Beasts, Foules, Fishes, Trees, Plantes, Stones, and such like; most pleasant and profitable; and not before committed to be printed in English. Newlie drawen out of divers Latine Authors into English; by Thomas Johnson." 22 leaves, Black letter. Oldys's Catal. of Pamphlets, &c. Nº 181. Quarto. 1595.

"Our Ladie hath a new Son. Doway, 1595." Catal. Bibl. Harleianæ, I; 2306. Octavo. 1595.

"An humble Supplication to her Maiestie. + Printed, Anno Do. 1595." My copy has in MS. 'Printed at Doway, or some other place in the Low Countrys.' At the end, "December 14. Anno 1595." Contains 86 pages. W.H. Sixteens.

"The most honourable tragedy of Sir Richard Grenvile knight." An 1595.

heroick poem, composed in stanzas of 8 verses, and consists of near 90 pages. It is dedicated to lord Monjoy by Jervis Markham. See Oldys's Life of Sir W. Ralegh, p. clxxvii, note e. Octavo.

1595. "A coppie of a recantation of certaine Errors, raked out of the dung-hill of Poperie, and Pelagianisme, publiquely made by Maister Barret of Kayes Colledge in Cambridge, the tenth day of May, in this present yeere of our Lord 1595, in the Vniuersitie Church, called Saint Maries in Cambridge: which Errors he did rashly hold, and maintaine: Translated out of Lattine into English. Anno 37. Elizabeth." Hereunto are annexed "The nine Assertions, or Articles of Lambeth, composed and agreed vpon at Lambeth-house on the 20. day of Nouember, in the yeere of our Lord, 1595, by Iohn Archbishop of Canterbury, Richard Bishop of London, Richard elect Bishop of Bangor, and sundry other reuerend and learned Diuines there present; for the determining of certaine Arminian points of Controuersie, that then arose in the Vniuersitie of Cambridge." These are in Latin and English. Both these little pieces were reprinted in 1630, at the end of an anonymous treatise entitled 'God no impostor, nor deluder,' but ascribed to William Prynne Esq; in a catalogue of his works published by his printer.

1595. Edward Dering his comfortable Letters full of Christian consolation, written unto sundry his friends; together with his words spoke on his death-bed, at Tokye, 26 June, 1576. Published 1595. Octavo.

1595. "Ovid's Banquet of Sauce, a coronet for his mistress Philosophy and his amorous Zodiac. Lond. 1595." By George Chapman. To which is added, "The Amorous Contention of Phillis and Flora, a translation by Chapman, from a Latin poem, written, as he says, by a Frier in the year 1400." Hist. of Eng. Poetry, III; 446, note m. Octavo.

1595. Florio's Italian dictionary. Ib. p. 465, note h. See p. 1213.

1595. Perry's Welch Grammar. Catal. Bibl. Harl. II; N° 15650. Quarto.

1595. "A plain Declaration or Description of Sin, Death, Devil and Hell. Printed for W. Bewley, 1595." T. Baker's Maunsell, p. 42. Octavo.

1595. "A pleasant Satyre or Poesie: wherein is discovered the Catholicon of Spain, and the chief Leaders of the League, finely laid open in their Colours. 1595." Quarto.

—— The history of the Bible, by Eusebius Paget.

1596. "A hundred and fourteen experiments" &c. as p. 1717.

1596. "A brief Apologie of Thomas Cartwright against all such slaunderous accusations as it pleaseth Mr. Sutcliffe in *his* seuerall pamphlettes most iniuriously to loade him with. A righteous man abhorreth lyes: But th'vngodly shameth him selfand is put to silence. Pro. 13. 5. 1596." Prefixed is an epistle "To the Reader." The head-title "A brief of Thomas Cartwright to the printed slaūders of Mr. D. Sutcliffe, Deane of Exeter, so farre as they concerne the same Tho. Cartwright." D 2, in fours. WH. Quarto.

1596. "De gestis Regum Anglorum. Edit. Savil. Lond. 1596." By William of Malmesbury. Warton's Gesta Roman. p. xlvii. Folio.

"The

"The Shield of Achilles; translated from Homer by George Chapman. Lond. 1596. This was followed by seven books of the Iliad the same year." See Hist. of Eng. Poetry, III; 441. Quarto. 1596.

"Tarquatus Vandermeres seauen yeares studie in the Arte of Magicke vpon the twelue months of the yeare, wherein many secrets are reuealed vnto the world." Beneath this title is a wood-cut of the author sitting at a table with a book before him; the Devil on the further side thereof pointing to the book as teaching him. Without, is another person taking an observation with a quadrant of the moon and stars. Under the said cut begins "Januarie 1596." Only 3 leaves. Quarto. 1596.

"Speculi Britaniæ pars. The description of Hartfordshire By John Norden." This title (over a small view of a Hart fording over the river Lea) is within a scroll compartment engraved on copper-plate. I have not seen the original edition, but copy from that annexed to Middlesex, in 1723. And as this description of Middlesex is closely copied from the original edition, probably this of Hartfordshire is also. It is dedicated "Amplissimo honoratissimoq; D. Edwardo Seamer militi, Baroni Beauchamp, Comiti Hertfordiæ literarum fautori maximo.—Io. Norden.—To Gentlemen well affected to this trauaile.—Thinges to be considered in the vse of this booke and Mappe." This map is larger than that of Middlesex, and on a smaller scale. The description, &c. on 31 pages. There seems to have been prefixed to this description of Hartfordshire "Norden's Preparatiue to his Speculum Britanniæ. Intended A reconciliation of sundrie propositions by diuers persons tendred, concerning the same." Dedicated "To—Sir William Cecill Knight, Baron of Burghleigh, Lord High Treasurer of England. *&c.*—Auctoris In Patriæ & Antiquitatis imperitiam Sententia." The Preparative is addressed "To all courteous gentlemen, Inspectators and Practitioners in Geographie, in Christo salutem." Dated at the end, "At my poore howse neere Fulham. 4. Nouember. 1596. Vnder your frendly reformations, John Norden." See p. 1723. Quarto. (1596.)

"The good huswives Jewell." A book of cookery. Sixteens. 1596.

Pro Andrea Bright, officium custodis bibliothecae reginae apud Palatium: And formerly Thomas Seex distiller, then Anthony Martyn distiller and bookkeeper, and now to Andrew Bright, with a stipende of 13l. 6s. 8d. per annum.

Pro Thoma Edmonds, secretario pro lingua Graeca constituto.

"ELIZABETH by the grace of God, *&c.* To all men, to whom these presents shall come, greeting. Know ye that wee, in consideration of the faithfull and acceptable service heretofore done unto us, by our well beloved servant Thomas Edmonds, esquire, of our especiall grace, certen knowledge, and mere motion, haue geven and granted, and by these presents for us, our heirs and successors we do give and graunt unto our said servant the office of secretarie for the Frenche tongue; which office our late servant Charles Yetsweirt deceased, held and enjoyed during his life; and by these presents, for us, our heires and successors, wee do make, ordeyn, Rymer, vol XVI. p. 264. 36 Eliz. p 5. m. 1. 1596.

deyn, constitute and appoynt the said Thomas Edmondes our secretarie for the Frenche Tongue, to have, occupie, exercise, and enjoye the said office of secretarie for the Frenche tongue, unto the said Thomas Edmondes duringe his naturall life, by himself, or by his sufficient deputie, or deputies; together with the wages and fee of threescore sixe poundes thirteene shillings and four pence of lawfull money of England by the yere, for the exerciseinge of the said office; the said wages and fee of threescore sixe pounds thirteene shillings and four pence, to be yerelie had and receaved by the sayd Thomas Edmondes, or his assigne, or assignes, to the proper use and behove of the sayd Thomas Edmondes, from the feast of saint Michael the Archangell last past, of our treasure, and of the treasure of us, our heires and successors, at the receipt of our Exchequer at Westminster, by the handes of the and chamberlaines of us, our heires and successors there for the time being, at four usuall termes of the yere; that is to say, at the feasts of sainte John Baptist, sainte Michaell the Archangell, the nativitie of our Lord, and the annunciation of our Ladie the Virgin, by even portions; together with all and singuler the proffits, commodities, advantages, preheminences, rights, priviledges, and emoluments whatsoever, to the said office belonging, due, incident, or any wise appertaining in as large and ample manner and forme as the said Charles Yetsweirt, or Nicasius Yetsweirt, father of the said Charles, John Mason, or Si Tuke deceased, or any other person or persons heretofore exercised, or enjoying the said office, had and received, or of right ought to have had and received, for the exercising of the said office; althoughe expresse mention, *&c.* In witnes whereof, *&c.* Witness our self at Westminster the seventeenth day of May."

Rymer, vol. XVI p. 290. "Commissio ad inquirendum de rebus ecclesiasticis." Where any three, or more of the commission had power to enquire, on the oaths of 12 men, of all and singular heretical, erronious, and offensive books, libels, writings, words, and sayings, published, invented, or set forth, or to be published, invented, or set forth hereafter, by any person or persons against us, or against any of our magistrates, *&c.*

—— "A Discoverie of certain Errours Published in Print in the much commended Britannia, 1594. Very prejudiciall to the Discentes and Successions of the auncient Nobilitie of this Realme. By Ralphe Brooke, Yorke Herault at Armes. Quam quisque norit artem, in hac se exerceat." It has neither date, printer's nor publisher's name; but very probably was published about this time. See Biogr. Brit. Camden. It was reprinted in 1723 with Camden's answer, and A second discovery with Brooke's reply to Camden. Quarto.

—— Mascall on planting and grafting trees.

1596. "A Treatise, shewing the possibilitie, and conueniencie of the reall presence of our Sauiour in the blessed Sacrament: The former is declared by similitudes and examples: the latter by the causes of the same." Device, IHS with a crucifix on the middle of the H, and over it I N R I. Under the H are three nails, their points meeting right over a heart; the whole encompassed with rays of glory, and this motto, " Man hath eaten the Bread of Angels. Ps. 77." Behind, appear the spear and spunge crossing each other, a hammer and pinchers crossing their handles at bottom. This is sometimes called the Jesuits' arms. " At Antwerp Imprinted by Ioachim Trognesius. 1596." On the back are two texts in Latin and English, viz. Iudic. 14. (14.) *and* Zach. 9. (17.) Then, " The Preface to the christian Reader.---A Copie of a Letter that the Author of this Treatise following, sent to his friend."---A Table of contents. The treatise on 121 leaves; then " An aduise for protestants and puritanes:" and the Errata. Neat White letter. W.H. Sixteens.

" The disposition or garnishmente of the Soule To receiue worthily the blessed Sacrament, deuyded into Three discourses, 1 Preparation. 2 Presentation before Christ. 3 Enterteinment. Qui timent Dominum, *&c.* Those that feare God, will prepare their heartes: and in his sight, sanctify their soules. Eccl. 2. At Antwerpe. Imprinted by Ioachim Trognesius. 1596." On the back are these two texts in Latin and English, from 4 Reg. 4. (6.) Sap. 16. (21.) Dedicated " To the vertuous & zealous Matrone Mistris S. H. and her Religious & feruent Sonne M. R. H. perfect deuotion in this lyfe to the Eucharist, & full possession thereof in the lyfe to come.—From my cell in the Charter house at Maclin.— T. N.---To the Reader.*---To the Catholique Reader.---To the Protestant reader, wherin is declared how we haue free-will to doo good woorkes.---To the Catholique-lyke Protestantes." The treatise on 293 pages: at the end, are affixed " A brief table of all the principall matters,—necessary to be committed to memorye.---A table of the contents of this Treatyse.---Faultes escaped in printing." Neat White letter, and all the pages enclosed in black lines. Hereunto is annexed " A conclusion, Conteining an Admonition to al the reuerend and religious Priests in England." This is on 8 leaves, a smaller type, and without black lines. W. H. Sixteens. 1596.

" A true confession of the faith, and humble acknowledgement of the alegeance, which we hir Maiesties subjects, falsely called Brownists, doo hould towards God, and yeild to hir majestie, and all other, that are ouer vs in the Lord. Set down in Articles or Positions, for the better & more easie vnderstanding of those that shall read yt: And published for the cleering of our selues from those vnchristian slanders of heresie, schisme, pryde, obstinacie, disloyaltie, sedicion, *&c.* which by our aduersaries are in all places given out against us. wee beleeue therfore haue we spoken. 2 Cor 4, 13. But, who hath beleeued our report, and vnto whom is the arme of the Lord reuealed? Isai. 53, 1. M.D.XCVI." The preface is addressed " To all that desire to feare, to loue, & to obey our Lord Iesus Christ, grace, wisdom and vnderstanding." The head-title repeats 1596.

* " In the firste ingresse to this discourse before I descended to any particuler Treatise, I preconceiued, that these my selender Meditations, shoulde come to the vew and censure of three sortes of persons; Catholicks, protestantes, & demi-catholickes, or catholique-like protestantes, or externall protestantes, & internall catholikes: some call them Church-papistes, others Scismatiques, whose mindes I thoughte good to prepare in particuler before I went any further."

repeats verbatim the title-page, and then, "Wee beleeue with our hearts & confes* with our mouths." This confession consists of 45 articles: the margins filled with texts of Scripture. The preface in B. L. the confession, Roman. C, in fours; the last leaf blank. See Catal. of Pamphlets in the Harl. Libr. N° 393. W.H. Quarto.

1597. "Bibliotheca Theologica: or A librarye theological, containing 1. A generall Analysis or Resolution: 2. A breife elucidation off the most sacred Chapters off Elohim his Bible: Drawen for the vse off yonge Christians, specially off the poorer sorte, vnable to purchase Variety off holy-men theyr wrytinges: By Henoch Clapham. Nihil primùm perfectum. Imprinted at Amsterodam, Anno 1597." Prefixed is "The proeme," wholly in double columns. The treatise consists of an analysis and elucidation of the first 14 chapters of Genesis, where it breaks off abruptly with this distich,

"Here businisse doth break me off. The Sequel do expect
What tyme or tymes, God giues the meanes: Mean-tyme this Mite
[accept."

Whether this work was ever taken in hand again, I cannot say; but at the end, by way of catch word, we have "¶ Chap. xv." The arguments, &c. are in long lines; the elucidations, &c. in double columns. The running title, BRESHITH. GENESIS. Besides the proeme, 28 leaves. Mostly Black Letter, much worn. W.H. Quarto.

1597. "Theological axioms or conclusions: publikly controverted, discussed and concluded by that poore English Congregation, in Amsterdam: To whome H. C. For the present, ad-ministreth the Ghospel. Togither with an Examination of the saide Conclusions, by Henoch Clapham. Here-vnto is added a little Tractate entituled, The Carpenter. Dej est, non errare: Hominis errare: Sapientis vitare: Insipientis perseuerare in errore. clɔ Iɔ xcvii." It is introduced with an "Epistle To al such in the church of Englande as vnfeignedly seeke Iesus Christ in incorruption, Grace & Peace be multiplied vnto their Consciences, Amen." The head-title, "xii Theological Axiomes or Conclusions, togither with their Examination." These occupy 14 leaves: "An end of the first XII Conclusions." The Carpenter is introduced with an "Epistle To Maister Abraham Breckman,—of Midlebrough in Zeland &c.—Amsterodam. 1597. 7 Mon. Iul.—Henoch Clapham." Head-title, "A litle Tractate, vtteringe the Truth of Christ his Two-Natures. Mark 6. 3. Is not this the Carpenter, Maries sonne?" F, in fours, B. L. W.H. Quarto.

1597. "An Epistle to the learned nobilitie of England. Touching the translating the BIBLE from the original, with ancient warrant for euerie worde, vnto the full satisfaction of any that be of hart. By Hugh Broughton. Iohn 1. The light shineth in darknes, though darknes doeth not comprehend it. Middelburgh, By Richard Schilders, Printer to the States of Zealande, 1597." Head-title, "To all the learned Nobilitie of England, Hugh Broughton wisheth all increase of knowledge, that they may esteeme the vnderstanding of Gods worde, and care for synceritie in

* Article 1. "That ther is but one God, one Christ, one Spirit, one Church, one truth, one Faith, one Rule of obedience to all Christians in all places."

in it, to be the head of wisedome and true Religion in Christ." Concluded on page 56. " From Middelburgh, in Sea-land, This 29. of May, 1597. Your Honours to commaunde H. Broughton." Hereunto is annexed " A request to the Arch. of Cant. to call in a corruption of a late English Cōmentation vpon Daniel, dedicated to the right H. Lordes." Concludes with, " I pray your Grace, that Printers be not allowed to disgrace my studies. Your Graces to commaunde, H. Broughton." H 2, in fours; Neat White Letter. W.H. Quarto.

" Seven sobs of a sorrowful soul for sinne." &c. See p. 965. 1597.

" Royall Exchange: To such worshipfull Citezins, Marchants, Gen- 1597.
tlemen, and other Occupiers of the Contrey, as resorte thereunto. Try to retaine, or send back again. The Contents ys after the preface. Seen and allowed here. At Harlem: Printed with Gylis Romaen. M.D. XCVII." A collection of Christian admonitions to the several degrees of persons who frequented the Royal Exchange; and dedicated to that worshipful and grave citizen of London Mr. A. T. from Harlem, by the author, John Payne. In 48 pages, Black Letter. Quarto.

" Grammatices Græcæ institutio compendaria." By William Camden, 1597.
for the use of Westminster school. See Biogr. Brit. article Camden.

" Theorique and Practise of Warre." &c. as p. 1258. 1597.

" The ancient state, authoritie, and proceedings of the Court of Re- 1597.
quests. 2. Octob. 1596." Device, An open book (the Bible), over which rays of glory appear issuing through the clouds, in an oval with this motto, DAT ESSE MANVS: SVPERESSE MINERVA. The whole enclosed in a compartment, on the sides of which are Minerva and Mercury; Minerva pointing up to the glory, Mercury supporting the book. In the upper corners are cupids on the wing holding festoons of printers' materials. Underneath, " Anno 1597." Prefixed, is a table, shewing the time when the several Acts, Orders and Decrees were made, proving the state,[f] authority, &c. of the Court of Requests. The head-title, " In nomine Domini nostri Iesu Christi. 13. Februarij. 1592. Actes, Orders, and Decrees made by the King and his Counsell, 9 H, 7. remaining amongst the Records of the Court, now commonly called the Court of Requests."

[f] Hence it appears that " the Court of Requests was parcell of the Kings most honourable Councell, and so alwaies called and esteemed. The Iudges of that Court were alwaies of the kings most honorable Councell appointed by the King to keepe his Councell board. The keeping of this Court was neuer heretofore tied to any place certeine; but onely where the Councell sate, the suitors were to attend: But now of late for the ease of suitors, it hath bene kept in the White-hall in Westminster, and onely in the terme time.——The forme of the proceeding in this Court, was altogether according to the processe of summary causes in the Ciuill Law.—The causes wherewith they deale, and whereof they iudge, are of all sorts: As Maritime, Ecclesiasticall, Temporall, but properly of Temporall causes, and onely of the other sort, as they are mixt with Temporall.—The maner of proceeding in the sayd Court. 1. By Priuy seale, Letter missiue, Iniunction, messenger, or bond. 2. By attachment. 3. By Proclamation of Rebellion. 4. By Commission of Rebellion. 5. By Sergeant at armes. Apparences by vertue of the Priuie seale." &c.

Requesta." These proceed regularly to the 23 of January, 27 Eliz: At the end are some instruments taken from an old book of precedents remaining among the records of this court;[s] the titles of which may be seen below. Ascribed to Sir Julius Cæsar. See Bibl. Legum Angliæ, I; 174. Contains 162 pages. W.H. Quarto.

1597. "The Trimming of Thomas Nashe Gentleman, by the hightituled patron Don Richardo de Medico campo, Barber Chirurgion to Trinity Coledge in Cambridge. Faber quas fecit compedes ipse gestat. London, Printed for Philip Scarlet,[a] 1597." On the back, "To the learned. Eme, perlege, nec te precii pœnitebit. To the simple. Buy mee, read me through, and thou wilt not repent thee of thy cost."---To the Gentle Reader.—Richard Lichfield.---To the polygrammaticall, parasitupocriticall, and pantophainoudendeconticall Puppie Thomas Nashe, Richard Leichfield wisheth the continuance of that he hath: that is, that he want not the want of health, wealth and libertie." Begins, "Mitto tibi Nashum prora N. puppi humque carentem.—Yours in loue vsque ad aras. Rich: Lichfield." On signature E 2 is Nash's portrait double-fettered. The copy before me is imperfect at the end. I find it licensed to Cuthbert Burby this year, and therefore very probably printed by or for him. 4°.

1597. "Vita Gul. Wicami Wintoniensis Episc. Lond. 1597." Ath. Oxon. I; 218. See Lowth's Life of William of Wykeham, Pref. p. 12. 4°.

1597. "A relation of the Stirrs in Wisbich Castle among the secular Priests and Jesuits." Strype's Annals, IV; 318.

1597. "The Frenche Chirurgerye, or all the manualle operations of Chirurgerye, vvith divers, & sundrye Figures, and amongst the rest, certayne nuefovvnde Instrumentes, verye necessarye to all the operationes of Chirurgerye. Through Jaqves Gvillemeau, of Orleans ordinarye Chirurgiane to the Kinge, and sworen in the Citye of Paris. And novv truelye translated out of Dutch into Englishe by A. M. Imprinted At Dort by Isaac Canin. M.D.XCVIJ."[t] This title printed within a compartment exhibiting sundry operations in chirurgery, neatly engraved on copper-plate. On the back are the queen's arms, supported by a lion and a dragon, and the Rose encircled with laurel supported by two angels, pendant thereunto, neatly engraved also. Dedicated "To the most high, mightie, Royalle, and Victoriouse Princesse, the most Christiane and Virtuose defendresse of the sincere & true Christiane Religione Ladye Elisabeth, By the grace of God, Queene of Englande, Fraunce, and Irelande &c.—Maximiliane Bouman Chirurgian at Dort.—To the King.—From Paris, the

[s] "21. H. 7. The oth giuen to the Kings Counsell Iudges of this Court.—5. E. 6. A priuie Seale to giue the partie possession of the lands of a man that doeth disobey all kind of Proceß to make the partie grieued satisfaction of his due.---An Extent.---1. & 2. P. & M. An Attachment and Extent.—3. & 4. P. & M. An Iniunction to a whole Towneship to refrein the abuse of their liberties.---2. Eliz. An attachment to the L. Warden of the Cinque ports, &c.

[a] Perhaps related to, and the successor of Thomas Scarlet; by or for whom we find no book printed after 1596.

[t] At the end, M.D.XCVIJ.

the 15. of Septembre, 1594.—Guillemeau.---The Epistle to the benevolent Reader.---To the gentle & curtiouse Reader.—Thyn as his owne, or els not worthye of vitall breath. A. M." The translator, as the former epistle by M. Guillemeau the author. This French Chirurgery consists of nine treatises, subdivided into chapters; and has prefixed "The Thesaurarye or Storehouse of Chirurgerye" on eleven copper-plate cuts, exhibiting "Four figures, or pertrayctures of mans bodye: Two of—the externall partes of the same: and the other tvvo, the most visiblest vaynes fit for phlebotomye," &c. These are on two plates; a back and front figure on each: the other nine plates are filled with instruments of chirurgery &c. with copious explanations on the opposite page. On the back of the last cut is a summary or table of contents of "The French Chirurgerye," which occupies 52 leaves, besides the prefixes, and an index at the end. "Inprinted At Dort by Isaac Canin. M.D.XCVIIJ."[a] W.H. Folio.

The Lady Ramsey's Pellican of her Almes deeds and Bounty to the poor. Octavo. 1597.

" A short Treatise of the Sacrament of Penance. With the maner of examining of Conscience for a general Confession. Wherunto is added another Treatise of Confession for such spirituall or deuoute persons as frequent that Sacrament. Sett forth in Italian by the Reu. Fa. Vincent Bruno of the Society of Iesus. 1597." Contains 124 pages, besides a table prefixed. Lambeth Libr. Sixteens. 1597.

" A Commentary upon the Epistles of St. Paul to the Thessalonians and Philemon, By Robert Rollock. Geneva, 1597." Mackenzie, III; 440. Octavo. 1597.

" Certaine of Ovid's Elegies by C. Marlow. At Middleburgh." 16°. ——

" All Ovids[1] Ellegies: Three Bookes, By C. M. *(Chr. Marlowe.)* Epigrams by I. D. *(John Davis.)* At Middleborough." Somewhat larger than the preceding edition. E. Malone Esq. These translations of Ovid's Elegies were burnt at Stationers' hall by order from the archbishop of Canterbury and the bishop of London, dated 1 June, 41 Eliz. See an account of Ancient Translations from Classic Authors prefixed to Johnson and Steevens's edition of Shakespeare's plays, p. 94. Edition 1778; Also, Hist. of Eng. Poetry, III; 420. ——

" A treatise of the sufferings and victory of Christ, in the work of our redemption: Declaring by the Scriptures these two questions: That Christ suffered for vs the wrath of God, which we may well terme the paynes of Hell, or Hellish sorrowes. That Christ, after his death on the crosse, went not into Hell in his Soule. Contrarie to certaine errours in these points publiklie preached in London Anno 1597." A vignette, and under it "1598." Contains 174 pages, neat White letter, and concludes with 1598.

[a] In the title-page M.D.XCVIJ.

[1] 'This translation of Ovid's Elegies was printed in or before 1598; for Davis's Epigrams, which are added at the end, are mentioned by Bastard in his collections of Epigrams, printed in that year.' E. M.

with "2 Cor. 2. 17. Wee are not as many which make marchandise of the Worde of God: &c. H. I." *(Henry Jacobs.)* On another leaf, the corrections of faults. See Ath. Oxon. I, 344. and 394. 395. W.H. Octavo.

1598. "A pithie exhortation to her maiestie for establishing her successor to the crowne. Whereunto is added a discourse, containing the Author's opinion of the true and lavvful successor to her Maiestie. Both compiled by Peter Wentworth Esquire. Prudens Princeps hæredem nominando Regno prospiciet, & si desit filius de successore serio cogitabit. Ex Spart. A wise Prince by naming his heire will provide for the safetie of his kingdome: and if he haue no sonne, he will be the more careful to establish his successor. Out of Spart. Imprinted. 1598." A prefatory epistle "To the reader;" at the end thereof, "Faults escaped in the printing." The exhortation on 121 pages. Then, on a separate title-page, "A treatise containing M. Wentworths iudgement concerning the person of the true and lawfull successor to these Realmes of England and Ireland. Wherein the title is briefly and plainlie set down: Dolmans objections refuted, and inconveniences remoued. Made two yeeres before his death, but published a yeere after his death for the publick benefite of this Realme. Imprinted 1598." This treatise on 95 pages, numbered afresh; but the signatures proceed regularly from the exhortation to P 7, in eights. W.H. Octavo.

1598. "A confession of the Faith of certain English people living in exile in the Low-countries. Dated from Amsterdam, the year of the last patience of the Saints. 1598." Mr. T. Baker's Maunsell, p. 24.

1598. Honour's conquest, or the history of Edward of Lancaster, and of his travels to Jerusalem, &c. Quarto.

1598. "Spirituall exercyses, and goostly meditations, &c. set forth by F. Willyam Perin, B. D. neulye imprynted at Caen by Peter le Chandelier, from the copie printed at London. Dedicated to the sisters of the order of St. Clare at Lovaine." Sixteens.

1598. "The syn against the Holy Ghoste: Made manifest from those grounds of Faith, which haue bene taught & received by the Faithfull in Englād, & that for those 40. y. togither vnder the prosperous raigne of my Soveraigne Lady & Quene Elishabet. Which may serue for a rayning in of the heady, & yet for a spur to slouthfull Spirits: By Henoch Clapham. Eccles. 7. 18. Be not just over-much, nor make thy self much wise: wherefore sholdst thou seeke to be desolate? 19. Be not wicked ouer-much, nor be thow foolish: why sholdst thow dy in thy vntyme? At Amsterdam: 1598." In a border of metal flowers. The treatise begins on the back, addressed "To his faithfull Brethren (a poore Remnant of the ever visible Catholike and Apostolicke Church) Abraham Crottendine, Iohn Ioope, Hugh Armourer, Christopher Symkins, Thomas Farrat, Abraham Wakefeild &c. Grace Mercie and peace be multiplied from God the father, through the Mediation of Je. Chr. his Son, by the instillation of his adopting spirit into their spirits, Amen."

At

At the end, the queen's arms, under which, "God preserve our quene." C, in fours. W.H. Quarto.

"A Treatise of the Holy daie and fasting daie in England, &c. By J. B. 1598." Mr. T. Baker's Maunsell, p. 49. Octavo. 1598.

"A Christian Directorie guiding men to their Salvation. Devided into three Bookes." &c. as p. 1667. "At Lovan, Imprinted by Laurence Kellam, cum priuilegio, 1598." Contains 718 pages, besides prefixes and affixes. The preface signed R.P. (*Robert Parsons.*) Octavo. 1598.

"A methode to meditate on the Psalter or Rosary of the Virgin Mary. Ant. 1598." Bodleian. Octavo. 1598.

"A Commentary upon 15 select Psalms. By Robert Rollock. Geneva, 1598." Mackenzie, III; 440. Octavo. 1598.

England's Heroical Epistles; by Michael Drayton. Octavo. 1598.

"De Turco-Papismo. Hoc est, de Turcorum & Papistarum adversus Christi Ecclesiam & fidem conjuratione eorumque in Religione & moribus consensione & similitudine. Lond. 1598, 99. By T. M. S." Ath. Oxon. I; 268. Quarto. 1598.

"Micro-cynicon, sixe snarling satyres." Sixteens. 1599.

"A temperate ward-word to the turbulent and seditious watch-word of sir Francis Hastinges knight, who indeavoreth to slaunder the whole catholique cause, and all professors thereof, both at home and abrode. Reduced into eight several incounters; with a particular speech directed to the lordes of her maiesties most honourable council. To whom the arbitriment of the whole is remitted, by N. D. (*N. Dolman, alias Robert Parsons.*) Imprinted with licence." Quarto. 1599.

"A Triall of Subscription: By way of a Preface unto certaine Subscribers. And Reasons for lesse rigour against nonsubscribers. Both modestly written, that Neither should offend." 28 pages, besides the preface of six pages. Sixteens. 1599.

"The pleasant history of the two angry women of Abington. With the humorous mirth of Dicke Coomes, and Nicholas Prouerbes, two Seruing-men. As it was lately playde by the right Honorable the Earle of Nottingham, Lord high Admirall his seruants. By Henry Porter, Gent. Imprinted at London for VVilliam Ferbrand, and are to be sold at his shop the corner of Colman streete neere Loathbury. 1599." On the back are "The names of the speakers," and "The Prologue," which is in prose. K. in fours. W.H. Quarto. 1599.

"The triall of maister Dorrell, or a collection of defences against allegations, not yet suffered to receive convenient answere. Tending to cleare him from the imputation of teaching Sommers, and others, to counterfeit possessions of devils," &c. 103 pages. Twelves. 1599.

"A Christian Letter of certaine English Protestants vnfained fauourers of the present state of Religion, authorised and professed in England: vnto that Reuerend and learned man, Mr. R. Hoo, (*Richard Hooker*) requiring resolution in certaine matters of Doctrine (which seeme to ouerthrow the foundation of Christian Religion, and of the Church among vs) vs) expresslie contained in his five Books of Ecclesiasticall Pollicie. 1599." On 49 pages, neat White letter. W.H. Quarto.

1599. Some account of Edward Squire, lately executed for treason, as actor; and Richard Wallpoole as deviser, in Spain. 1599. Quarto.

1599. A little book of Epigrams by John Weever. 1599. Octavo.

1599. "A Manuall of Praiers, gathered out of many famous & good authors, as well ancient, as of the time present. Distributed according to the daies of the Weeke. Whereunto is added a newe Calender, with the order to helpe at Masse. Printed at Calice. 1599." Contains 338 pages. Rev. Dr. Lort. Sixteens.

1599. "Dr. Dee's Apology, sent to the Arch-Bishop of Canterbury. 1595. Or, a Letter containing a most brief Discourse Apologiticall, with a plain Demonstration, and fervent Protestation for the lawfull, sincere, very faithfull and Christian course of the Philosophicall Studies and Exercises, of a certaine studious Gentleman: An ancient Servant to Her most Excellent Majesty Royall." Including a catalogue of Dee's writings printed and unprinted.*

1599. "A commentary upon the Gospel of St. John, with a Harmony of the Four Evangelists upon the Death, Resurrection and Ascension of Jesus Christ, at Geneva, 1599." By Robert Rollock. Mackenzie, III, 440. Octavo.

1599. "A briefe Treatise of divers plaine and sure waies to finde out the truth in this doubtfull and dangerous time of Heresie. Conteyning sundrie worthy motives vnto the Catholike Faith, or Considerations to moue a man to beleeue the Catholikes, and not the Heretikes. Set out by Richard Bristow Priest, Licentiat in Diuinitie." Device: IHS, with a cross patée over the H, with the nails and heart, as described in p. 1730-1; but without the motto, and the spear and sponge, and not so neatly executed. Printed at Anvverpe with Priuiledge. 1599." On the back is a small cut of the holy rood. On the next leaf, in Latin and English, "1. John. 4." and "August. de vtil. cred. Cap. 14."---To the reader.---The approbation of this Booke, according to the order of the Councell of Trent. Sess. 4.—Ita Censeo Guilielmus Alanus, S. Theol. apud Duacum Professor Regius. 30 April, 1574. Which is thus in English.—So doe I giue my censure, William Allen," &c. Besides; 176 leaves. W.H. 16°.

1599. "A Defence of the Churches and Ministery of England. Written in two Treatises, against the Reasons and obiections of Mr. Francis Iohnson, and other of the separation commonly called Brownists. Published, especially, for the benefit of those in these parts of the lovv Countries. Middelburgh. By Richard Schilders, Printer to the States of Zealand. 1599." This title taken from Mr. Johnson's answer: my copy wanting the

* Reprinted at the end of Mr. Casaubon's preface on 'A true & faithful Relation of what passed for many yeers between Dr. John Dee (a mathematician of great fame in Q. Eliz. and K. James their reignes), and some Spirits:' &c. Wherein he says, 'In the year 1595 he did write, (and was printed 1599, I am sure; but whether before that or no, I cannot certainly tell) A Discourse Apologetical, &c.'

the title-page. Prefixed is an epistle by "The publisher to the Christian reader.—* D. B." The first treatise begins with "An argument proving that the Churches of England are the true Churches of God.—H. Iacob. Against the Assumption of the said Argument Mr. Iohnson made 3. Exceptions and 9. Reasons, which hereafter follow in order: Together with Mr. Iacobs Replies vnto the same." This is concluded on p. 83; the back blank. Then, on a separate title-page, "A short treatise concerning the truenes of a pastorall calling in pastors made by prelates. Against the Reasons and Obiections of Maister Francis Iohnson, with others of the separation commonly called Brownistes." Vignette; a female head between two cornucopias. "1599." On the back, "An argument, shewing the trunes of a Pastorall calling in Pastors made by Prelates. Taken from a familiar * comparison, gathered out of the confessions of Maisters Iohnsons and others of the separation aforesaid. Against the said Argument, were brought Seauen Reasons by Maister Iohnson and others, which doe hereafter follow, together with Maister Iacobs Replies to the same." This on 4 leaves more. W.H. Quarto.

"The Boock of Physicke Wherin Through commaundement of the most Illustrious, & renoumned Duke & Lorde, Lorde Lodewijcke, Duke of Wirtenberghe, & of Teck, Earle of Mompelgart, &c. Most of them selected, and approued remedyes, for all corporall diseases, and sicknesses, which out of manye highe, and common Persons written Physick-bookes, are compacted, and vnited together. Through his renoumned Graces most famous Physition Mr. Doctour Oswaldus Gabelhouer. Faithfullye translated out of High-duche by the right worshipfull Mr. Doctour Charles Battus, ordinarye Physitione of the Citye of Dorte. And now nuelye translatede out of Low-duche into Englishe by A. M. Imprinted At Dorte by Isaack Caen, 1599. This title is printed within a very neat compartment engraved on copper-plate. The queen's arms at top, over the rose supported by angels; somewhat like the design at the back of 'The Frenche Chirurgerye,' p. 1734. At bottom, is a neat prospect of the city of Dort, having "Dordrecht" on a ribbon over it. "B. Dolendo fecit." Dedicated "To the most mightye vertuous and renoumned Princesse, and our most beneuolente, and gratiouse soueraigne, Ladye Elizabeth, 1599.

* Daniel Buck, a scrivener of London. See Fr. Johnson's Answer to this preface, prefixed to his Answer to Master H. Jacob his Defence of the Churches and Ministery of England.

* "The Argument of Comparison is this. As a couple of ignorant people not contracting, but meaning to marry, and yet thinking that vnlesse a Priest marry them, their marriage is nothing, whereas indeed their publique accepting each of other maketh the marriage: Now being married, (though vnlawfully *As themselues said*) by a Priest, yet their marriage is true and lawfull notwithstanding.

Even so, a Christian people, meaning to haue a sufficient man to their Pastor, yet thinking, that vnlesse a Prelate doe make him, he is no Pastor at all, neither can be theirs. Notwithstanding, he being made a Pastor, (though vnlawfully, *As they also doe acknowledge*) by the Prelate; yet by their mutuall accepting and ioyning together, he is now verely a Pastor, yea their Pastor, true and lawfull. H. Iacob." N.B. What is here printed in Italics is taken from the margin.

Elizabeth, *&c.*—Isaack Canine Bibliopola at Dorte.---To the most Illustrious, and right Honourable Ladye, Ladye Marie, borne Princesse of Orange, *&c.* Datum at Dort the 4. of Iulye A. D. M.D.LXXXVIIJ.—Abraham Canin.---Epistle of the Author to the beneuolent Reader.—Oswaldus Gabelhouer, His Grace of Wirtenberghs Physition, at Sturgarten.---To the beneuolent, and curteous Reader.—A. M.---Index," alphabetical and copious: on the back of the last page thereof, "The contentes of this boocke of Physicke:" divided into 6 parts. Besides: 393 pages. W.H. Folio.

1599. "A memoriall of a Christian life. Wherin are treated al such things, as appertaine vnto a Christian to do from the beginning of his cõuersion, vntil the end of his perfection. Deuided into Seauen Treatises: the particulars* whereof are noted in the page following. Written first in the Spanish tongue, by the famous Religious Father, F. Lewis de Granada, Prouinciall of the holy order of Preachers, in the Prouince of Portugall." Device; IHS, &c. very plain. "Imprinted at Rouen, by George Loyselet. Anno Domini. 1599." This is introduced with "The Translatours Dedicatory Epistle. To the right honourable, and vvorshipfull, of the foure principall Houses of Court in London, professing the studie of the Common Laws of our Realme.—From Roan, vpon the Holy Feast of the conuersion of S. Paul, in the yeare of our Lord. 1599.—Richard Hopkins." The IHS &c. as in the title-page, but set in a frame exhibiting the implements of the crucifixion. "The prologue to the christian reader." On the back of its last page is a rude cut of the holy rood. There are a few other wood-cuts, but very coarsely done. Contains together 762 pages and "A table of the contents." On p. 761, "The end of the first volume of the Memoriall of a Christian life. Deo Gratias. The second volume of the Memoriall *&c.* I haue already translated, and am preparing it towards the Print: which conteineth the three last treatises" *&c.* mentioned in the note below. Whereby it appears that the following article is the 2d volume of this Memoriall, though by another translator. W.H. *Octavo.*

1599. "A spiritual doctrine conteining a rule To liue vvel, vvith diuers Praiers and Meditations. Abridged by the reverend father Levvis de Granada of the holie order of Preachers. And divided into fiue treatises,

as

* "1.—an Exhortation vnto vertue and amendment of life. 2 Of the Sacrament of Pennance, and the three partes thereof:—contrition, confession, and Satisfaction: with a declaration of the Ten Commandements. 3 How we ought to prepare ourselues for the receauing of the most blessed Sacrament of the Alter. 4 Wherein are contained two principall rules of a Christian life. The one—fervseth for suche christians as begin newly to serue God, and haue a desire to be saued. And the other—for all professed Religious persons in Monastaries, and for such other Christians, as are not contented with the doring of all such thinges as they know to be of no necessitie for their saluation, but will indeuour to wade further, and to increase and profit more & more in the way of vertues. 5 Of Vocall prayer. 6 Of Mentall prayer: wherein is treated of the life of our Sauiour Christ. 7 Of the loue of God: wherein consisteth the perfection of a christian life, and therein is also treated of such things as do eyther help, or hinder the same."

as is to be seene after the prefaces. Nevvlie tranflated out of Spanifh into English. Pfalm 118. v. 35. Deduc me in femita mandatorum tuorum. Leade me (O Lord) in the path of thy commaundements. At Lovan, Imprinted by Laurence Kellam 1599." Dedicated "To the honorable syr vvilliam stanley Knight, Coranel of the English Regiment. &c.—From our college of the Societie of Iesus in Louan this 10. of March 1599. being the feast of S. Ioseph.—Rich. Gibbons.—The tranflatour to the gentle Reader.—At Louan the 25. of March, 1599.—Rich. Gibbons.---The author to the Christian Reader.—A spiritual doctrine devided into fixe [a] treatises." Besides: 397 pages, and a table of contents. W.H. 8°.

" Catechifmus Paulinus, in ufum Scholæ Paulinæ confcriptus." Ath. Oxon. I; 369. Octavo. 1599.

" Novum Testamentum [b] Syriacè, [c] Ebraicè, Græcè, [d] Latinè, [e] Germanicè, [f] Bohemicè, [g] Italicè, [h] Hifpanicè, [i] Gallicè, [k] Anglicè, [l] Danicè, & [m] Polonicè, ftudio Eliæ Hutteri. Norimbergæ, 1599." 2 vol. Folio. 1599.

" An explication of the article περὶ τῆ κατελθεῖν εἰς ᾅδε of our Lordes foules going from his body to Paradife, touched by the Greke, generally ᾅδε: The world of Soules, termed Hel by the old Saxon, & by all our tranflationes: with a defence of the Q. of Englandes religion: To, & againft the Archb. of Canterbury: who is blamed for turning the Q. auctority againft her owne faith. Sundry Epiftles are prefixed & affixed. By H. Br. Ἀδελφοί μου, &c. James, 2. 1. ΜDΧCΙΧ." Dedicated "To the mighty prince Elisabeth by the grace of God Quene of England, &c. defendour of the faith, &c.—Your M. moft carefull defendour of your faith, Hugh Broughton." Head title, "An explication of the Crede for the article κατελθεῖν εἰς ᾅδε: How that fpech hath bene vfed, of eaft & weft fynce tongues were vnto Plutarchs age beyonde the Apoftles vniforme in one tenour, for leauing this world: in fpech of foules departinge: & not more in the wicked which went to torment knowen, or in the vncerten, whether they went, then in the Godly which went prefently to Ioy: With a declaration how K. Ed. 6. fo held it: Whofe religion 1599.

 in

[a] 1. "Of Mental Praier. 2 Of Vocal Praier. 3 A rule of good life for all forts of men. 4 for Religious men. 5 Of The Sacrament of Penance. 6 Of receauing the bleffed Sacrament, with a proteftion of the Catholique faith, according to the holy Counsel of Trent."

[b] 'Secundùm editionem Tremellianam anni 1569; cui adjecit autor ex fua verfione quædam quæ in illa deerant.'

[c] 'Ex ipfa verfione Eliæ Hutteri.'

[d] 'Ex vulgata editione.'

[e] 'Ex interpretatione Lutheri.'

[f] 'Ex editione 1593.'

[g] 'Ex verfione Genevenfi anni 1562.'

[h] 'Ex Caffiodori Reyna tranflatione anno 1569, excufa.'

[i] 'Ex recognitione Genevenfi anni 1588.'

[k] 'Ex editione 1561, vel aliqua fimili.' See p. 796.

[l] 'Ex editione 1589.'

[m] 'Ex editione 1596.' Le Long, I; 45. Edit. 1723.

These 12 languages are inferted in 6 columns; two languages in a col. verfe by verfe: viz. In the 1st col. the Syriack (in Hebrew types), with the Italic under it. 2. The Hebrew, (having the fervile letters diftinguifhed, by being open, from the radicals, which are wholly black) and under it the Spanifh. 3. The Greek; and the French under it. These three col. are on the left-hand page, as the other three. viz. The Latin, with the English; the German, with the Danish; the Bohemian, with the Polish; are on the right.

in the same sense the Q. swearing to the Gospel, meant to defend: To the most reverend Ihon Whitgift D. in diuinity, Archb. of Canterbury, & Metropolitane of Englande." This occupies 78 pages. On the last leaf, " To all the lerned nobility of England.—Your honours most willing to haue bene employd for the Churches good: Hugh Broughton." W.H. Quarto.

1599. " A pleasant conceyted Comedie of George a Greene, the Pinner of Wakefield. Acted by the Earl of Sussex Servants." Reprinted in Dodsley's collection of Old Plays, I; 163. See Biogr. Dram. II; 136. Quarto.

1599. " Th'overthrow of Stage-Playes, By the way of controversie betwixt D. Gager and D. Rainoldes, wherein all the reasons that can be made for them are notably refuted; th'objections aunswered, and the case so cleared and resolved, as that the iudgement of any man, that is not froward and perverse, may easily be satisfied. Wherein is manifestly proved, that it is not onely vnlawfull to bee an Actor, but a beholder of those vanities. Whereunto are added also and annexed in th'end certeine letters betwixt the sayed Maister Rainoldes, and D. Gentiles, Reader to the Civill Law in Oxford, concerning the matter. 1599." This is introduced with an epistle from " The Printer to the reader." Head title, " Maister D. Rainolds aunswere vnto Maister D. Gager, concerning Theater-sights, Stage-playes, &c." This occupies 163 pages. Dated, " At Queenes College, the 30th of May. 1593.—Iohn Rainolds." Then follow the Latin letters betwixt Dr. Rainolds and Albericus Gentilis, which are concluded on p. 190. The whole B b 2, in fours. W.H. Again in 1600, printed at Middleburgh by Richard Schilders. Quarto.

1599. Ovid's Remedy of Love, by an anonymous translator. See Hist. of Eng Poetry, III; 420. Again 1600. See p. 1283.

1599. Novum Testamentum, the same as the edition in folio, above-mentioned. 4 Vol. 1599 and 1600. In the preface to St. Paul's Epistles; " Integrum Novum Testamentum in linguam sanctam convertendum suscepi; converti, correxi & annuo temporis spatio absolvi." Hutter also translated the four canonical epistles, the Revelation, and the history of the woman taken in adultery, from the Syriac. See Le Long, I; 45. I have the gospels by St. Matthew, and St. Mark, which i take to be the first of these 4 volumes, viz.

1599. " Sanctvs Matthævs, Syriacè, Italicè. Ebraicè. Hispanicè. Græcè, Gallicè. Latinè, Anglicè. Germanicè, Danicè. Bohemicè, Polonicè. Ex Dispositione & Adornatione Eliae Hutteri Germani. Noribergaae M D XCIX." The text begins on the back of this title-page; for the disposition thereof &c. see note d. The whole occupies 543 pages, including the title, numbered in the left-hand corner of every page. W.H. 4°.

1600. " Sanctvs Marcvs," &c. as to St. Matthew. " M D C." On 349 pages, numbered &c. as St. Matthew. These editions (folio & quarto) are peculiarly curious for the variety of modern translations. W.H. 4°.

1600. " The Nevv Testament of Iesus Christ faithfully translated Into English, out of the authentical Latin, diligently conferred with the Greeke" &c.

&c. at p. 1658. " By the English College then Resident in Rhemes. Set forth the second time, by the same College novv returned to Dovvay. VVith addition of one nevv Table of Heretical Corruptions, the other Tables and Annotations somevvhat augmented. Search the Scriptures. Ioan. 5. Geue me vnderstanding, &c. Psalm 118. v. 34.—Printed at Antvverp by Daniel Vervliet. 1600. VVith privilege." Concerning the authors of this translation, see Lewis p. 290 &c. W.H. Quarto.

" The Rosarie of our Ladie. Otherwise called our Ladies Psalter. With other godlie exercises mentioned in the Preface. Antverpiæ, Apud Ioannem Keerbergium. Anno M.D.C. Cum gratia et privilegio." This title is in a very neat engraved compartment, representing an altar-piece; over which is an appearance of the Virgin Mary, at half length, holding the infant Jesus before her, both crowned and irradiated. On the top of each jamb is an angel kneeling and adoring. In the middle, two lighted candles. On the dexter side is a bishop standing in a niche, with his hands clasped, and his eyes fixed on the vision, a crosier enclosed in his arms, and a mitre at his feet. On the other side is an abbot, in like posture, with a crosier only. " The preface, Containing diuers Annotations concerning the Rosarie of our Ladie: and the other Exercises here folovving: VVith the causes of composing and printing the same in this forme; and certaine commodities ensuing hereof.—25. of March, 1592. Your owne al and euer in Christ, T. W. P." This little book is adorned with variety of cuts, neatly engraved on copper-plates, by Ioan Collaert, from designs of M. de Vos; and contains the following pieces, viz. " The first rosarie of our Ladies psalter; resembled to a white Rose, containing fiue ioyful Mysteries.—The second Rosarie—resembled to a redde rose: containing fiue sorowful Mysteries.—The third Rosarie—resembled to a damaske rose:—fiue glorious Mysteries.—The Corone of our B. Ladie: with certaine particular points to be meditated, in saying the same.—The Corone of our Lord. With particular pointes to be meditated, in saying the same.—A briefe Rosarie of fiftene Pater nosters and Aues with one Crede: in memorie of the eight ioyes and seuen sorovves of the most B. Virgin Marie.—Litanies gathered out of the corone of our Lord.—Litanies—out of the corone of our Ladie.—The doleful state of our B. Ladie, vnder the crosse of her Sonne." Contains 128 pages, besides the preface. " The approbation. Libellum hunc, à viro Anglo, docto & pio, perlegendum curauimus; eiusque iudicio probatum, imprimendum duximus. 25. Ianuarij. 1599. Matthias Archiepūs Mechliniensis." F 4, in twelves. Neat White letter. W.H. Twelves. 1600.

" A detection of that sinnful, shamful, lying, and ridiculous discours of Samuel Harsnet, entituled: A discoverie of the fravvdulent practises of Iohn Darrell. Wherein is manifestly and apparantly shewed in the eyes of the world, not only the vnlikelihoode, but the flat impossibilitie of the pretended counterfayting of William Somers, Thomas Darling, Kath. Wright, and Mary Couper, togeather with the other 7. in Lancashire, and the supposed teaching of them by the said Iohn Darrell. 1600.

Psalme. 7. 14. Behold, He shall travaile with wickednes: for he hath conceiued mischiefe, but he shall bring fourth a lye. Imprinted 1600." Prefixed is an addresse "To the Christian and Well Affected reader, John Darrell minister of the Word, wisheth all Grace and Happines: with a iudgment to discerne betwixt thinges that differ," &c. The paging and signatures are very irregular and incorrect. At the end is a table of contents. W.H. Quarto.

1600. "A true narration of the strange and grevous vexation by the Devil, of 7. persons in Lancashire, and William Somers of Nottingham. Wherein the doctrine of possession and dispossession of Demoniakes out of the word of God is particularly applyed vnto Somers, and the rest of the persons controuerted: togeather with the vse we are to make of these workes of God. By John Darrell, minister of the word of God. He that is not with me, is against me: *&c.* Math. 12. 30. Printed 1600." My copy has in MS. 'Vid. Bp. Hall his treatise of Evill Angels, p. 342. He attests the truth of this story.' It is introduced with an addresse "To the Church of England.—I. D." Then, the narration, which occupies 23 pages more; printed 24 by mistake. The doctrine of the possession &c. with fresh signatures and pages. A—I, in fours; K—S, in twos; neat White letter. W.H. Quarto.

1600. "A true Discourse concerning the certaine possession and dispossessio of 7. persons in one familie in Lancashire, &c. By George More." Fasti Oxon. I, 108. Contains 85 pages. W.H. Octavo.

1600. "An answer to Maister H. Iacob his defence of the Churches and Ministery of England. By Francis Iohnson an exile of Iesus Christ. Though myne Adversary write a Book against me, would I not beare it vpon my shoulder, would I not bynde it for crovvnes vnto me? Iob 31. 36. Printed in the Yeare of our Lord. 1600." On the back, "The title and inscription of Mr. Iacobs book (because there is often relation vnto it hereafter, both in the Preface, and in the Book it selff, therefore) I thought good here to insert it at first. Thus it was, word for word as followeth, A Defence of the Churches." &c. as p. 1738. Prefixed is The preface, thus addressed, "To the Christian Reader, grace and peace from our Lord Jesus Christ." It is divided into 7 sections answering the epistle by D. B. (Daniel Buck, as we are herein informed) section by section. The head title, "An Aunswer to M. H. Iacobs arguments and replies concerning the Churches and Ministery of England." Mr. Jacob's arguments and replies are cited at length, and Mr. Johnson's answers thereunto, chapter by chapter, on 184 pages. Then, on a separate title-page, "An answer to Maister H. Iacob his treatise Concerning the Priestes of the Church of England, Made by the Prælates, Accepted and ioyned vnto by the people. Which he termeth a Pastorall Calling. By Francis Johnson an exile for the testimony of Iesus. Put yourselves in array against Babel *&c.* Ier. 50. 14. They shall not take of thee a stone for a corner, *&c.* Ier. 51. 26. 1600." This treatise proceeds in like manner as the foregoing, Mr. Jacob's arguments, &c. on White letter, and Mr. Johnson's son's answers on Black letter. The signatures and pages continued to p. 217, and "A Table of some particular things conteyned in this Book." W.H. Quarto.

"A Defence of a treatise touching the Sufferings and Victorie of Christ in the worke of our Redemption. Wherein is confirmed, 1 That Christ suffered for vs, not only bodily griefe, but also in his Soule an impression of the proper wrath of God, which may be called the paines of Hell. 2 That after his death on the Crosse he went not downe into Hell. For Answere to the late writings of Mr. Bilson, L. Bishop of Winchester, which he intitleth, The effect of certaine sermons, &c. Wherein he striueth mightily against the doctrine aforesaid. By Henry Iacob Minister of the worde of God. Iohn 7. ver. 24. Iudge not according to the appearance, but iudge righteous judgement. 1600." Contains 211 pages, including an epistle "To all the godly and religious Magistrates, faithfull Pastors, and other Christian brethren in England, Grace and peace be multiplied in the true sufferinges and victorie of Iesus Christ, our onely and most glorious Redeemer.—A Præface to the Christian Readers touching our 2. Questions and their Defence following." On the back of the last leaf is an analytical table of "The diverse Significations of the Greeke word Hades: which it hath according to the Circũstances of the places where it is vsed.—Whereunto the Hebrue Sheol may be rightly compared." W.H. Quarto. 1600.

"Reges, Reginæ, Nobiles & alii in Ecclesia B. Petri Westmonasterii sepulti usque ad Annum M.D.C. Lond. 1600." Quarto. 1600.

"Will. Kemp's 12 days Wonder, in a dance from London to Norwich. Lond. 1600." Cat. Bibl. Bodl. II; 47. Quarto. 1600.

XV books of Iliads of Homer. By George Chapman. See Warton's Hist. of English Poetry, Vol. III; p. 441. A thin folio. 1600.

"Pasquill's Mad Cappe. Lond. Printed by J. V. 1600." Ibidem, III; 445. Quarto. 1600.

"Pasquill's Fool's cap. Lond. 1600." Catl. Bibl. Bodl. II; 284. 1600.

"A Remedy against Schisme and Heresy, a treatise on Matth. XIII; 24. Lond. 1600." By Henoch Clapham. Ibidem, I; 284. Quarto. 1600.

"A Decacordon of ten quodlibeticall questions concerning Religion and State. Wherein the Authour framing himselfe a Quilibet to euery Quodlibet, decides an hundred crosse Interrogatorie doubts, about the generall contentions betwixt the Seminarie Priests and Iesuits at this present. Eccles. VII. Noli amare mendacium aduersus fratrem tuum, &c. Do not loue a lye against thy brother, neither do the like against thy friend." Device, a griffin sitting on a stone, &c. as p. 127. "Newly imprinted. 1600." Contains 361 pages, besides "The preface to the reader," and "Lenvoy." This work is ascribed to William Watson Priest. Ath. Oxon. I; 504. W.H. Quarto. 1600.

"Palestina: Written By Mr. R. C. P.* and Bachelor of Diuinitie." 1600.

* Query Robert Chambers, a secular priest, educated in the English College at Rheims, and who finished his studies at Rome.

nitie." Device, a phenix, &c. "Florence Imprinted by Bartelmew Sermartelli. 1600." Dedicated "To our most gracious and Soueraigne Ladie and Princes, whose dowrie is little England, and the largest heauens her fayrest inheritance, all happinesse and heauenly blisse." Contains 200 pages, besides 2 more of "Faults escaped." Quarto.

1600. "A position maintained by J. H. before the late Earle of Huntingdon: viz. Priests are executed not for Religion, but for Treason. Newly imprinted. 1600." In 15 pages. See p. 1082. Octavo.

1600. "A Midsommer Nights Dreame. As it hath beene sundry Times publikely acted, By the Right Honorable, the Lord Chamberlaine his Seruants. Written by William Shakespeare. Printed by Thomas Fisher. 1600." Quarto.

1600. "Approved experiments touching Fish and Fruit, to be regarded by the lovers of Angling, by John Taverner." Quarto.

1600. "Newes from Flaunders. A new ballad of the great overthrow, that the valliant captaine Graue Maurice, sir Frances Veere, and other of the queene of Englands friends, gaue to the archduke, and his army of Spaniards, vpon Sunday the 22d of June last past, 1600. To the tune of Lusty gallant."

It begins, "You that be desirous, and therein take delight," &c.

Ends, "Thus have you heard the service
Of these our English friends,
That still with losse of life and limmes
The Flemish state defends.
God banish thence idolatrie,
That Englishmen may say:
That still we haue in spight of Spaine
Some frendes beyond the sea. Finis.

"Captaines of the English slain. 1. Captain Yaxley. 2.—Honywood. 3.—Duxbery. 4.—Purton. 5.—Tirrell. 6.—Woodward. Prisoners of the enemy taken. The admiral of Arragon, Lewis de Villar, Jasper Sapena, With many other captains."

Books without either printer's name or date when printed: some of which were omitted in their proper places, whose dates might have been nearly ascertained by circumstances contained in them (as many such may be found in the foregoing part of this General History); some came not to hand in time; and others do not afford matter sufficient to indicate even nearly the time of printing.

—— "In this booke is Conteyned the names of ye baylifs Custos maiers and sherefs of the cyte of londō, from the tyme of Kynge richard the furst. & also thartycles of the Chartur & libartyes of the same Cyte. And of the chartur and libertyes off England wyth odur dyuers mat's good and necessary for euery Citezē to vndirstond and knowe. Which ben shewid ī chaptirs aftyr the fourme of this kalendir folowing." This title is at the head of the "kalendir" or table of contents, printed in double

1

double columns; as also is most of the book. It begins on signature A. ii. The leaf before it, of the same paper with the book, is blank. The said table is on three leaves, ending at the top of the second column of the last of them. Then, on signature A. i. begins the list of bailiffs, &c. with this head title "The names of ẏ balyss, Custos, Mayres. and sherefs of ẏ Cite of London from the tyme of kynge Richard the first called cure de lyon whiche was Crowned ẏ iij day of septēbre ẏ yere of oure lorde god xiC. lxxxix. Cap. pri°." Which concludes with "Anno xviij" Hen. 7, on the first page of A 8, the back thereof blank. My copy wanting this leaf, and the preceding table, i shall give the rest of the articles from the book itself. "The articles of ẏ charter & liberties of the Cite of london---Here folowyth the copy of the hole charter of london of the furst graunt, and the confirmacion of diuers kingis after. (112 *articles.*)---The acte for correciō of the errours and wrong Jugementis. in london.---The acte of parlemēt for tynthingis of trees aboue. xx. yere growingis. &ce.---The charg of euiri ward ī lōdō at xv---The Ordinaunce for the assise and weight of bred In the Cite of london---The copy of the bulle (*of pope Nicholas*) for the offring to ẏ curattis of the perisshens of the Cite of london in latin—date Rome apud scm'. petrum Anno incarnationis dnīce Millesimo CCCC. quinquagesimo tertio. Septimo Jd' Augusti. pontificatus nrī Anno septimo---The copy of the bulle of pope Nicholas for the same mator afore wryton. *In English: abridged.*---The letters of Jnnocent (*vii.*) Bisshopis.---The composicion of alle offeryngis within the cyte of london and Subirbis of the same—Beyt in mynde that thys bōde & arbitrement ys made ẏ xvij day of decembre—M.iiij C. lvij. *&c.*---The ordinaūce for brokers ocupiēg in london.---The nombre and the names of the perisshe chirches and alle odur chirches within london and the suberbis—Sōm of ẏ nombre of perish chirches amount. C.xviij.---The ordynaūce for wullē clothe with*in* london---The Articles desired by the comēs of the Cytee *for* reformacion of thingis preiudicall to the same off the mayer aldirmen and comen councell to be enacted.---The charge of the queste of ward*mot* in euery warde.—The articles of the good gouernaūce of the Cite of London.---Artycles of prestur[f] and other noyengis in the Citee of London.---Articles ageynst the parell of fyre.—The othe of the bedel of the warde & of the constables and sherefs sergeātis and francpledge and the othe of ẏ skauengers of euery warde.---The othe of euery fremā made in the cite---The othe for brokers in london.---The ordinaunce for the assise of talewod and belet in the cyte of london by the mair and aldirmen---The marchaundises wherof scauage ought to *be* taken in london. and how wyche (*myche or much.*)---Thoos thingis that longith to tronage and poūdage of our soueraine lord the kynge in the cite of londen.---The fourme of making of obligaciōs in dyuers man's.---*Item*, of quitaū*res*---Jtem billis of

[f] In the latter edition, "Artycles of prestres and other mounkes in the Cyte of London." Yet in the table of contents, the title agrees with this first edition, which is the proper one; there being no mention of either priests or monks in the article itself.

of payment.---*Item*, of lettres of atturnay.---*Item*, of Jndētors---*Item*, of lettres of lycence.---*Item*, of lettres of Sale---*Item*, of lettres of payment for mony made bee exchaūge from london to the martis ī braband.--*Item*, of award geuen out by arbytronent.---The copy of the kingis protection Ryal and protection graūted otherwyse than Ryall.---The copy of the kyngis chartour grauntyd for offencis of treson.---The fourme of makyng of supplicacions to ẏ king & to other lordis & estatis.—The fourme of complayntis made to the kynge and to odur lordis.---The ordynaunce of the Cite for tenauntis of houses what thingis they shall not remeue att theyr departinge.---Tecopy of ẏ othe yeuē to ẏ mayr and aldirmen ẏ tyme of kyng herre the vi.---The nombre of perish chirches. townes and bisshopriches and sherys in England [g] & ẏ cōpasse of the lande.—The copye a carete (*chart*) compasyng the circuit of the worlde and the compace of euery yland comprehendid ī the same---The hoole pardon of rome graūted be dyuers popes and the staciōs that ben there---Here folowith the knowlege what a karyne [h] ys.---The vij. ages of the worlde from adam forward.—The vij. ages [i] of mā lyuyng ī the worlde.---The copy of a letter sent out of the lande of messye in to ẏ lande of Garnade before ẏ cōquest therof.—Fro the cite of fesse ẏ x. day of march lxxxx. yeris machometi that is to sey M.iiij.C.lxxxvi---The copy of a letter sent frō the Sowdan of Babilon vnto the pope of Rome—Cair xxi day of Nouē. An. M.cccclxxxviij.---The oracion of the messanger to the pope. ---The craft of graffyng and plantinge of trees and altering of fruits as well in colours as in taste.---A tretise of the iiij. sesons of the yere and of the iiij. elementis which thei be and of what nature and of the caniculare daies [k]---The crafte to make a watir to haue spottis out of wullen cloth ---The fourme and the mesur to mete land by---The generall cursse to be declared iiij. tymes in the yere (*In 30 Articles.*)—The article conteyned in the byll of pope Nicholas purchached by the curatis of the same cite (*London,*) of oblacions---A prouision by acte of parlement to brynge

[g] Parish churches, 46822. Towns, besides cities and castles, 52080. Bishopricks, 17. Shires, or Counties, 36, &c. The length from Cateney in the marche of Scotland to Totnes in Devon, 420 miles. The breadth from St. David's in Wales to Dover, 300 miles. Compass about 4360 miles.

[h] "It is too goo wulward and barfott vij. yere. Jtem to faten bred & watter the frydday vij. yere. Jtem in vij yere. not too slepe oon nyght there he slepith another Jtem in vij yere. nott to com vndir noo couered place but yf it bee two here masse in the chyrch dore or porche Jtem in vij. yere nott to Ete nor drynke out of noo vessel but in the same that he made hys avow Jn. Jtem he that fulfilleth alle thes poyntis vij. yere duryng duthe and wynnethe. A. karyne that ys to sey A lenton."

[i] "The furst age is infancie, and lasteth from the byrth vnto vij yere of age. The ij. is Childhod, & endurith vnto xv yere *of* age. The iij age is adholocencye, & endurith vnto xxv yere *of* age. The iiij age is youthe, and Endurith unto xxxv yere *of* age. The v age is manhod, & endurith vnto l. yere *of* age. The vi age is & lasteth vnto last yere *of* age. The vij age of man is crepyll, and endurith vnto dethe."

[k] "Begynn the xv kalendas of august and endure to the iiij. nonas of september in which seson is gret perill to take syknesse and it is perillus to take drynkis or medecyns or too be lat blod but if it be for gret nede. and that must be aftir the middis of the day."

bryngе kynge Herry the vi. oute of the dett *of* ccc. lxxx. ij. M. li.—The crafte to make corke for diars---The reffaite to make ypocras.---Clarey.—The crafte to make ypocras and braket and clare---*Item*, to make gunepoudir.---*Item*, orchell *(for dyers)*---*Item*, a pigell to kepe freshe flurgen in---*Item* veneger fhortli if *you* haue nede---To make percely to growe in an our fpace---The mefurs of reynish wyne too be bought by in andwarpe and dordreight and *also* the mefurs and rekenyng of wyne to be bought at Burdeux and gawge of the fame---The weight and maner of beyng of Jrne, and the difference of ỳ weyghtes vfed in England.---The acte of parlement to compelle the Jugis of fpûall lawe to graunt ony party the copy of the lebel for any caufe.---The rate of the kyngis Cuftums fubfide of marchaundifes regiftred in the efcheker.---The compoficion betwene the marchauntis of england and ỳ towne of andwarp for the coftis of ther marchaundicis brought to the faid tuwne, and having thens." Then follows the ballad[h] of the Nut-brown maid, without any title, but there is one inferted in the table of contents. "The rekenyng to bey waris in flaundres.---The office that belongithe to a byfhop or to a priftis.---Here folowith the chartur of foreft.---The articles of the chartur and libarties of englãd called magna carta that is to fey the gret chartur---Narracio of thẽ that bien fhreuen and not contrite[i]—The valew and flynt of the benefyce of faint Magnus at londũ Brydge yerly to the perfon.—the fyeft day of decembre anno doĩ mcccc lxxxxiiij."[m]—The copy of faue conduyte.—Certificats.—Spycery.—Jtem a rekening for grocery ware.---The maner to make ynke"---The fervices, &c. at the inftallacion of Morton bifhop of Ely: without any title, but in the table of contents.—"The waye from Calice to Rome thorough fraunce."—The copy of a Teftament,[n] *1473*.—"The coefles to make Soep.—To brewe bere---Jn this chapiter is fhewid the patrons of alle the Beneficis in London.—And here begyneth the temperalities

9 U of

[h] It appears here, and in the fucceeding edition, in 30 ftanzas of fix long lines, each containing two, as printed among Prior's poems, and in Bifhop Percy's Reliques of ancient Eng. Poetry, II, 27, &c. Printed thus perhaps out of frugality of room. See Hift. of Eng. Poetry, I, 35.

[i] Which concludes thus, "& he fayd by caufe J had not a ftable purpofe & a trewe wylle to forfake all my livyng therfore alle my confeffion & all that J did in reffavyng my facramentis it avayled me not but J am perpetualli & wythouten ende dampned as J am wel worthy for our lord feyth in the gofpel of john qui manducat et bibit indigne iudicium fibi manducat & bibit &c." So little feem they to have been acquainted with the Scriptures in thofe days of darknefs and ignorance.

[m] In the lift of parifhioners, with their rents and offerings, Richard Arnold, the fifth perfon named, is charged, rent xli. offering xxxv f. The fum of all the rents £434. 11s. 8d. The fum of the offerings £75. 6s. 8½d. "The fhoppis in brig ftret. (17) with their rents and offerings." The fum of thefe rents £70. 3s. 4d. Offerings for them £12. 3s. 3d. The furplice fees, &c. £17. "The Somme of the hole retornes Cv. li. xxiijd. ob." i. e. (£105. 1s. 11½d.) The cofts and charges, £23. 5s. 10d. "Soo the fomme of the clere value of the benefice was this yere lxxxi li. xvi f. i d. ob."

[n] In which "Richard Arnholde, haberdafher," is nominated an executor.

of diuers archedekenys and other placis of rreligion—Here begynith the corodiſe of all the abbeyes in englande.—The weyght of eſſex cheſe and of ſuffolke in england and the weyght in andwerpe and in barough.—The coſtis for to make hering and ſprottis at the coeſte."---A letter without any ſuperſcription, but as it is entered in the table of contents, "The copy of a letter to my lord cardynall)* well made."---The lawes and beleue of the Saraſyns.---The yerely ſlint[p] of the liuelod belonging to london brydge.---The articles upon whiche is to Jnquyre in the viſitacions of ordinaries of chirches.—Tharticles founde by the Jnquiſitours at the viſitacion laſt done in the chirche of ſaint magnus.---A Complaynte[q] made to kyng herry the vi. by the duke of gloucester vpon the cardynal[r] of wynchesteri.---Here enſuen the articles as the kyngis councell haue conceyued ẏ which ẏ hygh and myghty prince my Lorde of gloucester hath ſurmyſyd vpon my Lorde of Wynchester chauncheler of England.—Here enſwen the anſueris and excuſaciōs made by mi lord of wĩcheſt' chauncelar of englōd vnto ẏ cauſis & materis of heuynes ayenſt hym by my lorde of glouſeter." This book is commonly called Ar-

* Mr. Warton, concluding the edition of this book printed about 1521 to have been the firſt, miſtakes this for cardinal Wolſey; but John Morton muſt evidently be intended, who was lord high chancellor at the beginning of Hen. viith's reign, archbiſhop of Canterbury in 1486, and a cardinal in 1493. As this letter addreſſes him only moſt reverend, and your grace, it ſeems to have been written before he was a cardinal; and as it complains of John Foſter, archdeacon of London, who, according to Leneve, was collated 6 Nov. 1490, it appears to have been written between that year and 1493. The table of contents, with ſufficient propriety, ſtiles him the cardinal, as the book was not printed till after that dignity had been conferred on him. He is herein ſupplicated by R. A. (Richard Arnold) as lord high chancellor, on a matter, ſays he, "yet hanging in Jugement afore your grace to myne intollerable coſt and charge."

Arnold, on a former ſupplication in the ſame cauſe, appears to have fled for his debts to the Sanctuary of Weſtminſter, and depoſited, in Foſter's hands, 40 fine cloths at 12s. a yard, and 12 cloths "engreyned" at 15s. a yard, in order to be divided among his creditors, ſhare and ſhare alike; but Foſter wanted to make gain by the cloths, and to pay ſuch creditors as he pleaſed their whole debts, and the reſt to have nothing. See fol. xlv, b. of this edition; the leaves of which are all numbered at the bottom of the firſt column.

p "The accompte of Willm. galle and hery Bumpſted wardeyns of London bredge from mihelmas A. xxij. E. iiij. Jnto myhelmas after and ij yeres folowynge" viz. the 1ſt and 2d of Rich. III.

q This complaint, by rights, ſhould have been inſerted after the two following articles, which precede it in chronology, the occurrence of them being in the 4th of Henry vi. this not till the 20th year of the ſame reign; and though no regard has been obſerved reſpecting the various foregoing articles, which appear to be a medley of anecdotes and memorandums, entered, perhaps, in a ſpare book, from time to time, occaſionally, as they occurred to the collector, and ſo printed; but it ſeems neceſſary to caution the reader of the laſt three articles in particular, leſt he be miſled by them, neither of them having any date, although it is from them principally that this miſcellany is denominated a chronicle.

r Henry Beaufort, ſurnamed the rich cardinal; by foreigners he was ſtiled the cardinal of England. He was inveſted with the habit, hat and dignity of a cardinal at Calais, 25 March, 1427, by the D of Bedford, regent of France, &c. See Hall's and Fabian's chronicles.

Arnold's* Chronicle; fometimes, The cuftoms of London. By whom, or when it was printed, does not appear: it feems to have been printed abroad; perhaps at Antwerp, as Arnold had correfpondence there, if he was living at the time of its publication, none of the precedents bearing date after 1494. The types are bold, or, as the printers fay, fat; rather larger than Englifh, N° 1, and ftand well in line: the blooming and initial capitals are of various forts and fizes, making but a mean appearance; the blooming II cuts the beft figure among them; and, being of the antique form, has a face between it's legs. The whole is unfkilfully or haftily, rather than incorrectly printed, feveral letters being reverfed, and having words fpaced in the middle inftead of the end, fo that part of fome words are blended with the next that follows, &c. The time of printing may be nearly gathered from the laft mayor and fheriffs inferted in the lift of them, which (in this edition) ends with thofe chofen the 18 Hen. VII. A.D. 1502. It is very remarkable of this edition, that the leaves, for the moft part, are numbered at the bottom of the front page, under the inner column to C.xviij, which fhould have been Cxix, as two leaves are numbered xvij, befides the table of contents, and that of the bailiffs, mayors, and fheriffs. The fignatures are irregular, viz. A 4, of which the firft is a blank leaf, the other three contain the table of contents; then another fignature A, with 8 leaves, containing the bailiffs, mayors and fheriffs; B 4, on the firft leaf of which begins the numbering of the leaves, as above mentioned; C 8—E 8; F 6—Q 6; R 8; S 6; T 6; V 5, the laft page of which is blank. The general title, and that of the bailiffs, &c. which my copy wants, are taken from that in the Bodleian. WH. Short folio.

" The Dialogues of Creatures Moralyfed, Applyably and edificatyfly/ to euery mery and iocounde mater/ of late trãflated out of latyn into our Englyfhe tonge right profitable to the gouernaunce of man. And they be to fell/ vpõ Powlys churche yard." Under this title is a wood cut of two Satyrs, male and female, half human and half goats, after the manner of the centaur, enclofed within four pieces of fret-work: the fame is at the head of the 90th dialogue, which is entitled, " Of a beafte callyd Satirus/ which weddyd a wyfe." On the back are two other converfation pieces; one, an old man and a young one; the other, an old man and a young king; half lengths: between thefe two cuts, " Here

* Not the leaft intimation of this appears in the book; only among its feveral mifcellaneous articles there are fome precedents of bonds, releafes, &c. with R. A. haberdafher of St. Magnus, London Bridge, as a party in them, and fometimes with Richard Arnolde, at length; fo that the principal authority for afcribing this collection to him is Hollinfhed, who, enumerating the learned men at the end of the reign of Hen. VIII. fays, " Arnold of London wrote certeine collections touching hiftoricall matters." Some of them, very probably, taken from Robert Bale, recorder of London, who " gathered as it were a chronicle of the cuftomes, lawes, foundations, changes, reftoring mageftrates, officers, orders, and publike affemblies of the citie of London, with other matters touching the perfect defcription of the fame citie;" as mentioned alfo among the learned men of the reign of Hen. VI.

afcir Folowith the Prologe of thys prefent volume." It is on one page, and concludes thus, "O lorde God (faith faint Auguftin) all thy Creaturis which thou hafte made/ crye to me and fece not that J owe to loue the my lorde god and maker aboue all othir thinge/ & therfore the autor & compofitor of this Boke for our holfome erudicyon & lernynge to auoyde flouth and fluggyffhneffe and to induce the myndes of the herers to quyckneffe & deuocyon/ hath compylyd this tretys that the more efyly we mowe vnderftonde the morall fenfe includyd in the fame." On the back of the prologue, "Here beginneth the table fhewyng the natures and effectys of all Creatures by the maner of perfuafyon." There are cxxii dialogues, with a cut at the head of each of them. Thefe fabulous dialogues contain much of Natural hiftory, according to the knowledge of thofe times; and the morals are exemplified by many hiftorical narrations, citing the authors from whom they are taken. As a fpecimen of the Natural Hiftory, the reader may fee in the notes, an extract from that "Of the Olefawnte[1] that bowyth not the kneys. Dialogo lxxxix." The leaves are not numbered, but the book contains T T, in fours, befides the prefixes. At the end, "Thus endith the Dialogus of Creatures Moralyfed." &c. as on the title page. See p. 345. The Rev. Dr. Lort, and W.H. Quarto.

— "True tidings of the wonderfull workes of the Rebaptifts of Minifters in Weftphalia, &c." Maunfell, p. 2. Quarto.

— "The Art of good liuing & of good dying. Alfo of the paines of Hell & of Purgatory, of the comming of Antichrift. 15 fignes going afore the iudgment generall, the ioyes of paradice, and of the iudgment generall. Printed at Paris with pictures." Ibid. p. 4. Folio.

— "The affault of Heauen, tranflated out of French by Thomas Paynell." Ibid. p. 5. Quarto.

"A Cate-

[1] "Thefe beaftis be very apte to batell: For the warryours of Perce and Medes vfe to fight in Towris of Tymbre fet vppon the backys of thefe beaftis/ and cafte downe fperys and dartys/ as from a wall/ and thefe Elephawntys haue greate mynde and vnderftondinge/ and they goo togider after ther manere/ and they fere the mows and flee from him/ and they goo two yere with whelpe, and they neuer gendir but oonys. Nor they haue neuer but oone whelpe at oonys. And they lyue ccc yeris/ as faith Jfydore Ethimol. xii. And fcripture that conteyneth the olde hiftoryes (*ancient MSS.*) tellyth that the Elefawnte is takyn in thys manere.. Two maydenes that be veray virgins theyr peeple beinge bare/ and the ouerpartys of ther bodyes alfo difclofyd and fhewyd goo both togider where thefe Elefawntys abyde, and one of them berith a potte The other berith a fword/ which maydyns with lowde voyce fyngynge the Elefawnte berith & comyth nere And by his naturall inftinccyon he knowith the innocencye of the virginall flefh, and goeyth worfhippe vnto the chaftite of them and as he is lyckynge the breftes and pappes of them/ he is merueloufly delytyd and fallyth afleape and withoute Taryinge the mayde with the fworde fmyteth him in to the fofte belye/ and fhedith his bloode and he fallyth down and the other mayde receyueth the bloode in the potte with the which is dyed a purple colowre that longyth oonly to a kynge to were." Pliny corroborates their affection for young perfons, efpecially young handfome women. Book viii; chap. 5.

"A Catechisme betweene the husband and the wife, whereunto is added a Dialogue betweene truth and the vnlearned man, translated by Rob. Legate." Ibid. p. 29. Sixteens.

"Cauteles preseruatory concerning the preseruation of the Gods, which are kept in the pixe. Printed in King Edwards daies. Ibid. p. 32. 8°.

"Mart. Kemnitius against the counsell of Trent, concerning Traditions." Ibidem.

"The Copie of an aunswere, made vnto a certain letter, wherein the answerer purgeth himselfe & other from Pelagius errours," &c. Ibid. p. 38. See p. 966. Quarto.

"The supplication that the nobles and commons of Ostericke made vnto kinge Ferdinandus, in the cause of christian religion, with the Kings answere &c." Translated by Miles Coverdale. Ibid. p. 39. Octavo.

"Declaration of the order that the Churches in Denmarke and many other places in Germany do vse, not onely at the holye Supper, but also at Baptisme. By Miles Couerdale. Printed beyond sea." Ibid. p. 39, and 93. Sixteens.

"Mich. Drayton his Harmonie of the Church, containing holy Himnes, and spirituall songes." Ibid. p. 46. Quarto.

"A Declaration what true praier is, how wee should pray, and for what we should pray." By John Knoxe. Ibid. p. 65. Sixteens.

"Of the lawful and vnlawfull vsurie amongst Christians, by Wolph. Musculus, translated by P. L." Ibid. p. 75. Sixteens.

"Debate betweene Pride and Lowlinesse." Anonymous. Ibid. p. 88.

"Preparation to the Lords Supper, by I. S." Ibid. p. 94.

"Jo. Tomkis his sermon on Ephes. 5. vers. 1, 2." Ibid. p. 105.

"A Tower of trustinesse, wherein euery Christian fighting vnder the banner of Christ may defend himselfe against the cruell assaults of his enemies, compiled in verse and prose by Leonard Gibson." Ibid. p. 115. Octavo.

"A treatise How by the Worde of God, Christian mens almose ought to bee distributed. Translated from M. Bucer De regno Christi, made for the blessed king Edward." Contains 28 pages, printed on Italics, besides an addresss to the reader, and an order for provision for the poor. Ibid. p. 116. Octavo.

The 17 preceding articles, taken from Maunsell, must have been printed before 1595, when his catalogue was published.

"A spiritual Almanacke/ wherein euery christen may se what they ought daylye to do/ or leaue vndone/ not after the lernynge of Ptolomy, &c: but out of the very true wholsome doctrine of God, &c: in his worde &c." Octavo.

"A brief Declaration of the fained sacrament commonlye called the extreame vnction, wryten by the godly learned man Mr. Jhon Caluine/ and translated out of ÿ Latine into Englysh by W. B."

"A

—— "A booke intituled the fantasies of Jdolatrie." Which consists of 50 stanzas; inserted at large in the first edition of Foxe's Acts and Monuments, p. 599, and in no other. It is introduced at the end of his narrative of Thomas lord Cromwell, as below.* As a specimen be pleased to accept the following extracts.

1. " All Christen people
Beyng vnder the steple
Of Jesu Christes faith,
Mark and drawe nere
And ye shall here,
What the holy scripture sayth.

2. First J wyll begyn
Your hartes to wyn,
With nother fable nor lye,
But with Gods testament
As is most expedient,
Concernyng idolatrie.——

11. This should suffise
All those that be wyse
But we of a stubbourne mynd
Be so harde harted
Wyll not be conuerted
But rather styll be blynde.

15. Roonyng hyther & thyther
We can not tell whether,
Jn Offryng candels and pence,
To stones and stockes
And to olde rotten blockes
That came, we know not from whence.—

28. Thus ran we about
To seke Jdols out
wandryng farre and nere,
Thynkyng the power
Of our blessed sauiour
Jn other places more then there.—

40. Yet haue we thought
That these Jdols haue wrought
Myracles in many a place
Upon age and youth
when of very truth
They were done by the deuils grace.—

43. Yet offer what ye wolde
were it Otes, Syluer or Golde
Pyn, Point, Breche or Rynge
The churche were as then
Suche charitable men
That they would refuse nothyng.—

45. Thus were we poore soules
Begyled with Jdolles,
with fayned myracles and lyes
By the deuyll and his doctors
The Pope and his Proctors,
That with such haue blerid our eyes.—

48. Besydes these stockes & stones
Haue we not had of late traytors bones
Thus their trompery to maintain;
which is a token verely
They go about moste earnestly,
To bryng in superstition again.—

50. And now to make an ende
Lorde we beseche thee to sende
Us peace and tranquillitie,
And that of thy mere mercy & grace
within short tyme and space,
to illumine vs with thi sincere veritie.

Thus ended this litle treatise made & compyled by Gray."

—— "The Declaration of the Fathers of the Councell of Trent, concerning the going into churches at such time as heretical Service is sayd, or Heresy preached." Pub. Libr. Cambridge.

—— "John Fisher his sermon upon this sentence of the Prophet Ezechiel, 'Lamentationes, carmen et væ', very aptly applyed to the Passion of Christ." Octavo.

A spiritual

* " This valiaunt Souldier and captayne of Christe the forsayde Lorde Cromwell, as he was most studious of hym selfe in a flagrant zeale to set forwarde the truthe of the Gospel, sekyng all meanes and wayes to beate down false Religion and to advaunce the true: So he always retayned vnto hym, and had about hym suche as could be founde to be helpers & furtherers of the same, in the nomber of whom were sundry and dyvers freshe and quicke wytter, pertaynyng to his famyly, by whose industrie and ingenious labours, diverse excellent both balladet and bookes were contriued and set abroade, concernyng the suppression of the Pope and all Popyshe idolatrie. Amongst the whiche omyttyng a great sort that we might here bryng in, yet this small treatise here followyng, called the fantasies of Jdolatrie, we thought not to passe ouer, conteinyng in it as in a brief some the great multitude of idolatrous pylgrimages for the posteritie hereafter to vnderstand what then was vsed in Englande.

"A Spiritual Consolation, written by John Fyssher bishop of Rochester, to hys syster Elizabeth, at such tyme as he was prisoner in the Tower of London. Very necessary and commodious for all those that mynde to leade a vertuous lyfe: Also to admonishe them to be at all tymes prepared to dye. Octavo.

"The Image of a very Christian bishop, and of a counterfeit bishop." Printed Cum priv. in Hen. 8. time. This is quoted as a very rare book by Mr. Prynn, in his Antipathie of Lordly Prelacie, p. 338-9. See The Ymage of bothe pastoures, &c. in p. 690.

"Orders taken Octo. 10. An. 3 Eliz. by Vertue of her Maiesties Letters to her Commissioners for Causes Ecclesiasticall." Quarto.

"John Ramsey his Corosyse to be layed hard vnto the hartes of all faythfull Professors of Christes Gospell." Octavo.

"A sermon of John Chrisostome of Pacience, of the ende of the Worlde, and of the last Judgment, translated into English by Tho. Sampson."

"A fruitfull sermon of D. Martin Luther, concerning Matrimony, taken out of the Epistle to the Hebrewes." Octavo.

"The Ballads or Canticles of Solomon, in Prose and Verse." Anonymous. Hist. of Eng. Poetry, III; 181, note c.

"An answere vnto Sir Thomas Mores Dialogue, made by Willyam Tindale." The Dialogue was printed in 1529: see p. 338; and this Answer about 1530. See The whole workes of W. Tyndall, &c. p. 247. W.H. Sixteens.

"Alexandri Gil. Linguæ Anglicanæ Logonomia. Lond." Quarto.

"The Boke for a Justice of Peace." See p. 153. Contains 28 leaves. Sixteens.

"Alexander Hume, Scot, his rejoinder to D. *Adam* Hill concerning the descent of Christ into Hell, wherein the answer to his sermon is justly defended, and the rust of his Reply scraped from those arguments as if they had neuer been touched with the canker." See p. 1274. Quarto.

"The Reformation of Religion by Josiah; containing a comment on 2 Kings, 23; 23—27." Octavo.

"A short and plaine Table orderly disposing the Principles of religion, and first of the first Table of the Law, whereby we may examine ourselues." Head title on signature A 1. Contains C, in eights. 16°.

A treatise on Predestination by Giles Wigginton. Also a kind of Ballad directed for advice to a young courtier. See Bancroft's Dangerous Positions; and Neal's Hist. of the Puritans, I; 472.

Bagford mentions in a letter to Hearne, which he has prefixed to Leland's Collectanea, "A description of a Roman camp, and place of exercise in the old artillery ground between Whitechapel and Bishopgate street, by a judicious author, whose name he had forgot, in the latter end of Q. Elizabeth's reign; a valuable quarto pamphlet. See Gough's Brit. Topogr. I; 718.

"The

—— "The Custumers Apology. That is to say, A generall Answere to Informers of all sortes, and their iniurious complaints, against the honest reputation of the Collectors of her Maiesties Customes, specially in the Out-Portes of this Realme. Written onely For Vnderstanding Readers And Wise in Highest Authoritie to Reade and discerne by. Alwaies prouided, In reading Reade all, or nothing at all." In a border of metal flowers. Contains A 3, B and C 4, D 3. Quarto.

—— "A briefe treatise of Oathes exacted by Ordinaries and Ecclesiasticall Iudges, to answere generallie to all such Articles or Interrogatories, as pleaseth them to propound. And of their forced and constrained Oathes ex officio, wherein it is proued that the same are vnlawfull." See An Apologie, &c. p. 1087. 58 pages; neat Roman letter. W.H. Quarto.

—— "St. Bernardyns Boke, entytuled, The Chrysten Relygyon," which had been translated out of Latin into French; reuised by some Doctors at Paris, and now translated into English by Henry Watson. Mentioned in the preface to "The Chirche of Euill men and women, whereof Lucyfer is the Head," &c. See p. 288. A severe invective against all kinds of gamesters. 38 leaves. Oldys's Harleian Pamphlets, N° 139. Quarto.

—— "A proper Dyaloge betwene a Gentileman and an Husbandman: eche complaynenge to other theyr myserable Calamyte, through the Ambicion of the Clergye." Written in verse, about the middle of K. Henry the eight's reign. In it is inserted a fragment of an old MS. treatise in prose, written, as the author says, above an hundred years since, and about the time of K. Richard the second. This he recommends to our

"Redynge, forthe to the end, seriously:
For though old Wrytynges apere to be rude;
Yet notwithstandynge, they do include
The Pythe of a Matter most fructuously."

Contains 24 leaves, black letter." Ibid. N° 173. Octavo.

—— "A princelie mirrour of peerles modestie." Head title on signature A 1, and seems not to have had any other. It relates the story of Susannah wrought into a novel. C 6, in eights. W.H. Sixteens.

—— "An Epittel exhortatorye, admonishing ãd warning all faithful Christiãs to beware of the false fained God of the aulter, and only to trust in the onelye lyuing God. Jhon iiii. (22) Ye worship ye wot not what we knowe what we worship." Head title; but as it contains only 4 leaves, and has no signatures, am apt to believe it to have been an affix to some other book. At the end, "Sent from verbo dei whose aucthour is in celo. Flee from worshipping of ydolles. i. Cor. x. Beleue the Scriptures. Marc. i. b. And require no more than is commaũded. Luc. iii. c." My copy is bound vp with "A proclamacyon of the hygh emperour Jesu Christe," &c. as p. 747; probably written by the same author; and though they are not the same types, nor the forms exactly of a size, yet as this book was printed by Rob. Redman, p. 394, and perhaps by others also, it might be an affix to those editions. W.H. 8°.

"The

"The Judycyall of vryns: Consyderynge that it is expedyent for euery man to know the operation and qualites of his body, and to know in what state and condicyon his body standeth in, whiche cannot be knowen so well as by the vryne. In consyderation wherof this worke is collected and gadered out of ỳ sentēcyals sayngis of al Auctours of Phisike, to the entent that euery man myght brefly come to the knolage of ỳ premisses, whiche sayd worke is diuided into. iii. seueral bokes, whereof the fyrst boke declareth pryncypaly how vryn is gendered in mans body, & of his qualites withall ỳ hole workyng of nature in mānes body. The second boke treateth of colours in vryn, & what they signifye. The thyrde boke treateth of cōtens in vryn & what they signifye, & suche sekenesses as they signifye is there declared, & also ther causes & qualites with many thinges moo, touchyng the scyens of Phisike, as brefly doth apere in a tabull, in the latter ende of this boke." This title is over a wood-cut of a doctor of phisic in his academic dress, holding up an vrinal in his left hand. Contains 63 leaves besides the title; B. L. with some Italic interspersed; the last page blank. "Here after foloweth a table to fynde quyckly euery Chapyter of this worke & also many other desesys & sekenesses & thynges here in expressed, & thynke not ỳ al thīges expressed in this worke to be noted in this table for ỳ wher to besy as by redynge you shall perceyue." Annexed to the forementioned table of contents is an alphabetical one. These are on two leaves, double columns: on the last page is only one column, from top to bottom. It has no date of time or place, nor any printer's name, but is supposed to be one of John Rastal's earliest performances, if not printed beyond-sea. I have not met with any treatise on the subject, in English, so full and particular, in so much that it seems to be a collection, at least an abstract, of whatever had been written about it. The compiler anonymous. W.H. Short folio.

"An Epistle of comfort, to the reverend priestes, and to th Honorable, Worshipful, & other of the Laye sort restrayned in Durance for the Catholicke Fayth. Matt. xi. Regnum coelorum vim patitur, et violenti, rapiunt illud. The Kingdome of heauen suffereth violence, and the violent beare it awaye. Deus tibi se, Tu te Deo. Jmprinted at Paris." Prefixed are a short address "To the reader, and a table of the principal chapters into which this epistle is divided, being 16 in number. At the end, "By one, that reuerenceth your prisons, beareth most dutiful affection to your persons & humbly craueth parte in your prayers. ISaiæ. 30. In silentia & spe, erit fortitudo vestra. In silence & hope shalbe your strength." Then, a table of faults with their corrections, included in the signatures. C c, in eights. W.H. Sixteens.

"A Most fruitfull, pithie and learned Treatyse, howe a Christian man ought to behaue himselfe in the danger of death: and how they are to be releued and comforted, whose deare freendes are departed out of this world. Most necessarye for this our vnfortunate age and sorrowfull dayes. John 6. Verily, verily, I say vnto you, he that beleeueth in me, hath

 euerlasting

euerlasting life. London Printed for William Blackwall, dwelling ouer against Guildhall Gate." Dedicated "To the right Worshipfull M. Iohn Mannors of Hadon, in the Countie of Darby, Esquier. And to the Wor. his Sonne and heire M. George Mannors, and the right vertuous Gentlewoman Mistres Grace Mannors, his Wife, W. B. wisheth all health and happinesse with increase of Wor." Wherein he says, "——I did long studie in what sort I might best shewe myselfe gratefull for the manifolde benefites which my poore father and his family haue found at your handes: who hauing been your ancient Tennants, haue suckt the sap of our liues out of your lands.——After I had long waited, at the last it was my good hap, to light vpon this most excellent, learned and godlye Treatise, which was written by a most vertuous and honorable personage, pure in life, and zealous in Religion: the Lady Iane Dudley.[1] A worke so full of consolation and comfort, as in my poor opinion neuer better was printed:" &c.---Acrostic verses on the names, Iohn Mannors, George Mannors, Grace Mannors.---The preface to the Christian Reader, addressed "Vnto all those that vnfeinedly desire to liue vnder the feare of God," &c.---A table of the contents; divided into two books, the first containing 40 chap. the second 2, and the third 12. Then, An Exhortation written by the Lady Iane, the night before she suffered, in ẏ end of the newe Testament in Greeke, which she sent to her sister the Lady Katherine." 260 pages, besides the prefixes; B. L. in borders of metal

[1] In this particular Mr. Blackwall must have been mistaken; misled perhaps by the treatise being anonymous, and Lady Jane's letter to her sister annexed at the end, bearing her name. He might have been better informed by consulting the author's preface, wherein he says, among other things, "in my bookes heretofore published, I haue set forth a general comfort concerning trouble, sicknesse pouerty" &c. and a little further, "I (though vnworthy and vnmeete) was called by authoritie, but specially by God, to teach, to exhort, to comfort:" &c. By which the author seems to have been in Holy Orders.

This appears to have been the same treatise with that mentioned in a contracted manner by Maunsell, p. 48. See p. 748. where it is said to have been translated out of High Dutch by M. Coverdale. Hugh Singleton in his epistle prefixed to "A spirituall and most precious perle," &c. says, ——I receiued at the hands of M. doctour Milo Couerdale, at whose hand I receiued also the copyes of three other workes of Otho Wermulerus, a German preacher in the city of Tigurie, who wrote them in the Germain tongue, as he did certain bookes mor, which are not as yet turned into the Englishe tongue. The names of those bookes which are translated are these: the precious perle, which the author calleth of affliction, another of death, the third of iustification, and the fourth of the hope of the faithful." See p. 744-5; also p. 787.

I have an edition of this treatise of Death, probably the same that Mr. B. printed the present edition from, without any dedication, but the preface addressed in the same manner, and is, with the whole treatise verbatim the same, differing only in orthography. Mr. Ames met with another copy, seemingly of this very edition, with a note in MS. thus, "This book was written by Rickard, son of William Tracy of Todlington in Gloucestershire Esq; who was one of the first that embraced the reformed Religion in this Kingdom. He died as of Henry the viii. and made a memorable Will, which was condemned in the Bishop of London's Court; his Body was dug up, and burned as a Heretick. This Richard wrote A preparation for the Crosse, lately ascribed to John Freeth. This present book was written in 1550." But Lady Jane was not beheaded till 12 Feb. 1554; besides, as the writer of this note quotes not his authority, I must prefer Singleton's account of the author, as he received it from M. Coverdale, the translator.

metal flowers. The running title, "The (1. 2. 3.) Booke of Death." See p. 742. W.H. Twelves.

"Generall matters to be remembred of (*by*) the Lord Maior throughout the whole year." In general, and month by month. Sixteens.

"Richard Smith D. D. &c. his confutation of Abp. Cramer's book on the Sacrament, entitled A Defence of the true catholike doctrine" &c. as p. 600. "This escaped the notice of the Oxford antiquary." T. Baker's Maunsell, p. 109. Octavo.

"An abstract of certain acts of parliament: of certaine her Maiesties Iniunctions: of certaine Canons, Constitutions, and Synodalles prouinciall: established and in force, for the peaceable gouernment of the Church, within her Maiesties Dominions and Countries, for the most part heretofore vnknowen and vnpractized. Cod. de Epis. & Cler. l. Nulli licere. Neither let them feare, to be called and suspected pickthankes, seeing their faythfulnesse, and diligent trauell carieth with it, as well praise, as honestie and godly zeale; hauing published the trueth to the eares of all men, and brought it to the open light. Proverb. 31. 8. Open thy mouth for the dumbe, in the cause of all the children of destruction." Prefixed are, an epistle "To the Christian Reader.---An Abstract of certaine Actes of Parliament: &c. viz. 25 Hen. 8. C. 19. intituled, An act concerning the submission of the Cleargie. &c.——This act is reuiued 1. Eliza. ca. 1.*" The subjects treated of are, "A learned Ministerie commanded by the Lawe.---Dispensations for many benefices vnlawfull." See these two reprinted, with answers to them, p. 958. "Excommunication by one alone forbidden.---It is vnlawfull for a Bishop, or any other Ecclesiasticall person by common right, to beare any ciuile office in the common weale.---Vnlawfull to ordaine a Minister without a Title.---The manner of Archbishops, bishops, and Archdeacons visitations, and what procurations are due for the same.---Fees for Letters of orders vnlawfull." Then concludes with certain interrogatories, as below.*

* "Out of this act (*says the author*) I conclude, that al Canons, constitutions, ordinances, and synodals prouinciall, made before this act: requiring and commanding a learned Ministery, prohibiting many benefices to be giuen to one man: prohibiting ciuil iurisdiction to be in Ecclesiasticall men, and prohibiting one man to excommunicate, for that such Canons, &c. cannot be repugnant to the lawes of this realme, nor hurtfull to the kings prerogative, are in force, & ought to be executed: and therefore by this act, all the Canons specified in any part of my treatise are in force, & so by vertue of this act, a learned ministerie commanded: Pluralities forbidden," &c.

* "And now generally to conclude: It were not amisse in my simple vnderstanding that the whole Church made humble supplication, vnto her excellent Maiesty, and her honourable Counsaylers, that the Judges of the Land, might be consulted, vppon the validity of the former act of Parliament, and that it might bee knowne, whether the forsayde Canons established thereby, or any of them, be in force: and if so that then her Maiesty woulde vouchsafe, graciously to take the Church affayres into her owne handes, and by his commission Ecclesiasticall, appoint such honorable and faythfull men as are not in the ministerie, to examine the bishops proceedings. Viz. Whether" &c. &c.

"" The pardon grauntyd to *(for)* the fraturnyte of Seynt Cornelys at Weſtmynſter *(to them)* that vicet *(visit)* gyue or ſende to it. ¶ Firſt the holy father ĩ god Thomas of ỹ title of ſeynt ſeſſelly cardinall preſt of Rome & Legat/ Archebyſſhop of yorke & chaunceller of Inglande &c. Alſo Lawrence of the title of ſeynt Thomas ĩ parione preeſt cardynall of Rome & legat. Alſo Mathewe of the title of ſeynt potencian preeſt cardynall of Rome/ hath grauntyd in the ſeell of ſeynt cornelys. cccc. dayes of pardon/ on ſeynt Barbaras daye. c. dayes/ in the natyuyte of our lorde. c. dayes/ in the firſt ſonday of aduent. c. dayes/ on aſſhe wednyſday. cc. dayes. The firſt ſonday ĩ lent. c. dayes. The firſt frydaye in clene lent. c. dayes. on palme ſonday. cc. dayes. on ſheerethurſdaye. cc. dayes on good fryday. c. dayes. on Eſter euyn. cc. dayes. on Eſterday. cc. dayes. the firſt ſondaye after Eſter. c. dayes/ the firſt ſonday after pentecoſt. c. dayes. on ſeynt Margaret's daye. c. dayes of pardõ. Alſo the reuerent father in god wyllyam archebyſſhoppe of Caunterbury hath graunted. xl. dayes of pardon. Alſo my lorde byſſhop of London. xl. dayes. Alſo my lorde the byſſhop of Rocheſter. xl. dayes. Alſo my lorde the byſſhop of Lyncolne. xl. dayes. Alſo my lorde the byſſhop of Ely. xl. dayes. Alſo my lorde the byſſhop of worſeter. xl. dayes. Alſo my lorde ỹ byſſhop of Cheſter. xl. dayes. Alſo my lorde the byſſhop of ſeynt Dauys xl. dayes. Alſo my lorde the byſſhop of Landaff. xl. dayes. Alſo my lorde the byſſhoppe of Salyſbury. xl. dayes. And alſo my lorde the byſſhop of Chicheſter hath graunted xl. dayes of pardõ. ¶ Ther is alſo founded an hoſpytall for the relyef of them that haue ỹ fallynge ſykenes. And is a bleſſyd thynge for women traueylynge with childe that guyueth or ſendeth any thynge in the worſhyp of God and ſeynt Cornelys. ¶ The ſume of this indulgence cometh in ỹ yere to M. M. viiC. & xl. dayes for euer to endure." It has a ſmall wood-cut of St. Cornelis indented at the beginning. Richard Gough, Eſq; A broadſide.

" Precepts of Cato: alſo Sage and Prudent Sayngeſ of the ſeuen wyſe men." Twenty-fours.

" Horæ beatiſſimæ virginis ad vſum eccleſie Eboracenſis. Lond. impreſſ. per Joh. Wright." Bibl. Rich. Smith, See Brit. Topogr. II; 426. Octavo.

" An expoſition on the v. vi. vii. chapters of Mathew, by W. T." &c. See p. 756. On Roman types. Sixteens.

" An Epistel or Moche learnĩg, ſent by ſaint Huldericus, Biſſhoppe of Auguſta, called Augſburgh, vnto Nicolas Byſſhoppe of Rome, the fyrſt of that name: agaynſt the vnmaried Chaſtitie of Pryeſtes." The head-title, " Unto Nicolas hys lorde and father, ãd mouſt vygylaunt Prouiſor of the holye Church of Rome, Huldricus by name onlye a Byſſhoppe, oweth Loue as his ſonne or chylde, and feare as hys ſeruaunt." 12 leaves. W. H. Sixteens.

" An Epiſtle of the perſecution of cathollckes in Englande. Tranſlated ovvt of frenche into Engliſhe and conferred vvith the Latyne copie, by G. T. To whiche there is added an epiſtle by the tranſlator to the right honorable Lordes of her maieſties preeuie councell towchynge the ſame

same matter. Psal. 105. Ver. 38. They shed innocent blood, euen the blood of theyr ovvne sonnes and of theyr ovvne daughters. Psal. 78. Ver. 2. They lay the deade bodyes of thy seruauntes (ô Lorde) for meate to the fovvles of the ayer, and the fleshe of thy saintes to the beastes of the fielde. Imprynted at Douay in Artois." The translator's epistle, which is prefixed, concludes on p. 42, with "Your honours humble oratour and vnfayned hartie Beadesman. G. T." The epistle touching the persecution is addressed "To his verie louinge frinde. M. Gerarde at Bononie in Italie." At the end of which is "An admonition sent by Gerard to the reader touching the former epistle." Then, "The copie of a letter sent from a priest, being prisoner in the Tovver of London, to the fathers of the Societie of Iesus in England," prefaced "To the deuoute reader;" and at the end a suffix by "The translator to the gentle reader;" beginning, "Since the printing of this epistle last rehearsed, I haue heard that the Author thereof vvas one Maister Briāt, who lately suffered (as is sayd) with Maister Campian, and Maister Shervvyn," &c. M 4, in eights: each signature set on the first page only. W. H. Sixteens.

"A consolatory letter to all the afflicted catholikes in England. Philip. 4. Sic state in domino Charissimi: So stand in our Lorde, my Dearest. Imprinted at Roan in Normandy." Superscribed "To his most deare countreymen all the afflicted catholickes in England. H. B. wisheth all comfort and strength and perseueraunce in Christ Iesus." Begins, "Right Noble Lordes, and worshippfull Gentlemē with other worthy Confessors of Christ his Church, and religion, & generally all ye that vnder the name of wilfull and obstinate Recusants," &c. Concludes on p. 111. To fill up the page. "Psalme. 30. Viriliter agite, &c. Behaue your selues mansullye, and let your hartes be comforted all ye that truste in our Lorde." W.H. Sixteens.

"Christmas carolles newely Jmprinted." This title is over a tolerably neat wood-cut of Joseph and Mary worshipping the child Jesus, lying on the ground before them. On the back, "A caroll of the byrth of Chryst.

"Come to Bethleem and ye shall se Puer natus est hodie."

See p. 164. Francis Douce, Esq. Sixteens.

Triplet's chronicle, or miscellaneous collection of useful memorandums, as it may be called; the only copy i know of it having no title; though very probably, in its original state, it had not only a title of some sort, but a calendar of the 12 months, preface, &c. However, it begins now on signature B, with this head-title: "Godly exercises of Prayer, to bee vsed Morning and Euening of euery housholder in theyr houses, or of any other, priuatelie." One morning, and one Evening prayer. Then, "A breef and necessarie Table for such as buie any kinde of merchandies—by the hundreth to retail by the pounde, &c. ----A discription of Waights and measures.--A briefe Rule shewing the iust payment of wages or expences by day, what it amounteth to in the whole yeere, &c.—-The beginning and ending of the Tearmes.-- The highvvayes highwayes *or distance in miles* from any notable towne in England, to the Cittie of London: newly collected and set foorth in a more larger and better manner then heretofore hath beene.---A Table of the difference of the [illegible] of Golde." It shews the value also of three different gold coins, from a pound to a grain; by which it appears that an ounce of Angel gold at that time was worth 3*l.* French Crown gold, 55*s.* and Sovereign gold, 50*s.* Then, on six pages are exhibited neat wood-cuts of the various gold coins then current in Europe, with their names and weights. After them, " A discription of Englande and VVales, vvith the commodities thereof, the names of the Bishoprickes and Shyres, with a briefe collection of the most notable Acts of the Kings of England since the conquest with the day of theyr entrance, death, and place of buriall." This abridgement concludes with the beheading of Mary queen of Scots, 1 Aug. 1587; it may be presumed therefore this little book was printed the latter end of that year, or the beginning of the next. Colophon: " Made at London by Robert Tripler, Stationer or Bookebinder, dwelling in Distaffe lane, at the signe of the Aqua vite Still, neere olde fishstreete, and are there to be sold." As John Wolf dwelt in Distaff-lane also, and about the same time, probably it was printed by him. Contains signatures B, C, and D, in eights; the page measures three inches and a half, by two inches and a quarter. It opens broad-ways, like music books, but reads short-ways. Francis Douce, Esq; Sixteens.

" A TREATISE OF CHRISTIAN RENVNCIATION. Compiled of excellent sentences & as it were diuerse homelies of Ancient Fathers: wherin is shewed how farre it is lawfull or necessary for the loue of Christ to forsake Father, Mother, wife and children, and all other worldly creatures. Against the enemies of the Crosse of Christ, who by temporall respects of obedience or other earthly bonds, withdraw themselues or others frõ the Confession of their faith and Religion. Wherunto is added a shorte discourse against going to Hereticall Churches with a Protestation." On the back, over a cross formed with metal flowers, are these texts, " Luc 14. Euery one of you which doth not renoũce all thinges which he hath, cannot be my Disciple. Mat. 16. If any man will come after me, let him deny himselfe, and take vp his Crosse, and follow me. Luc. 14. If any come vnto me and doth not hate his father and mother, and wife and children, and brethren and sisters, yea and moreouer his owne life, he cannot be my Disciple." The table of contents on one leaf. The whole occupies 170 pages. Hereunto is annexed " The Declaration of the Fathers of the Councell of Trent, concerning the going vnto Churches, at such time as hereticall seruice is saied, or heresy preached." Both in Latin and English, introduced with a preface " To the Catholicke Reader." The whole of this on 40 pages, with fresh signatures. Both pieces are anonymous, but apparently by the same Hand. Neither of them have printer's name, place, or date; but both neatly printed on Long Primer Roman, Nº I. Small Pica body. W.H. Octavo.

Towards

A declaration of the Bull of Pope Innocent VIII. for confirmation of the marriage between K. Henry VII. and Elizabeth daughter of K. Edward IV; and for the establishment of the crown to K. Henry VII. and his issue. Without date, or printer's name. The original, as in Rymer's Fœdera, XII; 297, is dated the 6th of the Calends of April, 1486: this declaration, therefore, may well be supposed to have been printed soon after the arrival of the Bull in England. See Acta Regia, III; 56—58, and Rapin's Hist. under 1486. The types resemble Caxton's, but query: however, being very scarce, i have transcribed the whole, for the curious reader, in the notes.* A broadside.

Towards

* " Our holy fadre the Pope Innocent the. viij. To the perpetual memory of this hereafter to be had, by his propre mocion without procurement of our soueraygn lord the Kyng or of any other person for conseruacyon of the vniuersal peas and eschewing of Sklaundres as shuld gendre the contrary of the same. Vnderstanding of the longe & greuous variaunce, discentions & debates that hath ben in this Realme of England betwene the house of the Duchre of Lancastre of that one party, And the house of the Duchre of Yorke on that other party. Wylling all suche diuysions in tyme folowyng to be put apart By the Counsell & consent of his College of Cardynalles approueth confermeth & stablisshyth the matrimonye & coniunction made betwene our sou'ayn lord King Henre the seuenth of the house of Lancastre of that one party And the noble Princesse Elyzabeth of the house of Yorke of that other partye with all thaire Issue laufully borne betwene the same.

And in lykewise his holines confermeth stablissheth & approueth the right and title to the Corone of England of the sayde oure soueraygn lorde Henry the seuenthe and the heires of his body lawfully begoten to hym & theym perteyning aswel by reason of his nyghest & vndoubted title of succession as by the right of most noble victory and eleccyon of the lordes spyrituales & temporales and other nobles of his Realme and by the aste ordenaunce & auctoritie of parlyament made by the iij. states of the lande.

Also our sayde holy Fadre the Pope of his proper mocyon by hyegh & holy commaundement chargeth & requireth eu'y inhabitant in this lande & euery subject in the same of what degree, state or condicion that he be. that non of theym by occasion of any successyon, or by any other colour or cause within this Realme by hym selue, or other mediate persones attempte in worde, or dede ayenst the sayd oure soueraygn lorde, or the heyres of his body lawfully begoten contrary to the peas of him & his Realme, vppon the payne of his grete corse and anathemе, the whiche thay & euery of thaim that so attempteth, fallyth in forth right by that selfe dede doyng. fro the whiche corse & Anatheme non man hath power to assoyle thaym: but our holy Fadre himselfe or his speciall depute to the same.

Forthermore he approueth confermeth & declareth. That yf hit pleaze god that the sayde Elizabeth the whiche God forbede shulde decesse withoute Issue bytwene oure soueraygn lorde & hir of their bodyes borne, that than suche Issue as bytwene hym & hir whome after that god shall ioyne him to, shalbe hade & borne right enheritours to the same croune & realme of Englande, Commaundyng that non man attempte the contrarie, opon the payne of his grete curse, which thay and euery of thaym soo doynge fallyth in, in the selfe dede doynge or may not be assoyled but by hym, or his specyall depute to the same.

Ouer this same oure holy Fadre yeueth his blyssing to all princes nobles and other inhabitantes of this Realme or outward that fauoureth aydeth & assisteth the sayd our soueraygn lorde & his heires ayenst hys or thaire rebelles, yeuing thayme that dye in his & thair quarrall full and plenarye Pardon and remyssyon of alle thaire synnes. Fynally he commaundeth alle Metropolitanes & Bisshopes vpon the payne of interdiccion of entringe the Chirche Abbotes Prioures Archydecones Paresshpriestes Priores & Wardeynes of the freres and al other men of the chirche Exempte and not exempte opon the payn of his grete curse whiche thay fallyth in yf thay do it not to denounce & declare or cause to be denounced and declared alle suche contrarye doers and rebelles accursed at suche time as thay ro the same in the name

"The vnlucklie Firmentie." B. L. Quarto.

"The booke in meeter of Robin Conscience." Mr. Ritson.

Towards the close of queen Elizabeth's reign, patents for almost every thing became so common, that the honorable House of Commons took them into consideration; and, amongst other patents and monopolies, you may find those mentioned in the note below,[p] taken notice of in the journals of the House of Commons, now printed;[q] and in a MS. formerly by Mr. Morrice, in his second part of a register, p. 307, and 531, in Dr. Williams's library.

Printers, in the earlier stages of the origin and progress of printing, made or cast their own letters. Such as wish to know the names and particulars of them who made a separate trade of it, may be satisfied by perusing a Dissertation upon English Typographical Founders and Founderies, written by the late Rev. Edw. Rowe Mores, A. M. & A. S. S. printed by John Nichols, 1778. The principal founderies at present exiling in England, are Caslon's, Jackson's, and Fry's, each of them abounding with characters for all known languages, and great variety of sizes.

name of the sayd o' sov'rayn Lorde shalbe requyred with aggravacion of the same curse yf the case shall so require So that if they for drede shall not move to publisshe the same; It is to them lefull to curse theire resistentis to the same and to oppresse theim by power temporally whiche they shalle calle for theire assistence to the same in the sayde our holy faders name.

And as touching the articles of this Bulle The Popys holines by this presente Bulle derogateth and maketh voide all maner grauntes, Privileges and Exempcions made by hym or his predecessoures to any persone or place where as thay shulde or myght be preiudiciall to the execution of this presentis and hath alle suche as expressely revoked by thys same as though they were written worde by worde within thies presentis Bulles as by his vadre leyde the more largely doith apere".

[p] To Edward Darcy, a patent for cards. On the mentioning of the monopoly of cards, sir Walter Rawleigh blushed. Upon reading of the patents, Mr. Hackwell, of Lincoln's-Inn, stood up, and asked thus; Is not bread there? Bread quoth one, Bread quoth another; this voice seems strange quoth another. No quoth Mr. Hacket, if order be not taken herein, Bread will be there before the next parliament, &c.

To John Spilman, a patent to make paper. See p. 1599.

To Richard Watkins and James Roberts, a license to print almanacs. See p. 1083, and 1030.

To Richard Wrighte, to print the history of Cornelius Tacitus. See p. 1718.

To John Norden, to print Speculum Britanniæ. See p. 1722.

To sir Henry Singer, touching the printing of school books.

To Thomas Morley, to print songs in three parts. Much like that to Bird and Talis, which may be seen in p. 1643.

To Thomas Wight and Bonham Norton, to print law books. See p. 1301, and 1303.

Others are mentioned by Mr. Rowe Mores, in his Dissertation on Letter-founders, &c. p. 77.

[q] I do not find that the printed copy of the journals of the House of Commons has any minutes after the year 1580; whereas this matter was taken into consideration in 1597, and again in 1601. See D'Ewes's Journals, p. 554, and 644.

THE END.

CORRECTIONS AND ADDITIONS.

PAGE 2, *l.* 16, *after* believe, that *add*, he printed Bartholomeus de proprietatibus rerum at Cologn; (See p. 71, and p. 199.) *Ibid. l.* 17, *dele* Alſo, *and after* this, *add*, laſt.

Page 3, *l.* 27, *after* Whitehill, *read* or Whetchill. *Ibid. l.* 28, *after* commiſſion, *add* (Rymer's Fœdera, 4 Edw. IV. Apud Wycombe, 20 die Octob.)

Page 4, *l.* 11, *for* extent, *read* extant. *Ibid. at the end of note* k, *add*, See it in p. 200.

Page 5, *l.* 9, 1571 *in the margin ſhould be in parentheſes, as the date mentioned in the title-page indicates only the time of beginning and ending the tranſlation. However, no doubt it was printed ſoon after the tranſlation was finiſhed; if not the ſame year, early in the next, and at Cologn. See Caxton's epilogue, p.* 7, 8.

Page 9, *l.* 6, *add*, It is without initial capital letters, ſignatures, catchwords, numerals, or figures to the leaves or pages; but it contains 778 pages, as told over by Mr. Randal Minſhull, library-keeper to the late Earl of Oxford, who publiſhed, about the year 1740, " Propoſals for printing by ſubſcription, an exact and ample account of all the books printed by William Caxton, who was the firſt printer in England:" &c.

Page 11, *l.* 9, *after* date, *read* whereby the *t* ſeemed to be an *x*. *Ibid. l.* 18, *inſert* about *before* 1471. *Ibid. l.* 25, *for* I find put, *read* is found; *and for* many, *read* ſome.

I cannot paſs over the device, or mark of Caxton, as it is called, without noticing ſome doubts communicated by an ingenious and worthy friend of mine, who poſſeſſes ſeveral of that Printer's works, and has examined many others, yet ſays he never ſaw this mark in any of them prior to the Doctrinal of Sapience; the type of which, as he obſerves, is materially different from any of thoſe exhibited among Mr. Ames's ſpecimens. The book named Ryal, he thinks, is alſo in the ſame character. From all which this Gentleman queſtions, whether theſe were really printed by Caxton; whether the mark has appeared in any book with either of thoſe types of which ſpecimens are given in the copper-plate, facing page 1, *or was ever uſed to any work of Caxton's own printing; and whether therefore, inſtead of attributing this device to Caxton, we may not conſider it as belonging ſolely to Wynken de Worde.*

It muſt indeed be owned, that W. de Worde was at leaſt very fond of this device, and has added it, in ſome ſhape or other, to moſt books of his printing. But in his folios he ſeems generally to have employed the very ſame block uſed in the Doctrinal of Sapience, even to the end of his life. Again, we muſt admit, that though Mr. Ames has ſuppoſed the type of this Doctrinal of Sapience to be the ſame with N° 1111 *of his plate, it is nevertheleſs certainly different; the letters more regular, better ſhaped, and approaching nearer to thoſe uſed afterwards by W. de Worde. And further, it muſt be obſerved, that neither this nor the Ryal-book ſhew abſolutely the date of printing them, but only declare the time of finiſhing their tranſlation; the firſt of theſe not till May, 1489, which was very late in Caxton's life. But however theſe circumſtances may furniſh matter of doubt, they certainly afford no proof. The type for printing the books above mentioned, might be a new letter, made for Caxton, by W. de Worde, his then ſervant, if not his ſon-in-law; and as a firſt attempt towards the improvement which he afterwards effected. A reaſon for not oftener finding the mark in queſtion among Caxton's books, has been offerred, page 25, 26. But admitting this mark, as uſually explained, to mean W. C. 1474, i think the device itſelf a ſufficient anſwer to all objections; for what could induce W. de Worde to invent ſuch a mark for his ſole uſe, with Caxton's initials? or to uſe it afterwards, with addition of his own name at length? Whereas, ſuppoſing it firſt adopted by Caxton, it was natural enough for him to continue it, as ſucceeding to Caxton's houſe and buſineſs: probably as a mark of pre-eminence in oppoſition to Pynſon, who was his fellow ſervant; and perhaps on marrying Caxton's daughter he might uſe her father's device, as an heireſs's coat armour, in the middle of his own. Time however may throw more light on the ſubject, and it is therefore ſubmitted to the inveſtigation of the curious.*

Page 17, *l.* 33, *after* Ex ſic eſt Finis, *add*, In the Pub. Libr. Cambridge is an edition with ſignatures; and has at the end, "Caxton me fieri fecit." *Ibid. l.* 42, *after* library, *add*, See Oldys's Brit. Librarian, p. 63.

Page 21, *bring down the date in the margin to the next article.*

Page 25, *l.* 38, *after* initials, *inſert* printed.

Page 26, *to note* x, *add*, The types are very like thoſe of the Speculum Chriſtiani, printed by Machlinia. *Ibid. note* y, *for* kaue, *read* knaue.

Page 30, *l.* 4, *dele* Tranſlated into Engliſh by the Earl of Worceſter. *Ibid. note* a, *for* in Norwich, *read* in or near Ludham, where large ruins are remaining.

Page 34, *l.* 35, *for* Ordinam, *read* Aldenham.

Page 35, *for* 1581, in the margin, *read* 1481.

Page 39, *after l.* 21, *inſert*, The Golden Legende, with cuts.—Wyllyam Caxton at Weſtmeſtre. 1481. Folio. Catal. Bibl. Rawlinſonianæ.

Page 41, *l.* 13, *after* ultimus *read*, which differs conſiderably from the Engliſh Chronicle he had printed in 1480.

Page 42, *l.* 14, *for* are *read* were. *Ibid. l.* 17, *after* be, *read* not. *Ibid. l.* 21, *for* deuoure, *read* deuoute. *Ibid. l.* 33, *for* writ, *read* written; *for* Pelerimage, *read* Pelerinage. *And read*, by Ant. Gerard, *after* Paris, *in l.* 34. *Ibid. l.* 41, *for* diſgreſſion, *read* digreſſion.

Page 44, *l.* 27, *read* Manuale. *Ibid. l.* 38, *read*, book and the firſt dyſtinction. *Ibid. l.* 40, *after* goodneſs, *add* &c.

Page 45, *l.* 30, *& ſeq. read*, "Orate pro anima Johannis Gower, quicunque enim pro anima ipſius Johannis Gower orauerit, tociens quociens mill.

Quingentos

Quingentos dies indulgencie ab ecclesia rite concessos misericorditer in domino possidebit. Enprynted at westmestre by me willyam Caxton and fynyshed the ij day of Septembre the fyrst yere of the regne of Kyng Richard the thyrd, the yere of our lord a thousand cccclxxxiij." Folio.

Page 49, *l.* 4, *add*, Query, whether it may not be found in the Archives of Westminster Abbey.

Page 52, *l. last*, *for* yore, *read* yere.

Page 56, *l.* 19, *for* no doubt, *read* probably.

Page 57, *l.* 13, *for* No. 1. of the specimen, *insert*, differs from any of the specimens in our copper-plate, and is much like, if not the same, as that of the doctrinal of sapience, p. 64. *Ibid. l.* 19, *read*, By Walter Hilton. *Ibid. l.* 25, *for* 1415, *in the margin, read* 1485. *And, instead of that and the six following lines, read*, "The Byrth, Lyf and Actes of Kyng Arthur; of his noble Knyghtes of the Round Table, theyr marvayllous Enquestes and Adventures; th'Achyeviyng of the Sang real; and in the end, le Morte D'Arthur, with the dolorous Deth and Departyng out of thys world of them Al. Whiche Book was reduced to the Englysshe, by Syr Thomas Malory, Knyght, and by me *(W. Caxton)* devyded into 21 bookes; chaptyred and enprynted, and fynysshed in th'Abbey Westmestre, the last Day of July, the Yere of our Lord 1485." Catal. Bibl. Harleianæ,* III; 372.

Page 63, *l.* 40, Liber festivalis, &c. *Since this sheet was printed, i have* 1486.
seen a perfect copy of it, with this colophon, "Here endeth the boke that is callid festivall. the yere of our lord Mcccc. lxxxvi. the day aftir seint Edward the kyng." *Being thus without printer's name, the types very rude, and not matching with any of Caxton's specimens, or any other contemporary printer we know of, it ought to be classed under that unknown printer in p.* 114, *&c. It contains* y, *in eights. folio.*

Page 64, *l.* 15, *add*, The Cambridge copy is divided into five parts; and contains H 10, in eights. *Ibid. against l.* 17, *insert, in the margin*, (1489.)

Page 65, *l.* 24, *add*, See the Emendations, &c. to the Ryal book, p. 57. *Ibid. l.* 25, *after* specimen *add*, according to Ames. *Ibid. l.* 27, *add*, His Majesty has a copy (i know of no other) to which is annexed the following curious injunction, or instruction to a priest about saying mass, entitled,

"Of the necligences happyng in the masse. and of the remedyes. Capitulo lxiiij.

"Lyke

* N.B. The compiler of this catalogue has evidently filed off some of the rust of this title, introducing the apostrophe mark, unknown at that time; also using the v for u, contrary to the then general practice; for though they had types for both letters, the v was used only at the beginning, and the u in the middle or end of words, whether for vowels or consonants. See p. 681, note c. The pointing and capitals are also evidently modernised; the orthography however, I doubt not, is otherwise exact. He acquaints us moreover, that this voluminous romance was drawn out of many volumes in French and Welch.

" Lyke as we haue seyd that thys boke is made especially for the symple peple· and for the symple prestes. whiche vnderstond not latin/ by cause that he is not so suffysaũt but that somtyme for necligence or other wyse he may faylle we wyll speke in thys chapytre of the necligences of the masse & saye the remedyes/ which ben assygned by maystres of dyuynyte/ and ben approued by auctorite of the lawe As yf by neclygence whiche god forbede the preest saye masse· and haue sayd the canon vnto the consecracyon without to leye the hostye vpon the aulter/ Anone as he shall apperceyue it. take a hostye and leye it upon the corporas· And begynne agayn the consecracion at ¶ Qui predie quam pateretur And yf he haue forgete to put in the wyne whyche ought to be sacred : anone as he shal apperceyue it that he put the wyn or water in the chalice. And begynne again the consecracyon at Simili modo postea quam vnto the ende. And yf it happen that he put but water in his chalice And that he had wende it had be whyte wyne/ Anone as he shal apperceyue it put he wyn in the chalice and begynne the consecracyon at Simili modo. vnto thende. And yf it happen that he had sayd all the consecracion. and he had forgoten to put water to the wyn· whiche thenne is sacred/ anone as he shal haue perceyued it/ put therin and begynne again at ¶ Oremus preceptis salutaribus moniti/ and saye the ¶ pater noster ¶ libera nos quesumus. But yf it happen that he now had made all the consecracyon of brede and wyne and that he had not sayd the canon but to Oremus preceptis and yf he had forgoten to put water in tothe chalice there where he shal apperceyue it. late hym put water in to the wyn whiche is thenne sacred And begynne agayn where as he lefte whan he apperceyued it/ And yf it happen that he had thenne sayd all the canon and all the consecracion & he had neyther wyn ne water in his chalice ne lete hym put it in the chalice/ and begynne agayn at Simili modo/ And saye all the canon in suche wyse that he make not the ij crosses. whiche he had made vpon the hostye after the consecracion vnto the second. ¶ Memento but saye all the remenaunt vnto the ende. And yf it happen that the preest made the sacrement of wyn without watre· it shal be reputed veri sacrament but the prest shold synne moche greuously yf he left the watre wetyngly. And yf he made it of watre without wyn/ that shold be noo sacrement/ The preest whan he will saye masse late hym take hede delygently that the hostie be hool & that it haue hool roundenes· and that it be made of whete. And knowe that the wyne ought not to be soure ne vergews. For it sholde haue noo consecracyon For the aygre wyne is no more wyn. but it hath be wyne And the vergews is not yet wyne but it shold be wyne yf it shold be suffred to ripe. Ther shold be put so lytil watre in the chalice, that yt shold not passe the wyne For yf the water passed the wyne the consecracyon shold be lette/ knowe the preest certaynely that yf in his conscience he knowe veryly that he hath synned dedely. of whiche he is not confessyd & repentaunt he synneth dedely/ For he gooth vnworthily to the aulter. He consacreth and holdeth vnworthily the body of our lord/ yf after mydnyght he haue ony thynge eten or dronken how wel that he hath slepte after : he ought not to saye masse that day ne receyue the body of our lord but yf he be

in.

in perill of deth· yf in alle the nyght by sekenesse or for ony good cause Juste & honeste he hath not slepte and hath not eten ne dronke after mydnyght. he may wel & sureli synge masse· yf in his masse after the consecracyon. he remembreth hym that he hath eten or dronken after mydnyght. or that he be in dedeli synne. or irreguler or excomyned or accursed. And of these thynges he remembred not hym self to fore ye masse Thenne especyally for the cause of excomynyng or for cause that he hath eten after mydnight. goo he nepasse no ferther forth but make an ende. And/ yf peraduenture he doubte to make ouer grete esclaundre to the peple yf he shold leue in suche estate So thenne yf he haue good contricyon. and purpose to confesse hym. & satysfie as sone as he shal mowe he may sureli procede & accomplisshe the masse For in so doyng at that hour/ by the Jnvysible bysshop/ that is ihesu criste he shal haue absolucion & dispensacōn as touching to accomplisshe the deuyne mistere whiche he hath bygonne· & not to saye masse vnworthyli. but to receyue worthily the holi sacrament· A doctour whyche is called. Bonauenture whyche saith that to fore the masse the preest ought to thynke of his estate & of his conscience. And ought delygently to make hym redy. And sayth that In sayeng his masse he ought not to thynke on hym self/ but onely on the sacrament that he maketh. yf to fore the consecracion. a flye or loppe or ony other venymouse beest were founde in the chalyce· it ought to be caste in to the piscine and the chalyce ought to be wasshen & to put other wyne & water in to the chalyce· And yf after the consecracyon were founde ony thīg as poyson or venymous beste in the chalyce it ought to be take wysely & wesshen and to brenne the beste. And the asshes & the wasshyng of the beeste to be put in the pyscyne. And by cause by adventure that the preest sholde doubte of the venyme· or sholde haue abhomynacion to receyue that which sholde leue in the chalice late it be put in to a fayr vessel & clene and late it be kept with the other relyques and anon to put other wyne or otheer water in the chalyce for to wasshe it and after to put in wyne & water and begynne agayn the consecracion of the blood at ¶ Simili modo. and after to receyue it to thende that the holy sacrament be accomplysshed whan the preest putteth the wyne & the water in the chalyce the dropes that abyde. somtyme without the chalyce be nothyng sacred ne crōmes of the hostye that other whyle abyde vpon the aulter/ whan the preest hath none entencion to sacre/ them. yf for colde or for ony necligence the hostye falle in the chalice. The preest ought not for that begynne agayn the thyng that he hath sayd to fore. but ought alleway procede forthon whan the preest sayth masse· yf in the hostye be ony fourme of flesshe or other fourme than brede/ he ought not to vse that hostye. but ought to synge agayn yf he haue no counseyll. ¶ And that for fere and for reuerence of the holy sacrament it suffyceth to hym to haue receyued it spyrytuelly/ ¶ Whan the preeste syngeth. and after the consecracyon he remembryth hym not yf he hath sayd or not sayd ony wordes whyche ben not of the consecracyon. the whyche he ought to saye/ he ought not to trouble hym self/ but ought to saye alleway forth wythout ony thing begynne agayn : ¶ But yf he knowe certeynly that he had lefte ony word

that.

that is of the conſecracyon. late hym begynne agayn alle the fourme of the conſecracyon. That is to wete/ ¶ Hoc eſt enim corpus meum/ or ¶ Hic eſt calix vnto. Ad remiſſionem peccatorum alle entirely/ And yf he knowe well that he hath forgeten ony wordes whyche be not of the conſecracyon/ he ought not to begynne agayn. but ought to procede alleway forthon yf ony thyng lytyl in quantyte abyde bytwene the teeth of the mete that thou haſt eten. and by the wyne or water wyth whyche thou haſt waſſhen thy mouth by ony aduenture thou haſt ſwalowed in lytyl quantyte as of ſpyttle that letteth no thyng to ſynge maſſe. yf for ony cauſe to fore the canon the preſte may not accomplyſſhe the maſſe an other preeſt may begynne agayn and may accomplyſſhe it and make an ende. and yf in the canon whan he maketh ony of the ſignes all way tofore the right ſubſtaunce. Another preeſte ought to bygynne there. where he hath left. And yf the preſte in ſayeng the wordes of the ſacrament faylled and myght not ſaye them all for ony thynge that myght happen to hym. ¶ Bonauenture counſeylleth that. that hoſtye ſhold be kept wyth the other relyques whych ben on the aulter. & that another preſte ſhold ſyng wyth an other hoſtie/ and ſaye another maſſe. But the pope Jnnocent ſayth. that in thys caas another preſte ought to begynne at ¶ Qui pridie quam pateretur. And whan the body of our lord is conſecrate. and not yet the blood/ yf the preſte may not ſaye the remenaunt for ony cauſe. or yf he haue forgeten to put wyn in the chalyce vnto in to thende of the maſſe yf he haue not receyued the hoſtie ſacred. thenne late hym put it reuerently and clenely wythin the corporas and put wyne and water in the chalyce and begynne at ¶ Simili modo poſtquam cenatum eſt. ¶ And ſaye all the canon vnto thende except that he make not the two croſſes whiche haue ben tofore made vpō the hoſtye bytwene the conſecracyon and the ſeconde memento ¶ And in the ende of the maſſe receyue the body and the blood of our lord/ And yf the preeſte fayleth for ony caas in ſayenge the wordes of the ſacrament of the blood and myght not accōplyſſhe them. ¶ Albertus counſeylleth that the wyne in the chalyce ſhold be put in to a clene repoſytorye/ and that it be kept wyth the relykes. and that another preſt put agayn wyne and water in the chalyce and begynne agayn at/ Simili modo. And that he accomplyſſhe alle the maſſe/ and receyue the body and the blood of our lord. Saynt thomas dalquyne ſayth that whan the preſte ſayth maſſe. and hath thenne receyued the body of our lord. and he fynde that in the chalyce is nothynge but water and he had ſuppoſed that it had be wyne he ought to take agayn another hoſtye. and put wyne and water into the chalyce. and begynne at ¶ Qui pridie quam pateretur. And ſaye alle vnto the ende of the canon. And in thende of the maſſe receyue yet the hoſtye whyche he hath ſacred wyth the bloode not wythſtondynge that he hath receyued the water whyche he had ſuppoſed that it had been wyne. ¶ For the commaundement to performe the ſacrament is more ſtronge. than is the commaundement to the preſte to receyue faſtynge/

" ¶ Otherwyſe ſhold not be kepte the ordynaunce of conſacracyon. Yf by ony neclygence fyl ony of the blood of the ſacrament on the corporas.

or

or vpon ony of the vestymentis. thenne ought to cutte of the pyece on whiche it is fallen: And ought wel to wasshen and that piece to be kept with the other relyques. And yf it fyl down vpon the therthe or. vpon a stone. or vpon wod· it ought to be wel scraped and raced the place where on it fylle and wel to be wasshen· and to put the wasshyng. & rasure or scrapyng in the sacrayre. And yf the body of Jhesu crist or ony piece fylle vpon the palle of the aulter or vpon ony of the vestymentes that ben blessyd· the piece ought not to be cutte of on whyche it is fallen. but it ought right wel to be wasshen And the wasshyng to be gyuen to the mynistres for to drinke/ or ellys drynke it hymself/

"This chapitre to fore J durst not sette in the boke by cause it is not conuenyent ne aparteynyng that euery laye man sholde know it Et cetera/"

Page 85, *l.* 38, *read* b to p, 6 each; *and dele all that intervenes.*

Page 96, *for the catch word* There, *read* I find.

Page 101, *l.* 26, *add*, Earl Spencer has a perfect copy, containing 45 pages and a half, besides the dedication of two pages. It has neither catch-words, signatures, paging, running-title, or colophon; nor any thing indicative of the printer, but a similitude of the types to Mr. Ames's specimen of Caxton's letter, No 11. *Ibid. l.* 33, *after* Royal library, *add*, See page 113. *Ibid. l.* 37, *after* "THE ACCIDENCE." *add*, This, which was the late Mr. Tho. Martin's, is now in my possession.[b] *And dele the rest of that article.*

Page 103, *l.* 1, *read* other edition. *Ibid. l.* 4, *after* one book, *insert*, See p. 190, &c. *Ibid. l.* 10, *read* ierom.

Page 105, *l.* 12, *after* in vain, *add*, Perhaps it might be deposited in the archives of Westminster-Abbey. *Ibid. l.* 32, *read* Vitas Patrum. *Ibid. note* o, *l.* 8, *for* 1492, *read* 1491; *and add*, See p. 108, note a.

Page 106, *l.* ', *read* The Vitæ Patrum. *Ibid. l.* 31, 32, *instead of* the Arte and Crafte to learne well to Deye, *insert*, The myrrour of the world. *Ibid. l.* 36, *add*, I take for granted this "Spousage of a Virgin to Christ" to have been printed by Caxton, being mentioned as such by Palmer, and by Lewis, probably from him; but it does not appear that either of them had seen the book. Mr. Warton mentions it as a piece of Bishop Alcock's, and dated 1486, but without the name of any printer, as to the other pieces of the same author, mentioned also by him: so that possibly it might be printed by Lettou, Machlinia, or the anonymous printer in p. 114. *Ibid. note* r, *l.* 2, *for* 2225, *read* 2255.

Page 108, *to note* a *add*, "This epitaph is introduced by M. Lewis (MSS. p. 2. penes me) in the following manner: "Here, (on his first arrival in England) by the favour of the abbot of Westminster, he set up his press in the abbey, where he printed many years, with great encouragement

[b] I find it was printed in Caxton's house, by W. de Worde, without date, and have given some account of it in p. 205. No doubt but it had been printed by Caxton, and frequently: the consumption of such books must have been very great, and of course they were consigned to the press as soon as well might be after the invention of printing became public.

ragement from the king, the nobility and gentry. He afterwards printed in his own house, in King-street, in the parish of St. Margaret, in Westminster, where he continued printing to the time of his death, A.D. 1491, when he was about 80 years old. He was buried in the parish church of St. Margaret, where, on his tomb-stone, was the following inscription, on a brass plate, I suppose, which is now lost: " Of your charitee" &c. Mr. Lewis indeed takes no notice of this inscription in his Life of Mayster Wyllyam Caxton, which was published in 1737; but as these his MSS. are dated 7 Dec. 1738, this anecdote doubtless was inserted on later intelligence; and as they appear to be memorials collected in order to compile A brief history of the origin and growth of printing in England, Mr. Ames, who adopted the plan, inserted the article in his Typographical Antiquities, p. 73, with the particulars from whence it was borrowed; and has written under it in his interleaved copy, " Since which I have seen it wrote in a very old hand in another old book, folio." The conjecture of this being a copy of the inscription on Mr. Caxton's tomb-stone is very rational. That he had one is highly probable. It is a pity but that the said MS. memorial had assured us of it.

I cannot take my leave of Master Caxton without intimating a doubt whether some of the foregoing pieces ascribed to him may not, on a strict scrutiny, by comparing the types, &c. be found to be the performances of some cotemporary printer, either at Oxford, Cambridge, or St. Albans; or even in London or Westminster, by Leton, Machlinia, or especially the anonymous printer mentioned in p. 114. These, however, are not many. All that bear his name as printer, or the words Caxton me fieri fecit, *may, I think, be depended on as the productions of his press: and those that express their being printed in " Caxton's house" may be presumed to have been after his death.*

At my first setting out in this arduous undertaking, I entertained hopes of being able to give a more correct and certain account of Mr. Caxton's works, having been informed that there were still existing complete copies of most, if not all, Caxton's books, collected and preserved by the late Mr. Chefwell, a very eminent bookseller of the last age, and that they were then in the possession of a gentleman, who, no doubt, would favour me with the perusal of them, and be glad of the opportunity of communicating materials so curious, and necessary to illustrate and authenticate the memoirs of our first printer. Without delay I waited on the gentleman, who very politely promised me the use of them, but said that they were sent over to Amsterdam, for the inspection of a friend there, but that he would write for them the first opportunity. A short time after, I took the liberty to write to him that I would with pleasure wait on him, in order to take extracts from his Caxtons, in such manner as should be most agreeable to him. In a few days I was indulged with an answer, informing me " he had received from Holland the very disagreeable intelligence, that all his fine Caxtons had met with the unfortunate accident (Heu lamentabile dictu!) *of being burnt, and totally destroyed, as he understood, by the neglect of a servant, in his master's absence, throwing down from a shelf a large bottle of aqua-fortis into the box where the said books were, and neglecting*

neglecting them in his fright, so that more mischief was done in the room." I am very much afraid my kind friend received but a Flemish account of his Caxtons.

Page 112, *l.* 6, *read* Londoniarum. *Ibid. l.* 16, *read* commonly.

Page 113, *after l.* 4, *add* The late John Baynes, Esq; of Gray's-Inn, had a copy with both his name and place, " Emp'nte p moy williã Maclyn en Holborn." *Ibid. l.* 10, *add* See p. 101.

Page 114, *after l.* 36, *add* Lyttleton's Tenures was printed by him jointly with Lettou, as p. 111; but it appears also to have been printed by Machlinia alone, and is now in the possession of Mr. Hargrave, of Boswell-court, or in Lincoln's-Inn library. *Ibid. insert* " Liber aggregationis seu liber secretorum Alberti magni de virtutibus herbarum lapidum & animalium quorumdam." This is the head-title on signature a ii, and has only a blank leaf of the same paper before it. It has neither direction-words, nor numbers to the leaves. Contains a—d 8, e 6, f 4. On the back of f ii is this colophon, " Albertus Magnus de Secretis nature Explicit Necnon per me wilhelmum de Mechlinia Jmpressus Jn opulentissima Ciuitate Londuniarũ Juxta pontem qui vulgariter dicitur Flete brigge." The two remaining leaves, or three pages (for the last is blank) consist of directions to find the changes of the moon, easter, &c. The paper-marks are the dog, the p, and the hand. Quarto. Brit. Museum, and WH. To my copy of this book is prefixed another, printed on the same types. It wants the title-leaf, but has this head-title, in ancient writing, " Albertus magnus de secretis Naturę et de miraculis Mundi." and at the end of the introduction, " Titulus. ¶ Jncipiunt Secreta mulierum & virorum ab Alberto magno composita." The text is commented on, paragraph by paragraph, but no intimation who the commentator was, unless perhaps in the title-page. Contains g 7, in eights. On the last page, " Finis huius tractatuli venerabilis Alberti magni, secreta expliciunt mulierum." It must have had another leaf, but whether blank, or not, i cannot say, knowing of no other copy. Quarto. W.H.+

Page 115, *l.* 8, *add* in the above account the statutes of Henry IV are omitted.

Page 119, *l.* 2, *for* who used it in 1518, *read* who used some Roman letter in 1509, and printed whole books with it in 1518.

Page 120, *insert* Liber sestivalis: printed in double columns. On 1493.
fol. 1, signature a ii, begins the " Prologus," of which see p. 43. " Incipit liber qui vocatur sestivalis." Contains fo. CC. " Finitum et completum in Westmonasteriũ Anno domini M.CCCC.Lxxxxiii." Over Caxton's small cypher, N° 2, See p. 236. Then follows, " Quatuor Sermones" 1494.
in double columns also, and contains fo. L. Has the small cypher, N° 2, and is dated " M.cccc.xiiii." These are in the Bodleian Libr. with this account by Mr. Hearne," Ex dono amicissimi ornatissimiq; juvenis Jacobi West è Collegio Baliolensi." Quarto.

Page 122, antepenult, *add NB.* This introductory poem was printed from Peter Treveris's edition 1527, my copy being imperfect.

Page 125, *l.* 24, *add* under it, "Meditacōns of Saynt Bernarde." *Ibid. l.* 35, *read* except y and z, which have only six leaves each.

Page 126, *l.* 1, *insert in the margin*, 1496.

Page 127, *l.* 17, *add* an edition of the Hunting only is in the Pub. Libr. Camb. Contains C 4. Quarto.

Page 128, *l.* 12, *add* These verses are not in the edition printed at St. Albans. *Ibid. l.* 15, *read* And tho ben' &c. *Ibid. l.* 18. *for* Thre, *read* There.

Page 129, *after l.* 33, *add* "¶ The companyes of bestys and foules.—¶ Explicit." This concludes the book of Hunting in the St. Alban's edition: but in this "¶ Here folowe the dewe termys to speke of brekynge or dressynge of dyuers beestys & fowles. &c. And the same is shewed of certen fysshes. &c.---Here now folowynge shall be shewed all the shyres & the byshopryches of the realme of Englonde.—Prouynces of Englonde. Caunterbury: Yorke: Stafforde: Derby: Notyngham: Northumbrelonde: Durham: Westmerlonde: Tyndale: Karlyle." Then follow the verses, as in p. 127 and 128.

Page 133, *l.* 1. *after* pages, *add* and a fresh set of signatures. *Ibid. against the last line, set in the margin*, 1498.

1498. *Page* 134, *insert* "Here begynneth the legend named in latyn legenda aurea That is to saye in Englysshe the golden legende. ffor lyke as passeth golde in value all other metallys so this legende excelleth all other bookes." This title is over a cut, as described in p. 303, which fills the remainder of the page. On the back thereof is Caxton's preface, as p. 46, &c. therefore am of opinion this is the general title, though sometimes set between the histories extracted from the Bible, and the feasts of the church, with the lives of the saints. However, the lives and histories taken out of the Bible, in all the editions, which have come to my knowledge, since that of 1483, are printed with separate folios and signatures. In this edition they occupy 52 leaves. Then, a separate leaf, with Caxton's cypher on one side, and a folio cut divided into two parts on the other, the uppermost representing the Salutation of the Virgin Mary, the undermost, the Crucifixion of our Saviour. After this, some copies have the large cut of saints, with Caxton's preface, as above. Then an alphabetical table for the feasts of the church, and the lives of the saints, the leaves of which are numbered afresh, and have fresh signatures. These conclude with "The lyf of saynt Erasmus," which ends on Folio CCClxxxxviii. "Thus endeth the legende named in latyn legenda aurea that is to say in englysshe the goldē legende. For lyke as golde passeth all other metalles/ *so this legende excelleth all other bookes.** wher in ben conteyned all the hyghe and grete festes of oure lord. The festys of oure blessyd lady/ The lyues passyōs and myracles of many other sayntes hystoryes and actes/ as all alonge here afore made mencion/ whyche werke J dyde accomplysshe and fynysshe att westmynster the viii. daye of Janeuer The

* These words in Italics are omitted in this edition.

The yere of oure lorde Thousande CCCC.lxxxxviii. And in the xiiii. yere of the reygne of kynge Henry the vii. By me wynkyn de worde." This colophon is over two cuts, one of the genealogy of the V. Mary, the other of the crucifixion. Then, on another leaf, the same two-fold cut as at the end of Judith, having on the back, "Tabula. Here foloweth a lytell Table conteynynge the lynes and hystoryes shortly taken out of the Byble. The lyf of Adam" &c. on one column. This evidently should be placed before the life of Adam. Folio. Bodleian Library, and Mr. Pitt.

Ibid. insert Missale secundum vsum Sarum. Mattaire's Index. My copy begins only on a ii: contains cclxxxvi leaves, in double columns. The last leaf printed on one column only. Colophon. "Jn laudem sanctissime trinitatis totiusq; milicie celestis ad honorē et decorē scē ecclesie. Sarū anglicane eiusq; deuotissimi cleri: hoc missale diuinorum officiorum vigilanti studio emendatum Jussu et impēsis prestantissimi viri winkin de worde. Jmpressum London. apud westmonasteriū per Julianum notarie et Johanem barbier felici numine expliciτuz est. Anno dnī. M.cccc.lxxxxviij. xx. die mensis. Decembris." On the back is Caxton's cypher, as p. 11. Folio. 1498.

WH.

Page 136, *insert* "Here begynneth a lytell treatyse or booke named Johan Maūdeuyll knyght born in Englonde in the towne of saynt Albone & speketh of the wayes of the holy londe towarde Jherusalem, & of marueyles of Ynde and of other dyuerse coūtrees." As this head-title is on signature A i and folio J, probably it had no other. This book contains 109 chapters, besides the introduction, with several ordinary wood-cuts. Contains S, in sixes. Colophon, "Emprynted at Westmynster by Wynken de worde. Anno dnī. M.CCCC.lxxxxix." On the back is Caxton's cypher, as N° 3, p. 236. John Chadwick, of Healey-Hall, Esq; About the size of a modern octavo. *Ibid. Note* r. *read* Harleianæ. 1499.

Page 144, *l.* 37, *read*, Henry the seventh.

Page 147, *insert* "The vii shedynges of the blode of Jhesu cryste." Over a cut of the crucifixion. B, in fours. "Enprynted.—M.ccccix." Quarto. *Ibid.* "Anno primo Henrici viii. Statuta." Title-page, WH. 4°. 1509.

Page 148, *l.* 35, *read* Again in 1511, and 1530. *Ibid. l. last, read* Galfridi.

Page 149, *insert* "The Justyces of peas." On a scroll over a cut of the king, sitting on a throne, &c. as p. 152-3. Contains 56 leaves. "Thus endeth the boke of Justyces of peas. Enprynted at Londō in ffletestrete at the sygne of the sonne. By Wynkyn de Worde. Jn the yere of our lorde god M.CCCCC. & X." On the back is his device N° 5. Quarto. In the Bodleian Library. *Ibid.* "Promtuarium paruulorum clericorum," &c. See p. 154. "Jmpressum—M.ccccc.x.xvii Januarii." Quarto. *Ibid. l.* 7, *read* Otterbourne. *Ibid. l.* 8, *for* 1508 *in the margin, read* 1510. *Ibid. insert* "The thre kynges of Coleyne. m.ccccc.xi." See p. 172." Device N° 5. Contains F 4. Quarto. *Ibid.* "Ortus Vocabulorum" &c. See p. 157.—" anno—1511. die vero 12 Augusti." Quarto. 1510. 1511.

Page 150, *l.* 10, *add* Again 1512, in the Bodl. Libr. Quarto. *Ibid. l.* 15, *for* Legendes of the Saynctes, *read* feestes of our lorde Jhesu cryst.

1514. *Page* 152, *insert* "Hore beate marie virginis ad vsum insignis ac preclare ecclesie Sarum." Device N° 7. Under "God be in my ehed," &c.

1514. as p. 165. At the end, 24 July, 1514. Long twelves. *Ibid.* "The deyenge creature." C 4, in sixes. 1514. See p. 145. *Ibid. l.* 26, *add* See Warton's Hist. of Eng. Poetry, II; 167.

1515. *Page* 153, *l.* 16, *read* florẽs. *Ibid. after l.* 22, *insert* "Alberti liber Modorum significandi.—1515." Quarto. Catal. Bibl. Harleianæ, N° 5352. *Ibid. l.* 26, *set in the margin*, 1516.

Page 154, *after l.* 12, *add* I since find Pynson used Roman Letter, with ȩ, æ, œ, in 1509, to Sermo Fratris Hieron. de Ferrara; also to The Ship of Fools, the same year. *Ibid. l.* 33, *after* comment, *add* Michael Wodhull, Esq.

1517. *Page* 155, *insert* "The noble and amerous aũcyent hystory of Troylus and Cresyde in the tyme of the syege of Troye. Compyled by Geffraye Chaucer." Over a cut of them at full length. There are cuts to each part; the title to the 5th part is over two cuts, 1. Two gentlemen riding on horseback. 2. A gentleman and two ladies on horseback also: the ladies ride sideways; one to the right, the other to the left. Contains Z, In eights. Colophon,

"Thus endeth the treatyse of Troylus the heuy
By Geffraye Chaucer/ compyled and done
He prayenge the reders/ this mater not deny
Newly correcked/ in the cyte of London
Jn Flete strete/ at the sygne of the sonne
Jnprynted by me/ wynkyn de worde
The. M.CCCCC. and. xvii. yere of our lorde."

On the last leaf is the same cut as on the title-page; on the back, his device N° 5. Quarto. Public Library, Cambridge.

1517. *Page* 155, *insert* "The remedy ayenst the troubles of temptacyons." With cuts."—M.CCCCC. and xvii." Device N° 5. Quarto.

Page 157, *l.* 29, *read* mensam, *and after* Sulpitii *add* Verulani. *Ibid.*

1518. *insert*, Multorum vocabulorũ, &c. 1518. *See p.* 142. WH. Quarto.

Page 158, *l.* 4, *read* Breuiloco. *Ibid. l.* 8, *insert* die vero *before* xxii. *Ibid. l.* 14, *after* in *insert* 1509; *and for* 1517 *read* 1511.

Page 171, *l.* 6, *for* Monmouthshire, *read* Brecknockshire.

1528. *Page* 177, *l.* 1, *set in the margin* 1528. *Ibid. l.* 9, *insert* Colophon: "Thus endeth the dystruccyon and vengeaunce of Iherusalem by Vaspazyan Emperour of Rome. Imprynted at Lõdon in the Fletestrete at the sygne of the Sonne by Wynkyn de Worde. Anno a partu virgineo M.D.XXVIII. die vero XXIII. Mensis Januarii." George Steevens, Esq; *Ibid. l.* 29, *after* Times. *insert* With cuts. *Ibid. l.* 32, 33, *dele* They are all embellished with wooden cuts, different from one another, but this last edition has most.

Page 179, *l.* 28, *read* appellatiuorum.

Page 181, *insert* "The assemble of foules." This title is on a ribbon, 1530.
under which "Here soloweth the Assemble of foules veray pleasaunt and compendyous to rede or here compyled by the preclared and famous Clerke Geffray Chaucer." Below this is a cut representing a student in his library, in a musing posture, his head resting on his hand. On the back is an address, by "Roberte Coplande boke prynter to new fanglers." This is in 4 octave stanzas, the first of which i shall transcribe, for the reader's amusement.

"¶ Newes/ newes/ newes/ haue ye ony newes
Myne eres ake/ to here you call and crye
Ben. bokes made with whystelynge and whews
Ben there not yet ynow to your fantasye
In sayth nay I trowe and yet haue ye dayly
Of maters sadde/ and eke of apes and oules
But yet for your pleasure/ thus moche do wyll I
As to lette you here the parlament of foules."

The poem, in stanzas of seven lines, then begins; and may be seen in any edition of Chaucer's works. At the end: "Thus endeth the congregacion of foules on saynt Valentynes day." After this follows the "Lenuoy of R. Coplande boke prynter." In three stanzas; concluding,

"And yf a loueuer happen on the to rede
Let be the goos with his lewde sentence
Vnto the turtle and not to her to take hede
For who so chaungeth/ true loue dothe offence
Loue as I rede is floure of excellence
And loue also is rote of wretchednesse
Thus be two louey scripture bereth witnesse. finis.

Imprynted in london in flete strete at the sygne of the Sonne agaynste the condyte/ by me Wynkyn de Worde. The 24 day of January/ in the yere of our lorde 1530." The type is very beautiful, much like to the Polychronicon, 1494; and is exceeding scarce. Folio. In the possession of Dr. John Billam, in Leeds. *Ibid.* "¶ Here foloweth a compen- 1530.
dyous story/ & it is called the example of vertu/ in the whiche ye shall fynde many goodly storys & naturall dysputacyons bytwene foure ladyes named Hardynes/ Sapyence/ Fortune/ and Nature. Compyled by Stephen Hawys one of ẏ gromes of the most honorable chambre of oure souerayne lorde kynge Henry the. vij. And prynted. xx. day of Apryll. Anno dnī. M.ccccc.xxx." This title is over a cut of Justice hearing the disputation of the four ladies: one listening behind. Contains A 6, B 4, C 6, D 4, E 6, F 4, G 8; with wood cuts. "Here endeth the example of vertue Imprynted: at London in Flete strete at the sygne of the sonne by me Wynkyn de worde. Anno dnī M.ccccc.xxx." Device N° 6. Quarto. George Mason, Esq. *Ibid. l.* 18, *for* vrbum *read* vrbem. *Ibid. l.* 20, *for* 121, *read* 117. *Ibid. l.* 25, *for* Alwater, *read* Atwater.

Page

1532. *Page* 184, *insert* " Guystarde and Sygysmonde. ¶ Here foloweth the amerous hystory of Guystarde and Sygusmonde, and of theyr dolorous deth by her father, newly trãslated out of laten into englysshe by wyllym Walter seruaunt to syr Henry Marney knyght chaunceler of ỹ duchy of Lancastre." This title is over a cut of Sygysmonde kneeling at the feet of a bed; a heart in a cup standing on a table before her; two maidens standing by her, one of them weeping. " Jmprynted—M.CCCCCxxxij." Over the same cut as on the title-page. His device N° 5. Quarto.

Page 185, *l.* 38, *read* the first five verses of the epilogue, *&c.*

Page 186, *l.* 20, *and elsewhere*, *read* picturesque.

Page 188, *l.* 4, *for* All *read* On. *Ibid. l.* 20, *dele* In the collection of George Mason, Esq;

1534. *Page* 189, *l.* 30, *for* M.D.XXIIIJ *read* M.D.XXXIIIJ. *Ibid. insert* " Whitintoni De Syntaxi, siue Constructione, opusculum." &c. 1534. Quarto.

1535. *Page* 190, *l.* 3, *for* MDXXXIII *read* M.D.XXXIIII. *Ibid. insert* " AESOPI PHRYGIS ET VITA Ex maximo Planude desumpta & fabellæ iucundissimæ: quarũ interpretes hi sunt. Guilielmus Gondanus. Hadrianus Barlandus. Erasmus Roterodamus. Aulus Gellius. Laurentius Valla. Angelus Politianus. Petrus Crinitus. Ioãnes Antonius Campanus. Plinius secũdus Nouocãnẽsis. Anianus. Guilielmus Hermanus. Nicolaus Gerbellius Phorcensis. Laurentius Abstemius Rimicius. Index omnes fabulas indicabit. Addite sunt his quædam iucũdæ ac honestæ, selecte ex omnibus facetijs Pogij Florentini, oratoris eloquentiss." Device N° 4. The life of Æsop begins on the back of the title-page. Contains M 4, in eights, besides the life and index. Colophon: " Londonij, Apud VVinandum de VVorde. Anno M.D.XXXV." On the back of the last leaf is his picturesque device. The whole printed on Italic types. Octavo. Francis Douce, Esq;

Page 192, *l.* 21, *for* black *read* blank.

Page 194, *l.* 33, *dele* pro.

Page 195, *after l.* 28, *add* Another edition without date is in the Public Library, Cambridge, with this colophon, " Here endeth the temple of Glas Enprynted in London in Flete strete in the sygne of the sonne by Wynkin de Worde." On the back is his device, N° 5. *Ibid. l.* 30. *for* Wharton's, *read* Warton's. *Ibid. Note* 2, *for* Pit's, *read* Pitsei.

Page 197, *l.* 17, *for* reum, *read* rerum. *Ibid. l.* 19, *dele* Caxton's original cypher, *and insert, instead thereof*, some verses, in stanzas of four lines. *Ibid. l.* 20, *after* page, *add* having at the head thereof, " Liber Primus. In noĩe patris & filii & spũssãcti. ã. Assit principio sancta maria meo."

Page 198, *l.* 28, *for* has, *read* as. *Ibid. l.* 32, *read* dyspendynge.

Page 200, *l.* 4, 5, 6, *dele* and here again is room enough for a colophon, on occasion. Doubtless there was another leaf; blank or not, is the question? *Instead thereof insert* On the last leaf is Caxton's cypher, and on the back page the title as at the beginning. *Ibid. l.* 9, *read* 00,6. Francis Douce, Esq; and. *Ibid. l.* 12, *after* of, *insert* its. *Ibid. l.* 21, *dele* the.

Page 205, *l.* 10, *read* in a somewhat larger form. *Ibid. l.* 39, *for* Wharton, *read* Warton.

Page

Page 206, *l.* 2, *after* Copland *add.* It was printed alſo by one Johan Nychol, without date. *Ibid. l.* 36, *after* Mr. Alchorne, *add* Another edition, without date, in the Bodl. Libr. which ends at the very bottom of the laſt page of A 8, " Amen. Explicit." *Ibid. for* Again *read* Alſo.

Page 208, *l.* 18, *read* Rhymes. *Ibid. l.* 24, *read* cõplaynt. *Ibid. l.* 25, *read* lokynge. *Ibid. l.* 27 *read* follows.

Page 211, *l.* 29, *read* (a thouſand four hundred fourſcore and twelve.

Page 216, *l.* 8, *read* emboſſed. *Ibid. l.* 10, *add* Another edition, with " Vulgaria ſtābrigr." in white letters on a black ground, over the cut of a ſchoolmaſter, &c. as p. 142. C, in fixes. " Enprynted at London in Fleteſtrete by Wynkyn de Worde at the ſygne of the ſonne." Without date. Device N° 5. Quarto. WH. I have another edition without date alſo, having " Vulgaria Stanbrigi" on a riband, and at the end, " Jmprynted at London" &c. In other reſpects like the forementioned. *Ibid. dele* all *l.* 11, *and inſtead thereof inſert* " Here begynneth a lytel treatyſe called the cõtrauerſe bytwene a louer and a Jaye lately compyled." In Skeltonic verſe. " Thus endeth the treatyſe of the louer and a Jaye/ lately compyled by me Thomas Feylde. Jmprynted," &c. Without date. *Ibid. l.* 26, *after* louers. *dele the reſt of that line, and add* " Here after foloweth a lytell contrauers dyalogue bytwene loue and councell/ with many goodly argumentes of good women and bad/ very compendyous to all eſtates/ newly compyled by Wyllyam Walter ſeruaunt vnto ſyr Henry Marnaye knyght Chauncelour of the Duchye of Lancaſtre." This title is over two cuts, of " Councell," and " Love." D, in fours. The whole concludes with a " Lenuoy of Robert Coplande.—Jmprynted at London" &c. Without date. *Ibid. l.* 28, 29, *read* " Here begynneth ẏ hyſtory of Tytus & Geſyppus tranſlated out of latyn in to englyſſhe by Wyllyam Walter," &c. as above. Over three cuts repreſenting " Tytus, Sophrone, *and* Geſyppus." The poem, in ſtanzas of ſeven lines, begins under thoſe cuts. A 6, B 4, C 6. With two cuts. " Thus endeth the frendly hyſtory of Tytus & Geſyppus. Enprynted at London" &c. Without date.

Page 218, *l.* 12, *for* xiii. *read* xiiii. *Ibid. l.* 13, *after* ſeptimi, *read* xi.^{m}. *Ibid. l.* 25, *read* hypotheſis.

Page 219, *l.* 5, *read* venerādi.

Page 221, *l.* 13, *read* begins. *Ibid. l.* 40, *read* inheritors,' *Ibid. l.* 41, *read* doomed.

Page 224, *after l.* 23, *add* Another edition, with the ſame title, on a ſcroll over the king's arms, is in the Bodleian Library. Quarto. *Ibid. inſert* " Modus tenend. Cur. Baron. cum viſu franc. plegii." Under this title is the king's arms ſupported by a dragon or Wivern, and a greyhound. Contains 14 leaves. Device, N° 5. Bodleian Library. Quarto. *Ibid.* A volume of law tracts, as in p. 344, and in the ſame order. Quarto. Bodleian Library.

Page 227, *l.* 11, *and elſewhere, for* foilage, *read* foliage. *Ibid. read* begins on the back thus:"

Page 230, *l.* 15, *read* that thou mayſt vp aſcende *&c.*

Page

Page 231, *l.* 9 *and* 10, *read* fagittary. *See p.* 237, Nº 8. *Ibid. l.* 25, *read* p. 233.

Page 234, *note b, col.* 2, *l.* 6, *after* See, *read* Ames's General History.

Page 236, *l.* 42, *and elsewhere, for* blafing, *read* blazing.

The following articles, printed by Wynken de Worde, came to hand too late to appear under his name. I give them here together, as they are without date, that the reader may insert them to his own pleasure.

—— " Here begynneth a boke of a Ghoostly fader/ that confesseth his Ghoostly chylde/ the whiche speketh fyrst of the. vii. deedly fynnes/ and after of the cyrcumstaunce that to them belongeth.——Thus endeth this profytable cõfessyon. Jmprynted at London" &c. Quarto.

—— " The castell of pleasure," On a riband, over a cut of a man, a woman, and a castle; with labels, " Desyre, Beaute, Pleasure." Beneath the cut, " The conueyaunce of a dreme how Desyre went to the castell of pleasure/ wherein was the gardyn of affeccyon, inhabyted by Beaute, to whom he amerously expressed his loue: vpon the which supplycacyon rose grete stryfe, dyspútacyon/ and argument betwene Pyte and Dysdayne. On the back begins a prologue, by " Copland the prynter to the author." At the end of the poem he addresses the author again, and concludes with " En passant le temps sans mal pencer. Quod Coplande. Enprynted at London" &c. Quarto.

—— " The Cõplaynte of a louers lyfe." On a riband, over a cut of an old man and a youth, with a tree between them. Begins,

" In maye whan flora the fresh lusty quene" &c.

In stanzas of seven lines. " Jmprynted at London" &c. Quarto.

—— " R. Whitinton De nominibus & epithetis Deorum, &c." Quarto.

—— " The Complaynt of the soule." On a riband, over a cut representing the separation of the soul from the body, as described in p. 143, &c. It begins on the back, with this head-title, " Here begynneth a lamentable complaynt that ỳ soule maketh of the wrethed lyfe of the body." On 14 leaves. " Here ende a lamentable complaynt—of ỳ wretched lyfe of the body. Emprynted at London" &c. Device Nº. 6. Quarto. WH.

—— " The vertue of ỳ masse." This title is over the cut of a priest, with attendants, holding up a wafer at the altar. In the octave stanza. A 8, B 4. " Here endeth the vertues of the masse. Jmprynted at London, by w. de worde." Quarto.

—— " The example of Euyll Tongues." In stanzas of seven lines. On four leaves, with the frontispiece. Quarto. Duke of Roxborough.

Page 237, *l.* 3, *after* centre, *add* supposed to be two roses on a stalk, for York and Lancaster. *Ibid. for* foilage, *read* 5 single leaves.

Page 240, *l.* 28, *read* it might not be, &c.

Page 248, *l.* 20, *for* 1449, *in the margin, insert* 1499.

Page 249, *l.* 1, *set in the margin* 1500. *Ibid. insert*, Joh. de Garlandia Equivoca. 1500. Quarto. *Ibid. insert*, " ¶ This is the boke of Cokery. ¶ Here beginneth a noble boke of festes royalle and Cokery a boke for a pryncis housholde or any other estates: and the makyage therof accord-

ynge

ynge as ye shall fynde more playnly within this boke. The feste of kynge Harry the fourth to the Henawdes and Frenchemen whan they hadde Iusted in Smythefelde.---The feste of the coronacyon of kyng Hearry the fyste. —-The fest of the Erle of Huntynton at Caleys.—-The erle of warwykes feste vnto the kynge at London.—-The stallacion of Clyfforde bysshop of london.---The fest of my lorde chaunceler archebysshop of yorke at his stallacion in yorke: the yere of our lorde. M.CCCC.lxv." After reciting the particulars of the three courses of this, as well as to the five preceding feasts, some other services are added, but without naming the occasion. "Here endeth the festes roiall of the kinge/ and other noble estates. ¶ And here begynneth the Calender of Cokery.—Here endeth the kalender of the boke of Cokery: And here begynneth the makynge." K 8, the rest in sixes. "¶ Here endeth a noble boke of the festes Ryall, and the boke of cokery for a pryncys housholde or euerye other estates housholde, as ye maye fynde in the chapytres & in the makynge accordynge. Emprynted without temple barre by charde Pynson in the yere of our lorde M.D." On the last leaf is his device, N° 4. Quarto. This scarce and very curious book was in the possession of the late dutchess dowager of Portland. The king's arms stampt on the covers.

"Here begynneth the Egloges of Alexāder Barclay prest, wherof the fyrst thre conteyneth the myseryes of courters and courtes of all prynces in generally The matter wherof was translated into Englyshe by the sayd Alexander in fourme of Dialogues/ out of a boke named in latyn Miserie curialiū/ compyled by Eneas Siluius Poete and oratour/ whiche after was Pope of Rome/ & named Pius." This title is over a cut of two shepherds, Coridon and Cornix, the interlocutors in these three eclogues. On the back is a cut of David and Bathsheba. Contains P 6, in fours; the last leaf blank. "Thus endyth the thyrde and last egloge of the mysery of court and courters/ Composed by Alexander Barclay preste in his youthe:" A cut of the two shepherds and a courtier fills the page. Without date, printer's name, or device. The fourth eclogue, which follows in my copy, is printed by R. Pynson. Whether W. de Worde printed a fourth, as he did the fifth, and who printed these first three, is at present uncertain. See p. 1783.

"The fyfte Eglog of Alexandre Barclay of the Cytezen and vplondysshman." This title is over the cut of a priest sitting in his study, &c. as p. 109. Under it, "Here after foloweth the Prologe." On the back of A.ii are the cuts of two shepherds, whole lengths, with "Interlocutoures be Amyntas and Faustus," over them. A 8, B 4, C 6. "Here endeth the. v. Eglog of Alexandre Barclay of the Cytezyn/ and vplondysshman/ Jmprynted at London in flete strete/ at the sygne of the sonne/ by Wynkyn de worde." His device N° 5. fills the page. W.H. Quarto.

Page 251, *l.* 6, *after* Jmprynted, *dele the rest of the article, and instead thereof insert*, at London in Fletestrete at the Sygne of the George by Rycharde Pynson, prynter vnto the Kyngis noble grace. And this boke made fynysshed the yere of our lord a. M.CCCCC. and. viij. the v daye of December." His device N° 4. *Ibid. l.* 32, *read* superadditis.

Page 254, *after l.* 15, *add* The Latin of this book is printed on Roman letter, with ƿ, æ, œ; the first perhaps used in this kingdom. *Ibid. insert* Ser-
1509. mo Fratris Hieron. de Ferraria. 1509. In Roman letter, with diphthongs also. *Ibid. l* 26, *read* euadant. *Ibid. l.* 27, *read* sepe vsiuenire.

1511. *Page* 256, *insert* "The chirche of euyl men and women/ wherof Lucyfer is the head/ and the members is all players dyssolute and synners reproued." Over a cut of our Saviour holding a cross within his right arm, and a spear within his left. G 1, in eights. This present treatye hathe made to be pryuted two venerable doctours of the facultie of theologye at Parys mayster thomas Varnet curate of saynt Nycolas of the feldes/ and mayster Nowell beda pryncypall of the ruled college of Moutagu The yere of our lorde. M.CCCCC.xj. the xxij. daye of Auguste." No printer's name, nor device. On the last page is a cut of our dead Lord on the Virgin's lap, as p. 276. See Oldys's Pamphlets, N° 139. Quarto.

Page 259, *l.* 25, *dele* all before the prologue, *and insert* only the title-leaf *in its stead.*

1518. *Page* 264, *l.* 25, *after* England, *add* This is the earliest book i have observed to be printed with Cum privilegio, &c. *Ibid. insert* "Roberti Whittyntoni—Editio de concinnitate grammatices & constructione. 1518. WH. Quarto.

1520. *Page* 266, *l. ult. for* ex *read* et. *Ibid. insert* "Whittintoni editio secunda Opusculum affabre recognitum et ad vnguem elimatum: De nominum generibus." &c. as p. 164. W.H. Quarto.

1521. *Page* 268, *insert* "Rob. Whitintoni Epistola respondens ad G. Hormani invectivas, & Dialogus cum eodem. 1521." Catal. Bodl. II, 680. 4°.

Page 270, *l.* 10, *after* 1502 *add* inadvertently omitted there as here proposed, but inserted in p. 1746. *Ibid. l.* 12, *after* account *add* omitted likewise under his name, but will be inserted in this appendix, under the omissions in p. 1442. *Ibid. insert* The admission of Edmund Husse into
1522. St. Mary's gild Boston, Lincolnshire. With an indulgence to him. See p. 310: also Brit. Topogr. I, 536.

Page 271, *to l.* 22, *add* Also without date. *Ibid. l.* 26, *for* p. 72, *read* p. 172. *Ibid. l.* 34, *add* Also without date.

Page 272, *l.* 20, *read* Mutius. *Ibid. l.* 27, *read* siue. *Ibid. dele the whole title of the first volume of Syr John Frayssart, on this page, taken from Mr. Beauclerk's copy, which I since find was supplied from W. Middleton's edition; and insert instead thereof,* "Here begynneth the first volum of sir Johan Froyssart: of the cronycles of Englande/ Fraunce/ Spayne/ Portyngale/ Scotlande/ Bretayne, Flaūders: and other places adioynynge. Trāslated out of frenche into our maternall englysshe tonge/ by Johan Bourchier knight lorde Berners: At the cōmaundement of oure moost highe redouted souerayne lorde kyng Henry the viii. kyng of Englande, and of Fraunce/ & highe defender of the christen faythe. &c." This title is enclosed with a border of metal types, and that within four odd pieces; on that at the bottom is a cross floree patent.

Page 273, *l.* 2, *read* chronycle, &c. *Ibid, l.* 8, *after* M.D.xxiii. *add* Cum priuilegio a rege indulto. George Mason Esq; a fine copy.

Page

Page 275, *l.* 19, *read* Porſenna. *Ibid. l.* 22, *dele* The whych two bokes, *with the remainder of that colophon, and insert instead thereof* " The whiche two bokes be cōpyled into one volume/ & ſynyſſhed in the ſayd towne of Calais the. x. day of Marche/ in the. xvi. yere of our ſaid ſoueravne lordes raigne. Imprinted at London in Fleteſtrete by Rycharde Pynſon/ printer to the kynges mooſt noble grace And ended the laſt day of Auguſt: the yere of our lorde god. M.D.XXV.[a] Cum priuilegio a rege indulto." On the back of the laſt leaf is the ſame coat of arms as at the end of the firſt volume. George Maſon Eſq; a fine copy. W.H.

Page 281, *after l.* 3, *insert* ¶ Natura breuiū/ &c. A ſubſequent edition to that in p. 280, having the table at the end in alphabetical order; whereas that is progreſſive: beſides, the additions noted in the table of that are inſerted in the text of this. Contains Fo. CC.XX. " Londini in edibus—M.D.XXVIIJ. Cum priuilegio," &c. Device N°. 2. as p. 242. W.H. Sixteens. 1528.

Page 285, *l.* 1, *after* leaf, *add* A, 8. *Ibid. l.* 21, 22, *read* The Shepheid's Kalendar appears from the laſt edition of it in 1656 to have been printed by him. *Ibid. l.* 23, *after* charges *add* of.

Page 287, *l.* 1, *read* ſuperciliouſly, *and after* caught *add* &c. *Ibid. l.* 28, *read* Cryſt.

Page 288, *after l.* 15, *insert* " Expoſitio. ſequentiarū ſcd'm vſum Sarum." Quarto.

Page 290, *l.* 10, *read* were received.

Page 291, *l.* 17, *after* dinner[b] *insert this note. Ibid. l.* 26, *for* matto *read* motto.

Page 293, *insert* " Here begynneth the Egloges of Alexāder Barclay preſt" &c. as p. 1781. Theſe firſt three being without date, printer's name or device, it does not appear quite clear to me whether they were printed by W. de Worde, or Pinſon; the fourth however was printed by him, and is entitled " ¶ The boke of Codrus and Mynaclus." Over the cut of a prieſt with a ſhaven crown, writing at a plutus; perhaps deſigned for the author. Contains 22 leaves with cuts. At the end, " Thus endeth the fourthe Eglogge of Alexandre Barcley, cōteyning the maner of the riche men anenſt poets and other clerkes. Emprinted by Richarde Pynſon prīter to the kynges noble grace." On the laſt leaf is

 his

[a] I have ſeen a copy with the date M.D.XXIII. agreeing with this of Mr. Maſon's, excepting the laſt leaf, which ſeems to have been recently reprinted.

I had alſo in my poſſeſſion an edition of W. Middleton's, the two laſt ſheets of which were ſupplied from another edition of Pinſon's, bearing his name, however, from which I copied in p. 275 of my firſt volume. The difference between that and Mr. Maſon's copy is as follows: The colophon of that edition is printed with types of the ſame ſize as the chronicle, and the lines diminiſh gradually to the date, in a line by itſelf, and the back page blank; whereas, in Mr. Maſon's copy the types are larger than thoſe of the chronicle, the lines are of equal length, and it has Pinſon's arms on the back page.

[b] A letter from H. VII. to the lord mayor and aldermen of the citie of London to make bonfires, &c. is in the Cotton Libr. See British Topography, I; 684.

his device N°. 5. Quarto. The 5th Eclogue was printed by W. de Worde. See p.1781.

— *Page* 296, *insert* " Here begynneth a lyttell treatyse cleped La conusaunce damours.—Thus endeth la conusaunce damours. Jmprinted by Rycharde Pynson, printer to the Kynges noble grace." Quarto.

Page 301, *insert these year-books*; " 27 Hen. VI.—prynter vnto the Kynges noble grace.---28 Hen. VI.—prenter vnto the Kyngis noble grace.---2 Edw. IV. sed'm Townsendis de nouo impressus in academia/ etc ac impensis honesti viri Richardi Pynsonis Regii īpressoris.---4 Edw. IV.—prynter to the Kyngs noble grace." Publ. Libr. Cambr. All in Quarto.

1498. *Page* 303, *l.* 78, *after* per *read* " Julianum notarie et Johannem barbier. M.cccc.lxxxxviij." *Dele* Probably in France, *and insert* See p. 1775.

Page 305, *insert* " Manipulus curatorum." This title is over a cut of the crucifixion, with the V. Mary and St. John. Colophon: " Cele-
1508. berimi viri dnī &c. as *l.* 27, 28. *After* feliciter *add* " Jmpressum per
egregium Julianum Notarium Jmpressorem commorātem extra temple barre sub Jntersignio sanctorum trium regum.—Anno domini milesimo. CCCCC. Octavo. xii. die Augusti." On the back, his small device. *After* 133 leaves, *add* besides the table at the end. W.H.

— *Page* 307, *insert* " The loue and complayntes bytwene Mars and Venus.—Explicit the compleyntes of Maris and Venus/ and of the broche of Thebes.—Here foloweth the coūceyll of Chaucer touchyng Maryag &c. whiche was sente te Bucketon &c.—Explicit.—The fyrst fynders of the vii. scyences artyficyall.—Amen. Thys in pryntyde in westmoster inkyng. strete. For me Julianus Notarii." Quarto.

Page 309, *l.* 9, *insert* Now (1789) in that of Francis Douce Esq; *Ib. l.* 10, *read* Statuta, *and set in the margin* 1504.

1527. *Page* 316, *l.* 1, *read* Scala, *correct also the catchword preceding. Ib. insert* " Horæ beatissimæ virginis Mariæ in verum vsum Sarum.—venun-
— dantur Londini apud cœmeterium S. Pauli. 1527." Quarto. *Ib.* " Le-
gēda maior beatissimi patris francisci a sancto Bonauentura suauissimo & religionis pietatem redolēte stilo cōposita." &c. A small neat wood-cut of St. Francis on his knees; our saviour on the cross in vision before him. " Venunditur vbi impressa est parisiis—& Londonijs in cœmeterio sancti Pauli sub signo sanctissime Trinitatis." At the end, " Bulla de stigmatibus Sācti francisci.—Datū Anagnie. vi. nonas octobris Pontificatus nostri (*Alexandri*) Anno primo. Bulla habetur in conuentu fratrum minorum parisiis.—¶ Jmpressū Parisiis opera Johīs barbier īpressoris necnō alme vniuersitatis bibliopole iurati." M 4, in eights. Francis Douce Esq; Sixteens.

Page 317, *l.* 10, *read* though mostly without date. *Ibid, l.* 11, *add* In 1555 &c. he printed at St. Andrews in Scotland.

— *Page* 318, *l. ult. read* " Here begynneth Nychodemus Gospell. Imprinted at London in saynt Leonardes Paryshe in Foster Lane by me John Skot."

Skot." *Ibid. insert The* Batayll of Eaynge courte, and the great sege of Rone." Quarto. Mr. J. Ritson. *Dele the same in p.* 892.

Page 319, *insert* "An Epistell of the famous doctor Erasm' of Roter-(1522.) dame/ vnto the reuerende father & excellent prince/ Christofer bysshop of Basyle/ cōcerning the forbedynge of eatynge of flesshe/ and lyke constitutyons of men. &c." In a compartment with Pinson's cypher at the bottom. R, in fours. Dated, "At Basyle on Ester monday/ The yere of our lorde god. M.CCCCC.xx.ii. Printed at London by—. Cū priuilegio regali." W.H. Sixteens.

Page 325, *insert* "A dyalogue bitwene the playntife and the Defendaunt. Compyled by Wylliam Caluerly/ whyles he was prisoner in the towre of London." On signature a ii "¶ To the kynges highnesse." In 6 octave stanzas. "¶ Thus endeth the supplication/" &c. The dialogue is in stanzas of 7 lines. C, in fours. Quarto. *Ibid.* "A treatise Against the possessions of the clergye, geddered and compyled by Jasper Fyloll.—Cum priuilegio regali." Octavo. *Ibid.* Enormytees vsed by ŷ Clergy, and specially agaynst ŷ Heresy of Simony vsyd by the Clergy. Impress.—cum priuilegio Regali." Octavo. —

Page 343, *l.* 19, *read* the bewte and good propertes of Women.

Page 346, *insert* "Here begynneth the introductory to write/ and to 1521. pronounce Frenche compyled by Alexander Barcley compendiously at the commaūdemēt of the ryght hye excellent and myghty prynce Thomas duke of Northfolke." On the last leaf, "Here foloweth the maner of dauncynge of base daūces after the vse of fraunce & other places translated out of frenche in englysshe by Robert coplande." C 4, in sixes. Jmprynted—M.CCCCC.xxi. ŷ xxii. day of Marche." W.H. Folio.

Page 353, *l.* 3, *read* Stationers. *Ibid, l.* 24, *read* Coplands. *Ibid. l.* 33, *dele* rose. *Ibid, l.* 34, *read* Rose Garland.

Page 358, *insert* "A Chronicle of yeres, from the begynnynge of the 1557. worlde—vnto the yere of our lorde M.D.lvii.—Imprinted at London in Fletestreate, at the—Rose Garlande," &c. Dr. Monro. Thirty-twos.

Page 366, *l. penult. after* Lidgate. *add* "Imprinted in Lothburi ouer against Sainct Margarytes church by me Wyllyam Copland."

Page 367, *insert* "The Hystorie of the mouste noble and worthy — Prynce Kynge Arthur, sometyme Kynge of great Brytayne now called Englande," &c. Folio. See Bibl. Westiana, N°. 2483. *Ibid.* "The Enterlude of youth." On 12 leaues. "Jmprented at London in Lothbury," &c. Quarto. *Ibid.* "Syr Tryamoure." F2, in fours. "Jmprinted—in Lothburye" &c. Quarto.

Page 374, *l. ult. for* 1542, *read* 1545.

Page 384, *insert* "This Boke is named the beaulte of women, trans- — lated out of Frenche into Englysshe.- Imprynted—in saint Martyns parysshe/ at the—faynt John Euāgelyst besyde charynge crose." Quarto. *Ibid.* "The Cessyōs of Parlyamēt of the imperyall Realme of Englande, And the assemblaunce of the same." Sixteens. *Ibid.* "As Jheronimus sheweth Jn this begynnynge, so wyll J wryte of the. iiij. Tokens, the whiche

whiche shall be shewed afore the dredefull daye of Dome, of our lorde Jhesu Criste. For there shall we shewe our self yonge and olde, &c." B, in fours. Colophon: "This translated out of Duche into Englysshe by John Doesbrugh. Jmprinted by me Robert Wyer." Sixteens.

1518. *Page* 378, *insert* "Olde teners newly corrected." B 7, in eights. 32°. *Ibid.* "The diversity of Courts." C 7, in eights. "¶ Expliciūt Diu'sitates curiarū cū iurisdictionib' earundem *&c.* Londini in edibus—— M.ccccc.xxviii. Cum gratia & priuilegio." 32°. *Ibid.* "Magna Carta in

1529. Fr. whereunto is added more Statutis than euer was imprynted in any one Boke before this tyme, with an Almanacke, *&c.* 1529." Sixteens.

1532. *Page* 390, *insert* The olde Tenures. 1532. B. in eights. WH. 32°.

1540. *Page* 397, *insert* "A commentary in Englysshe vpon Sayncte Paules Epystle to the Ephesyans. 1540." WH. 8°. *Ibid.* "The Natura Breuium, newly corrected in Englysshe: with dyuers addycyons of statutes, *&c.* 1540." *Ibid.* "The treasure of the Pore men. 1540." 16°. *Ibid.* The Bible in 5 parts, or volumes. 1540. 16°. *Ibid.* "This is the

—— Myrrour, or Glasse of Helth." 16°. *Ibid.* "Here folowith the Interpretaciō of goddes and goddesses, as is rehersed in this treatyse folowynge as Poetes wryte." With wood-cuts at the beginning and end. "Here endeth a lytyll treatyse namede the assemble of goddes and goddesses. Imprynted at London in Fletestrete by me Robert Redman." See p. 201.

—— *Page* 399, *l.* 7, *after* 387, *add* The title is set in the form of an hour-glass. *Ibid, after l.* 12, *insert* "¶ The boke of Justices of peas:— nouiter impressa et emendata." 16°. *Ibid.* "Lytylton tenures newly imprinted." On Roman types. Thirty-twos.

1526. *Page* 405, *insert under Richard Banks,* "Here begynneth a newe mater, ẏ whiche sheweth and treateth of the vertues and properetes of herbes" &c. J, in fours. "Jmprynted by me—a lytell from ẏ Stockes, in ẏ Pultry—M.CCCCC. &. xxvi." Quarto.

—— *Page* 411, *insert* "Here begynneth a newe boke of medecynes intituled or callyd the Treasure of pore men," &c. M. in fours. "Jmprynted—in the pultre at the longe shoppe by saynt Myldredys churche dore—Cum priuilegio." Quarto.

Page 413, *add to Laurence Andrewe* I have a fragment of Æsop's fables, bound with his Myrrour of the world, which seems to have been printed also by him.

Page 415, *l.* 2, *read* eclipses. *Ibid. l.* 17, *after* 1542 *add* on the sell. *Ibid, l.* 26, *read* prefixes.

Page 418, *l.* 11, *add* Again 1531. Michael Wodhull Esq; *Ibid, l.* 18, *add* In officina——

1533. *Page* 423, *insert* "Pasquil the playne" &c. as p. 435. "Anno 1533." Octavo. Francis Douce Esq.

1534. *Page* 425, *l.* 13, *add parentheses to the marginal date. Ibid. insert* "Psalmorum omnium juxta Hebraicam veritatem paraphrastica interpretatio authore Joanne Campensi: *&c.* Accessit Athanasius ad Marcellinum in in librum Psalmorum Capnione interprete. Paraphrasis in Concionem Salomonis Ecclesiaste succinctissima: *&c.* per eundem Joannem Campensem. Paris per Franciscum Regnault Expencis honestissimi viri Thome Bertheleti Londoniensi tipographii regii Anno 1534." 4°. See an English translation, p. 1545. *Ibid.* Diversite of Courtes, *&c.* 1535. 16. 1535.

Page 428, *insert* "Modus tenendi Curiam Baronis, *&c.* 1536." This is 1536. joined by signatures with "The Boke for a Justice of Peace" &c. in p. 425.

Page 431, *l.* 36, *insert* church of *before* England. *Ibid. insert* Olde 1538. tenures.—1538. 8°. *Ibid.* Articuli ad Narrationes—1538. Octavo.

Page 435, *l.* 16, *for* 1539 *in the margin set* 1540.

Page 441, *insert* The Castel of Helth, corrected and in some places 1541. augmented, by the first author therof, sir Thomas Elyot knight the yere of our lord 1541." In the compartment frequently used by him, having 1534 cut on its sill. Contains 90 leaves. Michael Wodhull Esq; 16°. *I have an edition having also* corrected &c. 1541, *printed by T. Powell, but without date of printing. See p.* 875. *I have also an edition in* 4°. *alike circumstanced; yet as the title is printed in the same compartment as the edition* 1539, *it probably was printed soon after it was corrected: is without the dedication, but has the arms at the end of the table; and contains* 94 *leaves, besides the prefixes.* "Londini in ædibus Thomæ Bertheleti typis impress. Cum privilegio—solum." *Ibid. l.* 19, *after* Eliotæ, *add* Eliotis librarie." Or,

Page 449, *insert* "The Defence of Good Women, devised and made 1545. by Sir Thomas Elyot knight. Anno M.D.XLV." In the compartment with 1534 on the sell. On the last leaf, D 8, the author's arms. Sixteens. Michael Wodhull Esq;

Page 450, *l.* 2, *add* Francis Douce Esq; whose copy has 1545 on the 1545. title, and at the end, "Londini in officina Thomæ Bertheleti Typis impres. cum priuilegio—solum." *Ibid. l.* 15, *for* p. 70, *read* p. 211. *Ibid. insert* "The ryght profytable Boke of husbandry" &c. 1546. See p. 423. 1546. *Ibid.* "SURVEYING. An. MD.XLVI." 60 leaves. W.H. Sixteens.

Page 453, *l.* 1, *read* of the histories. *Ibid. l.* 2, *read* countreis. *Ibid. l.* 3, *after* did *add* :. *Ibid. l.* 5, *after* wrales *for* ; *put* : *and for* auctours, fyrst *read* auctors, Fyrst. *Ibid. l.* 8, *and* 9, *dele* On the back is the cut of his sign, Lucretia Romana. *Ibid. l.* 10, *read* "To the right high and mightie Prince, Edwarde. *Ibid. l.* 11, *for* kinges *read* kynges. *Ibid. l.* 12, *for* & *read* and; *for* hyghnesse *read* highnesse. *I am obliged to Mr. Robert Loder of Woodbridge, Suffolk, for these corrections; as also for several others, which will be attended to in their places; and for intimating that under the year* 1542 *is inserted* "One named Johannes Faustiui fyrste founde the crafte of printyng in the citee of Mens in Germanie." My copy wants title and preface.

Page 456, *l.* 31, *read* Hadrianus Junius.

Page 460, *l.* 22, *for* 1555 *read* 1545.

Page 464, *l.* 17, *after* nor place; *read* but being bound up with two other tracts of Berthelet's printing, is my only reason for giving it a place here.

Page 466, *l.* 15, *dele* (1561) in the margin; and after *l.* 19, *add* I have also an edition in 4°. &c. as p. 1787. *Ibid. dele the first two lines of note* q, *and insert* This is rather the date of the author's revisal, than that of printing.

Page 468, *l.* 17, *for* Yhe *read* The. *Ibid. l.* 20, *for* which *read* and. *Ibid. l.* 21, *read* Hampstead. *Ibid. l.* 28, *read* appearance.

Page 472, *l.* 18, *for* boke *read* bukes. *Ibid. l.* 36, *add* See p. 178.

Page 474, *l.* 11, *for* 1596 *read* 1566.

Page 475, *l.* 4, *for* 1536 *in the margin, set* 1531. *Ibid. l.* 18, *set* 1531 *in the margin.*

Page 435, *l.* 8, *for* the *read* in; *and for* printed *read* prynted. *Ibid. l.* 11, *after* tongues. *add* Cum priuilegio regali."

Page 487, *insert* "The testament, and complaint of our soveraign lord James the 5th's Papingo." See Pinkerton's Scotish Poets, &c. p. ciii.

(1537.) Page 493, *insert* "How and whither a Christen man ought to flye the horrible plague of the pestilence *&c.* 1537.—James Nicolson for Jan. Gough. 16°. See p. 1447.

1543. *Page* 496, *insert* "An inuectyue agenst—swearing," *&c.* John Mayler for him. 1543. 16°. See p. 572.

Page 497, *l.* 25, *dele* back of the. *Ibid. note* e, *read* Psalm.

1550. *Page* 533, *insert* "A boke of Presidentes" &c. as p. 521. Contains x, in eights, besides prefixes. 1550. 8°. WH.

1552. Page 534, *insert* "Io Caius Doctor in Phisicke, his councell against the disease called the Sweat." 1552. Octavo.

Page 536, *l.* 15, *dele* book of the. *Ibid. l.* 16, *dele the first* then.

Page 540, *l. ult. for* 1551 *in the margin, read* 1541. *Ibid. note* h, *after* English *read* Dated 12 Mar. 1542; *rather than at the end of the note.*

1544. *Page* 541, *insert* Purtiforium, &c. as in p. 519.

1549. *Page* 546, *insert* "A Lesson of the Incarnation of Christ." See p. 580.

1550. *Page* 556, *insert* "The rates of the custom house," *&c.* Printed by Nicholas Hill for him, 1550. Octavo. See p. 709.

—— *Page* 557, *insert* "The Epistles and Gospelles" &c. as p. 410, 411. *Ibid.* "The epistles and gospels," &c. as p. 679. *Ibid.* "Thus endith the Boke of Nurture or Gouernaũce of Youth, with Stans Puer ad Mensam. Compyled by Hewe Rodes one of the Kynges Chapell. Jmpryntid—in Paules Chyrcheyarde by Thomas Petyt." 4°. Francis Douce Esq; Wants title-page.

1539. Page 559, *l.* 13, *and elsewhere, read* Litany. *Ibid. after l.* 22, *insert* An edition in 4°. "Jmprynted—by me Jhon Mayler" for him and others. 1539. See this Appendix under p. 571.

1550. *Page* 560, *insert* Bochas's Fall of princes, &c. by Lydgate. Folio. See p. 280.

Page

Page 561, *l.* 8, *read* a prynter. *Ibid. l.* 21, *for* 148 *read* 168. *Ibid. l. last*, *after* wors *insert* for richer,

Page 562, *insert* Our Lady's Psalter; and Rosary. By Bonaventure. 1555.

Page 570, *after l.* 5, *insert* " The Contention betwixte Churchyeard 1565.
and Camell, vpon Dauid Dycers Dreame sett out in suche order, that it is bothe wyttye and profytable for all degryes.—Imprinted—by Owen Rogers, for Mychel Loblee—M.D.LX," 4°. *Ibid. after l.* 9, *insert* The same again 1565. Bagford's Papers in the Brit. Museum. He had also license to print, In 1557-8, " The psalme of misererj, and in te Dmē speravij with the fountayne or well of lyfe; &c." In 1559-60, " An exortation to the knowlege and love of God." In 1560-1, " Davy Dycars Dreames, with the Reste." In 1562-3, " The sermonde in the wall, thereunto ānexed The cōmon place of Patryk Hāmylton.—Certayne Remydes agaynste the plage, translated out of the laten tounge practised by leonerde facions." In 1565-6, " Muskelus vpon the lj psalme, by Mr. Coxe."

Page 571, *after l.* 9, *insert* " *The Manuall* of prayers, or the prymer 1539.
in *Englyshe, set out at lengthe*, whose contentes the reader by the prologe next after the *Kalender* shal sone perceaue and there in shall se brefly the order of the whole boke. *Set forth by Jhon late bysshoppe of Rochester*, at the cōmaundement of the ryght honorable Lorde *Thomas Crumwel*, Lorde Priuie seale Vicegerent to the *Kynges* hyghnes.—*Cum priuilegio—solum*." In red and black. G g, in fours. Colophon, " Jmprynted in bottoll lane, at the—whyt beare by me Jhon Mayler for Jhon Waylande, and be to sell in powles churchyarde, by Andrewe Hester at the whyt horse, and also by Mychel Lobley,—1539." 4°. Richard Gough Esq;

Page 572, *l.* 32, *add* Again 1546.

Page 573, *l.* 1, *insert* splendidissimi *before* equitis. *Ibid. after l.* 12, *add* He printed also " The Christmasse Banckette," (running-title) and probably for John Gough. My copy wants title-page and the last leaf. 8°.

Page 574, *insert* " Jnstytutions or principall groundes of the lawes 1544.
&c. Wyllyam Myddylton. 1544." With his device. 8°. The late John Baynes Esq;

Page 575, *insert* "Flores aliqvot Sententiarvm" &c. as p. 407. 1547.
" Ex ædibus Wilhelmi Middilton Anno. M.D.XLVII." B 4, in eights. His device on the last leaf. W.H. *Ibid. insert* " A Frvtefull worke of 1547.
Lvcivs Anneus Senecæ. Called the Myrrour or Glasse of Maners and wysedome bothe in latin and in Englysshe lately Translated by Robert whyttynton, poet Laureate. And nowe newely Jmprynted." c, in eights." Thus endeth this lytle worke of Lucii Annei Senecæ—" Anno 1547. W.H. *Ibid. insert* " Lvcii Annei Senecæ ad Gallioneni de Remediis 1547.
Fortuitorum. The remedyes agaynst all casuall chaunces. Dialogus inter sensum et Rationem. A Dialogue betwene Sensualyte and Reason. Lately translated out of Latyn into Englyshe by Robert Whyttynton poet Laureat & nowe newely Jmprynted." c 4, in eights. " Anno 1547." W.H. *Ibid. l.* 5, after Borde, *add* See p. 345, &c.

Page 576, *insert* " The great boke of statutes cōteynyng all the statutes —
made

9 &

made in the parlyamentes from the begynnynge of the fyrst yere of the raigne of kynge Edwarde the thyrde tyll the begynnyng of the. xxxiiii. yere of the most gracious raigne of our soueraigne lorde kyng Henry the viii." This title is over the cut of a king sitting on his throne, &c. as p. 154. On the back, the king's arms and the Rose, as used by Pinson, p. 256. At the end of Ric. III. "Jmprynted—by Wyllyam Middelton. Cum priuilegio Regali." Concludes with cap. xxiiii. 9 Hen. vii. *N. B.* There are no acts of Hen. 8; neither does the table prefixed mention any. Folio. His Majesty's. *Ibid. add to note* w There appear to have been three editions of Froissart's Chronicle; one by Pinson himself; another with Pinson's name, but supposed to be a pirated edition; and a third by W. Middleton: of this it has been queried whether he ever printed any more than the first volume. I had a copy of it which had been Mr. Ames's; the title like the late Dr. Archer's copy, but had the king's arms, &c. as p. 256, on the back, and the colophon with Middleton's name, without date. The title of the 2d vol. had neither compartment nor border, and the back page blank. The remainder of this vol. to Fo. CCC.xii inclusive is printed on the same rude types as the 1st vol. except the last 8 leaves, which are on much neater types, with the colophon, in Pinson's name, printed on types of the same size as the chronicle, the lines gradually shortening, &c. This is supposed to be part of the pirated edition: the other edition, with Pinson's name, differs from it, particularly in this respect, that the lines of the colophon are of equal length, and of a larger size. I imagine there were no more entire editions than these three; but the making up copies from one or another of these, may seem to multiply editions greatly. I have seen Pinson's edit. with the last leaf reprinted on modern black letter, copied from the supposed spurious edition, but dated M.D.XXIII.

Page 577, *l.* 3, *for* 1537, 49 *read* 1534, 48.

Page 578, *l. ult. for* 1586 *read* 1546.

1548. *Page* 579, *insert* "The newe Testamente in Englyssh according to the translation of the great Byble.—Ex officina.—M.D.XLVIII." 24°. *Ibid.* "Here begynneth the Pistles and Gospels of the Sondays and festiuall holy dayes." Quarto.

Page 585, *l.* 18, *add*, Another edition without date in the Bodl. Libr.

Page 589, *l.* 12, *add* till 1569, when her son Humphrey paid iiij l. to the company as "the bequeste of Mrs. Elizabeth Toye Widowe."

—— *Page* 591, *insert* "A general free Pardon or Charter of Heuyns Blys, compiled in our old Englyssh Tong in 1400." Octavo.

Page 597, *l.* 20, *add* He died in 1573, Fr. Flower's patent being dated 15 Dec. 1573. See p. 1634.

Page 600, *l. ult. add* A copy is in the hands of Mr. Thorpe; and his letter on it to Dr. Ducarell in the hands of Richard Gough Esq;

1553. *Page* 602, *insert* "Liber Precum Publ.—Graece Latine." See p. 611.

Page 611, *dele l.* 1 *and* 2; *and add* Dedicated to Alex. Nowel, &c. *after* editus *in l.* 4.

Page

Page 627, *running-title, read* John Day.

Page 629, *insert* "The Staffe of Christian Faith" &c. as p. 662. 1557.

Page 636, *l.* 25, *add* A fine copy of this book is in Brasen Nose Coll. Libr. which has on the back of the title-page to Bassus, a table shewing names of the composers, and what psalms, &c. were set by each.

Page 639, *l.* 9, *set* 1564 *in the margin. Ibid. l.* 38, *for* 1563 *in the margin, read* 1564.

Page 644, *l.* 14, *add* I have now got a perfect copy, thus intitled, "Le Theatre auquel sont exposés & monstrés les inconueniens & miseres qui suiuent les mondains & vicieux, ensemble les plaisirs & contentements dont les fideles iouissent. Matiere non moins profitable, que delectable à tous amateurs de la parolle de Dieu, de la Poësie, & de la peinture. Par le Seigneur Iean Vander Noot." Among other prefixes is a dedication "A Tres-haute Tres-puissante, tres-noble, Tres-vertueuse Princesse, vraiemēt Chrestienne, Elizabeth, par la grace de Dieu Royne d'Angleterre," &c.

Page 646, *l.* 15, *read* altar. *Ibid. l.* 20, *read* riband. *Ibid. l.* 32, *read* p. 634.

Page 649, *insert* A Report—of the affairs of Germany, &c. 4°. See p. 677. Francis Douce Esq. *Ibid. l.* 34, *for* has *read* had. 1570.

Page 651, *l.* 37, *for* 1578 *in the margin, read* 1571.

Page 655, *l.* 39, *for* προλεγομενων *read* προλεγομένων. *Ibid. insert* "An Oration made to Q. Elizabethe, Lat. and Eng. Anno. 1573." Octavo.

Page 659, *l.* 32, *read* lesse. *Ibid. l.* 33, *read* Frenche. *Ibid. l.* 34, *read* scene.

Page 662, *l.* 19, *read* St. Augustines meditations and manuell. See p. 659.

Page 663, *insert* "The Testament of the Twelue Patriarchs." Octavo. 1577.
Ibid. "The Pöander of Prayers, by Thomas Becon." &c. Sixteens. 1578.
Francis Douce Esq.

Page 665, *l.* 28, *read* Iohannem. *Ibid. to note* t *add* See note r, p. 664.

Page 666, *insert* "The Schole Master,—By Roger Ascham. Anno 1579. 1579.
—Printed by Iohn Daye, dwelling ouer Aldersgate. Cum priuilegio &c. And are to be sold at his shop at the West dore of Paules."

Page 672, *catch-word, for* of *read* so; *and prefix the same to the first line of the next page.*

Page 676, *read the second article thus,* "A newe Dialngue, Vvhere in is conteyned the examinatiō of the Masse, and of that kind of priesthod, whiche is ordeyned to saye masse: and to offer vp for remission of synne, the bodye and bloude of Christ again." By W. Turner M. D. Printed with Seres. W. H. Also, by Day alone. —

Page 679, *insert* "De Maria Scotorum Regina," &c. 8°. *Ibid.* "Ane Detectioun of the duinges of Marie Quene of Scottes," &c. 8°. *Ibid.* "A Defence and true declaration of the thinges lately done in the lowe countrey," &c. *Ibid.* "The vpcheringe of the messe.—and Willyam Seres." 16°. *Ibid.* "A brief Sum of the Bible translated out of Dutch into Englysh by Anth. Scoloker;" with cuts. 16°. *Ibid.* "An Oration gratulatory made vpon the ioyfull proclayming of the moste noble Princes Quene Mary —

Quene of Englande. By Richard Tauerner. Sixteens. *Ibid. catch-word, for* RICHARD *read* Here.

Page 681, *l.* 11, *read* lilies. *Ibid. l.* 12, *read* LILIUM.

Page 683, *read* " TIMOTHY RIDER, The son of John Ryder of Wedenbet in Northamptonshire, husbandman, was bound apprentice to Richard Lynell for 7 years from the Purification, 1563; and made free 21 March, 1570. He appears to have soon stood in need of the Company's indulgence, and at length was appointed beadle, &c.

VOLUME II.

Page 685, *l.* 17, *after* deuices. *add* Also in April 1584 he had granted to him another copy of Hen. Disley's, called " The widowes treasorer," &c. as p. 683. *Ibid. dele* This, *and insert instead thereof* The Paradyse.

1576. *Ibid. l.* 18, *add* but he printed 3 editions of it; one in 1576, thus entituled, " THE PARADYSE of dainty deuises, aptly furnished with sundry pithee and learned inuentions: deuised and written for the most part by M. (*Master Richard*) Edwards,—: the rest by sundry learned Gentlemen, both of honor and woorshippe. viz. S. Barnarde. E. O. L. Vaux. D. S. Jasper Heywood. F. K. M. Bewe. R. Hill. M. Yloop, with others." Device &c. the same as to the edition 1577, except the date. This 4°. consists of one sheet unpaged, and 88 subsequent pages. George Steevens Esq; The other two editions, 1577 and 1578, follow. *Ibid. l. ult. after* losse. *add* 46 leaves.

Page 686, *l.* 4, *add* and another in 1585. I am informed also by George Steevens Esq; of two more editions of this book; one in 1596, the other in 1600, the latter in his own possession; but neither of them printed by Disle. In July 1582, the copy was granted to Tim. Rider, see p. 683, and the next year was put over to Edw. White, for whom probably the edition 1585 was printed, as those of 1596, and 1600, certainly were.

Page 692, *l.* 21, *set in the margin* 1559. *Ibid. l.* 28, *read* enclosed. *Ibid. l. pen. set in the margin* 1560.

Page 697, *l.* 13, *date in the margin*, 1565.

Page 701, *l.* 21, *for* 1750 *read* 1570. *Ibid. l.* 23, *add* Licensed.

Page 702, *l.* 28 & 29, *read after* prefixes, 190 leaves, numbered 191, N° 113 being omitted.

Page 704, *add* This first article was printed before in p. 690.

Page 707, *l.* 6, *read* nonnullis. *Ibid. l.* 7, *read* cuiusquidem. *Ibid. l. pen. for* MDXCVIII. *read* MDXLVIII.

Page 709, *l.* 27, *read* anatomie. *Ibid. l.* 33, *read* maye leme.

—— *Page* 710, l. 15, *add* Also without date. *Ibid. insert* " The Chartuarye in English, &c. For John Walley." Sixteens.

Page 711, *l.* 22, *dele* but. *Ibid. l.* 23, *dele* before 1565, nor after 1570. *And insert instead thereof*, but that he had a license to print two ballads in 1565. *Ibid. l.* 32, *dele* c *in* M.D.XLCVIII. *Ibid. read* eights.

(1559.) *Page* 717, *insert* " The declaracyon of the procedynge of a conference, begon at Westminster the last of March. 1559. concerning certaine articles of Religion and the breaking vp of the sayde conference by default and contempt of certayne Bysshops, parties of the sayd conference. Jmprynted

—by

—by Richarde Jugge and John Cawood prynters to the Quenes Maiestie Cum priuilegio Regiæ Maiestatis." 8 leaves. Sixteens. W.H. *Ibid. l.* 13, *date in the margin, read* 1559.

Page 721, *insert* " Statutes. Anno quinto Reginæ Elizabethæ." Folio. By Jugge alone. 1563.

Page 723, *insert* " A proclamation for calling in The admonition to the Parliament." See Neal, I; 295, &c. 1573.

Page 729, *l.* 8, *margin, read* 1580. *Ibid. l.* 9, *margin, read* 1584.

Page 732, *insert* " De Arte Concionandi," &c. as p. 970. *Ibid.* " The fables of Esope in Englishe," *&c.* as p. 940. 1570.

Page 734, *insert* " The Rocke of Regard, *&c.* By Geo. Whetstons Gent. 1576." 4°. *Ibid. insert* " Cometographia quædam Lampadis aeriæ quę 10 die Nouemb. apparuit Anno a Virgineo partu, 1577.—excudebat Robertus Walley.—1578. 4°.—Alexander Dalrymple Esq. 1576. 1578.

Page 736, *l.* 12, *for* another copy *read* an edition. *Ibid. insert* " The Justification of Man by Faith only: *&c.* By Ph. Melanchton, and translated by Nich. Lesse. *With*, A defence of the Word of God, by N. L." Sixteens. 1548.

Page 744, *l.* 30, *insert* See Brit. Topography, I; 932. *Also*, " An Exhortacion to the cariengе of Chrystes crosse;" &c. 32°. See Eccl. Memorials, III; 151.---" William Keth his seeing glasse, sent to the nobles and Gentlemen in England. "&c. 32°. Maunsell, p. 64.---" A plaine subuersyon or turning vp syde down of all the argumentes, that the Popecartholykes can make for the maintenaunce of auricular confession," &c. At the end, " Answere ye Popecatholykes." 32°.—" A confutacion of that Popishe and antichristian doctryne, whiche mainteineth ẏ ministracyon and receiuing of the sacrament vnder one kind, *&c.* by Graceyous Menewe." &c. At the end, " Be ashamed of your doings ye Papystes." N.B. This and the 3 preceding articles are without the printer's name, or device; but the types, manner & size are the same as The Hope of the faithfull, &c. A spirituall and most precious perle, &c. printed by Singleton. ——

Page 747, *l.* 12, *for* 1582 *in the margin, read* 1552. *and dele l.* 14, 15. *Ibid. insert* "—the boke of surveying and improuements." W. Copland for him. ——

Page 751, *l.* 12, *for* by *read* vp. *Ibid. insert* " Notable Textes of the scripeures which declare of what vertue, strength and holines the pixed or boxed God is:" &c. 16°. W.H. My copy is bound with " A Godly Newe short treatyse, &c. p. 750, by Rob. Stoughton, and as it is printed on the same types seems to claim a place under the same name. ——

Page 756, *l.* 34, *add* 8 leaves. Mr. John Notcutt.

Page 763, *insert* " The goodly history of the beautyfull Lady Lucres of Scene." 8°. *Ibid. l.* 37, *for* of *read* ys. *Ibid. l. ult. read* Phillip. 1560.

Page 766, *l.* 5, *for* 1551 *in the margin, read* 1553.

Page 767, *l.* 13, *add* Mrs. Gooch of Diss, Norfolk. *Ibid. l.* 14, *read thus*: " The firste syxe bokes" by the same. " Jmprinted for Rafe Newbery. Anno. 1561." Thomas Astle Esq. 1561.

Page

Page 782, *l.* 6, *add* Now newlie *before* imprinted. *Ibid. l.* 12, *add* Maunsell, p. 114. See it by T. East, 1581. *Ibid. l.* 20, *for* 1592 *read* 1590. *Ibid. l.* 35, *for* fist *read* fist.

Page 784, *l.* 11, *for* New *read* Newly. *Ibid. l.* 20, *read* 1588. *in the margin.* *Ibid. insert* "Phillip Sparrow: Colyn Clout:" and other poems by John Skelton, with his portrait. Octavo. W.H.

Page 786, *after l.* 6, *add* "Thursday, 1 Feb. 2. Eliz. Livery was granted to the Company of Stationers, by the Lord Maior and Court of Aldermen of London, at the prayer of John Cawood. To take place after the Pulters of the said City." *Ibid. l.* 11, *for* p. 125 *read* p. 356, 357.

1554. *Page* 790, *insert* "A copie of a Letter sent from the Counsell vnto the ryghte reuerende Father in God Edmonde (*Bonner*) Byshoppe of London —From Westmynster the xxvii of Nouember, 1.5.5.4. Your assured louing frendes, Ste. Winton Cancell. Henry Sussex. Arundel. John Bathon. John Huddylston. F. Shrewesburye. R. Ryche. R. Southwell. Edward Derby. Thomas Wharton. Excusum Londini in ædibus Johannis Cawodi Typographi Regiæ Maiestatis." *Ibid.* "A prayer made by D. Weston, Deane of Westminster, and deliuered to the Children of the Quenes maiesties grammar schole there, and sayd by them daily, morning and euening, for her maiestie." Latin and English. In the praier, "being nowe at the pointe of her deliueraunce." At the end, "Imprinted by John Cawoode." &c. Acts and Monuments, p. 1015. Edit. 1562.

Page 792, *l.* 3, *after* 1555. *add* By Hugh Rhodes. *Ibid. l.* 4, *add* Francis Douce Esq;

1559. *Page* 796, *insert* A Proclamation against bringing in unlawfull books.
1560. —A proclamation against breaking or defacing monuments in churches.
1569. *Page* 797, *l.* 9, *add* Mr. Robert Loder of Woodbridge, Suffolk, has a copy with "Imprinted—by John Cawood, Printer to the Queenes Maiesty. Cum privilegio Regiæ Maiestatis."

Page 799, *l.* 15, *for* Beddell *read* Reddell. *Ibid. l. ult. read* Marsh;

Page 800, *running title, for* BIDDELL *read* RIDDELL. *Ibid. l.* 5, *for*
1554. Beddell *read* Reddell. *Ibid. after l.* 13. *insert* "The Ballad of Joy vpon the publication of Q. Mary, Wife of king Philip, her being with child, Anno Do. 15--" Colophon: "Imprinted at London in Lombarde strete at the signe of the Eagle, by Wyllyam Ryddaell." This title and colophon are taken from a transcript of the said ballad in the Pepysian Library, Magdalen Coll. Cambridge, to which is annexed An extract of a letter from Mr. Michael Bull,[e] M. A. Fellow of Benet Coll. to Mr. Humphrey Wanley,[f] 12 June, 1701, with a copy of it, and acquainting him that a letter was sent from the Council to the byshop of London, to sing Te Deum for her majesty's being with child, and that a printed copy of that order was pasted on the back of the ballad, meaning the printed copy of it. They are still remaining in Benet Coll. From whence,

[e] See Masters's Hist. of Benet Coll. p. 256. Hasted's Kent, p. 361.

[f] Keeper of the Harleian Library.

whence, having lately been favoured with exact transcripts of them, i shall give a copy of the ballad,[g] which is extremely scarce, in the notes, for the curious reader; the letter was printed by I. Cawood,[h] and should have been given at large likewise under his name, but that i find it printed in Fox's Acts and Monuments, with small variation only in the orthography, p. 1014. Edit. 1562. Probably letters of the same purport were sent to the rest of the bishops, &c. However shortly after we are told that Te Deum was sung in the cathedral and other churches in Norwich, not only for the queen's being with child, but for her safe delivery of a PRINCE.[i]

Page

[g] "Nowe singe, nowe springe, oure care is exild,
Oure vertuous Quene is quickned with child.

Now Englande is happie, & happie in dede,
That God of his goodnes dothe prospir here sede:
Therefore let vs praie, it was neuer more nede,
God prospir her highnes, God send her good sped.

Howe manie good people were longe in dispaire,
That this letel england shold lacke a right heire:
But nowe the swet marigold springeth soo fayre,
That England triumpheth without anie care.

Howe manie greate thraldomes in englane were frene,
Before that her highnes was pwblyshed quene:
The bewtye of englande was banyshed clene,
With wringing and wrongynge and sorowes betwen.

And yet synce her highnes was planted in peace,
Her subiects wer dobtful of her highnes increse:
But nowe the recomfort, their murmour doth ceafe,
They haue their owne wyshynge, their woes doo relesse.

And suche as enuied the matche & the make,
And in their procedinges stoode styffe as a stake;
Are nowe reconciled, their malis dothe slake,
And all men are wilinge theyr partes for to take.

Our doutes be dyssolued, our fansies contented,
The mariage is ioyfull, that many lamented:
And such as enuied like foles haue repented
The Errours & Terrours that they haue inuented.

But God dothe worke more wonders then this,
For he is the Auther and Father of blysse:
He is the defender, his workinge it is,
And where he dothe fauoure they fare not amys.

Therefore let vs praye to the father of myght
To prosper her hignes, & sheilde her in ryghte:
With ioye to deliuer, that when she is lighte,
Both she & her people maie ioye without sight.

God prossper her highnes in euery thinge,
Her noble spouse, our fortunate kynge:
And that noble blossome, that is planted to springe,
Amen swete Jesus, we hartelye singe.

Blysse thou swete Jesus, our comforters three,
Oure kynge, our Queene, our Prince that shal be;
That they three as one, or one as all three,
Maye gouerne thy people to the plesure of the."

[h] See p. 1754.

[i] See Strype's Cranmer, p. 367; and Bp. Hopton's letter to the E. of Sussex, Norwich, 3 May, 1555. In the Appendix. p. 203.

1562. *Page* 802, *insert* "The Well Sprynge of Sciences, *&c.* by Humfrey Baker." Se p. 1001.

1563. *Page* 804, *l. pen. dele* head. *Ibid. insert* "A briefe Chronicle of the foure principall Empires.—by Iohn Sleidan, and englished by Stephan Wythers." Quarto. W.H.

Page 812, *l.* 6, *read* again 1560, and *before* frequently. *Ibid. l.* 11, *add* again xxx.—July, An. 1557. Quarto.

1570. *Page* 818, *insert* Quintus Curtius &c. as p. 813. Octavo. Francis Douce Esq;

1573. *Page* 820, *insert* "Les Plees del Coron," &c. *With* "An Exposition of the Kinges Prerogative,", &c. 4°. 1573.

1575. *Page* 821, *insert* "A treatise of Moral Philosophy," &c. 8°. 1575. Again 1579. See p. 814. *Ibid. l.* 32, *add* Again 1587. Francis Douce Esq;

Page 823, *l.* 14, *for* Barker's *read* Sir Fr. Walsingham's.

1591. *Page* 826, *insert* "The Accidence of Armorie," &c. 4°. 1591. See p. 813.

Page 827, *l.* 11, *add* It was however printed by Chr. Barker, in 1579, &c.

1554. *Page* 829, *insert* "A Sermon—at Paules 12 day of Nouember in the first year of our Soueraign Lady Queene Mary, *&c.* set forth at the requeste of such whole authority could not well be withstande.—M.D.LIIII." 16°. Gov. Pownall.---*Ibid. l.* 29, *add* Another edition of the same date, in 4to. George Steevens Esq.

Page 830, *l.* 15, *after* Christ *add* by Vincent Leriensis, and translated *After* by *add* John; *and after* Octo. *add* 4to.

Page 834, *l.* 14. *for* 1548 *in the margin, read* 1558.

1564. *Page* 836, *insert* "A Dialogue bothe pleasaunte and pietifull, wherein is a goodly regimente against the feuer Pestilence, *&c.* Newly corrected by Willyam Bulleyn," &c. 4°. See Appendix to the Sad Shepherd, p. 162, and 185, &c. Mr Waldron.

1581. *Page* 840, *insert* "The newe Attractiue," &c. 4to. 1581. *Ibid.* "A Discours of the Variation of the Cumpas" &c. 4to. 1581. See p. 1014, &c. *Ibid.* "A Glasse for Gamesters, *&c.* For Tho. Man. 1581." 16°. Francis Douce Esq.

Page 845, *l.* 1, *insert* 1559 *in the margin.*

Page 846, *l.* 1, *read* plow. *ibid. l.* 2, *for* the *read* then.

Page 852, *insert* "A Myrrovr for Magistrates.—Anno 1563." 4to.

(1567.) *Page* 856, *insert* "A new Almanacke and Prognostication for the yere of our Sauiour Christ M.D.LXVIII.—Published by John Securis Phisition, dwelling in Salisbury, in the New streete. Jmprinted" &c. In the Bodleian Library.

(1570.) *Page* 860, *insert* "A new and Pleasaunt enterlude intituled The mariage
1571. of Witte and Science." 4to. E. Malone. Esq; *Ibid.* "A Myrrour for Magistrates.—Newly corrected and augmented. Anno 1571." 4to. Again (1st and 3d parts) 1574.

Page 865, *l.* 43, *read* compacte. *Ibid. l.* 44, *read* hũdreth of. *Ibid. ult. for* thre *read* three.

Page

Page 866, *l.* 1, *for* hundred *read* hundreth. *Ibid. l.* 4, *add* Again 1577. *Ibid. l.* 5, *set* 1576 *in the margin*. *Ibid. l.* 17, *read* by Henr.

Page 867, *l.* 1, *read* V 7. *Ibid. l.* 3, *read* Fovre seuerall. *Ibid. l.* 21, *read* righte. *Ibid. l.* 27, *read* bee. *Ibid. l.* 33, *read* Marsh. Anno 1578. *Ibid. l.* 34, *read* Baron of Clinton.

Page 868, *insert* " The first and Chiefe Groundes of Architecture,— 1579.
Published By Ihon Shute,—1579." Folio. Colophon, 1580.

Page 870, *insert* " Iohn Heywoodes Works" &c. as p. 865. 4to. 1587. 1587.
At the end, " An Epilogue or Conclusion of this Worke by Tho: Newton" consisting of 30 lines, and signed " Thomas Newton Cestreshyrius," The orthography throughout much modernised.

Page 887, *l.* 23, *for* 1374 *in the margin*, *read* 1574.

Page 889, *l.* 30, *insert* Again 1568. *Ibid. l. ult. for* 1599, *read* 1569.

Page 891, *insert* " The Mirrour of Mutabilitie, or Principall part of 1579.
the Mirrour for Magistrates. Describing the fall of diuers famous Princes, and other memorable Personages. Selected out of the sacred Scriptures by Antony Munday, and dedicated to the Right Honnorable the Earle of Oxenford.—Jmprinted—and are to be solde by Richard Ballard, at Saint Magnus Corner. 1579."

Page 892, *l.* 9, *read* " A merry Jest of *(by)* Dane Hew." *Ibid. l.* 10, *add* See the tale of friar Peter and friar John. Hist. of Norfolk. *Ibid. l.* 11, *dele the whole, being printed by John Skot.*

Page 894, *l. pen. add* MDLX.—Jmprinted—by Thomas Hackette, and are to be sold at hys shop in Cannynge streete, ouer agaynste the thre Cranes." *Ibid. l. ult. after* Hooper's *insert* Exposition of the 23 Psalm, and his.

Page 898, *insert* " The true and perfecte Newes of the woorthy and va- 1587.
liaunt exploytes, performed and doone by that valiant Knight Syr Fraunci**s** Drake: Not onely at Sancto Domingo, and Carthagena, but also nowe at Cales, and vppon the coast of Spayne. 1587. Printed—by I. Charlewood, for *him*." Quarto.

Page 899, *l.* 11, *add* See p. 1311.

Page 904, *l.* 23, *dele* without the elephant. *Ibid. l.* 44, *add* with the same device; but a different block, without the elephant under it.

Page 906, *l.* 9, *read* dedicated. *Ibid. l.* 12, *read* p. 398.

Page 909, *read the first article thus:* " Ten Books of Homers Iliades translated out of French. By Arthur Hall Esquire.—Cum priuilegio."

Page 911, *l.* 27, *Set* 1584 *in the margin*; *and add* Again 1594. *Ibid. l.* 36, *for* historie *read* historie.

Page 915, *l.* 4, *for* 1589 *in the margin*, *read* 1590.

Page 918, *l.* 17, *for* Ja. *read* Jo. *Ibid. l.* 22, *read* Chr. Barker.

Page 920, *l.* 13, *after* Annexed is *insert* An epistle sent to the pastors of the Flemish Church in Antwerp, of. *Ibid. l.* 27, *read* lucubrationes. *Ibid. l.* 33, *add* Again 1587. *Ibid. l.* 34, *read* Dissertissimi.

Page 922, *l.* 7, *after* &c. *insert* By John Polman. *Under Wm. Griffith, insert* " Fyve Homiles of late, made by a ryght good and vertuous clerke, 1556.
called

called master Leonarde Pollarde, prebendary of the Cathedrall Churche of Woster, directed and dedicated to the ryght reuerende Father in God Rychard by the permissyon of God byshoppe of Woster his speciall good Lorde. Vewed, examined, and alowed by the right reuerende Father in God Edmonde byshop of London, within whose diocese they are imprinted. Cum priuilegio—solum. Anno. M.D.LVI." In the compartment with two boys riding in paniers on an elephant in procession; perhaps designed for Romulus and Remus. Colophon: "Imprinted at London in Fletestrete at the—Faucon agaynst saynt Dunstones Church by VVyllyam Gryffyth, and are to be solde at his shop a lyttle aboue the Condyte at the signe of the Gryffin. Cum priuilegio." 4to. W.H.

1570. *Page* 923, *insert* "—A discourse of Rebellion, drawn forth for to warne the wanton wittes how to kepe their heads on their shoulders. Imprinted —1570. The first of Maye." 16°. George Steevens Esq;

Page 925, *l. pen. for* Denham *read* Bynneman.

Page 926, *l.* 10, *insert* The colophon 1570, but the title-page 1571. *Ibid. l.* 28, *for* pages *read* leaves.

1577. *Page* 929, *insert* The last volume of Holinshed's Chronicle imprinted for Lucas Harrison. Francis Douce Esq; See p. 1155, &c.

1574. *Page* 932, *read the first article thus:* "The Notable Hystory of two faithfull Louers named Alphagus and Archelaus. Whearein is declared the true fygure of Amytie and Freyndshyp. Much pleasaunte and delectable to the Reader. Translated into English meeter by Edward Jenynges. With a Preface or Definytion of Freyndshyppe to the same.—Imprinted —in Fleetestreat—1574." *Ibid. l.* 25, *add* See p. 1451. *Ibid. l.* 26, *for* Holwell *read* Howell. *Ibid. insert* "A pretie and Mery new Enterlude called the Disobedient Child. compiled by Thomas Ingelend late student in Cambridge." 4to. Francis Douce Esq;

Page 933, *l. last, add* He died 16. October, 1577, and was buried in the church of All Saints, Bristol, as appears by the following epitaph, which was on a large monument supported with three fluted pillars, &c. at the upper end of the north aisle, but in the repairs 1782 removed. "Humfridus Toius, Londinensis, jacet in hoc tumulo, qui obiit 16 Oct. 1577.

Hunc mors peccati merces subtraxit amara
Qui Deo dives erat, religione pius:
Qui sibi pennultum coluit coelestes alumnos,
Fortunæque bonis pavit & ipse pius:
Christicola ut vivus fuit is, humilatus abibat,
Tum Christi posuit vulneribusque fidem.

Impensas egit in hoc tumulo Margerita conjux predicti Humfridi Toii." Barret's Hist. of Bristol, p. 442.

1564. *Page* 937, *l.* 20, *read* Thomas Powel's. *Ibid. insert* "An introduction to Wisdom" &c. as p. 446. "The Preface" is thus inscribed "To the right worshipful mayster Gregorye Crumwell, sonne to the ryghte honourable Lorde Crumwell, Lord pryuy seale, Rycharde Morisyne wisheth much

much wealth, wyth continual encreafe of vertue." Colophon: "Londini Excudebat Henricus VVykes. Cum priuilegio—folum. Anno M.D.LXIIII." 16°. A fragment. Francis Douce Efq.

Page 946, *note* b, *dele* This word Doni *&c.* *to* head title, *and infert inftead thereof* DONI is the name of the Italian tranflator. See the Italian verfes by G. B. prefixed. *Ibid. note* c, *l. pen. read* Burleigh.

Page 952, *l.* 23, *read* Tremellius.

Page 962, *l. ult. add* Again 1590. Printed for the Affignes of Willm Seres. With Denham's fign and motto at the end. George Mafon Efq. 1590.

Page 966, *l.* 5, *after* R. Newbery, *add* John Wyght, R. Tottle, T. Hacket, F. Coldock.

Page 972, *l.* 12, *for* view *read* vewe. *Ibid. l.* 30, *add* See Britifh Topography, II, 791.

Page 975, *note* r, *col.* 2, *l.* 7, *after* leaves, *add* lead. *Ibid. l.* 12, *for* pincers *read* pencils.

Page 976, *note*, *col.* 1, *l.* 2, *after* Colas, *add* or Kotoragna. See Viaggo in Dalmazia dell' Alberto Fortis. Vol. I, p. 150, &c. Edit. Ven. 1774, 4to.

Page 982, *l.* 22, *add* The third and laft voyage into Meta Incognita, was printed in 16°. A fragment. Francis Douce Efq.

Page 983, *l.* 12, *for* her *read* hir. *Ibid. l.* 31, *for* Military *r.* Militare.

Page 987, *infert* "The Grounde of Artes," &c. With John Harrifon. 8vo. 1582. Alexander Dalrymple Efq. 1582.

Page 989, *infert* "Oratio ad Pontifices, Londini A. D. 1553, in æde Paulina habita: per Nic. Grimaldum—1583." Octavo. 1583.

Page 994, *l.* 36, *read* A Chriftian Exhortation *&c.* *Ibid. infert* "A new and mery Enterlude called The Triall of Treafure, *&c.*—1567." 4to. Edmund Malone Efq. 1567.

Page 997, *infert* "Articles to be inquired of within the Diocefe of Norwich. The firft vifitation of Edm. Scamber. xx Eliz." 4to. *Ibid.* *l.* 20, *read* Ifocrates. 1581.

Page 999, *l.* 29, *add* Again 1588, and 1596. 4to.

Page 1001, *l.* 31, *add* Again 1598. W.H.+

Page 1002, *l.* 12, *after* Schoole-maifter; *add* with the hiftory of Arnalt and Lucinda, fet forth.

Page 1012, *infert* "The decree for tythes to be paid in London, anno 1580." For Gabr. Cawood. Brit. Topogr. I; 603. *Ibid.* "A Booke of Notes and Common places, *&c.* By John Marbeck.—1581." Mr. Denyer. 1580. 1581.

Page 1015, *l.* 1, *for* 1581, *read* 1585. *Ibid. l.* 21, *add* 1585 *in the margin*.

Page 1016, *infert* "A Regiment for the Sea, *&c.* 1587." 4to. See p. 783. *Ibid.* "Euphues and his England, *&c.* 1588." 4to. See p. 1012. 1587. 1588.

Page 1018, *l.* 2, *read* ætatis.

Page 1022, *l.* 21, *after* Foxe, *add* "The three firft Bookes of Ovid de Triftibus, tranflated by Tho. Churchyard." *Ibid. l. ult. read* Ballads.

Page 1027, *l.* 12, *read* Patauini. *Ibid. infert* "Bibliotheca Hifpanica, *&c.* By Richard Percyuall, Gent.—John Jackfon for him.—1591." 4to. W.H. Again 1592. 1591.

Page

1594. *Page* 1028, *insert* "Examen de Ingenios, *&c.* 1594." A. Islip for him. See p. 1286. Francis Douce Esq;

1597. *Page* 1034, *insert* "Devoreux. Vertues tears for the losse of the most christian King Henry, third of that name, King of Fraunce; and the vntimely death of the most noble and heroicall Gentleman, Walter Deuoreux, who was slaine before Roan in Fraunce. First written in French, by the most excellent and learned Gentlewoman Madam Geneuefue Petau Maulette. And paraphrastically translated into English. Jeruis
1597. Markham.—Printed—for Thomas Millington,—1597." 4to. *Ibid.* "The Voice of Memnons Image. Imprinted by I. R. 1597." George Steevens Esq;

1600. *Page* 1035, *insert* "Englands Helicon.—Printed by I. R. for John Flasket, and are to be sold in Paules Church-yard, at the signe of the Beare, 1600." 4to. George Steevens Esq; *Ibid. l.* 17, *add* Another edition, I. R. for Tho. Hayes.

Page 1037, *l.* 15, *read* "The xi bookes. *Ibid. l.* 18, *for* Guil. *read* Guli. *Ibid. read* Fulwod.

1573. *Page* 1040, *insert* "XII. mery Jests of the wyddow Edyth.—Finis. by Walter Smith. Imprinted at London. in Fleet-lane: 1573." 4to. George Steevens Esq;

1576. *Page* 1042, *insert* "The Princelye pleasures, at the Courte at Kenel-
1578. woorth.—In the year 1575. Imprinted—1576." 8vo. *Ibid.* "A gorgious Gallery of gallant Inuentions. Garnished and decked with diuers dayntie deuises, right delicate and delightfull, to recreate eche modest minde withall. First framed and fashioned in sundrie formes, by diuers worthy workemen of late dayes: and now ioyned together and builded vp. By T. P.—1578." *Ibid. l.* 16, *read* Deuided into two. *Ibid. l. pen. for* Sheets, N, 3, *read* N, in fours.

1587. *Page* 1046, *insert* "A Dutiful Invective Against the moste haynous Treasons of Ballard and Babington: with other their adherents latelie executed. Together with the horrible attempts and actions of the Q. of Scottes: and the Sentence pronounced against her at Fodderingay. Newlie compiled and set foorth in English verse: For a Newyeares gifte to all loyall English Subjects. By W. Kempe. Imprinted—dwelling at the—Rose and crowne, neere Holborne Bridge. 1587." 4to. In his Majesty's Library.

Page 1047, *l.* 16. *insert* Forbidden to be sold. Strype's Annals, IV; 46.

1591. *Page* 1048, *insert* "The Harmonie of the Church. Containing The Spirituall Songes and holy Hymnes of godly men, Patriarkes and Prophetes: all sweetly sounding, to the praise and glory of the highest. Now (newlie) reduced into sundrie kinds of English Meeter: meete to be read or sung, for the solace and comfort of the godly. By M. D.—Printed at the Rose and Crowne, neere Holborne Bridge. 1591."

1594. *Page* 1049, *insert* "A most pleasant and merie nevv Comedie, Intitled, A Knack how to knowe a Knave, *&c.* Imprinted—1594." 4to.

1595. *Page* 1050, *insert* "The Fisher-mans Tale: Of the famous Actes, Life and loue of Cassander a Grecian Knight, Written by Francis Sabie. —1595.

—1595. *Ibid.* "Floras Fortune. The fecond part and finifhing of the 1595.
Fifher-mans Tale. Containing The ftrange accidentes which chaunced to Flora, and her fuppofed father Thirfis: alfo the happie meeting with her defired Caffander.—By F. S.—1595." *Ibid.* "The Englifh Secretarie:" &c. as p. 1048. "For Cuth. Burbie" 4°. *Ibid.* "Quippes for Vpftart 1595.
New fangled Gentlewomen, or A Glaffe, to view the Pride of vainglorious women. Containing a Pleafant Inuectiue againft The Fantafticall Forreigne Toyes daylie vfed in Womens Apparell.—1595." White Letter. 4to. *Ibid.* "A Fig for Fortune. Recta fecurus. A. C.—Printed—for C. A. 1596.
1596." *Ibid. read the laft article thus:* "Brittons Bowre of Delights 1597.
Contayning Many, moft delectable and fine deuifes, of rare Epitaphes, pleafaunt Poems, Paftoralls and Sonnets. By N. B. Gent." The Earl of Leicefter's creft. "Imprynted—1597." Quarto.

Page 1051, *infert* "Phillis and Flora. The fweete and ciuil contention 1598.
of two amorous Ladyes. Tranflated out of Latine: by R. S. Efquire. Aut Marti vel Mercurio. Imprinted—by W. W. (*perhaps Will. Williamfon*) for Richarde Iohnes. 1598." 4to. Geo Steevens Efq;

Page 1056, *infert* "Morning and Euening praiers, with diuers Pfalms, 1574.
Hymnes, and Meditations, made and fet forth by the Ladie Elizabeth Tyrwhit."* Printed for Chr. Barker, 1574; with his rebus, as in the frontifpiece. On the back of the title-page are thefe arms; a lion rampant, double queued, in a bordure charged with 8 efcallops. This book, bound with "Prayers or Meditations,—Collected out of holy workes, by the moft vertuous and gracious Princeffe Katherine of England," &c. without printer's name, or date,[t] as p. 449; with part of a Litany, and fome other pieces of books, has lately come into the poffeffion of the rev. Mr. George Afhby, by the death of his mother. See p. 1076, note p. Since my publication of the 2d. vol. the faid gentleman has affured me by Letter, that the information that had been given me was vaftly *infra dignitatem* even of the outfides; and that along with the book has *always* been carefully kept a *bit* of paper with the infcription as below.* The proprietor very juftly obferves that fuch loofe notes without dates or fignatures are feldom exact, or deferve to be received implicitly. Though thefe devotional pieces are at prefent very imperfect, having feveral leaves together cut out, and the back parts left like guards, it can fcarcely be fuppofed that they were bound in fo elegant and fuperb a manner in that ftate. Why, when, or by whom they were fo caftrated, are queftions perhaps not now eafily to be refolved. The date of Lady Tyrwhit's prayers, and Q. Eliz. being

This title is taken from "The fecond Lampe of Virginitie," where they are reprinted. See p. 955. Not having feen the book.

[t] However as the prayer for the king, in the original edition 1545, fpecifies Hen. 8, this prays in the fame words for Edw. 6; therefore was not printed before 1547, nor after 1553.

* "This Book of *Private Prayer* was prefented by the Lady Eliz. Tirwitt to Queen Eliz. during her confinement in the Tower & the Queen Generally wore it hanging by a Gold Chaine to her Girdle & att her death left it by Will to one of her women of her Bedchamber."

being therein prayed for as queen, entirely confute the idea of these in particular having been presented to her in the tower. If any book in this miscellany was so, it might be the Litany, as p. 446; or the Prayers, &c. collected by Q. Catherine, as p. 449. But as they doubtless were prohibited at that time, must not the danger have been very great for them both, if discovered? There is however one conjecture more, and that not improbable: we know not what has been cut out from this famous little magazine. Mr. Ashby acquaints me in the P.S. of his letter, that he has got the concluding half sheet,* never bound or cut open, though somewhat damaged in the bottom lines of the text, but quite perfect and complete in the device, as described in p. 236; which shews it was printed by W. de Worde, and was very probably the book of prayers mentioned by Fuller, as printed by the joint command of Elizabeth consort of Hen. 7, and princess Margaret his mother. See p. 235. Here it may be objected, that then they must abound with Romish superstition: yet there is a salve for that sore. John Field, who set forth "An excellent treatise of Christian righteousnes," translated by him from the French of M. I. de l'Epine, dedicated it to Lady Eliz. Terwhit; wherein he says, "I have dedicated my labours herein, to your good Ladyshippe for sundry causes,—first that they may be a testimony to all posterity of your forvvardnes, fidelity and sincerity in the religion of Christ Iesus:—And I most humbly beseeche you in the eyes and sight of the vvhole vvorlde, that you constantly and inuiolably holde and keepe that blessed hope of your best inheritance. And as God in mercy hath dravven you out of the sinke and mier of Poperie, and of the false vvorshippe of God—to the true religion of Christ, so goe forvvards, and most humbly and continually thanke him for it." See p. 1070. Now, as Lady Tirwhit appears to have been sometime popishly inclined, no time more likely than in the reign of Q. Mary, when the princess Eliz. was in the tower; and then no danger in presenting to her such a book of prayers. When Elizabeth was queen, she naturally might have great regard for the book which had afforded her comfort in her affliction; and that Q. Eliz. highly respected Lady Tyrwhit, appears by her wearing her book of prayers at her side, whether it was presented to her bound in gold, or the queen had it bound afterwards with the other prayers; however, certainly they were not bound till after Tyrwhit's book was printed. It is not unlikely that Q. Eliz. and L. Tyrwhit might have contracted a friendship in their youth, which lasted during life. I have been the more particular in describing this article, as the worthy owner of it has taken extraordinary pains, by his hints and queries, to inform me concerning it.

Ibid.

* As this fragment evidently does not belong to either of the books of prayers specified as part of this collection, and yet was annexed unbound by some one of its possessors, who seems to have been persuaded that it appertained to some or other of them, it necessarily follows, that that person, whoever it was, concluded it to be a part of an edition of the book which had been cut out, (perhaps by some zealot) and was desirous to preserve so much of it as could then be obtained to manifest the original contents.

Ibid. insert " The Glasse of Gouernement. A tragicall Comedie so intituled, bycause therein are handled aswell the rewardes for Vertues, as also the punishment for Vices. Done by George Gascoigne Esquier. 1575." Colophon; " Imprinted at London By H. M. for Christopher Barker at the—Grasshopper in Paules Churchyarde.—1575." Another edition with this colophon, " Imprinted—in Fleetestreate at the—Faulcon, by Henry Middleton, for Christopher Barker.—1575." 4to. See p. 1076. 1575.

Page 1057, *insert* " The Hulie Historie of King Dauid, wherein is chiefly learned these godly and wholesome lessons, that is, to haue sure patience in persecution, due obedience to our prince without rebellion: and also the true and most faithfull dealings of friendes. Drawne into English Meetre for the youth to reade by John Marbeck. 1579.—for John Harrison." Quarto. 1579.

Page 1060, *l.* 20, *for* 1581 *in the margin, r.* 1582, *Ibid. l.* 24, *r.* 1581.

Page 1062, *insert* " Jesuitismi Pars secunda Puritano-papismi, &c. Laur. Humfredo.—excud. Hen. Midletonus. 1584." 8vo. *Ibid.* 1584.
" Richardi Sadleiri de procreandis eligendis, alendis frænandis et tractandis Equis Experientia.—1587." Quarto. 1587.

Page 1070, *insert* " Baptistes, sive Calumnia, Tragoedia, Auctore Georgio Buchanano Scoto.—M.D.LXXVIII." Octavo. 1578.

Page 1071, *l.* 45, *for* p. 1085, *read* 1058.

Page 1072, *insert* " Paraphrasis aliquot Psalmorum Davidis, Carmine Heroico. Scipio Gentili Italo Auctore.—Excudebat—1581." 1581.

Page 1074, *l.* 26, *for* Albercei *read* Alberici.

Page 1075, *l.* 11, " The copie of a letter" &c. and *l.* 19, Certaine Aduertisements" &c. were both printed by " I Vautrollier," probably his wife. See note i, in p. 1064. Their daughter was named Jakin, perhaps after the mother.

Page 1076, *l.* 29, *add* Printed by H. Middleton for him. Maunsell, p. 87. See p. 1801. *Ibid. to note* y, *after* Suffolk. *add* And since her decease in the hands of her son, the Rev. Mr. George Ashby.

Page 1080, *l.* 2, *for* p. 374, *read* p. 734.

Page 1082, *l.* 5, *insert* Mr. Gough has a copy with one leaf more, containing a colophon only. *Ibid. l.* 6, *read* Disputation. *Ibid. l.* 38, *add* Printed in Latin 1584. 1584.

Page 1083, *insert* " The true copie of a letter from the queenes Maiestie, to the Lord Maior of London, and his brethren: conteyning a most gracious acceptation of the great ioy which her Subiectes tooke vpon the apprehension of diuers persons, detected of a most wicked conspiracie, read openly in a great assemblie of the Commons in the Guildhall of that Citie, the 22. day of August, 1586. Before the reading whereof, maister James Dalton, one of the Counsellors of that Citie, in the absence of the recorder, made this speach hereafter folowing. Imprinted—1586." At the end, " Yeuen vnder our Signet at our Castell at Windsor, the 18. day of August 1586. in the 28 yeere of our reigne." In his Majesty's Library. Quarto. 1586.

Page

1595. *Page* 1088, *insert* "The New Testament" &c. as in 1553, p. 715; with the head of K. Edw. VI. but without Vivat Rex on the sides. 8°. Granville Sharp Esq;

Page 1093, *l.* 5, *for* token *read* tokens.

Page 1095, *l.* 18, *for* but has in the margin, *read* conditionally that it be printed. *Ibid. l.* 45, *for* himselse *read* himselfe.

(1686.) *Page* 1099, *insert* "An Epitaph vpon the death of Richard Price Esquier (the second sonne of Sir John Price Knight deceased) which
1587. Richard left this life the fifth day of Januarie 1586." A sheet Folio. *Ibid. insert* "The true and perfecte Newes of the woorthy and valiaunt exploytes, performed and doone by that valiant Knight Syr Fruuncis Drake: Not onely at Sancto Domingo, and Carthagena, but also nowe at Cales, and vppon the coast of Spayne. 1587. Printed by *him*, for Tho. Hacket." Quarto.

1588. *Page* 1100, *insert* "The Lamentations of Amintas for the death of Phillis: Paraphrastically translated out of Latine into English Hexameters, by Abraham Fraunce. Newlye Corrected.—Printed by *him* for Tho.
1589. Newman, and Tho. Gubbin. 1588." 4to. See p. 1679. *Ibid. insert* "A Farewell. Entituled to the famous and fortunate Generalls of our English forces: Sir John Norris and Syr Fraancis Drake Knights, &c. Doone by George Peele, Maister of Artes in Oxforde.—Printed by I. C. and are to bee solde by William Wright, at his shop adioyning to S. Mildreds Church in the Poultrie. Anno 1589." 4to. Brit. Museum.

Page 1109, *l.* 10, *for* 1583, *read* 1584.

Page 1112, *l.* 13, *read* have. *Ibid. l.* 14, *insert* Sold for 16 guineas.

1577. *Page* 1115, *after l.* 6, *insert* To which is annexed, "Trifles by Timothe Kendal deuised and written (for the moste part) at sundrie tymes in his yong and tender age." The whole contains S, in eights. On the last leaf "Imprinted—in Paules Churche Yarde, at the—Brasen Serpent by Ihon Shepperd. Anno 1577." Beneath, is the cut of a swan playing on a violin, and under it

"Martialis. Dulcia defecta modulator carmina linguæ
Cantator Cygnus funeris ipse sui."

In the collection of George Mason Esq. and Edm. Malone Esq. Sixteens.

Page 1117, *l.* 11, *for* 1759 *in the margin*, *read* 1579.

Page 1120, *l.* 37, *for* Wm. Woord, *read* W. Wood.

Page 1121, *l.* 6, *add* On Sunday the 12. March, in the hearing of such obstinate papists as then where prisoners there.

1582. *Page* 1123, *insert* "The Joyfull and Royal Entertainment of Fruuncis the Frenche Kings Brother at Antwerp.—For Wm. Ponsonby." Octavo.

Page 1131, *l.* 13, *for* the *read* sundry. *Ibid. l.* 17, *insert* "Herevnto are added for the more manifest proofe of the matters here reported, sundrie letters and confessions of the offenders, in the same maner as they are extant vnder the hand-writing of the offenders, without change of anie sentence or words." Richard Gough Esq.

Page

Page 1141, *insert* "Wonderfull and straunge sightes seene—over the 1583.
citie of London," &c. See Brit. Topogr. I; 692. *Ibid. l.* 24, *dele*
him, *and add* Henry Carre.

Page 1146, *l. penult. after* Query, *dele* whether the same as mentioned
above? *and add instead thereof,* Why his name was not inserted in the list
of benefactors set up in Stationers' Hall, as well as his wife's?

Page 1147, *insert* The first vol. of Holinshed's Chronicles has "Im- 1577.
printed for George Bishop," London, 1577. Folio. Francis Douce Esq;
His 2d vol. has "printed for Lucas Harrison." See p. 1798. My copy
has "for John Harrison," to both volumes. See p. 1155-6.

Page 1151, *insert* "Compendium Grammaticæ Græcæ Jacobi Ceporini 1590.
ex postrema authoris editione, nunc primum opera Ioannis Frisii Tigurini
castigatum & auctum. 1590." Contains 204 pages cyphered, excluding
title-page and dedication, followed by two leaves not cyphered; the first
of which has some Greek verses of Conrad Gesner, and some Latin ones
of Rudolphus Gualterus, in compliment to the author, and editor; the
last leaf is a table of contents. Michael Wodhull Esq;

Page 1159, *l.* 40, *prefix* A. *Ibid. l.* 43, *after* &c. *add* John Wolfe,
and after Licensed *add* Mr. J. Denyer.

Page 1163, *insert* "Lent Abell Jeffes on CC of his book of London's 1593.
complaynt by consent of our Master, 10 s. Stat. Register A. *Ibid. insert* 1594.
"The second report of Doctor John Faustus containing his appearances
and the deeds of Wagner. Written by an English Gentleman student in
VVittenberg, an Vniuersity of Germany in Saxony. Published for the
delight of all those which desire Nouelties by a frend of the same Gentleman. Printed by *him* for Cuthbert Burby,—1594." K 2, in fours.
Richard Gough Esq; *Ibid, l.* 32, *read* Marchecelsus.

Page 1166, *l.* 4, *for* Jack Wilson *read* Iacke Wilton. *Ibid. l.* 5, *for*
Nash *read* Nashe. *and after* Printed *dele* for G. &c. *and read* for C. Burby.
Ibid. l. 8, *after* shop, *read* the sign of the Unicorn.

Page 1167, *insert* "A Remembraunce of the well employed life and (1577.)
godlie ende of George Gascoigne Esquier, who deceased at Stamford in
Lincolneshire, the vij of Oct. 1577. Reported by Geo. Whetstones Gent.
an eye-witnes of his godly and charitable end in this world, 4to. then
printed." Biogr. Brit. III; 2139, note (25), Edit. 1750. See Ath.
Oxon. I; 190. Licensed to Edw. Aggas 15 Nov. 1577.

Page 1171, *l.* 2, *after* London *add* in 1593 *Ibid. l.* 3, *after* him *add* 1581.
in 1602. *Ibid. insert* "Sophoclis Antigone. Interprete Thoma Watsono
I. V. studioso. Huic adduntur pompæ quædam, ex singulis Tragœdiæ
actis deriuatæ; & post eas, totidem themata sententiis refertissima eodem
Thoma Watsono authore.—Excudebat—1581." 4to. *Ibid. l.* 18, *for*
Imperatore *read* Imperadore, *and add* Scritta in lingua Italiana da Petruccio Ubaldino, Cittadin Fiorentino." His device. "Londra, Appresso
Giouanni Wolfio Inghilese, 1581." George Stevens Esq; N.B. The
first Italian book printed in England.

Page 1172, *insert* "Scipii Gentilis in xxv. Davidis Psalmos Epicæ
Paraphrases—1584." 4°. George Stevens Esq;

Page 1173, *l.* 30, *after* England *dele* Running-title, my copy wanting the title-page. *and add inſtead thereof* Wherein is clearly prooued that the practiſes of Traitrous Papiſts againſt the ſtate of this Realme, and the perſon of her Maieſtie, are in Diuinitie vnlawfull, odious in Nature, and ridiculous in Pollicie." &c. *Ibid. l.* 33, *for* Octavo *read* Quarto.

1589. *Page* 1176, *inſert* "A notable and prodigious Hiſtorie of a Mayden, who ſundry yeeres neither eateth, drinketh nor ſleepeth, neyther auoydeth any excrements, and yet liueth: A matter ſufficiently opened and auerred, by the proceedings, examinations, and diligent informations thereof, taken ex officio by the Magiſtrate. And ſince by the order of the ſaid Magiſtrate Printed and publiſhed in high Dutch, and after in French, and nowe laſtlie tranſlated into Engliſh. 1589." Device: The hand and caduceus. "Printed—M.D.LXXXIX." 6 leaves. Quarto.

Page 1177, *l.* 14, *dele* Anti. *Ibid. l.* 15, *after* With *inſert* Antiſiatus.

1592. *Page* 1180, *inſert* "Four Letters, and certaine Sonnets: Eſpecially touching Robert Greene, and other parties by him abuſed: But incidently of diuers excellent perſons, and ſome matters of note. To all courteous mindes, that will vouchſafe the reading." Device: A palm tree. "Im-

1593. printed—1592." K 2, in fours. 4to. *Ibid. after* "Churchyards challenge." *inſert* As the works of no Engliſh writer are more ſcarce than thoſe of Churchyard, i have tranſcribed below,* for the curious reader, an enumeration of them, as prefixed to this collection of his pieces in proſe and verſe. George Steevens Eſq;

Page

* "Heare follow the ſeuerall matters contained in this booke.

"The tragidie of the Earle of Morton. The tragedie of Sir Simon Burley. A diſcours that a man is but his minde. A diſcourſe of the true ſteps of manhood. A diſcourſe of the honor of a Souldior. A diſcours of an old Souldior and a yong. A diſcourſe and commendation of thoſe that can make Golde. A diſcourſe & rebuke to rebellious mindes. A diſcourſe of hoſpitalitie & conſuming of time & wealth in London. A diſcourſe of misfortune and calamitie. A diſcourſe of law & worthy Lawyers. A diſcourſe of the only Phenix of the worlde. A praiſe of that Phenix & verſes tranſlated out of French. The tragedy of Shores wife much augmented. A diſcourſe of the ioy good ſubiects haue when they ſee our Phenix abroad. The tragicall diſcourſe of the hapleſſe mans life. The adue the writer made long agoe to the worlde. A diſcourſe of a fantaſticall Dreame. A tragicall diſcourſe of a dolorous Gentlewoman. A tragicall diſcourſe of a Lord & a Lady, tranſlated out of French.

"The bookes that I can call to memorie alreadie Printed, are theſe that followes.

"Firſt in King Edwardes daies, a book named Dauie Dicars dreame, which one Camell wrote againſt, whom I openly confuted. Shores wife I penned at that ſeaſon. Another booke in thoſe daies called the Mirror of Man. In Queene Maries raigne, a booke called a New-yeares giſt to all England, which booke treated of rebellion. And many things in the book of ſongs and Sonets, printed then, were of my making. Since that time till this day I wrote all theſe workes. The booke of Chips, dedicated to Sir Chriſtopher Hatton, after Lord Chancellor. The booke called Chance, dedicated to Sir Thomas Bromley, L. Chancellor then. The booke called Charge, to my L. of Sorrye. The booke called my Change, in verſe & proſe, dedicated to all good mindes. The book called my Choice, dedicated to the L. Chancellor ſir Chriſtopher Hatton. The book of the ſiege of Leith and Edenbrough Caſtell. The booke of ſir William Druries ſeruice, dedicated to ſir Drue Drury. The booke

called

Page 1186, *dele l.* 7, *and insert* "The EKATOMΠAΘIA, or Passionate Centurie of Loue. Diuided into two parts: whereof. the first expresseth the Authors sufferance in Loue: the latter, his long farewell to Loue and all his tyrannie. Composed by Thomas Watson Gentleman; and published at the request of certaine Gentlemen his very frendes.—for Gabriell Cawood" &c. to whom it was licensed in 1581." 4to. See p. 1328. George Steevens Esq;

Page 1194, *l.* 30, *for* 1595 *in the margin, read* 1593; *the same in l.* 34; *and to l.* 36, *add* Printed—for Henry Gesson and Francis Coules. Again 1595.

Page 1198. An edition of The Paradice of Dainty Devices 1585 is mentioned by Mr Warton, III; 285, note i; and as the copy was put over from Timothy Rider to Edw. White in 1583, it very probably was printed by, or for him. See p. 1201. 1585.

Page 1199, *l.* 14, *add* His Majesty has a copy having "for Thomas Nelson," &c. See p. 1350.

Page 1200, *insert* "The Paradice of Dainty Devices." *&c.* Device: a flower-pot. "Printed by Edw. Allde for *him*—1596." Capell's: Trin. Coll. 1596.

called the golden Nut, dedicated to the Qu. Ma. The booke of receiuing her highnes into Suffolk & Norfolke. The booke before of her highnes receiuing into Bristow. The booke of the Earthquake, to the good Deane of Paules. [1580.] The booke of the troubles of Flanders, to Sir Francis Walsing. [1578.] The booke called the scourge of rebels in Ireland, to my Lord Admirall. The booke called a rebuke to Rebellion, to the good olde Earle of Bedford. The booke of a sparke of freendship, to Sir Walter Rawley. The booke of Sorrows, to D. Wilson when he was Secretary. The booke of the winning of Macklin, to my Lorde Norrice. The book called the worthines of Wales, to the Qu. Ma. The booke giuen her Maiestie at Bristow, where I made al the whole deuises. The deuises of warre and a play at Awderly, her highnes being at Sir Thomas Greshams. The Commedy before her Maiestie at Norwich, in the fielde, when she went to dinner to my Lady Gernihgams. The whole deuises, pastimes & plaies at Norwich, before her maiestie. The deuises and speeches that men and boyes shewed with in many progresses. The book of King Henries Epitaph, and other princes and Lords, to Secretary Wolley. The book of my Deer adue, to M. Iohn Stannop. The book called a handfull of gladsome verses, to the Qu. M. at Wodstocke. The book called a pleasant conceite, a new yeeres gift, to the Queenes Maiestie.

"These workes following are gotten from me of some such noble freends as I am loath to offend.

Æneas tale to Dydo, largely and truely translated out of Virgil, which I once shewed the Qu. Ma. and had it againe. A booke of the oath of a Judge and the honor of Law, deliuered to a stacioner, who sent it the L. cheefe Baron that last dyed [1596] *(Query this date?)* A book of sumptuous shew in Shrouetide, by Sir Walter Rawley, sir Robart Carey, M. Chidly, and Mr. Arthur Gorge, in which book was the whole seruice of my L. of Lester mencioned, that he and his traine did in Flaunders, and the gentlemen Pencioners proued to be a great peece of honor to the Court: all which book was in as good verse as euer I made. an honorable knight dwelling in the black Friers, can witnes the same, because I read it to him. A great peece of work translated out of the great learned French Poet Seignior Dubartas, which worke treated of a Lady and an Eagle, most diuinely written on by Dubartas, and giuen by me to a great Lord of this land, who saith it is lost. An infinite number of other Songes and Sonets, giuen where they cannot be recouered, nor purchase any fauour when they are craued."

1600. Coll. Cambr. Again in 1600. Printed for him, but without the printer's name. George Steevens Esq. *Ibid. l. penult. after* maydes *add* Printed for him, and is in the Brit. Museum. The author, Tho. Salter.

1590. *Page* 1206, *insert* "A Canticle of the victorie obteined by the French King Henrie the fourth. At Yvry. Written in French by the noble, learned, and deuine Poet, William Salustius; lord of Bartas, and Counsilor of estate vnto his Maiestie. Translated by Josua Siluester Marchant-adventurer.—Printed by Richard Yardley, on Bredstreete hill, at the—Starre. 1590." 4to. George Steevens Esq;

1592. *Page* 1207, *insert* "The Triumph of Faith. The Sacrifice of Isaac. The Ship-wracke of Ionas. With a song of victorie obtained by the French king, at Yvry. Written in French, by W. Salustius" &c. as above. "Printed by Richard Yardley, and Peter Short.—1592." 4to. George Steevens Esq.

1595. *Page* 1208, *l.* 20, *add* Again 1598. *Ibid. insert* "A Commentarie vpon the Lamentations of Ieremy." &c. See p. 1250.—"For Tho. Man. 1595." 4to. Governor Pownall.

1597. *Page* 1029, *insert* "Tusser's 500 points of good husbandry." 4to. 1597.

1598. Francis Douce Esq; *Ibid.* "The First Fowre Bookes of the ciuile warres betwene the two houses of Lancaster and Yorke. By Samuel Daniel,—for Simon Waterson. 1598." Without prefixes: 88 leaves, figured. 4to. George Steevens Esq.

1600. *Page* 1210, *insert* "LVCANS First Booke, translated Line for line by Chr. Marlovv." Binnerman's device of the brazen serpent. "Printed by P. Short, and are to be sold by Walter Burre at the—Flower de Luce in Paules Churchyard, 1600." D 5, in fours. 4to. E. Malone Esq.

Page 1212, *l.* 37, *read* Ubaldino. *Ibid. l.* 38, *after* translated *add* by Robert Adams. *Ibid. l.* 42, *add* "Imprinted—for W. Holn." or Holme.

1595. See the Additions under his name, p. 1363. *Ibid. insert* "A Musicall Consort of Heauenly harmonie (compounded out of manie parts of Musicke) called Churchyards Charitie. Printed—for William Holme. 1595." 4to. George Steevens Esq.

Page 1215, *l. antepenult. for* Tables, *read* Fables.

1596. *Page* 1216, *l.* 3, *for* Printing *read* Poetry. *Ibid. insert* "Enchiridion morale opera Simonis Harwardi. Lond. Excud. Impensis W. Tailer." 16°. Trin. Coll. Cambridge. *Ibid.* "Chloris, or the Complaint of the passionate despised Shepheard. By William Smith.—1596." 4to. George Steevens Esq; *Ibid. l. antepenult. for* 1092 *read* 1392.

1599. *Page* 1217, *insert* "The Fortunate Farewel to the most forward and noble Earle of Essex one of the honorable priuie Counsel, Earle Marshal of England, Master of the Horse, Master of the ordinance, Knight of the Garter, & Lord Lieutenant generall of all the Queens Maiesties forces in Ireland. Dedicated to the right honorable the Lord Harry Seamer second sonne to the last duke of Sommerset. Written by Thomas Churchyard Esquire. Printed—for William Wood at the West doore of Powles. 1599." 4to. George Steevens Esq.

Page

Page 1220, *l.* 27. *read* Munstero. *Ibid. dele l.* 29, *wholly*. See p. 1372.

Page 1227, *l.* 8, *add* " Wherein against all the writings of the principall 1588.
maisters of that sect, those chief conclusions of the next page are (amongst sundry other matters, worthy the readers knowledge) purposely handled, and soundly proued. Also their contrary arguments and obiections deliberately examined, and clearly refelled by the word of God." See p. 1279.

Page 1230, *insert* " Sermons of Maister Iohn Caluin on the Historv of 1592.
Melchesedech: Wherein is also handled, Abrahams courage in rescuing his Nephew Lot: and his Godlines in paying tithes to Melchisedech: in three sermons. Also, Abrahams Faith in beleeuing God, comprehending foure Sermons. And Abrahams Obedience, in offering his sonne Isaack; in three Sermons. Translated out of French by Thomas Stocker. Gent. —and are to be sold at the shop of Andrew Maunsell, in the Royal Exchange. 1592." 8vo. Governor Pownall.

Page 1231, *l.* 14, *add* Allo for Thomas Man, seperately. George Steevens Esq.

Page 1232, *insert* The N. Test. for the Assigns of Richard Day. 1598. 1598.
24°. The late Sir John Hawkins. *Ibid. l.* 38, *add* See The Sad Shepherd, p. 143.

Page 1233, *l.* 1, *add* " By Samuel Lewkenhor."

Page 1239, *insert* " The Device of the pageant borne before Woolstone 1585.
Dixi, lord Mayor of the citie of London, an. 1585, Oct. 29. Imprinted —1585." At the end, " Done by George Peele, maister of artes in Oxford." One sheet, 4to. Brit. Topography, I; 675.

Page 1240, *l.* 29, *add* For Edw. White. *Ibid. l.* 41, *insert* and *before* deaths.

Page 1243, *insert* " Elizabetheis. Siue De Pacatissimo et Florentissimo 1589.
Angliæ Stato, Sub Fæelicissimo Augustissimæ Reginæ Elizabethæ Imperio. Liber secundus. In quo præter cætera, Hispanicæ classis profligatio, Papisticarumq; molitionum & consiliorum hostilium mira subuersio, bona fide explicantur. Chr. Oclando, Authore.—Ex Officina Calcographica. —1589."

Page 1245, *l.* 3, *read* the ministrie.

Page 1249, *l.* 11, *insert* 1593. *in the margin.*

Page 1250, *insert* " ZEPHERIA.—Printed—for N. L. and John Busbie. 1594.
1594." 4to. George Steevens Esq. *Ibid. l.* 29, *after* W. B. *add* (*Wm. Burton.*)

Page 1251, *insert* Prognostication for ever, &c. See p. 867. 4to. 1596. 1556.
Alexander Dalrymple Esq.

Page 1255, *l.* 22, *for* 1595, *read* 1593. *Ibid. l.* 35, *insert* 1593 *in the margin.*

Page 1257, *insert* " The Lives of the noble Grecians and Romanes 1595.
compared together by that graue learned Philosopher and Historiographer Plutarke of Chæronea. Translated out of Greeke into French by James Amiot, *&c.* and done into English by Thomas North. Printed—for Thomas Wight. 1595." Contains 1173 pages, besides the table. Folio. Francis Douce Esq. *Ibid. l.* 41, *add* Granville Sharp Esq.

Page

Page 1261, *l.* 4, *for* 1567-8 *read* 1576-7. *Ibid. l.* 11, *after* General History, *add* See p. 1337. *Ibid. l.* 16, *after* Hugh Corne, *add* See p. 1340.

Page 1264, *l.* 3, *read* continuall iudgement.

1598. *Page* 1266, *l.* 9, *for* 1583 *in the margin, read* 1582. *Ibid. insert* "Phillis and Flora. The sweete and ciuill contention of two amorous Ladies. Translated out of Latine: by R. S. Esquire. Aut Marti vel Mercurio. Imprinted—by W. W. for Richarde Iohnes. 1598." 4to.
1599. George Steevens Esq. *Ibid.* "The Famous Chronicle of king Edwarde the first, surnamed Edvvarde Longshankes, with his returne from the Holy Land. Also the life of Lleuellen, rebell in Wales. Lastly, the sinking of Queene Elinor, who suncke at Charing-crosse, and rose againe at Potters hith, now named Queene hith." Device the Pelican &c. as p. 715. "Imprinted—in Cow-lane. 1599." I, in fours. At the end, "By George Peele," &c. 4to. See p. 1163, and 1723. *Ibid. l.* 37, *read* lately.

1599. *Page* 1268, *insert* "Marcelli Palingenii Stellati, Poetae Doctissimi, Zodiacus vitæ: Hoc est, De hominis vita, studio, ac moribus optime instituendis. Libri XII. Opus mire eruditum," &c. 8°. 1599.

Page 1274, *l.* 43, *for* p. 1251, *read* p. 1256.

Page 1275, *l.* 15, *add* See p. 1380, &c. *Ibid. l.* 31, *set in the margin,* 1596.

1598. *Page* 1282, *insert* "The Famous Victories of Henry the fifth: Containing the Honorable Battel of Agin-Court: As it was plaide by the Queenes Maiesties Players.—Printed—1598." 4°. E. Malone Esq.

Page 1283, *l.* 29, *add* See p. 1380.

1594. *Page* 1285, *insert* "Sonnets to the Fairest Coelia.

Parue, nec inuideo, sine me liber ibis ad illam,
Hei mihi quod domino nō licet ire tuo. Trist. 1.

Printed—W. P. 1594." 4to. George Steevens Esq. *Ibid.* "Examen de ingenios, &c. as p. 1286.

Page 1286, *l.* 27. *after* Faulkener. *add*—sold by Richard Oliue." *Ibid. read note* g *thus*: Mr. Ames, thinking this to be Latin, corrected it accordingly.

1596. *Page* 1290, *insert* "The eleven Bookes of the Golden Asse, containing the Metamorphosie of Lucius Apuleius" *&c.* See p. 938. "Printed—
1597. 1596." 4to. Francis Douce Esq. *Ibid.* "The Wisdome of Solomon Paraphrased. Written by Thomas Middleton. A Ioue surgis opus. Printed—1597." 4to. *Ibid.* "Two Tales, Translated out of Ariosto: The one in dispraise of Men, the other in disgrace of Women. With certain other Italian Stanzas and Prouerbs. By R. T. Gentleman.—Printed—
1598. 1597." 4to. *Ibid.* "Orlando Inamorato. The three first Bookes of that famous Noble Gentleman and learned Poet Matthew Maria Boiardo Earle of Scandiano in Lombardie. Done into English Heroicall verse By R. T.
1598. Gent.—Printed—1598." 4to. *Ibid. dele the inverted commas at the end of l.* 30, *and add* One Booke cut into two Decads. Uno die consenui—Printed —1598." At the end of this English part is added "Tyronis Epistolæ: siue

Mus

Mus rampant in agro aureo. Liber vnus in duas decades partitus.—Ex Officina.—1598." To this is subjoined "The meane in Spending: Promising Praise to the Liberall, Pitie to the Prodigall, Mischiefe to the Couetous.—Printed—1598." 4to. These 3: George Steevens Esq. *Ibid.* "The trumpet of Warre, a sermon preached at Pauls Crosse, by Stephen Gosson. Printed by V. S. for I. O. 1598." 4to. See p. 1369. *Ibid. l.* 33, *add* V. S. for N. Ling. *Ibid.* "A pleasant Comedy entituled: An Humerous dayes Myrth. As it hath beene sundrie times publikely acted by the right honorable the Earle of Nottingham Lord high Admirall his seruants. By G. C. *(George Chapman)* Printed—1599." No division. H 2, in fours. 4to. *Ibid.* "A Warning for fair Women, containing The most Tragicall and lamentable Murther of Master George Sanders of London Marchant, nigh Shooter's hill. Consented unto by his owne Wife, aided by M. Browne, Mistress Drewry and Trusty Roger, agents therein, with their severall Ends. As it hath beene lately diverse Times acted by the Right Honorable the Lord Chamberlaine his Servants. Printed—for Will. Aspley, 1599." 4to. Licensed. See p. 1385. See Biogr. Dramat. I; 290: and II; 399. 1598. 1599. 1599.

Page 1291, *l.* 5, *for* a coat of *read* Sir Walter Raleigh's. *Ibid. l.* 6, *add* See Brit. Topogr. I; 312. *Ibid. l.* 11, Henry IV. Second part, *&c. read thus*: "The Second part of Henrie the fourth, continuing to his death, and coronation of Henrie the fift. With the humours of Sir Iohn Falstaffe, and swaggering Pistoll. As it hath been sundrie times publikely acted by the right honourable the Lord Chamberlaine his seruants. Written by William Shakespeare.—Printed by V. S. for Andrew Wise and William Aspley. 1600."† 1600.

Page 1294, *insert* "Thule, or Vertues Historie. To the Honorable and vertuous Mistris Amy Audely. By F. R. The first Booke.—Printed—for Humfrey Lownes. 1598." 4to. George Steevens Esq. 1598.

Page 1295, *insert* "A Godly Sermon before Edward Coke Esq; at Tittleshall, Norfolk." Sir John Fenn.

Page 1297, *l.* 20, *for* is *read* are.

Page 1299, *insert* "The Eagles Flight, Or Six principall notes, or sure markes for euery true Christian, to soare vp to the euerlasting nest of Gods Eternall kingdome. As it was deliuered in a most godly and fruitfull Sermon at Paules Crosse. By Maister Price at S. Johns in Oxford. Imprinted—for Iohn Busbie—1599." The text Luke 17; 37. Contains F 2, in eights. 16°. Licensed. *Ibid.* "Melancholike humours, In verses of Diuerse natures, set down by Nich. Breton, Gent.—Printed—1600." 4to. George Steevens Esq. *Ibid. note* p, *col.* 2. *l.* 3, *read* Stafford. 1599. 1600.

Page

† N.B. There are two copies of the same date; and in one of these the first scene in the third act is wanting: the Plays in all other respects are the same. It appears as if the defect was undiscovered till many copies had been sold; for only one, containing the addition, has hitherto been found. Signature E consists of six leaves: four of them (exclusive of the two additional ones) were reprinted to make room for the omission. This singular curiosity is in the possession of George Steevens Esq.

1600. *Page* 1301, *inſert* " A Pleaſant Comedie, called Summers laſt will and Teſtament. Written by Thomas Naſh. Imprinted—for Walter Burre. 1600." 12, in fours. Only the title leaf before ſignat. B. Quarto.

Page 1306, *l.* 8 *and* 9, *for* 1223, *read* 1213. *Ibid. l.* 12, *for* Bruſanius, *read* Bruſunus.

VOLUME III.

Page 1309, *l.* 21, *read* aſwell eaſtwarde as weſtwarde, *&c.*

Page 1311, *l. antepenult. after* Robert Ealie, *add* probably a miſprint for Robert Calie *(Caly.)*

Page 1319, *l.* 14, *read* ſomething.

Page 1323, *l.* 1 *and* 2, *dele* At this time *&c. and inſert* This title is taken from a MS. by Mr. Ames in his interleaved copy, ſeemingly from ſome catalogue; or there were two editions of it this year, my copy being
1584. entitled thus: " Campaſpe, Played beefore the Queenes Maieſtie on newyeares day at night, by her Maieſties Children, and the Children of Paules. ¶ Imprinted at London for Thomas Cadman, 1584." In a border of metal flowers after the manner of T. Dawſon; and perhaps may have a colophon, at the end, but my copy wants the laſt ſignature. It appears to have been played alſo at the Black fryers, having a prologue there as well as at the Court, and doubtleſs has two epilogues alſo, as to the edition 1591; p. 1203. The running-title of both editions " A tragical Comedie of Alexander and Campaſpe." W.II₄. *Ibid. l.* 19, *dele* 1588 *in the margin, and ſet it againſt l.* 21.

Page 1324, *l.* 12, *read* The Poeſies.

Page 1325, *running-title, read* Stirrvp; *and for* 1025, *read* 1325.

Page 1328, *l.* 15, *after* loue *add* See p. 1186, and p. 1807.

1580. *Page* 1330, *inſert* " The holie exerciſe of a true Faſt, deſcribed out of Gods word.—Printed for John Hariſon and *him.* An. 1580." *Ibid. l.* 25, *add* " Ihon Kyngſton for *him.*"

Page 1333, *l.* 16, *read* Philip. *Ibid. l.* 18, *add* Again 1595, & 1599.
1594. *Ibid. inſert* " Godfrey of Bulloigne. *&c.* And now the firſt part containing fiue Cantos, Imprinted in both Languages.—Imprinted by Iohn Windet for *him*—1594." 4to. George Steevens Eſq. Query, if the ſame as was printed for Chr. Hunt? See p. 1231.

Page 1337, *l.* 7, *add* Again for him only, 1588. *Ibid. l. ult. inſert* 1589 *in the margin.*

Page 1338, *l.* 2, *for* Ib. *read* Maunſell. *Ibid. l.* 9, *under T. Geſon, add* Again 1581. Francis Douce Eſq.

1599. *Page* 1341, *inſert* " The Silkewormes, and their Flies: Liuely deſcribed in verſe, by T. M. a Countrie Farmar, and an apprentice in Phyſicke. For the great benefit and enriching of England." A wood-cut repreſenting Silkworms &c. " Printed by V. S. for *him*, and are to be ſold at his ſhop at the Weſt ende of Paules. 1599." See p. 1290. George Steevens Eſq.

Page 1343, *l.* 9, *for* beyng *read* beyng. *Ibid. l. ult. add* It was printed in 1559, ſomewhat differently, and ſaid to be written by John Lydgate. See p. 876.

Page

Page 1363, *l.* 5, *after* wood-cuts. *add* See the note in p. 1362. *Ibid. l.* 6, *dele* 1596. *prefixed, and set in the margin. Ibid. insert* "The Mirror and manners of Men. Written by Thomas Churchyard Gent. Imprinted—for W. Holn. 1594." At the end is the following memorandum; "All the other bookes proposed comes out shortly wherein to take my leave of wrighting. The second part of the worthines of Wales shall be by Gods Grace dedicated to the Queenes Maiestie." 1594.

Page 1365, *l.* 5, *after* ver. 9. *add* By Hen. Arthington." *and dele the same in the next line. Ibid. l. ult. after* p. *add* 1341.

Page 1366, *l.* 3, *for* 1299, *read* 1300. *Ibid. l.* 34, *add* See p. 1734. *Ibid. l.* 38, *read* trivialibus.

Page 1368, *insert* "Thule, or Vertues Historie," &c. as p. 1811. *Ibid. l.* 26, *for* 87 *read* 85.

Page 1370, *l.* 16, *after* confession *add the note-letter* u. *Ibid. in note* w, *l. ult. for* notes *read* note s.

Page 1380, *l.* 7, *for* 1660 *in the margin, read* 1600.

Page 1381, *l.* 9, *for* llcensed *read* licensed.

Page 1382, *insert* "A fig for Momus: Containing Pleasant varietie, included in Satyres, Eclogues, and Epistles, by T. L. of Lincolnes Inne Gent. Che pecora si fa, il lupo selo mangia. London Printed for Clement Knight, and are to bee solde at his shop at the little North-doore of Paules Church. 1595." 4to. 1595.

Page 1391, *l.* 26, The next[t] book with a date, &c.

Page 1393, *l. ult. add* See Dr. Middleton's Dissertation concerning the origin of printing in England, p. 10.

Page 1397, *l.* 36, *for* Mcccc. *read* M.ccccc.

Page 1403, *l.* 12, *after* by *add* Tho. Sparke, and *This article is annexed to the foregoing one, and has the paging continued.*

Page 1404, *l.* 6, *for* notalis *read* notulis.

Page 1405, *insert* "Speeches delivered to her majestie this laste progresse, at the right honourable the Lady Russels, at Bissam; the right honourable lorde Chandos, at Sudbury; at the right honourable the Lord Norris at Ricorte. At Oxforde, Printed—1592. To the reader. I gather these copies in wore papers. I know not how imperfect; therefore must I crave a double pardon; of him that penned them; and those that reade them. The matter of small moment, and therefore the offence of no great danger. I. B." Reprinted by Mr. Nichols in his Collection of Q. Elizabeth's Progresses. *Ibid.* "VLISSES REDVX Tragœdia Nova. In aede Christi Oxoniae Publice Academicis recitata, octavo Idus Februarii. 1591." The university arms. "Oxoniae excudebat—M.D.LXXXXII." Dedicated "Illustrissimo viro D. Thomae Sackevilo Buckhurstiæ Baroni, Aureæ Periscelidis Equiti, Regiæ maiestati a consilijs, Academiæq; Oxoniensis 1592. 1592.

[t] "It is not easy to account for a press being set up here, and only employed in printing a single book, and then standing still eleven years.—And if it be objected that the press was stopped on account of the Civil War being renewed in 1469, yet all things were settled in 1471, and Caxton's press worked at Westminster." MSS. Lewis, p. 98, and p. 100.

niensis Cancellario, optimo atq; optatissimo. S.—Vale. Ex Æde Christi Oxoniæ sexto Idus Maij 1592. Honori tuo addictissimus, Gulielmus Gagerus." Prefixed are several commendatory verses. F 6, in eights. Francis Douce Esq.

Page 1411, *l.* 21, *for* and *read* the. *Ibid. l.* 30, In the Bodleian Library is a 'copy *&c.*

Page 1413, *note* i, *col.* 2, *l.* 11, *read* libertatibus.

Page 1415, *note* p, *col.* 1, *l.* 2, *read* humanas. *Ibid. l.* 10, *read* repetitionum.

Page 1416, *l.* 2, *read* "To the Christian reader". *Ibid. l.* 7, *read* Cantibrigiæ. *Ibid. l.* 16, *read* Academiæ.

Page 1421, *l.* 20, *for* ὑπὸ *read* ὑπὸ.

Page 1427, *l.* 5, *for* insulta *read* insula.

Page 1431, *l.* 24, *for* 1480 *in the margin*, *read* 1481. *Ibid. l. last*, *after* abovementioned *add* and p. 26, 27.

Page 1436, *l.* 35, *after* and *add* betweene. *Ibid. l.* 37, *read* furtherence.

Page 1438, *l.* 8, *& seq. read* I find in a Primer intituled "The Houres of our Ladie, after the vse of the church of York," printed anno 1516, a
1530. charm with this titling in red letters; "To all them *&c. Ibid. insert* "Missale ad vsum celeberrime ecclesie Eboracensis, *&c.* A. D. MCCCCC tringentesimo, die vero 2da Julii". 4to. See Brit. Topogr. II; 425. And a page or two further may be seen a curious form of bidding prayer, and another of cursing, for the church of York, from a MS. possessed by the late Sir John Hawkins.

Page 1439, *l.* 45, *under* TAVISTOCK, The Boke' of comfort called in laten Boetius, &c.

Page 1442, *insert* "In this boke is conteyned ẏ names of the baylyss Custose mayers and sheress of ẏ cyte of London from the tyme of kynge Richard the fyrst" &c. as p. 1746; but continued in this edition to "the

' On a blank leaf is written, "Decemb. 2°. 1634. Liber Bibliothecæ Bodleianæ ex dono Thomæ Clayton in Medicina Doctoris & Professoris Regii necnon Collegii Pembrochiensis Magistri Primi. Ipsissimum volumen, quod Doctissimus ille Linacer Medicus Regius et quondam Leonis Decimi condiscipulus, qui hunc Galeni librum Latinitate donavit Regio suo Henrico 8vo dono obtulit. Hunc librum dedit Henricus 8vus Cuthberto Tonstallo tunc temporis Episcopus Londinensis Ille viro cuidam amico suo nomine Speckefordo Anno Dni 1530. Quo mortuo (ut verisimile est) cum per diversos (ita ut fit) possessores pererrasset, tandem feliciter in manus præsentis Donatoris incidit, Qui Eum Thesauro Bodleiano (ipse Bibliothecæ Curator) tanquam κειμήλιον pretiosum perpetuo asservandum concredidit." This book is in its original binding, which is curious, having the King's arms and other ornaments stamped on each cover. For this anecdote I am obliged to the Rev. John Price, the present Librarian.

' In the Bodl. Libr. is a copy of this book which formerly belonged to Mr. Wanley, from whom it came to the late Earl of Oxford, and from thence to Mr. Hearne. In it are some MS. notes of Wanley's. In one of them he says, "The printing composer who set the types of this book seems to have been either a Dutchman or a German; many words being printed according to foreign pronunciation, rather than according to our old English orthography, not to mention his frequent mistakes, &c."

xii yere"* of Hen. 8. A. D. 1520; and therefore probably was printed the latter end of that year, or soon after. The types, as well as the booming initials, are the same as used by P. Treveris to The Great Herbal in 1526, and perhaps before. N. B. The leaves of this edition are not numbered either at top or bottom, but the signatures (after the register of mayors and sherifs) answer to those of the former edition; so that they differ only in the types and orthography, except in the article instanced in note f, p. 1747. This is the edition Mr. Ames made use of, and supposed to have been printed by Pinson, misled by the compiler of the Bodleian catalogue. See p. 270. Mr. Ames mentions also a 4to edition with wood-cuts.ˣ

Page 1448, *l.* 6, *for* readers *read* reader."

Page 1449, *l.* 2, *read* 3 masses for Christmas day.

Page 1452, *l. last*, *for* Elam *read* Elham.

Page 1453, *insert* " A comparyson betwene iiij Byrdes/ the Lark, the Nyghtyngale/ ẏ Thrusshe & the Cucko, for theyr syngynge who should be chauntoure of the quere. By Dan Robert Saltwood, Monke, and Imprinted by John Mychyel." A cut of four birds perched on a sprig. In seven-lined stanzas. D, in fours. " ¶ Thus endyth the comparyson of the byrdes compyled by Dan Robert Saltwood monke And imprynted by John Mychel." 4to. George Mason Esq.

Page 1456, *read the 2d article thus:* " A ryght notable sermon/ made by 1548.
Doctor Martyn Luther/ vppon the twenteth Chapter of John/ of absolution and the true vse of the keyes/ full of great cõfort. In the which also it is intreated of the mynysters of the Church/ and of the Scholemaisters/ what is dune vnto them. Ande of the hardnes and sustenes of the harts of menne. ¶ John. xx. ¶—Imprinted—1548. Cum priuilegio—solum." Ends on c 8. Octavo. Bodl. Library.

Page 1468, *l.* 12, to which he added a preface,ʸ *&c.* *Ibid. l.* 25, The first bookᶻ i have found mentioned by any, *&c.*

* Mr. Oldys thought it should rather be the 13th, one year being misprinted twice over. It is true " the iii yere" is printed twice; but the first year is by mistake printed " the ii yere", which should have been printed " the i year," and the first of the two iii years, " the ii year": the rest are all right. See Brit. Librarian, p. 23.

ˣ This is only a fragment, and was in the possession of the late Mr. Tutet.

ʸ This preface was written by Mr. John Spottiswood, an eminent author in the Law department of this country; and was an accurate antiquarian, as the variety of his tracts, &c. show, published since his death, under the inspection of his son, who possesses the same able talents. G. P.

ᶻ By the kindness of George Paton Esq; of Edinburgh, whose assiduity in procuring and transmitting suitable intelligence, towards perfecting this part of our labours, has never been wanting, i have, since this sheet was printed, been favoured with the following.

" Jottings taken at turning over an old book in Black Letter in the Advocates Library, sent to the faculty by a gentleman from Ayrshire in 1788: titled on the back Treatise of Noblenes.

After the first five leaves in prose, " Heir endes the Porteous of Noblenes translatit out of Frenche in Scottis be Maister Andro Cadiou. Imprentit in the South gait of Edinburgh be Walter Chepman & Androw Millar the xx. dai of Aprile the yhere of God mccccc & viii yheris."

After 20 leaves in verse, " Heir endis the Knightly tale of golagras, and Gawane in the South gait of Edinburgh be Walter Chepman and Androw Millar the viii day of of April the yhere of God MCCCCC & VIII yheris." Bp. Percy mentions 3 tales of Gawane &c. in his MS. This seems to be neither of them.

Follows Sir Glamor. 19½ leaves. Begins, Jesu Chryst hevinnis King." Sir Eglamore is in Bp. Percy's MS. And in print beginning as this.

Balade; one page. First line, "In all our Gardyne growes there no flowres."

"Heir begynnis an Litil tretie intitulit the goldyn targe compilit be Maister William Dunbar. *Begins* Ryght as the Stern of day begouth to Schyne." 5 leaves. "Walterus Chepman & Andro Millar." This has been often published.

"Ryght as all Strings are oewillit in ane
 harp
In ane Accord and twyne all with ane uthe
Quhilk is at king yan curiously y Carp
The found is Soete quhen that ye Sangis
 Suthe
Bot quhen yai ar discordant fals and mythe
Thar wit no man tak plesans in that play
Thai myght weill thole ye Menstrale wer
 away
Bot and ye Strings be not all trew and traist
Quhat Sal we do sall ye Menstrale Wite
Ye bot he bend and preve yam with a Wrast
Be yai untrew pull on and mak all quite
And other trew put in the Stede als tyte
And Change ay Sua quhile he fand trew
 Concorde
Than will men Say he is worht to be a lord
Than ryall king al yis fald real ye realme" &c.
4 leaves, with 4 stanzas in each page.

"Heir begynnis the Mayng or Disport of Chaucere." Begins, "In May quhen flora the fresche lusty quene" 10½ leaves. "Walterus Chepman—Andro Myllar."

Four leaves in verse: the beginning wanting. The last line, "Spink Sink with Stink e tartarum termagoratn." A. M.

The flyting of Dunbar & Kennedy. See the Ever-green.

Heire begynnes the traitie of Orpheus kyng and how he yeld to be wyn.' to hel to Seik his quene & other Ballad in the Latter end—The Nobilness & grete Magnificence. &c. W.C. A.M." 9 leaves.

"The Balade of ane right Noble Victorious & Myghty Lord Barnard Stewart of Aubigney Earl of Beaumont (&c. &c.) compilit by Mr. Wilyam Dunbar at the said Lords cumyng to Edinburg in Scotland Send in ane Hight Excellent Ambassiad fra the said Maist Crysten Kyng to our Maist Soverigne Lord and Victorious Prince James the ferde Kyng of Scottis W.C. Reuerende ryall right reverend and Serene &c. A. M." 2 leaves.

Seven leaves in verse: wants the beginning. Ends, "Quhilk wald waill to your Wiff gif ze fald wed ane." This is evidently The twa mariit wemen and the wedo. See Pinkerton's Ancient Scotish poems, I; 44 & 64.

"I that in heill was and gladnes" &c. 3 pages. Lament for the Deth of the Makkaris. Lord Hailes Collection, p. 74.

"My Gudame was agay Wif but she wes
 right gend
Sho dwelt forth fer I to france upon falkland
 fellis
Thay callit hir kind Killok quha sa hir welle
 kend
She was like a Caldrone bruke cler under
 kellys" &c. 1 page.

"I Master Andro Kennedy" &c. 2 leaves. Kennedy's Testament. Hailes, p. 35.

Fourteen leaves of Fitts, &c. of Robyn Hod. With a print of him on horseback; over which "¶ Here beginneth a gest of Robyn Hode." This wood-cut is like that used by Pynson, in his first edition of the Canterbury tales, for the Squire's yeoman.

This collection consists of a variety of pieces all in verse, except the first, but several of them imperfect; and beside such as are no where else to be found in print, they are valuable on account of the orthography for ascertaining the state of the language in Scotland at the time of their publication. The Bannantyne & Maitland MSS. are upwards of 60 years later, as the first began to be collected about 1568, and the other in 1585, they will be chiefly in the spelling of that period. What is here contained printed in the same place, by the same persons, has the appearance of being all published in *or about* the same year, viz. 1508, be Walter Chepman and Andrew Millar in the Southgait of Edinburgh. *This South-gait is certainly the Cow-gate, or South street from East to West as Maitland, in his Hist. of Edinburg, explains it, p. 185.* If these were the earliest, Poesy was the first fruits of the Scottish press. It may however still be doubted that they were not the first poems printed in Edinburgh: some of Dunbar's latest pieces are here; but his Thristle and Rose composed in 1503, on queen Margaret's coming to Scotland, is not in this collection. King James I. was murthered in 1436; so his poetical compositions preceded the commencement of printing, and would probably have been among the first publications of that

Page 1469, *l.* 4, but the title-page, *&c.* are wanting[a]. *Ibid. l.* 17, Mr. Professor Ruddiman.[b]

Page 1473, *add to note* k, See the acts of James I. parl. 3, ch. 67; also, James II. parl. 14, ch. 90.

Page 1477, *note* r, *col.* 2, *l.* 6, *add* See p. 1491.

Page 1483, *l.* 24, *add* See p. 1495, *note* w. *Ibid. l.* 31, *read* Calendas. *Ibid. after l.* 32, *insert* "---In Dominicam orationem pia meditatio," &c.

Page 1484, *l.* 13, *read* establiche. *Ibid. l.* 29, *after* seen, *add* See the edition 1574, p. 1497.

Page 1486, *insert* "The Confessioun of faith professit, and belevit be the 1561.
Protestantes vvithin the Realme of Scotland. Publisched be thaim in Parliament. And be the Estatis thairof. Ratifeit and appreuit, as hailsũ, & sound Doctryne groundit vpon the infallible treuth of Goddis vvorde. Math. 24. ☞ And this glaid tydingis of the Kingdome, salbe preached throuch the hoole warld for ane wytnes vnto all nationis: And than sall the end cum." Contains E 2, in fours, besides the title. At the end, "Thir Actis, and Artycles, ar Red in face of Parliament. And ratifiit be the three Estatis of this Realme. At Edinburgh ẏ 17. day of July. the zeir of God. Ane thosand fiue hũdreth three score zeris. And Imprentit be me Jhone Scott. 1561." Quarto. W. H.

Page

that sort. There are people alive who remember to have seen the Kings Quair in a printed pamphlet long before Mr. Tytler's copy, but now no where to be found. Gavin Douglas had translated the Remedy of Love before he wrote the Palace of Honor in 1501, and there were several impressions of this last poem "Set forth of auld among ourselves," before the London edition in 1553, as appears from the epistle to the reader in the copy "Imprinted at Edinburgh by John Ross for Henrie Charteris," now republished by the Morisons. The Walter Chepman above mentioned appears evidently to be the Walter Chapman mentioned by Maitland. "Walter Chapman, Citizen of Edinburgh in the year 1513, founded a chaplainry at the altar of St. John the Evangelist, on the southern side of the Church (of St. Giles) in honour of God, the Virgin Mary, St. John the Apostle and Evangelist, and all Saints, and indowed it with an annuity of twenty three marks." Hist. of Edinb. p. 271. *Also,* "*in the lower church yard, at present denominated the Back-stairs, stood the chapel of Holyrood, wherein on the 11th of August, in the year* 1528, *Walter Chepman founded a chaplainry at the altar of Jesus Christ crucified, and endowed it with his tenement in the* COWGATE". *Ibid. p.* 185. *Where it is observable that* SOUTH GAIT, *which Chapman prints as his residence, Maitland denominates* COWGATE.

[a] By the said Mr. Paton I have been favoured with a transcript of the title, viz. "¶ Breuiarij *Aberdonensis* ad percelebris ecclesie *Scotor.* potissimum usum et consuetudinem Pars *hyemalis:* de tp'e et de sanctis *ac* dauitico Psalterio congruenter per ferias diuiso: *cum* Inuitatorijs *hymnis* Antiphonis *capitulis* Respo sorijs *horis* feriar'. commemoracionib' p' anni *circulum* necnon *communi sanctorum* plurimarumq; v'ginum & matronarum ac *diversorum* sanctorum *legendis:* que sparsim in incerto antea vagabantur: *cum Kalendario et* Mobilium festorum *tabula* perpetua varijsq; *alijs* adiunctis *et de nove additis* sacerdotib' plurimum quam necessarijs in *Edinburgensi* oppido *Walteri Chepman* Mercatoris impensis impressa Februarijs idibus. *Anno* salutis nostre & gratie. *IX. M.* supra *et* quingentesimum." The words here printed in Italics are rubrics in the original. Many of the words are abbreviated which cannot be represented in this fount of types.

[b] Mr. Thomas Ruddiman never was a professor in any of the Scottish universities, but an excellent grammarian and adept critic in the Greek, but more particularly in the Latin tongue, as his admirable publications testify, having long justly gained universal approbation. G. P.

Page 1490, *l.* 6, *insert* Now in his Majesty's Library.

Page 1491, *l.* 31, *add* See p. 1477, *note* r. *Ibid. note* q, *l. last*, *for* 1557, *read* 1575.

Page 1492, *insert* " The Kingis complaint," in five-lined stanzas. A broadside. *Ibid.* " Maddies proclamation," in four-lined stanzas. A broadside.

Page 1495, *l.* 31, *for* Edinburgh *read* Edinburghi.

1573. *Page* 1496, *insert* " Ane breif commendatioun of vprichtnes, in respect of the surenes of the same to all that walk in it, amplifyit cheifly be that notabill document of Goddis michtie protectioun, in preseruing his maist vpricht seruand, and feruent messinger of Christis Euangell, Iohne Knox. Set furth in Inglis meter be M. Iohne Dauidsone, Regent in S. Leonards College. ¶ Quhairunto is addit in the end ane schort discurs of the Estaitis quha hes caus to deploir the deith of this Excellent seruand of God. Psalme xxxvii. Mark the vpricht man, and behauld the iust, for the end of that man is peace. ¶ Imprentit at Sanct Androis be Robert Lekpreuik. Anno 1573." On the back begins a dedication " To the maist godlie ancient and worthie Schir Iohne Wischart of Pittarrow Knicht, M. Iohne Dauidsone wissis the continual assistance of the Spreit of God, to the end, and in the end.—From Sanctandrois the xviii. of Febr." The Commendation in 47 octave stanzas; the lamentation of the States in 19 nine-lined stanzas. Concludes with a decastichon of Latin verses " Quam tutum sit propugnaculum Deo sine fuco inseruire, ex mirifica eximii Dei serui Ioannis Knoxii, in tranquillum vitæ exitum, illusis omnibus impiorum conatibus, conseruatione, & eius exemplum sequi monemur.—Finis. Quod. M. I. D." 4to. W.H.

Page 1499, *l.* 29, *add* In the Advocates Library.

Page 1500, *l.* 14, *after* fidelissimi. *add* Device: Truth &c. as p. 1498. *Ibid. l.* 15, *after* Charteris. *add* Anno Do. 1579. *and after* pages, *add* besides prefixes. Neat Roman types. W.H.

1581. *Page* 1501, *insert* The confession of the Faith of the Church of Scotland, subscribed by the King, &c. 1581. 8vo. See p. 1507. *Ibid.* " Ane Disputation concerning the Controversit Headdis of Religion, halden in the Realme of Scotland," &c. 8°. See p. 1654.

Page 1502, *l.* 23, *add* Contains 249 leaves, besides the prefixes. Ro-
1584. man types. Device: Jugge's Pelican, copied. *Ibid. insert* " A comfortable treatise of Justification, &c. By Henry Balnaves. 1584." See Knox's Hist. of the Reformation—of Scotland, p. 91.

Page 1508, *l.* 14, *after* Meluinum. *add* Pro. 16; 13. (12) Justicia stabilet thronum Regis. *Ibid. l.* 15, *after* Walde-graue *add* An. Dom. 1590.

1594. *Page* 1515, *insert* " Principis Scoti-britannorum Natalia." Device: Truth &c. as p. 1498; but the printer's initials omitted. " Edinburgi excudebat Robertus Walde-graue, Serenissimæ regiæ Majestatis Typographus. Anno 1594." This occupies 3½ pages, printed with Italics. To which is added another poem intituled " Amuletum," on 2½ pages. " Finis." Under it, " Hæc Andreas Melvinus." In Roman. 4to.

Page

Page 1520, *l.* 36, *read the date in the margin* 1599. *Ibid. insert* "Hymnes, or Sacred Songes, wherein the right Vse of Poesie may be espied be Alexander Hume. whereunto are added the experience of the Authors youth & certaine precepts serving to the practise of Sanctification. Edinburgh printed by Robert Walde-graue printer to the King's Majestie. 1599. Cum privilegio." Dedicated "To the faithfull & vertuous Ladie Elizabeth Mal-vill & Ladie Cumrie,—dated at Logie 16 Februarie 1598. Alexander Hume, Minister of the Evangell." 66 pages, B. L. except the dedication and preface, which are in Roman. 4to. 1599.

Page 1521, *insert* "The true lawe of free monarchies. Or, the reciprock and mutuall dutie betwixt a free King, and his naturall Subiects." Anonymous; but is placed in the collection of K. James VI's works. Without date. *Ibid.* "Ane Metaphoricall Invention of a Tragedie called Phoenix." On signat. K 1, begins "Ane Schort Treatise, Conteining some Reulis and cautelis to be obseruit and eschewit in Scottis Poesie." On signat. N 2, begins, "The CIIII. Psalme, Translated out of Tremellius." On signat. O ii, "Ane schort Poeme of Tyme." 2 pages. Then, "A Table of sume obscure wordis &c. I haue inserted for the filling out of their vacand pageis, the verie wordis of Plinius vpon the Phœnix, as followis." The whole contains P iiii. 4 . Trinity Coll. Cambridge. —— ——

Page 1528, *insert* "This is the dyalogus or Cõmunyng betwixt the wyse king Salomon and Marcolphus." Under it a cut of a king sitting on his throne with a sceptre in his hand, and two figures standing before him: the foremost with a three-pronged fork in his right hand; the other with a staff in his left hand: the same cut on the back of the leaf. 18 leaves. "Emprinted at Andewerpe by me Gerard leeu." 4to. Bodleian. *Ibid.* "Expositio hymnorum secundum vsum Sarum." With "Expositio sequentiarum —Sarum." Colophon: "Impressum per me Theodericum Martini in oppido Alosten. comitatus Flandrie. die xxii Marcii, anni MCCCCLXXXVII." 4to. Richard Gough Esq. *Ibid.* "Directorium sacerdotum" &c. as p. 87. Octavo. In the Bodleian; but wants the title-page. After the Calendar, "Incipit prologus" &c. At the bottom of the page is written "Antwerp, 1488." *Ibid.* "Missale secundum vsum ecclesie Sarum Anglicane." Colophon: "...Impressum Venetiis, per Joannem Bertzog de Landoia, felici nomine explicitum est anno Domini MCCCCXCIIII." 12mo. See Brit. Topography, under Hereford, Salisbury and York; where these and many other Service books according to the use of those churches, are more fully described. —— 1487. 1488. 1494.

Page 1529, *insert* "Breviarii secundum morem Sarum, &c. Impressum Venetiis, per Joannem Bertzog de Landoia, anno natiuitatis christianissimæ post millesimum quaterque centesimum nonagesimo quinto, kalendas Martias." 12mo. *Ibid.* "Missale ad vsum Ecclesie Sarisburiensis." Literis quadrat. Rothomagi. 1497." Folio. *Ibid.* Horæ B. Mariæ, &c. Sine loco. 8vo. 1497. *Ibid.* "Hore presentes ad vsum Sarum impresse fuerunt Parisius per Philippum Pigouchet, anno salutis 1498." *Ibid.* Bp. Burnet mentions a Mass book, *or Missal*, printed at London, 1500, in which "there is 1495. 1497. 1498. 1500.

is a Mafs for avoiding fudden death, which pope Clement made in the college with all his cardinals, and granted to all who heard it 270 days of indulgence," &c. Hift. of the Reformation. II, 61. I have not met
with that edition, but find the fame confirmed in all the Sarum Miffals in
my poffeffion, viz. from 1498—1557, except 260 for 270 days of indulgence. It is towards the end of the volume, and intitled "Miffa pro mor-
1501. talitate evitanda" &c. *Ibid.* "Miffale—Sarum." Over a cut of St. George
1502. flaying the dragon, and St. Catharine holding a lamb. *Ibid.* "Anno incarnationis dominice fecundo fupra quingentefimum atq; millefimum, die vicefima
prima menfis Septembris, opera et induftria M. Petri Oliueri et Johannis
Manditier, impreflorum Rothomagi, iuxta facellum diui apoftolorum
principis Petri commorantium. Impenfa vero Johannis Ricardi, mercatoris: hoc nouum et egregium opus facri Miffalis ad vfum famofe ac percelebris ecclefie Helforden. nuper inftanti ac peruigili cura vifum correctum
et emendatum, necnon autoritate reuerendi in Chrifto patris et domini eiufdem ecclefie epifcopi meritiffimi ac dominorum decani et capituli, eft in
propatulo venale facili precio coram cunctis productum et exhibitum."
The form of matrimony herein is more antique than any i have met with.
Though the prayers, pfalms, &c. were in Latin, the contracting part was
in English. "I, *N.* underfynge þe *N.* for my wedded wyf, for better, for
worfe, for richer, for porer, yn fekenes, and yn helþe, tyl deþ vs departe, as
holy churche haþ ordeyned, and þerto y plyzth þe my trouuþe. *Et iterum
accipiat eam per manum dextram in manu sua dextra, et ipsa dicat sacerdote docente.* I, *N.* underfynge þe *N.* for my wedded houfbunde, for better for
vvorfe, for richer, for porer, yn fekenes, and yn helþe, to be bouum to þe
tyl deþ vs depart, as holy churche haþ ordeyned, and þerto y plyzt þe my
trouuþe.—*Vel dicat in materna lingua hoc modo, sacerdote docente.* Wyþ
þys ryng y þe vvede and þys gold and feluer ych þe zeue and vvyþ myne
body ych þe honoure." The form of matrimony, as well as afking the banns,
was then celebrated at the church-door, the parties not entering the church
till that part of the office where the minifter goes up to the altar and repeats
the pfalm, Beati omnes qui timent Dominum, &c. But this was not peculiar to Hereford. See fimilar forms in p. 251, and 561. There is a
wood-cut of the king's arms and the George, at the beginning; fo that
probably it was printed for Pinfon as well as Ricards. At the end, "Finis
miffalis ad vfum celebris ecclefie Helforden. fumma cura et vigili opera
nuper impreffum Rothomagi. cum additione accentuarii legentibus in ec-
clefiis valde vtilis. Et hoc impenfis Johannis Ricardi eiufdem Rotham.
ciuis non immeriti iuxta ecclefiam diui Nicolaii commorantis." Folio.
Mr. Hearne had an imperfect copy of this book, now in the Bodleian, but
Mr. Ames had the ufe of a compleat one printed on vellum, then in the
poffeffion of the late Hez. Bedford, M. D. I omitted it under the name
of Henry Pepwell, intending it for the General Hiftory, where it properly
belongs, but it was forgot till too late. See Hearne's preface to his edition
1502. of Camden's Eliz. p. 27. *Ibid.* "Hore prefentes ad vfum Sarum impreffe
fuerunt Parifiis, per Philippum Pigouchet, anno Domini MCCCCCII, die vero

viii

viii Marcil pro Symone Voſtre librario, commorante ibidem in vico
nuncupato novo beate Marie in interſignio ſancti Johannis evangeliſte."
4to. *Ibid.* "Expoſitio hymnorum &c. Ant. per Mich. Hillenium. Se- 1502.
quentiarum.—Paris. 1502." 4to. Bodleian. *Ibid.* "Miſſale ad vſum in- 1503.
ſignis ac famoſe eccleſie Sarum: &c. Impreſſum Pariſiis per Thielmanum
Keruer in arte impreſſoria diſertiſſimum almeque vniuerſitatis Pariſienſis
librarium iuratum benemeritum. Anno ab incarnatione dominica quin-
genteſimotertio ſupra milleſimum. Pridie nonas Aprilis." 8vo. Richard
Gough Eſq.

Page 1530, *inſert* "Breuiariū ſecundū vſum hereford." This title, in 1505.
red, is over a cut of the portcullis, crowned and ſupported by a greyhound
& a vivern; on a riband at top, "Dieu et mon droit," and three roſes in
the foreground. Beneath the cut,

"Nō opis eſt clero que digna repēdere poſſit
Pro tantis meritis alma virago tuis
Eccleſie ſacris que margareta miniſtris
Conculiſy ethereo vive beata polo."

On the back page is a ſhort dedication to the clergy of Hereford, thus inſcribed; "Inghelbertus Haghe: illuſtriſſime viraginis: domine Margarethe:
comitis Richemonten. et derben atq; inuictiſſimi et longe ſereniſſimi Anglie
regis Henrici ſeptimi/ ſanctiſſime parentis: cliens et dedititius Herford-
enſis eccl'e prepoſitis et clero Salutem dicit." Concluding, "Valete ſancti-
tatis columina. Ex officina rothomagen. cum illic agerem ad Idus Julias
Anno ſalutis noſtre Milleſimo quingentiſimo quinto." After the calendar
are two leaves prefixed, containing the ſervice "Jn cōmemoratione ſ'cti
thome," and "Jn cōmemoratione ſ'cti ethelberti." Colophon: "Ad
benedictiſſimi ſemperq; ſacratiſſimi domini ac ſaluatoris noſtri ieſu chriſti
gloriam: et ad totius celeſtis curie laudē: atq; ſingularem illuſtriſſime comitis richemonten. commendationem: necnon ad toti' eccleſie hereford'
cleri vtilitatem et ſalutem: impreſſum eſt hoc breuiarium ſecūdum eiuſdem
dioceſis vſum in clariſſimo rathomagen. emporio: impenſis et cura Jnghel-
berti haghe dicte comitis Bibliopole ac dedititii Anno ſalutis chriſti Milleſimo quingenteſimo quīto. ii. non. auguſti." On the laſt leaf, the portcullis, as on the title-page, only. Hereunto is annexed another part, with
freſh ſignatures from AA to FF, in eights; the laſt leaf blank, as is the laſt
column of the preceding one. 16°. The rev. Dr. Lort, and Richard Gough
Eſq. *Ibid.* Horæ—Sariſburienſis. Paris. 1506. 8vo. *Ibid.* "Liber 1506.
Theodoli, ſiue Theoduli cum commento. Lond. 1508. Impreſſ. pro 1508.
Johanne Wright." 4to. *Ibid.* "Miſſale ſecundum vſum inſignis eccleſie 1508.
Sarum.—Anno incarnationis dominice quingenteſimo octavo ſupra milleſimum,—impenſa honeſtorum virorum Johannis huuin & Guillermi bernard,
mercatorum," &c. Folio. *Ibid.* John Huuin alſo printed "Miſſale in 1508.
vſum—Sarum. Rothomagi, 1508. Sept. 27. 8vo" *Ibid.* "Miſſale ad 1510.
cōſuetudinē inſignis eccleſie Sarum vna cum dicte eccleſie inſtitutis cōſue-
tudinibuſq. nuper elimatiſſime īpreſſu: additis pluribus que in ceteris
deſiderantur. In alma Pariſiorum academia. Anno domini virtutum

cōditorisq. mundi Millesimo quingentesimo decimo, die vero decimo kalendas mensis Aprilis,—1510." This title is in two rondeaux chained together, crowned and supported by eagles: over which, "Fortuna opes auferre: nō animū potest." underneath, an Hexastichon, "Ad sacerdotes exhortatio." The canon of the mass, printed on vellum, begins on Fo. clvj, with a folio cut of the crucifixion prefixed: many other neat wood-cuts are interspersed throughout the whole book. At the end is the cut of St. George slaying the dragon; and in the back ground is seen a royal virgin sitting on the ground, holding a lamb by a string with her right hand, and with her left hand supporting the arms of France and England quartered and crowned, a bright star appearing over her; on the opposite side are seen the king and queen looking over the city wall, as praying for the deliverance of their daughter. Folio. A very fine copy, W.H. *Ibid.* "Missale ad consuetudinem ecclesie Sarum: politissimis formulis (vt res indicat) emaculatissime impressum: additis plurimis commoditatibus modisatibus que in ceteris desiderantur." &c. A wood-cut of a priest between two assistants kneeling before an altar, over which is represented Christ between two angels, with the instruments of scourging: the same repeated at the beginning of the service. Colophon: "Missale ad vsum insignis ecclesie Sarum per Johanem Higmanum & Wolffgangum Hopylium in Parhisiorum academia emaculatissime impressum anno Domini virorum, saluatorisque mundi millesimo quingentesimo x kalendas Julii." and at the end, "J. B. G. H. me fieri

1510. fecerunt." Folio. *Ibid.* "Missale secundum vsum ecclesiæ Herefordensis.

1510. Rothom. 1510." Bodleian. *Ibid.* "Hore beatissime virginis Marie ad vsum Salisburiensis ecclesiæ," &c. Th. Kerver's cypher and name. Colophon, "Finit officium beate virginis Marie secundum vsum Sarisburiensis ecclesie. Impressum Parisiis per Thielmannum Keruer. Impensis ac sumptibus prestantissimi Wilhelmi Dauit ciuis et mercatoris Londoniensis et stapul' ville Calise. Anno Domini millesimo quingentesimo decimo: die vero quinta mensis Septembris." Borders of wood-cuts. 8vo.

1510. Bodleian. *Ibid.* "Manuale ad vsum celeberrime ecclesie Sarum, recentissime impressum Rothomagi optimis caracteribus atque completum. Anno salutis millesimo supra quingentissimum decimo,—finit feliciter. Deo gratias." 4to. Bodleian.

(1510) *Page* 1531, *insert* "Rudimenta Grammatices à Johanne Coleto, Decano Ecclesiæ Sancti Pauli London in Usum Scholæ ab ipso institutæ." Dedicated by the author to Lilye, the first head master of the said school, in a short elegant Latin epistle, dated 1 Aug. 1510. In the Pub. Libr. Cambridge, among the King's MSS. See Knight's Life of Colet, p. 124;

—— and the Appendix, N° xi. xiii. *Ibid.* "Hore beate Marie virginis ad vsum —Sarum—Parisiis, per Germanum Hardouyn commorantem inter duas portas palatii regis ad intersignium diue Margarete." 4to. *Ibid. l.* 7, *after* monsters, *add* Translated out of divers authors by Laur. Andrew of

1511. Calis, and printed at Antuerpe with pictures by Joh. Doesborow." *Ibid.* "The chirche of euyll men" &c. as p. 1782.

Page

Page 1522, *insert* " Officium B. M. V. secundum vsum Sarum. Ad finem 1512.
psalterium B. M. V. per Bonauenturum. Paris. 1512." 8vo. *Ibid.* " En- 1513.
chiridion preclare ecclesie Sarum cum deuotissimis precationibus ac venustissimis imaginibus. Paris 1513." Sixty neat cuts, with English descriptions in red. *Ibid.* " Portisorium seu breuiarium ad vsum insignis ecclesie 1514.
Sarum:" &c. Both parts. " Impressa Parisius per Thelmanum Keruer,
ad signum craticule commorantem in vico S'cti Jacobi. Anno Domini
MCCCCCXIIII. xxv die Januarii." On the back of the title-page, " Redemptoris mundi arma." A shield, with the instruments of the passion. See
p. 1308. On the title and last leaf Kerver's device, supported by two
unicorns. R. Gough Esq. *Ibid.* " Missale—Sarum nuper accuratissime
castigatum;—cum pluribus officiis nouis in fine additis. Imprime a
Rouen deuant sainct Lo. Magister Martinus Morin." At the end, " Finit
missale recentissime impressum Rothomagi iuxta ecclesiam sancti Viuiani,
ere & expensis Guillermi Bernard ibidem degentis ante atrium bibliopolarum maioris ecclesie. Anno Dnī. MCCCCC et XIIII. die vero XV mensis
Februarii." 4to. Bernard's initials and name, also ihs ☩, and R. A. D. N. F.
Ibid. Missale—Sarum, printed in the university of Paris, 1515. Octavo. 1515.
Bodleian. *Ibid.* Missale—Sarum, whose colophon has " in alma Parisiorum academia opera Wolfgangii Hopylii, impensis Fr. Byrckman,
1514. 28 Nov." Folio. Richard Gough Esq.

Page 1533, *insert* " Missale—Sarum, vna cum dicte ecclesie institutis 1516.
consuetudinibusque nuper elimatissime impressum, adiectis pluribus que in
ceteris desiderantur. Tabula etiam perpulchra &c. Consummatum in
alma Parisiorum academia, anno Domini virtutum conditorisque mundi
MCCCCCXVI." Colophon, " Missale ad vsum ecclesie Sarisburiensis optimis formulis (vt res ipsa indicat) diligentissime reuisum ac correctum,
cum multis annotatiunculis ac litteris alphabeticis, euangeliorum atque
epistolarum originem indicantibus. Impressum Parisius per Johannem
Kerbriant, alias Huguelin & Johannem Adam socios. Impensis eorun-
dem, necnon Johannis Petit atque Johannis Bienayse. Anno Domini
millesimo quingentesimo sexto, die vero xxii mensis Augusti." John
Petit's initials, and a fleur de lis on a shield supported by two lions seiant.
At the end, " Mater Dei" sitting. 8vo. Richard Gough Esq. *Ibid.* 1516.
" Hore—ad legitimum Sarisburiensis ecclesie ritum &c. Venundantur
Londoni a Francisco Byrkman, ciuis Coloniensis, in cemiterio sancti Pauli."
Colophon, " Hore—totaliter ad longum, cum (15) orationibus beate bri-
gitte, ac multis aliis orationibus et indulgentiis, cum tabula—ac in alma
Parhisiorum Academia, impensis et sumptibus—Francisci byrckman,—
impresse anno Domini MCCCCCXVI. Die vero xix Nouembris." 4to. Bod-
leian. *Ibid.* " Psalterium cum hymnis secundum vsum ecclesiæ Sarum. 1516.
Par. per Franciscum Byrkmanum. 1516." 4to. Bodleian. *Ibid.* " Mis- 1517.
sale ad vsum Ecclesiæ Eboracensis. Rothomagi. 1517." 4to. Catal. Bibl.
Bodleianæ, II; 186. *Ibid.* " Legende totius anni tam de tempore quam 1518.
de sanctis secundum ordinem Sarum." A cut, the virgin and child, and
the adoration: below, a female with a scroll, " Permutat breuis hora summis,"

and a number of women kneeling round her; and under her the martyrdom of the Maccabees: at the top, a shield with Birkman's arms, and another with a merchant's mark. At top and bottom, "Fortuna opes auferre non animum potest." Colophon, "Legende festivitatum tam temporalium quam sanctorum—Impresse Parisius, per Wolfgangum hopylium. Impensis honesti viri Franscisci Byrckman—Anno Domini MCCCCCXVIII."
1519. Folio. Richard Gough Esq. *Ibid.* "Missale ad vsum insignis ecclesie Sarum." Over the king's arms crowned and supported by angels; the rose, with IHS in the center, crowned; and St. George, &c. but somewhat different from that described in p. 1822. Colophon, "Explicit missale &c. Impressũ ĩpẽsis—Francisci regnault alme vniuersitatis Parisien. librarii iurati in vico s'cti iacobi ad ĩtersigniũ diui claudii cõmoran. Anno Dñi m. ccccc. xix. die xx martii". Folio. W.H.
1519. *Ibid.* "Hore beatissime *virginis Marie* ad legitimũ *Sarisburiensis ecclesie* ritum: cum quindecim orationibus *beate Brigitte* ac multis *alijs orationibus pulcherrimis* & indulgẽtijs, cũ *tabula* aptissima iã *vltime* adiectis." In black and red. The root of Jesse in a border of saints, and under it

"*Egredietur virga de radice Iesse;*
Et flos de radice eius ascendet."

On the back page of Fo. clxxxvj. "*Finis horarum. Hore beatissime v'ginis Marie* scd'm vsu Sarum totaliter ad longum: *cum orationibus*" &c. as the title. "ac ĩ alma Parrhisiorũ academia; impensis et sumptibus *honesti viri Francisci regnault* ciuis Parisiensis impresse in vico sancti *Jacobi* in intersignio sancti *Claudij* cõmorantis. *Anno Domini* M. ccccc.xix. Die v'o. xxiiij. mẽsis Octobris." Then, "*Contenta in his horarijs.*" 7 pages. "*Finis presentis Tabule. Hore*—Impresse Parisius per *Nicolaum hicqman allemanum;* Impensis—*Francisci* Birckmã ciuis Coloniensis. Anno dñi" &c. as above. On the back Regnault's rebus, and name. Every page enclosed in borders, adorned with neat wood cuts, of the apocalypse, dance of Death, and Julius Cesar's triumph, &c. On Fo. lxxxiiij, is a suffrage "De btõ rege* Henrico." With a cut of the king, whole length. Small
1519. folio. W.H. *Ibid.* "Missale ad vsum Sarum, seu missale ad vsum ecclesie Sarisburiensis, reuisum et correctum, cum multis annotatiunculis. Parisiis per Nicolaum Higman, almanum, sumptibus Fr. Regnault and
1519. Byrckman. 1519. 29 Oct." 4to. *Ibid.* "Breviarium—Sarisburiensis.
1519. Par. 1519." fol. Harleian cat. *Ibid.* "Processionale ad vsum—Sarum nouiter rursus castigatum per excellentissimum ac vigilantissimum & reuerendissimum in Christo patrem dominum nostrum dominum episcopum de Wynton feliciter incipit Parisius impressum per Wolfgangum Hopylium impensis honesti viri Francisci Byrckman,—Anno Domin MCCCCCXIX. die vero xxviii Octobris." Byrckman's arms; on a shield, Gutte de poix, in chief 3 crowns, supported by 2 eagles; over it, PERMUTAT BREVIS HORA IMA SUMMIS; below, FRANCISCUS BIRCKMAN. "Venun-

* "*Rex henricus sis amicus*
nobis in angustia,
Cuius prece: nos a nece
salvemur perpetua.

Lampas morum spes egrorum
ferens medicamina.
Sis iuorum famulorum
ductor ad celestia.

Par

"Venundantur Londonii apud Franciscum Byrckman, in cimiterio Sancti
Pauli." *Ibid.* "Hore B. M. V.—Sarum." Colophon: "Hic finem (1519.)
habent Hore &c Parisiis, per Fr. Regnault, in vico Sancti Jacobi, e
regione Maturinorum, ad signum elephantis." MS. date 1519. See
Gent. Mag. Jan. p. 13. *Ibid.* "Missale—Sarum, nuper accuratissime (1519.)
castigatum perpulchris caracteribus certisque biblie cotatiunibus etiam cum
alphabeti litteris super epystolas euangelia versiculos & gradualia impressum
officia omnium sanctorum totaliter ad longum (quod celebrantibus maxime
erit vtilitati) continens cum pluribus officiis nouis in fine additis." Jacques
Comin, with his device and motto, IN TE JESU SPES MEA. 4to. Richard
Gough Esq. A MS. note in his copy says, This was printed at Paris
1519. The Bodleian copy has a MS. date Rothom. 1521. *Ibid.* "EPI- 1520.
GRAMMATA CLARISSIMI Disertissimi'q; uiri Thomae Mori Britanni ad
emendatũ exemplar ipsius autoris excusa. Apud inclytam Basileam." This
title is in the compartment of Mutius and Porsenna by H. Holbein, afterward used by Pinson and others. 116 pages: on the last is Froben's device, a
caduceus held by two hands, on a shield richly ornamented; under it "Basi-
liae apud Ioannem Frobenium mense Decembri. Anno M.D.XX." 4to.
W.H. *Ibid.* Hore ad usum Sarum. Paris. (sumpt. Fr. Byrckman,
14. Jun.) Anno 1520. *4to.* Hist. of the Reform. II; Records, p. 143.
Ibid. Portiforium. Pars estivalis. The date in Extracta ex compoto is
1520 & 1521. 4to. *Ibid.* "Presens missale—Sarum nouissime extat 1521.
impressum Rothomagi opera magistri Petri Oliuier, impensis honesti viri
Jacobi Cousin, bibliopole Rothomagi moram agentis circumcirca cor-
digeros; et in atrio librariorum maioris ecclesie in regione curie ecclesi-
astice. Anno salutis M. D. XXI. die vero quinta mensis Septembris." 4to.
This is the colophon of a copy wanting the title-page, in the Bodleian.
The same appears to have been printed also for John Caillard of which
Mr. Ames had a copy thus entitled, "Missale ad vsum insignis ac preclare
ecclesie Sarum nuper accuratissime castigatum—cum pluribus officiis nouis
in fine additis." as above (1519). At the end, "Presens missale—impressum Rothomagi opera Magistri Petri oliuier Impensis—Johannis caillard
moram trahentis prope inter signium quattuor filiorum Edmundi Anno
salutis (*M.D.*) XXI. Die vero quinta mensis Septembris." 4to. The
late Mr. Ibbot had an imperfect copy, either of this edition or that in the
Bodleian, with a MS. date. Catal. Nº 2849. *Ibid.* A. Primer printed 1521.
by

Pax in terra non sit guerra
orbis per confinia.
Virtus crescat et feruescat
caritas per omnia
Nos sudore vel dolore
moriamur subito.
Sed viuamus et plaudamus
celis sine termino.
Vers. Ora pro nobis deuote rex henrice.
Resp. vt per te cuncti fiant inimici. *Oremus.*
Presta quesumus omnipotens et misericors
deus: vt qui deuotissimi regis henrici me-
rita miraculis fulgentia pie mentis affectu
recolimus in terris eius & omnium sanctorum suorum intercessionibus ab omni peste
febre morbo ac improuisa morte ceterisq;
erueamur malis et gaudia superna adipisci
mereamur. Per dominum nostrum iesum
christum filium tuum. Qui tecum viuit et
regnat deus. Per omnia secula seculorum.
Amen. Paternoster. Aue maria."

b. (for) Frances Bryckeman, in the yere of our Lord, 1521. Becon's
1522. Works, III; Fol. cci. (ccvii.) *Ibid.* "Aſſertio ſeptem ſacramentorum ad-
verſus Martinum Lutherum, edita ab invictiſſimo Angliae et Franciae
rege,—Heinrico eius nominis octavo, cum regiſtro nuper addito, atque
D. Eraſmi Rothe. epiſtola huius operis commendaticia. Impreſſ. Argentine
1522. per J. Brieninger." 50 leaves. 4°.* *Ibid.* "Contra Henric. Angliae
Martinus Luther. Longe alius eſt hic liber quam ille quem ante hunc ver-
1522. nacula lingua ſcripſit. Wittembergae". 4°.* *Ibid.* "Pſalterium, cum
Hymnis ſecundum vſum & conſuetudinem Sarum et Eboracen. with the
1523. cut of the Trinity. Paris. Fran. Birkman. 1522. 7 Jun." 16°. *Ibid.* "Pro-
ceſſionale—Sarum caſtigatum per epiſcopum Wynton. Antwerpie per Chr.
1523. Endouienſem. 1523." 4to. Bodleian. *Ibid.* "Aſſertionis Lutheranae
1524. Confutatio. Antv. ap. Mich. Hillerium. 1523." Bodleian. *Ibid.* "Hymnorum opuſculum cum notis muſicis ſecundum vſum eccleſie Sariſburienſis.
1525. Antv. per Chr. Endouium. 1524." 4°. Bodleian. *Ibid.* "Aſſertionum
M. Lutheri confutatio, per reuerendum patrem D. Johannem Roſſenſem
epiſcopum, &c. edita: ſuntque ſingulis confutationibus ſingulae Lutheri
aſſertiones praefixae, quo facilius, utrius ſententiae ſubſcribendum ſit, cog-
noſcatur. Acceſſit praeterea totius operis per eundem, praecipue tamen
annotationum additarum recognitio. Apud ſanctam Ubiorum Agrip-
1525. pinam." *Ibid.* "Prouinciale ſeu Cōſtitutiones Anglie:—rurſum reuiſe, atque impreſſe." See p. 312. A cut adapted to the clauſes of the Te Deum. Beneath: "Venales habētur Londō in cimiterio ſancti Pauli apud Fran. Bryckman." The whole in a neat architective compartment. Contains Fo. cclv. "Explicit preclarū opus wilhelmi Lindewode—ſumma cura atq; diligentia Chriſtopheri Endouien. Antwerpie impreſſum.—Impenſis vero Franciſci Brickman honeſti mercatoris Anno ſalutis noſtre Milleſimo quingenteſſimo viceſimo quinto. xx. die Decembris." Hereunto are annexed certain uſeful tables, with a preface by Jod. Badius Aſcenſius addreſſed to the clergy of the Church of England, dated, "Ex officina noſtra Parrhiſien. ad Idus Maias anni Milleſimi quingenteſimiſexti." Theſe have a diſtinct title-page: over the cut of St. George, &c. with the king's arms, and the roſe crowned,

"Moribus ingenuis: doctrina: opibuſq; potētes
Anglorum proceres: cleri: patreſq; britanni:
Qui ſanā colitis doctrinaz: ijs moribus equā:
Eccum quod totiens petijſtis nobile dogma.
Veſtib⁹ attalicis redimitū: omniq; redemptū
A vicio: & nullis per cuncta notabile mendis.
Exit: vt era ſuis referat condigna patronia."

The principal table, entitled "Tabula alphabetica annotatu digniſſimorum", has this colophon, "Explicit tabula compendioſa ſuper librum qui intitulatur Prouincialis, cōpilata per wilhelmū de Tylia nemore, cōpilata in feſto cōuerſionis ſcti Pauli. Anno Dnī. M.CCCCXXXIIJ." Which ſome have inadvertently taken for the date of printing. D 4, in eights. Folio. W.H.

Page 1535, *insert* " Manuale—Sarum. optimis typis—non sine singu- ——
lari industria Antwerpie impressum, *&c.* Venundantur Londini apud Petrum Kaetz." At the end a cypher, and under it, " Christopherus Endo- 1526.
viensis." Folio. Bodleian. *Ibid.* Horæ B. Mariæ Virginis. Paris. 1526. 1526.
Hist. of the Reform. II, Records, p. 138. *Ibid* " Missale—Sarum, in
alma Parrhisiorum academia nouiter impressum MDXXXVI." On the title-
page is the cut of St. George, &c. with the transactions of the passion in
the border, &c. The crucifixion on vellum, before the canon of the
mass, is in a superior style. Colophon, " Impressum impensis & sumptibus—Francisci Regnault librarii iurati alme vniuersitatis Parisien. commorantis in vico Sancti Jacobi in intersignio elephantis. A. D. MDXXVI.
die penultima mensis Octobris." Folio. Richard Gough Esq.

Page 1536, *insert* " Missale—Sarum, vna cum dicte ecclesie institutis, 1527.
consuetudinibusque nuper elimatissime impressum. Adiectis pluribus que
in ceteris desiderantur.—Consummatum in alma Parisiorum academia.
Anno Domini 1527. F. R." St. George &c. 4to. Richard Gough Esq. *Ibid.*
Horæ—Sarisburiensis. London. 1527. 4to. Catal. Bibl. Harleianæ, I; 1527.
N° 1768. *Ibid.* " Missale—Sarum". The frontispiece the same as to
the Legende &c. p. 1823. with the addition of six verses to the priests.
Colophon: "—in alma Parisiorum academia, opera industrii viri Nicolai
Prevost, impensis vero Francisci Byrckman: elimatissime impressum, quod
ceteris in multis excellit.—M.D.XXVII. tertio calendas Martias." At the
end, a round with a hen and chickens, and another with Birkman's mark,
initials and motto. Folio. Richard Gough Esq. *Ibid.* " Missale—Sa- 1527.
rum:—Antwerpie nouissime excusum.—Quod quidem tum prouidentie ac
honori ipsius Francisci Byrckman bibliopole eximii ascribendum est, cum
is quidem in hoc negotio haud pecuniis unquam pepercit, ac sumptibus,
tum et ipsi Christophoro Ruremundum, cuius quidem arte atque sedulo labore id exaratum constat. A. D. 1527, die vero 28 mensis Martii."
Folio. See Brit. Topography, II; 342-3. *Ibid.* " Horæ—in verum 1527.
vsum Sarum quamplurimis biblicis historiis decoratæ. *&c.* Impressæ
quidem Parisiis in officina industri calcographi Nic. Preuost: impensis
vero fidelissimi mercatoris Francisci Byrckman, ciuis Coloniensis & apud
eundem venundantur Londini, apud cœmeterium Sti. Pauli. Anno Domini 1527. die 18 Julii." 4to.

Page 1537, *insert* " Enchiridion preclare ecclesie Sarum, doctissimis pre- 1528.
cationibus ac venustissimis imaginibus, & iis quidem non paucis refertum.
Parisiis ex officina libraria vidue[4] spectabilis viri Thielmanni Keruer. Colophon, " Impressum est hoc orarium Parisiis in edibus vidue—in vico
diui Jacobi ad signum vnicornis:—anno salutis nostre millesimo quingentesimo vigesimo octauo, die ii Septembris." Printed on vellum in 24to.
Brit. Topogr. II; 343. *Ibid.* " Missale—Sarum, una cum eiusdem ecclesiæ consuetudinibus ac obseruantiis, suis locis insertis." &c. St. George
&c. with the hexastichon " Ad sacerdotes exhortatio. Colophon: " Explicit

[4] See Maittaire, II; 730, where he inserts " Biblia Latina: apud Thielman Kerver. fol. Paris. 1530." For which he quotes Le Long.

plicit Missale &c. Et sic prelo applicatum opere atque impensis Christophori Ruremundensis. Anno Domini MCCCCCXXVIII. die vero xiii Aprilis."
1528. Folio. Richard Gough Esq. *Ibid.* Processionale ad usum. Lond. 1528.
1528. 4to. Brit. Museum. *Ibid.* Horæ b. v. Mariæ. Paris. 1528. Octavo. Harleian catal. I; 1831. *Ibid. l.* 27, *for* M.D.XXIII. *read* M.D.XXVIII.
1529. *Page* 1538, *insert* "Missale—Sarum, una cum dicte ecclesie consuetudinibus & institutis, Accuratissime tersum. &c. Parisiis per Franciscum Regnault. M.D.XXIX." A cut of the elevation of the host, and 4 lines "Ad sacerdotem." The whole inclosed in a border of saints. Colophon: "—Parisiis, per Fr. Regnault, in vico Sancti Jacobi, e regione templi Maturinorum ad signum elephantis, 1529." 4to. Richard Gough Esq. *Ibid.*
1530. "Breviarium in usum Sarum." Colophon: "Finis partis estiualis breviarii insignis ecclesie Sarum mellifluis biblie concordantiis locupletate: & nuper Parisiis, arte & impensis vidue—Thielmanni Keruer impresse. Anno M.D.XXX. sexto calendas Nouembres." After the calendar follows an address to the English clergy from Constantinus Lepus, setting forth that he had undertaken to compile this Breviary at the desire of Fr. Byrkman, the bookseller who had generously relieved him in his necessities. 16°.
1530. Richard Gough Esq. Who has also an imperfect copy of the Winter part of the same date, but somewhat larger, having at the end a wood-cut of
1530. "Mater Dei, sitting with the infant Jesus. *Ibid.* "Hore beatissime virginis Marie ad legitimum Sarisburiensis ecclesie vsum, cum multis ac variis orationibus multum deuotis." Printed at Paris by Fr. Regnault. It has English rubrics; and the pages elegantly adorned. At folio c. is a print of a king with a leonine prayer addressed to him, printed by Hearne, Pref. to Otterbourne, p. 53, as from Horæ, by W. de Worde 1510; but query.
1530. but query. *Ibid.* Manuale. Fr. Regnault. Par. 1530. *Ibid.* Processionale
1530. in usum Sarum. Par. 1530. Bodleian catal. II; 141. *Ibid.* "¶ Julius Cesars commentaries. Newly translatyd owte of laten in to englysshe as much as cõcernyth thys realme of England sumtyme callyd Brytayne: whych is the eldyst hystoryer of all other that can be found/ that euer wrote of thys realme of England. 1530." Colophon: "¶ Here endyth the commentaryes of Julius Cesar as towchynge Brytayne now called Englande ∴ ¶ Cum priuilegio." Folio. Dr. Billam of Leeds. See p. 343. *Ibid.* Enchiridion—Sarum. Germ. Hardouyn. Par. 1530. 6 Maij. 16°.
(1531.) *Page* 1540, *after l.* 9, *insert* "This prayer of Salisbury vse is set out a long without ony serchyng/ with many prayers and goodly pyctures in the kalender/ in the matyns of our lady/ in the houres of the crosse/ in the vij. psalmes and in the dyryge. And be newly enprynted at Parys." A cut of the virgin surrounded with all her comparisons, under which are the ten lines, "God be in my hede" &c. as p. 467. The Calendar begins 1531. The cuts are very good: I. F. on that for June. On Fo. xv, "The manner to liue well/ &c. Cumpyled by mayster Johan quẽtin—translated in to englysshe by Robert Copland prynter in London." Y, in eights. At the end, "Parisijs per Franciscum Regnault. In vico sancti iacobi/" &c. On the last leaf is his device or sign only, the elephant and castle; on the castle is

is his mark, formed of the initials of his name, which is on a scroll at the bottom, Francois Regnault. The covers of my copy are stamped with the elevation of the host, and St. Barbara. 8vo. W.H. *Ibid.* Officium Beatæ 1531.
Mariæ Virginis in usum Sarum. 1531. 8vo. Harleian cat. II, Nº 1731.
Another in English of the same date. Ibid. Nº 1732. *Ibid.* "Horæ 1531.
btē marie virginis ad vsū ecclesie Sarū: cū multis ac varijs orationibus multū deuotis. 1531." The cut Te Deum &c. Under it, "Venundantur in cimiterio sancti pauli sub intersignio sancti Augustini." On the back, "An almanac for xv. yeres." Beginning m. d. xxix. At the end of the calendar "The pater noster* in englies.---The crede of the Aue.---Here foloweth te credo† as it ought to be sayd.—The. x.‖ commaundementes." The cuts are very neat, but no indication of the engraver. Prefixed to the Hours, which begin on Fo. xviij, are "The dayes of the weke moralysed.---The maner to liue well, &c. Compyled by mayster Juhan quentyn doctour of dyuinyte at Parys. Translated out of frenche —by Robert Coplād prynter at London." &c. &c. In Fo. xcv, is the anthem or leonine prayer entitled "De btō rege hērico. an." See p. 1824. Many of the rubrics in English. Contains Fo. cxcij. Colophon: "—Ex officina Christophori Ruremunden. Anno M. ccccc. xxxj. Die vero. xiiij. Maij." 4to. W.H.. *Ibid.* "The exposition of the fyrste Epistle of seynt 1531.
Jhon with a Prologue before it by W. T. 1531." 16º. *Ibid.* "This pry- 1532.
mer of Salisbury vse is set out along without ony serchyng, with many prayers, & goodly pyctures in the kalender, in the matyns of our lady, in the houres of the crosse, in the vij. psalmes, and in the dyryge. And be newly enprynted at Parys. M.D.XXXij." A cut of the Salutation, and under it signature A. On the back is an "Almanacke for xix. yeres." beginning 1530. GG, in eights. "Impresse Parisiis per Franciscū Regnault—

* "Our fader tat arte in heuen sanctifyed bethy name Thy kyngdome come to vs The wyll te done in erth as in heuen Our dayly breed gyue vs tho daye: et forgyue vs our dettys: as we forgyue our detters: And lede vs not in to tentacyon But delyuer vs from euil. Amen."

† "I Byleue in god fader almighty: creatour of heuen & of erth. And in his only sone our lorde: the wiche was conceiued of the holy goost. Borne of the vyrgyn mary The wiche suffred deth vnder pylate: and was crucyfyed deed & buryed. The wiche descended in to the helles & the. iij. day arose from dethe. The wiche ascended in to heuen: & set him on te ryght hande of god te fader almighty et from thens shall come agayne for to iuge the deed: and the quicke. I byleue in the holy goost And in the holy chirche catholike. And in te communion of all the sayntes of peradyse. And in te remissyon of synnes The resurreccyon of te fleshe. And the lyfe eternal: so be it," &c.

‖ "One god oneli thou shalte loue et worshyppe perfitely.
God in vayn thou shalt not swere nor by that he made truly.
The sondays thou shalt kepe in seruinge god deuoutly.
Fader and moder thou shalte honour: and shalt lyue longely.
Mansleer thou shalte not be in dede: ne wyllyngly.
Licherous thou shalte not be of thy body ne consentyngly.
No mannes goodes thou shalte not stele nor with holde falsly.
False wytnesse thou shalte not bere: in any wyse lyengly.
The werkes of the fleshe desire not but in maryage only.
The goodes of other couete not: to haue them vniustly."

nault—Anno dnī M.CCCCCXXXII. Die septima Augusti." 16°. W.H.
1532. I have another edition of the same date and size, better printed, and with
neater cuts, in the form of medallions, marked with the Lorrain cross, but
it wants the title. It has prefixed, tables for the full and change of the
moon, eclipses, &c. for the years 1533—1538.---An "Almanacke for xvii
yeres," beginning 1532. Towards the end, "Oratio dominica," in
Latin; then follows "The seuen petityons of the Pater noster, by Johā
Colet Deane of Poules.---Salutatio angelica," in Latin and English.--
"Duodecim articuli fidei.---The. xii. artycles of the fayth, the whyche
euery true christen man & woman be bounde to byleue." Paraphrastically
translated.---"The. x. commaundementes." In verse. N, in eights. On
the last leaf, "Expliciunt hore beatissime virginis Marie secūdum vsum
Sarum, totaliter ad longum, &c. impresse Parisiis, impensis quidem honesti viri Joannis Growte librarii, opera autem cōspicue matrone Yolande
Bonhomme vidue defuncti Thielmanni Keruer, sub vnicorni commorātis,
in vico diuī Jacobi. Anno dnī. M.D.XXXII. mense Augusto." On the
back is T. Kerver's device, with his name, and under it the date as above.
Hereunto are annexed "An inuocacyon gloryous named the psalter of
Jesus." With some other superstitious prayers, for saying one of which
pardon for "xlvi. M. yere. xii. yeres and. xl. dayes," was granted by pope
1532. Sixtus the fourth. ++, in eights. 16°. W.H. *Ibid.* Horæ beatæ Mariæ,
or Primer of Salisbury use, full of good cuts. Title wanting. Colophon:
"Expliciunt hore beate Marie—Sarum, totaliter ad longum cum multis
pulcherrimis orationibus & indulgentiis iam vltimo adiectis. Impresse
Parisiis in edibus Fr. Regnault, alme vniuersitatis Parisiensis librarii iurati.
Anno Domini millesimo quingentesimo trigesimo secundo, die vltima Octobris." Both in the title, and prefixed to the Completorium of the V. Mary,
is a beautiful cut of her funeral, with the legend of the Jew, who
attempting to obstruct it was deprived of the use of his hand. 8°. Ri-
1532. chard Gough. Esq. *Ibid.* "Manuale ad vsum ecclesie Sarisburiensis, iam
recens impressum ab erratis emunctissime vindicatum. Parisiis. per Fr.
1532. Regnault. 1532." 4°. Bodleian. *Ibid. insert* Graduale—Sarum.—Impress. per Nic. Prevost. Paris. 1532. Venundantur Lond. apud Rob.
Redman, et Par. apud Fr. Regnault.
1533. *Page* 1541, *insert* "Missale ad vsum insignis ac preclare ecclesie Sarum:
&c. Impressum Parisiis sumptibus Fr. Regnault—Anno Domini millesimo
quingentesimo trigesimo tertio, die vero xxvii Maij." 4to. See Brit.
(1533.) Topogr. II; 347-8. *Ibid.* "Enchiridiō preclare eccl'ie Sarisburiēsis devo-
tissimis precationibus ac venustissimis imaginibus: & ijs quidem non paucis
refertū." The printer's mark on a shield hanging on a tree supported by
two cupids. Under it, "God be in my hede." &c. as p. 467. On the
2d leaf, "Tabula ad inueniendum pascha:—incipiendo—M.D.XXXIII."
Every page in a border of pillars, &c. Contains x 4, in eights. Colophon, under the instruments of the passion forming a shield and crest, with
this motto, REDEMPTORIS MVNDI ARMA. See p. 1308. "Impressum
est hoc orariū Parisiis in edibus spectabilis viri Germani Hardouyn librarij
iurati

iurati vniuerſitatis Pariſien. apud palatiũ cõmorantis ad ſignũ diue Margarete." 16°. W.H. *Ibid. inſert* Portiforium ſeu Breviarium—Sarum. 1533.
Par. Fr. Regnault. 1533. Octavo.

Page 1542, *dele l.* 41, 42, *and inſtead thereof inſert* "The new Teſtament 1534.
as it was written, and cauſed to be written, by them which herde yt. whom alſo our Saveour Chriſt Jeſus commanded that they ſhoulde preach it vnto all creatures." This all in rubrics. "The Goſpell of S. Mathew. The Goſpell of S. Marke. The Goſpell of S. Luke. The Goſpell of S. Ihon. The Actes of the apoſtles. Joelis II. I will pour oute of my Spryte vpon all fleſhe, and your Sonnes" *&c.* On the back of this title-page is "An Almanacke for xviij. yeres," beginning m.d.xxvi, then, in 6 leaves, the kalendar; which with the goſpels and Acts of the apoſtles form the firſt part. After the Acts of the apoſtles is a title-page, "The Epiſtles of the Apoſtle S. Paul," with an enumeration of them, &c. all in Black-letter, incloſed in a fancy border: at the top is a repreſentation of St. Paul writing, and at the bottom the printer's mark. In the viij Chap. of the Acts, this edition has "and be holde a man of ethiophia, which was gelded, ãd of grete auctorite" &c. after the verſion of Wiclif, but which Tindal had tranſlated Chamberlain. See Lewis, p. 79, 80. Every book, and every chapter, begin with flouriſhed letters; and each evangeliſt has a cut of him indented at the beginning of his goſpel. At the end of the Revelation of St. John, "Here endeth the new Teſtament diligently ouerſene and corrected, and prynted now agayn at Antwerpe, by me Wydowe of Chriſtoffel of Endhoue In the yere of oure Lorde. M.CCCCC. and xxxiiij. in Auguſt." Then follows, "¶ This is the Table, wherein you ſhall fynde the Piſtelys & the Goſpellys after the vſe of Saryſbuery." 13 leaves. 16°. George Paton Eſq; of Edinburgh, a beautiful copy.
Ibid. "Miſſale ad vſum eccleſie Sariſburienſis. M.D.XXXIIII." On the 1534.
title-page, the king's arms, and roſe, over St. George, &c. as p. 1824; and the "Exhortatio ad ſacerdotes," in a border of 7 different compartments of the life of our ſaviour, the ſymbols of the evangeliſts at the corners, and at the top the deity ſurrounded by angels. Some of the cuts are dated 1525.
Folio. Richard Gough Eſq. *Ibid.* "Thys prymer of ſaliſbury vſe" 1534.
&c. as p. 1543-4. 16°. W.H. *Ibid.* "Hore beatiſſime virginis Marie ad 1534.
legitimum Sariſburienſis eccleſie ritum, cum *&c.* 1534. Venundantur Pariſiis a Franciſco Regnault, in vico" &c. In the title is a beautiful cut of the funeral of the V. Mary with the legend of the Jew, &c. as p. 1830. At the bottom, St. George and the dragon, with "Sancte Georgi ora pro nobis." The cuts have this monogram Colophon: "Impreſſe Pariſiis per Fr. Regnault,—opera & impenſis eiuſdem." Adorned with a great number of large & elegant wood-cuts: thoſe at the ſides are from the Revelations, and from profane hiſtory. Small folio. See Brit. Topography, II, 319, &c. The Harleian catalogue has one *(Officium)* of this date, octavo.

Page 1543, *l.* 8 *and* 11, *for* xxxxiiii *read* xxxiiii..

1535. *Page* 1545, *insert* " Psalterium Dauiticum ad vsum Sarisburiensis."
After which follow several services, and then, " Proprium sanctorum
tempore hyemale." Colophon: "—Parisiis per Fr. Regnault. 1535."
Has good cuts, with the monogram as above. 4to. Richard Gough Esq.
Who has also " Psalterium cum hymnis. 16°. Portiforium seu Breviarium ad Usum Eccles. Sarisburiens. 2 Vol. Paris. 1535. 4to. Harl.
cat. I, N° 1687. *Ibid.* Officium B. M. V. Lat. and Eng. for the use of
1535. Salisbury. 8°. Ibid. N° 1732. *Ibid.* The Prymer of Salisbury—F. Reg-
1535. nault—1535. 15. Oct. 4to. Bodleian. *Ibid.* " Hore—Marie" &c. as
the edition 1534, above, and has the same cut on the title-page. At the
bottom, the arms of England; and DEVM TIME. The calendar has good
cuts to each month. The cuts have the same monogram as those to the
edition 1534. " Venundantur Parisius, a Francisco Regnault, in vico
1536. Jacobi, sub signo elephantis. 1535." The colophon says, " Impresse Par-
rhisiis per Fr. Regnault: impensis & sumptibus eiusdem: alme vniuersitatis
Parrhisien. librarii iurati. A. D. millesimo quingentesimo tricesimo sexto,
die vero xxv Maii." Beautiful cuts. Small folio. See Brit. Topogr. II, 350.

1536. *Page* 1546, *insert* " The Newe testament yet ones agayne corrected by
W. Tyndale: and in many places amẽded/ where it scaped before by neglygence of the printer. Also a Kalender And a necessary table/ where
easily & lyghtly may be founde any story cõteyned in the foure Euangelystes/
and in the Actes of the apostels. Also before euery pystel of S. Paul
is a prologue very fruteful to the reder. And after the newe testament
foloweth the Epystels of the olde testament. *&c.* Newly printed/ in the yere
of our lorde M.D.XXXVI." At the end, " God saue the kynge/ and all his
1536. well wyllers." Rr 5, in sixes. Small folio. Mr. Joseph Parker. *Ibid.*
Officium B. M. V. Lat. and Eng. Lond. 1536. 8vo. Harl. cat. I,
1536. N° 1735. *Ibid.* Another in English undated. *Ibid.* " Rudimenta
Grammatices & docendi methodus, non tam Gypsuychianæ per Reuerendissimum D. Thomam Cardinalem Ebor. feliciter institutæ,
quam omnibus alijs totius Angliæ scholis præscripta. 1536." Card.
Wolsey's epistle to the masters is dated " Calend. Sept. 1528"; therefore
probably it was printed that year, or soon after. 8vo. The Rev.
Dr. Lort. Fiddes quotes an edition 1537.

1537. *Page* 1547, *insert* " This prymer of Salysbury vse is set out along wout
ony serchyng, with many prayers. And be newly emprynted at Rouen.
1537." At the end " Expliciunt hore beatissime V. M.—Impresse pro
Francisco Regnault commorante in vico diui Jacobi iuxta templum Matu-
1537. rinorum, ad signum elephantis." 16°. Brit. Topogr. II, 351. *Ibid.*
" An Introduction to lerne to rekyn with the pen and with Counters," &c.
1537. as p. 579. " Newly corrected," &c. 8°. 1537. *Ibid.* " The olde learning
and the new compared," &c. as p. 1448. 8vo. 1537. Maunsell, p. 77.

Page 1548, *l.* 2, *for* Contains *read* These contain. *Ibid. l.* 5 *and* 6,
dele " The Romaunt of the Rose." &c. Being meant of the French
1538. edition. *Ibid. insert* Officium B. M. V. Sarum. Lat. and Eng. 1538.
8°.

8°. Rothomag. Harl. cat. I; 1737. *Ibid.* "The newe teſtament of our 1538.
ſauioure Jeſu Chriſt, newly and diligently tranſlated in to Englyſſhe by
Thomas Mathew with annotations in ẏ mergent to helpe the reader to the
vnderſtãdyng of the texte. ✠ Set forth with the kynges mouſt gratious
lycenſe. Anno. M. D. XXXVIII." This title is in a compartment uſed by
P. Treveris to the Polychronycon printed by him for John Reynes, 1527.
Tyndal's prologue inſerted before the Ep. to the Romans, in the Bible 1537,
is here omitted. It has cuts only to the book of the Revelation, which
differ from any i have obſerved. Contains fol. c.xxxi, the title and table
to "fynde the Epyſtles and the Goſpelles after ẏ vſe of Saleſbury"
included. 4to. George Maſon Eſq. *Ibid.* "The new teſtament both
in Latin and Engliſh" &c. as p. 512. *Ibid.* "This Prymer of Saleſbury 1538.
vſe is ſet out a long woot any Serchyng with many Prayers and Goodly
Pyctures *&c.* Newly emprynted a Rouen. 1538." 8°. The late Rev.
Dr. Freind, Dean of Canterbury.

Page 1552, *inſert* Jo. Pilbarough his "Cõmemoration of the ineſtimable 1540.
graces and benefits of God infuſed through ẏ bright light of the knowledge
of his holy word, to our moſt dradde ſovereign Lorde Henry the eyght.
Lond. an. 1540." Ded. to lord Crumwell. 4to. T. Baker's Maunſell,
p. 80. *Ibid.* "A newe ballade made of Thomas Crumwel, called Trolle 1540.
on away." Printed at London in 1540. See it in Bp. Percy's Collection
of Ancient Poems, II; 64. *Ibid.* "A very godly defenſe full of lerning, 1541.
defending the marriage of preiſtes, gathered by Philip Melancton, and
ſent vnto the kyng of England, Henry the aight. Tranſlated out of
Latyne into Engliſh by Lewis Beuchame, 1541, in Auguſt. Printed at
Lipſe, by Vbryght Hoffe." 8vo. See Maunſell, p. 70. *Ibid.* "The defence 1541.
of the mariage of preiſtes, agenſt Steuen Gardiner biſhop of Wyncheſter,
Wyliam Repſe biſhop of Norwiche, and agenſt all the biſhops and preiſtes
of that falſe popiſh ſecte: with a confutacion of their vnaduyſed vowes. vnad-
uyſedly diſſned, whereby they haue ſo wykedly ſeperated them, whom God
cowpled in lawfull mariage. Made by James Sawtry. Prynted at Awryk,
by Jan Trooſt, 1541, in Auguſt." 16°. *Ibid.* "Hymnorum cum notis 1541.
opuſculum," &c. Colophon: "Explicit hymnorum opuſculum ad vſum—
Sarum *&c.* in officina vidue Chriſtopheri Ruremunden impreſſum ſumpti-
bus et impenſis Joannis Coccii. Anno a natiuitate Domini MCCCCCXLI.
menſe vero Julii." 4to. Bodleian. *Ibid.* Miſſale in uſum Sarum. Ven. 1541.
1541. Octavo.

Page 1553, *inſert* Manuale—Sarum. Antv. Anno Domini 1542. 4to. 1542.
Richard Gough Eſq. *Ibid.* "The names of books prohibited, delivered (1542.)
to the curates, anno 1542, to the intent that they ſhall preſent them, with
the names of the owners, to their ordinary, if they find any ſuch within their
pariſhes." Hiſt. of the Reform. Vol. I; Records, p. 240.

Page 1555, *inſert* "A bok of the office of Seruauntes Engliſhed by 1543.
Tho. Chaloner. Lond. 1543." 8°. Written by Gilb. Cognatus. Ded. to
Sir Hen. Knevet. See Ath. Oxon. I; 149. *Ibid.* "A Prophecie, or 1543.
Prognoſtication of the Emperour Charles the Fifth, made by Maiſter
Salomon.

Salomon a Jew. Printed beyond Sea, in 1543." 4to. Maunsell, II, 27.

1543. *Ibid.* The Practyse of Prelates &c. as p. 1578. A. D. 1543. 8vo. *Ibid.*

1543. A merry Prognostication, as p. 234. John Ritson Esq. *Ibid.* "Manuale ad vsum percelebris ecclesie Sarisburiensis: Rothomagi, recenter impressum,—typis Nicoli Rufi. MDXLIII." 4to. Bodleian.

1544. *Page* 1556, *insert* Manuale—Sarisburiensis. Par. 1544. 4to. Harl. cat. *Ibid. l. penult. read* Anno M.D.XL iij Nonas Octobris."

Page 1557, *to l.* 3, *add* Maunsell says it was printed beyond sea in 1540. It was however printed the same year by R. Redman; and also by his wife. In the Bodleian is a copy, printed at Marp. 1547. Octavo.

Page 1558, *l.* 12, *for* 1554 *in the margin, read* 1545. *Ibid. l.* 28, *for*

1545. —, *in the margin, read* 1545. *Ibid. insert* Processionale &c. as p. 415. The title is printed wholly in red, over the king's arms crowned, gartered, and supported by a wyvern and a greyhound, the rose and pomegranate over them, the flower de luce and portcullis beneath, a riband flying over all with *Dieu et mon droyt* like that used by J. Gowghe to a Salisbury prymer, 1536. Under these arms, printed in black, is the date 1545, in red; the whole enclosed in pieces forming a light compartment. On the back is a cut, having under it "Statio dum benedicitur aqua benedicta in omnib^{9} dominicis diebus: & fiat modo sequenti." At Fo. xj is another cut representing "Ordo processionis in die natiuitatis dnī ante missam." There are several other cuts representing the various stations, &c. on particular days, and occasions. D, in the 2d alphabet, in eights. The colophon as in p. 415, but ends with "iterum prelo applicatū absolutūq;" Quarto. W.H.

1546. *Page* 1561, *insert* "Manuale ad vsum ecclesie Sarisburiensis. Par. 1546."

1547. 4to. Harl. cat. *Ibid.* "An heauenly Act concernynge howe Man shall lyue, made by our Soueraygne Lord God the Father, &c. and all the whole Clergy of heauen. 1547." Sixteens.

(1548.) *Page* 1563, *insert* "An answer to a papystical exhortation pretending to auoyd false doctrine, vnder that colour to mayntayne the same." Beginning,

"Euery pylde pedlar Will be a medlar."

Ibid. l. 28, *set* 1548 *in the margin.*

1549. *Page* 1566, *insert* "A Dialogue or Cōmunycacyon to be had at a Table betwene two chyldren, gathered out of the holy Scriptures, by Johan Bale, for his 2: yonge Sonnes, Johan and Paule. printed at Lond: for Rich: Foster. an: MDXLIX." T. Baker's Maunsell, p. 6. *Ibid. l.* 19, *add* 3 and 4 of Edw. VI. cap. 10.

—— *Page* 1569, *insert* John Knoxe's sermon against the Masse, 4 April, 1550, in presence of the Counsell, &c. 16°. T. Baker's Maunsell, p. 101.

1551. *Page* 1570, *insert* Hore. B. M. V. Rothomagen.—Apud Rob. Valentinum. 1551. Twenty-fours

1552. *Page* 1571, *insert* "Psalterium dauidicum, cum aliquot canticis ecclesiasticis. Litanie. Hymni ecclesiastici." F. Regnault's device as p. 1829. Under it, "Parisiis. Apud Magdalenum Boursette, viduam spectabilis viri Francisci Regnault, via Jacobea, sub signo elephantis commoran. MDiij (M.D.lij.

(M.D.lij, as in the colophon.) On the back, "Psalmorum canticum multiplices effectus et virtutes habet diuo Augustino teste." Then, a calendar for the 12 months, and "Oratio multum deuota," are prefixed. Besides, Fo. CXXX, and an alphabetical table of the beginnings of each psalm, &c. 2 leaves more. Colophon as before, only after "elephantis" omitting "commoran." is added "circa Maturinos. Anno salutis nostre M.D.lij." On the last page is a cut of the creation. My copy has annexed "Hymni totius anni, &c. with fresh signatures and numerals. H 4, in eights. Colophon: "Hymnorum tam dominicarum quam festiuitatum secundum anni curriculum occurrentium finis: qui in officina libraria Magdalene Boursette vidue—via Jacobea sub signo elephantis circa Maturinos cōmoran. Anno nostre salutis. M.D.iij." (M.D.lij, as above.) The size of a modern octavo. W.H.

Page 1572, *l.* 13, *for* 1533, *in the margin, read* 1553.

Page 1574, *insert* "AN EPISTEL OF Moche learnīg, sent by saint Huldericus, Bisshoppe of Augusta, called Augsburgh, vnto Nicolas Bysshoppe of Rome, the fyrst of that name: agaynst the vnmarried Chastitie of Pryestes." 12 leaves. 16°. W.H.

Page 1578, *l.* 18, *add* W.H. my copy wants the title-page. Mr. T. Baker mentions a book with the same title in Skeltonic verse. Interleaved Maunsell, p. 32.

Page 1579, *l.* 1, *after* 1554 *add* "Ex officina Ricardi Hamilionis typographi." *Ibid.* The Prymer. Impensis Rob. Valentini. Impress. per 1554.
Johannem le Prest. Rouen. 1554. This is nearly the same as that of 1555, but the cuts are varied, and have the initials I. M.

Page 1580, *l.* 6, *after* 1554 *add (Mutatis mutandis.)* See p. 561. *Ibid.* 1555.
"Manuale London. 1555." The title compartment has a medallion of the heads at top, as described in p. 561. Query, if not designed for Philip and Mary? *Ibid.* "Processionale ad vsum insignis ecclesie Saris- 1555.
buriensis obseruandos accommodum" &c. as p. 415, to "tersum. Impressum Londini anno M.DLV." No printer's name, but the title is in the same compartment as the Manuale above mentioned; therefore both probably printed by J. Kingston and H. Sutton. *Ibid.* Processionale. 1555.
Colophon: "Explicit processionale ad vsum—Sarum obseruandos accommodum iterum prelo applicatum absolutumque. Londini—1555." The title border supported by two terms without arms. Another copy, the same year, whose terms have arms, and has at the bottom of the title T. R. 4°. See Brit. Topography, II, 357-8.

Page 1589, *l.* 27, *after* 1556 *add* The cut of the nativity has this 1556.
monogram 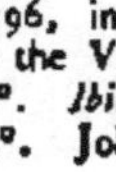. A large cut of St. Andrew has 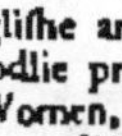.

Page 1596, insert "The Primer in Englishe and Latine, set out 1557.
along after the Vse of Sarum, with many godlie praiers, & pictures. 1557." 4°. *Ibid.* "——The defence of Women, &c. 1557." See 1557.
p. 763. 4°. John Ritson Esq. Again 1560. *Ibid.* "Constitutiones 1557.
Prov.

—— Prov. Angliæ; absque Comin. Lond. 1557." 8°. Bodleian. *Ibid.* "The primer in English for children, after the vse of Sarum." In a compartment. Without printer's name or date. 16°. W.H. *Ibid.*
1557. "Processionale &c. Rothom. Impensis Rob. Valentini. 15 Octob.
1558. 1557." Quarto. *Ibid.* "Processionale &c. Antuerp. apud Melchiorem Enalouiarum ad insigne mortis. 1558." 4°. Both, Richard Gough Esq.
(1559.) *Page* 1602, *insert* "A fruitefull Dialogue declaryng these wordes of Christ: This is my body. A learned Dialogue between Custome and
1560. Truth." See Strype's Life of Abp. Grindal, p. 313. *Ibid.* "Abraham hys Sacrafyce, or The Tryale of the Hearte. 1560." Biogr. Dramat. II; 1, 2. Probably a translation from Beza, but different from that by A. G. (Arthur Golding). See p. 1069.

1562. *Page* 1606, *insert* "Russiae, Moscoviae, et Tartariae descriptio. Authore Antonio Jenkensono Anglo, edita Londini 1562, et dedicata illustriss. D. Henrico Sydneo Walliæ præsidi. Cum priuilegio." This map was published in Ortelius's Theatrum orbis terrarum, No. 61. Edit. Antverpiæ, 1575.

1572. *Page* 1633, *insert* "The Schole house of Women. 1572." 4°. John
1573. Ritson Esq. *Ibid.* "The Pedigree of Sclander. A sermon." Dedicated to Mrs. F. B. without any name, 10 Aug. 1573. 8°. T. Baker's
—— Maunsell, p. 104. *Ibid.* "A compendious Treatise of Sclaundre." 8°.

Page 1647, *l.* 2, *add* Lately reprinted by Mr. John Nichols, with other progresses, &c. of Q. Elizabeth, in 2 vol. 4°.

Page 1650, *l. ult. add* See Gough's British Topography, I; 87, &c.

1578. *Page* 1653, *insert* "A TREATISE OF SCHISME Shewing, that al Catholikes ought in any wise to abstaine altogether from heretical Conuenticles, &c. By Gregorie Martin Licentiate in Diuinitie, DVACI. Apud Johannem Foulerum. 1578." On the back, "Hic Tractatus est planè Catholicus, & nostris imprimis hominibus hoc schismatis tempore pernecessarius. Ita testor Gulielmus Alanus S. Theologiæ Doctor & Professor." Then, "The preface to the Reader.—From Remes within the Octaues of Al Saintes. 1578. By your countryman G. M." The head title, "Reasons that Catholikes ought in any wise to absteine from heretical Conuenticles." Running-title, "A treatise of Schisme." L 2, in eights. 16°. W.H.

1582. *Page* 1661, *insert* "A Joyful and Royal Entertainment of Frauncis
—— the Frenche Kings Brother, at Antwerpe, 1582." *Ibid.* "An Epistle of the persecution of Catholikes in Englande. Translated vvt of frenche into Englishe and conferred vvith the Latyne copie. by G. T. To whiche there is added an epistle by the translator to the right honorable Lordes of her maiesties preuie councell touchynge the same matter.—Imprynted at Douay in Artois." The epistle to the Lords is concluded on

* This was reprinted by Wm. Carter in 1580, under the name of John Howlet, and dedicated to Q. Elizabeth; for which he was tried, cast, and condemned at the Sessions-house in the Old Baily, 10 Jan. 1584; and on the next morrow drawn from Newgate to Tyburne, and there hanged, bowelled, and quartered. See Holinshed, p. 1357.

on p. 42; the epistle touching the persecution is addressed " To his verie lovinge frinde. M. Gerarde at Bononie in Italie." This ends on p. 167. Annexed are " An admonition sent by Gerard to the reader touching the former epistle.—The copie of a letter sent frome a priest, being prisoner in the Tovver of London, to the fathers of the Societie of Iesus in England." With an introduction " To the deuoute reader." Lastly, " The translator to the gentle reader." 16°. W.H.

Page 1667, *insert* " Itinerarium Cambriæ, &c. Giraldo Cambrense. London, 1585." 8°. See Brit. Topogr. II; 481. *Ibid.* " An Answere to a certein Booke," &c. See p. 1416. " London 1585." Without Printer's name. 16°. *Ibid. l.* 30, *read* temperament. 1585. 1585.

Page 1688, *l.* 5, *after* F.N.B. *add (Franciscus Niger Bossentinus).* See Biogr. Dramat. II; 128.

Page 1708, *l.* 1, *dele* passages. *Ibid. l.* 21, *read* ductie? Againe.

Page 1712, *note* k, *l.* 3, *read* Magdalen.

Page 1732, *after l.* 5, *insert* " The Haven of Pleasure by J. T. 1596.
Dedicated to the bawling Wives and Mistresses. Lond. 1596." 4°.

Page 1742, *insert* " The famous historical Life of Robert, 2d. D. of 1599.
Normandy, surnamed for his monstrous Birth and Behaviour, Robin the Divell. Lond. 1599." 4°. Bibl. Rawlinsoniana.

Page 1765, *l.* 4, *for* Whitehill *read* Whetehill.

Page 1766, *l.* 31, *after* Ludham, *insert*, in Norfolk.

Page 1772, *l.* 23, *for Leton read Letton.*

Page 1773, *l. antepenult. insert* 1.

Page 1775, *l.* 9, *read* " Missale secundum vsum Sarum."

Page 1780, *after l.* 38, *should have been inserted,* " Here begynneth the Eglogues," *&c. as p.* 1781, *from l.* 21 *to l.* 43, *inclusive, rather than there.*

Page 1784, *l.* 12, *for* 78 *read* 7, 8.

Page 1798, *l.* 39, *for* humilatus *read* tumulatus.

Page 1799, *l.* 29, *for* Scamber *read* Scambler.

Page 1801, *note* m, *l.* 2, *for* Queen *read* Princess.

Page 1802, *l.* 18, *and l.* 27, *read* Tyrwhit.

Page 1804, *l.* 7, *for* (1686) *in the margin, read* (1586).

Page 1808, *l.* 24, *for* Binnerman *read* Binneman.

Page 1820, *l.* 8, *for* St. Catharine *read* Cleodelinde.

Page 1823, *l.* 34, *after* sitting, *insert* The first cut has this mark 

Page 1828, *l.* 19, *read* Richard Gough, Esq. who, &c.

Page 1830, *l.* 29, *for* hand *read* hands.

Page 1833, *to l.* 15, *add ibid.* " This prymer in Englyshe/ and in Laten is 1538.
newly translated after the Laten texte. M.D.XXXVIIj." With a copious preface concerning this new translation, and others, to the Hours, Penitential Psalms, Letany, Dirige, &c. To which is annexed, Jerom of Ferrara's Exposition, &c. as p. 1547-8. At the end, " Jmprynted by Nicolas le Roux."—" Here begynneth the Pystles and Gospels of euery Sonday/ and holy Daye in the yere. ✣ M.D.XXXVIIj." In a compartment

with I. G. on the fell: a cut of St. John on the back. 8°. Richard
1538. Gough, Esq. *Ibid.* Another primer, which wants the title and part of the kalendar. Colophon, "Jinpryntel in Rowen the yere of our Lorde. M.CCCCC.XXX.viij." This has the same prefaces as the primer above mentioned; and has annexed the Pystles and Gospels, &c. with a title-leaf very like that, with I. G. on the fell; but the text is set in a different form. No printer's name to either, though the last page to each is blank. 8°. Richard Gough, Esq. *Ibid. l.* 32, *for* Froost *read* Troost.

Page 362, *l.* 3, *&c. read thus*: "The Palis of Honoure Compyled by Gawyne dowglas Bysshope of Dunkyll." In the same compartment as his Virgil. Colophon. "Imprinted at London in fletstret, at the sygne of the Rose garland by wyllyam Copland. God saue Quene Marye."

1535. *Page* 426, *insert*, "A sermon made in the cathedrall churche of saynte Paule at London the XXVII day of June, anno 1535, by Symon Matthewe. Printed the XXX day of July." Text, 1 Pet. v; 6, 7. Sixteens.

1541. *Page* 554, *insert*, A Primer in English and Latin after Salisbury use, which wants the title. Colophon, "Prynted at London in Paules churcheyerde, at the sygne of the Maydens heade by Thomas Petyt. M.D.XLj." To which are annexed, An Exposition on the 51st Psalm, and a Meditation on the 30th Psalm, by Jerom of Ferrara; also the Pystles and Gospels—newly corrected and amended. Both these have the same colophons as the primer. Octavo. Richard Gough, Esq.

Page 1336, *l.* 6 *from the bottom*, *for* Printed *read* Printer.

Page 1395, *l.* 18, *for* Pharidis *read* Phalaridis.

*** Wherever the name of *Thomas Pownall, Esq.* or *Governor Pownall*, occurs in this Work, read *Mr. Thomas Pownall.*

☞ *There may be some other typographical errors, which the candid reader will please to correct where he finds them.*

INDEX of the PRINTERS contained in this VOLUME.

A.

B.

G.

H.

J.

K.

Kitson

Troost,

AN

INDEX of the NAMES

OF

AUTHORS AND TRANSLATORS,

AND THE

Subjects of the several Treatises inserted in these Volumes.

A.

Aurelio,

Bavande,

Caumpeden.

D.

E.

A. F.

F.

Frasie,

G.

Guivardo,

H.

I and J.

Luther,

Marulus,

Orlando,

P.

Perkins,

Pr.

T.

Tayre,

V and U.

V. and U.

W.

X.

Y.

Z.

www.ingramcontent.com/pod-product-compliance
Lightning Source LLC
Chambersburg PA
CBHW022126020426
42334CB00015B/779
* 9 7 8 3 7 4 1 1 8 2 0 8 2 *